Back to the Eighties

The 1880's

Through the Eyes of Three Country Newspapers

by Jerry Michael

HERITAGE BOOKS
2017

HERITAGE BOOKS
AN IMPRINT OF HERITAGE BOOKS, INC.

Books, CDs, and more—Worldwide

For our listing of thousands of titles see our website
at
www.HeritageBooks.com

Published 2017 by
HERITAGE BOOKS, INC.
Publishing Division
5810 Ruatan Street
Berwyn Heights, Md. 20740

Copyright © 2017 Jerry Michael

Heritage Books by the author:
Back to the Eighties: The 1880's Through the Eyes of Three Country Newspapers
Back to the Seventies: The 1870's Through the Eyes of Two Country Newspapers
It Was Different Then: 1870 to 1885 Through the Eyes of the Loudoun County, Virginia Press

All rights reserved. No part of this book may be reproduced or transmitted in any form or by any means, electronic or mechanical, including photocopying, recording or by any information storage and retrieval system without written permission from the author, except for the inclusion of brief quotations in a review.

International Standard Book Number
Paperbound: 978-0-7884-5778-4

Sometimes there is a defining moment in one's life which creates a lasting impression and influences a future course of action. During one summer over fifty years ago I had a Department of Agriculture job surveying the crops and measuring the cornfields of various Loudoun County farms. The work required plenty of walking and late one afternoon resting atop a hillside pasture near the historic hamlet of Waterford, I remember marveling at an exquisite patchwork of verdant crops and meadows resembling a Grant Wood pastoral painting. I fell in love with Loudoun that summer. Later when I made my home there I grew to appreciate its rich history as much as its physical beauty.

Loudoun is the northernmost county in Virginia, 35 miles west of Washington D.C. The eastern portion, sometimes referred to in the old deeds as the Salisberry plain, is relatively flat thus providing an ideal topography for the current Dulles Airport. Proceeding westward one encounters a series of undulating folds, a preview of the Appalachians, which occupy much of West Virginia. The Catoctins stretch through the middle of Loudoun but westerners would regard this as a mere foothill. Running parallel and a few miles back are the Short Hills which in the north dips in the Potomac and reforms in Maryland as South Mountain of Civil War fame. Finally, there is the Blue Ridge which proscribes the western limits of Loudoun and the beginning of West Virginia.

In between these moderate ranges are the valleys, gently rolling farmland drained by several streams which flow north to the Potomac. The soil for the most part is fertile, occasionally composed of Chester loam capable in the past of making Loudoun a national leader in orchard grass seed production and a state leader in dairying (today only one dairy farm remains)

Of course, there are many villages which dot the landscape. Examining the maps it seems that some of these settlements have simply disappeared and in some cases the names have been changed. Most however have expanded and prospered, particularly the county's centerpiece, Leesburg, which is now a small city.

The above paragraphs thus describe a setting for the following pages. The book, however, is less about a place than it is about the people in it and more than that what the people read from the local press more than a century ago. Editorials, current happenings, announcements, ads, obits, feature articles, jokes, etc. copied from the microfilm are arranged in a roughly chronological pattern.

The period itself was a rather benign one in our nation's history – twenty years after the great Civil War and over a decade before the next conflict. The so-called "gilded age" in this community it was not. The selected articles encompass the local as well as the national, the mundane as well as the significant, the humorous as well as the somber, the little guy as well as the important person. Hopefully with this approach the reader will gain a feel for the era as well as a simple knowledge of the incidents.

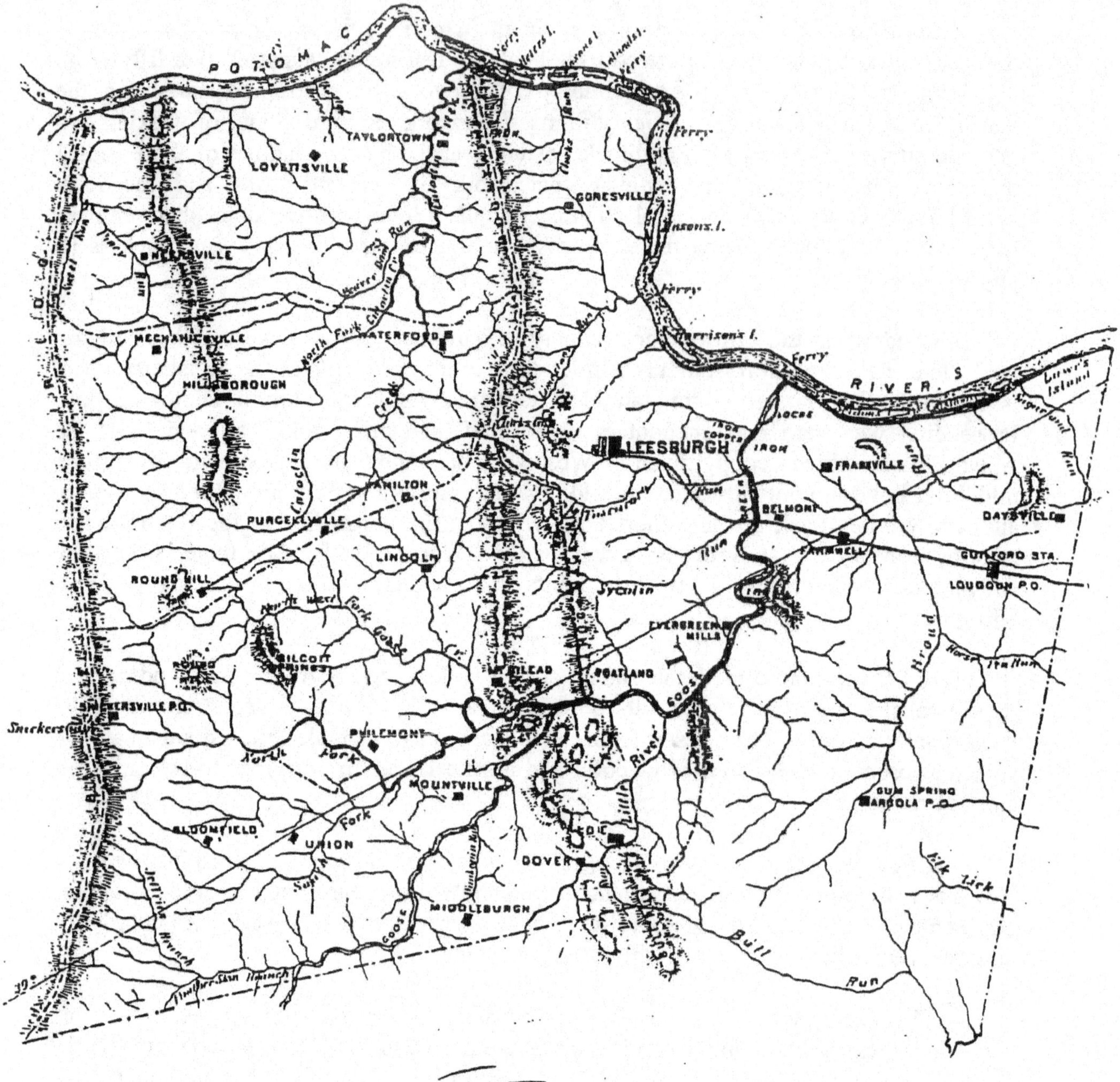

MAP OF LOUDOUN CO.
VIRGINIA.

1883. H.H.HARDESTY, PUBLISHER.

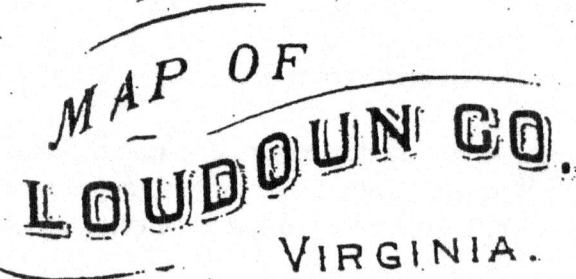

THE WASHINGTONIAN.

THE MIRROR.

The Loudoun Telephone

A description of the three local newspapers is in order. The oldest "The Washingtonian" first began publishing in 1808. It was edited in the 1880's by Captain William Lynch, a confederate veteran.

"The Mirror", like the Washingtonian, was published in Leesburtg and its editor was Benjamin Sheetz. It began in 1855, but both of these papers had to suspend operations in the Civil War due to a lack of paper and labor. These two were competitors but seemed to be on friendly terms and both voted faithfully the Democratic line. In those days, at least in Virginia, the Democrats were the conservatives and the Republicans, the liberals. Their editorials were usually sensible and well-expressed. Both papers were destined to join forces in 1903.

In nearby Hamilton in 1878 "The Telephone" began publication. It was of course named after the recent invention and was edited by a young Quaker Yardley Brown. In my opinion "The Telephone" is the most interesting of the three for it had an imaginative format, more modern graphics, an almost conversational relationship with the local news and superior outside sources. It was years ahead of its time in civil rights concerns. Most interesting of all were its editorials which were not at all subtle.

The Telephone was a Republican paper often expressing its partisan views in an "in your face" type of rhetoric. Its main focus, however, seemed to be the burgeoning temperance movement. It hated the Democrats (the bourbons) only a little less than the saloon keepers of Leesburg. Judging from most accounts of the day the alcohol problem was a genuine concern.

The news articles are copied from the microfilm and move in a rough chronological sequence. The ads, however, all from the same three newspapers and from the 1880's decade, are not necessarily from the same month as the accompanying articles.

The Country Newspaper

Before proceeding with the news of the 1880's, we should examine the opinions of two newspaper editors of that period. The first describes the rather unfortunate outcome of a local weekly, edited by a highly principled and passionate person whose experience was nil and whose business sense was apparently deficient. The second article by a big city editor provides a rather sympathetic overview of the small town press of that time.

April 1st, 1874 – The Mirror

A Touching Obituary.

The *Daily Argus* of Leavenworth, is no more. The editor of the *Argus* in writing the obituary of his paper, sums up the history of his enterprise in the following racy fashion.

"About four months ago we took possession of this paper. It was then in the very act of pegging out, and we breathed in it four months more life then it otherwise would have had had we not taken possession of it. Having neither friends, money, nor credit, we put into it all our surplus cash, and every dollar of our friends that we could get, but as everybody will see it is no go. We presume our enemies will rejoice, especially Simon Abide, D. R. Anthony, and W. McNeil Clough, but we have had the satisfaction of ventilating Simon and Daniel to our fullest extent. We did it because we believed them both to be villians of the deepest dye. Either the people of the city don't appreciate our efforts, or we don't know how to run a paper. We went into the business determined to run it or bust. We have busted. During our connection with the *Argus* we have made some friends and numerous enemies. The former will have our gratitude while life lasts; the latter are affectionally requested to go to hell. With these few remarks we take our leave of public life, and now propose to enter into a field of more usefulness and if God is willing we will never go into the newspaper business again."

JAN. 25, 1884.

THE COUNTRY EDITOR.

The country editor has a hard road to travel. He is the reporter, bookkeeper, mechanical-superintendent, business manager, collector, mailing machine and soliciting agent of the establishment. His work is hard, his receipts small and his creditors numerous. In a small town an editor has to steer his course so as to avoid giving offense to different circles of society, the religious denominations, the business community, and the rural population. If an influential old farmer wants a three-column notice of his new barn, it must appear or the editor may lose a hundred subscribers. Patchwork quilts, big beets and phenomenal eggs also clamor for space in the columns of the country paper. In the course of time the rural scribe becomes either jocose or morose; but in either frame of mind he continues to make friends who demand free advertising, and enemies who work against him.

The country editor is always getting ready to abandon journalism for something else, but he rarely carries out his threat. He generally dies in harness. In some wild communities editors occasionally meet with rough treatment. Sometimes they are driven out of the country, and when other methods of getting rid of they fail, they are sent to the legislature. The city editor gets a good deal of fun out of the country editor's work, but the man who bears the burden regards it as a serious business. And in the best sense it is serious. The little local weeklies scattered all over the country are in their way potential factors of civilization.— They develop their localities, bring their resources before the public and in a manner educate their readers. They are always on the side of the churches, the schools, progress and reform. Men who live and die working for such objects are public benefactors and deserve a substantial reward.—*Atlanta Constitution.*

January, 1880

THE MIRROR

BENJ. F. SHEETZ, Editor.

Thursday Morning, Jan. 1, '80

1880!

As we write, the old, old Chronicler in the belfry of Time, is tolling the funeral dirge of 1879. Slowly, sadly, sorrowfully falls the sound upon the midnight air. And as the mournful notes are borne across the broad bosom of mother earth, announcing to the children of men that the "old year is dying," there comes pealing forth from the same ponderous voice, a lighter, a merrier, and a more joyful refrain, which heralds the birth of a New King—that in genealogical order, is christened 1880.

1/1/80 Mirror

CHRISTMAS DAY was dark, rainy, and generally disagreeable. To many it was a day of festivity and joy—to others, a season of sadness and sorrowful recollections. There was no snow, no sleigh, no cold weather, no ice—and we have rarely witnessed a more quiet and orderly observance of the occasion. To day, every body has turned over a new leaf—which it is to be hoped they will keep unspotted through the year—and settled down to the realities of life 'till the return of another Christmas. We wish our patrons and friends a happy New Year.

1/1/80 Mirror

Mrs. Spronce of Augusta county, aged 102 years, started last week to walk to her sons near Ivy Depot in Albemarle. She walked from Buffalo Gap as far as Fisherville, sixteen miles, when the people of that neighborhood got up a sum of money and paid her fare on the railway to her destination.

1/8/80 Mirror

CAPT. H TUDOR TUCKER has recently returned from Richmond, where he had a very successful operation performed for cataract of the eye, by Dr. Hunter McGuire, Prof. of Surgery in the Medical College of Va. Captain Tucker's sight has been entirely restored to the eye operated on. He went to the Retreat for the Sick—the Hospital under the management of the ladies of the different Churches of Richmond—where he had the last attention possible, and fared sumptuously every day, upon very moderate terms, which, he says, are regulated according to the pecuniary ability of the patient, even to the bestowal of charity

Dr. McGuire's skill has given Capt. T. perfect sight from a state of total blindness. We need not leave Virginia to find the highest order of medical talent.

(Dr. Hunter McGuire was Stonewall Jackson's chief surgeon. Later he helped found the Medical College of Virginia and was President of the American Medical Association.)

January 1880

1/10/80 Washingtonian

THE FRIENDS of Mr. F. M. HENDERSON, who for a number of years has filled the position of Commissioner of the Circuit and County courts of this county, will regret to learn, that from some cause, his mind has become so much impaired, as to require his removal to the Asylum at Staunton.

He was a faithful and conscientious public officer, honest and true in every sense of the word. As a business man, he discharged as best he could, every duty assigned him, and as long as his health permitted, was an active, earnest christian worker in the church to which he belonged. We, with his many friends, lament his affliction, and hope he will soon be restored to health and his business again.

1/15/80 Mirror

THE last annual report of the Western Lunatic Asylum, at Staunton, shows that during the fiscal year ending Sept. 30, 1879, there were 532 patients of which 278 were females, the per capita cost of supporting whom was $135.97.

Of the patients admitted since the opening of the Asylum, five men are reported as "persons not insane," and the fact is thus explained in the report:

As some may be curious to know how sane persons get into the asylum, we state that one was an inebriate, one an opium eater, and another eccentric, all three being thought by their friends to be insane. The fourth was suffering with the delirium of typhoid fever, and the fifth, who had violated the law, was committed by advice of his counsel with a view to pleading insanity in his defence.

MILL PROPERTY
FOR SALE.

(being the first day of County Court) at about 12 o'clock, M., all the lands whereof the late J. T. Megeath died seized in the bill and proceedings mentoined, viz:

Gritland Mills

with about 30 ACRES OF LAND attached, situated about one and a half miles from Mountsvile, Va., on Goose Creek.
The MILL is a substantial, well finished structure, Gearing and Fixtures commplete and has a fine run of custom. The water power is excellent and there is a Comfortable DWELLING HOUSE, &c., on the premises.

1/31/80 Washingtonian

A Card from General Early.

Whenever it shall become necessary to defend my character against the aspersions of such creatures as Thomas B. Claiborne or his associates in or out of the Legislature, then that character will not be worth defending. As a matter of course, when I gave the written statement in regard to the character of that man, I expected the whole pack of his supporters—

"Both mongrel, puppy, whelp, and hound,
And curs of low degree"—

to open on me, and have not been disappointed. I think, however, I recognize in the assaults on me the inspiration of a man who has not the moral or physical courage to do that which he prompts his tools to undertake. The only response I have to make to the vituperation of the whole clan, from the head to the tail, is that whenever such men shall undertake to praise me my friends will have reason to begin to doubt me. I do not fear their denunciations.

(Typically old cantankerous Jubal.)

SLEIGH BASKETS!

LARGE STOCK! LOW PRICES!! These BASKETS are made with the lower half RATAN, consequently are much more substantial than when they are all Willow.
dec 12.   SHROFF & CO.

January, 1880

1/22/80 Mirror

THE CASE OF FITZ JOHN PORTER.—The committee on military affairs in the House of Representatives, have reported a bill for the relief of Gen. Fitz John Porter, who in 1863 was court marshaled for disobedience of orders, and dismissed from the service. The bill sets aside the sentence, and restores Gen. P. to his old position, or at the option of Porter, empowers the President to place him on the retired list with the rank of Major-General. The fifth section of the bill, which related to arrearages of pay, was stricken out and a new section inserted, which reads as follows:

"The Secretary of the Treasury shall pay to Fitz John Porter, late major general of volunteers and brigadier general of the United States army, out of any money in the treasury not otherwise appropriated, the sum of $75,000, which sum is hereby awarded him by the government of the United States as a measure of amends, in acknowledgment of the wrong done to and suffered by him," &c.

(Porter was court-marshaled by General Pope in the battle of Second Manassas. Down through the years he fought this decision through the courts and finally, at least officially, he won his reputation back and then some. The popularity of Porter and the unpopularity of the commanding General might had had something to do with this.)

1/22/80 Mirror

DEATH FROM HYDROPHOBIA.—Mr. R. G. Alexander, of Wilmington, Delaware, was a few weeks ago bitten in the face by a strange hound. Mr. A. was fearful at the time that the dog had hydrophobia, and at once resorted to various remedies. On Thursday morning, however, when he went to wash, he found that he experienced an aversion to water that he could not overcome. He ate a hearty breakfast, but could drink nothing, and stoutly maintained that nothing ailed him.— He refused to have a doctor called in until he had a spasm. The fangs of the dog had torn the cartilage of the nose and the first symptoms of the disease in such cases is a morbid feeling in the wound. Soon after this, the spasms became violent and to soothe the patient strong opiates were presented but he could not swallow. Toward evening he became very violent, but after the spasm begged to be killed and pleaded with those present to leave the room or he might unknowingly bite them. The spasms grew more pronounced and frequent and finally it required the united force of six men to hold him. He died in great agony just forty five days after being first bitten. A general outbreak of hydrophobia is feared in the neighborhood, as many dogs were bitten by the dog that caused Alexander's death

Just Out.

Hood's Great Book of the War

ADVANCE AND RETREAT,

Personal Experiences in the United States and Confederate States Armies,

BY GENERAL J. B. HOOD,

Late Lieutenant-General Confederate States Army, published for the

Hood Orphan Memorial Fund

THE entire proceeds arising from the sale of this work are devoted to The Hood Orphan Memorial Fund, which is invested in United States Registered Bonds for the nurture, care, support and education of the ten infants deprived of their parents last summer at New Orleans, (the melancholy incidents of which sad bereavement are still fresh in the public mind.)

For TERMS, RATES TO AGENTS, etc, Address with full particulars,

Gen. G. T. BEAUREGARD.

Publisher, on behalf of The Hood Memorial Fund NEW ORLEANS, LA.

John Bell Hood, who died the year before, had lost an arm at Gettysburg and a leg at Chickamauga. In the opinion of many, this very brave general was a not a good tactitian above the brigade level. Lee regarded him as "all lion, no fox." He later had 11 children in 10 years – 3 sets of twins. Sadly, he lost all of his money to poor investments and thus we have solicitations from former comrades and good citizens to support these children.

DAVIS SWING CHURN

Among the benefits to be derived from its use are:

It does not require one half the labor to use it that other churns do.

It makes more are better butter.

It is very easy to clean and is the most durable churn made.

Butter Workers,

are one of the *Greatest Labor-Saving Machine invented*. They save many minutes, working the butter quickly and more thoroughly than can be done by hand.

January 1880

MARE STOLEN.

I HAD Stolen from my Stable, near Farmwell Station, on Arundles Farm, on FRIDAY night, 16th inst., a small SORREL MARE, tolerable thin, hind feet White and a Blaze in her Face, and a small Scar in her right Flank, a lump on the top of head as if she had had Pole-evil.

FIVE DOLLARS REWARD will be given for recovery of this Mare, or for information which will enable me to get her, or Ten dollars for the Mare and Thief.

CHARLES J. GREEN,

jan. 24 3t*   Farmwell, P O.

1/24/80 Washingtonian

☞ The bill for the erection of a Free Bridge, across the Potomac, at Georgetown, which has been managed by Gen. Eppa Hunton, passed the House of Representatives, on Wednesday last. This will form an important improvement to this section of Virginia.

1/22/80 Mirror

A MEAN THEFT.—Last Tuesday night, a thief or thieves entered the kitchen of PATRICK GILL, a worthy old man living on the suburbs of town, and cleaned out his meat barrel. The old man recently slaughtered and salted down four nice hogs, and the rogues carried off all but three pieces—together with the offal, sausage, and about four gallons of lard. The man mean enough to rob Patrick would steal his blind grandmother's dinner.

1/1/80 Mirror

HOW TO GROW RICH.—Nothing is more easy than to grow rich. It is only to trust nobody—to befriend none—to get all you can and save all you get—to stint yourself and everybody belonging to you—to be the friend of no man, and have no man for your friend—to heap interest upon interest, cent upon cent—to be mean, miserable and despised for some twenty or thirty years—and riches will come as sure as disease, disappointment and death.

1/24/80 Washingtonian

A story is told of a clergyman in a Massachusetts town who forgot his notes on a Sabbath morning, and as it was too late to send for them, he said to his audience, by way of apology, that this morning he should have to depend upon the Lord for what he might say, but in the afternoon he would come better prepared.

THE UNEQUALLED

Excelsior Hot Blast Cook!

Go To J. E. Brenner's

MIDDLEBURG, VA.,

AND EXAMINE his Mammoth Stock of STOVES—the Largest and Finest Assortment in Loudoun or adjoining counties! Over ONE HUNDRED to select from!—including the following IMPROVED STYLES—

THE IRON KING, CAMBRIDGE, EXCELSIOR and ROSSMORE,
with Reservoirs and Double Ovens;

THE FARMER GIRL, CHAMPION, ELMORE, EXCELSIOR and ORANGE.
with Single Ovens

THE PARLOR SUN AND SUNLIGHT,
(Fire-place Heators.) Handsomely Nickle-Plated

THE ARGAND, STAR KING, ST. NICHOLOUS, DUPLEX, and TRIPLETTE,
Plain and Nickle-Plated;

—ALSO A FULL LINE OF—

OFFICE, STORE & CHAMBER STOVES.

FOR WOOD OR COAL.

☞ Before purchasing elsewhere, please call and examine my Stock and Prices, (or send for List,) which will compare with any house in the city.

☞ STOVES DELIVERED and put up, at short notice.   Very Respectfully,

J. E. BRENNER.

January, 1880

1/29/80 Mirror

ANOTHER JAIL DELIVERY—TWO PRISONERS MAKE THEIR ESCAPE, AND TWO OTHERS ON THE EDGE OF DELIVERANCE.—About 12 o'clock Tuesday night, as Mr. WILLIAM NIXON, the jailor's son, was entering the house, his attention was attracted by a noise in the jail yard, as of some one jumping. He aroused other members of the family and upon repairing to the cell occupied by Page Wallace, awaiting trial on the charge of attempted rape—Samuel Robinson, for murder, and two others for minor offences, they discovered a hole in the wall, through which Wallace, and a man named Adams, had emerged into the jail yard, from whence, by means of two or three blankets tied together, they had scaled the brick wall surrounding the yard, and made their escape. Robinson and another prisoner, were found in the cell, but the impression of Mr. Nixon is that they, too, had gotten into the yard, but were frightened back by his accidental arrival.

It seems that the cell in which the prisoners were confined is lined with two inch oak plank, the joints of which had shrunk, leaving an opening of about half an inch. Into this crack they had inserted the leg of the stove and prized off the board; behind this lining was an old door opening into the yard and with the board they had wrenched off, they had broken the hinges of the old door and walked out. Once in the yard the scaling of the wall was comparatively an easy process, and up to the hour of this writing nothing has been heard of the fugitives.

The frequency with which prisoners escape from our county prison indicates a want of security that should be speedily remedied by the authorities, even to the erection, if necessary, of a new building.

$50 REWARD

WILL be paid for the apprehension of PAGE WALLACE, recently escaped from the County Jail of Loudoun Co., Va.

PAGE WALLACE is a copper colored negro, face slightly bleached by confinement in Jail, and with many pimples on it—no beard; about five feet eight inches tall, and thick set—was poorly clad when he escaped.

☞ The above Reward is offered by the Governor of Virginia in the name of the Commonwealth.

J. W. FOSTER.
Commonwealth's Attorney, for Loudoun Co.
January 30, 1880-tf.

1/15/80 Mirror

One of the pluckiest men in the medical profession is Dr. South, of Western Texas.— He was warned some time ago that he would have to pay with his life the forfeit of having voted as a member of a grand jury for the indictment of a certain band of desperadoes. One night a man rode up to his ranch and informed him that the wife of the ringleader of the gang was ill, and that he must attend her. He naturally thought that it was a trick to get him out and kill him, but he got his horse and rode away with the messenger right among the gang of desperadoes, and, dismounting, entered the tent of the woman. There lay the sufferer, while the men who had promised to kill the physician stood near by. The doctor drew his revolver, placed it on the pillow, and remarked that he would "attend to professional calls first and personal ones afterwards." The desperadoes were impressed with his courage and his humanity, and trebled his fees instead of shooting him.

Pro Bono Publico!

HAVING recently purchased the

Eagle Hotel

adjoining the EAGLE RESTAURANT, we have removed our stock and business thereto. In our

New Place of Business

we have a commodious and elegant DINING ROOM, where MEALS, TO ORDER, will be SERVED AT

All Hours.

OYSTERS, and other delicacies, in every style, during their seasons!

We continue to be Agents for the celebrated.

POP CORN WHISKEY,

and shall keep constantly on hand, for sale on draught,

Milwaukee Beer.

We shall be happy to receive calls from our old patrons and friends.

GEO. H. NIXON & BRO.

T. T. HAYDOCK
CINCINNATI, O.

1/29/80 Mirror

Does Farming Pay?

Mr. John W. Grantham, of Jefferson county, West Virginia, answers the above question in the following letter, which we find in the Shepherdstown *Register*:

"I have heard so much about agricultural depression, and land not yielding more than 3 per cent., that I am inclined to send you statement of our farming for 1879. Land properly cultivated will yield as much profit as any legitimate business we can engage in ; much better than banking, as I know from experience. But for the statement. My son and I have a small farm that cost us $7095.00. Last year we had 58 acres in wheat and 34 in corn, and raised 1314 bushels wheat and 220 barrels corn. We sold from the farm as follows:

998 bushels wheat at 98c.,	$978.00
105 bushels wheat at $1.50,	157.50
30 lambs, at $3.00,	90.00
4 lambs, for	7.00
268 pounds wool, at 28½c.,	75.91
44 barrels corn, $2.25 per bbl.,	99.00
11 fat hogs,	126.92
Profit on 4 cattle sold,	30.00
Profit on one horse sold,	53.00
Rent of tenant house,	30.00
Total,	$1,647.35

EXPENSES.

Hire of 1 hand 10 mo., $10,	$100.00
Hire of 1 hand 10 mo., $7,	70.00
Hire extra labor,	3.00
Harvesting 26 a. with reaper,	15.00
Harvesting 27 a. with cradles,	36.00
Threshing and cleaning wheat,	20.50
Taxes,	80.65
2 tons offal for sheep,	34.00
Blacksmith bill,	39.50
Wheelwright bill,	14.30
Fertilizer,	154.00
4 tons plaster,	26.00
Total,	$593.55

Besides, we kept 110 bushels wheat for bread ; salted up over 4,000 pounds of pork, and had the milk, butter, eggs and poultry—I do not count hay and oats because we fed them.

(Farms in this area, at this time, were mostly general farms with little specialization. There were, however, over seventy mills in Loudoun County which would provide outlets for the surplus grain raised. Dairying was just a few years in the future for Loudoun County. Newly completed rail facilities would foster the building of creameries and the resultant shipping of milk products to Washington city.)

1/29/80 Mirror

"Bob" Ingersoll Before a Jury.

"Bob" Ingersoll is said to be exceedingly effective before a jury, and many stories are told of his triumphs as a special pleader when he was a criminal lawyer in Illinois. On one occasion, years ago, he was engaged in that State as counsel for a farmer who had quarreled with a neighbor and shot him dead.— The evidence was plain and direct on that point, though there was nothing to show that the prisoner had not believed that he was acting in self-defense. When Ingersoll was addressing the jury he drew a pathetic picture of the prisoner's wife and children—he had declined to allow them to be present at the trial, as a less sagacious advocate might have done—waiting in eager expectation for his return, confident that he would be acquitted of a crime which he would not and could not have committed except to save his own life.

"I see the wife now," continued the shrewd barrister, "standing at the door of her home, the sunlight on her hair, straining her eyes after the figure of the man dearer than all the world to her. I see his little boys swinging on the gate, with smiles about their lips, gazing down the road, watching for their beloved, innocent father, and sure that he is coming.— They are all ready, the dear little fellows, to jump down, run after him, leap into his arms, and kiss away the sadness—the shadow of his unfortunate deed—while they cry : "Dear, dear father, we knew you would come!"— And, gentlemen of the jury, you who are yourselves husband and fathers, won't you let him go home?"

The members of the jury were listening with wet eyes, and leaning toward the eloquent advocate. The foreman, a big, brawny, simple-hearted farmer, the tears on his sunburned cheeks, was so carried away that, thinking the question addressed personally to him and demanding an answer, exclaimed in a choking voice, "Yes, Bob, we'll let him go home!" Ingersoll had not half completed his argument, but he knew that was the supreme moment, and so down. The prosecuting attorney made a long speech in reply, but it was, of course, entirely vain. The jury, after being out five minutes, returned a unanimous verdict for acquittal.

(Ingersol was probably the most famous agnostic of the day. The local papers at times referred to him as the "infidel Ingersol.")

HORSES BROKEN

TO RIDE AND DRIVE.

I desire to announce that I am prepared to break colts to ride and drive—in single and double harness, at

From $10 to $15 Each.

Apply to   J. W. LOVE,

4-jan-tf.   1½ miles South of Hillsboro, Va.

February, 1880

2/5/80 Mirror

COMMONWEALTH vs. SAMUEL J ROBINSON.

For the Murder of Edward Thomas,

Who Was Shot in this County, on the night of the 23d of October, on the road from Lincoln to the Aldie Turnpike.

Found Guilty of Murder in the Frst Degree.

Sentenced to be Hanged, in the Jail Yard on Friday Morning April 9th 1880, between the Hours of Six and Eight o'clock.

The Trial Commenced on Wednesday last.

After motions for continuance, on the part of the accused, had been submitted and overruled, the jury was empaneled and sworn, the indictment read, and the prisoner pleaded "not guilty."

Capt. Foster, Attorney for the Commonwealth, in his opening remarks to the Jury, informed them that this was a case of murder by lying in wait, that he expected to establish the guilt of the prisoner at the bar, by circumstantial evidence, the only kind of evidence usually attainable in such cases, circumstances which, slight in themselves, like single strands formed when united, a rope that would completely enclose the prisoner and establish the proof. He expected to show to the jury; the corpus delicti, that Thomas had been shot on the night of Oct. 23d, that the prisoner had a motive for the murder, and malice towards the accused having had a previous quarrel with the deceased, and harboring purposes of revenge, that the prisoner was near the place of the murder at the time of the murder, that he had in his posession a gun showing evidences of having been recently used, that he gave a false account as to the discharge of the weapon, and his whereabouts, that tracks made at the place of the murder corresponded to the shoes of the accused, and that the prisoner was confronted with the dying man, and that he, the dying man, there in his dying declaration declared that this man murdered him, and gave the particulars and minutiæ. Capt. Foster then commented upon the kind of conviction of the prisoners guilt necessary for a verdict against him.

Maj Orr for the defence, commented upon the responsibility resting on the jury and council for the defence, begged the jury to be careful to put away that unconscious impression, that one accused of crime is guilty, until he establishes his innocance. Said that the more serious the charge the more careful should be the investigation, and the fuller and clearer the proof. That circumstantial evidence is the most perilous sort of evidence, that circumstances were often misunderstood and misinterpreted and exhorted the jury to examine every strap of the rope of evidence as rigidly as if their own lives depended on this trial. He said further that it would be shown to the jury, that Edward Thomas was engaged in the business of gambling and in the illicit sale of whiskey, and must have many enemies, that Thomas was a convicted felon, his oath would be inadmissible and so his dying declarations. He dwelt upon the point that the prisoner's guilt must be established free from a reasonable doubt, and that he must not be convicted on what was at best but a strong suspicion.

THE EVIDENCE.

J. W. Logan, for the commonwealth, testified that he last saw Ed Thomas, on the 23d, Oct, lying on the road where he had been shot, on the North Fork road a short distance from the Snickersville Turnpike, he was perfectly helpless, lying flat on his back, without use of himself from his shoulders down, still had use of his voice, sent for Dr. Chamblin, got blankets and made him more comfortable, left him in charge of the Doctor There was a bag with him, but I do not know contents. His wounds, were bleeding but little but there had been considerable loss of blood.

Dr. L L Chamblin, physician, saw Ed Thomas on Oct. 23d. about sunrise, he was mortally wounded, shot in the back of the neck, a little to the left. It was a gunshot wound, the charge was a little scattered, some shot were close together, counted 26 in the region of the spine. The man who shot him must have been to the left and behind him. There was with him a bag containing a small lot of whiskey, containing about two gallons.

Albert Cockrille, was on the night of murder riding home about 10 o'clock, after passing place of murder, 200 yards, met a man going that way, the man was walking along openly and didn't seem to be hiding, spoke to him, but the man did'nt answer, asked Henry Furr with whom he was riding who it was and he said Sam Robinson, three quarters of a mile beyond met another person, supposed to be Ed Thomas; can't swear to the identity of either party, knew Robinson,

February, 1880

Joseph Ball (colored,) Sam was playing cards until too dark to see in Otley's field, then went to Ed. Thomas,' Sam and Ed. had some conversation, didn't know what, nothing in their manner showed any difficulty between them. Witness knew of none, Ed. said he must lock up his house, everybody knew Ed. was going to Snickersville, witness went in the house to play cards, Sam did not—witness did not know where he went. Sam had on light suit of clothes like the ones he is now wearing, don't remember the hat.

The prosecution then closed its case with leave reserved to introduce one more witness to-morrow.

For the Defence, the first witness was too drunk to testify, and was sent to jail to sober off.

Walter Osburn testified that dec'd left his store after buying 2 gallons of whiskey about seven o'clock, the night of the 22d, did not look at watch, it might have been 8 o'clock, but he thinks it was not much after 7.

Henry Stewart, Robinson had on that evening the clothes (light)—that he has on now He has been wearing them ever since we commenced to gamble together, more than a year ago. We don't dress up, because we don't go to church like all good people do.

Ann Eliza Robinson, child of the accused aged 9 years, was next put upon the stand. She testified that her father came home a little after dark, went up to Uncle Harry Jackson's stayed a few minutes, came back home ate his supper, and went to bed, that she stayed awake *five hours* after that, that she sleeps by the side of her father's bed. The cross examination then asked who told her to say so and so, she said her mother told her when asked to talk loud, and to say that her father came home, went to Uncle Harry's ate and went to bed—that she sat up.

The Judge then told the jury that they were sole judges of the credit to be given to the child's story, but cautioned them, if they should disbelieve her, against letting her story prejudice them against the prisoner.

So closed the 1st day's proceedings.

J. Taylor recalled by prosecution, exhibited a Gun found in the posession of prisoner when found looked as if it had been recently discharged, judged from the appearance of the tube; prisoner said he had shot it at a squirrel that morning; he knows the gun by certain marks, will swear to identity of the gun as one he gave to the Commonwealth Attorney. Capt. Foster swore that it was the identical gun Taylor brought him.

Harry Jackson (col), brought back from the jail after having sobered off lives 200 yards from prisoner, saw the prisoner come into his house, I think about 7 o'clock, stayed a short time, four or five minutes, he was sober—didn't notice his clothes, tolerably light night—moon under clouds. It was about an hour after dark

Jesse McIlhenny (col'd) for prosecution. The week before the killing, heard Robinson say that as sure as he was a living man he would get him; it was during a quarrel between Sam and Ed. Thomas said clear out I want no more to do with you. Both were angry Told Stuart that he knew nothing worth coming to court about, didn't consider this worth coming to court for.

Henry Stuart (recalled)—Jesse McIlhenny said to witness that he knew nothing about it.

J. W. Garrett—For last three years prisoner has been living on my land and behaved well, paid his rent punctually—his general reputation is that of a man of peaceful and quiet demeanor, doesn't have company loitering around his house have seen him under influence of liquor, never beastly drunk.

J. L. Chamblin has known prisoner, his general reputation in the neighborhood is not good, said to be addicted to cards, bad company, doesn't think he lived over 50 yards from Harry Jackson, prisoner lived a little over 2 miles from scene of murder, knows nothing about his temper when drinking.

Commonwealth in rebuttal.

Henry Furr, (colored,) reputation as a peaceable and orderly man, not good associates with bad company, and drinks and plays.

Greg Furr (colored,) reputation as a peaceable &c. not very good, drinks some, sometimes seen drunk—said to be a bad tempered don't know whether he beats his wife.

Alfred Bell (col.) Cant say he is peaceable drinking and gambling raises h—ll when he is drunk—don't know his Honesty.

At the conclusion of the evidence, the council, Mr. Orr for the defence and Capt. Foster for the State, presented the case to the jury in able speeches, fully reviewing all the facts bearing upon it.

The case was given to the jury about 8 o'clock, Thursday night, on Friday morning when the jury was called, they stated that they did not understand that the case had been given them for the verdict and had not agreed upon one.

About half past two o'clock, the jury returned, and after the usual forms, answered that they had found the prisoner guilty of murder in the first degree. The jury, at the request of prisoner's counsel, was polled, and each answered "guilty of murder in the 1st degree."

The Judge then said 'You have had a fair and impartial trial by a jury of your country, and found guilty of murder in the first degree as alleged in the indictment, and the sentence of the Court is 'That you be taken to the jail of this county and confined there until the 9th day of April 1880, and then between the hours of 6 and 8 o'clock A. M. be taken to the jail yard, and hung by the neck until dead. May the Lord have mercy on your soul.'

PAGE WALLACE.

PARTICULARS OF HIS BRUTAL LUST

HIS PURSUIT AND CAPTURE.

His Confinement in the Hagerstown Jail, Awaiting the Requisition of the Governor of Virginia.

A DARING SCOUNDREL.—Last week we announced the breaking of the jail in this town and the escape of PAGE WALLACE, a somewhat notorious colored character, confined therein, and awaiting trial under an indictment for attempted rape upon a white woman. The Governor offered a reward of $50 for his apprehension, and strong hopes were entertained that he would be speedily captured; but before it was generally known throughout the county that he was at large, news was received that on Thursday night he had assaulted another white woman on this side of the river opposite the Pt. of Rocks, accomplished his hellish purpose, and then escaped into Maryland. We understand that a band of determined men have for the past few days been scouring the country for him, and have once or twice been warm on his trail—among them two or three near relatives of the outraged woman.

THE PARTICULARS OF HIS CRIME

It seems that a white woman living near the Old Furnace in this county, had on Thursday gone over the river into Maryland. Returning in the evening, she reached the Virginia shore between 7 and 8 o'clock, and was proceeding alone to her home, a mile and a half distant. When about a quarter of a mile from the river "she was caught round the arms from behind by some one, and thinking it was John Ambrose one of the ferry men, whom she had left at the ferry, exclaimed: "Why, John, what do you mean?" The unknown person told her to keep quiet or he would kill her. Turning her head, she discovered it was a negro. She screamed out, "John, come here quick, some one has got hold of me." The negro then struck her several severe blows in the face, threw her down and threatened to kill her and throw her in the river if she made any further noise.—Under this threat she desisted but continued to struggle, until her strength failed, and she sank back exhausted. He then accomplished his purpose, and left her lying in the road.—

He made his way to the ferry, broke loose a boat and rowed to the Maryland shore and made his escape. When the woman recovered she proceeded to a neighbor's house, and was soon afterwards joined by Ambrose, to whom she related the affair. The next morning several persons visited the spot where the ravisher had accomplished his deed and tracked him to the river and up the canal to the first lock. He had on a pair of boots with heel taps and rough nails on the sole, and wore a white hat with spots on it, his hat and boots corresponding with the ones he had on when he broke jail.

His victim, it is said, was badly bruised, one eye being entirely closed, and she was for several days confined to her bed from the injuries received. The mountains and surrounding country was scoured by armed men, until Monday morning, when the following story of

HIS CAPTURE, AND NARROW ESCAPE FROM LYNCHING

was furnished the Baltimore GAZETTE of Tuesday, by a correspondent who wrote from Sharpsburg, Md., on Monday night:

"Intense excitement was occasioned here to day by the unexpected capture of Page Wallace, the colored man who outraged Miss Mary Morman, living in Virginia, near the point of Rocks ferry. Early this morning a brother of the outraged lady accompanied by a man named Reynolds while walking along the river bank near Harper's Ferry, saw Wallace on the opposite bank and fired several shots at him. He succeeded in escaping and made his way to this place. About 3 o'clock in the afternoon, while a number of men were congregated in a saloon, Wallace entered and proceeded to drink heavily. He was soon in a state of intoxication, and in the midst of a burst of drunken hilarity boasted of his terrible crime. He was at once seized by the bystanders to whom he admitted his guilt and removed to jail. Later in the evening, when news of his capture became known the greatest indignation against him was manifested, and threats of lynching were freely made. Finally, the authorities, fearing that violence would be resorted to, sent him under a strong guard to Hagerstown, where he was lodged in jail.

IN JAIL IN HAGERSTOWN

Immediately upon the arrival in Leesburg of the GAZETTE containing the above, Sheriff Carruthers telegraphed to the Sheriff of Washington county, Md., and on Wednesday morning received the following answer:

HAGERSTOWN, MD., Feb. 3, 1880.

J. E. CARRUTHERS, *Sheriff of Loudoun County, Va:*

Page Wallace is in jail here. Will hold for requisition. F. K. ZEIGLER, Sheriff.

February, 1880

HAGERSTOWN, MD., Feb. 3, 1880.
J. E. CARRUTHERS, *Sheriff of Loudoun County Va:*

Page Wallace is in jail here. Will hold for requisition. F. K. ZEIGLER, Sheriff.

REQUISITION FROM THE GOVERNOR.

Gov. Holliday was at once notified, and will no doubt promptly issue his requisition on the Governor of Maryland for the rendition of Wallace into the hands of the Virginia authorities, when he will, probably be returned to the jail of this county to await a criminal prosecution.

2/12/80 Mirror

PAGE WALLACE is still held in the Hagerstown jail, awaiting the requisition of the Governor of Virginia for his delivery to the authorities of this State. The apprehension at first entertained that the prisoner would be taken from the jail there and forcibly dealt with, has subsided, and the law will probably be observed on both sides the river.

DIED:

Suddenly at his mother's residence, Hamilton Va., February 8th, 1880, of consumption, J. C. JANNEY, in the 29th year of his age.

This great destroyer of thousands in their prime had been preying upon him for years. Serious results were, more than a year ago, anticipated, but under kind and judicious treatment he rallied, and his friends began to think that he might be spared to them for many years. But all the while, the disease was slowly drinking up his life, which, quite recently, became manifest, yet no one thought that he would so soon follow his remains to the tomb. But, on Friday last, the sun shone with such warmth and beauty, and the air seemed to be so calm that he ventured out, to feast upon nature, as she looked so lovely in her snowy robes, not for a moment thinking it the last time he would view his native hills, yet it was true. The exposure was too great. He sank rapidly from that time until Sunday evening at 9 o'clock, when he expired.

The funeral services took place at his home, Tuesday, at 11 o'clock, A. M. Rev. P. H. Miller, who was his college and classmate for five years, officiated. From thence quite a number of sympathizing friends accompanied the bereaved family to Union Cemetery, Leesburg, where the lifeless form was laid in the silent dust, to await the trumpet blast that shall awake the sleeping natives of the earth. M.

Feb. 11th, 1880.—*Mirror Copy.*

2/12/80 Mirror

A Scant Ice Crop.

NEW YORK, Feb. 4.—The ice crop which bade fair to come out of the cold weather of the first days of February, is again a matter of doubt. All that the nipping weather had done was neutralized by the fall of snow, which, melting yesterday, and resting as part snow and part water on the thin covering formed during the few cold days will be incorporated in the ice should freezing weather ensue, and would appear next summer as that fast selling commodity that makes consumers unhappy and keeps up a perpetual quarrel between the delivery men and their customers. The prospects for the ice crop are indeed gloomy, and while the situation was serious enough several weeks ago, and there was yet time for the crop to grow and be harvested, the outlook now is dubious.

A superintendent of one of the ice companies, who has been hopeful hitherto, said to a reporter yesterday: "I regard the prospect as gloomy beyond expression. The people along the North River who in winter depend upon their labor at the ice houses are suffering more than anybody has any conception of and unless ice or charity comes soon to relieve them their sufferings will be terrible. I was up along the river this morning, looking for ice that might be cut in the 'bights' and behind the islands, but I couldn't find four inches anywhere. This snow, if it all melts away, will carry off the ice. If it only melts partly, and there is freezing weather, the ice will be of such an inferior quality that the companies cannot harvest and sell it at a profit, nor can the consumers use it with comfort.

(Before modern refrigeration, a few cold days were important for those who lived in the country. Ice could then be cut and stored. Properly insulated, it could last for the coming year. In the city, ice was shipped commercially from the northern states.)

2/26/80 Mirror

THE Legislature of Maryland has passed a bill imposing a fine of one dollar upon each person who shall "curse, swear or use obscene language on or near any street or highway within the hearing of any person passing." The *Bulletin* thinks, if the law is rigidly enforced, there need be no more taxes imposed, and that in a short time they will not only pay the State but the National debt as well.

February 1880

THE MIRROR.

THURSDAY.................... Feb. 19.

We understand that for several years past an organized band of rogues, with headquarters in the mountains beyond Hillsborough, have been rendering themselves particularly annoying to the neighborhood, stealing everything they could lay their hands on, on both sides of the river. Their depredations became so bold and outrageous that the citizens organized for their own protection and a few days ago succeeded in capturing three of the party, white men, who C. C. GAVER, convicted of some petty larceny, and ordered thirty stripes each. After sentence, one of the party turned state's evidence, and told of various other thefts perpetrated by the gang, and implicating and giving the names of some four or five others who are yet at large. The three originally caught, were lodged in the jail here on Monday afternoon, to await the action of the grand jury, while officers are in pursuit of the missing rogues.

As Sergeant ATTWELL was making his round about 3 o'clock last Friday morning, he found HENRY DOVE, an old colored man, lying in the branch near the depot. The railroad crosses the stream, and the old man, walking on the track, missed his footing and fell, the distance being about ten feet. When picked up, he was considerably bruised and almost unconscious from the fall and exposure. Luckily, the water was shallow. He was properly cared for, and the next day sent to his home.

DEATH OF A CENTENARIAN — BETSY HOPKINS, (colored) died in Waterford last Sunday night, at the advanced age, according to the most reliable data, of *one hundred and six years*.

Gov. HOLLIDAY last week forwarded to Governor HAMILTON, of Maryland, his requisition for the body of PAGE WALLACE, a fugitive from this State, and at present confined in the jail at Hagerstown. The requisition was honored by Gov. Hamilton, and on Tuesday morning Sheriff CARRUTHERS and Deputy W. W. NIXON went to Hagerstown for the prisoner, and we may be able, before going to press, to announce the return of Wallace to his old quarters in the jail of Loudoun.

NOTICE TO REPAIR JAIL.

SEALED Proposals will be received at the Clerk's Office of the County Court of Loudoun, Leesburg Va., at 11 o'clock, a. m. on the 26th day of April, 1880, for lining the two lower rooms of the Jail of said County —with Sheet Iron 3-10 inch thick, supposed to require about 750 feet of Iron and furnishing and putting in place 4 Iron Windows to be done according to plans and specifications to be found at the Clerk's Office.

PROPOSALS to be addressed to the Clerk of the County Court, marked, "Proposal for Lining County Jail." Committee reserve the right to reject any and all bids.
JOSEPHUS CARR,
N. B. PEACOCK,
J. M. HOGE,
 Committee.

Our Fourth Season

since first introduction by us in 1876, of this VERY LIGHT and

Cheap Pruner.

Makes Smooth Cut. Pruning can be done from the ground without ladder or climbing.

Sold at manufacturer's price, $2, by Agts

CLINE & SONS.

(Also three or four other good styles PRUNERS at low prices.)   (mar. 4, 1880.

Home-Made Wheels!

MADE right here in the County for us. Good quality and low price; will have but few Sets; call and secure a bargain indeed Also, Rims, Hubs, Spokes, Shafts, Swingletrees, Yokes, Double-trees, Tongues, Bows, Boxes, Rubber and Enam Cloths, Corduroys Linings, Tufting Buttons, Carriage Knobs Whip Sockets, Back Lights, Shaft Tips Swingletree Plates, Pole Tips, Axle Clips Ferrubs, Cockeyes, Clamps, King Bolts, Lazy Back Irons, Steps, Pole Eyes, Shaft Couplings, Stump Joints, Fifth Wheels, Hub Bands, Shaft Gums, Gum Spring Blocks, Carriage and Tire Bolts, Felloe Plates, Springs and Axles, and many other Goods, making a very large and most complete assortment in this (one of our special lines.) *Prices low and satisfaction assured.*

CLINE'S Hardware Hall.

February 1880

THE WASHINGTONIAN.

LEESBURG, LOUDOUN COUNTY, VA
SATURDAY.................February 21, 1880

THE THIRD TERM—THE GRANT BOOM.

Those constituting the leaders of the Grant party have determined to press him for the nomination. They believe their success depends upon his popularity, and are determined to set at defiance the practice of this country since the formation of our government, and the known wish of a vast majority of our people, that no man shall fill the executive chair more than two terms. While the leaders may plan his successful nomination, the people, in whom dwell the love of liberty and a determined purpose to guard against every innovation looking to the change of our Republican system of Government, will decide whether they will risk the consequences of this change, in the traditional practice of the country, to flatter the ambition of a leader, or gratify the cupidity of a horde of office holders and seekers.

2/26/80 Mirror

THE LASH.—The three white men noticed in these columns last week, as having been arrested, convicted, and committed to jail under a sentence of thirty lashes each for roguery, had the measure of their sentence duly administered in the jail yard on Monday morning. That is two of them received thirty stripes each—and are retained in custody to answer before the grand jury, for another and higher grade of offence. The third man, upon whose testimony the others were convicted, was given twenty stripes, and released from custody.

1/24/80 Washingtonian

A bridal couple from Washoe Valley, at breakfast the other morning conversed as follows:
He. 'Shall I skin you a pertater honey?'
She. 'No, thank you, dearie, I have one already skun.'

ROUND HILL, Feb'y 16th, 1880.

This country has been very much excited over some wholesale stealing that took place last week, down between the Hills, where hog-pens, hen roosts and meat houses were robbed without stint. A man by the name of Dillo was captured who "squealed" upon the gang, implicating four white and four colored men in the depredations. A vigorous, but unsuccessful search was made of the mountains by fourteen or fifteen citizens.

2/12/80 Mirror

INVESTIGATING A POSTMASTER.—The Washington correspondent of the Alexandria *Gazette* writes to that paper on Monday, that—

"Special agent Shellcross, who was sent to Hamilton, Loudoun county, Va. to investigate the charges against the postmaster there has returned. The charges were that the postmaster at Hamilton was in the habit of reading books and papers sent to subscribers at his office, before delivering them to the persons to whom they were addressed, and also reading aloud in the presence of the loungers about the office postal cards addressed to people served with mail at that office. The postmaster asked to be allowed to defend himself against these charges before the department. His request has been allowed, and he will come down on this afternoon's train for that purpose."

SCROFULA

can only be cured by a thorough purification of the blood. If this is neglected, the disease perpetuates its taint through generation after generation. Among its earlier symptomatic developments are Eczema, Cutaneous Eruptions, Tumors, Boils, Carbuncles, Erysipelas, Purulent Ulcers, Nervous and Physical Collapse, etc. If allowed to continue, Rheumatism, Scrofulous Catarrh, Kidney and Liver Diseases, Tubercular Consumption, and various other dangerous or fatal maladies, are produced by it.

Ayer's Sarsaparilla

Is the only powerful and always reliable blood-purifying medicine. It is so effectual an alterative that it eradicates from the system Hereditary Scrofula, and the kindred poisons of contagious diseases and mercury. At the same time it enriches and vitalizes the blood, restoring healthful action to the vital organs and rejuvenating the entire system.

February 1880

2/26/80 Mirror

HARVESTING ON A LARGE DAKOTA FARM.—Ride over these fertile fields of Dakota, and behold the working of this latest triumph of American genius. You are in a sea of wheat. On the farms managed by Oliver Danrymple are 15,000 acres in one field.— There are other farmers who cultivate from 160 to 6000 acres. The railroad train rolls throughout an ocean of grain. Pleasant the music of the rippling waves as the west wind sweeps over the expanse. We encounter a squadron of war chariots, not such as once swept over the Delta of the Nile in pursuit of an army of fugitive Israelites, not such as the warriors of Rome were wont to drive, with glittering knives projecting from the axles to mow a swath through the ranks of an enemy, to drench the ground with blood, to cut down the human race, as if men were noxious weeds, but chariots of peace, doing the work of human hands for the sustenance of men. There are twenty-five of them in this one brigade of the grand army of 115, under the marshalship of this Dakota farmer. A superintendent upon a superb horse, like a brigadier directing his forces, rides along the line, accompanied by his staff of two on horseback. They are fully armed and equipped, not with swords, but the implements of peace—wrenches, hammers, chisels. They are surgeons in waiting, with nuts and screws, or whatever may be needed.

This brigade of horse artillery sweeps by in echelon—in close order, reaper following reaper. There is a sound of wheels. The grain disappears an instant, then reappears; iron arms clasp it, hold it a moment in their embrace, wind it with wire, then toss it disdainfully at your feet. You hear in the rattling of the wheels the mechanism saying to itself, "See how easy I can do it."

An army of "shockers" follow the reapers, setting up the bundles to ripen before threshing. The reaping must ordinarily all be done in fifteen days, else the grain becomes too ripe. The first fields harvested, therefore, are cut before the ripening is complete. Each reaper averages fifteen acres per day, and is drawn by three horses or mules.

The reaping ended, threshing begins. Again memory goes back to early years, to the pounding out of the grain upon the threshing floor with the flail—the slow, tedious work of the winter days. Poets no more will rehearse the music of the flail. The picture for February in the old *Farmer's Almanac* is obsolete. September is the month for threshing, the thresher doing his 600 or 700 bushels per day, driven by a steam-engine of sixteen horse-power. Remorseless that sharp-toothed devourer, swallowing its food as fast as two men can cut the wire bands, requiring six teams to supply its demands! And what a cataract of grain pours from its spout, faster than two men can bag it!

The latest triumph of invention in this direction is a straw burning engine, utilizing the stalks of the grain for fuel.

The cost of raising wheat per bushel is from thirty five to forty cents; the average yield, from twenty to twenty-five bushels per acre. The nearness of these lands to Lake Superior, and the rates established by the railroads— fifteen cents per bushel from any point between Bismarch and Duluth—give the Dakota farmers a wide margin of profit.

Since the first furrow was turned in the Red River Valley, in 1870, there has been no failure of crops from drought, excessive rains, blight, mildew, rust, or other influence of climatology. The chinch-bug has not made its appearance; the grasshoppers alone have troubled the farmers, but they have disappeared, and the fields are smiling with bounty. With good tilth, the farmer may count upon a net return of from eight to ten dollars per acre per annum. The employment of capital has accomplished a beneficent end, by demonstrating that the region, instead of being incapable of settlement, is one of the fairest portions of the continent. Now is it a wonder that the land-offices are besieged by emigrants making entries, or that the surveyors find the lands "squatted" upon before they can survey them; that hotels are crowded; that on every hand there is activity. During the months of May, June, and July, 1879, the sales of government land were nearly 900,000 acres, and the entries for the year will probably aggregate 1,500,000, taken in homestead, pre-emption and tree claims. There are other millions of acres, as fair and fertile, yet to be occupied.—C. C. COFFIN.

February, 1880

NICHOLS, SHEPARD & CO., Battle Creek, Mich.

Established in 1848.

ORIGINAL AND ONLY GENUINE "VIBRATOR"
Threshing Machinery and Portable and Traction Engines.

THE STANDARD of excellence *throughout the Grain-Raising World.*

MATCHLESS for Grain-Saving, Time-Saving, Perfect Cleaning, *Rapid and Thorough Work.*

INCOMPARABLE in *Quality of Material, Perfection of Parts, Thorough Workmanship, Elegant Finish,* and *Beauty of Model.*

MARVELOUS for *vastly superior work in all kinds* of Grain, and *universally* known as the **only successful** Thresher in Flax, Timothy, Clover, and all other **Seeds.**

Astonishingly Durable and *wonderfully simple,* using less than half the usual gears and belts.

PORTABLE, TRACTION, and STRAW-BURNING STEAM-ENGINES, with special features of Power, Durability, Safety, Economy, and Beauty entirely unknown in other makes. **Steam-Power Outfits** and **Steam-Power Separators** a specialty. Four sizes of Separators, from six to twelve horse power; also two styles **Improved Mounted Horse Powers.**

Thirty-Two Years of Prosperous and Continuous Business by this house, without change of name, location, or management, furnishes a strong guarantee for superior goods and honorable dealing.

CAUTION! The wonderful success and popularity of our VIBRATOR Machinery has driven other machines to the wall; hence various makers are now attempting to build and palm off inferior and mongrel imitations of our famous goods.

BE NOT DECEIVED

by such experimental and worthless machinery. If you buy at all, get the "**Original**" and the "**Genuine**" from us.

☞ **For full particulars** call on our dealers, or write to us for Illustrated Circulars, which we mail free. Address

NICHOLS, SHEPARD & CO., Battle Creek, Mich.

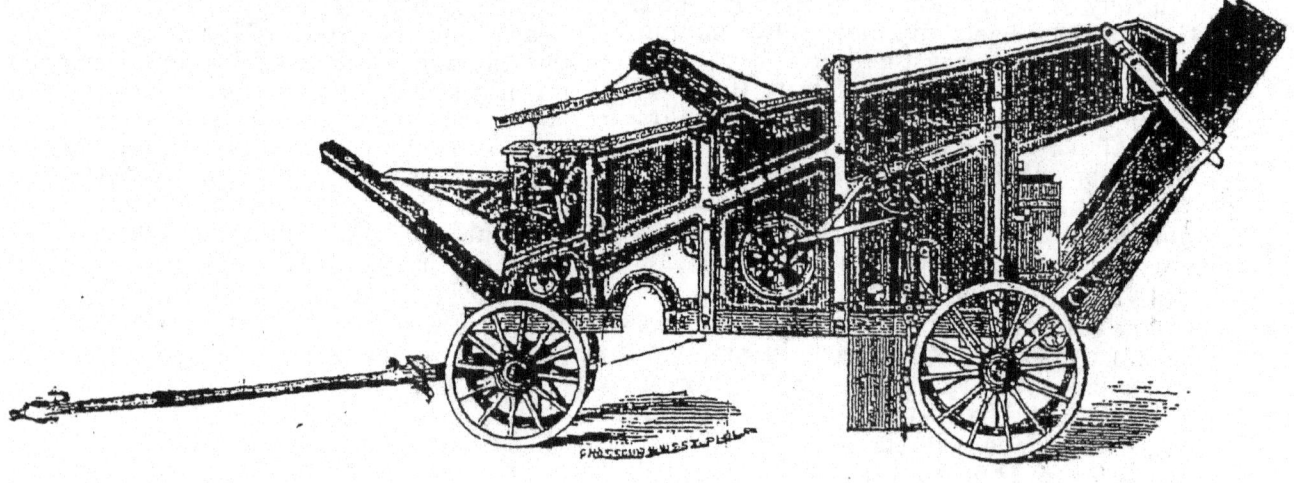

February, 1880

2/19/80 Mirror

Lynching in Loudoun

PAGE WALLACE HUNG!

HIS VICTIM WITNESSES HIS DEATH!

Over Two Hundred Men Participate in the Execution.

HIS RESCUE FROM THE HANDS OF THE SHERIFF.

HIS BODY LEFT HANGING ON A SYCAMORE TREE!

The usual peace and good order of this community was disturbed on Tuesday last by one of those violent outbursts of public indignation begotten of one of those too frequent infringements of the laws of God and man.— At the January term of the County Court of Loudoun,

PAGE WALLACE,

a negro, and a somewhat notorious character, was indicted by the grand jury, for an *attempted* rape upon the person of a white woman of this county— the penalty for which is imprisonment in the penitentiary. After his indictment he was committed to jail to await trial for the alleged offense

HE BREAKS JAIL.

On the night of January 27, he broke jail, and a reward was offered for his apprehension. On the Thursday night succeeding his escape, another white woman, living near the Point of Rocks Ferry, in this county, was assaulted and her person outraged by a negro man, whom she recognized as

PAGE WALLACE.

As soon as the fact became known, intense excitement was created throughout the county, especially in the neighborhood where the outrage was committed, and for several days the surrounding country was scoured by a band of armed men looking for the fiend.

HIS ARREST.

Finally he was arrested at Sharpsburg, Md., where in a drunken revelry he boasted of his hellish exploit, and was lodged in the jail at Hagerstown, and on Tuesday last, under

A REQUISITION FROM GOV. HOLLIDAY,

Sheriff CARRUTHERS and Deputy W. W. NIXON proceeded to Hagerstown for the purpose of claiming the prisoner and bringing him to Leesburg for trial. They were driven to the Pt. of Rocks by Mr. F. P. LEWIS, who was to remain there with the vehicle until the return of the officers on the evening train.

Arrived at Hagerstown, the Commonwealth's Attorney for Washington county told the Sheriff that if he would wait until Wednesday morning, he would furnish him a posse of men to see him safely to the Virginia shore, but as no trouble was apprehended up to that point, the offer was declined, and the Sheriff and his Deputy proceeded with Wallace on their return trip, with no other interference than the angry shaking of fists at the prisoner and a few harmless threats of lynching.

SCENE AT THE PT. OF ROCKS.

During the day, however, unusual commotion was visible at the Point of Rocks. Large numbers of quiet but determined looking men assembled there, and when the train arrived at six o'clock in the evening having aboard the two officers and their prisoner, not less than 300 people greeted their landing. All was serene, and the party was permitted to land and proceed to the river, where a boat was in readiness to bring them across the Potomac. But it was the ominous quiet that almost invariably precedes a storm. When the boat containing the officers and their charge left the shore, a half dozen other boats were launched, loaded down with men and a coil of rope. As soon as the

VIRGINIA SHORE WAS REACHED,

a rush was made for the prisoner. Sheriff Carruthers at once asserted his authority, and cocking his revolver, expressed his determination to defend his prisoner. Instantly, the muzzles of a dozen pistols were levelled at his head,—and he was coolly informed that no harm was intended him unless he forced it upon himself; but that they were determined to have WALLACE. He was at once pinioned in the embrace of a half dozen stalwart arms, others of the now infuriated mob disarmed the deputy and took him in charge, while the crowd seized the unfortunate negro, and hurried him up the bank, uncoiling the rope as they went.

THE PLACE OF EXECUTION.

When they reached a point in the road about 300 yards from the river, and within a few steps of where the outrage for which he was

ABOUT TO SUFFER DEATH

had been committed, a halt was ordered. A noose was made in one end of the rope and placed around the prisoners neck—the other end was thrown over the limb of a sycamore tree, and just then the victim of his hellish lust, the woman whose person he had outraged,

APPEARED UPON THE SCENE,

when Wallace fell upon his knees, and it is supposed was about to plead forgiveness. Whatever his intentions, they were abruptly cut short by a prompt and vigorous jerk at the other end of the rope, and in the twinkling of an eye the body of the ravisher was dangling in the air—perforated by a dozen pistol shots.

The hanging took place about 7 o'clock and in less than ten minutes after the work was done, the crowd had dispersed, and nothing remained to tell the story of the terrible transaction, save the lifeless form of Page Wallace.

The most of the men engaged in the lynching wore masks, those who did not were strangers, and to the officers unknown. The body was left hanging, until Wednesday morning, when an inquest was held over it.

Thus ends the last act in the sad drama—a fearful retribution for a terrible crime;—and however deeply all good citizens may and do deplore such acts of violence, it should nevertheless serve as a warning, that there are offences in which the verdict of an outraged community will sometimes usurp the prerogatives of the law.

On his way from Hagerstown to the Point, the doomed man, according to those having him in charge, apprehended no immediate harm. He denied having been at the Point of Rocks after his escape from jail, and said that he crossed the river at Harper's Ferry, but those who compared the tracks, say that those tell-tale iron-heeled boots worn by Wallace, are too plainly impressed on the beaten ground where the assault was made to admit of a doubt of his presence, even if the woman herself had not fully identified him. He remarked to one of the Sheriffs that he supposed he would be carried to Leesburg, tried, and hung, as Miss Morman would swear that he was the man who committed the offence, and he was unable to prove where he was the night of its occurrence.

HIS DEMEANOR IN THE PRESENCE OF DEATH.

At every station they passed on their journey a curious crowd peered through the car window at the prisoner, and no harm came of it, so that when he stepped from the platform of the car at the Point, and beheld a large number of persons assembled, and no immediate demonstration was made against him, he appeared to think that they too had been attracted thither by an idle curiosity.— It was not until they had gotten well out into the river, and he observed that the boat in which he was crossing was flanked on either side, by other boats, in one of which lay an ominous coil of rope, and a half dozen more boats followed in their track, laden to the waters edge with groups of stern looking men, that it seemed to flash over his mind that there was

DANGER IN THE AIR.

He asked the Sheriff the meaning of the rope, who told him he didn't know. Wallace said, "They are going to hang me." The Sheriff replied, "Not if I can prevent it." He then requested that the manacles be taken from his wrists that he might have a show for his life. But by this time the boats had reached the Virginia shore, and the result is already detailed above.

The verdict of the jury was, that on the evening of February 17th, 1880, Page Wallace came to his death by hanging by parties to the jury unknown.

We understand that when the body was cut down, nine bullet holes were found in it.

February, 1880

2/21/80 Washingtonian

Since February 3 Wallace has been in Hagerstown jail, closely guarded, for fear that an attempt might be there made to wreak summary vengeance upon him. A requisition from Governor Holiday for his transfer to Virginia was given a few days after his capture, but it was not sent to Governor Hamilton until a day or so ago. This morning Sheriff Caruthers and Deputy Sheriff Nixon, of Loudoun county, went to Hagerstown to take the negro to Leesburg. Wallace was immediately turned over to them by the Hagerstown authorities, and securely handcuffed was taken to the depot. They started from Hagerstown on the 3:10 P. M. train, and arrived at Point of Rocks at 5:46 P.M. Along the route there was no demonstration; but as soon as the Point of Rocks was reached it was found that a crowd of about one hundred men had gathered, and by their actions they showed what their object was. Before the train had stopped several boarded it and passed through the cars to make sure that the man they wanted was there. When the sheriff and his deputy stepped from the car with their prisoner, a cry went up, 'There he is!' but it was hushed by those who seemed to be superintending the affair, which had been prearranged with great nicety of detail. Quietly the crowd followed the three to the river, the negro being handcuffed to the Deputy. The three took a boat across the ferry and the crowd followed as fast as they could secure boats. On the Virginia side were about one hundred and fifty masked men who waited the sheriff's coming in quiet, but as soon as his boat touched the shore they made a rush for it. The Sheriff drew his revolver and attempted to the best of his ability to drive them back, but all his resistance was useless. He was speedily overpowered, and searched, and the keys of the handcuffs taken from him. The deputy was also overpowered, the handcuffs unlocked, and Wallace was in the hands of the lynchers. All this was the work of a very few minutes, and they dragged their prisoner in haste three hundred yards up the Leesburg road, to the very spot where he committed the crime upon Miss Morman. There they strung him up with a rope to the limb of a sycamore tree.

The excitement over the affair has now quieted down considerably, and the people dispersed to their homes, though the body still swings from its tree by the road.

2/19/80 Mirror

The Masher's Mistake.

"Here comes the masher," the fat passenger said: "How much he travels this winter.— His coat is dark, his trousers are light, his collar is high and his manly throat is bared to the breeze. Let us look at him and admire him. See how he sits graceful as Apollo new lighted on a rail fence, to talk politics with the neighbors. But, soft, here comes a girl seeking a seat. Maiden, our prayers are all for thee. Too late; all is vain; the masher has caught her eye, her fate is sealed, her heart is lost." "Sir," she said; and the music of her voice thrilled the car; "sir, is this seat engaged?"

He looked up at the vision of glowing cheeks and laughing eyes, marble brow and clustering curls, and he relented; even the masher's heart warmed toward the lovely girl, the latest victim of his manly charms, "Oh, certainly not," he said, and his bow was a study of grace for the stern man; "oh, certainly not; you are entirely welcome; I shall be only too happy——" "Then," cried the charmed victim, "mother, you can sit here beside this gentleman."

And an old woman, seventy-three if she was a day, with no teeth and only one eye, a small box a big band box in a bag, a green reticule and an umbrella, two paper bags, and a piece of calamus root, tottered into the proffered seat and sat down and piled her things into the young man's lap. And the girl, the beautiful girl, went and sat down beside the passenger with the sandy goatee who was so bashful that he couldn't and didn't say a word to his companion all the way to Newark, and blushed to his ears every time the fat passenger winked at him.

(A masher was an obnoxious equivalent of what was called a wolf sixty years ago.)

FOR RENT.

A NEW FRAME DWELLING HOUSE, located in Waterford, Va., just opposite the dwelling of C. L. Hollingsworth, built in modern style with good Cellar, 4 Rooms and a commodious Pantry on first floor, 4 Rooms on second floor, and two finished Rooms in attic, all conveniently arranged. About

2 Acres of Ground

attached, with New Stable and Ice House on same, and a good deal of FRUIT.

For further particulars and terms, apply to
J. T. McGAVACK, Trustee,
Waterford, Va.

March, 1880

MARCH COURT—THE NEW JUDGE—THREE RECRUITS FOR THE PENITENTIARY.—THE CROWD, &C.—Last Monday was March Court—a day that in ye olden times was memorable, because it inaugurated the Spring canvass for candidates and fine horses. But all that is changed now. The voice of the former is hushed in the land, and the neighing of the latter is visibly diminished. But notwithstanding this—a bright sun and a bracing atmosphere, coupled with the fact that a new form was that day to fill the judicial bench, and a half dozen or more criminals were to be tried for divers offences; formed an incentive for visiting the county seat that the average Loudoun citizen couldn't well resist, and as a consequence the crowd in attendance was unusually large.

At 10 o'clock the Court-House bell was rung, and His Honor, Judge McCABE, ascended to the bench, and for the first time proceeded to the discharge of his official duties. Before transacting any business, the Judge said—

I feel to-day a degree of humility I have seldom, if ever, experienced before. Being, perhaps, the youngest Judge ever elected by the General Assembly of Virginia, I am called upon to preside over the Criminal Court of one of the largest and richest counties of the Commonwealth. I feel, to an appropriate extent, the responsibilities of the duties of that position. But, relying upon your gentle forbearance and accustomed courtesy, I enter upon the discharge thereof with an humble boldness.

I know I shall make mistakes. I know that some of my decisions will be reversed—but those of you that know me, I think, know that each and every time I shall decide according to my interpretation of the law fearlessly, honestly, conscientiously, in the sight of God.

If I thought it necessary, I would ask you for your forbearance and for your courtesy.—But knowing you, I know that these, at your hands, I shall receive.

Those of you that may have business to transact in this Court, I ask you to be here promptly as may be at ten o'clock; for as near that hour as can be this Court each day will open.

At the very beginning I would say to the Sheriffalty of the County, that though there sits in this Court-House a higher Court than this—a Court with appellate jurisdiction—I know of no Court that should be conducted with more solemnity than this. Here criminals are tried—here men's liberties are taken away or given back—here the majesty of the law is vindicated in the eyes of offenders. I ask you, then, gentlemen of the Sheriffalty, to preserve, while this Court is in session, that degree of decorum and solemnity that is appropriate to the time and place.

And to you, gentlemen of the bar, I have simply to say, that I hope our relations towards one another may at least be as pleasant in the future as they have been in the past.

HARD IS THE WAY OF THE TRANSGRESSOR.—A few weeks ago, three white men were arrested in the Hillsborough neighborhood charged with sundry offences against the possessions of various citizens. The Justice found them guilty of petty larceny, mainly on the testimony of one of the three, who "squealed." For that—the petty larceny, we mean—he ordered the "squealer" to receive 20 lashes and the other two 30 each—and committed all hands to jail to answer other charges beyond his jurisdiction. The lashes were administered, as we stated last week—On Monday the grand jury found true bills against them for house breaking and burglary in two cases, and on Tuesday they were put upon trial, and plead guilty. The trial of the younger of the three, who turned State's evidence, was continued. The other two were tried, found guilty, and their punishment fixed at seven years in the penitentiary on one indictment, and five years in the same institution on the second—making twelve years in all.

We are glad to learn that neither of the three are citizens of Loudoun, but belong to an organized band, with headquarters on the (we blush to say it of our native county—but she's in West Virginia now,) Jefferson side of the Blue Ridge.

EWELL ATTWELL offers a reward of $50 for any information that will enable him to discover the party who fired his stable, on the night of the 2d inst. The information, he says, can be given confidentially, and the reward will be paid if the guilty party is found.

April 1880

4/22/80 Mirror

GRANT'S OPINION OF THE SOUTHERN PEOPLE. — Gen. Grant's latest speech was at Cairo, Illinois, where he is thus reported —

"It has been my good fortune," he said, "to have just passed through a little bit of the Southern states lately in rebellion, and it is gratifying to me, and I know it will be to you, that in every one of them scenes, speeches and decorations were made, the same as you see here. The stars and stripes floated everywhere. A great portion of the speakers in every instance were men who in conflict wore the gray, and the speeches which they made showed their present devotion for the flag for which we fought, which is all we ask of them that they should respect and honor the flag and be good citizens, and hereafter if it should be assailed by a foreign foe, that they should unite with us as one people.

4/24/80 Washingtonian

MR. TALMAGE COMES BACK FROM THE SOUTH AND TELLS WHAT HE SAW.

Mr. Talmage directed his congregation Sunday to sing "My country, 'tis of thee," said his text — Judges, 1, 15 — and continued as follows: "To meet engagements in nine of the South land in the spring-time, I made a trip two weeks long below Mason and Dixon's line. I went equipped with questions and hungry for information on moral and religious and political subjects. I found while South the most perfect proof that the bulk of the stories we get here in the North, distilled by special correspondents, are sheer fabrications and most persistent attempts to misrepresent the real character of a large section of our people. There is no more need of governmental espionage at Charleston or Savannah and the other Southern cities than there is in New York or Boston. Some people have an idea that the sentiment in the South leans towards the reestablishment of negro slavery. Ah! the people are all heartily glad to get rid of it and the plains now are placed under a better system of cultivation because it is gone. Old planters told me that the worry and anxiety and the care of looking after a plantation of negroes are all gone, and now all they have to do is to pay the wages at the end of the month. Put it to ballot in the South whether or not you would have again the system which prevailed before the war and you would get a thundering negative. The fight for slavery closed sixteen years ago and those Northern politicians who keep the subject of American slavery still rolling might as well try to make the Dorr rebellion in Rhode Island or the attempt of Aaron Burr to found an empire a test for our fall election.

"Another impression is that there is an hostility to Northern men who come to the South to settle. The impression is that they are to be kukluxed or otherwise made uncomfortable. It is a lie. They want all the help they can get from the North. They want the cotton spindles near the cotton fields and Northern men to manage and Northern girls to tend them. Of course, there is no more admiration for fools and braggarts there than here. A man may go down to a Southerner as he works in the field and begin his self-exultance. I'm from Boston, I am, Yes, I marched through this very section with my regiment; I remember killing a heifer on your front stoop. What a good thrashing we gave you, didn't we, now?" Such a man as that, to say the least, would not get a very hearty welcome.

Cancer Hospital

Established in Washington, D. C.

FOR THE CURE of CANCERS, TUMORS, CATARRH, DYSPEPSIA AND PILES, WITHOUT THE USE OF KNIFE, OR LOSS OF BLOOD.

ALSO, all forms of Female Complaints, so common to our best female population, including Prolapses, Displacement, Ulceration, and Female Weakness.

☞ If we do not Cure, no charge will be made for our service.

Good Board can be had at $1 per day, and at the United States Hotel (next door to Hospital) at $2 per day.

Dr J. H. BACHELER and
J. S. PALMER,
Proprietors.
No 325, between 3d & 4½ Streets.
Pennsylvania Avenue,
Washington, D. C.

April, 1880

4/8/80 Mirror

THE EXECUTION TO-MORROW —Between the hours of 6 and 8 o'clock to-morrow morning, (April 9th) in the jail yard in this town, SAMUEL ROBINSON, (colored) will undergo the severest penalty imposed by our laws for the commission of any crime, viz: *death on the scaffold.*

Every preparation has been made for the execution, and made in such a way as most likely to render the operation as humane as the painful occasion will permit.

Up to the hour of this writing, the condemned man has uttered no word either in the way of denial or confession of his guilt. He sleeps well—eats heartily—enjoys good health, and seems almost joyous over the near approach of the fatal hour that is to waft his soul into the immediate presence of its God. He converses freely, and talks of his tragic end, and his glorious hopes of the future, with as much composure and confidence as the ordinary man would do over an anticipated pleasant journey.

Before this paragraph will have reached many of our readers, the soul of SAMUEL ROBINSON will have explored the boundless realm "from whence no traveller e'er returns." Whether he will maintain his present reticence, and enter eternity, with his lips sealed as to his knowledge of the fearful crime for which his life is the forfeit, a few brief hours will determine.

4/22/80 Mirror

—A good "drive" was perpetrated upon a Connecticut Western conductor a few days ago. A man boarded the train at a way station and paid his fare to a point a few miles distant. On reaching his destination he concluded to proceed to a further station, and finally continued on until he reached Winsted. Each time he paid his fare in cash to the conductor, instead of buying a ticket at the station, although by this means the passage cost him considerably more. At last the conductor spoke of this, and suggested that it would be economy for him to buy a ticket and asked him why he didn't. "Well," said the passenger, "I'll tell you. Some time last summer I got into a little trouble with this company and they used me mighty meanly, so I just said to myself, 'That Connecticut Western Company won't never get another cent of my money if I live a hundred years;' and they won't, and that's why I pay my fare to the conductors." The conductor dropped the conversation at that point.

WM. H MAY & SON,

MANUFACTURERS OF

Agricultural Implements
AND
Standard Fertilizers,
AND DEALERS IN
Field and Garden seed.

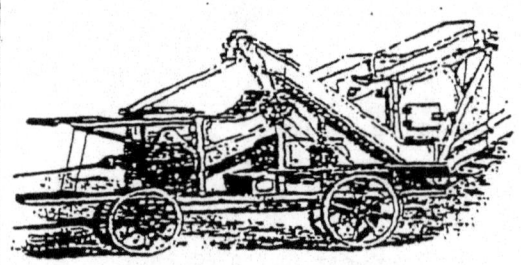

GENERAL AGENTS FOR
Buffalo Pitts Endless Apron Threshers, Vibrating Threshers, Pitts Farm Engines, &c., Watertown Steam Engines, McCormick Twine Binders, Reapers, Mowers, Meadow King Mower, Kemp's Manure Spreader, Ithaca Rake and Plaster Sower, Superior Force Feed Grain and Fertilizer Drill.

BAKER VIRGINIA WHEAT FAN

Studebaker Wagon, Tennessee Wagon, South Bend Chilled Plow, best Chilled plow made, and fully guaranteed. We have the largest stock of any house in the State, of the following implements, Plows, Dirt Scoops, Cultivators, Corn Shellers, Cutting Boxes, Harrows, Wheat Fans, Cider Mills, Animal Pokes, Water Drawers, Leather and Gum Belting, Cucumber Pumps, Canal Barrows, Seed &c. Warehouse and Fertilizer Factory, No. 38 UNION ST., Foundry and Plow Works, FAIRFAX ST., between Queen and Princess, Store and Office, 11 NORTH FAIRFAX ST.,
ALEXANDRIA, VA.

Orders left with W. C. Benton near Middleburg, will have our prompt attention.

April 1880

[From the Mirror Extra of Friday, April, 9.]

Death on the Scaffold.

EXECUTION OF
SAMUEL ROBINSON,
FOR THE MURDER OF
EDWARD THOMAS!

HISTORY OF THE CRIME!

Appearance of the Prisoner.

SCENES AT THE GALLOWS, &c.

Although the courts of Loudoun are not unfrequently called upon to try cases of crimes, it is a noticeable fact that the dread sentence of death has been pronounced but four times since the formation of the County in 1753.— The first was so long ago that the name of the victim, as well as the offence for which he was hung, have long since passed from the memory of the "oldest inhabitant."

Samuel Robinson.

FRIDAY, THE 9TH OF APRIL, 1880, between the hours of 6 and 8 o'clock in the morning, as the time, and the jail yard as the place of execution.

THE PRISONER IN JAIL.

After his conviction and sentence, Robinson bore himself with great fortitude, and soon appeared to be entirely reconciled to his fate. He was visited by several ministers during his incarceration, but his chief spiritual adviser was the Rev. R. T. DAVIS, under whose instructions and earnest labors he professed conversion, and about ten days ago received, at the hands of Dr. D., the ordinance of baptism.

IN HIS CELL.

A few days before his execution, this reporter visited Robinson in his cell and learned from him that he was in the 28th year of his age, having been born on the "Piggott farm," near Philomont, in 1851. Both his parents were at that day free people. He is a bright mulatto, and weighs about 150 pounds. He said that he rested well, ate heartily, and enjoyed good health, and was rather anxious for the fatal day to arrive. Drinking whiskey, playing cards, and keeping bad company, he said, were vices that every young person should shun, as they were the fruitful source of untold misery in this world. He said he had a wife and six children, and the bitterest drop in his cup of woe was parting with them.

The gallows consisted of a platform 6 by 8 feet, with a double-leaf drop, three feet square, in the center, and worked by a treadle. The entire structure was 14 feet high, and the platform seven feet from the ground, which was reached by a flight of eleven steps. The rope, a 1 inch hemp cord was the same used for the hanging of Winter Payne, (colored), at Warrenton, Va., in 1879.

AGAIN IN THE CELL.

On Thursday afternoon, our reporter again visited Robinson, in his cell. He found him composed—rather more nervous that on his former visit. The workers were engaged in erecting the scaffold in the jail yard, and the sounds of their hammers rung through the cell like voices of approaching doom, but the prisoner smiled and talked, seeming undisturbed by the melancholy reverberation.

He said he knew what was going on—and knew precisely what it meant, but it had no terror for him. While in the cell a friend sent him some cigars and fruits. He counted the cigars, fourteen in number, and laughingly remarked, that he thanked him for his kindness, but that they might as well have been kept in the store—that if he had a week to stay he couldn't consume them. Among the fruit were some bananas, which were strangers to him. Upon being told what they were he replied, that he would try one of them before he left. He expressed himself as ready and anxious for the fatal hour to arrive—said he had no ill feelings against a solitary human being, but hoped to meet them all in heaven, where he felt confident he was going. He was again asked if he had anything that he wanted to say in reference to the crime of which he had been convicted, and his answer was

NOTHING—I HAVE NO CONFESSIONS TO MAKE, and with that assurance ringing in his ear, the reporter bid him a last farewell. A suit of clothes lay folded up in one corner of the cell, and when the warden of the jail opened the door to let us out, Robinson, with a ringing laugh, asked him if he didn't think he had better put them on, as there might be some difficulty about it if he waited until after he was hung.

His wife was with him all day Thursday, until 5 o'clock in the evening, when she bid him farewell. The parting is represented by those who witnessed it as most affecting.

Later in the evening Rev. Mr. Cannon, visited him and held appropriate services. Still later, Rev. Wright and Tilghman, (colored), were with him for some time, engaged in singing and praying.

During the early part of the night, he laughed and talked to his guards, and smoked several cigars.

About 11 o'clock he laid down, and his guards say slept well and soundly until twenty-five minutes before five, when he arose and immediately engaged in prayer, continuing his devotion for seventeen minutes. He then sang "Arise my soul, arise."

HIS LAST MEAL.

At 20 minutes past five on the fatal morning his breakfast was set before him, consisting of stewed oyster, broiled shad, ham and eggs, biscuit, hot rolls and coffee. He left it, however, almost untasted.

In a few minutes thereafter, Revs. Cannon, Wright and Tilghman entered the cell and engaged the prisoner in religious exercises—the latter leading in prayer, and all joining in singing "There is a fountain filled with blood."

At 20 minute past six, the ministers retired, leaving Robinson for a short time, at his own request, in private devotion.

At 6½ the officers of the law entered the cell. Sheriff Carruthers proceeded to read the death warrant to the condemned man, immediately after which his arms were pinioned, and he was led forth to the scaffold, preceded by the Sheriff and Rev. Mr. Cannon, and Revs. Wright and Tilghman, who together with all the Sheriff's Deputies ascended the scaffold with the prisoner.

Robinson was dressed in a suit of brown cassimere—wore a white collar and black neck-tie, and a pair of well polished heavy shoes.

On the scaffold Rev. Mr. Tilghman read the 23d Psalm and Rev. Mr. Cannon offered a fervent prayer, the prisoner kneeling with as much composure as if in a Church. At the close of the prayer, the Sheriff asked him if he had anything to say. He responded in the negative, and his limbs were then bound and the noose adjusted about his neck—he all the time being apparently as calm as any one of the 60 odd spectators who stood around. The black cap was adjusted, and at 25 minutes before 7 o'clock

THE TRAP WAS SPRUNG,

and the body of Robinson hung suspended between earth and heaven. The body was given a drop of 4½ feet, and for a second after it fell the toes barely touched the ground. It was speedily elevated, and the heart continued to pulsate for 13 minutes. After hanging 23 minutes, Drs. Edwards, West and Leith, pronounced life extinct, the body was lowered, when it was found that the

NECK HAD BEEN BROKEN.

The body was placed in a neat coffin, and at once forwarded as he requested, to old Ebenezer church burying ground, near Bloomfield. Thus ends the last act in this sad drama—its counterpart, let us hope, never to be enacted in Loudoun during the life time at least, of the present generation.

Robinson died without either openly denying or acknowledging his guilt. And up to the last moment, bore himself with remarkable coolness. Even while the Sheriff was pinioning his arms, he requested that some cigars lying in the window should be handed to the prisoners in the opposite cell. In going to the scaffold his tread was firm and steady.

A number of persons congregated on the outside the jail wall, but there as well as in the enclosure, everything passed off quietly, and in an hour after the execution, the town bore its usual quiet aspect.

May, 1880

5/22/80 Washingtonian

THE DUTY OF CENSUS TAKERS.

The enumerators of the Census have all been appointed. They will commence their work the 1st day of June. The duties of the enumerators are simple and require only ordinary intelligence and a conscientious performance. They are required especially to visit each abode and obtain the age, sex, race, color and condition of each occupant, including births and deaths to June 1 only, of which daily reports are to be made to the local Supervisor and the General Superintendent at Washington. The compensation of enumerators is: For each death returned, 5 cents for each establishment of public industry on the general schedule of manufactures, (No. 3,) 15 cents; for each establishment of productive industry reported on special schedules of manufactures, 25 cents.

5/6/80 Mirror

Remarkable Fate of Four Boys.

In 1853 four gentlemen entered their sons at a boarding school at Cokesbury, N. C.— They had been for years intimate friends and clergymen in the Methodist Church. These boys remained at this school, room-mates and class-mates, and entered Wofford College, standing relatively first, second, third and fourth in a large class. They remained at this institution four years, were room-mates all the time, graduating relatively first, second, third and fourth. They then entered a law office at Spartanburg and studied law under the same chancellor. The war broke out and at the call for troops they all entered Jenkins' rifle regiment from South Carolina and were mess-mates in the same company. Being near the same height they stood together as comrades in battle in this regiment. At the second battle of Manassas, August, 1864, a shell from the enemy's batteries fell in the ranks of this company, killed these four boys and none other in the company. They are buried on the same battle field and sleep together in the same grave. Their names were Capers, McSwain, Smith and Duncan.

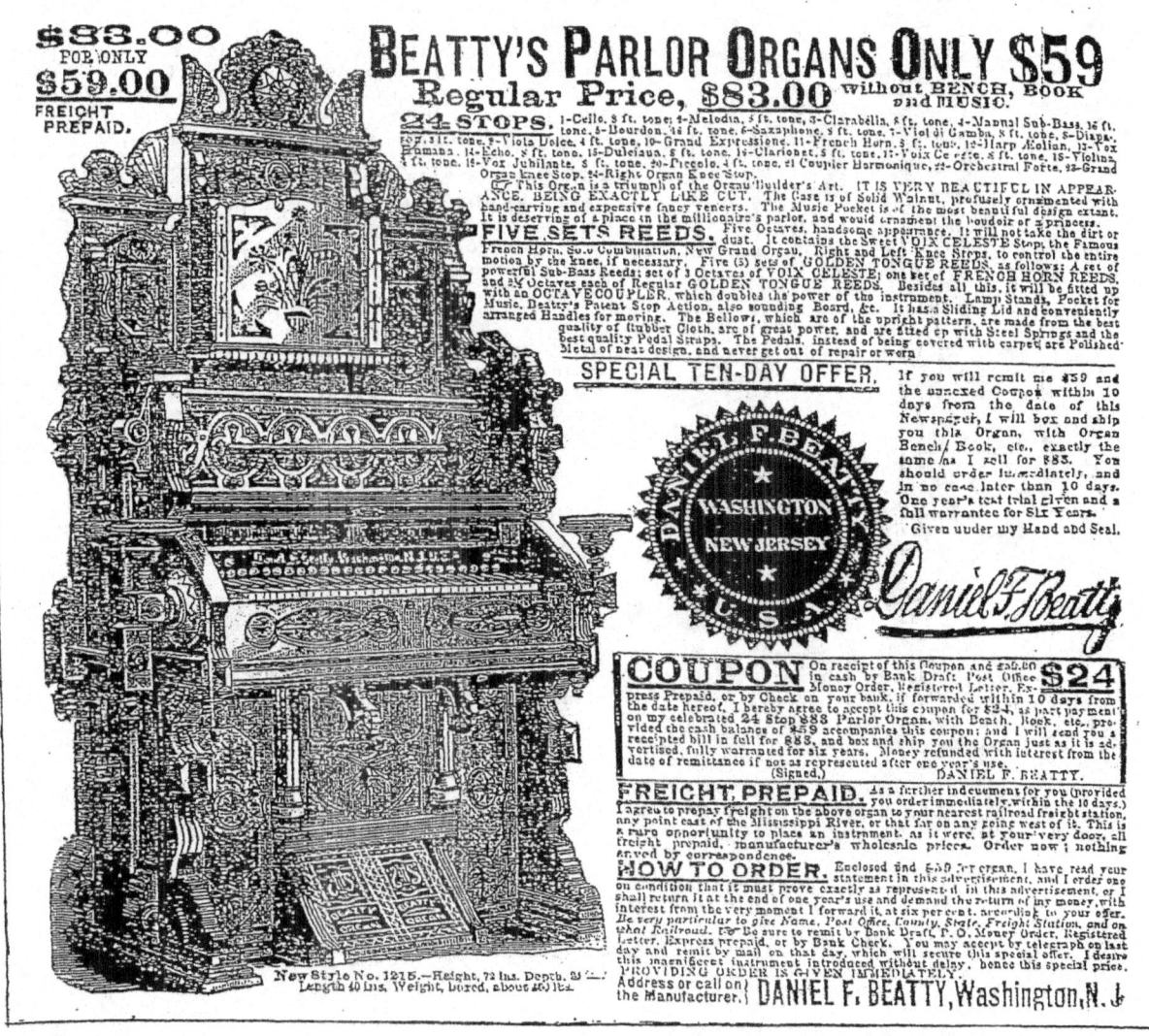

June, 1880

Prof. E. Hamilton's
GREAT NEW YORK CIRCUS
AND GOLD BAND!

Leesburg, Wednesday, June 30, 1880.

One Exhibition Only, in afternoon. Doors Open at 1 o'clock P M.

"TRIUMPHANT WE COME."

33 Artists, 5 Female Riders, 3 Clowns. Three times its former Size. All New. Now on its

20 Annual Tour. Only Artists of Recognized Ability Engaged

We value reputation above a few dollars saved on salary. Every act and artist mentioned in any of our publications will be here as advertised. No Menagerie, no Side Show no Gamblers or Confidence Men, no Peanut Men on the seats to annoy our customers, but the oldest and only

LEGITIMATE SHOW IN AMERICA.
PROF. E. STOWE'S GOLD BAND!

We take pleasure in announcing the engagement for the season of Prof. E. Stowe's Gold Band. The best band of instruments that ever traveled, as well as the finest set of instruments ever made, costing $135.00.

THE STREET PARADE.

will take place at 12:00 by Prof. Stowe's Gold Band, followed by the artists of the Company:— At 1 o'clock. Madame FREEMONT will make a Mid-Air Assension to the top of the centre-pole, eighty feet high. FREE FOR ALL.

Prof. Hamilton will introduce his six trained horses, two of which will teeter on a plank, balancing themselves, and will perform the dying horse trick. Over 100 separate tricks performed by them.

Mrs Laveley, the Iron Jaw Lady, will hold by her teeth, a cask containing forty-two gallons of water, and will be drawn to the dome of the canvas, carrying heavy weights with her, by the teeth, having no equal.

Doors open at 1 P. M., one Exhibition Only.
Admission 50 & 25c.

LOVETTSVILLE, TUESDAY, JUNE 29th, 1880.
SNICKERSVILLE, THURSDAY, JULY 1st, 1880.

Chicago Convention!

STAMPEDE on THE THIRTY SIXTH BALLOT.

Republican Nominees,

GARFIELD AND ARTHUR!

This Convention, which assembled in Chicago last Wednesday, and closed its labors on Tuesday night of this week, was the longest and stormiest of all its predecessors. It would be useless, in the circumscribed space of a weekly journal, to attempt anything like even an abstract of the proceeding. Besides, the work for which it was called together has been accomplished, and the proceedings now would read like the literature of last year's almanac.

The various committees completed their reports, which were adopted on Saturday morning—a synopsis of the platform will be found in another column.

Throughout the day the most intense excitement prevailed, especially when the committee on credentials seated or unseated delegates from contested States and districts.

The contested seats were all disposed of by three o'clock, and a motion was then made to take up the report of the committee on rules. Gen. Sharpe, of New York, the particular friend of Senator Conkling, moved as a substitute that the convention proceed to ballot for President. The motion was vigorously opposed by the Blaine elemen. who were not willing that the Grant men should have the advantage of proceeding without rules, and particularly the rules reported. The Sherman and the Edmunds strength went over to Blaine, and with their aid the motion was defeated.

At 7 o'clock in the evening the convention again came to order with at least 15,000 people present, and the nomination of candidates was announced as in order.

The announcement of Mr. Blaine's name was the signal for another wild scene of confusion and excitement—the nomination was seconded by Mr. Pixley, of California. Minnesota being called, Mr. E. F. Drake presented the name of William Windom. Mr. Conkling nominated Gen. Grant in a speech of some length.—''

The nominating speeches having all been made, Sunday was devoted to a repetition of the disgraceful and uproarious scenes of the preceding Sabbath, only to a more moderate degree, and betting was not near so common. It appeared to be generally realized that the time for bluff and bluster had passed, and the managers on both sides evidently issued orders to the boys to keep quiet. The managers themselves were busy as bees all day.— Trading and dickering was in full progress. Both sides were giving out statements plainly intended for effect.

Monday's Proceedings.

CHICAGO, ILL., June 7.—Eighteen ballots for the nomination for President were taken during the first session of the convention today. So suspicious were the Grant and the Blaine men that in some way there might be fraud in the summing up of the ballots that each employed an expert calculator to keep the count, and these two were unknown to each other and to the secretaries. They sat where they had the latter in full view, and kept tally of every vote that was recorded.— Before the balloting was proceeded with the chair made an earnest appeal to the delegates and the spectators to maintain at least a decent show of decorum, and the appeal had considerable effect, for although there were frequent demonstrations of applause, there were no scenes of disgraceful disorder, such as have been the rule during the entire session of the convention. Grant on the first ballot led Blaine twenty votes, and this difference was pretty much preserved during all of the eighteen ballots that were taken.

Tuesday Morning.

The Convention reassembled at 10 o'clock, and the balloting was at once proceeded with, resulting as follows:

THIRTY-SECOND BALLOT.

Grant, 309; Blaine, 270; Sherman, 117; Edmunds, 11; Washburne, 44; Windom, 3; Garfield, 1;

THIRTY-THIRD BALLOT.

Grant, 309; Blaine, 276; Sherman, 110; Edmunds, 11; Washburne, 44; Windom, 4; Garfield, 1.

THIRTY-FOURTH BALLOT.

Grant, 212; Blaine, 275; Sherman, 107; Edmunds, 11; Washburne, 30; Windom, 4; Garfield, 17. Garfield refused use of his name.

THIRTY FIFTH BALLOT.

Grant, 313; Blaine, 257; Sherman, 99; Edmunds, 11; Washburne, 23; Windom, 3; Garfield, 50.

THIRTY-SIXTH BALLOT.

JAS. A. GARFIELD NOMINATED.

June, 1880

6/10/80 Mirror

Thirty-five ballots having convinced the friends of Blaine and Sherman that there was no chance for either of these gentlemen, as is usual in such contingencies, they cast about for a "dark horse," and found him in the person of JAMES A. GARFIELD, of Ohio. Mr. Garfield is no stranger in the political world and his political opponents must not flatter themselves with the idea that in his candidacy they have not a "foeman worthy of their steel." He is a native of Ohio, having been born in Cuyahoga county, on the 19th of November 1831—and is consequently in the 49th year of his age. He is a graduate of William College Massachusetts, and a lawyer by profession, though we believe he occasionally indulges in Campbellite preaching. He served in the Ohio State Convention of 1859-'60. In 1861 he entered the Union army as Colonel of the Forty-second Ohio Volunteers—was promoted to the rank of Brigadier General in 1862—was Chief of Staff of the Army of the Cumberland, and in 1863 was promoted to the rank of Major General— he does not appear to have been a success in that capacity, as he was that year elected a member of Congress from the nineteenth Ohio district, where he has served ever since. He is a bitter partizan—a man of ability, and popular with his people. He was a member of the celebrated Electoral Commission in 1876, and voted every time with the immortal eight in seating R. B. Hayes. At the last session of the Ohio Legislature he was elected United States Senator to take the place of Allen G. Thurman after the 4th of March 1881. He was smirched with the Credit Mobilier stick, and had an unpleasant association in the DeGolyer claim; but these and other short-comings of the Chicago nominee, will be fully ventilated as the canvass progresses.

His associate on the ticket, Mr. Arthur is so far as we can call to mind just now, a great "unknown."

He is a protege of Conkling, and through the influence of that gentleman held for a time the position of Collector of the port of New York—from which he was ejected by President Hayes for alleged delinquences in office. Conkling labored hard for his retention, but was finally beaten, and Arthur went to grass. His nomination to the second place on the national ticket now, is clearly thrown out as a sort of peace offering to the Conkling wing of New York Republicanism, and outside of that it has no significance whatever.

6/26/80 Washingtonian

AGRICULTURAL.

ENSILAGE.

This is attracting great attention and as far as we can see, is destined to be a discovery of great value to the farmer, and may almost revolutionize agriculture, particularly in sections not adopted to grass growing. To those of our readers who may not have seen a description of ensilage, we state that it is the preservation of green forage in silos, or pits. Corn fodder has been principally used for the purpose. Various depths have been adopted for the pits, varying from 5 to 15 feet. Where water is easily reached, a part of the receptacle is put above ground, being bricked up. It is best to dig the pits under shelter, but they are frequently located in the open air. The system was first practiced by M. Goffart, of France. After many years of experiments, he seems to have perfected it, and has described it in a little work (which has been translated) entitled "The Ensilage of Maize." We quote from a letter recently addressed to "The Tuckahoe Farmers Club," of Henrico, by Dr. Banister of Amelia, on this subject; "Happily there has recently been introduced to us from Europe, a mode of providing winter food for stock of all kinds, which is comparatively inexpensive, and capable of supplying in abundant quantity a forage of a high order of excellence. It is accessible to any farmer who can command the services of a feed-cutter, driven by horse or other power. Such is the ensilage of green vegetation, but especially of corn,

(It was indeed a revolutionary procedure but Loudoun farmers were quick to adopt it as evidenced by the numerous silos still standing all over the county. These are vertical or upright silos, but ironically about sixty years ago the original pit silo, now called the trench silo, became popular again. Today, plastic is increasingly used to make insilage airtight.)

June, 1880

(From the Richmond State of Monday.)

AT TEN PACES.

The Duel Which Took Place Yesterday Morning Between Messrs. M. C. Elam of the Whig, and Col. Thomas Smith of Fauquier—A Meeting on Historic Ground—Mr. Elam Shot in the Face—The Offensive Article which Caused the Meeting—All Parties Reticent

Yesterday morning about sunrise a duel was fought between Mr. William C. Elam, editor of the *Whig*, and Col. Thos. Smith, of Fauquier, a son of Ex Gov. William Smith. All the preliminaries were so quietly arranged and carried out so secretly that it has been a difficult matter to get possession of the facts.

THE CAUSE OF THE DUEL.

The meeting had its origin in an editorial article which appeared in the Whig last Tuesday, headed "Political Pirates," which denounced, in unmeasured terms, the funders, or so much of the conservative party as had "utterly repudiated the old names under which it had masqueraded, and assumed a new style, the democratic party of Virginia." This denunciation embraced all the leaders in 1869, and included the Governor (William Smith) who was chief magistrate of Virginia at the close of the war, who were described as having "grabbed the remaining swag and sneaked away in humiliating disguise and shameful trepidation."

Friday night Col. Smith, accompanied by Gen. William H. Payne, Captain Alexander Payne, and Mr. Bernard P. Green, came to this city. The party spent the interval at the residence of Mr. William L Royall. They left his house yesterday morning at 4 o'clock in two buggies and drove straight to Oakwood Cemetery to which place it is understood that Mr. Elam, Mr. James B. Walters, of the *Whig*, and another gentleman (whose name has not been learned) went in a hack.

THE PLACE.

It was stipulated that the parties should proceed to a line near the fence of Oakwood Cemetery and there agree upon the spot where the duel should be fought. The place selected was a grove east of Oakwood and near the York River railroad, and in the immediate vicinity of the spot where the Mordecai-McCarthy duel was fought.

It was also stipulated that no person should be on the ground, save the principals and their seconds. Two surgeons are said to have been near the field, but in fact only one surgeon was near.

THE DUEL.

The two principals, accompanied only by their seconds, then went to the field, leaving the other parties near the line of the Oakwood cemetery fence. The two men were put in position. At the first fire Mr. Elam fell to the ground.

Mr. Walters, upon seeing his principal wounded and bleeding, went in search of the surgeon, who was found some distance from the place. When the doctor arrived on the field Mr. Elam was the only person there.

His wound was temporarily dressed, and he was carried to the residence of Mr. James B. Walters, No. 566 Sixth street, when Dr. Hugh M. Taylor was called in and rendered the necessary surgical attention.

MR. ELAM'S WOUND.

Mr. Elam was struck in the centre of the chin, the ball splitting the bone and embedding itself under the tongue. The counter stroke broke the jaw-bone on the right side of the face. The physicians are of opinion that the wound will heal very rapidly and Mr Elam will soon be out again.

It is understood that after the fight Colonel Smith and his friends drove from Richmond to the White House, from which place they walked to Lester Manor. It is also understood they expected to go from that point to Baltimore on a freight boat. The sudden appearance of the party at Lester Manor and their hurry to get away excited the suspicions of some of the people there, and it was surmised that a duel either had been or would be fought.

POLICE INVESTIGATIONS

On Monday morning, Major Poe instituted proceedings looking to the arrest of the dueling party, and warrants were issued for the arrest of Jas B. Walters and Wm H. Payne, and Thos. Smith and Wm. C. Elam.

ARRESTS.

Sergt. Daniel Wren found Mr. Elam at Mr. Walter's residence, and served the warrant upon him. Mr. Elam's condition being such as to preclude his removal he was paroled—Mr. Walters was arrested and taken before Justice William Hall Crew and bailed in the sum of $1,000 for his appearance at the Police Court next Saturday morning, Mr. John Booth surety.

The duel grew out of the *Whig's* article, and the point of special offence was the paragraph touching Gen. William Smith, late Governor of Virginia, a paragraph charging him with sneaking off with swag and with disgraceful trepidation.

July, 1880

THE WASHINGTONIAN.

LEESBURG, LOUDOUN COUNTY, VA

SATURDAY............... June 26, 1880

DEMOCRATIC TICKET.

FOR PRESIDENT,
GEN. WINFIELD S. HANCOCK,
OF PENNSYLVANIA.

FOR VICE-PRESIDENT,
WILLIAM H. ENGLISH,
OF INDIANNA.

GEN. HANCOCK FOR PRESIDENT.

The Cincinnati Convention opened on Tuesday last. The best feeling prevailed, and but one spirit actuated and governed the body. They met to make a nomination which would have the confidence of the country, and which would receive the enthusiastic support of the party.

Upon the third Ballot GEN. WINFIELD SCOTT HANCOCK was nominated, receiving the most remarkable vote ever cast in a National convention, showing the wonderful unanimity in the country for his nomination.

He was a distinguished General during the late war, and among the first to recognize the civil rights of the Southern States, by the announcement of sentiments which drew down upon him the anathamas of the Republican party at that time. He stands without reproach before the country, pure and noble in all that constitutes a great man—conservative and national in his views, and true alike to all sections—the man above all others to settle sectional agitation and restore a political and national good feeling in the country.

WM. H. ENGLISH, the candidate for Vice President, is a man of public distinction in the Northwestern States, having served eight years in Congress, and governed at all times by the liberal national sentiments which recognize the rights of all sections as equal.

The old flag which was furled and laid away at the close of the Tilden canvass, has been brought out, and will soon be unfurled to call the conservative party, in this locality, to rally around it.

THE MIRROR

BENJ. F. SHEETZ, Editor.

Thursday Morning, July 1, 1880.

HANCOCK AND ENGLISH

With a harmony and unanimity almost, if not entirely, unprecedented in National Conventions, the Democrats at Cincinnati last week nominated a ticket for President and Vice-President of the United States, that is receiving the unqualified endorsement of men of all parties and every shade of political opinion. From all sections of the country, North, South, East and West, it has been hailed with delight by the Democracy, while the Republicans themselves stand appalled at its grandeur and assured success.

What Gen. Grant is Reported to Have Said.

Chicago, June 25.— A despatch to the *Times* from Galena says: "It is not true, as reported, that Gen. Grant has declared his intention of supporting Gen. Hancock. The report doubtless grew out of the many favorable comments he has made on the action of the Cincinnati Convention. He does not hesitate to say that in his opinion the Democrats have in Gen. Hancock nominated their best and strongest man for the office of President, and that neither his public nor private character can be successfully assailed. This is the substance of the ex-President's public statements on that subject; but it is no secret to his intimate friends that he declares Hancock will be elected our next President.

General Sherman said to a newspaper man in Washington: "If you will sit down and write the best thing that can be put in language about General Hancock as an officer and gentleman, I will sign it without hesitation." General Joe Johnston said: "It pleases me better than any other could have done. It is a very strong nomination, and will win."

TURNER ASHBY.

During that period of suppressed excitement in Virginia after the John Brown incident at Harper's Ferry, and before the outbreak of the war, a young man from one of the northern States passed a week or two as a guest in the house of one of the oldest and most distinguished families of Northern Virginia.

The young man was frankly a Republican in politics, but the fact made no difference whatever in the courtesy or kindness of his host, or in the treatment given to him by the gentlefolk of the surrounding country, to whose houses he was freely invited, as a gentleman visiting in the house of a gentleman, a neighbor. His business in the neighborhood was social, not political—he was, in fact paying his addresses to his host's daughter—and his political opinions, though perfectly well known, were not discussed and perhaps were scarcely thought of at all.

One evening during his visit this young man, C. D——, was invited in company with his host's family to attend a reception given by Turner Ashby on the occasion of a tournament. He went, of course, mingled freely with the other guests, and found nothing in his reception to mark any difference between himself and the other gentlemen present, until the supper was served. Then a disagreeable incident occurred.

A young man of the neighborhood who, as C. D—— afterward learned, was a rejected suitor for the hand of the woman to whom he was himself laying siege, approached him as he stood talking with her, and without speaking to C. D—— at all, said to the lady:

"Isn't it a sublime piece of impudence for a Yankee and a black Republican to come down here now and accept the hospitality of a Virginia gentleman, after all that has happened?"

The young woman replied, quickly:

"Mr. B——, you should be the last person to criticise the catholicity of my father's hospitality—you have profited by his indisposition to draw social lines too sharply. You have been received by him as a guest upon several occasions."

The reply was so stinging that the youth straightway withdrew from the supper-room, and C. D——, thinking it better to retire from a company in which he might be less welcome than he had supposed, went to the cloak-room for his hat and coat. He had scarcely entered the door of the room when B—— approached him saying:

"What I said just now had reference to you, and was meant to be insulting."

Young C. D—— had not been used to encounters of this kind, and had little disposition to engage in affairs of honor; but he seriously intended to prosecute his suit for the hand of his host's daughter, and he knew instinctively that all hope of success there must be abandoned if he failed to resent an insult of so gross a nature.

This was the signal for the persons present in the room to interfere to prevent a brutal fight with fists. A challenge in regular form was quickly given and accepted, and C. D—— anxious to have the affair ended as speedily as possible, insisted that the duel should be fought at once in a grove near the house, by the light of torches.

All the persons concerned prepared themselves immediately and were about to quit the room for the appointed place, when Turner Ashby, white with rage, burst through the door. A whisper of what was going on had reached him.

He entered the room, paused a moment and then advanced to B——, quivering as he went forward so violently that half the persons present supposed that he meditated an assault upon B——. His voice, however, was low, and his speech very deliberate.

"What is the time fixed for our meeting, Mr. B——?" he asked.

"I am to fight Mr. C. D—— immediately," answered B——.

"I beg your pardon," replied Ashby, "but Mr. C. D—— has nothing to do with this affair. He came to my house to-night as my guest. When I invited him to come the invitation was Turner Ashby's word of honor that he should be treated here as a gentleman; it was my voucher for his character to my other guests, and for the character of my other guests to him. I am sorry to have to explain these points of good breeding to you, Mr. B——, but you have shown your ignorance of them by insulting my guest. That insult is mine, not his, to resent. He is here under my invitation, and that is my pledge of protection. If you are not prepared to make a proper and satisfactory apology at once, both to my guest and myself, you must fight Turner Ashby, and the time and place already agreed upon will answer as well as any other. What do you say, sir?"

Now, fighting a duel with a young stranger wholly unused to firearms and fighting of any sort was one thing; fighting a duel with Turner Ashby in a rage, was very well understood to be another and a much more serious thing, and young B——'s consciousness of this difference wrought a complete change in his mood. He pleaded in excuse for his conduct the fact that he had been drinking too freely, and signed the pair of apologies which Turner Ashby wrote.

C. D—— ended his visit soon afterward, and the war came on to prevent its repetition. Turner Ashby's gallantry in war and courage and command over men, and the story of his death, are all matters of history now; "but his high character, says C. D——, "never impresses me so strongly in reading of his military exploits as it does when I look at that faded slip of paper written by his hand and signed by B——

Turner Ashby was an iconic figure to Confederates particularly in the Shenandoah valley. Colonel Ashby was the head of Jackson's cavalry and was killed early in the War.

THE SOUTH CAROLINA DUEL.

Denounced in Darnington.

INCIDENTS OF THE COMBAT—DESCRIPTION OF THE GROUND.

TIMMONSVILLE, July 8.—During the past two days I have passed through the greater part of Chesterfield and Darlington counties and talked with more than one hundred persons of every class and condition about the fatal duel between Col. Cash and Col Shannon, at DuBose's bridge, on Monday. There is one universal sentiment of regret at the horrible affair, and with only a few exceptions have I heard a kind word for Col. Cash or any approval of his part in this terrible tragedy. The feeling throughout this county is most intense, and so shocked was this community when the news of the result of the duel reached Darnington Courthouse that some of the more impulsive citizens endeavored to organize an indignation meeting on Tuesday to express the public disapprobation of the "appeal of Arms,', and especially to denounce the practice of making Darlington county the theatre of such preformances. The public was more deeply incensed on this account because this made

THE THIRD HOSTLE MEETING

in the county within a period of two years. The better counsels of more prudent men prevailed, however and the indignation meeting was abandoned. During the day the entire community wore a preoccupid air and the duel was in the mouth of every man, woman and child. The merchants talked about it over their counters, the lawyers at their desks, on the street corners in the hotels, barber shops and barrooms, from white and black alike, there came a wail of genuine regret that the exigency of the code had caused the sacrifice of the noble and chivalrous Shannon. Since the stirring times of 1876 I do not remember to have ever seen such unanimity of public sentiment upon any subject.

MR. M'COWN'S STATEMENT.

At 11 o'clock last night, by a forced drive, I called on Mr. G. J. McCown, one of Col. Cash's friends in the affair on Monday, at his residence, ten miles distant from Darlington Courthouse, and secured the following statement of what he witnessed on the duelling ground, McCown said:

'I was off at some distance from the seconds when they met in the field to make arrangements. They stepped off the distance—I think Mr. Saunders did the stepping. In about twenty minutes the principals walked and took their positions, Col. Cash standing down the river, which was South, and Col. Shannon up the river. The principals stood parallel with the river, Col. Shannon's second being stationed to the right in his rear, and Col. Cash's second standing on the left opposite Col. Shannon's second. Col. Shannon wore a black alpaca sack coat, white vest and light pants. Col. Cash had on a black frock coat, white vest and white pants.

BEFORE THE WORD.

was given the principals bade their seconds good bye, shaking hands with them Col. Shannon kissed his wife's picture, which he carried in his pocket. At the word one Col. Shannon fired, his ball striking two thirds of the distance between himself and Col. Cash, on a direct line with Col. Cash's body. At the word two Col. Cash fired, his ball striking Col. Shannon in the right breast, about the nipple, and passed into the body about two inches above the heart. Col. Shannon stood some two seconds or more in an erect position, and turning to the right dropped to his knees. After the usual formalities Col. Cash and his party left the field. Both parties seemed very cool and collected. Col. Shannon looked pale but exhibited no fear. Drs. Wallace, Calloway and Lee at once rushed to Col Shannon after the firing, and about five minutes after he had fallen the wound was probed. He did not struggle, he seemed to die without any pain. I was in about twenty steps of the parties when the duel took place. There were about

ONE HUNDRED PEOPLE STANDING AROUND.

from one to five hundred yards from the duel, nearly all of whom rushed to the ground on the discharge of the pistol and the fall of Col. Shannon. Col. Cash's son was stationed about five hundred yards from the field and watched the fight through his glasses. When the firing was done he at once repaired to the scene, meeting his father as he left the ground.

AFTER THE DUEL

I stayed on the ground for perhaps ten or fifteen minutes. It was a very sad scene, and I never care to witness another. The fact that the duel would take place was known in the community the evening before (Sunday), and every one who heard of it went to the ground. So far as I know there were no officers of the law on the ground.

THE DUELLING GROUND

is a kind of sandy barren with a stunted growth of trees and bushes near Lynch's creek or river which runs almost due north and south. The day of the meeting was very pleasant and the sky was overcast with clouds which shielded the combatants from the fierce heat of the sun. On the morning of the duel it is related that Col. Cash and his son practiced with their pistols, firing wads at each other at fifteen yards. Col. Shannon is also said to have stopped with his party within two miles of the ground and tried his pistols. So it seems that both parties went into the fight with a determination to kill his antagonist, and

A DOUBLE TRAGEDY

was only prevented by a lack of proper deliberation on Col. Shannon's part, who fired without taking aim, but upon a line with Col. Cash's body. Col. Cash is said to have drawn a fine bead on his opponent, and was in most excellent practice. He is a very expert shot, and can cut a string with his pistol or hit a coin at an almost incredible distance. He comes from fighting stock, and does not know what fear is. Col. Shannon was also a man of most remarkable nerve and unimpeachable courage. He was at one time affected by a kind of nervousness or paralysis of the wrists which made his hand somewhat unsteady, but I have heard had entirely recovered from the affliction during the last year or two.

In company with his friends Col. Cash went to Mr. R. D. Lee's house, near Du Bose's Bridge, in his carriage on Sunday, arriving in the afternoon, where he spent the night. Col. Shannon and his party left Camden on Monday morning in a carriage. He left home without informing his family of his destination, but told his son to let them know that he had gone out to fight a duel with Col. Cash.

DURING THE RIDE.

to the fatal field he seemed to be fine spirits, and laughed and talked in his usual cheerful way without once alluding to the approaching meeting. So well concealed was the duel that the colored man who drove the carriage thought that Col. Shannon was going out into the country to attend a pic-nic until the party stopped and tried the pistols.

7/24/80 Washingtonian

THE RECENT FATAL DUEL.

A Letter from Senator Butler—He Does not Regard the Tragedy at Dubose's Bridge as Defensible Even Under the Code of the Duello.

EDGEFIELD COURTHOUSE, July 13, 1880.
Editors Charleston News and Courier:

Dear Sirs,—I want to say to you that you have my hearty endorsement in the position you have taken in reference to the Cash-Shannon tragedy. It is no reflection upon the memory of the gallant gentleman of the past who resorted to the duello to settle their personal differences to ask that the law be vindicated in this case. In former days the most punctilious decorum and chivalrick courtesy distinguished the conduct of gentlemen in "affairs of honor," and coarse ribaldry and gasconade in correspondence was as odious as the brand of cowardice; but now the "swash-buckler style" appears to be fashionable

The issue is very sharply made between those who trample law defiantly under foot and those who execute it, and I do hope the courage enough may be found to execute it.

It will be a sad day for South Carolina when a gentleman, who feels it to be his personal or professional duty to vindicate private rights in our courts, is first to be insulted pursued, vilified, and goaded to desperation, and then shot. If that is to be the place which our civilization is to occupy, we shall all be sleeping on our arms. And there must be something radically wrong in a public sentiment which can *force* a man of Shannon's high character and acknowledged courage to fight a duel under the circumstances which surrounded him. It is about time we were finding out where we are, and ascertain whether "border ruffianism" is to govern this country, or whether civilized institutions shall be maintained.

> (Duels seemed to be very prevalent about this time, but they were about to go on the wane due to popular revulsion and increased enforcement penalizing seconds as well as principals.)

8/5/80 Mirror

Racing in Loudoun County.

Some horse racing took place in Loudoun Co., last week. The first race which came off on Wednesday and which has attracted much attention, was a two mile dash between Mr. Robt. Neville's Satan (the same was ridden in the gentleman's steeple in Washington by Mr. Bartel.) and Mr. H. Grafton Dulany's Champ. Both horses are well bred, though Mr. Neville's flyer had the advantage in youthfulness. The stakes were for $500 a side. At the appointed time half the people in Loudoun and Fauquier were on the track. Mr. Neville rode his own horse, and Mr. R. D. Rozelle rode Mr. Dulany's. The pace was a hot one twice around the mile course, but on the last quarter stretch Satan put on a spurt which won him the race by a half dozen lengths.

On the ground at this event was Captain Cotten, a gentleman from England, who is in Virginia buying horses for an English hunting club, and the gentleman immediately challenged Mr. N. to run Satan against a thoroughbred which he had recently purchased. Mr. Neville accepted, and high stakes were put up. The Englishman, however, had reckoned without his host, for when the race came off his "racer," which was really a very handsome horse, was badly distanced by Satan, who kept up a marvelous stride, and won the race in his own time. Both gentlemen rode their own horses.

FERTILIZERS
Manufactured by
F. L. MOORE,
GEORGETOWN, D. C.
FALL SEEDING,—'80.

Moore's Half-and-half	$45 00
Moore's One-Third	40 00
Moore's One-Fourth	34 00
Moore's I X L	38 00
Moore's Ammoniated Bone Phosphate	38 00
Moore's Bone and Meat Fertilizer	35 00
Moore's Pure Raw Bone	35 00
Ammoniated Dissolved Bone	35 00
A No. 1—Peruvian Guano, (Guanape)	60 00
" " (Lobos)	48 00
Best Ground Blue Windsor Plaster	$6 50 to 7 50

POOLESVILLE, MD., July 21, 1880.
MR. F. L. MOORE.

DEAR SIR: I used last fall on my wheat your One-Third Fertilizer at the rate of one hundred and forty pounds to the acre. I have threshed and made on one field between 24 and 25 bushels to the acre.
GEO C. SLIFER.

(This ad continued to the bottom of the page and halfway into the next column with twenty-one more testimonials.)

PUBLIC SALE
OF
STOCK,
Farming Implements, &c,

Thursday, Aug. 12, '80.

I WILL sell, to the highest bidder, at my residence on the "Ruse" farm, adjoining the town of Hamilton on the day mentioned, all my STOCK, FARMING IMPLEMENTS &c., embracing

4 Good Work Horses
1 TWO-YEAR OLD COLT,
2 One-Year Old COLTS, 2 last Spring do.

5 GOOD MILCH COWS,
(all fresh and young; 7 Yearling Steers and Heifers. Spring Calves. 6 Essex Hogs; 2 Brood Sows and 4 Shoats, (Berkshire): A No. 1 Southdown BUCK;

1 Keller WHEAT DRILL,
(little used;) 1 LIGHT
FOUR-HORSE WAGON (new);

2 TWO OR THREE HORSE WAGONS, (one right new, 1 One Horse Spring Wagon; 1 Telegraph Cutting Box, (large size;)

ONE WHEAT FAN

1 Double Corn Sheller, (Pennock, new.) 1 PLANET MOWER; 2 pairs Hay Frames; HARNESS for four Horses; 2 sets Single Harness; 3 sets Plow Gear; 1 Three-Horse Harrow, 3 Taylor Plows, new; 3 Double and 2 Single Shovel Plows, 2 Grain Cradles, 2 Mowing Scythes, 6 Cow Chains, Forks, Shovels, Single and Double Trees, 1 Log Chain, 1 Fifth Chain, &c., &c.

8 BARRELS VINEGAR.

3 STAND BEES, besides numerous other unmentioned articles.

☞ Most of the above property is new, or very little used and is all in good condition.

TERMS.—All sums under $10 cash. All sums over that amount, notes for Six Months required with approved security with interest from date. No property to be removed until terms are complied with.

T. H. VANDEVANTER,
aug. 4, 1880   J. H. Clapham Auc'r

The Modern Livery Horse.

There has been a great change in livery horses within the last twenty years. Years ago, if a young fellow wanted to take his girl out riding, and expected to enjoy himself, he had to hire an old horse, the worst in the livery stable, that would drive himself, or he never could get his arm around his girl to save him. If he took a decent looking team, to put on style, he had to hang on to the lines with both hands, and if he ever took his eyes off the team long enough to look at the suffering girl beside him, with his mouth, the chances were that the team would jump over a ditch, or run away, at the conclusion. Riding out with girls was shorn of much of its pleasure in those days. We knew a young man that was going to put one arm around his girl if he did not lay up a cent, and it cost him over three hundred dollars. The team ran away, the buggy was wrecked, one horse was killed, the girl had her hind leg broken, and the girl's father kicked the young man all over the orchard, and broke the main spring of his watch. It got so that the livery rig a young man drove was an index to his thoughts. If he had a stylish team that was right up on the bit, and full of vinegar, and he braced himself and pulled for all that was out, and the girl sat back in the corner of the buggy, looking as though she should faint away if a horse got his tail over a line, then people said that couple was all right, and there was no danger that they would be on familiar terms. But if they started out with a slow old horse that looked as though all he wanted was to be let alone, however innocent the party might look, people knew just as well as though they had been it, that when they had got out on the road, or when night came on, that fellow's arm would steal around her waist, and she would snug up to him, and—O, pshaw, you have heard it before.

Well, late years the livery men have "got onto the racket," as they say at the church sociables. They have found that horses that know their business are in demand, and so horses are trained for this purpose. They are trained on purpose for out-door sparking. It is not an uncommon thing to see a young fellow drive up to the house where his girl lived with a team that is just tearing things. They prance and champ the bit; and the young man seems to pull on them as though his liver was coming out. The horses will hardly stand still long enough for the girl to get in, and then start off and seem to split the air were open, and the neighbors say, "Them children will get all smashed up one of these days." The girl's father and mother see the team start, and their minds experience a relief as they reflect that "as long as John drives that frisky team there can't be no huggin' a going on." The girl's older sister sighs, and says, "That's so," and goes to her room and laughs right out loud. It would be instructive to the scientists to watch that team for a few miles. The horses fairly foam, before they get out of town, but striking the country road the fiery steeds come down to a walk, and they mope along as though they had always worked on a hearse. The shady woods are reached, and the carriage scarcely moves, and the horses seem to be walking in their sleep. The lines are loose on the dash board, and the left arm of the driver is around the pretty girl, and they are talking low. It is not necessary to talk loud, as they are so near each other that the faintest whisper can be heard. But a change comes over them. A carriage appears in front, coming towards them. It may be some one that knows them. The young man picks up the lines, and the horses are in the air, and as they pass the other carriage it almost seems as though the team is running away, and the girl that was in sweet repose a moment before acts as though she wanted to jump out. After passing the intruder, the walk and conversation is continued. If you meet that party on the Whitefish Bay road at ten o'clock at night, the horses are walking as quietly as oxen, and they never wake up until coming into town. If the driver seems to be asleep, one of the horses will kick the single-tree and wake him up, and then he pulls up the team and drives through the town like a cyclone, and when he drives up to the home the old man is on the steps, and he thinks John must be awful tired trying to hold that team. And he is.

It is thought by some that horses have no intelligence, but a team that knows enough to take in a sporadic case of buggy sparking has got sense. These teams come high, but the boys have to have them.

SOMETHING NEW
— AT —
Woodburn, Va.

A NEW CIDER MILL—capacity One Hundred and Twenty Bushel an hour. Come one, come all, and make your Cider for 40 cents a Barrel. A Screw-press Power, 15 tons, and buy anything you want while the apple juice is running. Come, we will be glad to wait on you. Respectfully,

sept 3-tf. O. M. BUSSARD

Letter from the Frontier.

KIOWA, COMANCHE & WICHITA AGENCY, I. T.

DEAR SHEETZ: When I saw you last I promised occasionally to let you hear from the Indian Territory. This is about the first leisure evening I have had, and although the thermometer is standing at a little over one hundred I will jot down a few things, observed within the last few weeks, which may interest some of your Loudoun readers.

Some months since, a very pious and very noted old Delaware Chief, by the name of Black Beaver, conceived the idea of building a Church near here, and his high character among all the whites of this country enabled him to raise the necessary funds to accomplish the desire of his heart, and although he died some two months since, the Church is completed, and was dedicated about one month since. Being invited to attend this meeting, I went and found the Church building a neat and substantial frame structure, located in a deep, broad canon, at the head of which is a fine spring, (a very rare article in this country). Around the Church and up and down the canyon the more civilized Indians, belonging to the Wichita, Caddo and Delaware bands, were encamped in regular camp-meeting style.— They treated myself and other whites who attended their meeting, with great hospitality and kindness.

When I first got on the ground I met a delegation of wild Kiowas, whom I knew very well. They were dressed in the unique costume of the plains, and told me that they had come to find out what was meant by christianity; they had never heard of it before and were anxious to learn something about it. They were met and cordially entertained by the more civilized bands, and in the evening, after engaging the necessary interpreters, an educated Choctaw preacher endeavored to explain to them what it meant. The wild Chiefs are very inquisitive and frequently interrupted the preacher with questions, but the best order prevailed and everything passed off pleasantly. I was invited by Jumper, a Seminole Chief and preacher, to a seat where I could see and hear all that passed. This Seminole preacher will be recollected by some of your readers as one of the leading and most prominent spirits of the Florida war. He is a fine looking man, was an able warrior, and is said now to be accomplishing much good among his people as a preacher. After listening to all the Choctaw minister had to say, these wild Kiowas returned to their camps, and in a few days called their various bands together to discuss the white man's religion, as they term it, and the conclusion reached was this—that according to their doctrine none could go to the happy hunting ground except those who believed in the white man's God, and while all this might be true they knew that their fathers, mothers and friends who had died heretofore had never heard of this religion, and consequently if the doctrine was true, had gone to the bad country, and that upon the whole, they thought it would be better for them to go to the bad place, where they would meet all of their relatives and friends, than to the good place where all would be strangers.

While the more civilized of the affiliated bands were enjoying their meeting, another portion, under the leadership of a Caddo and Delaware Chief, were having their grand annual dance, and being pretty well acquainted with most of these Indians, curiosity led me to the dance also, where I found several hundred Indians engaged in dancing or looking at others. They danced a great variety of dances to the dull, monotonous music of the drum, but the regular war dance was the only one that interested me. In this they were dressed in the most grotesque style in many cases, while in others they were scarcely dressed at all. Some of them wore war bonnets upon which were arranged horns. Their faces were painted in the most hideous style, and everything about their whole rig was designed to be as frightful as possible and during the progress of the dance they frequently brandished their weapons and with the wildest and most hideous yells dashed upon their imaginary foes, and went through all the forms of killing, scalping, &c., &c. They consider all this very grand and frequently asked me how I liked it. While the dance was in progress a band of some two hundred Cheyennes came suddenly upon the camp — Everything looked a little *squally* and many of the Indians themselves thought trouble was at hand, but the Chief of the Caddoes stepped out from his band and, by signs, asked what was wanted, when the Chief of the Cheyennes came forward and told him they came as friends to witness the dance and to give them a specimen of the Cheyenne dances. They were then shown a camping ground near our trading house, and after they were settled and when it had grown dark, I concluded to go down and see what was to be done. I found the warriors were painting and making various other preparations for a big dance, while the squaws were equally busy in preparing a grand feast of dog meat. All of these Indians are quite hospitable, and they regard a refusal to partake of their delicacies by their visitors as a breach of etiquette, and I therefore quietly withdrew without saying anything to my white friends who had gone with me. When the meal was ready all of my friends were invited to partake, and sooner than give offense they all had to eat dog. They say it was very good but they had poor appetites and ate lightly—which I think probable.

We have at this time a large number of Shawnees, Osages, Kickapo and Pawnee Indians visiting the Indians of this reservation, and therefore have a complete round of frolicing all the time.

Yesterday, while very busy in my counting-room, I heard the sound of a drum, accompanied by the wild singing and piercing yells of savages, and looking out over the prairie I saw some thirty warriors on foot, at the head of whom was a kind of leader dressed in a magnificent war bonnet of eagle feathers which hung down behind and swept the ground. The Indians were dancing, leaping and yelling as they approached, while some fifteen or twenty Indians, mounted on horseback, with lances in their hands and their horses very richly caparisoned, dashed to and fro through their lines in every conceivable style. I wondered what it meant, but soon found that they were visitors to this reservation from other agencies, and had come up to our house to entertain us with a dance. They always expect to be treated to cakes, candies, nuts, &c., on such occasions; this, of course, we gave them, when, after finishing the dance and enjoying the treat, they quietly withdrew in fine humor. But I have already written more than I intended and will close.

Yours, &c. * * *

Cathartic Pills

AYER'S PILLS are an effectual cure for Constipation or Costiveness, Indigestion, Dyspepsia, Loss of Appetite, Foul Stomach and Breath, Dizziness, Headache, Loss of Memory, Numbness, Biliousness, Jaundice, Rheumatism, Eruptions and Skin Diseases, Dropsy, Tumors, Worms, Neuralgia, Colic, Gripes, Diarrhœa, Dysentery, Gout, Piles, Disorders of the Liver, and all other diseases resulting from a disordered state of the digestive apparatus.

As a Dinner Pill they have no equal.

While gentle in their action, these PILLS are the most thorough and searching cathartic that can be employed, and never give pain unless the bowels are inflamed, and then their influence is healing. They stimulate the appetite and digestive organs; they operate to purify and enrich the blood, and impart renewed health and vigor to the whole system.

Prepared by Dr. J. C. Ayer & Co.,
Practical and Analytical Chemists,
Lowell, Mass.
SOLD BY ALL DRUGGISTS EVERYWHERE

OPIUM EATERS EASILY CURED By one that used it 13 years. Address JOS. A. DUNN, Elizabeth, N. Y.

Uncle Remus,

AND OTHER LATE BOOKS, at the

LOUDOUN BOOKSTORE.

THE FALL TERM

Of Lincoln Academy begins September 13, 1880. Those wanting a good, substantial, and cheap School, in the healthy valley of old Loudoun, will do well to address the Principal, J. S. WILSON at Lincoln, immediately.

DAY'S HORSE & CATTLE POWDER,

A sure preventive of Lung Fever and a certain remedy for Glanders, Yellow Water, Distemper, Founder, Heaves Slavering, Fevers, Coughs, Worms, Loss of Appetite and Vital Energy, &c.

Cures Hoove x, Scouring, Hollow Horn, Wolf, Hidebound Loss of Appetite, Staring Coat, Distemper, will increase the flow of Milk and Cream and make the Butter firm and sweet. It prevents all diseases in Sheep and Lambs, improves their condition and assists in fattening. It cures Rot, Coughs, Colds, Spots, &c. It is especially recommended for ewes when giving milk to lambs. It prevents Hog Cholera, cures Ulcers in the Lungs and Liver, Swelled Necks, Coughs, Measles, &c. and promotes the growth of stunted Pigs. Each package contains 1 pd., full weight.

Price 25 Cents.

August, 1880

8/7/80 Washingtonian

Messrs. HARRY WOODSON and RODIE C. ALLEN, the former late of the Dixie Minstrels, Philadelphia, and the latter of Charley White's Minstrels, New York, gave two entertainments at Hammerley's Hall Leesburg, this week, greatly to the satisfaction and amusement of their audience. The performance is amusing and entertaining to the most refined audience. Mr. Allen is a superior banjoist and Woodson is a most admirable imitator in the characters he represented. The "Old Darkey's return to Dixie" was remarkably fine and touching.

8/12/80 Mirror   COMMUNICATED.

BOARDERS IN LOUDOUN.—Loudoun County is becoming quite a summer resort—and why not—(the writer has travelled over the greater part of the U. S., and has never as yet seen any place that surpassed Loudoun in natural beauty. Situated several hundred feet above the sea and between two mountain ranges, she possesses pure air, fertile soil, clear and wholesome water, and plenty of that good article mostly desired by boarders—shade. Her people are honest, intelligent, industrious and hospitable. When right minded folks come or go to the country, they neither look for, nor expect the cookery of a Breemont Hotel or a Parker House, nor do they expect to recline upon velvet lined sofas, or walk on Axminster or Brussel's carpets, &c., &c., &c. No; but you will get an airy room, clean beds, excellent water and good, wholesome and well-cooked food, and attention and kindness thrown in, and I know (from experience), that health will follow; it is worth a trial at any rate.

But Mr. Editor there is another class of people I would speak of: They are the ones that are never satisfied—I will cite a true case that occurred at Hillsboro' in this county.— These people drove to the place of a gentleman in Hillsboro' who keeps boarders, and instead of going to the residence of the gentleman, they went to the stable. The looks, &c., of the stable were reported to the 'Boss' man (and at this juncture of the proceedings, which had been witnessed by the proprietor and his boarders and friends,) the gentleman of the boarding house drew near and asked if the ladies and gentlemen were 'looking for a boarding place, &c., when the chief of the unceremonious arrival,—said "your d—d house, much less your stable,—is not good enough for my horses. The gentleman addressed, simply said 'If you don't like my house you can go elsewhere." Whenever a set of Shoddys or Veneerings are looking for a place into which they wish to retire and display their vulgarity and ignorance, I would advise them to give Loudoun the "go-by," as we don't want them and will not have them.   CATO.

8/19/80 Mirror

Hancock and English Club.

At a meeting held in Aldie, on Saturday, August 14th, 1880, for the purpose of organizing a 'Hancock and English Club. Chas. B. Adams Esq., was called to the Chair, and Clarence Thomas elected Secretary.

Upon motion, Capt. John R. Hutchison stated the object of the Club to be: The erection of a Hancock and English pole and flag, surmounted with a ball and revolving chicken cock—the procurement of a band of music—a barbecue and a regular old-fashioned Democratic love-feast generally.

On motion, the following Vice-Presidents were unanimously elected: Wm. H. Rogers, J. S. Redd, Dallas Furr, Capt. J. R. Hutchison and William Gaines.

Moved and agreed the following standing committees be appointed.—

Committee on Pole.—Jos. L. Norris, Chairman; David I. Lee, E. A. Tyler, Robert Whitlock, Richard Garrett and A. J. Redd.

Committee on Flag.—Capt. J. R. Hutchison, David L Lee, Wm. H. Rogers Wm. Gaines and Jno. T. Laws.

Committee on Invitation.—Clarence Thomas, Robert Adams, Chas. Matthews, J. M. McVeigh and J. F. Brawner.

Committee on Music.—Dr. R. D. Leith, David L Lee, R. L. Moore, J. S. Laws and J. P. H. Green.

Committee on Barbecue and Dinner.—Whole neighborhood.

Committee on Table.—Capt Jno. R. Hutchison, Humphrey Lynn, Milton Gulick, J. J. Currell, Dr. R. D. Leith, Thomas Gaines, Jno. Adams, B. P. Brawner, Jno. F. Simpson, Edward Potts, J. F. H. Green, Newton Palmer and James W. Ferguson.

Committee on Seats.—Williamson Skinner, Humphrey Lynn, E. A. Tyler, Ned Ish, A. M. Cridler, Geo. Bodner, Robt. Riticor, Wm. F. Gulick, Robert Gulick, Richard Garrett and Andrew Norman.

Committee on Water.—J. M. McVeigh, Robert Adams, F. A. Ish, J. S. Redd, Joshua Riticor and J. F. Riticor.

Committee on Printing.—Same as the Committee on Invitation.

Committee on Horse Feed.—Andrew J. Redd

8/14/80 Washingtonian

THE MAN WHO LOOKS LIKE HANCOCK.—A special dispatch to the Cincinnati *Commercial*, dated Zanesville, O. Aug. 13th, says :—The B. & O. train from the east pulled out of the depot this morning bearing a large number of knights for Chicago. Having a few minutes to stop, a gentleman resembling Gen. Hancock appeared on the platform of the rear car, and was introduced with great gravity as the democratic candidate for President. The crowd cheered lustily, and when the noise had subsided the gentleman spoke as follows :

"Fellow-citizens— I am delighted at this demonstration. I am glad to see so many democrats in Ohio who are going to vote for me. I passed through West Virginia yesterday, and similar scenes greeted my eyes at every station.—At one place they presented me with a number of chickens in the shell, and '—

Here the crowd saw the joke and began to laugh and yell, in the midst of which the train pulled out.

August, 1880

7/29/80 Mirror

LAST WEEK, in digging the pit in which to plant the HANCOCK and ENGLISH pole at Orrison's corner on Saturday, the workmen came upon the hickory stump, several feet under ground, of the POLK and DALLAS pole reared at the same point in 1844. Notwithstanding it had been buried in the earth for *thirty-six years*, the wood was in a perfect state of preservation, and as a relic of the past was eagerly seized upon by those curious in such matters, and converted into walking sticks, &c.

8/12/80 Mirror

POLE RAISING AT ALDIE.—The Hancock & English pole raising at Aldie last Saturday was not attended with the good luck that was expected. The pole originally, we understand, measured about 80 feet, but when partially elevated, the splice broke and nearly one-half of it came crashing to the earth. The flag was speedily attached to the "better half" and that portion of the staff duly planted, after which Col. R. H. LEE delivered a most telling and inspiring speech in behalf of Hancock, English, and the National Democracy.

8/26/80 Mirror

Hancock and English Pole Raising and Grand Mass Meeting at Snickersville, August 28th, 1880.

The pole raising will commence at 10 o'clock a. m.

9/9/80 Mirror

Pole-Raising and Public Speaking at Upperville.

NORTH FORK, VA., Sept. 6th, 1880.

MR. EDITOR:—On Thursday last, the Hancock and English Club, of Upperville, had a gala day and a grand demonstration, which was the unfurling of a beautiful flag, beneath a Hancock and English streamer, on a pole about 90 feet in height. The flag was run up to its position by W. S. Peach, Chairman of the Hancock and English Club. The Silcotts Springs Band played a national selection.

9/23/80 Mirror

Pole Raising at Waterford.

The Wheatland Hancock and English Club, propose raising a pole in Waterford, Sept. 18th, 1880 at 2 p. m.

The members of the Democratic Clubs, of Loudoun County, and the public are respectfully invited to attend.

8/19/80 Mirror

THE GARFIELD DEMONSTRATION IN LEESBURG—POLE RAISING—SPEECHES, &c.—Several weeks ago, just after the erection of the Hancock and English pole in Leesburg, the colored Garfield Club of this town concluded that they must have a pole, and made the necessary preparation for the occasion. It seemed to be entirely under the auspices of the colored Republicans, and nobody paid much attention to it, (the malicious canard so widely circulated to the contrary notwithstanding.

It was finally announced that the pole would be raised on Saturday last, at which time special trains from Washington and Alexandria were to bring vast numbers of sympathizing Republicans from those cities and the intervening country, to participate in the proceedings. It was published far and wide that the first Republican pole in Loudoun would be raised in Leesburg at the time indicated—and naturally our people awaited developments.

During the morning of Saturday a few wagon loads of darkies from the upper portion of the county drove into town, and before ten o'clock the pole was planted at the south end of King street. A negro band had arrived the evening previous from Alexandria, which kept up an almost incessant blowing of horns until about 4 o'clock when the train arrived bringing hither the expected guests. Instead of two trains there was but one, and the arrivals, embracing men, women and children, numbered 300. Simultaneously with their arrival the flag was run to the pole mast, the procession was formed, and after parading the streets for awhile, proceeded to Court-House square, where, after a few words of welcome from Mr. EDWARD NICHOLS, speeches were made by A. M. CLAPP, editor of the *National Republican*, J. M. SYPHER, of Washington, and one or two others whose names we did not learn. We think we are safe in saying that the crowd did not number over 500, nine-tenths of whom were colored men and women.

September, 1880

THE MIRROR

BENJ. F. SHEETZ, Editor.

Thursday Morning, Sept. 30, 1880.

PRESIDENTIAL TICKET.

FOR PRESIDENT,
WINFIELD SCOTT HANCOCK,
OF PENNSYLVANIA.

FOR VICE PRESIDENT;
WILLIAM H. ENGLISH,
OF INDIANA.

ELECTORS,
At Large.—JOHN ECHOLS, of Augusta.
P. W. McKINNEY, of Farmville
1st District.—THOMAS CROXTON, Essex County.
2d   "   L. R. WATTS, Portsmouth.
3d   "   HILL CARTER, Hanover County.
4th   "   SAMUEL F COLEMAN.
5th   "   JAMES S REDD, of Henry.
6th   "   SAMUEL GRIFFIN
7th   "   F. M McMULLEN, Green County.
8th   "   J. G. MENEFEE, Rappahannock Co.
9th   "   H. H HENRY, of Tazewell.

For Congress---Eighth District,
Hon. JOHN S. BARBOUR,
OF ALEXANDRIA.

Attention Young Democrats.

All young men who have become of age since the 1st day of February, 1879, and have not registered, should do so at once. None of such is required to pay a capitation tax before voting, but if any fail to register he cannot vote.

Hancock and English Tournament.

A Hancock and English Tournament will be held a ½ mile West of Belmont Station, on

SATURDAY, SEPTEMBER 4th, 1880.

The prize will be A BRIDLE AND WHIP
CAPT. J. W. FOSTER, will deliver the address to the Knights.
The Riding will commence at 10 o'clock. A. M. General invitation extended to all.
A spacious pavilion will be prepared for dancing, and every preparation for the comfort and pleasure of those who may attend.
A good STRING BAND will be in attendance.
WM. PEACOCK,
Chief Marshal.

9/30/80 Mirror

The Demonstration at Lincoln.

MR. EDITOR: In accordance with their previously advertised intention, the Democracy of Lincoln and surrounding neighborhood, met in that quiet little village on Saturday, the 25th, for the purpose of raising a flag-pole, from which should float the names of our glorious candidates and standard bearers— Hancock, English and Barbour. The pole, a beautiful one, was raised without trouble or accident, and the banner unfurled amid the cheers and huzzas of the hundreds who had aided in its erection. In a beautiful and shady neighboring grove, a stand had been erected, for the occupation of the speakers who had been invited to address their fellow citizens upon this occasion), and the comfortable seats spread out in its front, gave conclusive proof that the committee had not been unmindful of the comfort of those who were to listen— be instructed and entertained. These seats the many assembled speedily occupied, and Mr. Jno. T. Shuey in a short, but pleasant and pertinent address, introduced to them as the first speaker of the day, Col. Henry E. Peyton, a citizen of Loudoun and a gifted one, of whom we may well feel proud. It would be gross injustice to that gentleman (as, indeed, to those who followed after,) in attempting here anything more than the most brief and cursory report of the many good and all-sufficient reasons he gave for the Democratic faith that was in him. He seemed pleased, in many views, to stray from the familiar and beaten path, and moved upon a higher and more elevated plane of political discussion. The dangerous and pernicious principles of strong, and centralized government, desired by our Republican friends, met with their merited rebuke; and the fraud of 1876, perpetrated by that christian statesman (?) James A. Garfield, et al, by which the expressed voice of fifty millions of people had been stifled, received such denunciation as only the accomplished rhetoricians might hope to give it.

(And so the speaker continued, lambasting in good partisan style the Republican opponents and connecting Garfield to the Credit Mobilier scandal and other sins. Unfortunately, we can't quote an effective rebuttal because the Republican newspaper "The Telephone" has no records on microfilm for 1880.)

September, 1880

9/16/80 Mirror

THE SO-CALLED CODE OF HONOR.

DEAR SIR.—The frequency with which attempts have been made of late to fight duels in the State of Virginia, is not adding anything to our reputation as a highly civilized people. We are becoming the bye word and reproach of States and people where such flagrant and shameful breaches of the peace are hardly ever known. In England duelling is well nigh extinct. The press and public sentiment frown it down as a relic of barbarism, while the law threatens its heaviest penalties against such misdemeanors. But here in Virginia the public are often treated through the Press to the blood-thirsty proceedings of 'an affair of honor' (so-called) with all its atrocious and murderous wickedness, and no legislation thus far has been able to check the cold-blooded tragedies. Public men—men whose business is to make and execute laws for the prevention of crime—are sometimes the daring spirits who over-ride the law and all its officers. They set an example in the adjustment of difficulties between men which, if followed, would resolve society into a state of chaos, and make human life of no more account than the life of a brute. These men are great sticklers for the *Code*. They put *their* code above that of God and the Commonwealth, and they are ready to stigmatise any man as a coward and poltroon who refuses to accept a challenge to fight a duel.

9/16/80 Mirror

DISTRESSING ACCIDENT.—A most sad and melancholy accident occurred on the W. & O. Railroad last Tuesday morning, the first of the kind, we believe, that has ever happened on that road—by which a worthy citizen lost his life. As the early morning train was coming from Round Hill, when in the cut just beyond Hamilton depot, the engineer discovered a man walking down the track a few hundred yards in front of the engine; the brakes were immediately put on and every signal sounded that could be, but to no purpose, and soon the dashing train was upon the unfortunate victim, who met with a horrible death. As soon as could be the train was stopped, and the dead, mutilated body proved to be that of Mr. Jos L. DAVIS, a deaf mute. Mr. D. had gone out in search of his cows, and walking on the track, with his back to the approaching train, of course could hear none of the warning sounds, and met his death as stated above. Coroner H. O. CLAGETT visited the scene of the accident but did not deem it necessary to hold an inquest. It was apparent that the train-men had done everything that could be done to prevent the accident, which was occasioned by the infirmity of hearing of the unfortunate man. Mr. Davis was about 50 years of age, and leaves a wife, also a mute, but no children.

THE GENUINE YOUNG AMERICA Corn and Cob Mill.

MANUFACTURED BY D. Whitman Sons & CO.

"We have seen a variety of Corn and Cob Mills, but believe the Young America to be the best and most reasonable in price that is made. J. H. PANCOST. S. B. NICHOLS, Silcotts Spring, Va.
We recommend it to all who have Stock or Poultry to feed. J. W. GARRETT, Philomont, E. FENTON, Lincoln, Va.
I am delighted with the Young America Mill bought of W. T. Shoemaker. R. C. LITTLETON, Bloomfield, Va.
I have been using one for about 25 years and recommend them to farmers and stockholders. ISAAC NICHOLS, Lincoln, Va.
It took special Premium at Montgomery county, Md., Fair, Sept. 11th, 1878, and at Loudoun county Fair, Sept. 19th, 1878, and at the Alexandria Fair, Oct. 2nd 1878. Send for circular. For sale by
Price, $40. W. T SHOEMAKER, Lincoln, Va.

September, 1880

GENERAL HUNTON

9/4/80 Washingtonian

We believe we state the sentiments of a decided majority of the conservative voters of this district, when we express our regret at the loss in congress of the valuable service of this gentleman. But his declaration, that he would not be a candidate again, thus expressing his wish to retire from public life, left no chance for his friends to press him for renomination. His retirement is a loss to this district and State.

It has rarely been the fortune of any member from Virginia to gain a more influential position in that body, than he had won by the display of sound judgment, admirable good sense, and a faithful and unflinching discharge of his duty as he understood it. While not brilliant on debate he was strong in argument, and thoroughly fortified in every essential, to a full discussion and vindication of every question he espoused, and always won the attention and made his influence felt over that body. By reason of the nearness of his district to the capital, he had a vast amount of business to attend to in the District, and we are sure of his effort to accommodate the wants of his constituents, be fairly judged, with a knowledge of the vast number of cases with which he was daily besieged, he will be found to have done his full duty in that line. We regret that his services are lost at this important period in the march of the party to ascendency, and wish that it could have been otherwise.

He retires to private life bearing a splendid public record.

(Eppa Hunton's retirement proved to be premature as he later was appointed to fill a vacancy in the U.S. Senate.
As an attorney from a neighboring county, he practiced often in the Loudoun courts. In the Civil War, he commanded the 8th Virginia Regiment composed of many local soldiers and rose eventually to the rank of Brigidier General. Wounded like many of his comrades in Pickett's charge (up to 90% killed, wounded or captured) he re-recruited the decimated 8th to be an effective force. General Hunton was the only southerner appointed to the commission to settle the 1876 Hayes-Tilden election.)

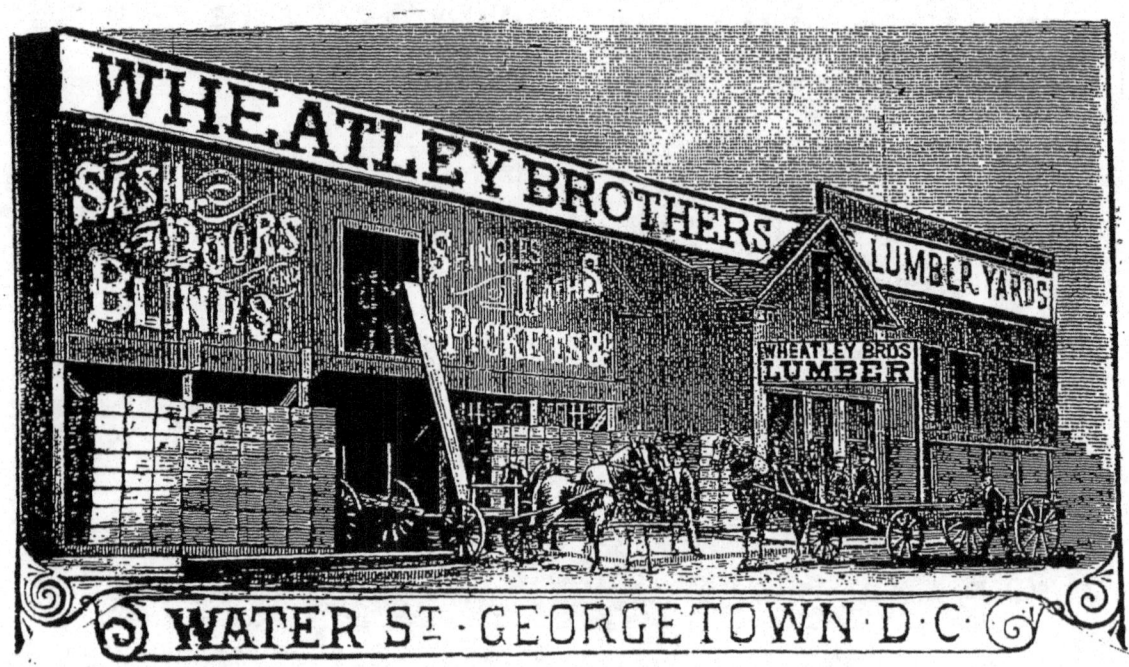

—ALL KINDS OF—
Building and House Furnishing Material!
LUMBER DELIVERED ON CARS OR BOATS FREE OF CHARGE.

September, 1880

Belmont for Sale.

BY virtue of authority in them vested by decree of Loudoun Circuit Court, entered in the cause of Warner vs. Kephart, on the 7th day of May, 1880, the undersigned will offer at public auction, to the highest bidder, in front of the Court-House, in Leesburg, at about noon, on

MONDAY 13th SEPTEMBER, 1880,

that fine old Homestead of the Lees, known as "BELMONT," now occupied by the Hon. F. P. Stanton, and is situated in Loudoun county, Va., about five miles East of Leesburg, on the Washington turnpike, and within less than a mile of the W. & O. R. R., containing about

400 ACRES.

The IMPROVEMENTS consist of a large and

Handsome Brick DWELLING,

occupying a remarkably healthy and commanding position, with all necessary outbuildings.

There is FINE FRUIT upon the place and its easy access from Washington would make it a desirable home, as well as a profitable investment for any one, whose business is in the city, but who would prefer to live in the country.

TERMS OF SALE:—Ten per cent. of the purchase money to be paid in Cash, and the residue in four equal instalments, payable respectively, on the confirmation of the Sale, in one, two, and three years from the day of Sale, the purchaser to give his bonds, bearing interest from the day of Sale, for the deferred payments—and the title to be retained till payment in full.   LOUIS H. POWELL,
HENRY HEATON,
L. W. FOSTER,
Commissioners of Sale.

Historic Belmont is still standing, but is part of a country club complex.

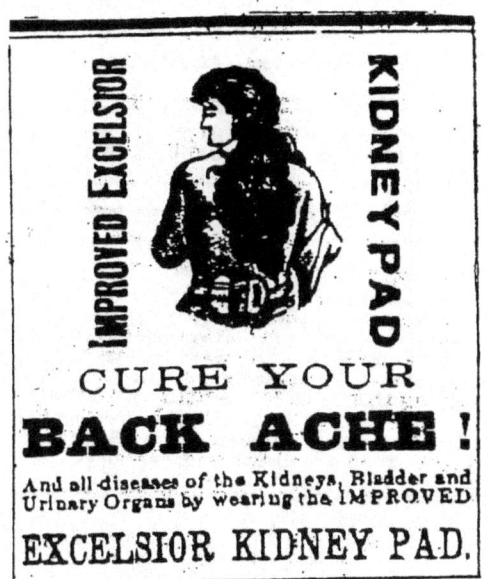

9/30/80 Mirror

An Old Ringmaster's Experience.

Ringmaster Robert Ellingham, a veteran showman who has been connected with the circus business since 1836, stood by as the tents were packing, gazing thoughtfully on the busy scene.

"Things have changed a little since my days," he said. "They didn't use to do things in this way when I was young. They didn't have any big tents and electric lights and special cars and gilded chariots and advance agents. We used to play by the light of oil lamps, and sometimes by scarcely any light. We didn't travel by rail, and as for advance agents they were altogether unknown.

"I first entered the show business, continued the ringmaster, "in 1836. There were some shows in this country before that time, as early as 1833—Howe's and Brown's and a few others. The show I went with was called Aaron Turner's Circus. Aaron Turner was the owner and P. T. Barnum was the treasurer. I entered the show as a singer—a delineator of negro character. There were no minstrels in those days, but minstrel singers used to travel with the shows. They were performing in New York city when I joined the show, and after that they travelled through the Eastern cities, through Pennsylvania, New Jersey, Maryland and the South. There were altogether about forty or fifty horses in the show. We had no menagerie. Such things were unknown in those days in connection with circuses, although some showmen travelled about with wild beasts which they exhibited in the rural towns. The principal performers in our circus were Napoleon and Timothy Turner, son of the proprietor.— They both were riders: one of them rode a single horse and the other rode two and sometimes four horses. There were no bareback riders in those days and the Turner boys always used saddles. The other attractions were Signor Vivalli, the plate spinner, whom Barnum mentions in his book, and Joe Pentland, the clown. There was also a man named Helcheser, a remarkable delineator of negro character, who used to give concerts in a tent outside, and sing old plantation and negro songs. Were there any trapeze performances? Oh, no! There were no aerial performances, no jumping or leaping in those days. All they did in that way was to walk and dance and leap over hurdles on stilts.

"When we got to Richmond, Va., late in the fall, we encountered another show belonging to Derious & Hopkis. I don't know what the trouble was, but the proprietors failed and the show was sold under the hammer. They bought in the outfit, however, and started Barnum, our treasurer, in the show business. He travelled through the South with Vivalli, the plate spinner; Joe Pentland the clown from our show and a minstrel man from Philadelphia named Jim Sandford. He left the show before the end of the season and I took his place.

September, 1880

9/18/80 Washingtonian

FATAL AND DISTRESSING ACCIDENT.

On Saturday evening last Miss Bertha Edmiston, a pupil of the Episcopal Female Institute, was fatally burnt by her clothing taking fire, and died the next morning at 11 o'clock. Miss Edmiston, of Weston, West Va., went up to her room, which was on the third floor for some purpose at 7½ o'clock. She took in her hand, a kerosene oil lamp. After she had gotten in her room the chimney which had been insecurely fastened on the lamp fell off, which startled her and caused her to drop the lamp on the floor. She turned and ran out of the room, but some of the oil which ran out of the mouth of the lamp caught in the flame and set fire to her dress— a thin lawn. She flew along the hallway down two long flights of steps defying the efforts of one of the young ladies on one of the landings who tried to stop her but could not, only succeeded in throwing a small shawl over her face which protected it from the fire. When she reached the lower floor Mr. Wheat having in the meantime heard her screams met her and in an instant threw something around her and put out the flames.

She was carried into a room and had the tender care of physicians and nurses, but no effect could save her life. The accident occurring just at the beginning of the session has thrown a gloom over the whole school; and Dr. Wheat, who is proverbial for his watchful care and kind interest to his pupils, is heavily bowed down by this great calamity. It is proper to state that the whole building is lighted with gas, but finding the bracket in the room Miss Edmiston occupied leaked a little she was advised until it was repaired to use a lamp.

Miss Edmiston was about sixteen years old. Her remains were sent to her home on Monday morning.— *Winchester Times.*

(The old oil lamps caused many fires, some similar to this.)

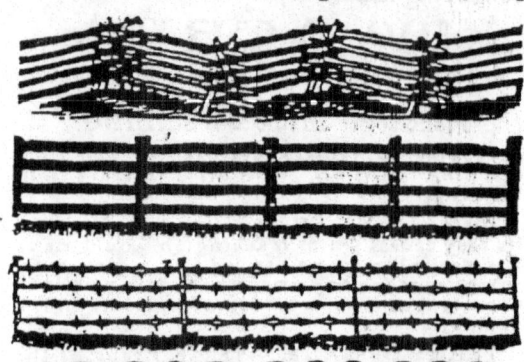

Supposedly, the invention that helped spell the end of the western cattle drives.)

October 1880

10/14/80 Mirror

A PORTION OF A CATTLE TRAIN WRECKED.—About eighty three car loads of cattle, collected from along the line of the Virginia Midland Railroad passed through here over that road Saturday night for Baltimore. Just north of the tunnel near Four Mile Run, between this city and Washington, a portion of one of the trains of twenty two cars was thrown from the track about half past eleven o'clock, by the breaking of the axle on one of the stock cars. The detached cars rolled into the river on the right hand side of the road, and several others were telescoped, causing the loss of all the cattle and sheep they contained. About eighteen head of cattle and one hundred and sixty-five sheep were killed outright, while a number of others were so badly maimed that they were slaughtered on the spot by Washington speculators who made their appearance as soon as the character of the accident became known.

10/26/80 Washingtonian

The *Maine Farmer* sees with regret the disuse of oxen and the diminution in their number. It admits that horses perform the work better and quicker than oxen; that they are more fit for use on roads or to encounter bad weather; that they suffer less from extraordinary exertion and from heat than oxen, and that they are adapted to many purposes for which oxen are unfit.

But it says, is not the argument in favor of oxen equally forcible? Oxen cost less at first, and the annual expense for harness, finery and food is much less for oxen than for the horse; they increase in value from the beginning of work; g: are worth more at last than at the first; going at last to the butcher at a price varying from one to two hundred dollars per yoke, while the skin of the dead horse is all that is worth anything. There are some ox-teams that will do as much work on the farm as horses, team for team; but we are aware that such instances are rare. On the contrary, as a general rule, horses will perform about twice as much work on the farm as oxen. English farmers, after carefully experimenting, have arrived at the conclusion that while it takes eight oxen to do the work of five horses the balance of cost would be from twelve to fifteen dollars per annum in favor of ox-teams.

(The Washingtonian had an article on farming in every issue; not surprising in a rural community like Loudoun.)

OLD DOMINION SPOKE AND WHEEL FACTORY,

SNICKERSVILLE, VA.,

Manufactures the Superior "STERRICK" WAGON WHEEL.

THE PROPRIETORS of this Factory call the attention of the people of Loudoun and adjoining counties, to this Superior WAGON WHEEL they are manufacturing. For Strength, Durability and neatness of construction, it has no equal, and will prove the MOST ECONOMICAL AS WELL AS THE SAFEST WHEEL that can be had. This Wheel has had a severe and thorough test by the United States Government, and its merits are fully endorsed at the Quartermaster's Department at Washington, D. C.:

☞ Those who want to try this Wheel will please address
MONROE, GRAHAM & CO.,
Snickersville, Loudoun Co., Virginia.

Manhood:
How Lost! How Restored,

JUST PUBLISHED, a new edition of Dr. CULVERWELL's CELEBRATED ESSAY on the *radical cure* (without medicine) of Spermatorrhœa, or Seminal Weakness, Involuntary Seminal Losses, Impotency, Mental and Physical Incapacity, Impediments to Marriage, etc.; also, Consumption, Epilepsy, and Fits, induced by Self-Indulgence, or sexual extravagance.

The celebrated Author, in this amiable Essay, clearly demonstrates, from a thirty years' successful practice, that the alarming consequences of self-abuse, may be radically cured without the dangerous use of internal medicine or the application of the knife; pointing out a mode of cure at once simple, certain, and effectual, by means of which every sufferer, no matter what his condition may be, may cure himself cheaply, privately, and *radically*.

☞ This Lecture should be in the hands of every youth and every man in the land.

Sent, under seal, in a plain envelope, to any address, *post-paid*, on receipt of six cents, or two postage stamps. Address the Publishers,

The Culverwell Medical Co.,
41 Ann St. New York, N. Y.; Post Office Box, 4586. [ap. 22, 1880

10/21/80 Mirror

'Why are you in such a hurry?' said a man to an acquaintance. 'Sir,' he replied, 'I have bought a new bonnet for my wife and fear the fashion may change before I get home.'

October, 1880

"Stonewall Jackson's Way."

ANECDOTE OF A CONFEDERATE GENERAL WHO HAD A WAY OF HIS OWN.

As is well known, Jackson was careless in dress, in gait, and when astride a horse he was just as apt to have his No 9's dangling out of the stirrups as in them. A thoughtful man, with oblong features, kindly gray eyes, sombre in looks, with a mind never at rest, he appeared often in what may not inappropriately be termed "fits of abstraction," and apparently oblivious to everything passing around him, but at the whistle of a minnie ball, or the boom of a cannon, how his whole face lit up with expectency! He was suddenly alive to coming events." Of Jackson's rigid discipline I will here put on record an instance. While a boy, I was coming out of the postoffice in Lexington, Va., one morning, and as I came out, a youth of some seventeen summers passed in, clad in a black suit. I stopped for a minute on the pavement at the postoffice door, with my face toward the Virginia Military Institute, of which Jackson was then a professor. Jackson was coming up the street at the time, and only a few yards from the door. The cadet was in citizen's dress, and had "run the blockade" to get a letter from "his girl," and had thus violated two rules—come to town in citizen's dress, and without leave! He was coming out, unconsciously, into the "snare of the fowler" but he chanced to spy Jackson within a few yards of the office, and instantly sprang back, jumped over the counter, flew past the postmaster, and leaped out of the back window, cat style, on "all fours."

Jackson took in "the situation" at a glance, for, as the cat's heels were disappearing out the back window, Jackson's stern countenance darkened the door, and he cried out in a stentorian voice: 'I recognize you sir! Go to the barracks and report yourself under arrest!" Many a mentor would have been blind to the escapade, would have tried not to have seen his pupil, would have winked at it, but not so with Jackson; on the contrary he quickened his pace and was an interested spectator to the lively movements of the pupil's heels. But it has been a mystery to me ever since, how in the world Jackson recognized that cadet by his No. 7 boots as his heels were disappearing out of the window.

PERSONAL.—We were glad to greet on the street a day or two ago, our old friend Mr. F. M. HENDERSON. He is looking remarkably well, and it is a real pleasure to see him once more in our midst.

An Incident of the Seven Days.

A battery of the First Artillery halted that night in a little clearing. The men lay down, unhitching their horses, but leaving them in harness. The First Sergeant now an honored officer of the Third Artillery, told me he got up and walked toward one side of the clearing. He was halted and turned back by a sentinel. Going toward the other side he was again challenged.

"Who comes thar?"

"The voice struck him. He replied, 'Friend' and said, "What regiment is that?"

The answer came, "Seventh Alabama"

"What regiment is that on the other side?"

"Fifth Georgia." replied the sentinel.

"What battery is that?"

Here was a situation. The sergeant naturally didn't know the name of a battery in the rebel army. Hesitation would have been fatal. By a lucky inspiration he replied, "One of Stuart's batteries," knowing that Jeb Stuart commanded their cavalry.

"Oh," said the other, "then you's a boss battery?"

"Yes," said C——. "Good night."

"He immediately awoke the captain, who rather angrily said, "What the deuce is the matter now?"

"Excuse me, captain," said the sergeant, "but we're camped between a Georgia and an Alabama regiment."

It is needless to say that the captain got up. Horses were hitched in quietly, and the battery withdrew from between the sleeping regiments, who never knew of the prize that was within their grasp.

Dr. R. H. Edwards,

DRUGGISTS AND APOTHECARY
LEESBURG, VA.,

KEEP constantly on hand, a complete stock of Drugs and Medicines, Patent Medicines, Soaps, Perfumery, Combs, Brushes, (Tooth, Hair and Nail,) Knives and Scissors, Tobacco—Chewing and Smoking, Cigars Pipes, &c.

PRESCRIPTIONS CAREFULLY COMPOUNDED.

Stimulating Liniment,

INVALUABLE FOR
Rheumatism, Neuralgia, Spinal Affections
Chilblains, Sprains. Stiff Joints,
Bruises, Enlarged Glands
Swellings of all Sorts
Sore Throat,
Toothach,
&c.,

IN MAN OR BEAST.

October, 1880

10/7/80 Mirror

DARING CLIMBING — When the North Danville Hancock and English and Cabell Club raised their flag pole they surmounted it with the figure of a cock, but somehow in the erection of the pole the cock's position became deranged. The pole lacked but a few feet of being one hundred in height, and to alter the position of the cock became a matter of much concern to our neighbors over the Dan. Several attempts were made by men to ascend the pole, but in every instance the hearts of the climbers grew faint, and before more than half of the pole was scaled they turned back. Yesterday, however, Mr T. J. Corbin, the impulsive and energetic president of the North Danville Club, offered a colored man employed by the Western Union Telegraph Company $10 if he would climb to the figure that tipped the top of the pole and place it in proper position. The man accepted the offer, and was soon at the top of the pole. The wind was blowing briskly at the time and the slender pine pole swayed beneath the weight of the daring climber, who nothing daunted, performed his task while the lookers on stood with their hearts in their mouths as they watched him. He asked if he had finished the work right, and an affirmative reply was shouted him back. Whereupon the colored man removed his hat and at nearly one hundred feet from the earth, waved it in the air and hurrahed for Hancock and English.

The Bonanza for Book-Agents is selling our SPLENDIDLY *illustrated* book, Life of

GENERAL HANCOCK

written by his life-long friend Hon. J. W. FORNEY, and author of *national fame*, and an *ardent* admirer of the "superb soldier"; including the Life of Hon. WM. H. ENGLISH. This work is officially endorsed, low-priced, *immensely* popular, and selling beyond precedent. Outfits 50c. Act quick and coin money. For the best book, *best terms*, and full particulars, address HUBBARD BROS., Atlanta, Ga.

AGENTS WANTED AT ONCE to sell the lives of our next President and Vice-President,

GEN. HANCOCK AND Hon. W. H. ENGLISH

Thousands are waiting for the book. It contains steel portraits of the Candidates and other full-page engravings. Extra inducements offered to those selecting territory now. Douglass Bros., 55 W. 5th st., Cincinnati, O.

10/28/80 Mirror

"OUR FLAG IS (NOT) THERE" — A few weeks ago the gallant little band of Waterford Democrats, erected a handsome Hancock and English pole in that town, from the mast of which floated a streamer bearing the names of their standard-bearers, and a beautiful national flag. About the same time the Democrats of Lincoln erected a similar pole at that point. A few weeks ago, as has been already noted, an effort was made to destroy the latter with powder. The effort failed, but the animus of the deed remained. And now we have to chronicle a more successful outrage on the Waterford pole. Last Monday night some miscreant cut the rope by which the stars and stripes were run up. At the time the pole was raised the municipal authorities of the town exacted a $600 bond before they would allow it to go up, and it was given. Now, the first and only injury sustained has been by the pole itself — will these patriotic city fathers take the proper steps to ferret out the guilty party, and visit upon them the condemnation uttered by Gen. Dix against the first man that tore down the American flag, "shoot him on the spot." But all badinage aside, isn't it contemptable? — Thank heaven the streamer with the names of H., & E., was *nailed* to the top of the pole, where they still float in triumph — it was the national emblem alone that was made to trail in the dust.

9/16/80 Mirror

LOUDOUN'S FIRST HANCOCK — A correspondent from Bloomfield, Loudoun county, Va, writes: "The first male child born in our neighborhood since Gen. Hancock's nomination, is a colored or negro child, and it has been named Winfield Scott Hancock Talliaferro. The father, Edward Talliaferro, has been voting the Democratic ticket ever since the war. Among the hardest workers at the Snickersvile flag-raising were three colored men. One of them put the iron bands on the splice of the pole but says he will not do it for a Garfield flag that is to be raised there."—

It is astonishing how completely some people can be absorbed in their own thoughts. A prominent candidate, who gives up the whole of his mind to politics, met a prominent church member who remarked that his church had just got a new organ. 'I hope it will support the regular nominees, was the absent minded reply.

ATTENTION

Democracy!

COME TO THE GRAND

BARBECUE,
—AND—
TORCHLIGHT

Procession!

TO BE GIVEN AT

LEESBURG,

on the Day and Evening of

WEDNESDAY,

OCT. 20th, 1880.

Provision has been made TO FEED

10,000 PEOPLE.

THE LADIES ARE ALL COMING!

Hancock and English Clubs

from this and adjoining Counties,

AS ALSO, FROM

Alexandria, Washington and Georgetown, to be invited.

Speeches, Speeches

Men of National Reputation,
and many of this Country's Greatest and
MOST FAMED ORATORS,
will address the multitude

HANCOCK
—AND—
JOHN S BARBOUR

invited and expected to be present.

MUSIC MUSIC!

SIX BRASS BANDS

will be in attendance,—including the

MARINE BAND,

OF WASHINGTON, D. C.

8,000

TORCHES, BANNERS

TRANSPARENCIES.

THE TOWN WILL BE

Brilliantly Illuminated,

EXTENSIVE FIRE-WORKS

are to be provided, and HANDSOME
ARCHES here and there,
MADE TO SPAN THE STREETS, having
inscribed thereon the names of our
STANDARD-BEARERS,

Hancock, English, & Barbour

Let our WHOLE COUNTY turn out!

An Extraordinary

Demonstration

is determined upon, and WILL BE HAD.
It is understood that THIS IS TO BE A

GRAND RALLY

OF THE DEMOCRACY!

We know in this house no FUNDERISM,
no READJUSTERISM. We will be called
upon in November next, to meet our old and
common political enemy—Republicanism.
Let us meet it with Unbroken Column.

JAS F. DIVINE,
JNO. Y. BASSELL,
HENRY HEATON,
oct. 7, 1880.   Committee

November, 1880

11/4/80 Mirror

TUESDAY'S WATERLOO.

There was an election last Tuesday all over the United States, for President, and we, like thousands of others throughout the land, sat up until 5 o'clock Wednesday morning, waiting for the returns. And we got 'em. To say that we were surprised, disappointed, and fairly disgusted, hardly expresses our chagrin. Under the leadership of the pure and gallant Hancock, notwithstanding we knew that the enemy held us at a disadvantage at almost every point, we had fondly dreamed of victory and a disenthralment from the rest of Republicanism—but from the first dispatch to the last, we saw our fondest hopes decay until at this writing an inglorious defeat.

Throughout the campaign just brought to a disastrous close, we conscientiously believed that the election of Hancock and a change of administration, would rebound to the good of the whole people, and restore and continue to us the government in the purity, simplicity and honesty with which it was handed down to us from the fathers. A majority of the American people thought otherwise, and however much we may deplore their action, we are too good a Democrat and too sincere a lover of our free institutions, to do aught else than bow with as good grace as we can command under the circumstances, to their verdict.

From the Washington Post of Wednesday.

GARFIELD ELECTED

New York, Indiana, Pennsylvania, Connecticut and Maine Carried for Him.

HANCOCK SECURES NEW JERSEY AND THE SOLID SOUTH WITH THE PACIFIC STATES CLOSE AND DOUBTFUL.

A Small Democratic Majority Claimed In the House of Representatives, Based on Relative Gains and Losses.

The Legislatures in Connecticut, New York and Pennsylvania with the other States Democratic or Doubtful

Full and Complete Returns from Each State, County and City of This Great and Glorious, but Awfully Depraved Country.

The country voted yesterday for a President and Vice President to hold office for four years from the 4th of March next. The result was the election of the Republican candidates, James A. Garfield, of Ohio, and Chester A. Arthur, of New York. Returns received up to 4 30 o'clock this morning show them to have surely carried seventeen States representing 205 Electoral votes, twenty more than the Constitutional majority

November, 1880

LOUDOUN OFFICIAL.

Districts	FOR PRESIDENT.		
	Hancock.	Garfield.	Hancock Readjuster Ticket.
Leesburg District			
Leesburg	488	225	12
Goresville	183	48	000
Lovettsville Dis.			
Lovettsville	107	268	1
Waters'	56	50	000
Luckett's Store	59	100	000
Jefferson Dis.			
Waterford	102	147	000
Hillsborough	146	77	7
Pursellville	65	75	000
Woodgrove	67	17	000
Mt. Gilead Dis.			
Mt. Gilead	60	87	22
Hamilton	115	118	000
Hughesville	82	81	5
Snickersville	132	45	13
Silcott's Springs	101	87	2
Mercer Dis.			
Middleburg	130	81	16
Unison	149	95	16
Powell's Shop	76	28	1
Aldie	94	56	20
Broadrun Dis.			
Farmwell	156	83	1
Guilford	105	75	16
Gumspring	209	54	6
Total	2635	1793	145

11/25/80 Mirror

—An eloping couple were married on the bridge over the Potomac at Harper's Ferry, on Thursday last. The stern parent had brought his daughter from Newmarket, Va thus far on his way west to take her out of the reach of a poor, but deserving admirer — The P. and D. A., had, however, stolen a march on the old man and got a train ahead of him Procuring a license at Frederick and the services of a clergyman he kept the latter awaiting him on the Maryland side of the State line, and stole the girl away while her father was busy writing a letter home telling of their escape from the lover. After the ceremony all hands returned to Newmarket.

10/21/80 Mirror

Emerson and His New Lecture.

One evening when Ralph Waldo Emerson was engaged in preparing his new lecture Mrs. Emerson, who had that moment flattened her finger while trying to drive a nail with the smoothing iron, thrust her head into his study, and said,

"See here, sir! I want you to drop that everlasting pen of yours for a minute or two at least, and go down to the grocery and get a mackerel for breakfast."

"My dear," replied Mr Emerson, looking up from his work. "my dear, can't you go? You see, I'm billed in a dozen places to deliver this lecture on 'Memory,' and it isn't half finished yet"

"And that's what you call your infernal lecture, is it?" said Mrs. Emerson, sharply. "A nice party you are, to deliver a lecture on 'Memory.'"

"And why not, my love?" said Mr. Emerson, meekly.

"You never go out of the house that you don't forget to put on your hat or boots, and you never take a letter of mine to mail that you don't carry it in your pocket for six months or a year unless I happen to find it sooner. During the past thirty days you have carried out of this house and forgot to bring back no less than seventy five or eighty umbrellas; and you know yourself the last time you went to church, you took out your false teeth, because, as you said, they hurt your corns, and came away and left them in the seat. I say you are a nice man to talk to a cultured audience on 'Memory,' and if you don't trot right off to the grocery, I'll expose you before you're twenty four hours older."

Mr. Emerson started on a jump for the grocery, and when he got there he couldn't for the life of him recollect what he had come for.

John Norris & Son
Steam Saw and Planing
MILLS,
DEALERS IN
LUMBER, SHINGLES AND LATHS,
AND MANUFACTURERS OF
Sash, Doors, Blinds, Frames, Mouldings, &c.
ON hand and for sale a large quantity o Building LUMBER, of all descriptions comprising 4-4, 5-4, 6-4 and 8-4 White Pine Yellow Pine, Poplar, Ash and Walnut.

November, 1880

THE MIRROR.

THURSDAY.................. Nov. 25

THANKSGIVING DAY.—Services will be held in St. James Episcopal Church on Thursday, (this morning), at 11 o'clock. Collection for the Poor.

COLD SNAP.—For several days past the weather has been extremely cold. On Monday and Tuesday mornings the thermometer stood at ten degrees above zero. Monday night ice formed across the Potomac at White's Ferry; and the ponds and small streams in this vicinity are covered with ice from three to four inches thick. Active preparations are going on among ice gatherers to "take it in."

On Wednesday as the Sheriff of Albemarle was crossing the Blue Ridge near Waynesboroh with a posse to arrest a criminal, they were intercepted by a black bear, to which they gave chase, and captured. The mountains are said to be "full of bears" this season.

Speaking of bears reminds us that one of these shaggy monarchs of the forest made his appearance in the streets of Leesburg on Monday and after prowling around for an hour or two to the alarm of some and the amusement of many, he climbed one of the elms in the court house square—from which however, he was finally dislodged.

THE HAMILTON POST OFFICE.—The Washington correspondent of the Alexandria Gazette in his letter of the 22d. says:

As stated in this correspondence last week Mr. Y. T. Brown was appointed postmaster at Hamilton, Loudoun county, Virginia vice J. M. Hoge, removed "for cause." Mr. Brown however though has applied for the position has declined it upon the ground that though Hoge deserves to lose it, he (Brown) hopes to get something better." Mr. Hoge has been reappointed.

(The postmaster's job was often a plum of political patronage, with positions changing with every new administration.)

11/18/80 Mirror

Mark Twain, describing the beauty of a certain morning in the Bermudas says it was sufficient to have directed his thoughts heavenward had there not been just enough amateur piano music to keep him reminded of the other place.

LYDIA E. PINKHAM'S
VEGETABLE COMPOUND.

A Sure Cure for all FEMALE WEAKNESSES, Including Leucorrhœa, Irregular and Painful Menstruation, Inflammation and Ulceration of the Womb, Flooding, PROLAPSUS UTERI, &c.

According to "Last Call," a celebrated history of the temperance and prohibition periods, Mrs. Pinkham's medicines tested out to 20.6% alcohol. Some other patent medicines at that time were even more potent.

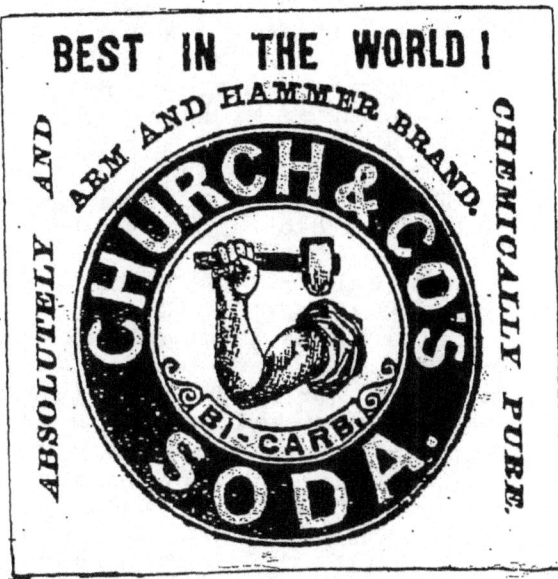

Look familiar?

12/30/80 Mirror

HAVING HIS HAIR CUT.

From the Staunton Vindicator.

A man may be a Superintendent of a railroad, may order whole trains of cars about, may say to one man, "go" and he goeth, and to another "come" and he cometh, but when he comes to having cut the hair of his three year old son in a barber shop, he is as one against whom the wicked may shoot out the lip. The Superintendent dropped in last Wednesday to have the hair of the junior boss trimmed. It must have taken an hour to get the rooster into the chair, during which time he managed to kick over two perfume bottles and a shaving cup and plant his heel in the barber's eye. The miserable father said meekly that if he had known it was going to be so bad he would have brought the boy's mother along, and then added with timid confidence, "She always manages him first-rate." A chronic growler who sat by the stove remarked amid the howls of the youngster that it was "—— pity he hadn't brought her along." Then commenced a great warfare. The boy under the impression that a surgical operation was about being performed on him, yelled from the word go. He cried out that there was hair down his back, which was the fact; and his eyes, which wasn't far from wrong, and his ears, which was correct, and then screamed out that it had got down in his socks which was no error.

"You don't have his hair cut often do you?" said the growler by the stove.

"Oh we don't have this trouble when his mother is along. She can manage him I tell you," said the superintendent mending his hold on the strugling patient.

"I hope so," said the growler, "for this thing is worse than shoeing a mule."

"I hope it doesn't disturb you," said the anxious father.

"Oh no!" said the man by the stove. "It ain't much worse than a mustard plaster on my back. I reckon I can weather through it."

Just here all the arts and rules known to barbers were being praticed on the young demon. He was promised untold wealth next Christmas, but it would'nt do. At last an artifice was agreed upon between the wretched parent and the barber by which the patient was made to believe that "Pa" was cutting his hair, that unhappy official dancing behind the chair while the barber plied the scissors. This transparent device was betrayed by the looking glass and its discovery was heralded by renewed howling.

The miserable parent looked at the man reproachfully and went on holding his offspring down in the chair. At last the keen witted barber thought up something that would work. He said:

"Lookit dere. Keep quiet. Dere ees a beautiful leetle mowse on der floor—"

The mouse did the business. The young fiend gave a howl and threw himself clean over the back of the chair. The hair cutting was ended for that day. As the unhappy father left he remarked that the next time he would bring the boy's mother along, "She could manage him."

"Yah" said the barber looking at him sternly. "I dinks it mauch better as you pring dot woomans along," and as the door closed he turned to the man at the stove and said "Un I kinks it better as he don't come some more at all. I shoost os leaf cut an eel's hair as dot child's."

FINE YOUNG MILCH COW
AND CALF,
FOR SALE CHEAP BY

S. J. JOHNSTON.

FOR SALE.

I HAVE for Sale 1 Champion Reaper and Mower, (self Rake) nearly new, and in first rate order; also, 1 good HEAVY WAGON with new Bed and Hay-Frames. As I have no use for either, I will sell low, and on easy terms—or would trade for a good horse.

Apply to   S. A. CAMPBELL,
              Near Ball's Mill.

12/9/80 Mirror

DIED.

At the house of Burr Hamilton, in Loudoun county, Va., on the 28th ultimo, JOHN R PIERPOINT, after a short sickness, in the 83d year of his age. The deceased was a native of Loudoun. His early life was devoted to teaching, and was much valued for his ability and success in that direction. He afterward engaged in the drug business in Alexandria, and did a good business, but owing to the war it was suspended and his means lost. Soon after he lost his eyesight, and a little later his wife was removed by death. He then returned to his friends in Loudoun to await the summons of his Heavenly Father He accepted what seemed his hard lot, was favored with great patience, and was often quite cheerful. "Mark the perfect man and behold the upright; for the end of that man is peace."—*Alex. Gazette.*

December, 1880

12/30/80 Mirror

THE WEATHER.—Last Sunday was a stormy day, and told heavily on the various religious assemblies, whose worshippers, in most instances, could almost be counted on one's fingers. Snow fell to the depth of about four inches, which, added to that already on the ground, measures over twenty inches, and has seriously impeded travel in many portions of the county, the drifts in some instances, for half a mile at a stretch, being over the tops of the fences. On Monday and Tuesday the Road Commissioner in Leesburg District, had a force of about twenty hands employed in removing the obstruction on the Point of Rocks road, about a mile from town. Perseverence, however, on the part of the traveling public, has to a great extent overcome the difficulties, and the number of sleighs, sleds, &c., that have appeared on the streets during the past day or two, indicate that "where there's a will there's a way," even though it leads through a six foot snow drift.

AND THE CRY IS, STILL IT COMES.—Snow began falling Tuesday night, gently, 'tis true, but nevertheless it come, and is still coming at the hour of going to press, Wednesday afternoon. The mail train from Alexandria, due here at 11:30, has not put in an appearance at 3 p. m. What the end will be "no fellah" can predict.

12/25/80 Washingtonian

NEARLY PERISHED IN THE SNOW.

Yesterday afternoon officer Columbus found a white man who gave his name as Herbert Vansickle, of Leesburg, Va., in a bank of snow in the White lot. He was almost frozen to death, and upon being taken to the Fifth precinct station he so far recovered as to be able to leave on the evening train for his home. But for the timely arrival of the officer he would have perished in the snow —*Wash. Post.*

A week later: From the Loudoun *Telephone,* January 6, 1881

—WEATHER. Well yes, we have had weather enough right here in Loudoun County, to cool all the left hand side of eternity. It snowed! and our people crawled out on top! then it snowed, and the original program was played with barn shovel costumes; then it snowed, and we repeated the operation. Then it snowed again—and again &c. etc,—Then it blowed and we cleared the walks— some of them— then it blowed and we shoveled snow. For variety it rained a little, and froze some—yes some!—that is, water refused to run and mercury backed into its hole—it touched "30" below the elliptical figure. Finally, it rained some more, and froze; then it froze some more and rained. It snowed, rained, hailed, blowed and froze.

12/25/80 Washingtonian

SNOW DRIFTS—OBSTRUCTION OF ROADS.—The question has been raised, whether or not it is the duty of the Commissioner of Roads to have the snow drifts opened on the roads in their respective districts, so the roads can be traveled. The 5th section of the Loudoun Road law, in stating the duty of the Overseer of Roads, says:

"His duties shall be to see that the roads in his district are kept in good repair; that the bridges are in safe condition; that the roads are kept *free from obstructions,*" &c.

This clearly makes it the duty of the Road officers to keep the roads in a condition for travel and transportation. They are not in that condition now.

January 1881

1/6/81 Mirror

THE WEATHER in this vicinity continues cold, but there has been a marked change during the past few days. Last week was the coldest snap known here in many years.— For several mornings the thermometer hanging at our office door fell to 13 degrees below zero, and at other points in Leesburg it is reported to have gone as low as 20—while reliable information from Waterford represents it even lower than that—some say 28. But be that as it may, the number of frosted feet and ears—some of them badly so—that are met with, attest the severity of the cold.

Many of the county roads, owing to snow drift and ice, are and have been impassable during the week, necessitating the driving through orchards and fields, in travelling from point to point. In the town the supply of wood is barely sufficient to meet the necessary requirements of the people, and we fear in some instances partial suffering has been the consequence.

The trains on the W. & O. Railroad were for several days almost entirely blockaded — Trains leaving Leesburg at 12 o'clock one day not reaching Alexandria until noon the next. On Sunday a train left Alexandria drawn by three engines which reached here about 5 o'clock in the evening, bringing us the first mail we had had since Thursday.

1/13/81 Mirror

THE COLD IN LOUDOUN.—A friend has furnished us the following item with reference to the recent cold snap in this county: At Jas Hoges, near Hughesville, the thermometer was 32° below zero; at Wm. Hoge's, same neighborhood, 32 degrees below zero; Joshua Hatchers, 29½ degrees; at Janney's Mill it was said to be, 38 degrees; at Waterford I did not hear what it was Saturday—on Friday it was 25 degrees.

> Extraordinary cold for this region. Having lived in this area for 83 years, I have witnessed only a handful of zero degree nights.

A dispatch from Berryville, Clarke Co. last night says: "The weather is colder than ever known here before. The thermometer at 6 o'clock this morning stood 26 degrees below zero." Advices from "The Plains," in Fauquier county, state that the snow is 33 inches deep, undrifted, in the woods in that vicinity, and from 9 to 12 feet in drifts.

THE TELEPHONE.

FRIDAY............... JAN. 7th.

—The snow blockade, of the railroad, was raised on Wednesday. Two engines with a number of hands pushed and shoveled through to Round Hill, relieving us along this end of the road of our isolation of more than a week.

—TAYLORTOWN ITEMS. Ice on the Potomac from six to ten inches.—— Mercury stood at 23 degrees below zero last Friday morning, and on Saturday at 28.——Flowers are frozen.——Snow much drifted.

—No school at Lincoln this week, as the late assistant teacher decided to leave, and her successor, a Miss Ogden, from Ohio, got snow bound.

—When the snow is two or three feet deep it is no fun to meet a large drove of cattle.

MORRISONVILLE.

MR. EDITOR:—Christmas, with all of its festivities has gone and is now numbered with the things of the past. Christmas, the long looked for holiday of the year, though a season of meriment and rejoicing, has passed almost unnoticed by many, on account of the terrible snow, which fell a few days previous, and drifted up many of our roads, making it next to impossible to travel over them; some of them have been harrowed down and travel has commenced. I commend Mr. A. B. Merchant for the excellent manner in which he has opened most of the roads on which he is overseer. Give us a few more such men! I have heard of several sleighs being turned over in the snow drifts, but none happened to be serious.

The New Year morning of 1881 dawned as clear and bright, with as beautiful sunshine as ever lent its rays to the beautiful snow capped mountains of the far North, making it a scene of rare beauty; but it brought with it so little warmth, that it was scarcely preceptable until about the middle of the day, when, under its gentle warming influence some little thaw was noticed. The intense cold of the night brought the mercury down to 30 degrees below zero and in some localities as low as 35.

January, 1881

1/13/81 Mirror

[From the New York Sun.]

A VILLAGE BURIED IN SNOW.

HEROISM AND SUFFERING IN THE VIRGINIA MOUNTAINS.

A Thrilling Story of Escape from a Tomb of Snow—300 Persons Imprisoned in the Mountains—A Messenger for Aid found Half-Frozen—A Relief Expedition Sent Out.

BERRYVILLE, Clarke County, Va., Jan. 6. This evening about dusk Mr. Richard A. Ward, residing on the outskirts of the village, found a man lying in the snow near the roadside, partially insensible from cold and terribly emaciated. The stranger was at once removed to Mr. Ward's residence, where, after he had been revived and had been supplied with food which he devoured in a ravenous manner, he startled his preserver by one of the strangest and most thrilling narratives of human distress that has ever been chronicled. The man stated that his name was Roger S. Cooper, and that he resided in the village of Paris, a small town near the summit of the Blue Ridge Mountains, on the dividing line between Clarke and Loudoun counties. He had volunteered to come to Berryville to urge the residents by all the ties of humanity and manhood to organize a relief party and go to the assistance of the villagers, who were literally buried in the snow, and to the number of about 300 were in danger of death from both cold and hunger.

(The two paragraphs to the right tell the true story. A big city reporter creates an account, half truth and half fable, demonstrating that an occasional lying journalist was present even then.)

1/15/81 Washingtonian

THE SNOW-BURIED VILLAGE OF PARIS.—The inhabitants of Paris, a village on the Blue Ridge mountain, about two miles west of Upperville, have been waked from the usual monotony of village life, since the snow storm, to find themselves the subjects of newspaper lamentations, and the objects of untold verbal expressions of sympathy, from all parts of the country. The snow presented the theme, and the fertile imagination of a correspondent of the New York Sun supplied the sad and heartrending scenes which the snow-buried village presented when reached by tunnels through the mountainous drift, which the correspondent's imagination had thrown over this doomed village. The truth is, Paris is in the condition of the surrounding country, well supplied with snow but with plenty to eat, and the mountains around them with plenty of wood to keep them warm; no deaths nor serious injuries have occurred to any of its inhabitants as we have heard.

1/14/81 Telephone

An Improbable Story Disposed Of.

Newspapers of the sensational class have, within the past few days, published a long and improbable story, in which the little village of Paris, in Fauquier county, Va., was asserted to be buried under the snow, some of its inhabitants frozen to death, seventy-five of its couple of hundred population lying on beds of sickness, and others starving, together with a graphic description of how a relief party from Berryville, Clarke county, after much suffering, reached the suffering villagers and succored them. The Alexandria Gazette published this story on Monday, and added the following, which is doubtless reliable: "A gentleman just from Upper Fauquier, near Paris, states that the above, if not altogether incorrect, is at least greatly exaggerated, and that while there is a great deal of snow nothing like covering up of villages or freezing to death or starvation really exists, except in the fertile imagination of the writer of this really thrilling romance."—Balto. Sun.

February, 1881

THE WASHINGTONIAN.

LEESBURG, LOUDOUN COUNTY, VA.

SATURDAY............February 12, 1881.

THE WINTER.

From the beginning of this year the Storm-King has put forth his power, and reigned with a severity unknown for many generations, in all parts of the world. No latitude has been peculiar in receiving his attentions. The tropic, temperate and cold regions have all felt the force of his fury. Snow has fallen where formerly the mild reign of summer was unbroken, and the flowers bloomed perpetually. The orange groves of the South, as well as the pine forests of the North, have felt the severity of the winter's winds, and all the countries of Europe, and sections of our own continent, bear testimony to its general severity. Within the last few days the southern winds and warm sunshine, have moderated the temperature here.

1/27/81 Mirror

LONG FASTS IN LOUDOUN.—Last week a correspondent from Round Hill, informed the *Washingtonian* that—"Mr Edgar Ballinger, of that neighborhood, lost a "sow" on the 20th of December, the day the big snow fall, and she was found under a snow drift near the side of the road on Monday, the 17th of January, apparently in good health, but very much reduced in flesh, having fasted twenty-eight days."

1/28/81 Telephone

—The immense weight of snow has proved most too much for some buildings in this locality. It came near crushing the Depot building at our station and but for the timely efforts of Mr. Berry and some assistants the building would have been wrecked — The old blacksmith shop near Mr. Wm. Tavenner's house fared worse. The walls spread and tumbled and the roof fell in a heap of ruins.

2/17/81 Mirror

THAT THAW.—The mild weather which prevailed during the closing days of last week, and the heavy rain of Friday night, brought about the expected results on Saturday, in a general breaking up of the ice, the melting of snow drifts, and the overflowing of water courses. For a few hours the smaller streams in this vicinity, Tuscarora, Goose Creek, Big Spring, Limestone Branch, etc., presented quite formidable appearances, their rush and roar of muddy water, bearing on their bosoms floating debris of various sorts, admonishing the luckless wights who approached either shore, to beware. They soon exhausted their fury, however, and in a little while offered no resistance to being crossed, and without, so far as we have been able to learn, inflicting any serious damage to person or property while rolicking in their mad tantrum.

The Potomac river was unusually high.— Crossing was out of the question, and serious consequences were apprehended at Edward's, White's, and the other fords along its banks, while the dwellers on the Islands, with painful recollections of the freshet of 1877, were, as may be imagined, in anything but a comfortable frame of mind. Fortunately, as the day wore on Mr Vennor's "mild, spring like weather," succumbed to the chilling breath of a keen nor-easter —abandoned for the time, its sporting with the elements, and allowed the blue waves to roll onward in comparative quiet, until, freighted with their heavy cargo of floating ice, they came in contact with that great national highway—the Long Bridge,—where they "played such high fantastic tricks" that if they didn't make angels weep, they at least caused men to see sights, an epitome of which will be found in another column.

February, 1881

2/17/81 Mirror

WASHINGTON CITY INUNDATED

The Potomac Breaks its Banks and Floods the City.—Six Feet of Water From the Monument to the Capitol.—Property Destroyed.—The Long Bridge Broken.

The immense quantity of ice which covered the Potomac river in the vicinity of Washington city, has for some days past led to serious apprehension should a sudden thaw take place, and blockade the current at Long Bridge. But the worst fears were more than realized on Saturday.

A heavy, strong frost, which made mountains of ice and was held by snow, succumbed to a thorough and extensive thaw. The river gave way, and in giving way carried all before it. Never was such a scene witnessed in this section. The rapidity of action on the part of the current was marvelous. On Friday night the city turned out its gas and went to sleep quietly; on Saturday morning it awoke to call for ferry-boats and canoes to carry it from its residence to its place of business.

The heavy rain of Saturday morning aided to a certain extent in startling the business.

Early yesterday the south side of the city was submerged. The Potomac walked over its banks with the noisy insolence of a politician, and began to crowd water upon the people of Washington, whether they wished it or not. It struck first at the Washington Monument, rapidly metamorphosing that portion of the city into an island. Following in its course, it started creeks and rivers along the tributary streets to Fourteenth, south of the Avenue, and engulfed that section.

As early as 10 o'clock it tackeled Pennsylvania avenue, and, visiting the Center market in a perfect flood, drove the occupants thereof from the buildings. It continued to rise, and by 11 o'clock one half of the handsomest and most extensive thoroughfare in America was a river.

Seventh street was a sea for several squares below the boulevard, and the cars were flooded as they passed along. The water was up to the horses' necks and the occupants of the cars necessitated to stand in the windows or to climb upon the roofs.

Fourteenth street was, if possible, still worse, carriages and cars in danger of being swept away, a perfect river running over that section of the town; and on some occasions wayfarers on the cars were compelled to call for boats and, climbing through the car windows, saved from death by drowning.

The water rose rapidly about Sixth street and Ninth early in the day. The Baltimore and Potomac Depot and Ford's Opera House were both cut off from communication with the outer world before noon. The market house was a dense sea of swimming vegetables. Several of the energetic butchers improvised stands along the framework of the seats for the inaugural procession, and dealt out their uncooked stomachies from that point.

An odd sight it was, at this stage of the game of the nation's life, to see in the heart of its capital city skiffs, canoes and bateaux paddling around its streets—and worse still, mud-scows, actually mud-scows, carrying passengers from place to place.

DAMAGE TO THE LONG BRIDGE.

Large crowds of people were collected in the vicinity of the Long Bridge all day Saturday, waiting for the expected destruction of the bridge. After the 6:32 train from Alexandria passed over, all travel on the bridge was stopped. The ice from above washed upon the bridge and seemed to threaten it with instant annihilation.

During the day the railings on the causeway and telegraph poles were carried away by the ice and swept over the bridge. The great crash did not come until about nine o'clock at night, when a section of the trestle work between the District side and the causeway was carried off the stone piers, leaving a gap of about 800 feet. The section was carried entire to a point about 300 feet, where it landed with its head down stream. The water rose along the Washington river front until the roadway of Water street was completely submerged.

The necessary lumber to reconstruct the damaged causeway is already on the ground. This morning, if possible, a tug will be secured in Alexandria, and a corps of engineers will be brought to the Virginia side of the bridge, to make a thorough examination. As soon as possible the work of repair will be begun, and it will certainly be finished by the 4th of March.

HOW TRAVELERS WILL GO SOUTH.

Transfer coaches will leave the Baltimore and Potomac depot and transfer passengers for the South and their baggage via the Aqueduct Bridge to Fort Runion, on the Virginia shore, where trains will stop until the repairs of the Long Bridge are completed.

February, 1881

2/19/81 Washingtonian

A Wild Waste of Waters Covering the Entire Country

WASHINGTON INUNDATED AND THE LONG BRIDGE WASHED PARTLY AWAY.

WASHINGTON, February 12.—Nothing has ever been witnessed here in the memory of the oldest inhabitant to compare with the freshet and flood of yesterday and to-day. The break up commenced at Georgetown at 1 o'clock yesterday morning and the river began to rise rapidly. The dammed ice at the long bridge was a magnificent but fearful sight, and as thousands of tons of it came crushing and breaking down the river the water swept over the banks and through the city. It came pouring through the long stretch of land between the observatory and the Washington monument, and following the bed of the old canal spread through the streets. At 5 o'clock the carp ponds were flooded over, and at 10.30 the freshet had reached the Center market, and the water was rising so rapidly that the people escaped from their homes with difficulty and were compelled to leave their effects behind. It was only a very brief time before the water had reached the Baltimore and Potomac depot, and as far as Missouri avenue to the Botanical Gardens, at the foot of the capitol, and spread over that ground. This was the eastern limit. Pennsylvania avenue was submerged from Second street to Seventh and from Ninth to Tenth streets, the water at the latter place reaching above the curb on the north side and being about two feet deep on the south side. All the cellars of the stores on both sides were flooded, and the floors in a number of establishments on the south side were covered with a foot of water.

The damage is immense and cannot now be calculated. At the Baltimore and Potomac depot the water was six feet deep.

At 8.30 p. m. three spans at the west end of long bridge gave way before the pressure of the ice and passed off down the river. A man, whose name is unknown, attempted to cross the low ground between the city proper and South Washington at Sixth street. His horse fell and threw the rider, who was drowned. A colored man was also drowned at Seventeenth-street wharf by falling into the river while gathering driftwood.

THE LONG BRIDGE, 300 feet of which has been swept away by the recent flood, has had quite a varied experience. The Bridge was erected under an act of Congress, passed January 5, 1808, incorporating the Potomac Bridge Company. In 1829 a freshet occurring sweeping away a greater part of the structure. The company not being able to repair the bridge their right and title was sold to the government for $20,000. The bridge was again rebuilt at an expense of $200,000. In 1840 the bridge was again destroyed.

2/17/81 Mirror

CUT OFF.—The closing days of Congress—the usual excitement attendant upon an early change of administration—the appearance of Joe Jefferson in his famous Rip Van Winkle, these, and perhaps other inducements, last Friday attracted some fifteen or twenty ladies and gentlemen from Leesburg to Washington, all full bent on coming home Saturday. But lo, and behold, Friday night the wind blew, the rain descended, and the flood came, and there they were, surrounded by water, forty miles from home, and some of them, no doubt, without a change of linen; while in other instances the plaintive voices of anxious friends and "young children," were mournfully ringing in their ear "come home, dear father, come home." But they couldn't. Monday was County Court. Duty demanded that the Judge; a half dozen counsel and other Court officials, should at least be in place, but an element, which when aroused, is of all things the most uncontrolable, and bids defiance to the power and ingenuity of man, said stay a little longer; while yet others, with nothing particular to call *them* home, complacently "waited," like Micawber, "for something to turn up," but doubtless more than one wearied form fell asleep mentally sighing, for some contrivance to "carry me back to old Virginia." The old maxim, however, of "where there's a will there's a way," found verification in this instance. Sunday morning dawned bright, bracing and clear, and about 8 o'clock that night twelve of the party were safely landed in Leesburg, thanks to the accommodating spirit of a Georgetown liveryman Mr Darnes—who sent them over land, via Chain Bridge, in a four horse ambulance. Later in the day another of the party made his way to Alexandria and reached home next morning on the freight train; another crossed the river at Shepherds, opposite Alexandria, in a tug, while yet others crossed on the acqueduct bridge at Georgetown and intercepted the train on the W. & O. R. R. at Arlington. "But all's well that ends well,"

February, 1881

2/26/81 Washingtonian

A WAR REMINISCENCE.

Making a Bed for President Lincoln.

We were at Harrison's Landing, after the Seven Days' fight, and, as may be imagined, felt pretty badly. True, the final and bloody repulse of the rebels at Malvern Hill had cheered us up somewhat, but it was plain to enlisted men as well as officers that the occupation of Richmond would have to be deferred for a long time.

It was during our first week's occupation of this pre-historic spot that I enjoyed the first and only opportunity I ever had of seeing President Lincoln, who visited the army shortly after its arrival in order to ascertain its exact condition and decide upon its future movements.

As the writer of this was the orderly of Major General Sumner, whose guest the President was during his brief stay, he had more than ordinary good advantages for observing his peculiarities, which, it is needless to say, he improved to the utmost.

What first impressed me about President Lincoln was the excessive awkwardness of his figure and the fact that his clothes didn't seem to fit him. Tall, gaunt and ungainly, he certainly looked like a rail splitter going about in his Sunday suit or an undertaker temporarily out of business. This latter resemblance was intensified by the melancholy character of his features, and the coat, vest and trousers of funereal black in which he was habitually attired. The expression of his face was an odd mingling of shrewdness, sagacity and native kindliness; and, despite its sadness, there continually lurked about the corners of his mouth gleams of quaint humor, of which none of his pictures give the slightest indication.

Mr. Lincoln wore what is commonly called a plug hat, and although it may have only been of conventional length, it appeared to me extraordinarily tall. Although it may well be doubted if any other species of hat would have better become him, I remember thinking at the time that the stove pipe added greatly to the oddness and grotesquerie of his appearance.

The troops were to be reviewed on the day of his arrival, and I remember the General was very much perplexed as to the character of the President's mount and finally consulted him as to the kind of a charger he would prefer. I remember his answer as plainly as if it were only yesterday:

'General,' said he, 'any kind of a quiet beast will do. I don't think I was cut out for a cavalryman, and I am afraid a high-spirited war steed might prove a little too much for me.'

In the General's stud was a little sorrel mare called Bonnie, the soul of gentleness and good temper, and he at once proposed her for Mr. Lincoln's use.

'All right,' said the President; 'I guess the mare will suit me to a T. Besides, among horses, that sex is much the easiest to manage. This remark, however, he added, with a sly twinkle in his eye, 'does not hold good of humanity.'

When Mr. Lincoln was mounted on Bonnie his appearance was more peculiar than ever. The little mare was not more than fourteen hands high, and so great was the length of the President's legs that, once fairly settled in his saddle, his feet nearly touched the ground. As he ruefully remarked, glancing at his extremities:

'If I was only two inches longer, I think I'd get off and walk.'

Mounted by his side on a splendid stallion, prancing and rearing, and surrounded by a brilliant staff, Gen. Sumner looked like a veritable cavalier of old, while the Chief Magistrate of the Republic, by comparison, had the appearance of some quiet country parson who, in ambling to morning service, had fallen in among military men by mistake.

However, the enthusiasm of the men for the plain-looking civilian was tremendous, and the President was much pleased with the review. Particularly was he delighted with the spirit of the troops, which was evidently much better than he expected.

As he rode back he said to the General, gleefully, 'Those boys seem as if they were willing to go in again to-morrow,' a sentiment to which that officer heartily assented.

After our return to camp the President dined heartily, and towards evening went away to visit some of the other generals.

It was about eight o'clock, and getting dark, when General Sumner ordered me to send his colored servant to him. This was a sprightly contraband, whom the men had christened Stonewall Jackson, but on the present occasion Stonewall belied the promptness of his namesake and was not forthcoming.

As it turned out afterwards, he had been attacted by the playing of the bands of some New York regiments about a quarter of a mile on our right, and, of course could not leave while there was a horn blowing.

I saw the General was getting anxious and finally he spoke.

'Davis,' said he, 'do you know how to make a bed?'

I confessed that my experience in that line was somewhat limited.

'So is mine,' said he, 'but something must be done. I am expecting the President every moment and he retires early. As that black rascal hasn't turned up yet, I suppose that we must try and prepare his bed ourselves.

The General had surrendered his own cot for the use of the President, and we at once proceeded to arrange it as best we could. We had hardly gotten fairly under way when in walked Mr. Lincoln.

'Hello! Sumner,' said he, 'making your bed? This is the first time I knew that corps commanders acted as their own chambermaids.'

The General replied in the same vein, telling him that the cot was for him, and explaining the circumstances under which we had felt obliged to do the work of the derelict Stonewall.

'All right,' said the President, good-humoredly, as he took his seat on a camp-stool in the corner, 'go ahead; do not mind me. I'll merely watch you and take a lesson, so that if you ever come to the White House I shall be able to reciprocate, should it prove necessary.'

We were getting along nicely, and had nearly finished, when suddenly an idea seemed to strike the General. He glanced fertively out of the corner of his eye at the President and then at the cot. After repeating the operation several times I perceived his meaning.

The awful fact had dawned upon him that there was a marked discrepancy in the length of the cot and the person who was to occupy it.

In vain did we re-arrange the blankets and fiddle-faddle with the pillows—the result remained the same. The man was unmistakably longer than the bed.

Mr. Lincoln had been watching us closely and enjoying the scene intensely. At length he seemed to take pity on the General's perplexity, and spoke.

'What's the matter?' said he, as a quizzical smile played over his features; 'anything wrong with the bed?'

'I'm afraid,' said the General, as he wiped the perspiration from his brow, 'I'm afraid that it's a little short.'

'Or I'm a little long,' chuckled the President; 'but can't you fix it in no way?'

'I really don't see how,' returned the General, despondently. 'It's very annoying.'

'Well, I'll show you,' said Mr. Lincoln, good-humoredly, as, jumping up, he seized two camp stools and placed them at the foot of the cot. 'There, that will give the the necessary six or eight inches. Just put the blankets over them, and everything will be all right.'

We did so, and the General, radiant with delight, congratulated Mr. Lincoln upon his ingenuity.

'Oh,' said the President, modestly, 'it's an old trick of mine. When I was a country lawyer, traveling on the circuit in Illinois, twenty years ago or more, the beds were uncommonly short, and had to be pieced out with whatever was handiest. When Douglas and I stumped the State together I had to do the same thing at least half a dozen times. He (Douglass) was never tired making fun of it, and told me that whenever I left home I ought to take my bed along with me; 'and,' continued the President, musingly, 'I rather think he was right.'

On the following night Mr. Lincoln was not obliged to use the camp stools, as we managed to procure a longer cot for him, and doubtless the whole affair soon passed out of his memory, but for my own part I shall always retain the liveliest recollection of my little experience in Presidential bed making.—*An Eye Witness, in the Boston Times*

FRAZER
AXLE GREASE.

Best in the world. Lasts longer than any other. Always in good condition. Cures sores, cuts, bruises and corns. Costs but little more than the imitations. Every package has the trade mark. Call for the genuine, and take no other.

February, 1881

2/18/91 Telephone

GUILFORD FLASHES.

Editor Telephone—I have reported to the Telephone from time to time some of the doings of the consumers of the liquid damnation, which is sold in Guilford, under the name of whiskey. In consequence, I have received various threats mixed with much vulgar profanity and abuse. I have a few explanations to offer concerning my course in the matter.

In the first place the subject of rumselling and dramdrinking is one that is perfectly legitimate to discuss.

It is proper and right to show the injury done to body, soul, mind and estate of the drunkard or moderate drinker. The man who gets drunk in public, puts himself on exhibition, and any person has the right to tell the fact to others or to publish it as widely as he pleases. I am told that it is none of my business how many get drunk, or what they do when they are drunk; that I must stop talking about it or I will get whipped &c.

I maintain that it is my business and I do not propose to stop talking about it!

I have reported only here and there an item out of a mass which no man can number. Very few matters of the kind come to my notice as I do not frequent their gates of Hell myself, but I know that there are few days without a drunken man in Guilford.—There are few weeks without a disgraceful fight. The times are frequent when a lady cannot traverse the streets with freedom, for fear of insult. We have heard, for years, temperance orators rehearsing these glittering generalities, concerning the lives, the property, and the happiness destroyed by drink and it falls upon unheeding ears. What we need to talk about is how many of our young men are becoming drunkards, how much of our happiness and prosperity is being ruined.

Why is there not a fight every week in Herndon or Farmwell? Why are those places being built up and improved while Guilford is stationary?

And now if there are any more who think this discussion can be stopped by bulldozing, I have a word to say to them. I have reported no persons name thus far, but if I am treated any more with abuse and threats, I shall publish all the circumstances including the names of the parties.

G. C. Wells.

2/26/81 Washingtonian

[Communicated.]

Guilford, Loudoun Co., Va., Feb. 18, '81.

Mr. Editor: The wise man says: "Answer a fool according to his folly," and this is my apology for asking space in your paper to notice a scurrilous and slanderous communication printed in the last issue of a paper published at Hamilton, in Loudoun County, bearing the euphonious name of "*Telephone*." It is headed in large capitals, "Guilford," and signed "G. C. W." It purports to give a true picture of society in and around the village of Guilford, and with one grand flourish of his rhetorical pen, he assails the whole population, placing them in the same category as a nest of petty gamblers and dram-drinkers, Church members, magistrates, school and road officers, gray heads and beardless youths, ebony and alabaster, all absorbed in a primitive game, the details of which, by early training, the writer seems to be more familiar with, than he is with the lesson of the Ninth Commandment.

There is an old adage which reads thus:—"People who live in glass houses should not throw stones at their neighbors' residences." "G. C. W." is a pronounced political gambler, and struts beastfully in rags won by betting on the late Presidential election in violation of the laws of Virginia (vide Code of Va). Perhaps by a strain upon his metaphysical acumen he might enlighten the readers of the "*Telephone*" as to the difference between the moral quality of a wager upon the result of the ballot box and the number of points made from the "Hus-l-cap." The astute writer above alluded to, evidently had no desire to conceal his personal identity he wears no *nom de plume*, but gives his proper initials that all the people of Loudoun may know that this reprobate Sodam has one righteous man and prophet amongst them. But this was unnecessary. The Ass might don the garb of the lion, but the ears and brays would betray his *genus*. Like the adder, he stings the bosom that warms him; stigmatizes and maligns his neighbors and patrons. If the people should elect to let him serenely alone in the future he will have no reason to complain of social, political, or business ostracism. The people of Virginia will welcome, with open hearts and hands, all who come among them, from whatever quarter, irrespective of political or religious complexions, who conduct themselves with propriety; but when they come as political emissaries, as moral crusaders, as spies and crimminators—when they come like the locusts and frogs of Egypt, to eat out the substance of the land and deposit their slime, we would be wanting in decency and proper self-respect, if we did not say plainly to these interlopers and would-be dictators: Attend to your own business, and we will endeavor to attend to ours.

Vindicator.

3/10/81 Mirror

THE FOURTH OF MARCH IN WASHINGTON

President Garfield Inaugurated

A Gala Day at the Capitol.

Last Friday was a gala day at the National Capitol, the like of which was never before seen by the "oldest inhabitant." The preceding evening emptied into the city an influx of people far in excess of her ability to accommodate, and as if to make the situation more intensely disagreeable, the windows of heaven were opened, and rain hail, snow, and wind swept over the modern Mecca with a fury well calculated to disgust the tens of thousands of pilgrims who had flocked thither from the four corners of the great Republic, to participate in the scenes incident to a Presidential inauguration. Of course it is not expected that we should do more in the limited space at our command, than tell our readers who were not present, that despite wind and weather the great event was fully carried out according to programme, and in all its appointments was a huge success.

The early hours of Friday morning were dark, dreary and foreboding; but by 10 o'clock the misty veil was rent asunder—the storm abated, the sun shone with spring like fervor, revealing to the astonished gaze of the 200,000 people who had arrived during the prevalence of the storm and the darkness of the night, a city magnificently attired in her holiday garb, with public buildings, private residences, and stately arches, radiant with flags, banners and bunting, evergreens, flowers and appropriate mottoes, while the motley crowd that thronged the Avenue, jammed and jostled each other after the most approved Democratic fashion.

At about 11 o'clock two four-in-hand carriages drove into the White House grounds. General Garfield and President Hayes stepped into one and took the back seat, President Hayes being on the right.

The procession then started at the sound of a signal gun. As the two carriages came out of the gate there was a loud cheer from the crowd, which ran almost continuously down the avenue, as the Presidential party moved along.

While the Presidential party was moving toward the capitol, the Senate assembled to receive them, and while thus waiting, Gen. Hancock, clad in full military dress, entered the hall escorted by Senator Blaine. The moment he was recognized, the scene that followed is represented by those who witnessed it, to have been without precedent inside those dignified old walls. Senators rose in a body and clapped their hands, the enthusiasm reached the galleries, and found expression in more boisterous demonstrations, which lasted for full ten minutes.

In the gallery was seated Mrs. Garfield, mother of the President elect, his wife and daughter, and Mrs. Hayes—and the wives and daughters of members, &c. The Diplomatic Corps to the number of about 100, nearly all of them dressed in full official costume, occupied seats on the floor of the Senate, as did also the Judges of the Supreme Court.

Finally the Presidential party reached the chamber, and Vice-President elect Arthur was conducted to the Chair and introduced by Mr. Wheeler. Mr. A. made a short speech, after which the oath of office was administered to him by the retiring Vice President, who also uttered a brief farewell address. The members of the House of Representatives next made their appearance, and when quiet had been restored, the Senate was called to order by the new Vice President, and the first executive session of the XLVII Congress was opened by prayer by the Chaplain, Rev. Dr. Bullock. The roll of new Senators was then called, and all responded except "Mahone, Virginia."

The Vice President having been duly installed and the new Senators sworn in, a procession was formed of those inside the Chamber, headed by the President elect, and proceeded to the platform at the East front of the building, where President Garfield read to at least 25,000 people his inaugural address, the full text of which will be found in another column.

At the conclusion of the inaugural ceremonies the entire procession proceeded up the Avenue to the President's House, in front of which a grand stand had been erected, and from which the newly made President reviewed the troops as they passed before him.

Virginia had several military companies in the procession,—the most of them colored

March 1881

3/17/81 Mirror

Garfield's Yellow Dog

WASHINGTON March 4 — A little yellow dog which followed Garfield's carriage in the procession to-day, has a history. About a year ago the same dog followed General Garfield from where he got off a street car to his house, corner of Thirteenth and I streets. The General noticing the dog, threw him a piece of meat and forgot the occurrance until he met the same dog on the same corner the next day.

Following him home again he was rewarded by another piece of meat. Finally the dog made General Garfield's house a kind of a temporary headquarters. When General Garfield went to Chicago as a delegate to the convention that nominated him the dog followed him to the depot. Before the news reached here of the nomination of General Garfield the dog set up a joyful barking that was almost unbearable.

"Something has happened," said one of the ladies in the house, "and here is a telegraph messenger." The message contained the information of his nomination. When General Garfield came here, some weeks after his nomination the story was told him, and he said he would take the dog to Ohio with him, but when the time for starting arrived the dog could not be found, the animal, being of a roving nature. General Garfield never saw the dog since until yesterday, when, riding out with a friend, there he was. Calling him by his name, "Bob," the dog recognized the voice and appeared to be happy. As the General arrived at the Riggs House the dog again disappeared. He saw nothing of him until to-day as the procession was moving from the White House. The dog followed the carriage all the way to the Capitol.

troops.

Gen. Hancock reached the stand considerably in advance of the head of the procession, and his appearance was again the signal for the wildest applause by the multitude in waiting.

The procession was disbanded about five o'clock. At night came the pyrotechnic display and the inauguration ball. The former was grand, almost beyond description. "The display consisted of continuous flights of rockets, parachutes, with changing colored illuminations, bombshells, &c., forming great jeweled clouds in the heavens. Among the set pieces was a magnificent tree with golden foliage, a superb sun, with coruseating radiations, the national coat of arms, an emblem with the letters of "Army and Navy," around which revolved the national ensign; the grand cataract of Niagara the whole ending with a gorgeous device, in which appeared lifelike portraits of the President and Vice-President elect."

THE INAUGURAL ADDRESS of President Garfield is published in full in another column. It is a paper of no mean pretentions and as a literary production is in striking contrast with many of its predecessors and marks its author a man of comprehensive thought. Should President Garfield prove to possess the nerve to perform as well as he plans, the country will profit and prosper under his administration.

But inaugural speeches, like political platforms are not always observed when the object for which they have been prepared, has been attained. It will therefore be wiser to wait and judge the tree by its fruit.

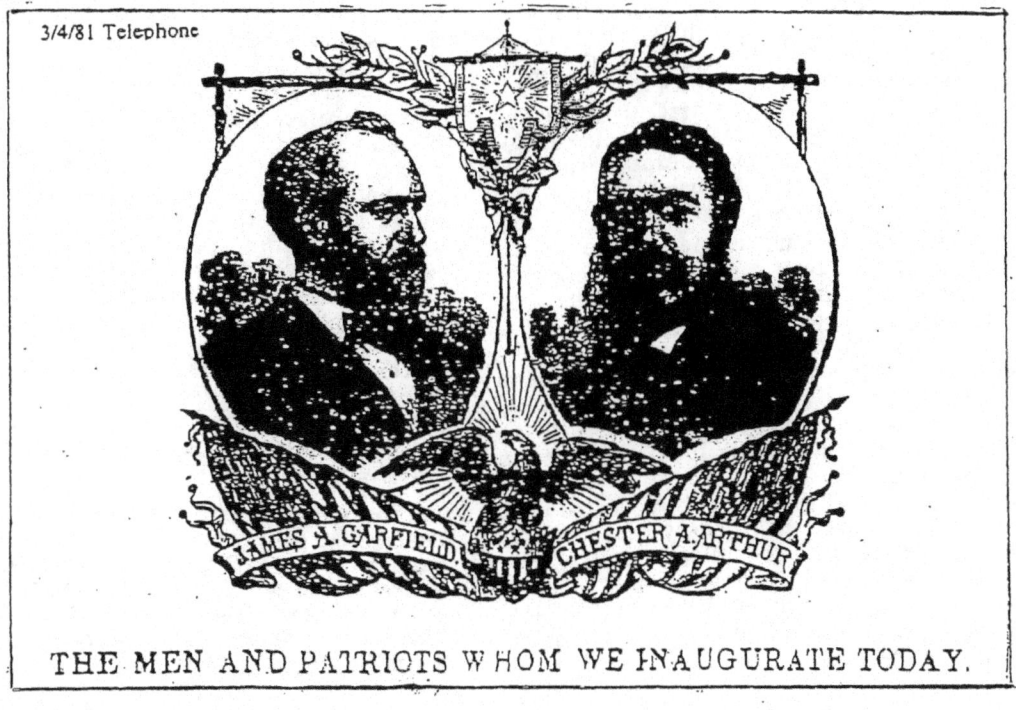

3/4/81 Telephone

THE MEN AND PATRIOTS WHOM WE INAUGURATE TODAY.

[From the Washington Post of Tuesday.]

MAHONE TO THE FRONT.

HE TAKES HIS STAND WITH THE REPUBLICANS.

A Remarkable Scene in the Senate — The Virginian, Excoriated by Senator Hill, Is Forced to Declare Himself — The Debate in Detail.

Senator Mahone, of Virginia, was formally introduced to the American public yesterday in one of the most memorable scenes ever witnessed in the United States Senate chamber. In a desperate combat between the Representatives of two great parties for the control of a high legislative body he appeared as the umpire. The struggle raging around him finally centered on him and he was forced to disclose his political position, and having disclosed it to defend it. It was a field day in the history of Senatorial debates. Pendleton and Hill led the Democrats, and Conkling the Republicans.

When Mr. Conkling had finished his speech Senator Hill, of Georgia, took the floor. Mr. Hill seldom speaks without commanding the attention of the Senate. He has a rarely logical mind, is quick of perception and cannot be deviated from the course he maps out for himself in advance by the incidents of discussion. There is no man in the Senate, unless it be Mr. Conkling, who can use words more adroitly than the Senator from Georgia. Mr. Hill's speech was as follows:

MR. PRESIDENT — For the first time in the history of the United States Senate the regular, orderly, timely, proper organization of the committees is resisted, resisted by an entire party, resisted by a great party.

Mr. President, let us come to the point. The Senator from New York has repeated over and over again in language too plain to be misunderstood, (he has not stated it as his opinion; if I understand his language he has affirmed as a fact), that within a few days the Republicans will control a Constitutional majority of the Senate, and that the Constitutional majority will have it in its power to select the committees.

Let us come to the fact; it is a great fact. I have believed that when every seat shall be filled, the Senate will be Democratic precisely as it is now. If I am wrong in that belief, I have been deceived; if the Senator from New York is correct in his statement, I have been deceived.

Yet in the face of this high presence, in the face of the nation, the leading Senator on the other side, the great Senator from the great State of New York, rises and repeats over and over again that when the Senate shall be full it will have a constitutional majority of Republicans. How has that been accomplished? That is the question. For what purpose has that wonderful coalition been accomplished by which somebody, sent here as a Democrat, has been seized on — no. I will not say seized; I will imitate the words of the distinguished Senator from New York — taken and carried away to the Republican party?

Who did it? The Senator from New York did not; I acquit him; I know him too well. Who did it? Who has seized, who has taken and carried away? How is it that we on this side have no right to act on the assumption that thirty-eight members who were sent to this body as democrats are not still Democrats? Sir, I say they are, and I stand here to vindicate the honor, the integrity, the fidelity to State, to people and to principle of all the thirty-eight who were sent here as Democrats, and I deny that either has proved treacherous to his constituents or has falsified the commission that lies upon your table.

Sir, I concede the right of every man to change his opinions; I concede the right of every man to change his party affiliations; I concede the right of any man who was elected to the high place of a seat in this Senate as a Democrat to change and become a Republican; but I deny in the presence of this Senate, I deny in the hearing of this people, that any man has a right to accept a commission from one party and execute the trust confided to him in the interest of another party.

Manhood, bravery, courage, fidelity, morality, respect for the opinions of mankind, requires that whenever a man has arrived at the conclusion that he cannot carry out the trust which was confided to him, he should return the commission and tell his constituents "I have changed my mind and therefore return you the commission you gave me." Sir, I do not believe that a single one of the thirty-eight gentlemen who were elected as Democrats and whose names are before me there, will hold in his pocket a commission conferred by Democrats, conferred on him as a democrat, and without giving notice to his constituency, without giving notice to his associates, will execute that commission in the interest of the adversary party and go and communicate his conclusions, first of all, and only, to the members of the adversary party.

Sir, who is it that has changed? Who can he be? Do you receive him with affection? Do you receive him with respect? Is such a man worthy of your association? Such a man is not worthy to be a Democrat. Is he worthy to be a Rebulican? If my friend from Illinois, my friend from Kansas, or my friend from New York, were to come to me holding a Republican commission in his pocket, sent here by a republican Legislature, and whisper to me 'I will vote with the Democrats on organization,' I would tell him that if he so come he would be expelled with ignominy from the ranks of the party.

(As Hill neared the conclusion of his speech Mahone left his seat on the sofa and moved over to his desk. He was evidently intending to reply, and it being his maiden effort he appeared somewhat nervous. After remaining in his chair for a moment he stepped down one row towards the front and seated himself beside Senator Don Cameron. Mr. Cameron whispered a few words in his ear. Mr. Hill's peroration was as terrible an arraignment as could well be imagined, and when he sat down Mahone was standing by Gen. Hawley's side on the front row, calling 'Mr. President' After a moment's delay he was recognized. The chamber was as silent as the tombs and all eyes were fastened upon the Virginian. Mr. Hill, lolling back in his chair, looked him squarely in the face. A scene of the most dramatic character followed. Mahone was terribly in earnest. He had not uttered two sentences before he had passed the first row of seats and entered the semi circle in front of the Vice President's desk. Clear, crisp and sharp fell the words from his lips. He never faltered save once, when he sent for a glass of water to moisten his lips. The spectacle was dramatic and unique. The speaker had no thought of himself. He was emersed in his subject. Regardless of the customary decorum of the body, which really confines a Senator to the space in front of his desk while talking, unless he wishes to do something unusual, Mahone paced back and forth the length of the space between the northeast door of the lobby and the head of the main aisle. His gestures were rapid and effective. In the excitement of the debate he crouched like a tiger and thrusting his hands before him, arms extended full length, towards the Senator from Georgia he defended himself. There was nothing abject or servile in the speech. It was bold, defiant and even menacing.)

Mr President, I do not propose to detain you and the Senate more than a few minutes The distinguished gentleman from Georgia has manifestly engaged in an effort to disclose my position on this floor.

Mr. Hill, of Georgia—I do not know what your position is. How could I disclose it?

Mr Mahone—Sir, you might have been a little more direct, as you might well have been, in asking my position; and that I will give you.

Now, Mr. President, the gentleman has assumed not only to be the custodian here of the Democratic party of this Nation, but he has dared to assert his right to speak for a constituency that I have the privilege, the proud and honorable privilege on this floor of representing [applause in the galleries] without his assent, without the assent of the Democratic party, on whose behalf he would undertake here to speak. [Applause in the galleries.] I owe them, sir, I owe you [addressing Mr. Hill] and those for whom you undertake to speak nothing in this Chamber. [Applause in the galleries.] I came here, sir, as a Virginian to represent my people, not to represent that democracy for which you stand. [Applause in the galleries.] I come with as proud a claim to represent that people as you to represent the people of Georgia, won on fields where I have vied with you and others in the cause of my people and of their section in the late unhappy contest; but thank God for the peace and the good of the country that contest is over, and as one of those who engaged in it, and who has neither here nor elsewhere any apology to make for the part taken, I am here by my humble efforts to bring peace to this whole country, peace throughout the sections, not here as a partisan, not here to represent that Democracy which has done so much injury to my section of the country. [Applause in the galleries.]

Now, sir, the gentleman undertakes to say what constitutes a Democrat. A Democrat! I hold, sir, that to-day I am a better Democrat than he, infinitely better—he who stands nominally committed to a full vote, a free ballot, and an honest count. I should like to know how he stands for these things in the State of Georgia where tissue ballots are fashionable. [Laughter and applause in the galleries.]

Now, sir, I serve notice on you that I intend to be here the custodian of my own democracy. I do not intend to be run by your caucus. I am in every sense a free man here, sir, I trust able to protect my own rights and to defend those of the people whom I represent, and certainly to take care of my own.—I do not intend that you, sir, on this floor shall undertake to criticise my conduct by innuendoes, a measure not becoming this floor or a straightforward legitimate line of pursuit in argument.

I wish the Senator from Georgia to understand just here that we may get along in the future harmoniously, that the way to deal with me is to deal direct. We want no motions of discovery. Now, sir, you will find out how I am going to vote in little while. [Applause.]

I regret that so early after my appearance here I should find it necessary to intrude any remarks whatsoever upon the attention of this body I would prefer to be a little modest; I would prefer to listen and to learn, but I cannot feel content after what has passed in this presence when the gentleman by all manner of methods, all manner of insinuations, direct and indirect, has sought to do that which would have been better done and more manly pursued if he had gone directly to the question itself. He has sought to disrequire that I should state either that I was a Democrat or anything else. I suppose he could not get here from Georgia unless he was to say he was a Democrat anyhow. [Laughter.] I come here without being required to state to my people what I am. They were willing to trust me, sir, and I was elected by the people, and not by a Legislature, for it was an issue in the canvass. There was no man elected by the party with which I am identified that did not go to the Legislature instructed by the sovereigns to vote for me for the position I occupy on this floor. It required no oath of allegiance, blindly given, to stand by your Democracy, such as it is, [laughter] that makes a platform and practices another thing. That is the Democracy they have in some of the Southern States.

Now, I hope the gentleman will be relieved. He has been chasseing all around this Chamber to see if he could not find a partner somewhere, he has been looking around in every direction; occasionally he would refer to some other Senator to know exactly where the Senator was who stood here as a Democrat that had the manhood and the boldness to assert his opinions in this Chamber free from the dictation of a mere caucus.

AN UNEXAMPLED EXHIBITION.

Mr. Hill.—Never before has there been such an exhibition in the Senate, where a gentleman shows his democracy by going over to the republicans. I will not defend Virginia; she needs no defense. She has given to the country and the world and humanity some of the proudest names in history. She holds in her bosom to-day the ashes of some of the noblest and greatest men that ever illustrated the glories of any country; and I say to the Senator from Virginia that neither Jefferson nor Madison, nor Henry, nor Washington, nor Lee, nor Tucker, nor any of the long list of great men whom Virginia produced ever accepted a commission to represent one party and came here and represented another party.

(Mahone is an interesting study. He comes across today as irascible and arrogant, yet able, much like some other demagogues of diminutive physical stature. The newspapers continually predicted his demise but yet he persisted. This former Confederate General (the hero of the Crater) had a home base near Petersburg and continually carried the black vote there. He was elected; like his fellow senator, Riddleberger, (quite a character himself) due to a controversy over how to pay for the state debt. He become eventually a Republican senator in a democratic state and yet the Republican paper The Telephone hated him. With an equally divided U.S. Senate his switching parties was momentous.)

The Lowell Industrial Works
HAMILTON, VIRGINIA.

Superior Plows

Farmers, Millers, and others, in want of Castings or Machine work, look to your interests:

Lowell's Improvement

Come where you can get the most work for the least money, and get it done promptly.

BEING A PRACTICAL MECHANIC, of over twenty-five years' experience in this business, and having first-class machinery, I can do work at shorter notice and at less expense than any other shop in Loudoun. I shall make a SPECIALTY OF PLOW WORK

BROWN WAGONS. G. T. DUNLOP General Agent, West Washington, D. C. new styles with Stiff and Falling Tongues. 1, 2, 3 and 4 horse, barrow and broad tread. DouglasForce Pumps. Cucumber Pumps. Fence Wire a specialty and at low prices, Silver & Deming Feed Cutters. Sinclair feed cutters. Rife's Patent Grind Stone for grinding Reaper knives.

Horse Rakes, Young American Corn and Cob Mill, Harrows, of all kinds and sizes. Farm Bells. Wheel Barrows, Lightning Hay Knife. Monumental Churns, Cylinder Churn, Staff Churns. Well Buckets, Measures, Horse Buckets, Trace Chains, Curry Combs, Horse Brushes, Hames, Whitewash Brushes, Forks, Picks, Shovels, Spades, Hoes and Mattocks, Grind Stones and Grind Stone fixtures. Hay Rakes, Plow handles, Back Bands, Axes, Hatchets &c. A full stock of LANDRETHS GARDEN SEED, fresh and Genuine. Large stock of choice Field Seed at Market Prices. Choice Western early Clover Seed. Mammoth or Sappling Clover Seed. Timothy Seed, white Clover Seed, Red Top Grass Seed. Orchard Grass. Kentucky Blue Grass, English Lawn Grass. Hungarian Grass Seed American and German Millet. POTATOES early Rose, (Second crop) used by all Truckers for first early planting. More productive and earlier than the regular stock Early Rose. Vermont genuine Early Rose, Beauty of Hebron, Snow Flake, white Peach Blow, Burbank, Peerless. Sweet Potato Roots. Seed Corn, white and yellow, Cotton Seed Meal, for feeding stock. Heavy western Seed Oats, (Fine).

G. T. DUNLOP, West Washington.

Georgetown, or West Washington, as it was sometimes called, was at this time home to cattle stock sales as well as some stores catering to farmers. These stockyards in just a couple of years would move across the river to property close to where the Pentagon is today.

April, 1881

4/21/81 Mirror

THE DELUSIONS OF OFFICE SEEKERS.—A Washington letter in the New York Sun says:

The present hunt for office is beyond precedent. There is actually not a place for one in a thousand of those who apply. For weeks not less than two thousand persons have been waiting for less than two hundred places.

The man who nominated Garfield has gone home. He went by the swearing train. The man who started Garfield for President went home, too. Both came to Washington for something handsome, not doubting they would get it. The former wanted to go to China or Brazil; the latter, having a large family, had decided to content himself with the marshalship of his district. Having spent about $200 apiece, and got only admission to the White House along with the crowd, and a two second shake of the President's hand, they began to smell a rat. A sense of the delusive character of their expectations suddenly dawned on them. Desperately they pushed themselves into Garfield's presence with their stories. He didn't know either of them. Hope then went out like a candle. Their wrath rose, and terrible oaths mingled with their demand for through tickets. Neither knew the other's business till they met on the train. When last heard from they were drinking from a black bottle over a solemn agreement never again to make a President.

The effort to depose Rev. Chas. B. Ramsdell from the pulpit of the North Presbyterian Church of this city is the absorbing topic of the day. The "trial," so far as the Washington Presbytery are concerned, has come to an end, with a victory by a bare majority for that portion of the congregation which stood by the pastor and insisted that his relation with the church should not be disturbed. But the end is not yet. The large party of church members who urged the pastor's withdrawal or expulsion are not willing to rest under the defeat; they maintain that they are right in their position; that the pastor by his marriage with a lady of the Roman Catholic faith, has so impaired his usefulness and so disturbed the peace and harmony of the church that a severance of the pastoral relation is essential to its prosperity. They will take the case, by

4/28/81 Mirror

OUR GREAT INVENTIONS.—The fifteen great American inventions of world wide adoption are: 1. The cotton gin. 2. The planing machine. 3. The grass mower and reaper. 4. The rotary printing press. 5. Navigation by steam. 6. The hot-air engine. 7. The sewing machine. 8. The india-rubber industry. 9. The machine manufacture of horseshoes. 10. The sand blast for carving. 11. The gauge lathe. 12. The grain elevator. 13. Artificial ice making on a large scale. 14. The electric magnet and its practical application. 15. The composing machine for printers. A sixteenth must be added—the telephone.

4/23/81 Washingtonian

ON last Saturday morning, a two horse team belonging to a Mr. Simpson, of Aldie, while standing in front of the Machine shop, near the depot, became frightened at the cars, and ran away, causing considerable damage to the wagon, but fortunately the horses were not hurt.

THE new and handsome residence of Col. Henry E. Peyton, 2 miles from Waterford, in this County, was completely destroyed by fire, on Saturday night last, nothing being saved but a few articles from one room, and they in a damaged condition. A number of valuable papers, (among them a "diary" kept by Col. P. during the war, from April 1, 61 to September 1, '65,) were also burned.

A TELEPHONE line is being erected from White's Ferry, on the Potomac, to connect with White & Wooton's grain Ware house, in Leesburg, a distance of about 4 miles.

FOR SALE!

A NO TOP BUGGY. As good as new, having been thoroughly repaired. Can be seen at Schooley's shop in Waterford, Va.
1881-3t.   CHESTER COLT.

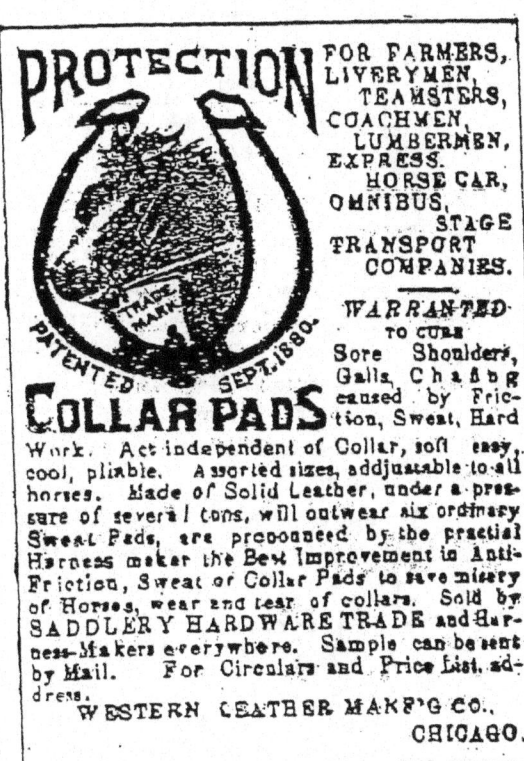

PROTECTION

FOR FARMERS, LIVERYMEN, TEAMSTERS, COACHMEN, LUMBERMEN, EXPRESS, HORSE CAR, OMNIBUS, STAGE TRANSPORT COMPANIES.

COLLAR PADS

PATENTED SEPT. 1880.

WARRANTED TO CURE Sore Shoulders, Galls, Chafing caused by Friction, Sweat, Hard Work. Act independent of Collar, soft, easy, cool, pliable. Assorted sizes, adjustable to all horses. Made of Solid Leather, under a pressure of several tons, will outwear six ordinary Sweat Pads, are pronounced by the practical Harness maker the Best Improvement in Anti-Friction, Sweat or Collar Pads to save misery of Horses, wear and tear of collars. Sold by SADDLERY HARDWARE TRADE and Harness-Makers everywhere. Sample can be sent by Mail. For Circulars and Price List, address

WESTERN LEATHER MAF'G CO., CHICAGO.

May 1881

THE TELEPHONE.

FRIDAY.............. MAY 13TH

—Already are the summer boarders coming in. Hamilton is becoming quite a retreat for our city cousins. And still there is room for more.

—A MRS. HAYES TEA PARTY.—The members of the Lincoln W. C. T. U., and Triumph Lodge will jointly hold a Temperance tea party at Lincoln, soon.

—Mr. David Hess, left our Town on Tuesday morning, enroute for Bishmark, Dakota, to seek success among the wilds of the frontier— May he have abundant success.

—Behold the candidate cometh. He pauseth in the highway among the rabble; he contendeth with no man; he eateth with publicans and sinners; he humbleth himself altogether, he giveth his hand to the poor and doeth homage to them that are of low estate; he prayeth in secret (for votes,) and exhorteth the people to go not after vain things. Surely he will be exalted in the day of—— election.

FRIDAY.............. MAY 27TH

—Candidates saddles will now have a chance to cool off.

—You must now speak of it as the New New-Testament.

—A gentleman of our vicinity who has patronized the famous faith doctor, John Miller, writes us that Miller is permanently located at Big Lick, Roanoke Co., Va. where he hopes to see all invalids who wish his treatment.—Board can be had there for 75 cents per day—$4. per week.

The corn is willing, but the cut worms are so.

—It will soon be announced that Samuel A. Gover is to be retained as post master at Waterford.

Mr. T. Vandevanter, of our Town, was so unfortunate as to have a car load of hay, valued at $140., burned on the track near Leesburg last Monday. As soon as the fire was discovered the trainmen backed the car to the Leesburg water tank and let a flood on it, but without effect. Mr. Vandevanter fears that there is poor chance to recover damage from the R. R., as it is in the hands of a receiver; but we hope he will not have to lose his property because of the carelessness of the Road's employees or inefficiency of the Road itself.

—Died on the 21st inst, at the residence of H. R. Holmes, Robert Hunter, aged about 15 years. "Bob" had been a faithful fellow, and was a splendid specimen of horse-flesh, up to within three months of his demise. At that date he was attacked with what developed finally into heart disease. His fine constitution gradually yielded to the ravages of this enemy of all life and at the moment when it had been settled, that for the safety of his comrades Bob must be shot, he gently laid down and breathed his life out without a struggle.

5/26/81 Mirror

THE REVISED NEW TESTAMENT.—Last Friday and Saturday, the first copies of the Revised New Testament were placed in the hands of the people of Boston, New York, Baltimore, Washington, and the larger cities, and on Sunday most of the pulpits had something to say about it.

5/14/81 Washingtonian

Mark Twain, in speaking of canibalism, grows serious for once, and solomnly declares that, for his own part, he would rather go hungry for two days than eat an old personal friend.

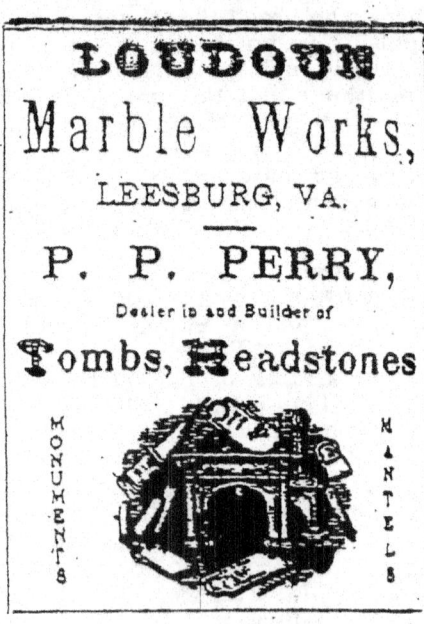

LOUDOUN
Marble Works,
LEESBURG, VA.

P. P. PERRY,
Dealer in and Builder of
Tombs, Headstones

MONUMENTS   MANTELS

5/19/81 Mirror

THE SENSATION OF THE HOUR.

Senators Conkling and Platt Resigned.

Its Effect Upon the Senate.

The United States Senate met in session on Saturday, having adjourned over from Friday until Monday. On that day the body assembled as usual, at 12 o'clock, everything, seemingly, as serene as a May morning. But scarcely had members taken their seats, and the usual formalities of opening been completed, when the Vice President laid before the Senate the following communications:

WASHINGTON, D. C., May 16, 1881.

Sir:—Will you please announce to the Senate that my resignation as Senator of the United States from the state of New York has been forwarded to the governor of the state.

I have the honor to be with great respect, your obedient servant,
(Signed) ROSCOE CONKLING.
To Hon. C. A. Arthur, Vice-President.

This communication was received with great sensation, which was heightened when the Vice President laid the following before the Senate:

SENATE CHAMBER, May 16, 1881.

To the Hon. C. A. Arthur, Vice-President of the United States

Sir:—I have forwarded to the governor of the State of New York my resignation as Senator of the United States for the State of New York. Will you please announce the fact to the Senate. With great respect your ob't serv't T. C. PLATT.

The reading of these communications fell upon the ears of Senators like the sound of a fire bell at midnight, and almost took their breath.

(These two who represented the Stalwart faction of the Republican party were arguably the two most powerful men in the Senate. Their retirement was a bombshell and also a tremendous miscalculation. The prescient comments by the Loudoun papers pretty well tell what happened. Ego seemed to play a role in this as well as the factional antagonism which was a residue of the Garfield election.)

6/2/81 Mirror

THE NEW YORK SENATORS.—It is not often that U. S. Senators, and politicians of the order of Conkling, find themselves so completely impaled on their own pickets, as Conkling and Platt. After an unsuccessful fight of two months against a President whom they assisted in elevating to power, they resigned their places in the Senate, evidently expecting to be returned before their seats could get cool. But alas for the uncertainty of things temporal. The lordly Roscoe had reckoned without his host, and for the past two weeks he has been hanging around the suburbs of Albany, at first bold and threatening, next imploringly, and finally, obsequiously trying to coax the Legislature of his own creation, to give back to him the gilded toy which he, in his childish obstreperousness, cast from him. But his usual power of persuasiveness and fascination don't seem to pan out worth a cent, and the strong probability at this writing is, that the Legislature on Tuesday, refused to return either of the retiring Statesmen, Conkling and Platt.

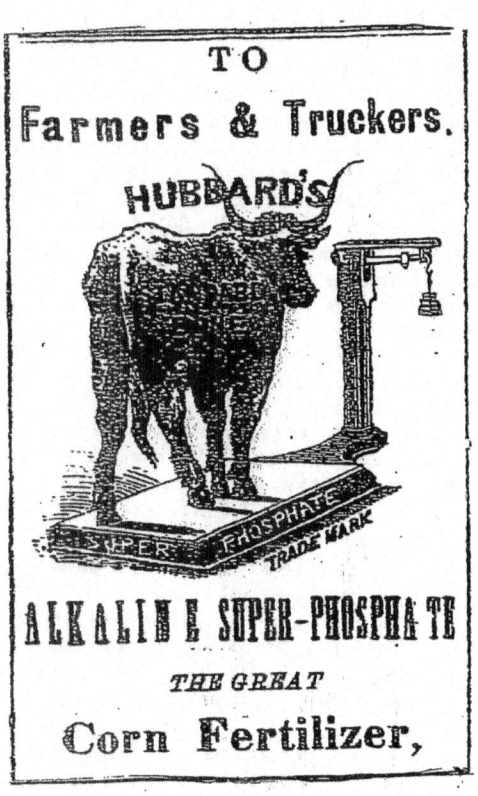

POSTOFFICE ESPIONAGE.

HOW IT GOT A PLAIN SPOKEN VIRGINIAN INTO TROUBLE.

Carmichael Held to Answer for Writing His Opinion of Mahone on a Postal Card—Yesterday's Proceedings in the Case at Alexandria.

These plain Anglo-Saxon words, on the back of a postal card, addressed to "Senator Z. Vance, N. C., U. S. S., Washington, D. C.," have furnished the groundwork for one of the most amusing prosecutions in the history of the Postoffice Department.

Please send me your speech on that damn dog Mahone, Resp'y
JOHN CARMICHAEL.
Middleburg, Loudoun County, Va.
March 31, 1881.

The sender of the card, a farmer of the Old Dominion, and a graduate of the Virginia Military Institute, was arrested on the affidavit of one William T. Henderson, as an inspector of the Postoffice Department, charging that "one John Carmichael did deposit, or cause to be deposited, in the postoffice at Middleburg, Loudoun county, Virginia, a postal card addressed to Senator Z. Vance containing language against a Senator as follows: 'Please send me your speech on that damn dog Mahone,' which is an indecent epithet, and in violation of Section 3,893 of the Revised Statutes of the United States, and against the peace and dignity of the United States." The preliminary examination came off yesterday morning, in Alexandria, before United States Commissioner Fowler. The court room was well filled with the proud sons of the sacred soil; many staunch Democrats, quite a number of respectable straight Republicans, very few Ethiopians and Readjusters.

Mr. Lewis, the United States Attorney for the Eastern district of Virginia, a gentleman and a lawyer, conducted the prosecution. The accused was represented by Ex-Congressman Eppa Hunton, of Virginia; United States Senator Morgan, of Alabama, and Maj Scott, of Fauquier county, one of Virginia's most brilliant advocats.

Awaiting the arrival of the tardy Commissioner, there was a general run of conversation. One old Virginian, well known to national fame, said, "This case, seemingly insignificant, has two important bearings: In the first place, Mahone is at the bottom of this prosecution. He has been so damnably abused that he wants a victim In the second place comes the question of the right of a gossipy postal attache to read the private communications on postal cards. This last point is of national significance."

The prosecution opened with James E. Bell, the superintendent of the city delivery of the Washington Postoffice.

Gen. Hunton—By what authority did you read that postal card? Do you not know that it was indecent to do so and positively prohibited by law?

Postal Agent Bell—Yes, but I considered it my duty.

Gen. Hunton—Why did you read it, sir? Did you not know that officials have been discharged for such illegal reading?

Mr. Bell—I considered it my duty, and took the risk. In my opinion, the law sustained me.

Gen. Hunton—I see by the Washington Post, a most reliable newspaper, that the postal card trade is immense. Do you read them all?

Mr. Bell—The Post's figures are correct. The business is simply enormous. In the city of Washington alone our monthly delivery averages over 50,000 annually. Now, as to my reason for withholding this postal card, the postal law, by which I am guided, told me to do so because it was scurrilous

Maj. Scott—Are you aware of the fact that the word "scurrilous" has been eliminated from the statute and that now only 'indecent' words are pronounced unmailable?

Here a third lawyer, a stranger, appeared for the prisoner. He quickly drew out the fact that the postal card written by Carmichael had been forwarded to headquarters and obtained the earnest consideration of the Postmaster General, but he failed, despite his strict cross-examination, to bring to light the man who was pulling the wires. The witness was stubborn and insolent until the lawyer announced himself a United States Senator—the Hon. John T. Morgan, of Alabama.

Senator Morgan—Is it your habit to suppress postal cards?

Mr. Bell—Frequently. For example: abusive postal cards are almost daily received against the President, but they never reach him; we burn them up.

Senator Morgan—What right have you to keep the President from knowing what some of the people think of him? The President has the same rights as any man to obtain the popular sentiment. We are not living in a despotism.

Mr. Bell—Senator Mahone has received very many scurrilous postal cards.

Senator Morgan—"Well, I don't know of any special guardianship in the Postoffice Department over Senator Mahone.

Mr. Bell—We aim to protect all Senators from these scurrilous postal card writers. We

June 1881

don't want to lacerate their feelings.

District Attorney Lewis concluded the argument. He said that he had no desire to vindicate Senator Mahone from the epithets of "dastard," "traitor," or "damn dog." The defendant had a right to say what he pleased of Mahone, but he had no right to send an indecent expression on a postal card through the mails. He had violated the statute, and should be held for trial.

United States Commissioner Fowler decided that the words "damn dog" were offensive to the fine delicacy of the public, and he therefore, held Mr Carmichael to appear under $500 bonds, before the United States Circuit Court, to convene in Alexandria on the 5th of July. The bond was promptly filled.

6/16/81 Mirror

Last Thursday, for the space of about three hours, rain fell in torrents, and without intermission. All the smaller streams in this vicinity swelled out of all proportion, doing considerable damage to wheat, corn, and grass, growing along their banks, and playing smash with water-gates and fencing generally, and by their treachery came near luring several human beings to destruction. Mr. J. J. Hogeland, attempted to cross Tuscarora, a mile or so from this town, and was compelled to cut his horse loose from the wagon and make his escape on the animal's back, leaving the wagon to its fate, which, however, sustained no serious injury. We also learn that Mr. Gus. Loughborough, attempted to cross a little stream in the neighborhood of the Trappe, with a four horse team, he sitting in the body of the wagon. The current proved too strong—the wagon body with Mr. L. in it, became detached from the running gear and was giving that gentleman a merry ride down stream, when he plunged into the water and swam ashore. The horses, with the remainder of the wagon, after floundering in the water for sometime, succeeded in safely reaching the store.

Fortunately, no damage was done in either of the above cases, but they should serve as warnings to deter others from making similar attempts to cross these treacherous little streams when they are on the rise. In their angriest mood, a few hours delay, at farthest, renders them perfectly harmless.

6/17/81 Telephone

—Of all the mean and disgusting affairs which have yet happened at Guilford, the last was the lowest. A certain set have for some months been persecuting and annoying Mr. G. C. Wells, simply because he had the independence to speak his mind. One night last week miscreants visited Mr. Well's wheelwright shop and broke the window glass and some new work which was in process of construction, then smeared the door with filth. We sincerely hope Mr. Wells will "Hunt the rascals down," and make them suffer for their demonly devilment.

6/24/81 Telephone

—GUILFORD FLASHES:—No cause but whiskey can boast of such champions as those who so valiantly attacked unprotected property to vent their rage against "Guilford Flashes."— Without brains to argue the case and without courage make an attack when any person is about to defend it, they have no resort but to sneak around after dark and do a little damage and cause a little annoyance. To call such creatures beasts would be a libel upon the whole brute creation; to call them reptiles would insult the whole slimy kingdom. It is only those creatures who bear the outward semblance of humanity that can descend to so low a level. These must be the Yahoos of Gulliver's Travels, which were heretofore supposed to be imaginary. It is possible that sufficient evidence may be obtained to identify at least a part of them.— Should such be the case, "Guilford Flashes" will promptly illuminate the subject. In the meantime the "Flashes" will not be deterred from keeping the public posted by any such petty annoyance.—The war horse does not stop for a hissing viper.

(Guilford, VA is now Sterling, VA.)

June 1881

Thursday Morning, June 23, 1881.

HARVESTING has pretty generally commenced throughout this county; those who have not already done so will be busily engaged by the close of the week. The harvest is fully ten days later than it was last year.— So far as we have heard an expression, the yield promises to be a good one.

HARVEST is engaging the attention of every body. Consequently, the old town is as quiet as a graveyard, and there is not so much as a good sized dog-fight to break the dull monotony, or afford a local paragraph.

GEN. LONGSTREET, who has been appointed United States marshal for Georgia, has been interviewed concerning Mr. Davis's History of the Civil War. For the most part Gen. Longstreet was non-committal, but in some points coincided with Mr. Davis, and notably in his opinion that Washington could have been captured after the first battle of Manassas.

WAITING FOR THE END OF THE WORLD.— Last Sunday was the day designated for the world to come to an end, and a despatch from Quebec states that several people set up all Saturday night waiting for the grand conflagration. They were disappointed in that, but considerable consternation was created by the shock of an earthquake, many supposing that it was an evidence of the fulfilment of the prophecy that time was to be no more.

6/30/81 Mirror

SELF BINDERS —There have been two of these machines at work, during harvest, in this neighborhood. We saw the one run by Mr. Jno. Titus on the Temple Hall farm; it did its work admirably, cutting and binding the wheat as rapidly as an ordinary reaper cuts. Mr. T. seemed much pleased with his machine, declaring he would not be without it for twice its cost. We understand the other machine which is owned by Mr. J. B. Beverley, gave equal satisfaction. One misses the thwack of the rifle and the sweeping swash of the swathe, but the thorough and expeditious work of these wonderful machines cannot fail to commend them to our farmers.— Their capacity is said to be eighteen to twenty acres per day.

These machines were of the "Buckeye" pattern and were sold by Messrs. Shrof & Co. of this town.

Crampton's
IMPERIAL SOAP,

THE BEST and most Economical Soap known. No family that ever tries it can afford to do without it.

Chemically pure, and is undoubtedly the best Laundry soap in use. "Full Weight," pressed bars, in substantial wrappers, at 10 cts., each, or three bars for 25 cts.

The Price of the IMPERIAL SOAP is $5.25 per box of 100 ¾ lb. bars. 75 lbs. in the box.

Lamp Lighting

MAYOR'S OFFICE,
Leesburg, June 1st, 1881.

SEALED PROPOSALS will be received at this office until 12 o'clock, M., SATURDAY, JUNE 25th, 1881, for LIGHTING, EXTINGUISHING and CLEANING the TOWN LAMPS, Furnishing OIL, WICKS, CHIMNEYS and LAMPS, should any be broken, and Keeping in Repair the Lanterns for ONE YEAR from the 1st day of July, 1881. The said proposals to be at so much for each lamp in use. The Council reserves to itself the privilege of rejecting any or all proposals offered.

The successful bidder will be required to execute a bond in the penalty of $250, to be satisfactorily endorsed, to ensure the faithful performance of his contract.

Proposals must be addressed to the Mayor of Leesburg, and marked "Proposals for furnishing Oil, Lighting Lamps, &c."

The Oil must be of best quality Coal Oil.
GEORGE R. HEAD,
June 1, 1881.   Mayor.

FOR SALE!

A VALUABLE DAIRY FARM

In Fairfax County, Va., containing 180 acres, 6 miles from Washington, 20 minutes' walk to the Washington and Ohio Railroad Station. The land is well located, watered and productive; all the conveniences for keeping a large dairy; also, buildings necessary for the place; fine well of water to the dwelling; plenty of fruit of all kinds. The dwelling is commodious for summer boarders; will accommodate 60. For further information address Mrs. L. BAILEY, Bailey's Cross Roads, Fairfax Co. Va.

July, 1881

THE MIRROR

BENJ. F. SHEETZ, Editor.

Thursday Morning, July 7, 1881.

On Saturday morning last, the 2d of July President Garfield came to the Baltimore & Potomac Depot, Corner 6th and B. streets, in Washington, about 9 o'clock, to take the northern train, intending to go to Long Branch where his wife and children were, and then to go to New England on a short trip for relaxation.

As the President and Mr Blaine were passing out of the ladies waiting room, in the large saloon on the way to the train, a man behind the President, and near the B street door, fired a shot out of a large calibre revolver at the President, which inflicted a slight wound on Gen. Garfields right arm, and advancing, the assassin fired a second shot, which struck the President on the right side above or behind the hip, in the short ribs.

The President fell bleeding profusely Medical aid was at once summoned. He was taken first into an upper room of the depot, and afterward to the White House.

The would be assassin was at once seized and proved to be a man named Charles Guiteau, hailing from Chicago, a dead beat who has been persistantly importuning the President and officials for a place, without success. Mrs. Garfield was at once telegraphed and came to Washington that afternoon and has been constantly in attendance on her husband ever since.

The wires sent the news to all parts of this land and to the uttermost parts of the earth, in a few short minutes. It caused a thrill of horror, pain and indignation, over the whole civilized world; responses, expressions of the deepest and most sincere grief and sympathy, came from every corner of this Union. All personal, and party, and sectional feeling was forgotten and disappeared like frost before the sun.

Message after message came from England, the whole continent of Europe from Australia, Japan, and the Isles of the Sea, in a few short hours.

ASSASSINATION!

President Garfield Shot!

THE TWO SHOTS FIRED.

WHAT THE ASSASSIN SAID.

HIS INTENTION TO KILL!

A thrill of horror rung throughout the land last Saturday morning when the telegraph wires flashed over the continent the soul appaling announcement that JAMES A. GARFIELD, President of the United States, had been assassinated in the Depot of the B. & P. Railroad, in Washington city, by a disappointed office seeker named GITTEAU, and received such wounds as would probably result fatally. We condense from our exchanges, the following history of the most brutal and damnable outrage.

As is known, the President's wife had been spending a few weeks at Long Branch, for the benefit of her broken health. On Saturday last the President proposed to join her, and together pass a few days in travel through New England, visiting friends and scenes of early life. For that purpose he had repaired to the depot of the Baltimore and Potomac depot accompanied by Secretary Hunt and Mrs. Hunt, Secretary Windom and Mrs. Windom, Postmaster James and Mrs. James and some others. The most of the party had taken their seats in the car. The President alighted from his carriage, at the B Street entrance of the depot, and being informed that he had ten minutes before the train started, arm in arm he and Secretary Blaine walked through the ladies' parlor and had entered the large reception room in the main portion of the depot, when two pistol shots were fired in rapid succession. The crowd screamed "He's shot the President. Arrest the man." The assassin was making his way as fast as possible out through the ladies parlor tow'rd the B street door, a carriage being there to take him away. Depot officer Kearney threw himself before him, seized him by both arms between the elbows and shoulders and held him as with a vise The pistol was in his hand when he first saw him and he had just put it into his coat pocket when the officer nabbed him The would be assassin said: "Yes, I have finished Garfield; now Arthur is President. I am a stalwart" Kearney secured the pistol, a heavy five barrel "English bull dog," and hustled the man to police headquarters.

71

July, 1881

Mrs. Garfield who was adjourning at Long Branch, was first notified of the husbands condition by the following telegram.

Mrs. Garfield, Elberon, Long Branch

"The President wishes me to say to you from him that he has been seriously hurt. How seriously he cannot say. He is himself and hope you will come to him soon. He sends his love to you.

A. F. ROCKWELL

She arrived in the city about 7:30 o'clock, on Saturday evening, accompanied by her daughter, Miss Mary, and her oldest son, Harry. On entering the room of the President he recognized them, and moved as if he would embrace them. Mrs. Garfield with suppressed emotion passed swiftly to the bedside where she knelt and tenderly embraced her husband in silence. Her presence seemed to brighten him wonderfully, as his brave, sanguine heart was cheered by the love that had never failed him.

Says a watcher by the bed side: "Mrs. Garfield did not close her eyes in sleep throughout all of that night. She spoke but little, and would flit from side to side, first resting for a moment on one chair or sofa; and then hovering about the door of the sick chamber. During the President's most painful moments she was constantly at his bedside.

Recognizing the necessity for composure on her part, she has not given way to tears but once since her arrival. That occasion, let it be stated in all tenderness, was shortly after midnight. She was resting in an easy chair, and a brief, fitful slumber came. It was only of a few minutes duration, but sufficient to allow the saddest of dreams. A sob was breathed forth from her tired lips, and tears crept out of her partially closed eyelids. She awoke with a start, and wept for a few moments as she supposed unobserved. Then controlling her emotions she arose and walked swiftly into the President's presence, stooped over him, pressed a kiss upon his forehead and said with simple fervor, "My poor husband."

7/15/81 Telephone

Some cry "Crucify him! crucify him! others say imprison him! while some agree that the place for him is in an insane asylum; but we would suggest a different plan.

Station the Villain as nearly as possible in the position where the President stood when shot; then get Buffalo Bill or some other "dead shot" and station him where Guiteau stood and give him that same "bull dog" pistol, and have him put a ball into the diaphragm of the fiendish assassin in a spot corresponding to the wound of the President; then put Guiteau upon the dissecting table and go for that ball with a knife—"in the interest of Science," of course.

7/8/81 Telephone

FRIDAY.................JULY 8TH.

OUR STRICKEN PRESIDENT.

At this late day it would be an insult to our readers to offer an account of the late awful tragedy, for it is an insult to patriotism, on the part of any man, who, living here so near the National Capitol, has not already learned the particulars of this fearful calamity;—especially so, when we contemplate that in foreign lands, beyond the seas, the people have watched with eagerness and seized with devoted earnestness, every symptom and change in this fearful woe of our great Nation. For nearly a week has elapsed since that dark cloud of impending calamity first settled over our beloved Country; and the awful suspense of these six days has made them weeks. And in every part of our Nation—aye! it is a Nation now!—the plow has stopped in the furrow, the fire lay smouldering on the forge, the hod carrier stood still on the ladder, aye! the very reapers paused in the ripening grain, while the people poured forth into the streets and from the countryside to hear the tidings of good or ill from our beloved and stricken President. Verily, the Nation was one vast audience—bowed in prayer for the life that hovered "between two worlds" "like a star upon the horizon verge."

July 1881

7/8/81 Telephone

He is a man about five feet seven inches high, and weighs apparently about 130 pounds. He was dressed in black coat, pants and vest and low-quarter shoes. His collar had long points, which were turned down at the ends, and he wore a black tie — He held a black slouch hat in his hand. His head is small and covered by a heavy suit of brown hair, which is closely cropped, not being over a fourth of an inch in length — His face is thin and long, the lower part of it being covered with a thin growth of whiskers of light brown color. His forehead is high, but very narrow. His nose is of the aquiline form, very thin—at the end a little hooked. The nostrils are compressed and the base narrow. His eyes, which are his most peculiar feature, are small and sunken in his head under heavy eyebrows.

7/8/81 Telephone

That the man desired to prepare the way for the plea of insanity is evinced by this letter which was found on his person at police headquarters:

JULY 2, 1881.

To the White House:

"The President's tragic death was a sad necessity, but it will unite the Republican party and save the Republic. Life is a flimsy dream and it matters little when one goes. A human life is of small value. During the war thousands of brave boys went down without a tear. I presume the President was a Christian, and that he will be happier in Paradise than here. It will be no worse for Mrs Garfield, dear soul, to part with her husband this way than by natural death. He is liable to go at any time anyway. I had no ill will toward the President — His death was a political necessity. I am a lawyer, a theologian, and a politician. I am a stalwart of the stalwarts. I was with Gen. Grant and the rest of our men in New York during the canvass. I have some papers for the press, which I shall leave with Byron Andrews and his cojournalists at 1420 New York avenue, where all the reporters can see them. I am going to the jail.

CHARLES GUITEAU."

THE MIRROR
BENJ. F. SHEETZ, Editor.

Thursday Morning July 14, 1881.

THE PRESIDENT'S CONDITION.—The latest advices from Washington are to the effect that all the symptoms in President Garfield's condition, are of the most encouraging and hopeful character

LATEST BULLETINS.

EXECUTIVE MANSION, Washington, July 13, 1.15 A. M.—At this hour (1.15 A. M.) the President is sleeping. During the early part of the night he was considerably weaker, though it is hoped that the sleep he is obtaining, will refresh him.

EXECUTIVE MANSION, July 13, 2 A. M.—At this hour the President is resting quietly. The two attending physicians at the mansion tonight—Drs. Bliss and Reyburn—are both sound asleep in the room adjoining the President's.

Interview with Dr. Bliss.

WASHINGTON, July 10.—"The President is better than he has been at any time since he was shot," said Dr. Bliss, the physician in charge, this afternoon, "and every day and hour adds to the hopes of his recovery.

"Do you consider," your correspondent inquired, "that the danger period has passed?"

"Oh, no; it will not pass. I think, for a week. Yesterday we were somewhat disturbed by the increase in temperature, as we did not know what change there might be in the internal conditions to cause it; but the temperature was soon reduced, and by very simple means. To-day it is much better. He is of course, very weak. If you could see that strong man in his present condition you would realize how severe his hurt is. He is doing better continuously—very much better than we would have dared to hope."

"The physicians who are not in this case and who have not seen the patient, doctor, seem to know more about it than you do.— They say now that the diagnosis was all wrong; that the wound is not so severe as it has been made to appear, and that it is very doubtful whether the ball pierced the liver or entered the ventral cavity?"

"I know they do, and I do not understand why medical gentlemen are willing to put themselves in that position. It might do for laymen. We have been taking careful notes of the case every half hour for the benefit of the President, for the sake of science and for ourselves. These notes will constitute the record, and the result will show that the original diagnosis was perfectly correct.

> The legacy of Dr. Bliss is not good. He had difficult relations with his fellow doctors and he was arrogant and deceptive with the press. Worse than this, he misdiagnosed the path of the bullet. Unfortunately, the x-ray machine was developed just a few years in the future.

"CRANKS" IN WASHINGTON.

WASHINGTON, July 6.—In connection with the arrest of McNamara, who threatened to shoot Secretary Blaine, an attache of the police department said on Tuesday:

"I am not much surprised at this fellow turning up. Indeed, I shall not be surprised if a half dozen more of them come this way, or will develop from the material already in Washington. We have plenty of the stuff here out of which at least a dozen full fledged assassins could be made, provided some one excites or starts their minds in that direction. Just now their minds are occupied in their efforts to get their imaginary grievances righted. For instance, there is a 'Colonel' Pinchover, who has been the guy for congressmen and others about the Capitol and departments for years with his famous Lake Tahoe Canal scheme and his war against the railroads. He and all such as he should be locked up somewhere or sent out of town.— The slightest thing will start such men off, and make them commit the greatest of crimes. The hobby that Pinchover is now riding happens to be a harmless one, but who can tell where it may end if he is permitted to roam about?

"Then again there is the long-haired Greek, 'Doctor' Tachmintis, who thinks the Pope of Rome is conspiring against him. That fellow visits the White House daily, and is allowed to go about the rooms. He, too, has annoyed the President at times.

"Mahommed Dean Conn, another one, a Persian, is harmless enough in his way, but there is the germ of disorder in him. I could name a dozen more of them, if I wanted to, who to-day are just as bad mentally as Guiteau. Even he did not do any harm for a long time, but what he did do shows the danger in such people. Guiteau never talked anything but office until two weeks ago, and just think what a change occurred. There are more of these characters, or 'peculiar people,' as some call them, about this city than in any other. Their minds are not balanced, and they are liable to go off like a sky-rocket, on the slightest pretence. The magnitude of this event has excited and overwhelmed people of sound minds. Who can imagine then, the effect it has on the crack-brained, and will continue to have for several days? This crime is to day the all absorbing topic, and Washington city is, of course, the centre of it. This city, then, is the great attraction, the central idea, and we must expect visitors of this kind. As they can be easily recognized, they won't be able to do much harm, because there is a government insane asylum here. It is the custom of some cities to send all their cranks this way."

"Is that done often, do you think?"

"Dozens are sent during the year and we have to provide for them To illustrate what I mean, the authorities of some cities think it cheaper to pay the transportation here than to pay for their keeping in their own institutions Insane people are often dumped in on us in that way. Then, again, all who have money don't have to be sent They come quickly enough during excitement.

"At the inauguration of Mr. Garfield four insane men turned up here who wanted to be inaugurated, each claiming to have been elected Seven were arrested on the day Mr. Hayes was inaugurated. An equal number wanted to take General Grant's place at the first and nearly a dozen on the occasion of his second inauguration. Don't you remember what an excitement the marriage of Nellie Grant created? Well, five or six 'cranks.' one of whom paid about $50 for his railroad ticket, ranging in age from thirty to sixty years, came on here, each claiming to be the groom. Two of them were sent to the insane asylum the same day in the same ambulance, and they fought all the way over as to which of them was the real groom. During the excitement that followed the Nathan murder mystery sixteen persons in all in different parts of the country confessed

August 1881

to being the murderer. In the excitement that took place during the consideration of the Inflation bill, as it was called, we had over a dozen financial 'cranks' to come, and over a hundred were already here. They all kept reasonably quiet, except a demented New York Congressman, who rode about the streets increasing the circulating medium by throwing greenbacks out of his carriage in the streets. In the insane asylum there are four men who claim to be presidents, one or two kings, one queen and three men who have financial theories that they claim will save the country."

The officers have been instructed this evening to pick up and "run in" all of the known "cranks" if they are heard to talk on this subject at all.

"Can you remember any other crazy men?"

"Not by name. Well, yes; have you ever heard of John Biggins?— No? Well, he was a big Irishman about six feet four, and as strong as a yoke of oxen. He was a rough-looking chap, too, and had a hand like a leg of mutton. He was as crazy as a loon, but only on one point, and that he never showed until the occasion arrived. He was one of President Grant's visitors. One day he called, looking as sober as a judge and as quiet as a lamb, and asked to see the President. His name was sent up stairs, and, after waiting awhile, he was shown into the President's reception room.

"'What can I do for you, Mr. Biggins?' asked the President.

"'President Grant,' said Biggins, his craziness breaking out for the first time, 'I wish you to understand that I don't want you peeping thrugh the keyhole of my bedroom door any more. If you do it again I'll shoot you dead, as sure as my name is Biggins.'

"'So would I if I were you,' replied President Grant, not a muscle of his face moving; 'and I can assure you it will not occur again.'

"The coolness of the President probably saved his life, for Biggins was armed and desperate. He is now in the insane asylum."

THE TELEPHONE.

FRIDAY............Aug, 5th.

"God reigns and the [President] at Washington still lives!"

The Bush Meeting was a success; bloated faced men bent their heads to the convincing words of the able speakers, even unto conviction; saloonatics glanced furtively over their shoulders and started at every sound —alarmed by the very presence of Temperance and Purity;—now open the ballot box and we will hurl the Rum fiend from Loudoun's green wall and fertile fields.

—Rev. Mr. Schooley, of Berryville, who had passed over the road, gave us information regarding the condition of the turnpike, on the Mountain, which was so fearfully ripped up, by a storm last Saturday. He says that from the grocery (?) located on the mountain, for nearly forty rods westward the pike is terribly torn —from one foot to fifteen feet deep, leaving a gorge piled with huge rocks as though they had been dumped there from a thousand carts; making it impossible to pass along the road, even on horseback.

ESTRAY HOGS!

LOUDOUN COUNTY TO WIT:

To the Clerk of the County Court of said county, we, Rodney Janney and Thomas Gore, freeholders of said county, do hereby certify that by virtue of a warrant to us, directed by E. B. Powell, a Justice of said county, we have this day, on our oaths, viewed and appraised 5 HOGS, or Shoats, taken up by T. L. Worsley on his land, as Estrays, and assess said 5 Hogs at 4½ dollars each— say $22.50. The said Hogs are black and white spotted, with crop on right ear, weighing about 90 lbs each, of the sex two sows and three barrows.

Given under our hands this 18th day of September, 1881.

T. H. GORE,
R P. JANNEY,
EDGAR LITTLETON, Clerk.

August, 1881

THIS SPEAKS OF THE BIG SHOW!
AND THE ONLY SHOW THAT WILL EXHIBIT AT
LEESBURG, THIS YEAR!
UNDER NO CIRCUMSTANCES WILL ITS DATE BE CHANGED!
Monday, August 22, 1881

NO SOONER! NO LATER! NO LONGER!

Old Jno. Robinson's Great Show

CIRCUS, MENAGERIE,
Museum, Aquarium.

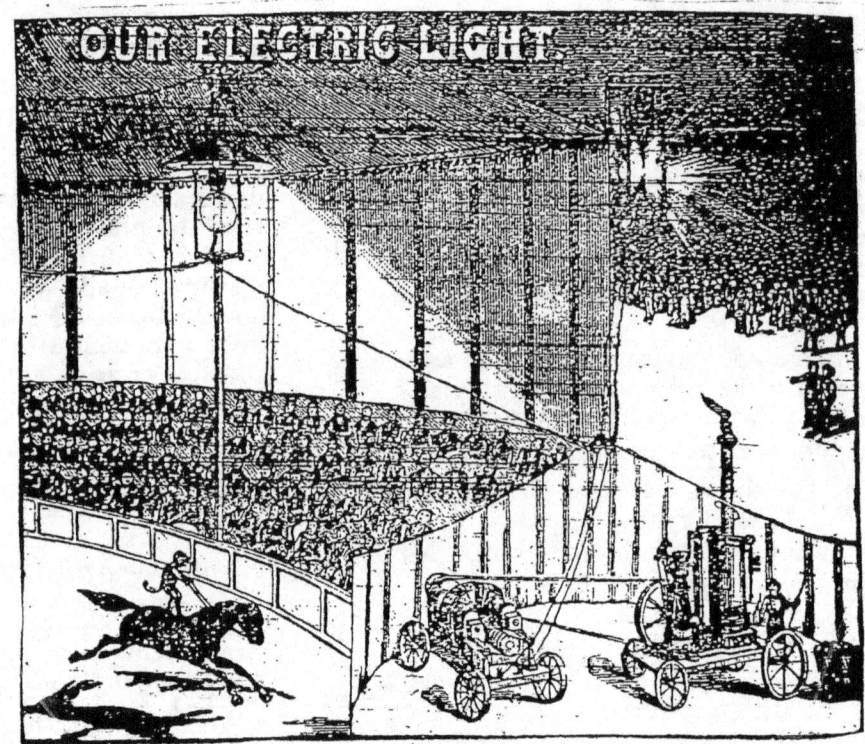

The Sensational Features Are:

The Great Electric Light. A Herd of the Largest Elephants. The Largest Rhinoceros in America, weight 4,000 lbs. A Giant White Polar Bear. A Drove of Bactrian Camels. Musk Ox. A Colossal Living Alligator. Egyptian Valpus. One Hundred Different Kinds of Monkeys. Pair of Sacred White Peacocks, worshipped in India as Gods. The Man-eating blue-faced Mandril. The Great Taminur or Ant Bear. One Hundred different kinds of Plumage Birds.

August. 1881

The Startling Novelties are

100 Performers, Male and Female,

50 Dens of Rare Animals,

100 Diminutive Shetland Ponies,

smaller than Newfoundland Dogs.

A Cortege of Golden Chariots.

A School of Sea Lions.

A Troupe of Hindoo Jugglers

The Circus Embraces

More Equestrians,   More Vaulters,

More Gymnasts,   More Clowns,

More Athletes,   More Specialties,

Than Any Show in America!

And now a few words to the People of LEESBURG AND VICINITY:

You all know the Show! It has Always been Known as a Big

Show! It is now Bigger and Better than Ever!

It is Larger and Grander than Ever. The Pictorial Bills of the OLD

JOHN ROBINSON SHOW are correct representations of

the WONDERFUL FEATURES which can be witnessed

in the CIRCUS and MENAGERIE.

Just Added, a Giant Ox, 20 hands

High, is Larger Than an Elephant.

More Lions, More Camels, More Tigers, More Cages, More Elephants, More Monkeys,

THAN ANY SHOW IN AMERICA

The Extraordinary Attractions are a

TROUPE OF Hindoo Jugglers,

The Anatomical Wonder! The Samson of the Nineteenth Century! The Human Meteor!
A Woman shot from a Cannon loaded with Powder, and whirled through
the air with terrible force and speed.

The Best Troupe of Educated Dogs and Monkeys in the World!

The Grand Street Parade is Bright, Beautiful and Brilliant.
There will be no combination with any other shows—the time is fixed. The OLD
JOHN ROBINSON SHOW never changes or postpones and his
show is too big to need a combination with any other
Two Thousand RESERVED CUSHION CHAIRS at but a small advance.

August, 1881

8/11/81 Mirror

AUGUST COURT.—Monday last was August Court, and we were not disappointed in our expectations of a large crowd—it reminding us of an old fashioned August Court day. The fine rain on Sunday evening had laid the dust and cooled off the hitherto sweltering atmosphere, and when the sun rose clear and cloudless we had a day perfect, as far as weather could make it. The crowd began to gather early, and it was steadily on the increase until, by noon there were decidedly more people in town than there had been on a similar occasion for a good many years past. The proceedings in Court were brief—Judge McCabe adjourning about twelve o'clock in order to give the delegates to the County Convention the use of the Court House; during the sitting of the Convention, Col Blair, the Readjuster candidate for Attorney General addressed a restless crowd from the portico, and after the Convention made its nomination it was addressed by Col. Peyton and Judge H. W. Thomas, in stirring speeches. By the time all this was over it was getting late; the crowd began to disperse and by dusk the old town had sunk into its wonted quiet with nothing save the trampled appearance of the streets and the court green to indicate the recent presence of a great crowd. The order throughout the day was excellent, and whilst on Monday there were several arrests for small offences, there were no disturbances of anything like a serious nature. The occasion was much enlivened by the presence of the Tankerville Band, which arrived in town early in the day and discoursed through the streets some very excellent music; and just here we would express our thanks to the gentlemen of the Band for the courtesy of a serenade rendered in front of the *Mirror* office—the sweet strains of which fell with soothing effect upon ears wearied with the din of a busy, surging crowd.

Determined to find the existence or the remains of this town that was large enough to support a popular band, I recently drove down Tankersville Road. There were high banks on both sides which suggested this rather narrow lane had once borne the tread of animals, wagons and humankind for a couple of centuries. Except for one lonely country church, there was no sign of a possible village. Like Bolington, Waters, Goresville, Dover, Mechanicsville, Willard, and few other extinct Loudoun settlements, Tankersville and its music had ceased to exist.

8/12/81 Telephone

AUGUST COURT.

AN IMMENSE CROWD.

POLITICS, WHISKEY, MELONS.

REPUBLICAN(?) CONVENTION(?)

DEMOCRATIC CONVENTION.

READJUSTER SPEAKING.

O! what a crowd! It seemed that the vales of Loudoun had verily disgorged their contents of Humanity into the old Burg.

Everything was lively except August Court. Everybody was busy doing nothing or what amounted to nothing, or worse than nothing—with a few exceptions.

The old time genuineness of the occasion was evidenced by the fact that

RUM RUM RIOT,

and well sustained the boast that "This is our bush meeting." Every little while loud voices and a rushing crowd indicated that another of "the boys" was being "sent up;" men with bleared eyes and bloated faces staggered among the crowd with rude oaths and foul language; men who were Created in God's own image," bowed to the scourge of the Satanic King; wandered about annoying people and disturbing the peace; and if they escaped the lock-up, they went reeling to that mockery of man's earthly heaven—a home—to make of it a hell.

We do not take pleasure in these declarations—far from it! We would rejoice to chronicle the fact that our people were the most orderly in the land; but so long as this curse of drink lurks in our midst, as a duty to God and Humanity, the voice of the TELEPHONE will be heard crying out against it.

Away with this rum traffic, and August Court will be a small affair; for men would not only cease to go there to get drunk, but the work of the Grand Jury will be light, there will be fewer sheriff's sales, fewer cases in court and men will realize that they can do themselves and families more good by staying at Home.

September 1881

9/1/81 Mirror

Old-Time Nevada Jurors.

"Mining suits ain't what they used to be. There's been no real live litigation to speak of since the Raymond & Ely suit with the Hermes in Pioche.

"Were you in town?"

"Well, rather; I traveled 400 miles on a mule to get to the jury box. I struck the town about 6 o'clock at night, and walking into the leading bar room inquired if the suit had begun. Inside of half an hour a man came up and asked me what my name was. He wrote it down on his shirt cuff, and then he said: 'Pard, if you want to stay and see the suit, let me see you through on your expenses; and he handed me $500, remarking that he thought the R. & E. had the bulge on the law. I said that I thought that myself, and then I sauntered off. In about an hour a man came to me and told me I was drawn on the jury. I said I didn't mind, and agreed to stand in. About 9 o'clock a man tapped me on the arm and handed me five hundred, remarking that the Hermes had about all the law and facts on their side that was necessary. He thought I might need a little money for expenses. Of course I took the money, he seemed so anxious to get rid of it, and then I slipped into a back room, put on a pair of false side whiskers, a thin duster I had been carrying under my coat, and I was a changed man. By 10 o'clock I was on a good horse that I paid $300 for, and started off on a prospecting trip. I couldn't bear the idea of holding the scales of justice in a case like that. I was fearful of further corruption, you see.

9/1/81 Mirror

Whatever may be thought of Vice President Arthur's fitness for the responsible position to which he would be elevated in the event of Gen. Garfield's death, it must be admitted that all through the trying hours of the President's illness, Mr. Arthur has borne himself with the greatest propriety, in the face of the impending responsibility, and the embarrassing situation that confronted him.

Chair Factory,

AT HAMILTON, LOUDOUN COUNTY, VA

D. G. CORBIN, proprietor and Manufacturer of SUPERIOR HICKORY

Splint Bottom Chairs.

He asks an inspection of his stock, which for style of finish and durability, will compare with any work on the market. Orders solicited.

☞ The highest price paid for good Hickory Timber. D. G. CORBIN,
Hamilton, Loudoun County, Va.

aug. 20, tf.

9/9/81 Telephone

FROM WASHINGTON TO LONG BRANCH.

The President delighted with the trip and improves all the time

"WHY, THIS IS BETTER THAN THE WHITE HOUSE."

NEWARK, DEL., Sept. 6, 10 40 A. M, The President's train, which started from Washington at 6.30, arrived at Charles Street depot, Baltimore, at 8.03 A. M.—a slight delay having occurred at Patapsco while the engine was taking water and the attendants were changing the position of the patient. The train arrived at Bay View at 8:10, and left at 8:17, and when the B. & P. officials left Mr. Brown said that there was a decided improvement in the President's condition since he left the White House.

INCREASING THE SPEED.

By the time the first ten miles were passed, a speed of 25 miles per hour was reached, and Mr. Sharp sending to the President's car to know how the President rode, received answer, "Excellently, you may increase your speed." The speed was thereupon increased to 35 to 40 miles per hour. Along the road at the stations small knots of people had gathered to see the train pass, and the trains which under orders had taken the sidings, were lying as dead trains, there being no escape of steam from the engines. The engine of the special worked efficiently, but with the least possible noise, using neither bell nor whistle, and the windows having been gummed there was no rattling.

MRS. GARFIELD,

when the train started was somewhat nervous, but by the time the train reached Odenton she had recovered, and Col. Corbin stated at Bay View that she was perfectly delighted with the trip thus far.

THE ARRIVAL AT LONG BRANCH.

LONG BRANCH, Sept. 6.—The train bearing the President reached Elberon station at 1 o'clock precisely. There was no delay in adjusting the switch, and five minutes later he was in the front of his quarters, the entire train being backed up almost to the very door. The assembled crowd, and there were thousands, made no attempt to invade the line of soldiery deployed about the house.

September, 1881

9/15/81 Mirror

PRESIDENT GARFIELD has been doing well ever since his removal to Long Branch. He has had several periods of unfavorable symptoms; notably on Sunday, when it was feared an abscess was forming on the lungs. But that, the doctors think, has been gotten rid of, and the patient's condition on Tuesday was quite encouraging—that morning he was lifted from his bed and placed in an invalid or reclining chair, where he remained for nearly an hour. "There were no ill effects from the change of position. The physicians say they will allow him to sit in the chair at least once a day so long as his present favorable condition continues.

THE TELEPHONE.

FRIDAY................SEPT. 16th.

—Showery yesterday.

—Fair next Tuesday.

—The coal trade is lively.

—Farmers are getting ready for seeding.

—Too much hard cider in Town for the reputation of our Place.

—Now is the time to "Go West."— Tickets from Washington to Chicago only $7.

—Wanted, to trade a bran-new Estey organ for a good young horse. Apply at TELEPHONE office.

—Wanted, a good Horse, for which a superior new sewing machine will be taken as part pay.— Apply to TELEPHONE office.

—The *National Republican* says:

Mr. J. F. Dodd, formerly of the Arlington Mills, of Georgetown, D. C., is running a mill at Waterford, Loudoun County, Va., and he is doing well.

That's so! Mr. Dodd has transformed the Waterford Mill from a rat harbor to a first-class country establishment, having expended much money and time in so doing, and he certainly deserves creditable mention.

9/29/81 Mirror

EDITORS MIRROR AND WASHINGTONIAN.— There seems to be a necessity for me to beg the use of your columns again in behalf of Mr. A. L. Saunders. Some time ago I gave notice that I would be in Leesburg on August Court day to solicit funds to buy an artificial leg for him. Well, I was there on that day, and was informed that there had been money raised at Leesburg and sent to him for that purpose, and that he had said he did not want a leg, and could not use one if he had it. So I made no further effort, till I saw Mr. Saunders. He did receive $50 per Mr. T. W. Edwards, shortly after the loss of his leg, and being more in need of family supplies at that time, he used the money for that purpose. Of course he wants and needs a leg, and has never said anything to the contrary and I am trying to raise enough to buy a good article of the kind for him.

I expect to get the leg made by Mr. H. D. Reinhardt, No. 63, S. Sharp St., Baltimore, Md., and it will cost $75. A good, India rubber spring leg. Now I hope this will be sufficient to explain all that is necessary, and that the people at large will help me in this matter, without further trouble to publishers and readers of your papers.

Respectfully, F. W. FOUCHE.

9/15/81 Mirror

A FOUNDLING.—A colored child, well-dressed, with a bundle of clothing by its side, was left in Mrs Glover's yard, in this town on Thursday night last. It was taken in and cared for, and if the heartless mother is not found it will be sent to the poor house.—*Ib*

THOMAS STEADMAN. | ALBERT ORRISON.

New Livery Stable.

Fresh Stock!

COMFORTABLE & STYLISH VEHICLES

Charges Moderate

WE beg to announce to the citizens of Leesburg, and the public generally, that we have opened at the 'REAMER HOUSE' Stables, A NEW

LIVERY

AND FEED STABLE,

where we will be pleased to see our friends, and furnish them with a stylish TURN OUT, at prices as moderate as the times will admit.

☞ Travelling Salesmen, and others desiring Horses or Vehicles, for a length of time, will receive special rates. HORSES FED.

Give us a call.

STEADMAN & ORRISON

aug. 4, 1881-3m.   Leesburg, Va

September 1881

9/15/81 Mirror

Here and There in Virginia.

A correspondent of the Norfolk *Ledger*, writing from Upperville, which he reached by private conveyance from Washington city, says of

FAIRFAX, LOUDOUN AND FAUQUIER.

The rich scenery of the Valley of the Potomac fully compensated for the roughness of the old turnpike. That old pike had borne on its back for nearly a century the immense trade from the Valley of Virginia, and through this valley the trade of Tennessee. The huge old wagons, with their teams loaded with bells (to scare away the bears as we boys were told) are things of the past. This road leads through Fairfax, (not Poorfax, as it used to be called), a country regenerated by modern agriculture from the miserable broom-sedge state. I remember having been offered some forty years ago a farm in Fairfax for $2.50 per acre, which could not be bought to-day for less than $50.

As we leave Fairfax we enter the poorest part of Loudoun, which of late has been improved as highly as such soil (a cold, clammy clay) could be. Fortunately, this is but a narrow strip, for we soon enter the land in which the conglomerate limestone abounds, the constant disintegration of which restores to the soil what its heavy crops rob from it. This is the finest agricultural region I have ever seen. Loudoun was, and I believe still is, the largest tax paying county in the State, and this is one among the many evidences of her wealth. It used to be said that there was less litigation in Loudoun and more in its neighbor (Fauquier) than in any counties in the State. If this is so, it is probably due to the peculiarity of the people. Loudoun is peopled with a steady, slow-moving, industrious and hard-working race, while the inhabitants of Fauquier are a quick, sprightly, frolicking set, valuing more the saddle horse than the plow-horse. Indeed, by their horses you could know them.

9/29/81 Mirror

Friday evening last an old colored woman, on crutches, entered a railroad car, in Washington, for the purpose of coming to this city. The car was crowded and the old woman requested a colored man to give her his seat, as it was impossible for her to stand. The man refused. Gov. Holliday, of Virginia, who was in the car, overheard the conversation, and promptly tendered the old woman his seat, which was accepted with thanks. The act was looked upon by those in the car as a most graceful one.—*Alex. Gazette.*

9/16/81 Telephone

DAY BY DAY

MONDAY.

Another crisis has arisen in the President's case. A new but not an entirely unexpected complication is reported, involving one of the patient's lungs. It is thought probable that an abcess has already formed, in which case the President's chances of recovery will be materially lessened.—

TUESDAY.

The condition of the President was considerably more hopeful yesterday than on Sunday. The Postmaster General, who paid him a brief visit, was agreeably surprised to find him looking so well. During the interview the President spoke in a clear voice, and made several inquiries in regard to the business of the Postoffice Department, showing that his mental faculties remained unimpaired. His pulse during the day averaged six beats less than on Sunday, and his temperature was a little over a degree lower. The physicians now hope that the inflammation of the right lung will not culminate in an abcess, but time alone can determine the issue of the latest complication in his case.

WEDNESDAY.

Yesterday marked a pleasant and interesting episode in the history of the President's long illness. At his own request he was placed in a reclining chair near a window in his chamber, where he remained—apparently enjoying the change of position and a view of the ocean—for over half an hour, without experiencing the slightest ill effects. His pulse at the morning, noon and night dressings was 100. His temperature in the morning was 99.4, at noon 98.8, and at 5:30 P. M. 98.4. The President's physicians continue hopeful.

THURSDAY.

The news from Elberon continues cheering. The President occupied his reclining chair for an hour and a half yesterday, took an extra quantity of nourishment, and passed what his physicians call a comfortable day. It now seems probable that the lung complication is under control and fast disappearing, while the wound is doing as well as could be expected. At the morning dressing his temperature was 98.4 and pulse 100. At the evening dressing, at 5:30 o'clock, his temperature was found to be 99.2 and his pulse 112, both being higher than on the previous evening. The physicians assert that this rise indicates nothing, as temporary fluctuations must be looked for for some time to come.

THE UNINVITED GUEST.

An Episode of a New Orleans Banquet.

Some years ago when John McCullough was in New Orleans a complimentary dinner was given him, to which Robson and Crane, the commedians, were invited. Robson tells the following story of an incident which occurred:

"It was a private affair, so that when I saw, sitting between Crane and myself, a very seedy-looking old gentleman, my attention was arrested, and I began to eye the old chap with suspicion. By and by he began to attract the attention of the company. He was a man of, say sixty or thereabout, unshaven and very shabbily dressed. The night outside was bitterly cold, and yet the old fellow wore a thin summer coat buttoned up to the throat. What first drew my attention to him was his appearance, and after that his appetite. He ate voraciously, and his drinking kept pace with his eating. Again and again did Crane and I replenish his plate and fill his glass, and again and again were they emptied. I confess that a barbarous sense of the humor of the thing came over me, and I gave way to it. From my 'pride of place' I deliberately plied the ancient marine the wine, and made a point of inviting the attention of the whole table to him. They all went into the joke and insisted, one after another, upon drinking wine with the old man. The idea, of course, was to get him tipsy, but here we all failed, for the old gentleman had a head as hard as Socrates, and moreover, seemed to know when he had enough. The quiet whisper and nudge was going around the festive board, 'Who's our friend? Who brought him in?' etc. But it was quickly suppressed, for at last, with quiet dignity, but firm courtesy, he declined to drink any more, and no entreaty could move him from his resolution. None of our party seemed to know him, so we concluded that he was a poor relation or acquaintance of some of the givers of the banquet, who had kindly run him in for a good feed. In the meantime speeches were made, toasts were drank, and a slightly inebriated individual sung out: 'Say, mine ancient friend, won't you give us a speech? Something about Shakspeare, you know—he's the fellow.'

"Nobody, of course, imagined that the old man would have the nerve to get up and say anything, but he did. Well, sir, in the course of my experience I have heard a great many clever people talk about the immortal bard, but on this occasion I heard in fifteen minutes the most intelligent exposition of Shakspeare's genius that it has ever been my fortune to listen to. And the whole thing was done so easily, and with such an entire absence of effort, that it was not until he had finished that we all began to realize that we had been under the spell of a profound critic and an accomplished orator. And those who came to scoff remained to praise. John McCullough rushed over and grasped his hand enthusiastically, and thanked him for the honor of his presence, and begged his name that the company might know to whom they were indebted. For the first time the old man seemed to lose his self-possession. He articulated a few words, but it was plain his emotions were getting the better of him. Crane filled him up a glass of wine, and the old man drank it, and after a little pause, rose slowly and with difficulty. His manner had been changed. He no longer looked the keen critic and fluent orator, but a weak, infirm old man, who in spite of every disadvantage of appearance, still retained a certain dignity, an elusive but unmistakable something that pronounced him to be a gentleman.

"Said a friend to me as the old man got upon his feet, 'Bob, this don't look like art; this is nature.' 'Gentlemen,' said the unknown, in a voice tremulous and full of pathos, 'I owe an apology to you all. I have no excuse to offer for having intruded upon your festivity, but I can at least make the amend of confessing that I am no intruder. I came to this house this evening on the invitation of a man I once knew, and I stumbled by accident into your banquet. I came here hungry and cold (and I thought I could hear the wind whistling outside as he intoned rather than pronounced the words 'hungry and cold') and I could not resist the temptation. I wanted to eat and drink and get warm.'

"And the old man's eyes dropped on the table, as if overpowered with a sense

September 1881

of his degradation.

"'I know this is shameful,' he continued, 'but physical weakness sometimes begets mental weakness, and I have eaten nothing for three days. For three weeks past I have not slept in a bed, but stole a rest in doorways or in a chair in the office of some hotel. Sometimes I have walked the streets till daylight. Such things, gentlemen, tell heavily upon a man of my age. Otherwise no man with a remnant of pride left could have acted as I have done to night. But I thank God I have at least retained courage enough to tell the truth. And now, gentlemen,' said the brave old man, straightening up with wonderful dignity of manner, 'accept my gratitude for what I have received. I have eaten and drank with you, and am refreshed and grateful. I trust you will pardon my infringement of hospitality and common honesty and permit me to depart.'"

The dinner party immediately raised a purse of $68 for their needy friend. Robson will not tell his name, but says that twenty-five years ago he was a Congressman from Ohio, and he was once a candidate for the Vice-Presidency of the United States."

LOUDOUN POMONA GRANGE.
Meets at various places on the first Monday in February and the fourth Saturdays in April, August and November.

SUBORDINATE GRANGES.
MEET MONTHLY.
Snickersville, Snickersville,
Third Saturday.
South Fork, Union,
First Saturday.
Loudoun Valley, Hamilton,
Fourth Saturday.

I. O. O. F.
No. 36—Loudoun, Leesburg,
Saturday.

KNIGHTS OF PYTHIAS.
No. 32—Katoctin Lodge, Leesburg
Tuesday.

I. O. R. M. IMP.
No. 38—Katoctin Tribe, Hamilton,
Wednesday.
No. 34—Shenandoah, Lovettsville
Thursday.

W. C. T. U.
Meets on the last Friday of each month, at Lincoln Lyceum Hall.

(Meetings of clubs, lodges, political and church groups, etc. seemed to be surprisingly prevalent in the days of the horse and buggy. Several of the most active were the Grangers composed of farmers and the WCTU and the Good Templar whose main focus was on the temperance issue.)

AGENTS WANTED FOR BORDER OUTLAWS
By J. W. DUEL

The New, Authentic and Thrilling History of the Lives and Wonderful Adventures of America's great Outlaws,

The Younger Brothers, Frank and Jesse James,

And their bands of highwaymen, down to the present moment. More than 40 illustrations, late Portraits of the principal characters, including Frank James, never before published, and 12 **FINE COLORED PLATES.** Interviews and letters from Cole Younger—Startling Revelations. All about the Black Flag, the Black Oath, the Secret Cave, and hundreds of other wonderful things. Most exciting book ever published. Full history of the late robbery and double murder at Winston, Mo., with illustrations. 65,000 copies sold in six months. Nothing like it!—beats everything! 616 pages, price $1.60. Agent's canvassing outfit, 50 cents. Write immediately for full particulars to HISTORICAL PUBLISHING CO., 516 N. 4th St., St. Louis, Mo.

DR. CLARK JOHNSON'S **Indian Blood Syrup.**

CURES FEVER AND AGUE AND SKIN DISEASES.
CURES SCROFULA, CURES BILIOUSNESS.
CURES HEART DISEASE, CURES RHEUMATISM AND DROPSY.
CURES NERVOUS DEBILITY.

(TRADE MARK.)

CURES Dyspepsia, Liver Diseases, Fever & Ague, Rheumatism, Dropsy, Heart Disease, Biliousness, Nervous Debility, etc.

The Best REMEDY KNOWN to Man!

12,000,000 Bottles
SOLD SINCE 1870.

September, 1881

THE LOUDOUN FAIR.

BEGINS ON SEPTEM'R 20,
AND CONTINUES FOUR DAYS.

THE Managers of the Fair have made extensive improvements in buildings, such as a handsome and commodious

GRAND STAND AND PRESIDENT'S STAND.

They offer an unusually attractive programme of

RACES — FOUR for EACH DAY

There will also be a
CREASED PIG RACE,
FOOT-HURDLE RACE,
BARREL RACE, and
SACK RACE,—one each day.

Hon. James G. Blaine

will be present during the Fair, and deliver an address.

The services of

PROF. JOHNSON,

of Florida, (an Aeronautical Engineer) have been engaged at considerable expense to make a

BALLOON ASCENSION,

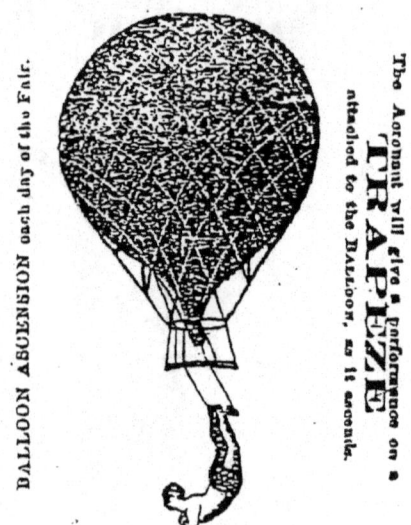

BALLOON ASCENSION each day of the Fair.

The Aeronaut will give a performance on a **TRAPEZE** attached to the Balloon, as it ascends.

The Society is determined to make this the most entertaining and attractive Exhibition ever held on the grounds. Send for circular.

Sep. 8, 1881.

9/23/81 Telephone

THE FAIR.

The exhibition of the Loudoun Agricultural Society was not as good this year as the unusual exertions on the part of the managers, warranted us to expect —*the blight of the drouth was laid upon it.* But it had a number of new and novel features which gave it unusual attractions. The improvements on the grounds in the way of buildings &c., were very commendable and there was evidence that the managers had exerted themselves to make this exhibit an unusually good one.

THE DISPLAY OF STOCK

was smaller than usual, but the quality was good. Among the prominent cattle exhibitors were Sellman & Fadeley, J. B. Beverley, of Fauquier, and J. B. Beuchler. The display of

AGRICULTURAL IMPLEMENTS

was good, some new features being added. Shroff & Co. had their usual fine collection of reapers, mowers, drills &c. Thomas Brown exhibited and took premiums on the Studebaker wagons, Mr. Fouche and Geo. C. Thomas displayed carriages. There were also many other commendable exhibits.

FARM PRODUCTS

were very scarce. It is a lamentable fact, that the farmers do not take enough interest in enlarging and making attractive this feature of the Fair.

THE LADIES' PAVILION

was, in most respects quite well sustained. The displays of butter bread, cake, preserves, jellies &c. and various kinds of needlework were very good. But everything that the late dry weather could affect was scarce and poor. The display of flowers consisted of a single floral plow, which was a very fair piece of work.

THE BALLOON ASCENSION,

except on the first day was quite a success and an interesting feature.

September 1881

9/29/81 Mirror

COMPLETE.

List of Premiums Awarded by the Loudoun Agricultural Society at the Fair of 1881.

HORSES—QUICK DRAFT.

For the Best Stallion, Sellman and Fadeley	$15
2nd Best Stallion, Sellman & Fadeley	c m
For Best Brood Mare and Colt, R. Ferguson	10
2nd Best Brood Mare and Colt,	
For " Stallion, 3 year old, R Ferguson	10
For Best Gelding or Filley, 3 years old, J. Vansickler	5
For Best Stallion, 2 years old, J S Silcott	5
" Gelding or Filley, 2 years old, J W Foster	5
For Best Colt foaled in Spring 1881, Walter L Furr	5
For Best Double Team of Horses, Henry Harrison	10
For Best Horse for Single Harness, Dr J H Moore	10

THOROUGH BREDS

For Best Thorough bred Stallion, S. D. Long	10
For 2nd Best Thorough-bred Stallion,	
For Best Thorough-bred Mare, S D Long	10

SADDLE HORSES.

For Best Stallion, Geo Y Dodd	15
" Filley, 3 years old, G W Fling	5
" 2 year old Stallion, J S Silcott	5
" Riding Mare	10
" 2 year old Gelding or Filley, E. B. Harrison	5
For Best Colt foaled in Spring, 1881, J. M. Hoge	4

HORSES—HEAVY DRAFT.

For Best Stallion, Fadeley & Co., (Clydesdale)	15
For 2d Best Stallion owned in Loudoun County, Fadeley & Co.,	10
For 2d Best Stallion, Singleton & Bayley	c m
For Best Brood Mare and Colt, J. M. Hoge	10
For Best 3 year old Stallion Thos. E. Taylor	5
For Best 2 year old Stallion, S. A. Campbell	5
For Best 2 year old Gelding or Filly, J. M. McVeigh	5
For Best 1 year old Colt, S L Moore	4
" Colt foaled in spring 1881, J. M. Hoge	4
For Best 2-Horse Team, J. M. Hoge	8
For Best Brood Mare and Colt, J. M. Hoge	10
For Best 3 year old Stallion Thos. E. Taylor	5
For Best 2 year old Stallion, S. A. Campbell	5
For Best 2 year old Gelding or Filly, J. M. McVeigh	5
For Best 1 year old Colt, S. L. Moore	5
" Colt foaled in spring 1881, J. M. Hoge	5
For Best 2-Horse Team, J. M. Hoge	6
" Mare or Gelding, open to all ages, J B Beverly	5

HORSES—GENERAL UTILITY.

For Best Stallion, Sam'l W George Jr	8
" 3 year old Gelding or Filly Douglas Tyler	4
For Best 2 year old Stallion, J S Silcott	4
" 1 year Colt, William Hough	4
" Colt foaled in Spring 1881, Walter L Furr	2

JACKS AND MULES.

For Best Mule 3 year old and upwards, Thos Brown	4

NEAT CATTLE.

2nd Best Yoke Oxen, James Wortman,	$5

Natives or Grades.

Best Bull Edgar F. Birch,	$10
" Milch Cow, J. B. Beverly,	10
2nd Best Milch Cow, J. R. Beuchler	c m
" Heifer two yr's. old or under E. B. Harrison,	5
Best fatted Steer J. B. Beverley,	5
" " Cow or Heifer J B Beverley	5

Short Horns.

Best Bull 5 yr's. old or upwards J B Beverley,	15
Best Milch Cow J B Beverley	10
" 2 yr. old Heifer J B Beverley	5
" 1 yr. old " J B Beverley	3

Alderneys.

Best Bull 2 yrs. old or under, Sellman & Fadley	5
Best Milch Cow, Sellman & Fadley	10
" Heifer 2 yrs. old Sellman & Fadley	5
" " 1 yr. " Sellman & Fadley	3
" Herd Alderney Sellman & Fadley	10

Holsteins

Best Bull 3 yrs. old or under Stirling Murray,	10
Best Bull 2 yrs. old or under J R Beuchler	5
Best Milch Cow J R Beuchler	10

SHEEP.

Southdown.

Best Buck, Edgar F. Burch	$4
2nd Best Buck, Jas Alfred Jones	c m

Shropshiredown

Best Buck, T M C Paxson	$4
2nd Best Buck, A H Rogers	c m
B 1 Pair Ewes, A H Rogers	4

Merinos.

Best Buck, Sellman & Fadely	$5
" 1 yr old Buck, Sellman & Fadely	2

Mixed Breed.

Best Buck, T. M. C Paxson	$4
" Pen Mutton, Edgar F. Burch	4
" Pair Ewes, E F Burch	4
" Pair Ewes, 1 yr. old, E. F. Burch	4

SWINE.

Best Grade Boar, James Thomas	$4
" " Sow and Pigs, T M C Paxson,	4
" Chester Boar, Geo W. Fling	4

September 1881

" Poland China Sow and Pigs, W. H. Wise......

POULTRY.

Best pair Plymouth Rock Fowls, Miss Eliza Paxson..... 2
Best Seabrights, Geo T Beuchler...... 2
" Bantams, Thos Mason...... 2
" Brown Leghorns, Geo T Beuchler..... 2
" Shanghai, Miss Janet Harrrison..... 2
" Silver Pheasants, Miss M B Riticor 8
" Mixed Breeds, Miss Ellen Thomas 2
" Pair Ducks, Miss Eliza Paxson.... 2

HAMS AND PORK.

Best Ham—Mrs. Wm. B. Lynch....... $3
2 " Miss C. Mason......cer. merit

NOTE.—The committee would have awarded the first premium for best cured ham to Mrs. R. E. Furr, if it had been accompanied with recipe for curing.

AGRICULTURAL IMPLEMENTS.

Best Implement for cultivating corn, Shroff & Co............ 1
Best Harrow, Shroff & Co......... 1.50
" Wheat Drill (Willoughby) Shroff & Co........ 5
Best Reaper Mower combined (Buckeye Table Rake), Shroff & Co..... 5
Best Mower (Buckeye,) Shroff & Co..... 5
" Horse Rake, Shroff & Co..... 2.50
" Straw and Hay Cutter, Shroff & Co. 3.50
" 2 Horse Wagon, Thos. Brown... 2.50
" Four or Six Horse Wagon, Thomas Brown........ 3.00
Best Three Horse Plow (Oliver Chilled) Shroff & Co.......... 3.50
Best Two horse Plow (Oliver Chilled) Shroff & Co........ 2.50
Best Double Shovel Plow, Shroff & Co. 1.00
" Corn Sheller (Pennock,) Shroff & Co............ 2.50
Best Wheat Fan (Baker) Shroff & Co.... 2.50
" Churn (Davis Swing, E. J. Northrup. 1.00
" Display Agricultural Implements Shroff & Co............ 2.50
Best Display manufactured in County, Cockey & Co........ 5
Best Grain Cradle, Shroff & Co.... 50c.

WINES.

Best Blackberry Wine, Mrs Wm. H Cummins........ $1
Best Blackberry Cordial, Mrs Bessie Rogers............ 1
Best Currant Wine, Mrs Wm B Lynch... 1
" Grape " Mrs Mollie Hempstone..... 1
Best Brandy Peaches, Mrs Tunis Titus... 1
" Cider in bottles, Miss M V Riticor 1
" Gooseberry Wine, Mrs E H Trundle 1

STEAM ENGINES.

Canton Monitor, Threshing Engine & New Model Vibrator, Thresher, Shroff & Co. $5

AGRICULTURAL PRODUCTS.

Best bushel Red Wheat, J. W. Wortman $2
" " White Corn, R. E. Furr..... 2
" " Yellow do Jonah Nixon 2
" " Clover Seed, Tunis Titus..... 2
" " Timothy Seed, Geo. W. Fling 2
" Barrel Flour, J. F. Dodd...... 2

DAIRY FRUITS.

Best lot potted Butter not less than 5 lbs. put up before 1st Sept., $3
" Miss F. A. Mead........ 1
" Fresh " Mrs. J. Tyler....... 1
" Cheese, Miss Sallie B. Nixon. 1
" ½ bushel apples, S. A. Campbell... 1
" lot Grapes, (3 lbs or more,) Mrs. Arch Hammerley..... 1
" lot Pears, Miss C. Mason...... 1
" display fruit not less than 5 varieties, Sarah M. Titus....... 5

VEGETABLES

Best ½ doz. Beets, Mrs. M. E. White.... $1
" " Carrots, " Geo. Carter.. 1
" " Parsnips, S. A. Campbell.. 1
" " Cabbage, S. A. Campbell.. 1
" 3 Egg plants, Mrs Geo. Carter..... 1
Best ½ dozen onion, J. W. Wortman..... 1
" Celery, Geo. Carter..... 1
" Salsify, Mrs. C. T. Hempstone 1
" Squash, Miss Mary L. Thomas 1
" ½ bushel Irish Potatoes S. A. Campbell 1
" " Sweet " J. W. Wortman 1
" lot Tomatoes, Mrs. J. H. Alexander 1
" quart Lima Beans, Mrs. Ann S. Wood 1
" lot Pumpkins, Jonah Nixon, 1
" Gourds, G. G. Corbin...... 1
" display Vegetables, (not less than 5 varieties, Geo. Carter...... 3

DOMESTIC MANUFACTURES.

piece white homemade flannel, Mrs. Jno. Williams....... $3
Striped Linsey, Mrs. Jno. Williams 2
Carpeting, Miss Maggie E Williams 2
Blankets, Miss Lula Moore....... 2
Yarn Counterpane, Mr. Jonah Nixon.......... 2
Homemade cotton Table cloth, Mrs. W. H. Thomas....... 2
Homemade Linen Table Cloth, Miss Mary E. Williams...... 2
pair Homemade Linen Sheets, Mrs. Jno. J. Tyler....... 2
display linen Fabrics, Miss Eva B. Williams......... 2

HOUSEHOLD FABRICS.

Oil Paintings, Miss Kate Carter.... $1
Water Color " Miss Mary B. Wildman........ 1
Piece Embroidered Silk, Miss Sallie Whitmore....... 1
" Cotton, Miss Belle Curry 1
Speciman Worsted work, Miss F. A. Mead......... 1
Monochromatic drawing, Mrs Ann S. Wood........ 1
Crayon drawing, " " 1
Lead Pencil Drawing, Miss Jennie Chamber......... 1
Piece Pellis work, Miss Alice Zimmerman........ 1
Wax flowers, Mrs C. M. Gingrich, 1
Hair " Mr. C. E. Evard..... 1
Worsted work, Ellen Thomas...... 1
Shirt, Miss Virginia Littleton..... $1
Cotton Quilt, Miss Sallie Brabham 1
Hearth Rug, Mrs. J. R. Walker.... 1
pair Silk Stockings, Miss Belle Curry 1
Yarn " Mrs Frank Thrift 1
Silk and cotton Stockings, Miss Jannie Furgerson........ 1
display of child's clothing, Miss May Sellman........ 1
worsted Quilt, Mr. J. J. Tyler.... 1
Lady's Dress, Miss Virginia Mott.. 1
Crochet Quilt " Kate E. Price.... 1
Speciman needle work, Mrs. C. 1

September 1881

R. Ferguson, "Belmont,"   1 1.
  Time: 4:10, 4:05.

Races—Second Day.

BICYCLE RACE—Purse, $50.

H. S Owen,   1. 1.
J. M. Borden,   2. 2.
George Cook,   3. 3.
P. M. Smith,   4.
  Time—4.00, 4.38¼.

4-YEAR OLD TROTTING RACE—Purse, $40

L T Jacobs, s. m., Mollie Bawn,   1. 1. 1
T T Taylor, b. g., Polk Taylor,   2. 3. 2
J C Vansickler, b. m., Dolly Young, 3. 2. 3
  Time—3.33, 3.38, 3.32.

COUNTY RACE—TROTTING—Purse, $115.

Sellman & Fadely, b. s., Castleman,   1: 1: 1
A Shreve, b. g., Little Mac,   2: 2: 2
J C Vansickler, g. g., Harry,   3. 3. 3
  Time—2:55, 2:47, 2:48.

(Considering the transportation and other difficulties of the time, the fair was an amazing venture surpassing in many ways the fairs of today. Consider the effort in getting a show herd across county with no modern trucking. The emphasis primarily was on agricultural and home life achievements with entertainment only an adjunct. Notice the number of awards and in particular, those for women who in most cases worked just as hard as the men. But there was a cloud on the horizon.

10/1/81 Washingtonian

Our Loudoun County Agricultural Society.

As the annual exhibition of this Society has just passed, it is probably the fittest time to make some comments upon its general management.

After what has been witnessed this and other years, but more particularly this year, we will certainly have to admit that the Society has not an appropriate title when we style it "Agricultural." A stranger or a native would conclude from the word that the exhibits from the farm predominate, or rather that the products of the farm were the important leading features. I suppose every visitor from other counties or states or perhaps half of the people of our county, are ready to testify that the products of the farm certainly are not the leading features of the Society of to day. Consequently the society would never be recognized by the name it bears. I have reason to believe the intentions of the President and Executive Board have been good, and their chief purpose and effort have been to promote the varied interests of the farm. Now, while I grant their intentions have been good, I am also ready to say that the means used to accomplish the end, have been, in my opinion, their sad and shameful mistake. Of course you at once see to what I refer. I mean your admitting the Devil himself and his corps of assistants to enter upon your grounds and set their demoralizing, degrading, damnable, devilish traps in the shape of Fortune Wheels, Ball-Rolls, Soap Money, and a lot of other kindred inventions that have proved so successful in corrupting, contaminating, and destroying the moral principles of the unsophisticated country man, and even occasionally taking in the more cultivated and enlighted of some of our towns. Now I do not presume to elevate myself to a lofty seat among the saints, and so feel that I am high and dry above the unwholesome stench, so that I should have to stoop to sniff a scent of the putrid, corrupt things to which all mortal flesh is heir. I do not raise myself to any such high position, but with sorrow and shame confess that I act a full part in other and perhaps more sinful ways. I have heard this matter discussed before the Executive Board, where arrangements were being made for the exhibition, and the argument advanced and which soon prevailed, was that the very existence of the society hung upon the heavy receipts from the sources of which I have just spoken.

These gamblers, even of the lowest type and of the higher, more fashionable and more popular type pay high prices for the consent and protection of our Board of Managers. I have heard some good men remark somewhat after this. Admit them, admit them by all means, we can't do without the money they pay for the privilege or the crowds they help to attract. So far as I know, the premiums are awarded in a fair and square way. I am ready to say for my own part, if the Society is to be kept alive in the way just named, I had rather take a part in knocking it in the head and killing it outright than to see its good features gradually eaten out by a contageous cancer.

Respectfully yours,
D. H. VANDEVANTER.
Waterford, Sept. 26th, 1881.

GEORGETOWN CATTLE Market.
Drover's Rest, Sept. 27, 1881.

320 Cattle up and sold,	
Very best,	5 a5½ c
Good,	4½ a5 c
Medium fair,	3½ a4 c
Thin Steers, Oxen and Cows,	2½ a3 c
200 sheep and lambs sold,	5 a6¼ c
sheep	3½ a4 c
Clipped	c
20 cows and calves sold from $25 to $50.	

(One must remember that in those days cattle were driven over the roads to market, hence the name drover.

September, 1881

9/24/81 Washingtonian

DEATH OF THE PRESIDENT.

HIS LAST HOURS;

A SUDDEN DEATH AFTER ALL.

Heart Trouble.

At 10 o'clock Monday evening the President was resting quietly. The physicians had retired, and Attorney General Mac Veagh had just forwarded a favorable despatch to Minister Lowell. Thirty-five minutes later the President breathed his last. Shortly after 10 o'clock he was seized with acute pains in the region of the heart, and Dr. Bliss, on being summoned to the bedside, found that the pulse was no longer distinguishable. The catastrophe so much dreaded had arrived, the pus had found its way into a vein and obstructed the circulation, so that death was inevitable. Mrs. Garfield was hastily summoned, and spent the fleeting moments that remained at her husband's side. The members of the Cabinet were also notified, but did not reach the cottage until after his death. After conferring together a telegram was sent to Vice President Arthur at the Fifth Avenue Hotel, New York, announcing the sad intelligence, and requesting him to come to Long Branch by the first train in the morning.— Below will be found the latest despatches relating to the mournful event:

HE PASSES PEACEFULLY AWAY AT 10:35 LAST NIGHT.

ELBERON, September 20—1:15 A. M.—The following official bulletin has just been issued:

"ELBERON, N. J., September 19—11:30 P. M.—The President died at 10:35 P. M. After the bulletin was issued at 4:30 this evening the President continued in much the same condition as during the afternoon, the pulse varying from 102 to 108, with rather increased force and volume. After taking nourishment he fell into a quiet sleep about thirty five minutes before his death, and while asleep his pulse rose to 120, and was somewhat more feeble. At 10.10 o'clock he awoke complaining of severe pain over the region of the heart, and almost immediately became unconscious, and ceased to breathe at 10:35 o'clock.
(Signed) "D. W. BLISS,
"FRANK H. HAMILTON,
"D. HAYES AGNEW."

THE CLOSING SCENE.

Attorney General MacVeagh came to Elberon Hotel from the Franklyn cottage at 11 P. M. and made the following statement. "I sent my dispatch to Minister Lowell at 10 P. M. Shortly before that Dr. Bliss had seen the President. I found his pulse at 106 beats per minute, and all the conditions were then promising for a quiet night. The Doctor asked the President if he was feeling uncomfortable in any way. The President answered, 'Not at all,' and soon afterwards fell asleep, and Dr. Bliss returned to his room, across the hall from that occupied by the President. Colonels Swaim and Rockwell remained with the President. About 10:15 the President awoke and remarked to Col. Swaim that he was suffering great pain, and placed his hand over his heart. Dr. Bliss was summoned, and when he entered the room he found the President substantially without pulse, and the action of the heart was almost indistinguishable. He said at once that the President was dying, and directed that Mrs. Garfield be called; also the other doctors. The President remained in a dying condition until 10:35, when he was pronounced dead. He died of some trouble of the heart, supposed to be neuralgia; but that, of course, is uncertain. I notified Gen. Arthur, and sent a dispatch to Messrs. Blaine and Lincoln, who are en route from Boston to New York. The Cabinet, at 11:30 P. M., went into consultation."

ANNOUNCING THE NEWS AT ELBERON.

Another correspondent telegraphed as follows: Allusions had been made to the fact, as stated by all the physicians, that the afternoon and evening had been spent quietly by the President, and Dr. Boynton said: "I do not, under the circumstances, regard the quiet and comfortable evening as by any means a good indication. He is not at all relieved from the danger which may at any moment prove fatal." He had scarcely finished the sentence, which was a summing up of the conversation, when Mr. Rickard, one of the confidential doorkeepers at the cottage, put his head in at the east door of the Elberon reception room and quietly, but with an evident underlying and deep excitement, beckoned to the doctor, who, accompanied by the reporter, followed the messenger. Once outside the hotel, Mr. Rickard said: "The President seems to be sinking fast." All three hastened towards the lines, and this, seven minutes after life had departed, was the first whisper of immediate danger, and it was sent out as a bulletin several minutes before it was known from any other source. At the guard line the three gentlemen met Capt. Ingalls, in charge of the troops, and asked, hastily:

"Is it as bad as reported?"

"It is, I am afraid," was the answer.

September, 1881

AT THE BEDSIDE.

The same correspondent sent a dispatch later, saying when Mrs. Garfield entered the bedroom and was told that the President was dying, she maintained her calm exterior and gave no evidence of breaking down. She is now bearing her affliction with all the fortitude for which she was so remarkable during her long and terrible trial. She is now as well as possibly could be expected. The President's remains have, for the present, been placed under the charge of Mr. Morris, the village undertaker, and will remain until the arrival from New York to-morrow morning of a New York undertaker and embalmer who has been telegraphed for.

[New York Herald Special.]

"OH! SWAIM, WHAT A PAIN."—SEARCHING FOR A REMEDY—WHO WERE PRESENT.

At fifteen minutes to ten o'clock General Swaim and Col. Rockwell were in the room together. They were preparing for a quiet watch, when the President said, putting his hand to his heart:

'Oh! Swaim, what a pain!'

General Swaim came immediately to him and said 'Where is the pain?' He exclaimed 'Oh! oh!' and Col. Rockwell taking his pulse in his hand said to Swaim, 'I can't find it.' Swaim immediately ran to Bliss' room and the alarm spread. Dr. Bliss came to the room. Mrs. Garfield, Mrs. Rockwell, Miss Mollie Garfield, Mr. C. O. Rockwell, Dr. Boynton and 'Dan,' the faithful colored servant, were summoned at once. Dr. Bliss came in quicker to the summons than could easily have been expected considering the small sleep he has had for the last three months.

Hardly a minute it seemed, to the anxious waiters, elapsed before the doctor was in the room. His practical eye saw the immediate condition of affairs at once. There was an immediate necessity for raising the temperature. If it should fall beyond the point science had indicated there was no hope of another hour of the precious life that for the moment lay in his hands.

'Bring ammonia and mustard instantly,' he said.

Search was made for the two things that might, perhaps, have prolonged life a little while, but there was no mustard in the room and there was no ammonia there. A messenger ran across the darkened lawn to the Elberon hotel, perhaps a hundred and fifty yards away. He stumbled up the low porch of the hotel almost exhausted in his breathless haste and waited for the precious medicaments to be got. Warren Young, the military messenger, meanwhile galloped at headlong speed to camp, almost a half mile away, for the mustard and ammonia, while those in the room stood breathless. There was not a word to say. There was only one thing to do. It could not be done.

'Oh, how it hurts there!' said he again, with his hand still on his heart. Modern science was powerless. The man at last was dying. There were by his bedside those who had at their fingers' end the utmost appliances of skill, the utmost resources of modern knowledge; yet death was there, and General Garfield was his victim.

Mollie Garfield was close beside him. Drs. Bliss and Agnew were there; so were Col. Rockwell, Gen. Swaim, Dr. Boynton, Mr. J. Stanley Brown, private secretary; Mrs. Rockwell, Miss Lulu Rockwell, two messengers, Mr. H. L. Atchison, Mr. John Ricard, Mr. Lancaster, Mr. Spriggs and two other faithful attendants.

'Oh, how it hurts here!' the President said once more, then, with an uneasy motion, he seemed to try to turn over, and, drawing one long breath that was almost a gasp, his tortured lungs refused their service. The heart was stilled, and life was gone.

A NATION'S SORROW.

HOW THE NEWS RECEIVED AND ANNOUNCED IN OTHER CITIES.

At midnight last night throughout the country the bells tolled a doleful dirge, announcing the death of the President, who had come by reason of his long suffering so near to the people, that to each one his demise seemed to bring a sense of personal loss.

In New York Trinity church bells began to toll at 11:17 p.m., when the news of the death of the President was confirmed. The bells in the upper part of the city were also tolled.

At Albany the bells were tolled by order of Mayor Nolan on the announcement of the death, and the public buildings were draped in mourning.

The news was received at Cleveland at 11 o'clock and created great excitement, although it was expected. The cathedral bell was tolled and was followed by the other churches of the city.

The news was received in Boston at 11:20 p.m., and at 11:30 the fire alarm bells struck the first peal. All the theatres announced no performances for to-night.

The news was received at Titusville, Pa., with spontaneous and involuntary demonstrations of sorrow. At midnight the bells of all the churches were tolled.

The news was received in Baltimore at 10:50 and not a moment hardly had elapsed before the big bell of the city began tolling in its sonorous tones, whilst the thirteen bells of various engine houses accompanied it. Mayor Latrobe determined to call a meeting of the city council for this afternoon, to take appropriate action.

The tolling of bells throughout the city aroused the people of Richmond, Va., from their beds.

The death was announced in Cincinnati at 10:20 p.m., creating a profound sensation. Theatre audiences were dismissed with the announcement of the death, and the tolling of bells carried the news to the people.

VICE PRESIDENT ARTHUR NOTIFIED OF THE DEATH.

Attorney General MacVeagh has just sent the following to Vice President Arthur: "It becomes our painful duty to inform you of the death of President Garfield, and advise you to take the oath of office as President of the United States without delay. It it concurs with your judgment, will be very glad if you will come here on the earliest train tomorrow morning."

(Signed) WM. WINDOM, Sec'y of the Treas'y.
W. H. HUNT, Sec'y of the Navy.
THOMAS L. JAMES, Postmaster Gen.
WAYNE MACVEAGH, Attorney Gen.
S. J. KIRKWOOD, Sec'y of the Int.

LONG BRANCH, N. J., Sept. 20—The single telegraphic wire at the Elberon has been employed all day conveying official messages and bringing replies. The trains today brought new representatives from all sections of the country, until, with those already here they constituted an army by themselves. Early in the morning the details of the last few minutes of the life of the dead President were obtained, and when it became known that Mrs Garfield had sat by the bedside of her dead husband from half-past eleven o'clock until near two o'clock, saying nothing, but giving vent now and then to her pent up sorrow by suppressed sobs, the hearts of all were touched in the deepest manners and eyes filled with tears. There was an early report that Mrs Garfield had broken completely down, but this was soon after corrected by Dr. Boynton. The Doctor said that while Mrs Garfield was suffering the deepest of affliction, yet she was exhibiting wonderful heroism, fortitude and self-control. Only once during the day did she completely succumb to the great sorrow, and that was when her son, James Garfield, who had been summoned from Williamstown, came into her presence. Then her pent-up grief could no longer be controled, and she yielded to her feelings for several minutes. The boys were still left to her, and this gave her great comfort.

Special Dispatches to the Evening Star.

THE FUNERAL TRAIN ON ITS WAY TO WASHINGTON.

AT ELBERON THIS MORNING.

LONG BRANCH, Sept. 21, 8:20 a. m.—Colonel Corbin watched last night with the Presidents remains. They were laid out in the casket, ready for burial, and at 8:30 will be placed in the parlor of the Francklyn cottage.

THE REMAINS AT FRANCKLYN COTTAGE.

LONG BRANCH, Sept. 21.—The President is laid out in the suit of clothes which he wore on Inauguration day. His left hand is laid across his breast, after the manner he had in life. This was done in order to make his resemblance as near to life as possible.

APPEARANCE OF THE REMAINS.

The body is so greatly shrunken that artificial means had to be resorted to give the clothes the appearance of fitting. In addition to the natural shrinking from his illness the operation connected with the autopsy has left the body in an even more emaciated state. The autopsy was very thorough, and the fluids of course have left the body.

THE FUNERAL CAR IN WHICH THE REMAINS ARE TO BE BROUGHT TO THIS CITY.

LONG BRANCH, Sept. 21.—The train has been brought round upon the special track to the front of the cottage. Car No. 248 is the baggage car, which also carries a large quantity of ice for the undertakers.

The last car on the train as it leaves the cottage is the mourners car, occupied by Mrs. Garfield. It is the car of President Roberts of the Pennsylvania road, which has been so often described. At 9:40 o'clock the governer of New Jersey with his staff and a delegation of citizens arrived at the cottage. Immediately after the body was placed in the car by the undertakers. Passing through a file of soldier attendants at about the same time the Cabinet, Chief Justice Waite, of the U. S. Supreme court, the Judges of the U. S. court in this vicinity, the governor of the state entered the train. Mrs. Garfield then entered the car assigned to her. The guard of soldiers, with reversed arms, were the last to enter, and everything was in readiness to start. A few minutes before ten o'clock the casket was removed from the cottage by six strong men, and, passing through a guard of soldiers formed in parallel lines, was placed in the third coach. The attendants and others who accompanied the party took seats in the fourth car. Dr. Reyburn is the only surgeon who went on the special train. At exactly 10 o'clock the funeral train started from the Francklyn cottage, moving from the grounds very slowly. The train reached Elberon station at 10:8 a. m., and stopped up the road about a quarter of a mile from the station. To this point the special train which brought President Arthur and Gen. Grant

ARRIVAL AT WASHINGTON.

On Wednesday the remains of President Garfield were, after brief funeral services at the cottage at Elberon, taken by special train to Washington and placed temporarily in the rotunda of the Capitol. Less than three weeks ago the President left the White House for Elberon, the whole nation breathing the hope that the balmy air and the pure breezes from the ocean that he loved so well might bring back health and bloom to his sunken cheeks and vitality to his wasted frame.— Loving hands tended him then on his journey professional eyes watched him, ready to note and overcome any indication of weakness;

September, 1881

science was brought to his aid to banish all discomforts of travel, and his passage to the sea was smooth and gentle. Yesterday he came back to the capital in shroud and coffin. All along the route there were evidences of the gloom that has fallen upon the nation. Every station which the train passed was hung with solemn drapery; men stood with uncovered heads until the procession was lost to sight, and when it reached Washington the surging crowds on the streets showed how deeply the heart of the nation has been touched. The way to the Capitol was strewn with flowers; the soldiers of the army in which he had fought guarded his bier, the knights whom he had once commanded came to do him reverence, muffled drum beat out in hollow tones, bands played solemn dirge, and up the broad steps of the Capitol he was carried gently into the rotunda to lie there until taken to his last resting place. Crowds of people for hours filed in silence to view the remains, and when midnight came and the lights grew dim nothing was heard but the regular tread of the guard of honor, while high overhead and crowning the massive dome the figure of Liberty looked down, as if guarding the city where he met his death wound at the hands of an assassin.

The Oath Taken at His Residence before a Few Friends

NEW YORK, Sept. 20—1:45 A.M.

General Arthur was sworn in a quarter past two this morning at his house. Two Judges of the New York Supreme Court had been sent for, J. R. Brady and Charles Donohoe. Judge Brady arrived with Messrs. Rollins and Root, at ten minutes before two, but the ceremony was out of courtesy deferred until Judge Donohoe's arrival a little after 2 o'clock, with Ex-Commissioner French. On John Donohoe's arrival General Arthur rose from his seat in the library and advanced to the front parlor. General Arthur stood behind his table, facing the window. He had gained his composure; his eye was clear and his manner dignified. The gas in the library was burning dimly and his fine, tall form stood out grandly from the dark background. Old allegorical pictures loomed out from the darkness—pictures of conquests and of triumphs, of defeat and despair—and above all was the white marble bust of Henry Clay. Judge Brady stood on the other side of the table, facing General Arthur. Grouped around the two men were Judge Donohoe, Elihu Root, Commissioner French, Daniel G. Rollins and General Arthur's son. Judge Brady slowly advanced a step and slowly raised his right hand. General Arthur did likewise. A moment of impressive silence followed. General Arthur's features were almost fixed. Then Judge Brady administered the oath. General Arthur, speaking in a clear, ringing voice, said:

I do solemnly swear that I will faithfully execute the office of President of the United States and will to the best of my ability protect and defend the Constitution of the United States.

10/1/81 Washingtonian

THE REMAINS LAID TO REST.

LAST RITES OVER THE BODY OF THE DEAD PRESIDENT.

The Bereaved Family all Present at the Funeral Services.

CLEVELAND, September 26.—The body of the late President Garfield has been carried to the grave with so great a funeral display and attended by such a multitude of mourners as must ever make the event memorable. It is certainly the chief day in Cleveland's history, as it is also the saddest. Garfield was regarded with great admiration and affection in northern Ohio, and his body has been followed to the tomb to-day by sincere mourners. Over 800,000 persons have taken part in this demonstration. Fully 60,000 people were in in the procession. The rest were spectators.

The marvellous exhibition in the square went on all night. Silver reflectors threw the rays of electric lights full upon the towering pavillion from all sides. A light hung from the ceiling directly over the bier.

Every train in the early morning deposited its hundreds in the city. The excitement in the streets and especially about the overwhelmed eating houses and hotels was great. Many persons who had no lunch baskets went without breakfast. At 9 o'clock the guards at the square crossed bayonets, and the line, which had been moving for twenty four hours at the rate of 5,000 an hour, was stopped. Hundreds were standing in line in Superior street at the time awaiting their turn. Even at this early hour the line of march was cleared by the military pickets. The sun was excessively hot and the air was close. The guards, who had had long hours of vexatious duty, stood at their posts quite worn out.

At the south of the pavillion was a stand for 1,500 people. Gens. Sherman, Hancock, Sheridan and others of the guard of honor; the Justices of the Supreme Court, the Congressional escort, the Governors of States and Mayors of cities sat there; and besides them there were the singing societies and the newspaper correspondents. The funeral car was drawn into position near the western entrance to the pavillion at 9:30. The bier upon it was draped in black, and white plumes were upon its top, while at the four corners were the tattered battle flags of Garfield's old

September, 1881

regiment, the Forty second Ohio. The car was drawn by twelve black horses, four abreast, wearing black covers, silver fringed, and led by six black grooms in mourning dress.

The family arrived shortly before 10. They were preceded by Bishop Bedell and the Episcopalian and Presbyterian clergymen of the city. Mrs. Garfield walked with Harry, her oldest boy, and Irwin, her youngest. James supported the feeble steps of his venerable grandmother. The brother and two sisters of the late President followed, and Miss Mollie walked with Gen. Swaim. Other friends and relatives followed, and then ex-Gov. Hayes, Wm. M. Evarts, and the members of the Cabinet entered the pavilion. The family sat by the casket.

Two armchairs draped in crape designated the seats to be occupied by the wife and the mother of the dead President. The brother of the President who was seated near Mrs. Garfield, and the mother, who was on her left, were convulsed with grief as the mournful ceremonies proceeded, but the wife, whose name has become the synonym of fortitude, was calm and heroic through it all.

The Rev. Dr. Charles S. W. Pomeroy delivered the closing prayer. Immediately afterward the red-coated Marine Band, which stood without the pavilion, played with sweet and touching effect "Nearer, my God, to Thee." The band then played "There's a beautiful land over there" and "Safe in the arms of Jesus."

THE PROCESSION TO THE CEMETERY.

When the casket was lifted from its resting place and borne on the shoulders of the guards, there was a surpressed moan which seemed to come from the lips of Mrs. Garfield but it was choked back as if to calm the sobs of the child Mollie, who wept convulsively.

The marines under Lieut. Walker, carried the casket slowly to the funeral car. The carriages then filed up, and Dan, the President's faithful body servant, mounted the coach in which Mrs. Garfield and her boy Irwin entered. Mrs. Garfield walked firmly to the carriage upon Harry's arm, showing signs of breaking down in her grief-stricken but brave face. The aged mother of President Garfield tottered feebly as she leaned on the arm of her grandson James and Gen. Swaim. She appeared to be overcome with her sorrow. Miss Mollie and the brother and two sisters of the dead man followed. Then came the others of the family relatives and friends. The Generals of the army (among them Gen Hancock, who attracted much attention) and the Cabinet Ministers, followed. The ceremonies at the tomb were brief, but impressive.

A Soldier Attempts to Kill Guiteau.

WASHINGTON, Sept. 11—Another sensational incident in connection with Guiteau's imprisonment occurred this evening. As Sergeant Mason, of the second artillery, which is doing guard duty there, was being relieved, he took deliberate aim at Guiteau and fired. He missed Guiteau, however, the ball passing six inches from his head. The affair created the most intense excitement at the jail. A couple of hours after the news of the shooting reached the city in an exaggerated form to the effect that Guiteau had been killed. Mason was thought to be intoxicated by the officer in command of the guard. He says he was sober, but having been sick for some days had taken a deal of quinine, which may have affected his mind. Mason was placed under arrest and sent to the arsenal, where he was placed in confinement. It is said he threatened on several occasions that he would kill Guiteau the first time he had a good chance. He regretted to night that he failed to do so, saying that he tried hard, but had to shoot at him through two windows from the outside of the jail

9/19/81 Mirror

A SPECIAL train of cars that left Washington on Friday, with a number of members of the press and Commandary of Knights, en route for Cleveland, when between Youngstown and Petersburg, and running at the rate of about a mile a minute, ran into a hand car containing nine employees of the road, seven of whom were killed. The foreman of the gang had not only been warned by the section boss, but told in person by the engineer of the pilot train, which was running ten minutes ahead of the special, to look out for it. With utter recklessness he declared he would risk it, and he had but reached the middle of the trestle before the special struck the hand-car, with the frightful consequences stated above.

10/7/81 Telephone

It will be gratifying to all who love the memory of James A. Garfield, that the dismembered section of his vertebra will *not* be placed on exhibition in the Medical Museum, as was reported. At least the Washington *Star* asserts that this statement is authoritatively made.

September, 1881

9/29/81 Mirror

President Arthur's Inaugural.

"For the fourth time in the history of the Republic its Chief Magistrate has been removed by death. All hearts are filled with grief and horror at the hideous crime which has darkened our land, and the memory of the murdered President, his protracted sufferings, his unyielding fortitude, the example and achievements of his life and the pathos of his death will forever illumine the pages of our history. For the fourth time the officer elected by the people and ordained by the constitution to fill a vacancy so created is called to assume the executive chair. The wisdom of our fathers, foreseeing even the most dire possibilities, made sure that the government should never be imperiled because of the uncertainty of human life. Men may die, but the fabric of our free institution remain unshaken. No higher or more assuring proof could exist of the strength and permanence of popular government than the fact that though the chosen of the people be struck down, his constitutional successor is peacefully installed without shock or strain, except the sorrow which mourns the bereavement. All the noble aspirations of my lamented predecessor which found expression in his life, the measures devised and suggested during his brief administration to correct abuses and enforce economy, to advance prosperity and promote the general welfare, to insure domestic security and maintain friendly and honorable relations with the nations of the earth, will be garnered in the hearts of the people, and it will be my earnest endeavor to profit and to see that the nation shall profit by his example and experience. Prosperity blesses our country; our fiscal policy is fixed by law, is well-grounded and generally approved; no threatening issue mars our foreign intercourse, and the wisdom, integrity and thrift of our people may be trusted to continue undisturbed the present assured career of peace, tranquility and welfare. The gloom and anxiety which have enshrouded the country must make repose especially welcome now. No demand for speedy legislation has been heard, and no adequate occasion is apparent for an unusual session of Congress. The constitution defines the functions and powers of the executive as clearly as those of either of the other two departments of the government, and he must answer for the just exercise of the discretion it permits and the performance of the duties it imposes. Summoned to these high duties and responsibilities, and profoundly conscious of their magnitude and gravity, I assume the trust imposed by the constitution, relying for aid on Divine guidance and the virtue, patriotism and intelligence of the American people."

After the reading of the address by the President Secretary Blaine stepped forward and grasped the President's hand, and after him his fellow members of the cabinet and others present shook hands with the President.

9/29/81 Mirror

IN MEMORIAM.

Last week President ARTHUR issued a proclamation, requesting that Monday, the 26th of September, 1881, be observed by the people of the United States as a day of "humiliation and prayer," and that the pastors of the various Christian churches throughout the land, open their respective houses of worship for that purpose.

In obedience with this request, the pastors of the churches in Leesburg, agreed to hold union services in the M. E. Church, South, at the time indicated, and Mayor HEAD issued a proclamation requesting the citizens of the town to close their places of business and suspend all secular employment, between the hours of 10½ and 1 o'clock—which suggestion was strictly observed, and during the hours named a calm Sabbath-like silence, pervaded our streets.

JOS. PRATHER,

—OF—

WASHINGTON, D. C.,

Announces that he has opened a

WHOLESALE

Commission House,

No. 939. Louisiana Avenue.

And respectfully solicit Consignments of

GRAIN, HAY, STRAW,

BEANS, PEAS, SEED, DRIED FRUITS,

Lumber, Hides, Leather,

Dressed Hogs, Poultry. Butter and Eggs,
Game and Fish.

CATTLE, SHEEP AND HOGS A SPECIALTY.

REFERENCES.—Banking House of Riggs & Co.; Banking House of Lewis Johnson & Co.; Hill & Duvall, Grocers; 928 Louisiana Ave. W. H. H. Cissell, Grocer, 1014 Seventh Street N W.

J. R. SMOOT, General Agent.

A Matter of Business.

"You were out late last night, dear," said Mrs. Breezy, taking her seat at the breakfast table and fumbling nervously with her fork.

"Oh, no," said Mr. Breezy. "It wasn't late. You see, darling, you were asleep when I came in, and—"

"No, Mr. Breezy. I was not asleep; but as you say, it was not late for you. Nothing would convince you that the clock struck three as you closed the hall door. Of course business detained you, my dear. It is wonderful how much business a man will find to transact after midnight, but of course we women know nothing about such things. We never can understand you men, can we, dear? We are always imagining all sorts of horrible things when you happen to stay away a day or two without sending us a line. Women are so nervous, are they not, dear? What silly creatures we are, to be sure. If we would only go to bed and go to sleep, it would save us a world of trouble, wouldn't it, dear? We might know that you great, strong men can take care of yourselves. If you are obliged to sit up until two or three o'clock in the morning talking business with your customers, it is really ungrateful in us to complain, for of course you have the worst of it, don't you, darling? How it must have bothered you and how tired you must get, and think that it is all for our sakes. When you come tottering home so tired that you can hardly get up stairs, and throw yourself on the bed without even strength to remove your boots, we should appreciate your devotion in thus laboring to support us. Now, last night, dear, when you stumbled over the rocking-chair, and found yourself obliged to cling to the head board to support your weary form, you presented a really sad example of the overworked husband and father. When your shattered nerves caused you to upset my fresh bottle of cologne and scatter the contents of my work-basket over the floor, you really looked the typical martyr of married life. Of course you do not remember it, dear.— You were too tired and worn out with that horrid customer to remember anything. What a dry, stupid time you must have talking business up to three o'clock in the morning, and you look so sleepy and tired and used up this morning. I would really imagine you had experienced a severe illness if I didn't know it was those terrible racking business cares which pull you down so. I see you have quite lost your appetite, dear. You haven't even touched your steak. Now, dear, this will not do.— You must not apply yourself so closely to business. It is killing you," and Mrs. Breezy's mouth curled into a decided sneer, as she dug a tablespoon into the fried potatoes.

"But, my dear," said Mr. Breezy, making a heroic effort to swallow a little of the steak. "It was a most important engage—"

"Of course it was," said Mrs. Breezy, as she poured out a cup of coffee with trembling hand. "Of course it was, love. Your engagements are always important. They will never keep over until morning, never. What if these engagements—these very important engagements—do occur five or six nights out of the week. It is a sign of your prosperity. Should I complain if you find yourself obliged to meet your customers at theatres and concert halls and at poker parties in out of the way hotels? No, dear, you are obliged to adapt yourself to your customers' mode of life. It is all in the way of business and we short-sighted wives are very unreasonable to suppose for a moment that you frequent such places out of choice, when even instinct should teach us that you would much prefer being home in the bosoms of your families.— You dear, abused husbands! How patient you are, to be sure, with us fidgety, unreasoning creatures," and Mrs. Breezy pushed back her chair with a jerk and left the room.

October, 1881

10/14/81 Telephone

A LETTER WHICH MR. BLAINE WROTE TO PRESIDENT GARFIELD.

My Dear Garfield:—Your generous invitation to enter your Cabinet as Secretary of State, has been under consideration for more than three weeks. The thought had really never occured to my mind until, at our late conference, you presented it with such cogent arguments in its favor, and with such warmth of personal friendship in aid of your kind offer. I know that an early answer is desireable, and I have waited only long enough to consider the subject in all its bearings, and to make up my mind definitely and conclusively. I now say to you, in the same cordial spirit in which you have invited me, that I accept the position. It is no affectation for me to add that I make this decision not for the honor of the promotion it gives me in the public service, but because I think I can be useful to the country and the party—useful to you as the responsible leader of the party and the great head of the government. I am influenced somewhat perhaps, by the shower of letters I have received, urging me to accept—written to me in consequence of the unauthorized newspaper report that you had been pleased to offer me the place. While I have received these letters from all sections of the Union, I have been especially pleased, and even surprised, at the cordial and widely-extended feeling in my favor throughout New England, where I had expected to encounter local jealousy, and perhaps rival aspiration. In our new relation I shall give all that I am and all that I can hope to be freely and joyfully to your service. You need no pledge of my loyalty in heart and in act.— I should be false to myself did I not prove true both to the great trust you confide to me and to your own personal and political fortunes in the present and in the future. Your administration must be made brilliantly successful and strong in the confidence and pride of the people—not at all directing its energies for re-election, and yet compelling that result by the logic of events and by the imperious necessities of the situation.— To that most desirable consummation I feel that, next to yourself, I can possibly contribute as much influence as any other one man. I say this not from egotism, or from glorious merely as a deduction from a plain analysis of the political forces which have been at work in the country for five years past, and which have been significantly shown in two great national conventions. I accept it as one of the happiest circumstances connected with this affair that in allying my political fortunes with yours—or rather, for the time, merging mine in yours—my heart goes with my head, and that I carry to you not only political support, but personal and devoted friendship. I can but regard it as somewhat remarkable that two men of the same age, entering Congress at the same time, influenced by the same aims, and cherishing the same ambitions, should never, for a single moment in eighteen years of close intimacy, have had a misunderstanding or a coolness, and that our friendship has steadily grown with our groth, and strengthened with our strength. It is this fact which has led me to the conclusion embodied in this letter, for however much, my dear Garfield, I might admire you as a statesman, I would not enter your cabinet if I did not believe in you as a man and love you as a friend.

Always faithfully yours,

JAMES G. BLAINE.

October 1881

10/14/81 Telephone

WORSE THAN BAD WHISKEY.

THE POISONOUS COMPOUNDS SOLD IN LOCAL OPTION COUNTIES.

It is well known that in the counties of Maryland in which "local option" prevails, and the sale of spirituous liquors is prohibited, the enfeebled health of the inhabitants, and sometimes the malarial tendencies of the climate, create a great demand for "tonic bitters." One of these compounds was recently submitted to the judgment of the Commissioner of Internal Revenue, to determine whether it could pass muster under a revenue stamp as a proprietary medicine, for use in localities where pure whiskey could not be had. His reply will be of interest to those who are in the habit of using the "medicines" which are furnished as a substitute for old rye. His decision was as follows:

TREASURY DEP'T OFFICE INTERNAL REVENUE,
September 29, 1881.

R. M. Proud, Esq., Collector of Third Dist.:

SIR—I have received your letter of the 28th concerning a formula. It appears that a druggist residing in your district is putting up bottles of whiskey and water, and adding to each pint bottle, with other ingredients, a grain of strychnine, and labeling it "tonic bitters." Such a compound is regarded by a most competent druggist to be dangerous to life, and if dispensed by a regular druggist, should be labeled "poison," so as to protect the unweary persons against its too free use. Under these circumstances it would, in my opinion, be improper to give the sanction of this office to the sale of this compound of medicine.

Respectfully,
GREEN B. RAUM, Commissioner.

9/29/81 Mirror

THE post mortem examination of the body of the late President, developed the fact that the surgeons in charge of the patient after he was shot, had entirely mistaken the course of the ball, that their probing for the same had been in a pus cavity, while the bullet was lodged in an opposite portion of the body. It is also stated, that so bungling was the autopsy, that they missed the deadly missile altogether, and only found it accidentally in the basin with the removed intestines, to which it had become encysted.

A despatch states that Dr. Boynton continues freely to denounce the treatment of the case and the report of the autopsy, and indicates that he will soon make public a full statement of the true nature of the case from the beginning to the end on his own responsibility. The physicians officially in charge say that in a short time they will make a supplementary report on the autopsy, covering every point and feature in detail. It is said also, and on the authority of those who had every means of knowing, that many of the statements given out as to the favorable condition of the President and the bright remarks attributed to him were, to put the most favorable construction on it, erroneous; that for thirty or forty days before his death the President was either delirious or unconscious most of the time. These facts, with many others equally strange and important, will, it is understood, soon be made public through the medium of those who stand responsible for them.

GRAY'S SPECIFIC MEDICINE
TRADE MARK The Great English Remedy; An unfailing cure for Seminal Weakness, Spermatorrhea, Impotency, and all diseases that follow as a sequence of Self-Abuse; as Loss TRADE MARK
BEFORE TAKING of Memory, Universal Lassitude, Pain in the Back, Dimness of vision, Premature Old Age, and many other Diseases that lead to Insanity or Consumption, and a Premature Grave. AFTER TAKING.

☞ Full particulars in our pamphlet, which we desire to send free by mail to every one. ☞ The Specific Medicine is sold by all druggists at $1 per package, or six packages for $5, or will be sent free by mail on receipt of the money by addressing

THE GRAY MEDICINE CO.,
Mechanic's Block, Detroit, Mich.

☞ Sold in Hamilton and everywhere by all druggists.

October 1881

10/14/81 Telephone

GUITEAU'S CONFESSION.

The New York Herald on Thursday contained seven closely printed columns of what purports to be an autobiography of Guiteau, as dictated by him to a stenographer. His story of the assassination or, as he prefers to style it, "the removal of the President," is one of the most cold-blooded accounts of a dreadful crime that has ever been put on paper. "My idea, simply stated," he remarks, "was to remove as easily as possible Mr. James A. Garfield, a quiet and good natured citizen of Ohio, who temporarily occupied the position of President of the United States, and substitute in his place Mr. Chester A. Arthur, of New York, a distinguished and highly estimable gentleman. Mr. Garfield I intended to quietly remove to Paradise, (which is a great improvement on this world,) while Mr. Arthur saved the republic." And he adds: "Not a soul in the universe knew of my purpose to remove the President. If it has failed I shall never attempt it again. My motive was purely political and patriotic, and I acted under Divine pressure. It was the same kind of pressure that led Abraham to sacrifice his son Isaac."

After giving an account of his application for either the Austrian mission or the Paris consulship, and the little satisfaction he obtained either from President Garfield or Secretary Blaine in respect to these appointments, he asserts that the rebuffs he met with "had not the slightest influence on him either one way or another in reference to his removing the President." He came, he said, to the bloody determination pending the answer to his request for the Paris consulship, and for several weeks after being denied an interview with the President he did not press his application either to him or to Mr. Blaine. In the meantime, according to his story, he was brooding over the quarrel that had broken out between the stalwarts and the half-breeds in consequence of the resignation by Mr. Conkling of his seat in the Senate.

"My conception of the idea of removing the President was this: Mr. Conkling resigned on Monday May 16, 1881. On the following Wednesday I was in bed. I think I retired about 8 o'clock. I felt depressed and perplexed on account of the political situation, and I retired much earlier than usual. I felt wearied in mind and body, and I was in my bed about 9 o'clock, and was thinking over the political situation, when the idea flashed through my brain that if the President was out of the way everything would go better. At first this was a mere impression. It startled me, but the next morning it came to me with renewed force, and I began to read the papers with my eye on the possibility that the President would have to go, and the more I read the more I saw the complication of public affairs, the more was I impressed with the necessity of removing him. This thing continued for about two weeks. I kept reading the papers and kept being impressed, and the idea kept bearing and bearing and bearing down upon me that the only way to unite the two factions of the republican party and save the republic from going into the hands of the rebels and democrats was to quietly remove the President.

"Two weeks after I conceived the idea my mind was thoroughly settled on the intention. I never mentioned the conception to a living soul. I did most of my thinking in the park and on the street, and I used to go to the Arlington and Riggs House daily to read the papers.

"After I had made up my mind to remove him the idea when I should remove him pressed me, and I was somewhat confused on that. I knew that it would not do to go to the White House and attempt it, because there were too many of his employees about, and I looked around for several days to try and get a good chance at him, and one Sunday (the Sunday before he went to Long Branch) I went to his church in the morning. — It is a small frame building, and I stood there at the door a moment. I was a little late; the services had progressed about one-third. I noticed the President sitting near an open window about three feet from the ground, and I thought to myself. — 'That would be a good chance to get him.' I intended to shoot him through the back of the head and let the ball pass through the ceiling, in order that no one else should be injured, and there could not possibly be a better place to remove a man than at his devotions. I had my revolver in my possession when I first went to the church, having purchased it about 10 days before the President's going to Long Branch. This was the Sunday prior to his leaving for Long Branch on Saturday. During that whole week I read the papers carefully. I thought it all over in detail. — I thought just what people would talk, and thought what a tremendous excitement it would create, and I kept on thinking about it all the week. I made up my mind that the next Sunday I would certainly shoot him if he was in church and I got a good chance at him. Thursday of the same week I noticed in the papers that he was going to Long Branch, and on the following Saturday he did go to the Branch for Mrs. Garfield's health. I went to the depot all prepared to remove him. I had the revolver with me. I had all my papers nicely prepared. I spoke to a man about a carraige to take me, as I told him, over near the Congressional Cemetery.

"'I got to the depot about nine o'clock, and waited there until the President's White House carriage drove up.' He did not kill him at that time, he says, 'because he had not the heart to fire while Mrs. Garfield was with him, clinging tenderly to his arm.' Learning that the President was to return on the following Monday Guiteau went again to the depot to watch for him, but when the President reached there so many persons were about him that the time did not seem opportune. All that week, however, he says he watched for him and tried at various times to get a shot at him but did not succeed. How he dogged him everywhere, day by day, is minutely told. Finally he heard from the papers that the President was going to Long Branch on Friday, and we give at this point his own narrative of what befell.

"'I took my breakfast,' he says, 'at the Riggs House about eight o'clock. I ate well and felt well in body and mind. I went into Lafayette Square and sat there some little time after breakfast, waiting for nine o'clock to come, and then I went to the depot, and I got there about ten minutes after nine. I rode there from the park in a 'bob tailed' car. I left the car, walked up to a bootblack, got my boots blacked, and inquired for a man named John Taylor, whom, two weeks before I had spoken to about taking me out toward the Congressional Cemetery. They told me that I will take you out there for $2.' — 'All right,' said I, 'if I want to use you I will let you know.'

"'I then went into the depot and took my private papers which I intended for the press, [including a revised edition of my Book, The Truth, a Companion to the Bible,] and stepping up to the news stand asked the young man in charge if I could leave those papers with him for a few moments, and he said 'Certainly; and he took them and placed them up against the wall on top of some other papers. This was about twenty minutes after nine, and I went into the ladies' waiting room and I looked around; saw there were quite a good many people there in the depot and carriages outside, but I did not see the President's carriage. I examined my revolver to see that it was all right, and took off the paper that I had wrapped around it, to keep the moisture off. I waited five or six minutes longer, sat down in a seat in the ladies' room, and very soon the President drove up. He was in company with a gentleman who, I understand, was Mr. Blaine, and I am satisfied that he was Mr. Blaine, though I did not recognize him. This gentleman looked very old, and he had a peculiar kind of headgear on, that I did not recognize as that of Mr. Blaine. The President and this gentleman drove up in a plain single seated carriage, with one horse. This gentleman, I think, was driving. It was a single carriage—ident seemed to be in a very earnest and private conversation with this gentleman, who evidently was Mr. Blaine. They sat in the carriage I should say some two minutes; they had not completed their conversation when they reached the depot, and during the interview of two minutes they finished their conversation— During this time they were engaged in very earnest and private conversation, as I have said.

"The President got out on the pavement side and Mr. Blaine on the other side. They entered the ladies' room; I stood there watching the President, and they passed by me.— Before they reached the depot I had been promenading up and down the ladies' room between the ticket office door and the news stand door, a space of some ten or twelve feet. I walked up and down there I should say two or three times working myself up, as I knew the hour was at hand. The President and Mr. Blaine came into the ladies' room and walked right by me; they did not notice me, as there were quite a number of ladies and children in the room.

"There was quite a large crowd of ticket purchasers at the gentlemen's ticket office in the adjoining room; the depot seemed to be quite full of people. There was quite a crowd and commotion around, and the President was in the act of passing from the ladies' room to the main entrance through the door. I should say he was about four or five feet from the door nearest the ticket office, in the act of passing through the door to get through the depot to the cars.— He was about three or four feet from the door. I stood five or six feet behind him, right in the middle of the room, and as he was in the act of walking away from me I pulled out the revolver and fired. He straightened up and threw his hand back, and seemed to be perfectly bewildered. He did not seem to know what struck him. I looked at him; he did not drop; I thereupon pulled again. He dropped his head, seemed to reel and fell over.

WANTED,

A VERY SMALL AMOUNT of MONEY FOR A VERY LARGE AMOUNT OF GOODS! Having a very complete assortment of Goods in my line, purchased for "CASH, DOWN," from parties in the cities who needed money badly, I can now show some of the Greatest Bargains in Virginia, for first-class goods at rates so LOW as to astonish the best informed. After many years of experience in the science of Business, founded upon the sound basis of TRUTH, JUSTICE, and NO misrepresentation, I can positively say, 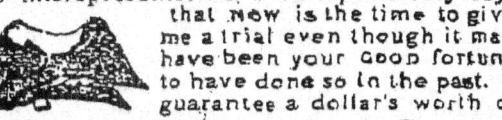 that now is the time to give me a trial even though it may have been your GOOD fortune to have done so in the past. I guarantee a dollar's worth of goods for every dollar received. First-class goods from first-class hands. A splendid lot of SADDLES AND

HARNESS,

at very low prices; Bridles, Martingales, Collars, Halters, Girths, Blankets, &c.
A beautiful assortment of TRUNKS, VALISES at panic prices; Whips, Spurs, Bits, Stirrups, Rings, Buckles, Hames, Pads, &c.
Every description of LEATHER of sound quality, very cheap.
Lap Covers, Horse Boots, Saddle Trees, Web, Deer Hide, &c. low.
A complete stock in SHOE TOOLS, SHOE FINDINGS, LASTS, &c. nov
☞ All kinds of REPAIRING attended to promptly, and in a first-class manner, at moderate rates.

ALFRED CLINE,
(one door north of Reamer's Hotel.)

Victor Liver Syrup.

(Formula of Dr. P. D. Fahrney.)

This great Liver and Blood Renovator has been used by the Drs. Fahrney for nearly one hundred years, in the form of tea. It acts direct upon the Liver and Kidneys through the medium of the blood. No home is complete without it, scores are testifying to it wonderful effects in curing diseases originating from impure blood, Torpid Liver and diseased Kidneys. Get a circular from your merchant. Sold by all medicine dealers. Price $1.00 per bottle, sample bottle 25 cts.

Victor Remedies Co., M'f'rs & Prop's,
FREDERICK, MD.

10/20/81 Mirror

EARLY VS. MAHONE—THE LATTER ARRESTED—HE PUBLISHES A CARD.—One night last week the Democrats had a torch-light procession, and public speeches in Richmond. Among the speakers was Gen. JUBAL A. EARLY, who in the course of his remarks, quoted from the Richmond *Whig* the following paragraph, and then uttered what follows; as reported by the *Dispatch*:

"Jube Early is for Daniel! Surely that is sufficient reason why everybody else should be against Daniel."

Gen. Early read the quotation calmly, and quite as calmly said: "This is sufficient reason why Mahone and those who wear his collar should be against Major Daniel or anything I am for; for he knows that I know him to be a miserable coward and a base liar.

"Mahone cannot, therefore, be for anybody or anything that I am for; and this, no doubt, is the reason why he did not want to fight the enemy at Spotsylvania Courthouse when he was under my command, and I wanted him to fight."

What subsequently took place is not known, until the papers of Monday last announced

THE ARREST OF SENATOR MAHONE.

Senator Mahone was arrested in Washington city Saturday night, about 8 o'clock, upon a warrant sworn out by a party named Strong of the District, charging him with intent to violate District law in his purpose to leave the city for the object of fighting a duel with Gen. Jubal A. Early, of Va. The warrant was placed in the hands of Detective Coombs and Capt. Vernon, who served it upon Senator Mahone at his rooms in the Portland Flats, on Fourteenth street. The Senator seemed greatly surprised at the course affairs had taken, and at first was reluctant to go, but expressed his willingness to accompany the officers if it was necessary. He was therefore placed in a hack and, with the officers, was driven to Judge Snell's residence, where the party alighted. The Judge was greatly surprised to see a Senator of the United States under arrest, but asked the party to be seated. Col. Strong then stated the reasons that influenced him in swearing out the warrant. Senator Mahone said that he had no thought of leaving the city, and that the idea that he would fight such an old man as Gen Early was absurd. Judge Snell then took Senator Mahone's personal recognizance that he would not leave the city for the purpose charged in the warrant.

Gen. Mahone left Washington for Richmond on Sunday morning, the *Whig* of Monday contained the following card:

To the Public: The speech of Gen. Jubal A. Early in Richmond, October 11, 1881, has been read by me so far as it refers to myself. The rank of Gen. Early in the Confederate army entitled the speech to that much. It brings me to decide whether I shall demand satisfaction from Gen. Early for what was intended by him as an insult. After years of unprovoked malice and indirection he presents the issues squarely and grossly. It admits of no discussion and would neither be met nor evaded by recrimination. I so accept it. My decision, arrived at advisedly and maturely, is, that the rank of Gen. Early, which is his sole claim to recognition, does not outweigh the other considerations which forbid such recognition. The public of Virginia need no specifications of the facts concerning General Early, on which I rely for this action. I only desire to make it known that I am neither ignorant or neglectful of his speech. He could give me no satisfaction, and I can have none, even in describing him as he is known of all men. He may therefore proceed with his falsehoods and would be insults, assured of immunity so far as I am concerned. WM. MAHONE.

(It seemed inevitable that somehow William Mahone and Jubal Early would go to war. Neither were shrinking violets.)

THOS. W. BIRKBY.   GEO. W. RUPP

LOUDOUN COACH FACTORY.

BIRKBY & CO., would inform their old friends and the citizens of Loudoun generally, that they keep constantly on hand, and make to order,

Carriages, Buggies,

and all work pertaining to the trade, which they guarantee equal, if not superior, both in durability and style of finish to that manufactured at any establishment in this county or elsewhere, and at as low prices.

REPAIRING promptly attended to as usual, and upon the most reasonable terms.

We have also a *FINE LOT* of *HARNESS* for sale, CHEAP.

SHOPS on the corner of Loudoun and Liberty streets, Leesburg, immediately in the rear of the residence of T. W. Birkby.

They solicit a call from those needing anything in their line.

October 1881

10/21/81 Telephone

THE AMATEUR LAWYER

The young lawyer conducting his first case before a jury is worthy of the deepest commiseration. Take him, for instance, in the criminal court, before which he has a case.— While the prosecuting attorney is trying the first witness into bow-knots and untying him again, the amateur sits listening intently, endeavoring to look as unconcerned as a marble statue in a thunder-storm. He throws in timid objections every time he sees a hole, and as each one is overruled by the court he puts on a stern look, as much as to say:

'I'll knock the wind out of that in the Supreme Court.'

When the prosecutor, usually an old and able attorney, dryly says:— 'Take the witness,' the youthful aspirant trembles a little and endeavors to swallow something that is sticking in his throat. He feels that every eye in the room is upon him and that they are as hot as stove lids. He fires a few initiatory questions at the witness and warms as he proceeds until he is brought up standing by: 'Oh! your honor, we object to such irrelevant questions,' followed by a few scratching remarks from the prosecutor. The court sustains the objection and advises the young lawyer to keep within the bounds which sets him to wondering where in thunder the bounds are. Objection follows objection, and each one is promptly sustained.

He tries to remember what the witnesses swore to, but cannot recall their evidence to save his life. The prosecutor finally winds up with a grand peroration, and he says: 'And in conclusion, gentlemen of the jury,' the youth nervously fingers his moustache, if he happen to have one about him, and wishes he had never begun the abominable business. Cold chills are fingering him over the back, as if measuring him for a new shirt, and his spinal column acts like it was tired and wanted to sit down awhile. Like Banquo's ghost, the lump in his throat won't go down by an obstinate majority, and he swallows at it and wonders what he is going to say and how long it will take him to say it. As the prosecutor calmly takes his seat the young lawyer rises and moves to the front. He dare not look at the audience and tries to imagine there is no one in the room but himself and the twelve sphynx like forms in the jury box. The eyes of each juror are fixed upon him.

'Gentlemen of the (swallows) ury.'

Very good. He then surveys them for a moment and every man in the box thinks he is endeavoring to read their thoughts; but he isn't. He is wishing to gracious he could read his own thoughts. At last he strikes out and goes for them about their intelligent looks and how he feels that his client's interests are safe in their hands. At the same time he feels serious doubts as to their safety in his own hands. He worries through his speech with an average of two swallows at that lump to the sentence.— The prosecutor closes the argument and the case goes to the jury, who retire to a room to chew tobacco and ask each other what they thought of it. It so happened that the flimsy testimony against the accused warrants a verdict of not guilty, whereupon the amatuer grasp his client's hand, whispers: 'It was a hard fight but I got you out of it.' Then he rises, loads up enough law books to swamp a mud scow, casts a triumphant look at the prosecuting attorney, who smiles pleasantly in return and walks slowly and majestically down the aisle to the door with as much dignity as if he owned a western railroad. Oh, you can't deny it, even you old veteran— you've all been there.—

October, 1881

10/13/81 Mirror

The Largest Farm in the World

The farm of Mr. Dalrymple, in Dakota Territory, has a wheat field containing 30,000 acres. A correspondent of the Chicago *Inter Ocean*, August 18, thus reports an interview with Mr. Dalrymple:

We asked for Mr. Dalrymple, and he came down from some room above; a slender, quiet-looking man, with a pen behind his ear, whom you would judge to be a schoolmaster or clergyman at sight. His hands were soft and white,—more accustomed to the book or pen than the plow—and his face, were it not covered with beard, was not so much burned as mine. He met us cordially, invited us to spend the day and dine, and suggested that he would have a team hitched up to drive us over the place. I noticed he always called it "the place."

In the meantime I asked him a few questions. The first one was as to the yield this year.

"It was a late spring," said Mr. Dalrymple. "At the time when we are usually putting in a crop the place for miles around us here was covered with water from the melted snow, and you could have sailed a boat over a field where now there is wheat that will yield. I feared at one time that the crop would be a failure, but I am very positive now that the average per acre will not be below twenty bushels."

"Have you sold your wheat?"

"Our plan is different from the ordinary method. We are sending about three train loads a day to Duluth."

"How many bushels is that?"

"About 30,000 bushels. We load a vessel at Duluth every two days and send it to Buffalo, where it is sold on arrival at the market price."

"What is that?"

"The price to day," said Mr. Dalrymple, consulting a telegram, is "$1.27 at Buffalo. Freights are about 27 cents, so it nets us about a $1 a bushel."

"What will your crop amount to?"

"I am expecting about 600,000 bushels.— Besides this we have about 90,000 bushels of oats, which we keep for our stock."

"Do you keep stock enough to eat up 80,000 bushels of oats?"

Mr Dalrymple smiled pleasantly and remarked that eight hundred horses and mules eat a good many oats.

"How much does your crop cost you?"

"It costs us about $6 an acre to produce a crop when we use our own stock and pay our men by the month, but when we hire men and teams by the day it costs us about $8 an acre."

"What do you pay your men?"

"We pay $30 a month for regular hands and $2 per day for extra hands during harvest."

"What machinery have you going to-day?"

"Two hundred self binding harvesters and thirty steam threshers. These 200 harvesters cut an average of 2,800 acres a day, and the threshers turn out about 80,000 bushels a day. As fast as it is threshed we bag the wheat, cart it over there to the cars, empty the sacks and send away three train loads daily.

"Where do you keep your men?"

"If you had been here at 5 o'clock this morning you could have seen 800 men at breakfast. We keep forty cooks."

Mr. Dalrymple explained at length how this enormous business is conducted. The 30,000 acres under cultivation are divided into five divisions of 6,000 each, under superintendents, who are responsible directly to Mr. Dalrymple, the commander-in-chief. Each of these regiments is divided again into battalions, with a foreman or major, who has charge of 2,000 acres. Under him are three companies, each having a captain and cultivating a section, which is 640 acres of land. Each superintendent plants his crop and harvests it, reporting from time to time to Mr. Dalrymple, who directs and oversees the whole, but spends the greater part of his time at the office, planning and calculating for the best results from the smallest outlay. The superintendents are responsible for the good order of their men, stock and machinery, and there is a decided rivalry between them as to which can produce the biggest crops. When the ploughing commences in the spring the men go out in gangs, each taking 540 acres, under the direction of a foreman, who rides along on horseback to see that the work is done properly. Everything is in the military style.

HARVEST 1881!

The BUCKEYE TABLE RAKE REAPER,
Manufactured by C. AULTMAN & CO.,
Canton, Ohio.

THE Reaper Frame is a model of beauty and power. Rake and Platform are right under the driver's eye. The Table Rake is the easiest Reaper to bind after, because it delivers sheaves in the best shape. In reaping tangled crops it has no equal. Light draft, no side draft, no weight on horses' necks.

October, 1881

Wanted, a good Carriage Smith and horse shoer to rent a shop in a good location. There is a wheelwright shop adjoining, and the rent can all be paid in work.
5-20-4t] C. G. WELLS, Guilford, Va.

For sale, one good three horse wagon. Apply to G. W. COMPHER, Taylortown, Va. 5-20

For Sale, a good feather bed. Inquire at the TELEPHONE office.

FOR SALE.—A 3-year old heifer. Apply to R. L. Myers, tinner, Lovettsville, Va.

For Sale.—A good heavy four-horse wagon. Apply to A. F. Johnson near Mt. Gilead, Va.

For Sale.—A "Steinway" Rosewood PIANO, nearly as good as new. Apply to CARRIE HAMMERLY, Leesburg Va.

For Sale.—CHEAP, a two-horse wagon, nearly new, made by Sam'l Lewis.
W. A. STROUD, Lincoln Va.

For Sale.—A good riding and driving mare, Telegraph Stock. W. A. STROUD, Lincoln Va.

FOR SALE. A Clough & Warren, Cabinet Organ, five stops and in good condition. Inquire of or address J. Z. Shugert, Hamilton, Va. 3-4.

Wanted—At the Hillsboro Factory, in large or small lots, smooth, evenly cut and sewed carpet rags, reeled on skeins--white ones to themselves. Will pay from 6 to 10 cents per lb. according to quality. C. C. GAVER,
3d 4t. Hillsboro, Va.

For sale, 2,000 chestnut rails and a few timber lots on Short Hill.
E. A. LOVE, Hillsboro, Va.

For Sale,—A House and Lot in Hamilton, Va. It is good sized, in good condition and convenient. Inquire at Telephone Office.

10/21/81 Telephone

THE CHAMPION PATENT MAN.

In the weekly issue of patents on Tuesday Edison, the phenomenal inventor, had granted him twenty-two. Of these twenty relate to devices connected with his electric system of light, making, according to the records of the patent office, sixty now issued to him relating to that system. Edison has taken out more patents from the patent office than any single inventor. Including the twenty-two issued Tuesday he has in all been granted two hundred and nine patents on all subjects, including, of course, the electric light, and the records show he has over one hundred additional awaiting the decision of the commissioner of patents, a majority of which will, no doubt, be allowed.

HALL'S VEGETABLE SICILIAN HAIR RENEWER

Has been in constant use by the public for over twenty years, and is the best preparation ever invented for RESTORING GRAY HAIR TO ITS YOUTHFUL COLOR AND LIFE.

It supplies the natural food and color to the hair glands without staining the skin. It will increase and thicken the growth of the hair, prevent its blanching and falling off, and thus AVERT BALDNESS.

It cures Itching Eruptions and Dandruff. As a HAIR DRESSING it is very desirable, giving the hair a silken softness which all admire. It keeps the head clean, sweet and healthy.

The State Assayer and Chemist of Mass. and leading Physicians endorse and recommend it as a great triumph in medicine.

10/22/81 Washingtonian

A RUNAWAY AND SMASH UP.—Last Monday morning as Mrs. M. P. MINIS, with a nurse, three children and the colored driver, were coming to town, in her carriage, just as they were descending the hill in the lane leading from her house to the Pt. of Rocks road, the tongue broke, and the horses dashed off at a furious speed. The driver clung to the lines and managed them as best he could until they reached the main road near the Big Spring, where he ran them into the fence and thus checked their "mad career." The carriage and harness were considerably damaged, but fortunately, beyond a terrible fright, the occupants of the vehicle escaped almost without a scratch.—Mirror

103

November 1881

11/4/81 Telephone

ANOTHER CRANK.

A well-built and powerfully-built man appeared at the White House yesterday afternoon and demanded to see the "accounts of the President." Mr. Dinsmore, the doorkeeper on duty, at once recognized the visitor as a "crank" who had called there in May last and was sent home to his friends in Pennsylvania, and with a view to delivering him into the custody of the police suggested that the "account." could be seen down street, and that he would accompany him. The man, who gave the name of John Walling, of Pennsylvania, then presented a letter which he insisted gave him the right to enter the Mansion, and endeavored to force his way in. Mr. Dinsmore seized him and a desperate struggle ensued. Walling attempted to draw a revolver, but Dinsmore, who had grasped him by the throat, choked so vigorously that he was unable to use it. Steward Crump and another employee of the house hurried to Dinsmore's assistance and the lunatic was with some difficulty, overpowered and his revolver taken from him. It was a large sized seven-shooter, with every barrel loaded. The police were notified and Walling, or Dr. Noetling, was taken to the station and locked up. The letter which he presented read as follows:

JOHN WALLING: You are hereby informed that Dr. John Noetling is lawfully elected President of the United States and occupies the White House every day.

ALMIGHTY GOD.
Communicated by the Holy Spirit.

FRIDAY............ Nov. 18th.

Mosby was seldom defeated and never outwitted to my knowledge but once. He had crossed the mountains with a few men into Clarke county, when he was informed that a Federal officer, with a squad of cavalrymen, was in the vicinity. The officer had stopped at "Clay Hill," the residence of Mr. Whiting, and Mosby made up his mind to capture officer and men. His action was prompt, as usual. He went to "Clay Hill," captured the Federal officer while he was seated at supper, and carried him off prisoner to Upperville, east of the Blue Ridge. There had been nothing at all unpleasant about the whole affair.— Mosby and his prisoner were on the most friendly terms The partizan had ridden his favorite gray mare on the scout, and at Upperville was standing beside her, ready to mount, when the Federal officer said:—

"That's a superb animal, Colonel?"

"Yes," was the gratified reply of the partizan, as he patted the mare's neck.— The officer sauntered closer.

"A very fine animal!" he repeated. "I'll try her paces!" And, throwing himself into the saddle, he disappeared at full speed, and Col. Mosby never again saw his favorite grey mare or his prisoner.—

Agent for Loudoun County, of the CELEBRATED

Bickford & Huffman Drill.

July 7, 1881-1y.

REPAIRING

of Saw Mills, Engines Threshers, Reapers, Mowers, Horse Rakes, Wheat Drills, and Farming Implements generally, shall receive prompt attention.

J. P. LOWELL, Prop'r and Supt.

November 1881

11/19/81 Washingtonian

Guiteau's Trial:

The trial of this assassin commenced in Washington, on Monday last. Mr. Leigh Robinson, one of the counsel for the defence, asked for further time, in order to obtain additional counsel and witnesses; but Mr. Scoville, the other counsel, said he did not want any further delay, and Guiteau, insisting on being heard, also desired the case to proceed. Judge Cox stated that the case should proceed, as far as the swearing of the jury was concerned, and then he would consider the question of extension.

Guiteau made several efforts to make a speech, but was prevented by the Court. He is making a strong effort to make out a deranged mind in his case. He had written out his speech, and we have it published in full in the daily papers. Although the production of an unbalanced and erratic mind, he says some things which, we think, some of the Stalwarts endorse, and who secretly wished consummated. The pacific and national course which Garfield and Blaine had foreshadowed was death to their sectional animosities, and the removal of the President, as Guiteau terms it, was not a very grievous occurrence to them. In his address the assassin says:

To-day I suffer in bonds as a patriot, because I had the inspiration and nerve to unite a great political party to the end that the nation might be saved another desolating war. I do not pretend war was immediate, but I do say emphatically that the bitterness in the republican party last spring was deepening and deepening hour by hour, and that within two or three years or less the nation would have been in a civil war. In the presence of death all hearts were hushed; contention ceased. For weeks and weeks the heart and brain of the nation centered on the sick man at the White House. At last he went the way of all flesh, and the nation was a house of mourning. To say I have been misunderstood and vilified by nearly the entire American press; nay, more by nearly the entire American people, is a true statement. But Providence and time rightens all things, and to-day, by the gradual change of public opinion, I am justified in passing with laudable contempt the continual venom of certain newspapers. Let the newspapers change from "Guiteau the assassin" to "Guiteau the patriot!"

READ THIS AND SAVE MONEY.

Harness Saddles and Collars.

We beg leave to inform our friends and patrons, that we are not unmindful of the kind and liberal patronage extended to us in the past, and our motto is still to live and let live, by still *Lowering* our prices, at the same time maintain our high reputation for selling the Best

Harness, Saddles and
COLLARS,

in this State or any other We have now 15 Sets of

Single and Double

Buggy & Carriage Harness,

made up of OUR OWN MANUFACTURE—made of the Best Material and Workmanship, and BEAUTIFULLY MOUNTED, at Prices much Lower than ever, besides, Heavy WAGON and TEAM HARNESS, all our own make and Warranted, besides a large stock of cheaper

grades of Harness, as low as $7.00 a Set, also Whips, Lap-Dusters, Horse Fly-Nets, Riding Bridles, Mens' and Boys' Saddles, (in great variety,) Saddle Blankets, Plow Gear, and the very best

HORSE COLLARS,

made, Kip Skin, and warranted to never gald, and every article worn by a Horse, in great variety, and as good as the best, and inferior to none sold here or elsewhere. "ENCOURAGE HOME INDUSTRY." Call and see us.

A P BRECKINRIDGE, Leesburg, Va.

Guiteau, the Murderer.

Happening in Washington last Saturday morning, we followed the train of pedestrians until we found ourselves at the City Hall, within the walls of which, Guiteau was undergoing trial for the murder of President Garfield. A deputy marshall politely assigned us a seat inside the bar, and for the space of three hours we watched the proceedings in this already historic trial. The jury is composed of twelve sturdy looking, well-meaning men, who appeared to have a full appreciation of the gravity of their situation. Col. Corkhill, surrounded by Judge Porter, of New York; Mr. Davidge and Mr. Smith, counsel for the prosecution, presented quite an array of legal learning, while opposed to them, sat Mr. Scoville, brother-in-law of Guiteau, and Mr Leigh Robinson, counsel for the defence. The government counsel had the advantage, at least in number, and harmony of action, as subsequent events proved. The prisoner, Guiteau, sat beside his brother in law, Scoville, while on his right sat Mrs. Scoville, his sister, with his brother John a little in the background. The prisoner himself is, we should judge, about five feet seven or eight inches in height—weighs 135 or 140 pounds—is about forty or forty five years of age, with a round, bullet shaped head, the hair and whiskers of which were cropped short, presenting altogether rather a repulsive appearance for an "Agent of Deity." During the earlier stages of the morning's proceedings, he frequently interrupted the witnesses, taking exceptions to their testimony, which he contended was not admissible, &c. And once he interrupted the proceedings to say "That he understood that there are one or two disreputable persons hanging around this court room intending to do me harm. The Chief of Police has very kindly furnished me with an escort, and I have a body-guard. Now I want to inform all disreputable persons that if they attempt to injure me, they will probably be shot dead by my body guard. [Laughter.] I have no fears as to my personal safety. There has been considerable loose talk on this subject for a week, and I wish to let the public understand it."

He finally became quiet, and during the remainder of the session of the court he looked the least interested person in the building. During the examination of Dr. Bliss, who was kept on the stand for over an hour, explaining the course of the ball, and the general character of the wound, the Dr. exhibited an actual section of the back-bone of President Garfield, showing the hole made by the bullet. The section of bone exhibited was about six inches in length, and was carefully examined by the jury, and the counsel on both sides, Guiteau himself viewing it with as much cold blooded indifference as if it had been a child's toy.

If Guiteau is not crazy, he is the most consummate villain, and most thoroughly trained scoundrel that ever faced a jury.— The system with which he planned his murder—the cool deliberation with which he executed it—the fear that he has ever manifested of bodily harm from a mob,—indicating his reasoning faculties and his own sense of the enormity of his offence; and even the aptness of all his interruptions in court, tend to repel the idea of the presence of that species of insanity which should shield him from the vengeance of outraged justice; still, there is something in the manner and general bearing of the creature, that so indicates an unbalanced mind that one scarcely knows what ought to be done with him.

We are putting up at reduced prices, the

GALVANIZED
Star Lightning Rods,

with Wood and Glass Insulators. The Rod does not come in contact with anything but glass until it enters the ground, and is the most desirable rod in use. They may be seen on the house of Maj. C. H. Lee, and J. Y. Bassell, Leesburg, Judge Murray and Rev. L. B. Turnbull, at Farmwell Station. These Rods have been in use for years and do not fall down as some other rods have done.

ROOFING, SPOUTING, &c., promptly and well done, in town or country. Water-Coolers, Cream Freezers, Preserving Kettles, and Fruit Jars of all kinds constantly on hand.

TINWARE—Wholesale and Retail.

W. H. THOMAS,
Leesburg, Va.

December, 1881

THE MIRROR.

VOL. XXVI.   LEESBURG, VA., THURSDAY, DEC. 22, 1881.   NO. 28

Clark Mills and his son, sculptors, last Saturday took a plaster of paris cast of Guiteau's head. The prisoner objected at first, but when he found that it was intended to perpetuate his features for the scrutiny of future generations, he readily consented. Mr. Mills says that "In his examination of the prisoner he found that the faculties on the left side of the head appeared to be normal and well developed, but the right side was almost flat, as though diseased.

Mr. Wm. F. Norman, a worthy young farmer of this county, fell into the hands of a gang of sharpers in Washington, one day last week, and was fleeced out of $200. Under pretence of showing him the spot where Mrs. Surratt was hung, he was drawn to the neighborhood of capitol hill, where, by a preconcerted arrangement, the villains inveigled their new found friend into some sort of confidence game with the above result. One of the accomplices is in jail where he is held to await trial. Mr. Norman returned home a poorer, but we'll warrant a wiser man.

1881.   1881,

Christmas.

Opening of *Christmas Goods* at

Loudoun Book Store

ON MONDAY, DEC. 12TH, 1881.

Gift Books, Fancy Goods, Stationery, Children's Books in great variety, beautifully illustrated ; Toys, Fifty different Games for children, Beautiful Christmas Cards, Wagons, Sleighs, Fancy Chairs, Brackets and Mirrors.

Handsome Assortment of Japan Goods

Bibles,
Prayer Books,
and Hymnals,
Writing Desks and Work Boxes, Window Rods and Fixtures, Shades, &c., Fancy Boxes, Paper, Envelopes and Cards, Large Supply of Fine Pocket Books, Portmonuals, Velvet Frames, China Ornaments

☞ Full stock of Blank Books, Diaries for 1882, Wrapping Paper, Paper Bags for meat, as well as other kinds.

A Judge's Charge, With Variations.

The following comes from Georgia, and its accuracy is vouched for by the stenographer who took it down :

Judge ———, was noted for the way he got mixed in his charges to the jury. On one occasion a case was tried before him the points of which may be briefly stated thus: Smith brought suit against Jones upon a promissory note given for a horse. Jones's defense was failure of consideration, he averring that at the time of the purchase the horse had the glanders, of which he died, and that Smith knew it. Smith replied that the horse did not have the glanders, but had the distemper, and that Jones knew it when he bought.

The judge charged the jury : "Gentlemen of the jury, pay attention to the charge of the Court. You have already made one mis-trial of this case because you did not pay attention to the charge of the Court, and I don't want you to do it again. I intend to make it so clear to you this time that you can not possibly make any mistake. This suit is upon a note given for a promissory horse. I hope you understand that. Now, if you find that at the time of the sale Smith had the glanders, and Jones knew it, Jones can not recover. That is clear, gentlemen. I will state it again. If you find that at the time of the sale Jones had the distemper, and Smith knew it, then Smith can not possibly recover. But, gentlemen, I will state it a third time, so that you can not possibly make a mistake. If at the time of the sale Smith had the glanders, and Jones had the distemper, and the horse knew it, then neither Smith, Jones, nor the horse can recover. Let the record be given to the jury."

THE WASHINGTONIAN,

LEESBURG, LOUDOUN COUNTY VA.

SATURDAY .... Dec. 31, 1881

THE NEW YEAR.

"*The clock strikes one. We take no note of time, save by its loss.*

A *New* Year means that the *Old* Year has ended—that another has been added to the long list of the years that are gone—have passed beyond recall, from all control or influence of ours, for good or evil, for making or mending; that with all which men have inscribed on it, it has been put away among the records of creation, to be brought up in unimpeachable evidence, for weal or woe, in the final judgment which each mortal must meet, to whom its hours have been intrusted.

☞ Guiteau's trial is drawing its slow length along, and it may, like all things earthly, reach its end in the immediate or distant future. He still persists in his offensive course towards the witnesses for the prosecution, but has sufficient method in his madness to be very respectful to the witnesses on his side. Judge Cox, we think, has been unjustly censured for his management of this trial, but we cannot see how he could have properly done otherwise, with the erratic creature he has to manage. Dr. A. C. McDonald, Medical Superintendent of the New York Asylum for the Insane, after a long examination, stated that he believed Guiteau a sane man. In response to a question from the District Attorney, the Doctor said—

"In my judgment the man has been playing a part all the time in court. I base that opinion on my observation of him in the jail, and of his conduct during my visit to the jail as contrasted with his conduct here. I base it also on my observation of him extended all through the trial, and on the gradual development of the changes which, I think, I have detected in his action and behaviour. In the first place, his conduct in the jail was in marked contrast with his conduct in court. During the trial I have noticed that the prisoner had access to newspapers, and that he has read them in court; but I have noticed that he has not been always reading newspapers or books when he pretended to be, but that he has been sometimes looking over the top of the book or newspaper, either at the witness or jury. I have noticed that he has shown a keen interest and appreciation in the progress of the trial, such as I do not think an insane man would show, especially an insane man who was convinced of the care of the Almighty. I have noticed that his conduct in court, the mode and manners and ways of his interruptions have varied as the comments of the newspaper press have varied. I have noticed that the interruptions have been made when the evidence was telling against him, and not when the evidence was in his favor."

12/29/81 Mirror

Guiteau's Christmas.

WASHINGTON, Dec. 25.—Guiteau spent Christmas very quietly at the jail to day. Very few persons are permitted to enter the jail on Sundays, and nobody excepting his brother and sister is allowed to visit the prison unless by consent of Judge Cox or Mr Scoville.

J. W. Guiteau, accompanied by a few acquaintances, called and had an interview with his brother. Late in the afternoon, after these visitors had gone, Guiteau ate a hearty Christmas dinner, which some friends sent to the jail for him. He has prepared another statement for publication which he intimates contains important and interesting revelations bearing on his case. He does not propose however, to distribute this gratuitously, but is waiting for a customer who will pay him $100 for it.

January, 1882

1/6/82 Telephone

Horrors! Horrors! Horrors! all over the country, on that most sacred of all days of the year—Christmas—caused by the unchained demon of Rum. And from many parts of our own State come the sad tidings of debauch and crime, on that day which should be wreathed in "Good will toward men." Is it not time that men who are too weak to flee from its fearful presence should be snatched from the jaws of this monster by the strong hand of the law?

1/7/82 Washingtonian

Wailing Ice Men.

The Most Unfavorable Prospect in all the Experience of the Knickerbocker's President.

"My experience in the ice business covers a period of twenty five years," said Augustus Hunt, president of the Knickerbocker Ice Company, yesterday afternoon, "and I have never before known the prospects of the ice crop to be so unfavorable at this season of the year. Of cours the weather in our immediate vicinity has frequently been so mild that no ice has been formed until the beginning of the year, but even the rivers and lakes of Maine, the main source of our supply, which have always before been frozen thickly over by this time, now seem likely to fail us. Twice thi swinter ice about two inches in thickness has formed upon the Kennebec, but it has quickly melted, and from our agents in that region I on Saturday heard that the river was absolutely clear. The cold weather of to-day is somewhat encouraging, but even if it should continue and intensify, the season must necessarily be a very short one, if wintry weather be not continued unusually far into the spring.

If the lakes and rivers of Maine should freeze now, at least two or three weeks of cold weather would be required for the ice to attain the thickness which we desire, and the cutting and storing away of the crop, even when hastened by the employment of a large extra force, would occupy at least three weeks more. We have never yet been forced to draw upon the Canadian fresh waters for our ice, as the Maine supply has always been ample.

1/13/82 Telephone

HE WANTED REVENGE.

Too "Green" for a horse Thief.

The rumor published in the last issue of the TELEPHONE, that the thief who had stolen Mr. Washington Haines' horses, was arrested in Winchester, was founded on fact. The thief, "Green," is the same chap who stole one of the same horses about two years ago. It is stated that he took the horses up the Valley and crossed the Shenandoah, near Ashby's Gap, thence to Winchester, where he was about to sell the horses to a buyer, for $300.; but before he concluded the bargain, intelligence of his thieving act reached Wincester, and he was taken into custody by a constable, who, (while probably waiting for authority to commit him to jail) kept him in the livery stable where he was arrested; and thinking there was no possible way of egress in the rear part of the building, gave his prisoner the liberty of the stable, and was soon surprised to find that Green had crept through a hole—and was'nt.

After getting away the thief started southward and twice boarded trains on the Valley Railroad, but, not having any money, was put off both times. He then quit railroading and turned his attention to Agriculture—engaging in bailing hay, where he was overtaken by the authorities who were in pursuit. When he recognized the approaching officers, he ran, but after dodging three bullets, he stopped and gave himself up—Sheriff Carruthers and others went to Winchester for him and arrived at Leesburg Jail with him on Wednesday evening.

Green says that he committed this second offense because Mr. Haines promised (when he was arrested before) that he would not inform Green's mother of his crime, and afterwards violated his promise.

A SHREWD TRICK FOR A LUNATIC.

Some years ago, in one of the counties of Southern Indiana, a wealthy and prominent gentleman showed such marked symptoms of insanity on the subject of business that his family and friends decided that to send him to an asylum or in some way confine him was the only way to prevent his wrecking his fortune by the most foolish schemes of speculation. The authorities ordered him sent to the State Hospital for the Insane. But all knew that to get him there without trouble it would be necessary to keep the matter a profound secret from him. This was thought to have been done, but, as the sequel shows, he was fully informed of the benevolent purpose of his friends. The sheriff, a friend of the insane man, invited him to go with him to Indianapolis on a pretended business trip. He readily agreed to go, and did go. Arriving in the afternoon, the official thought to wait till the next morning before going to the asylum, and after dinner he left the hotel to make some business calls, saying to his patient that he would be in by half-past seven and they would go to the theatre together. The moment that the sheriff was out of sight the insane man ordered a hack and drove to the asylum, and asking for the superintendent he informed him that he would be over there the following day with a patient. He said: "One of the most marked peculiarities of this subject is that he insists that I, and not he, am insane; hence when we arrive he will be very likely to tell you that he came to bring me to the asylum." He returned to the hotel and was in his room when the sheriff returned in time to start for the theatre. After breakfast next day the sheriff proposed a drive, and, of course, took his friend to the asylum. Arriving there, the superintendent met them, and greatly to the astonishment of the sane man, greeted the other most cordially. His astonishment increased when the crazy man introduced him to the doctor as the gentleman to whom he had referred on the day before. He began to explain to the doctor that he had brought him a patient, but was cut short by the remark of that gentleman, that he knew all about the matter.

The result was that the sheriff was taken in charge, and being furious at such treatment, he was put in a straight jacket, had his head shaved, and was locked in one of the strongest cells of the institution, while the insane man drove back to the city, took the train home, where, when he arrived, he told the story as a capital joke

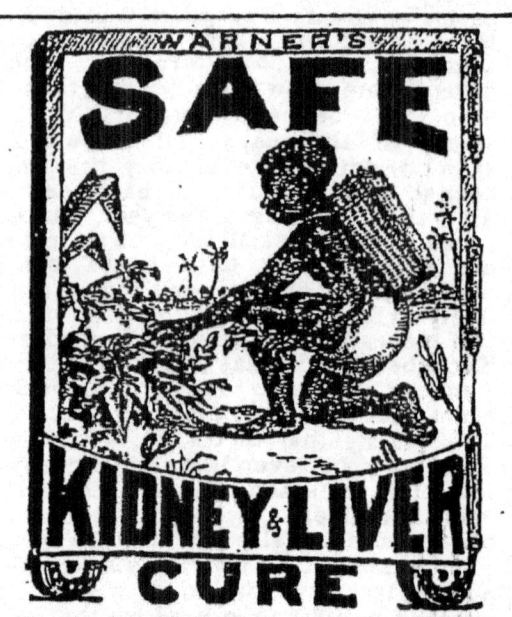

The leading Scientists of to-day agree that most diseases are caused by disordered Kidneys or Liver. If, therefore, the Kidneys and Liver are kept in perfect order, perfect health will be the result. This truth has only been known a short time and for years people suffered great agony without being able to find relief. The discovery of Warner's Safe Kidney and Liver Cure marks a new era in the treatment of these troubles—

January, 1882

1/5/82 Mirror

The *Telephone* of Thursday, says: "The sad news comes to us that the second son of Thomas E. and Mary P. Taylor, aged about four years, died of Dyphtheria on Wednesday morning, and it is reported that their oldest child, a boy six or seven years of age is very sick with the same disease."

1/14/82 Washingtonian

LETTER FROM FREDERICK.

FREDERICK, MD., Jan. 11, 1882.
Probably one of the most distressed families in Frederick at the present time in consequence of the ravages of diphtheria is that of Rev. Osburne Ingle, the popular pastor of All Saints' Protestant Episcopal Church, in this city. Since Friday last three of his interesting children have been carried to the grave and two or three more are now lying seriously ill of the same dread disease. One lovely daughter died during the past year, making four within the space of one year.

The total number of deaths from diphtheria to date in this vicinity during the past few months will probably aggregate one hundred and twenty-five.

1/28/82 Washingtonian

Diphtheria.

To us it appears that fresh air is the first necessity; we should allow a diphtherial patient to be near an open window. Next, we should use hot malt vinegar for flannel wraps round the throat, gargles, of the same dilated with water, and the most tonic diet possible. Neither quinine nor mineral tonics, but hot, strong wines, yolks of eggs beaten up in strong beef tea; warm baths made of chamomile flowers; feet placed in mustard water, and flannel wraps soaked in hot vinegar around the stomach. The juice pressed from raw beef, heated in a farina boiler and given constantly, but, above all, hot red wine.

MESSRS. EDITORS:—I ask that you will publish the following recipe for that terrible scourage, Diphtheria, which seems to threaten our community.

Take equal portions of Flowers of Sulphur and Glycerine; mix to the consistency of cream, and give one teaspoonful every three hours. C.

1/7/82 Washingtonian

THE small-pox is prevailing in many parts of the country, and in some parts of this State. While we are exempt from it in this county, we should take the necessary precautions against it, by having all the members of our families vaccinated, who have not been, and those who have not been vaccinated for a long time should try it over again.— It might save you from an attack of that dreadful disease. It is in possible to confine contagious diseases to any one locality, when so many of our population are continually traveling over the country, and for that reason we should endeavor to guard against them as we are liable to be brought in contact with them at any time.

1/12/82 Mirror

THE prevalence of the smallpox, in the larger cities, and the reported sporadic cases in various portions of the country, should warn the public to lose no time in fortifying themselves against the attacks of this most loathsome of all disease, by prompt and general vaccination. "An ounce of preventive is worth more than a pound of care," says the old maxim, and no matter how often you may have been vaccinated in the past, it will do you no harm to try it again. The most, if not all of our physicians, have provided themselves with a supply of *pure vaccine matter*, and a timely resort to it may save untold *suffering* and annoyance in the future. In the meantime, we publish for the benefit of all interested, the following recipe that we and going the rounds, and which is said to be unfailing even in the worst cases not only of small-pox but also of scarlet fever. Here it is—

Sulphate of Zinc, one grain, Foxglove, (digitalis) one grain; half a teaspoonful of suger, mix with two tablespoonfuls of water. Take a tablespoonful every hour.

DIPHTHERIA Croup, Asthma, Bronchitis, Neuralgia, Rheumatism. JOHNSON'S ANODYNE LINIMENT (*for Internal and External Use*) will instantaneously relieve these terrible diseases, and will positively cure nine cases out of ten. Information that will save many lives sent free by mail. Don't delay a moment. Prevention is better than cure.

JOHNSON'S ANODYNE LINIMENT CURES Influenza, Bleeding at the Lungs, Hoarseness, Hacking Cough, Whooping Cough, Chronic Diarrhoea, Dysentery, Cholera Morbus, Kidney Troubles, and Diseases of the Spine. Sold everywhere. Circulars free. I. S. JOHNSON & CO., Boston, Mass.

1/5/82 Mirror

FIRE—THREE HOUSES NEARLY DESTROYED.—About three o'clock Wednesday morning, this community was aroused from their slumbers by the alarm of fire, which, from the quiet hour of the night when first discovered, had already made rapid progress, and for awhile threatened the most serious consequences, not only to the property immediately involved, but to that of the surrounding neighborhood. As it was, the fire was confined to the three one and a half story brick and frame dwelling houses on Wirt street, occupied respectively by Samuel Grimes, John Evans and Philip Harris. The most, if not all, of the furniture in each house was saved, and the buildings themselves though badly burned, were preserved from total destruction by the active exertions of our citizens, and the effective work of the engines—after they were gotten in working order. Fortunately, the night was comparatively calm, and the destruction was confined within the limits indicated. The fire is supposed to have originated from a lot of hot ashes deposited during the early evening in the rear of one of the buildings destroyed.

1/5/82 Mirror

THE fire of Wednesday morning demonstrates the necessity of our Corporate authorities paying more attention, especially during the winter season, to the proper management of our fire apparatus. It is too late when a fire breaks out to be wasting time in endeavoring to get the "machines" in working order, which could be so easily obviated, if the engine room was kept warm, and the engines dry.; and this can only be accomplished by keeping a constant fire, during the winter season, in the engine house, which would prevent water freezing in the engines, and thus delaying their usefulness in the hour of necessity. The council should lose no time in adopting this or some other method for the accomplishment of the object to be arrived at. Fortunately for this community, it is not often that we have practical use for a fire engine, but when we do want it we "want it bad," and every reasonable precaution should be taken to have it in readiness at a moment's warning.

1/13/82 Telephone

GUITEAU.

We sat in the court room and watched and listened to the occasional remarks of the notorious criminal for several hours and from our observations deduced the following conclusions:

Guiteau is naturally endowed with sufficient ability, both intellectually and physically, to make an honest living.

He has plenty of brains and is sane enough to be entirely responsible for his actions, before the law; but it may be admitted that he is unstable and incoherent.

He is sane but morbidly debased and reckless—the natural result of having given unlicensed liberty to the lower instincts of his nature.

He has the most contemptibly mean expression and the most arrogant and audacious manners that we ever saw in any individual.

He is the smartest man that we ever knew to set up a claim of having been insane within six months.

His impudence is too caustic to emanate from the brain of a fool.

His plea of inspiration is absolutely incompatible with his past life; for *there is positively no good about him*—"do men gather figs of thistles?" Does God inspire men who do not possess his spirit.

He killed our beloved President and we believe he is as absolutely responsible for his acts as the average of his fellow-citizens, therefore should suffer the penalty of unvarying justice.

WITH a view of making a change in our business, we will, for 60 *DAYS*, offer at or near *COST*, our entire Stock of

Woolen Goods, &c

embracing in part for the Ladies:
Cashmeres, Delaines, Alpacas, Plaids, Ginghams, Calicoes, Shawls, Cloaks, &c.

FOR THE GENTLEMEN

We have Cloths, Cassimeres, Tweeds, Corduroy, Flannels and Full Linsey, Boots, Shoes, Hats, Caps, Gloves and Hosiery,

in great variety, together with a nice assortment of *FANCY NOTIONS* and *UNDERWEAR*, for both sexes. Bleached and Brown *MUSLINS, GROCERIES* and *HARDWARE*. Will be sold at a small margin above cost.

☞ Our Terms will be *STRICTLY CASH*, or trade at *Cash Prices* at the above rates.—Come early and often if you wish to procure bargains.

☞ All persons knowing themselves indebted to the present, or late Firm, are requested to come forward and make settlement. Respectfully,
J. W. PLASTER & CO.,
Hughesville, Va.

(Mirror copy.)

Feed, Board,

—AND—

Commission Stables!

Horses Trained.

DRIVE IN!

HAVING Leased the Large and Comfortable Stables of the Loudoun Hotel, on

MARKET STREET, LEESBURG, VA.,

and refitted them in a complete manner, I take pleasure in informing the public that I am prepared to

FEED, BOARD and
TRAIN HORSES,

at a Fair Price, and to SELL HORSES ON COMMISSION.

For further particulars, call at the Stables.
H. WHITZELL,
jan 7-1y.] Leesburg, Va.

GUITEAU'S DOOM.

END OF THE GREAT TRIAL ON THE SEVENTY-FOURTH DAY.

"Guilty as Indicted,"

A Verdict Rendered by the Jury After a Retirement of Fifty-Six Minutes.

Judge Porter concluded his argument in the Guiteau case Wednesday evening. Judge Cox then delivered his charge to the jury, occupying about one hour and fifteen minutes in its delivery.

When the Judge had finished all eyes turned to the jury.

The court took a recess. The prisoner sat up stairs and was very nervous. He was confident of acquittal. He refused to eat.

The court told the jury they could retire — They arose to go. Mr. Scoville asked that they be instructed as to the form of their verdict. Judge Cox said that if they found the accused not guilty by reason of insanity, they should say so in their verdict. The jury then, at 4:38 P. M., retired.

Presently the Judge returned to the bench, Mr. Scoville took his old seat by the table, and counsel for the prosecution were also in place. The jury entered. The twelve stolid faces that defied had interpretation still betrayed no sign, though their early return was taken as evidence of their decision. Foreman Hamlin and the Clerk of the Court arose as soon as the panel had all answered to their names.

It was 5:36 P.M., when the clerk asked the usual question: Gentlemen of the jury, have you agreed upon a verdict?"

"We have," said foreman Hamlin.

"Guilty as indicted?" asked the clerk.

"Guilty as indicted."

Some one in the audience started applause, and a cheer was heard in a corner, but it was quickly suppressed.

"If the Court please," said Mr. Scoville, but he was interrupted by the clerk, who proceeded, saying, "Gentlemen of the jury, hear the verdict as rendered. Your foreman says that you find the defendant, Charles J. Guiteau, 'Guilty as indicted.' So say you all?"

"So say we all," replied the jury.

Guiteau sat immovable and uttered not a word. Mr. Scoville desired to have the jury polled.

"John Hamlin," called the clerk.

"Guilty," came the response, and so on down through the panel—each one answering without hesitating.

The fatal word made many shudder; among them who did not shudder, however was the prisoner. He kept his position intact, and as the twelfth juror answered he called out in an ordinary tone of voice, "God's blood will be on the head of that jury; that's my answer to that." He evidently intended to say "my blood," but the mistake was unheeded by him.

The Court then turned to thank the jury, but Guiteau's voice was heard again. "God will avenge this outrage," said he. That was all. There was no further scene. The prisoner prepared to go out. The Court thanked the jury for their patience and attention.

THE COMMON SENSE
LIFT AND FORCE PUMP

Makes a complete Fire Department for any Country Home out of common wood pump, at a very small cost. WORTH FIFTY TIMES ITS COST if you need it to put out a fire, and extremely handy for lots of other things.
Ready for action in ONE-EIGHTH OF A MINUTE.
Energetic business men who will give it proper attention are wanted to handle this pump in every town in Pennsylvania, New Jersey, Maryland, Delaware, Virginia and North Carolina, and will be accorded control of suitable territory not already occupied.

CHAS. G. BLATCHLEY,
MANUFACTURER

February, 1882

2/9/82 Mirror

COMMUNICATED.

A Plea for Local Option.

"Wine is a mocker, strong drink is raging; and whosoever is deceived thereby is not wise."

I am a woman, and I touch not, taste not, handle not, neither have I husband or brother to fall victims to this terrible monster; yet, for the sake of those who have, would I plead that this curse be removed from our midst. It is sweeping broad spread over our land, and each sun that rises, sinks to rest, seeing some poor, deluded soul conquered by King Alcohol. We see it in our midst each day of our lives, and are powerless to help it. We can only bow our heads in submission, and pray for strength and courage to fight on. We know it is a bitter contest, but one in which we hope yet to come off more than conquerers. I could tell of the brave little band that joined hands in the old church at Aldie on the 7th of April, 1876, with the determination to fight the enemy to the death. Since that time, many have been our struggles, and our little army, heart-sick and sore, have at times almost given up the fight, believing King Alcohol had conquered. But not so. Though the King's forces have been doubled in the past year, we are still to the front, and are fighting on with renewed strength and vigor. We are determined to dethrone this monster King; he shall not destroy the bravest and best of our land, without an effort to put him down,—and the only effectual way to do this is for each son of our land, whether he be the King's subject, or whether he be fighting to dethrone the King, to come forward and vote for Local Option. If you will cast your vote with us my brother, it will remove from our community this terrible plague, worse by far than the taint of leprosy. O, my brother man, you cannot look upon this matter in the light that I do; if you did, there would be no more liquor license in Virginia.

Why was the temperance movement rapidly expanding at this time so much so that it eventually culminated in the 18th amendment? Perhaps Newton's axiom "for every action there is an equal and opposite reaction" could apply to our social history. The alcohol problem seemed to be very serious. The stronger drinks were continually referred to while the weaker ones, even beer, were barely mentioned. Reportedly, Leesburg had 12 saloons and a saloon was several degrees worse than the sports bar of today.

2/9/82 Mirror

CHICKEN STEALING.—For several weeks past a perfect chicken stealing mania has raged among certain of our colored fellow citizens, and a score or more of hen roosts have been depopulated by the marauders; the latest raid being upon the premises of Maj CHAS. H. LEE. The Major immediately had a hand bill printed and circulated, offering a reward of Ten Dollars for the conviction of the thief. A few days thereafter, information was obtained, which led to the discovery, beneath the floor of a house occupied by a colored family, of a bag full of chicken feathers, heads, entrails, &c., and to the subsequent arrest of two colored boys, George Johnson and Charles Veeney. At a hearing of the case before Justice POWELL on Monday, some of the chicken heads, especially that of a white faced, Black Spanish, one eyed rooster, were identified by one of the owners of the lost fowl, which, coupled with the direct and positive testimony of a colored girl, that Johnson and Veeney, had brought the chickens to the house and dressed them for market, secreting the offal where it was found by the officer, made a plain case, which the Justice was not slow in punishing. Veeney is a new comer in this section, and to him was ordered nine-and-thirty lashes, with twenty more if found in the County after the expiration of ten days. Johnson was awarded nine-and-thirty stripes, and four months in jail.

2/23/82 Mirror

Tommy was a little rogue whom his mother had hard work to manage. Their house in the country was raised a few feet from the ground, and Tommy to escape a well deserved whipping ran from his mother and crept under the house. Presently the father came home, and, hearing where the boy had taken refuge, crept under to bring him out. As he approached on his hands and knees Tommy asked, "Is she after you, too?"

The Patent Self-Acting Cow Milker M'f'g Co.

Every one who owns a cow should have one of our wonderful Milkers. Sent free to any part of the United States on receipt of $2. Send for our Illustrated Pamphlet on the Cow, containing sectional views of a cow's teats and bag dissected and scientifically explained, by Drs. White and Wilson of this city. Sent free to any address.

GEO. E. KING, President.

Office, 575 Broadway, New York.

2/11/82 Washingtonian

Important Discoveries.

M Pasteur, the distinguished French chemist and naturalist, is pushing his researches in a direction and with a thoroughness which not only will secure him lasting prominence in the world of science, but which bid fair to serve the double purpose of benefiting his fellow men in the alleviation and prevention of disease, and in also showing other scientists that their right road runs through the field of physical investigation.

M. Pasteur has discovered that diphtheria, typhus and typhoid and splenic fevers in man and in brutes, are due to the presence of these organic germs. He went further, and found that it was possible to prevent these diseases by vaccination. In the case of splenic fever—a deadly disease communicable to man—in France, thousands upon thousands of sheep have been carried off by it, and the farmers ruined. One of Pasteur's experiments was very striking. Twenty-five sheep having been vaccinated, they and twenty-five others were inoculated with the strongest virus. The twenty-five that had not been vaccinated all died on the day after, while the protected sheep were in perfectly good condition.

2/23/82 Mirror

BEECHER VISITING A LOW RESORT OF VICE IN PARIS.—"When I was in Paris I went to hell," said Mr. Beecher yesterday morning. His vast congregation held its breath during the pause of a minute that followed, then he continued: "With my companions, I had heard of the Jardin Mabille, a sort of garden to which the courtezans flock at night, and where virtuous citizens traveling from afar go to look at them as they walk and talk. I saw there men paid, as I understand it, by the city government, for the purpose of making frolic, and if ever I saw hell in the form of lust it was in the faces of some of those men. They were faces utterly devoid of goodness, sentiment, and conscience. They looked like burnt out craters—there wasn't any soul in them."

(Beecher, the most prominent liberal preacher of the day had his own brush with sexual scandal. A long and widely published court trial in the 1870's alleged an affair with a parishioner. Though he was acquitted, it forever clouded his legacy.)

Willard's Hotel
WASHINGTON, D.C.

The elegant, popular, and historic Hotel of the National Capital.

O. G. STAPLES, proprietor
Late of the Thousand Island House.

2/17/82 Telephone

Last Friday, two men (?) by the names of Sullivan and Ryan, (accompanied by about two thousand men(?) went out to a rural town in Louisana and pounded each other till one of them, Ryan, was nearly dead, and Sullivan got a small fortune for the job.

Now we think it is about time for Congress to enact a law inflicting severe punishment on all parties participating in these low, brutal affairs. We do not tolerate bull fights, but allow men to behave a great deal worse than bulls.

— PHILOMONT FLASHES. A colored man, formerly a slave of Wm. Benton dec'd., recently died at the county poor house, at the advanced age of 105 years.

2/17/82 Telephone

The murderer of President Garfield has been treating himself to a high toned suit of clothes paid for with the money sent him by autograph-hunting jackasses and jackassessesses. On the 30th of June next the government will supply him with a necktie which "will fit him like the paper on the wall."—*Baltimore American.*

2/23/82 Mirror

The quiet town of Alexandria has had its sensation in the way of a broken-off wedding, and, perhaps, a broken heart or two. A few days ago on Asaph St., the guests were all invited, the bride arrayed, and the minister ready book in hand, but the bridegroom tarried. At last in his place came a brief note to the expectant fair one in which her delinquent groom briefly stated "that he could not marry her, as his mother said that it would cause her to go to the poor-house, as he could not support a wife and mother both, and that he thought as his mother did, and hoped the young lady would not think hard of him for breaking off the match." Not think hard of him! Of course not. She ought to have got down on her knees and thanked heaven for saving her from such a cowardly milksop. A man who is afraid his mother will go to the poorhouse if he takes a wife will be very apt to wind up in that institution himself.—*State.*

February, 1882

2/24/82 Telephone

FROM THE SEAT OF WAR.

Oystermen Ousted.

SEVEN VESSELS AND SIXTY-ONE MEN SURRENDER TO THE VALIANT CREW UNDER COMMAND OF THEIR GALLANT LEADERS.

[Special Telegram to the Whig]

NORFOLK, VA, February 18th.

Governor Cameron and General V. D. Groner, who left here Thursday night with the City Guard and Blues for the Rappahannock river, in response to the request of the civil authorities of Mathews county, to attempt the capture of the invading oyster fleets, arrived at the mouth of the river about 8 o'clock Friday morning, after a stormy and rough voyage.

By a ruse suggested by Gen. Groner, who had the Reed to pass a tow-line to the steamer Louisa, the dredgers thought we had a disabled vessel in tow and thereby enabled us to get within a half mile of them, while they were at work dredging.

Gen. Groner, who was in command ordered the Blues to fire one solid shot across the bow of the Creswell, the nearest one, which immediately hove to and the captain surrendered the vessel and crew of nine men.

The schooner J C., of Norfolk, was then fired over, and she, too, surrendered without resistance; as did the other vessels, except the Philip Kirkwood, who we had to chase for three hours down the bay, overhauling her after firing eight shot and shell. The schooner Alice and Annie Johnson (nine men), Fashion, Chandler (eight men), Pungy, Mary, Pauline, Kellum (nine men), and the sloop Hamberg, were taken and turned over to the sheriff of Mathews county, who locked them up in the jail of his county.

(The oyster war continued for many, many years.)

2/24/82 Telephone

Piratical oyster dredgers have been a great annoyance and terror to Virginia fishermen along the Chesapeake and its tributaries, and Gov. Cameron deserves the thanks of his people for the vigorous and successful raid which he recently made upon them, thus giving these marauders a lesson which they will not forget for some time; at least those sixty-one men, will have that days instruction brought forcibly to their minds, as they toil upon the public works for the benefit of the Penitentiary. Sixty-one men under competent bosses can make several miles of railroad in from "one to three years"

2/23/82 Mirror

GOV. CAMERON'S prompt action against the oyster dredgers in Virginia waters, is generally commended, and if it puts a stop to these piratical raids on the oyster beds of the State, it will have accomplished a great good. An exchange thus recites the grievances—to arrest which Gov. Cameron last week employed the military power of the State:

"For fifty years this war has been waged on both shores of the Chesapeake Bay and hundreds of lives have been lost in the engagements that have taken place between the dredgers on one side and the tongers and officers of the law, on the other. Four years ago a fleet of seventy five strange vessels appeared in Virginia waters and in defiance of the authorities dredged on forbidden ground and fought skirmishes with the tongmen until the vessels were loaded. At the present time Virginia has no oyster navy to protect her beds and the inhabitants take the law into their own hands. Now whenever a piratical craft comes within range of the shores it is treated to a broadside of buckshot from the ducking swivels of the infuriated landsmen."

March 1882

3/16/82 Mirror

Gen. Grant's Condition.

A REPORT THAT HE HAS BEEN RUINED BY STOCK SPECULATION.

NEW YORK, March 9.—It was pretty openly declared on Wall street to day that Gen Grant, who has been loaded up with a variety of stocks ever since the break of last month—prominent among which are Wabash Pacific and Denver and Rio Grande—"laid down" on his brokers yesterday, being unable or indisposed to make good his dissipated margins. The steadily accumulating losses which he has been obliged to submit to is what led him to deed his Long Branch property to Mrs. Grant a week or more ago At present it is declared the General is without any personal income worth speaking of. It is even reported that the $250,000 raised for him by George Jones was all invested in Wabash securities which have fallen from par to nearly fifty cents on the dollar. This is doubtful, however, as by the terms of the subscription Mr. Jones was made the trustee of the fund and would not have been likely to invest it in a shifting stock like Wabash. Nothing that Gen Grant has gone into lately has been very successful, and his name has at last ceased to be of much importance to big enterprises. In other words he is no longer a drawing card on Wall street. His son "Buck," however, is said to have made "a pretty big pile."

(Though a notoriously poor judge of some of his associates, Grant would have some true friends like General Sherman who would come to his aid.)

3/23/82 Mirror

The oyster war in the Chesapeake has ended with the conviction of the fifty eight captured pirates and their sentence to a year's imprisonment in the Virginia penitentiary— The piratical fleet of seven vessels is confiscated to the State, and for the present the business of stealing oysters seems to be rather at a discount. The Judge and jury had no sooner got through with their part of the work than they were seized with a spasm of soft heartedness and petitioned the Governor to remit the sentence of imprisonment, and if he wishes a repetition of the oyster war next winter he will probably let the pirates off.— Times

3/23/82 Mirror

Strong influences are being brought to bear on President Arthur for the pardon of Mason, the would be assassin of Guiteau, and subscriptions for the relief of Mason's family are pouring in from various sections. The sentence may seem to be harsh—but when it is remembered that Guiteau was in the hands of the law, threatened with mob violence, and that Mason was placed over him to defend him from the violence of the mob; and that taking advantage of the opportunity given him, he not only disobeyed orders, but betrayed the trust reposed in him, by seeking to murder the man he was in honor bound to protect, the severity of the sentence is greatly mitigated. It is no justification of Mason's conduct to say that Guiteau was a cold blooded assassin who richly merited death. It was to vindicate the majesty of the law that the civil authorities rescued him from the hands of the mob and threw him behind the bars of a prison, and placed around these prison walls a cordon of soldiers to make their precaution doubly sure. And yet Mason, one of the chosen agents of the government to maintain the supremacy of the law, was the first to raise his hand with murderous intent against the defenceless, imprisoned criminal. Guiteau will soon be hung, as he deserve to be, and Mason, with proper discipline, may in a short time emerge from the Albany penitentiary, where he is now engaged in the shoe shop, a more discreet man and soldier.

(Mason's unsuccessful attempt at Guiteau is somewhat remindful of Jack Ruby's successful attempt at Kennedy's assassin, Lee Harvey Oswald.)

3/25/82 Washingtonian

THE WILL OF THADDEUS STEVENS.

Under the will of Thaddeus Stevens his favorite nephew, Thaddeus Stevens, Jr., was to receive the bulk of the estate at the end of fifteen years if he overcame his dissipated habits; if he did not, however, he was to receive $800 per annum during his life, and the residue of his estate, provided it amounted to $50,000, was to be devoted to the founding of an orphan asylum. His nephew not complying with the requirements of the will, the executors were about arranging for the transfer of the estate to the Children's Home, of Lancaster, Pa., when Dr. Thaddeus N. Stevens, of Indiana, stepped in and filed a bill in equity, claiming the estate on the ground that it does not reach $50,000. Able counsel have been retained on both sides.

April, 1882

4/6/82 Mirror

A Desperado Killed by One of His Gang.

The notorious bandit and train robber, Jesse James, who has been a terror to Missouri and the southwest since the close of the rebellion, was shot dead by one of his associates at St. Joseph, Mo., yesterday morning. The large rewards offered by the State of Missouri for the body of Jesse James, "either dead or alive," tempted the cupidity of one of his confederates in crime named Ford. The latter, taking advantage of a moment when James had disarmed himself preparatory to washing his hands, sent a bullet through the head of the desperado. There is good reason to believe that the killing will result in the breaking up of the gang of robbers he has headed. He was the master-spirit of those lawless ruffians and had so successfully defied the law that they seemed to regard him as invincible. The manner of his taking off will no doubt also have a discouraging effect upon those of his gang who survive him. They will feel that they cannot trust each other, now that one of the band has assassinated the chief for the sake of the blood money. If the state can now convict Ford, the murderer of James, as an accomplice of the latter in his deeds of violence and bloodshed and send him to the gallows, or penitentiary for life, it will derive a double benefit from one shot which killed James.— A man who would shoot down a confederate in crime for the price set upon the head, would murder the traveller for the money in his pocket, and is therefore dangerous in any community.—*Star*.

The Ford brothers were members of Jesse James gang, and at the time of the murder were inmates of his family, and enjoying his confidence. The heavy rewards offered for the body of James, dead or alive, is supposed to have led to the horrible tragedy. James was a miserable outlaw, and his taking off, no doubt is a "consummation devoutly to be wished for," but his murderer has proven himself possessed of all the villainous instincts of the chief, without his courage, and merits being summarily disposed of. A despatch from St. Joseph, gives the following particulars of the shooting of Jesse James.

"After having eaten breakfast Jesse James and Charles Ford went to the stable to curry the horses, and on returning to the room where Robert Ford was, Jesse said: "Its an awfully hot day." He pulled off his coat and vest and tossed them on the bed. Then he said: "I guess I will take off my pistols, for fear somebody will see them if I walk in the yard." He unbuckled the belt in which he carried two 45. caliber revolvers, one a Smith & Wesson and the other a Colt's, and laid them on the bed with his coat and vest. He then picked up a dusting brush, with the intention of dusting some pictures which hung on the wall. In order to do this he got on a chair, his back being now turned to the brothers who silently stepped between Jesse and his revolvers, and at a motion from Charley both drew their guns. Robert was the quickest of the two. In one motion he had the long weapon on a level with his eye, with the muzzle not more than four feet from the back of the outlaws head. Even in that motion, quick as thought, there was something which did not escape the acute ears of the huntsman. He made a motion as if to turn his head to ascertain the cause of that suspicious sound, but too late. There was a quick flash, a sharp report, and the well directed ball crashed through the outlaws skull. There was no outcry; just a swaying of the body, and he fell heavily, back upon the carpeted floor, the ball having entered the base of the skull and made its way out through head over his left eye. It had been fired out of a Colt's "45" improved weapon, silver-mounted and pearl-handled, which had been presented by the dead man to his slayer only a few days ago."

4/7/82 Telephone

A number of men have identified the body, and there is no question about its being that of Jesse James. A look at the body at the undertaker's showed that he was a fine-looking man apparently forty years old, with broad forehead, and his physiogomy was that of an intelligent, as well as a resolute and daring man. The house where James lived and in which he was killed has the appearance of an armory. A number of guns and pistols, including a repeating rifle, a needle gun and navy revolvers, with a good store of ammunition, were found there. Jesse was in the habit of wearing two belts, with a brace of very fine revelvers and twenty-five extra cartridges. In a small stable, near the house, were discovered several fine horses, the property of James.

The Ford brothers claim that they are detectives, and that they have been on James tracks for a long time. It is believed they were with James in the Blue Cut train robbery, and that they were influenced in killing him by the hope of getting the big reward, which has been offered for James, dead or alive, by the Governor and by the express and railroad companies.

It is learned that Ford, who is believed to be a member of the gang, was under the control of Police Commissioner Craig, of Kansas City, and has been used as an instrument for James' destruction. Ford is a young man about 22 years old, and looked like a verdant youth from the country. In appearance he is a mere boy, and is the last person in the world to be taken as the slayer of the famous outlaw.

April, 1882

4/21/82 Telephone

THE JAMES GANG.

A Gradual Extermination of the Band

Sometimes it has seemed as if there was no retribution for these men, who shook their bloody hands in defiance of justice while they shouted over their work. A recapitulation of the manner in which they have, one by one, met a terrible fate, will go very far toward establishing the correctness of the idea that, every now and then, Time takes hold of these matters himself, and, in his own way, gets even.

Dick Little, who was one of the saddle gang, tired out, killed Hite, his most intimate companion, and then turned over the whereabouts of Jeff Hite, a brother, to the authorities. This Hite was sentenced, a few days ago, to a term of twenty-five years in the Missouri penitentiary. Little has come off lucky by resorting to the process known as "squealing."

John Younger was shot to death by Capt. Lull.

Bub McDaniel, who was at the Winston Robbery, was handed over to the Kansas authorities and escaped from jail. He was secreted in a swamp by an old negro, who gave him away, and he was shot down like a mad dog. He fought until he fell. His brother, Tom McDaniel, was tracked by two Kentucky farmers and killed for a part he took in a bank robbery.

Bill Berry was killed in Mexico, Mo., by a sheriff's posse and one of Pinkerton's men.

A squad of soldiers and a deputy United States Marshal overtook Joe Collins and Bill Hoffren near Buffalo, Kan. A fight ensued and the two outlaws were left dead on the grass.

Arkansas Johnson was snapped up by a bullet fired by a citizen of Denton, Tex.

Sam Bass had a shot that cut off his existence in Round Rock, Tex.

Henry Collins was overtaken in Sherman, Tex., and killed on the street by the sheriff.

On the northern boundary line of the United States Billy Collins came face to face with Deputy Marshal Anderson. The two fired and fell simultaneously.

In the raid into Minnesota, where the Youngers were captured and where Frank James received a wound from which he has never recovered, Bill Chadwell, Charlie Pitts and Clel Miller were killed.

Ed Miller, as stated, was left for the coffin by Jesse James; and now the leader of the most fearless banditti of modern times is plucked by one of his own company.

There are in the penitentiary Pipes and Herndon for ninety-nine years, in Albany, for robbing the mails in Texas. Jack Keene, serving out a fourteen years' sentence for a bank robbery in West Virginia, Jeff Hite, twenty-five years in Missouri for a train robbery, and Tucker Bashall and Billy Ryan, twenty-five years each for the same offence. Four are on trial in Independence, Mo., for train robberies and two are awaiting trial in the same place. Arthur McCoy is the only one of this band who has died a natural death thus far.

Frank James, it is believed, is not in Kentucky, but in the pan handle section of Texas, where he and Jesse invested in a ranch some years ago.

The bank and train robberies committed by this gang are as follows:

Columbus, Ky.	$15,000
Elizabethtown	20,000
Huntington, W Va.	19,000
Liberty, Mo.	12,000
Corydon, Iowa	9,000
St. Genevieve, Mo.	17,000
Corinth, Miss.	9,000
Jewelry at Corinth	5,000
Gads Hill	20,000
Muncie	20,000
Big Spring, gold	60,000
Total	$206,000

This does not include stage and other robberies, which are estimated at over $50,000.

April 1882

4/21/82 Telephone

JESSE JAMES AT HOME— FROM AN INTERVIEW WITH THE FORDS.

"What sort of a man was Jesse in his home—was he kind to his children?"

"Yes, he was kind, but he had no control over them, and would get mad at his wife if she corrected them."

"Was he inclined to read much?"

"Yes; he read a great deal, but only the papers. He talked about his robberies when we were alone. He said often that he should never quit the business as long as he lived.— We were to have robbed the Platte City bank last Monday night. Jesse was to take Bob into the bank with him, and I was to guard the outside. He told me to kill every damned man who came near. He always confided in me and didn't seem to want to trust Bob with his plans, but depended on him to do as he was told."

"Did you ever see any visitors at Jesse's house?"

"No, never. H's house was so situated that he could keep off 100 men until he could get to the stable and ride away from pursuit, should it occur."

"His horses were said to have been especially trained for his dangerous work. Is that so?"

"No; that story is all bosh. He never cared anything for them so they were good travelers. He rode hard and soon killed his horses."

No Whiskey!

BROWN'S IRON BITTERS is one of the very few tonic medicines that are not composed mostly of alcohol or whiskey, thus becoming a fruitful source of intemperance by promoting a desire for rum.

5/4/82 Mirror

A TRAMP, an imbecile looking old couger, created quite a stir in this town last Saturday afternoon, by striking with a cane that he carried in his hand, two ladies who happened to pass him on his journeyings in and near town. Neither lady was hurt by the blow, but the insolence of the act aroused a strong feeling against the offender, who was promptly arrested and lodged in jail; but as there was no law which seemed exactly to fit the case, he was detained until Monday morning, when an officer escorted him outside the corporate limits and ordered him to go, which he did without standing upon the order of his going. The old creature *may be* a harmless imbecile, but if he is not careful a broken head will be the reward of his impertinence.

WASHINGTON ADVERTISEMENTS.
WASHINGTON
Horse & Carriage
BAZAAR.
938 and 940 Louisiana Avenue.
AUCTION SALE OF
Horses, Buggies, Carriages, Express Wagons, New and Second Hand Harness, every
TUESDAY, THURSDAY & SATURDAY
COMMENCING AT 10 O'CLOCK.
S. BENSINGER, Auctioneer.
feb 4-3m

ONLY 75 CTS.
a year to single subscribers.

ONLY 50 CENTS
a year to clubs.

HANDSOME PREMIUMS
ADDITION TO CLUB RAISERS

THE CHEAPEST PAPER IN THE WORLD

THE POST IS THE GREAT NATIONAL WEEKLY.

A SILVER OR GOLD WATCH
In one day by raising a club for THE POST.
Address   STILSON HUTCHINS,
WASHINGTON, D. C.

May, 1882

5/19/82 Telephone

TAR AND TERROR.

A NEGRO DRAGGED FROM HIS BED, COATED WITH TAR AND TURNED LOOSE.

Last Friday night, about ten or eleven o'clock, the peaceful denizens of Purcellville were aroused by a few pistol shots and cries of "murder," in the vicinity of a house owned by a white woman, who, for a long time has had a colored man living with her. When they arrived at the house they found the negro in a sorry plight, being stripped, his shirt tied over his head and his body coated with tar. He stated that a company of about twenty men, about half white and half colored, came to the house a short time before, and after breaking down the door, dragged him out of bed, took him out of doors, stripped him and tarred him, then turned him loose with a warning to make himself scarce in that locality. He says he recognized two of the party. After spending most of the night in getting rid of the tar, the Negro left on Saturday morning.

It was reported a short time ago that the woman had driven the negro away; and probably his return was the cause of the violence. The woman is supposed to possess considerable money, which she inherited from an honorable father.

LATER.—We learn that the Negro was spending the night at a neighboring house, to escape capture, as he had been warned, a few days previous, to leave the vicinity. It is stated that there were no white men in the crowd that mistreated the man.

---

200 BUSHELS CHOICE EARLY CLOVER SEED; 100 BUSHELS SAPLEY CLOVER SEED; 100 BUSHELS CHOICE ORCHARD GRASS SEED; and a full supply of Prime

TIMOTHY SEED,

at the Lowest market rates.
feb. 2. HOUGH, GRAY & CO.

5/5/82 Telephone

USEFUL HINTS.

DANDRUFF.—The annoyance from dandruff can be prevented by dampening the scalp three or four times a week with sulphur water, made by putting one-half of an ounce of flour of sulphur into a pint of water, shaking occasionally for two days; then pour off into a clean bottle.

REMEDY FOR BALDNESS.—Glycerine, four ounces; tannin, one drachm; tincture of cantharides, two drachms; oil of capsicum, ten drops. Apply to the bald spots night and morning.

TOOTH POWDER.—Prepared chalk, four ounces; orris root (powdered), two ounces; green myrrh (powdered), one-quarter of an ounce; oil of cinnamon, twenty drops.

SUPERFLUOUS HAIR.—These are best let alone. Shaving only increases the growth and depilatories are dangerous and sometimes disfigure the face. The only sure plan is to spread on a piece of leather equal parts of golbarium and pitch plaster, lay it on the hair as smoothly as possible; let it remain there three or four minutes, then remove it with the hair, root and branch. This is severe but effective. Kerosene will also remove them. If sore after using rub on sweet oil.

HOUSE PAINTING.—This should be done early in winter or spring, when it is cold and no dust flying. To mix paints for different coats; Outside—1st, 2d and 3d coats, mix the lead to proper consistency with boiled oil, showing time between to dry hard. Inside—1st coat, mix lead and paint in mixture one-half boiled oil, one-half turpentine; 2d, one-fourth oil, three-fourths turpentine; 3d, mostly turpentine with a little oil to hold color. No dryer required. Inside paint must have light.

BROOMS.—It is not economy to have too few brooms; one for the sleeping-room upstairs, one for parlor and sitting-room and one for the kitchen are not too many. As they are worn they may be passed down a grade at a time, the new one always going to the parlor. If the new broom is allowed to stand in cold water for twelve hours, afterward thoroughly drying it, it will last much longer. A broom should never be allowed to stand on its brush, as it makes it permanently one-sided and ill-shapen. Hang it up by a loop in the handle.

6/16/82 Telephone

THE TELEPHONE.

—Bloomfield has gone to seed.

—The land is full of drummers.

—Sorenuf Summer has struck us.

—Eggs are unusually high for this season of the year.

—Mr. L. Dow Hess has packed up his samples and goeth forth on the war path as drummer for a Baltimore grocery house.

—Mr. Charlie Tavenner of Leesburg, was quite badly hurt by his horse running away, near Hughesvill, on Tuesday. His buggy was wrecked.

—It is reported that two men named Clendenning and Dyer were recently found lying in the road near Hillsboro, having fought each other until both were entirely exhausted. It seems that they had previously had some trouble, and meeting in the road they proceeded to settle their accounts with the above result. They were both badly bruised, especially about the heads.

—There arrived here on the train over the Washington and Western (late W. & O.) Railroad from Loudoun a young woman, in charge of two officers, madly deranged. The unfortunate, upon landing from the train, was at once placed in a hack, which was in waiting, and driven rapidly through the streets to the Virginia Midland Railway depot, where she was forced on the cars — Her destination was the Staunton Insane Asylum. The wild shrieks of the woman as she passed through the streets, and at the depot, and her haggared look and disheveled long black hair made a sad scene. The deranged lady was Miss Foley, of Gum Springs, Loudoun county.—

It is said that there is a wild man in the forests of the Potomac, not far from here; but we do not indulge in ghost stories.

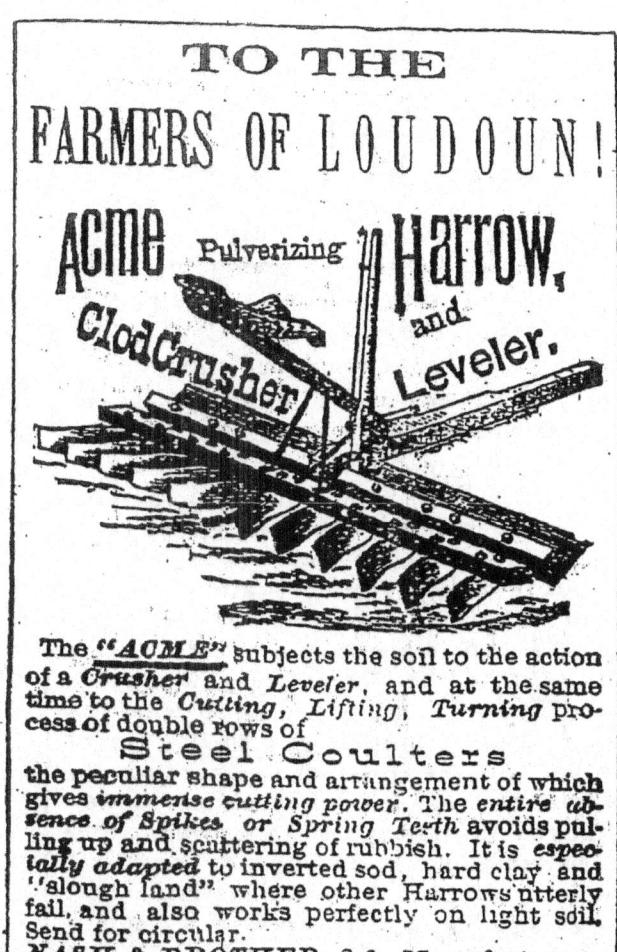

TO THE FARMERS OF LOUDOUN!

ACME Pulverizing ClodCrusher Harrow, and Leveler.

The "*ACME*" subjects the soil to the action of a *Crusher* and *Leveler*, and at the same time to the *Cutting*, *Lifting*, *Turning* process of double rows of **Steel Coulters** the peculiar shape and arrangement of which gives *immense cutting power*. The *entire absence of Spikes* or *Spring Teeth* avoids pulling up and scattering of rubbish. It is *especially adapted* to inverted sod, hard clay and "slough land" where other Harrows utterly fail, and also works perfectly on light soil. Send for circular.

NASH & BROTHER, Sole Manufacturers. HARRISBURG, and 22 COLLEGE PLACE, Penn. NEW YORK CITY

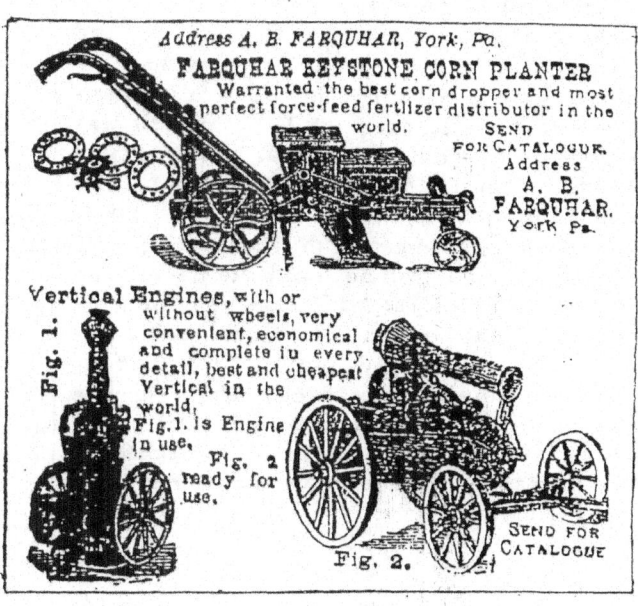

Address A. B. FARQUHAR, York, Pa.
FARQUHAR KEYSTONE CORN PLANTER
Warranted the best corn dropper and most perfect force-feed fertilizer distributor in the world. SEND FOR CATALOGUE. Address A. B. FARQUHAR, York Pa.

Vertical Engines, with or without wheels, very convenient, economical and complete in every detail, best and cheapest Vertical in the world.
Fig. 1 is Engine in use.
Fig. 2 ready for use.
SEND FOR CATALOGUE

THE MIRROR

BENJ. F. SHEETZ, Editor.

Thursday Morning, July 6, 1882.

To-Day we copy so much of the published incidents of the execution of Chas. J. Guiteau as will serve to assure our readers of his death; and convince them of the savage-like blasphemy with which he met the grim monster.

Guiteau was the principal actor in a drama that has been before the country for just a year. It began with the crack of the murderer's pistol in the depot at Washington, and ended with the thud of his body as it shot from the scaffold a year, less two days, afterward. At the beginning there went up a wail of sorrow and pity from the whole nation, at its end there arose a shout of exultant joy from the crowd who surrounded the scaffold. Between the prologue, "It is done—Arthur is President, I am a stalwart of the Stalwarts," and the epilogue, "I am God's man—Arthur is a coward and an ingrate," came many scenes of darkness and gloom.—First the lingering illness and death of the President, then the "law's delay," in the preparation for the trial, the ten long, weary weeks of the trial itself—the conviction, sentence, and last scene of all, the execution. All along this time, were the relatives of the murderer striving to prove first his insanity then to gain a pardon, a reprieve or commutation of the sentence; while he himself was striving to make it appear that he was inspired and therefore then he was not responsible, thus travestying the character of the Apostles to excuse a cowardly murder. All efforts however, failed, and he paid the penalty of his act. And whilst there may be some who think still that he was not a responsible being, we judge that it would be hard to convince the majority of people that he was insane, or inspired, or that his execution was not lawful and right. They will rather think that his vanity and egotism were his madness, and his malignity his inspiration. So let his memory perish.

GUITEAU HANGED.

PRESIDENT GARFIELD'S ASSASSIN MEETS HIS DOOM.

His Death a Swift and Painless One.

Last Friday, just one year lacking two days from the date of the assassination of President Garfield, the miserable wretch who fired the fatal shot, was hanged in the jail in Washington city, in the presence of about 250 persons. Our city exchanges for the past few days have been filled with the details of the last scenes in the melancholy drama, but now that it is over, the name of Guiteau should be permitted to sink into its merited oblivion.

The condemned man seems to have borne himself with much fortitude to the last, and met his final doom very much like murderers generally do. At 10 o'clock Friday morning having expressed a desire to take a bath, the facilities for were promptly furnish him, and he plunged in; he then busied himself for an hour or so in writing, after which, at 11:35 he partook of his last meal, which consisted of a pound of broiled steak—a dish of fried potatoes, four slices of toast and a quart of coffee, all of which he consumed with seeming relish. Soon after he had finished his meal, the door of his cell was thrown open and Guiteau, attended by his spiritual adviser, Dr. Hicks, and the officers whose duty it was to execute the law made his appearance, and with a firm step, walked to and ascended the scaffold, without flinching. When everything had been arranged on the scaffold, Dr. Hicks made a fervent prayer. At its conclusion Guiteau read a selection from the tenth chapter of Matthew, from the 28th to the 41st verses inclusive. The manuscript which the doomed man had written that morning was produced by Dr. Hicks, and Guiteau, looking over the upturned faces before him announced his intention to read his dying prayer, which he did in a loud, distinct voice, as follows—

PRAYER FROM THE SCAFFOLD.

My dying prayer on the gallows. Father, now I go to Thee and the Savior. I have finished the work Thou gavest me to do and I am only too happy to go to Thee. The world does not yet appreciate my mission, but Thou knowest it. Thou knowest Thou did inspire the removal of Garfield and only good has come from it. This is the best evidence that the inspiration came from Thee and I have set it forth in my book that all men may read and know that thou father, didst inspire the act for which I am now murdered. This government and nation by this act I know will incur Thy eternal enmity, as did the Jews by killing Thy man, my Saviour. The retribution in that case came quick and sharp and I know Thy Divine law of retribution will strike this nation and my murderers in the same way. The diabolical spirit of this nation, its government and its newspapers toward me will justify Thee in cursing them and I know that Thy Divine law of retribution is inexorable. I therefore predict that this nation will go down in blood, and that my murderers, from the executive to the hangman, will go to hell. Thy laws are inexorable, oh, Thou Supreme Judge. Woe unto thee, men that violate Thy laws. Only weeping and gnashing of teeth awaits them. The American press has a large bill to settle with their Righteous Father for their vindictiveness in the matter. Nothing but blood will satisfy them, and now my blood be on them, this nation and its officials. Arthur the President is a coward and an ignate. His ingratitude to the man who made him and saved his party and land from overthrow has no parallel in history, but Thou Righteous Father, will judge him. Father Thou knowest me, but the world hath not known me, and now I go to Thee and the Savior without the slightest ill-will toward a human being. Farewell ye men of earth.

A "POEM" BY THE ASSASSIN.

He then commenced to chant these verses in a sad, doleful style:

I love the Lordy
Glory hallelujah!
And that is the reason
I am going to the Lord.
Glory hallelujah! Glory hallelujah!
I am going to the Lord.

Here Guiteau's voice failed, and he bowed his head and broke into sobs. But he rallied a little, and went on with his chant.

I saved my party and my land.
Glory hallelujah!
But they have murdered me for it,
And that is the reason I am going to the Lordy.
Glory hallelujah! Glory hallelujah!
I am going to the Lordy.

Here again his feelings overcame him and he leaned his head on the shoulder of Dr. Hicks and sobbed pitifully. Still he went on.

Glory hallelujah.
I am with the Lord!

This closed the chant and then Rev. Mr. Hicks gave to Guiteau his final benediction and farewell, saying: "God, the Father, be with the, gives thee peace forevermore."

ALL IS OVER.

The attendants then pinioned his legs, placed the noose over his head and carefully adjusted it about his neck. Mr. Strong placed the black cap over his head, and as he did so Guiteau called out in loud tones, "Glory, glory, glory!" Instantly the spring was touched the drop fell at 12.40, and Guiteau swung in the air. The body turned partly around, but there was not the slightest perceptible movement of the limbs or any evidence of a conscious effort to move them. When the drop fell a yell was sent up by some persons in the jail. This was echoed outside by the voices of a thousand or more people, who hurrahed lustily. There was a general onslaught by the populace upon the door, which was so powerful that the officers were unable to withstand it. Hundreds of people crowded into the office, and there was a terrible crush at the doors. For at least forty seconds after the drop fell the body hung motionless. Then there was a slight motion of the shoulders and legs, due to muscular contraction. Three minutes after the trap fell the body was lowered to be examined by the physicians. There was a decided action of the heart for fully fourteen minutes, and the pulse fluttered two minutes longer. When the body had hung with the feet just touching the ground for over half an hour it was lowered into the coffin which was waiting for it under the scaffold. The physicians decided at once that the neck had been broken.

VIEWING THE REMAINS.

When the body was lowered the black cap was removed and the face exposed. The features were pallid and composed. About the mouth there was considerable moisture After the body had been arranged in the coffin. Warden Crocker ascended the steps of the scaffold and addressing the crowd, which was kept back from the scaffold by a line of officers, said that those who desired could pass along the side of the scaffold and view the body. Then the crowd of spectators was formed into line and passing between the scaffold and the wall of the jail viewed the dead face. Some jail officers, two or three physicians and Dr. Hicks stood about the coffin. John W. Guiteau joined this company and fanned his dead brother's face to keep away the flies. John W. Guiteau did not go upon the scaffold but stood during the scene just within the line of officers at the bottom of the steps. When liberty was given to the crowd to view the remains the scaffold was at once filled with people, who curiously examined every joint and bolt. At 1.40 p. m. the lid of the coffin was put in place and the body was borne to the jail chapel.

After the body was taken to the jail arrangements were made to let Mrs. Scoville view it. Guiteau just before the trap was sprung dropped a piece of paper from his hand. This paper was given him by Warden Crocker to be dropped by the condemned man as a signal that he was ready.

HIS BURIAL.

On Saturday afternoon Guiteau's body was buried in the northeast corridor of the jail. The brick flooring was taken up and a grave seven feet deep was dug, into which the remains of the wretched assassin were deposited, far beyond the reach of the body snatchers. Six of the jail prisoners acted as pallbearers. There was no ceremony.

Temple Cafe,
604 Ninth Street Opp. U. S. Pat. Office
WASHINGTON, D. C.

A TEMPERANCE CAFE
FOR LADIES AND GENTLEMEN
Regular Meals 30 cents. Lunches at all hours.
MRS. S. D. LA FETRA, PROP'R.

THE TELEPHONE.

FRIDAY .... JULY 7TH.

— Ye Editor is under the weather.

— Nearly all Tuesday forenoon was devoted to a fine big rain—a good, square cold-water celebration of the "Glorious Fourth."

— Reports from all parts of the State are to the effect that the wheat crop is excellent—probably the best since the war, both in quantity and quality.

— HARVEST SERMON. A harvest sermon will be preached at the Lutheran Church, near Lovettsville, on Sunday July 9th, at 10 P. M., by the pastor, Rev. P. H. Miller.

— We have received a copy of the *Herald* a Democratic paper recently started at Fairfax C. H., by Mr. S. R. Donohoe, formerly of this County. Excepting its politics, the *Herald* is a good paper.

— More communications unaccompanied by the names of the writers received this week. They go to the waste basket as usual. Will people *never learn* the regulation of publishers in this respect.

— Now that the farmers have a fine wheat crop to sell we hope that those who have been owing us little bills for a long time, will send in the lucre.

— On Monday our town was awakened by the shrill whistle of a locomotive which seemed to turn our streets into a railroad; it proved to be a traction engine sent to Mr. Jas. B. Pengh, from Waynesboro, Penn., with which he expects to run a threshing machine. It walked through our town as proud as a war horse, and seeming conscious of its mysterious power.

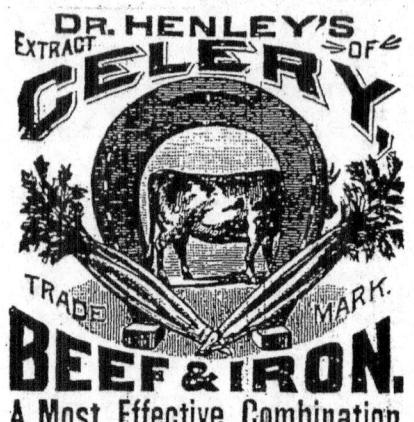

A Most Effective Combination.

This well known Tonic and Nervine is gaining great reputation as a cure for Debility, Dyspepsia, and NERVOUS disorders. It relieves all languid and debilitated conditions of the system; strengthens the intellect, and bodily functions; builds up worn out Nerves; aids digestion; restores impaired or lost Vitality, and brings back youthful strength and vigor. It is pleasant to the taste, and used regularly braces the System against the depressing influence of Malaria.

Price—$1.00 per Bottle of 24 ounces.
FOR SALE BY ALL DRUGGISTS.

July 1882

7/14/82 Telephone

AN INVENTOR'S COURTSHIP.

How Edison Was Married and Forgot all About the Occurrence.

[From the Buffalo Commercial Advocate.]

Griffin, Edison's private secretary, once told me a familly characteristic story of the manner in which Edison came to get married. The idea was first suggested by an intimate friend, who made the point that he needed a mistress to preside over his big house, which was being managed by a housekeeper and several servants. I dare say the idea had never occurred to him before, for be it known he is the shyest and most bashful of men; but he seemed pleased with the proposition, and timidly inquired whom he should marry. The friend somewhat hastily replied, "anyone;" that a man who had so little sentiment in his soul as to ask such a question ought to be satisfied with anything that wore a petticoat and was decent, and concluded by saying: "There are a number of nice girls employed in your factory over yonder. They aren't especially refined or cultivated, I must confess; but are respectable, and that is the main consideration after all."

Edison looked them over, and after making his selection, put the question plumply to her. It was Edison's way of doing business, but it embarrassed the young lady all the same. She asked time to consider, and Edison granted her a week. At the end of that time she accepted him, and they were married without delay. They had decided to visit the New England States and Canada and make quite an extensive tour. As a bridal party drove to the station they passed his laboratory. Turning to his wife, Edison excused himself for a few minutes, saying there were some matters that needed his attention, and that he would be at the station in time for the train. The train came and went, and so did several others, but no Edison. The bride, who knew his peculiarities, drove back to the house and awaited her liege lord's pleasure. She never saw him again for forty-eight hours.— Immersed in some idea that had suddenly occurred him, he became oblivious to brides, honeymoons or anything else.

☞ Epitaph said to be copied from a tombstone in the cemetery Montmarte "Here lies Joseph X who for twenty years after the death of his wife lived in the society of his mother in law, and died in the certain hope of a better world beyond."

THE BEST REMEDY
FOR
Diseases of the Throat and Lungs.

AYER'S CHERRY PECTORAL.

Diseases of the pulmonary organs are so prevalent and fatal, that a safe and reliable remedy for them is invaluable to every community. AYER'S CHERRY PECTORAL is such a remedy, and no other so eminently merits the confidence of the public. It is a scientific combination of the medicinal principles and curative virtues of the finest drugs, chemically united, to insure the greatest possible efficiency and uniformity of results, which enables physicians as well as invalids to use it with confidence.

WIND ENGINE
AND BUCKEYE PUMP,

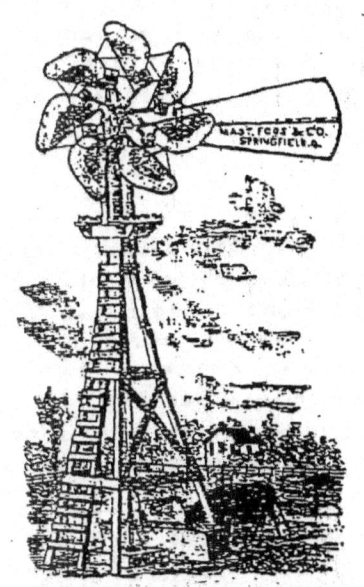

THE BEST ARRANGEMENT for Raising Water from Deep Wells ever invented. See the one at work in Messrs Wildman & Harrison's field, near Leesburg.

SHROFF & CO., Agents for Loudoun County.

July 1882

7/20/82 Mirror

CAVE, CANIS.—Some citizen, whose slumbers, probably, have been disturbed by dogs, took his revenge on Saturday night last by strewing around loose, some "cold poison." On Sunday the effects began to be apparent in the forms of several "dead dogs," and since, then canines of high and low degree, have been "shuffling off," numerously, causing the owners of dogs to keep their pets under pretty close confinement. We suppose that no one will deny the fact, that there are scores of worthless curs that were better dead than alive, yet most persons will condemn this mode of "removing" them—for in nine cases out of ten, where poison is spread promiscuously, it is the good dogs that get it and the mean ones escape.

Some ten or twelve dogs have fallen victims to the poisonous bait, since Sunday, among them several valuable ones, upon whose heads their owners regularly paid State and corporation taxes, and who prized them as highly as they would their horse. But this promiscuous throwing around of poison, where it is liable to be taken up even by children, is not only highly reprehensible in morals, but it is a criminal offence as well—as will be seen from the following extract taken from the criminal laws of Virginia, chapter III, section 27, acts of 1878:

"If a person maliciously administers poison to, or expose it with intent that it should be taken by any horse, cattle, or other beast of any person, * * * he shall be confined in the penitentiary not less than two nor more than ten years."

Should the future reveal the author of the recent poisoning, he'll probably have a merry time of it.

7/1/82 Washingtonian

An Englishman named Green, living in Chesterfield county, Va., had been missing from his home for more than a week, until last Thursday, his dead body was found in the woods some distance from his home.— When found a setter dog, in an emaciated condition, was lying by his side. "There never was a better friend than old dog Tray."

7/27/82 Mirror

A DOG IN A WHEAT STACK.—Last Monday morning week, a favorite dog belonging to Mr. CHRISTIAN HEMPSTONE, residing near town, was missing, and so continued until noon on Wednesday, when the hands at the stack-yard, heard queer sounds proceeding from one of the ricks of wheat. They were speedily set to work, and in a short time the entire stack was torn down, and at its very base they found, "poor dog tray," thin, thirsty and hungry. Unlike the fabled dog in the manger, he offered no resistance at being led from the straw he could not masticate. It seems that early in the morning on Monday, the dog had ensconced himself in an ordinary wheat shock; subsequently, that particular shock was selected as a nucleus around which to build, and without disturbing either that or the sleeping canine, the rick grew and was completed before noon, so that for two nights and nearly three days the poor dog had been imprisoned in his narrow confines, without food or water, and precious little fresh air.

LIGHT ! LIGHT
Gaslight!

PORTABLE !   ECONOMICAL !!
CLEAN !!!   CHEAP !!!!

DANFORTH'S SIX JET NO-CHIMNEY BURNER with Vienna Shade and Ring, a Brass Lamp and DANFORTH'S FLUID, nearest *Perfect Light and Safety* found; with ordinary care lasts years. Free from grease, smoke, soot. Lamp *always* clean. Flame of a match vaporizes the Fluid, same as steam is formed in a tea-kettle, which, escaping through small holes in head of burner, gives *the light*, and like steam depends upon heat. Hence, when light is blown out vapor stops forming, and there is *no* more light until you again create vapor by applying flame. This burner fitted to *all* lamps. Does not heat collar of lamp. *Light* pure. Combustion *perfect*. Bottom of a white China plate *cannot be smoked* if held one inch above the flame. All this without a chimney.

DANFORTH'S FLUID cannot be exploded. All are earnestly urged to call and see these goods. No one asked to buy.

$173.75 for a SQUARE or UPRIGHT ROSEWOOD PIANOFORTE, with Stool, Book and Music. Only $80 for an Eight Stop, Sub-Bass and Octave-Coupler ORGAN. Chapel Organs $65, Pipe Organs $94. OTHER BARGAINS fully described in Illustrated Catalogue which is sent FREE with full particulars. VISITORS ARE ALWAYS WELCOME. Address or call upon DANIEL F. BEATTY, Washington, New Jersey

GRAND TEMPERANCE RALLY AND BUSH MEETING

TO BE HELD
IN THE WOODS AT PURCELLVILLE,
Loudoun County, Va.

TUESDAY, WEDNESDAY and THURSDAY, AUG. 8th, 9th, and 10th.

GRAND EXCURSION!

OVER THE

WASHINGTON & WESTERN R. R.

From WASHINGTON, ALEXANDRIA And Intermediate Points.

ROUND TRIP TICKETS

FROM WASHINGTON	- $1.65		FROM HERNDON	- $ .75
" ALEXANDRIA	- 1.40		" GUILFORD	- .65
" CARLIN'S	- 1.25		" FARMWELL	- .55
" FALLS CHURCH	- 1.15		" LEESBURG	- .35
" VIENNA	- 1.00		" CLARKS GAP	- .25
" HUNTERS	- .90		" HAMILTON	- .20
" THORNTONS	- .85		" ROUND HILL	- .20

Trains will leave Washington at 7 o'clock A. M. and connect at Alexandria Junction with trains from Alexandria, which will leave that city at 7 o'clock. Returning, the trains will leave Purcellville at 6 P. M., and arrive in the cities early in the evening.— Excursionists will have but a short walk from the depot to the grounds.

Many Eminent Speakers

Will be in attendance. Hon. W. W. Berry, G. W. C. T., I. O. G. T. of Va., Rev. W. W. Bennett, Pres. of Randolph Macon College, Ex-Gov. Wm. Smith, Rev. Thos. L Poulston, Hon. Hiram Price, of Iowa, Commissioner of Indian Affairs, and many others have promised to be present.

REFRESHMENTS FOR MAN AND BEAST will be for sale on the grounds, and, in fact, every effort will be put forth to make this one of the most pleasant, interesting and profitable occasions of the season. All persons who have never seen the BEAUTIFUL LOUDOUN VALLEY, with its grand old mountains and green vales, should not lose this opportunity to do so, and at the same time attend this occasion, which will be full of interest to everybody. By order of the Committee,

JOS. H. JEWETT, Pres.

(Circus ad in the The Mirror.)

THE VERY FIRST VISIT
OF THE FAVORITE
ORTON SHOWS!
TO LEESBURG.

MONDAY, AUGUST 7th, 1882,
IS THE FIXED, ABSOLUTE AND UNCHANGEABLE DATE OF THE

The Biggest in the World.

Make no mistake, be sure of the date of the coming of

Miles Orton's New Mastodon Shows
...AND...
Royal German Menagerie!
3 Great Circus Troupes 3
A CONGRESS OF WONDERS,
MAMMOTH TRAINED WILD BEAST SHOW,
ALLEGORICAL STREET PAGEANTS,
AND A VAST MENAGERY

(Circus ad in The Washingtonian.)

The Only Big Show Coming!
The Celebrated Orton Shows

Leesburg, Monday, August 7th, 1882
IS THE FIXED, ABSOLUTE AND UNCHANGEABLE DATE OF THE

The BIGGEST IN THE WORLD!
Make no mistake; be sure of the date of the coming of
MILES ORTON'S NEW MASTODON SHOWS,
AND
Royal German Menagerie.

Admission, 50 Cents; Children under Nine Years, 25 Cents.
DOORS OPEN AT 1 and 7 P. M.

A CONGRESS OF WONDERS.
Mammoth Trained Wild Beast Show,
Allegorical Street Pageants,
And a Vast MENAGERIE.

A Thousand Triumphs of the Track. The New Show of the Period. A Convocation of Rarities, a Freshet of Wild Beasts. A Synod of Surprising Beauties, and a Trinnity of Arenic Champions, engrossing all the Greatest Bareback Riders in the world.

Miles Orton, the Hero,

Champion of all ages, in his Duo Carrying Act, with the Earth's Infant Prodigies riding on top of his head. He has no equal.

THE SPANISH CIRCO, THE SCHOOL OF
CANINE GRADUATES, and
$20,000 RIDING DOG, "HECTOR."

Allie and Bernard,

The 4 and 5 year old Midget marvels in Heroic Mid-Air Sensationalism, and danger-defying Aerial Gallantry, concluding with a Tremendous Headlong Dire from a great height, representing to the excited imagination the rapid descent of a Fiery Comet

— SHOT — from the Dread Immensity of Space.

Georgeous Sunbright Chariots and Sumptuous Golden Tableau Cars. Swaying Mastodons, Monsters and Mammoths. The Titanic BUBALIPUS, fettered and Chained in an Iron-Bound Den. The Juvenile Circus. A Most Enormous Menagerie of Living Rare Wild Beasts. 100 Famous Favorites, and the Best Riders, Leapers, Gymnasts, Jugglers, Calisthenists, etc., in the Great Triple Circus Company. Free Parade daily at 10 o'clock.

August, 1882

8/10/82 Mirror

AUGUST COURT, a day memorable in the history of Loudoun, comes off next Monday. That it will be well attended we do not doubt, but whether it will exhibit anything like the "pomp and circumstance" of ye olden time, is problematical.

THE CIRCUS.—Miles Orton's Celebrated Show exhibited in Leesburg on Monday, and notwithstanding they spread their canvass at three different points in this county, quite a large crowd was attracted here on the day named. The street parade was quite creditable the collection of animals was not very large; but the entertainment in the ring was fully equal to the average travelling circus. The bare-back riding, the trapeze performance by two little children, and the "high and lofty tumbling," of the company, &c., &c., were all excellent, and gave general satisfaction to all who witnessed it.

THE TEMPERANCE BUSH MEETING at Purcellville, was commenced on Tuesday, and will close to-day, Thursday. The attendance, we understand, has been quite large, and the speaking excellent. The weather has been good, a trifle too warm, perhaps, but otherwise everything seems to have conspired to render the occasion pleasant, and we hope beneficial to the cause.

8/18/82 Telephone

On Aug 2nd Barnum's Show exhibited in Troy, and after the performance the animals were driven to take cars on Green Island, and while attempting to cross a bridge the main body went all right but four elephants turned back, escaped from the attendants and started down the street. Three were speedily brought back, but the fourth, a large male elephant, refused to be "coaxed" and went on a little bender, injuring ten persons, two of them fatally and destroying a large amount of property, including a number of tomb-stones. We are told that the genial Mr. Hutchinson was around early next morning and settled all damages, to the tune of $4,000.

8/24/82 Mirror

NEW CISTERN.—For once our city fathers have taken "time by the fore top," and anticipating what some day might happen, have prepared for it by digging another large cistern on the court-house square, just below the Reamer House. This is just in the heart of the town and the buildings on the opposite side of the street are all built adjoining one another, some of them being old and inflamable, so that in the event of a fire, the old cistern, which is a small one, would be totally insufficient for the needs of the Fire Department; and almost certainly would the whole row be doomed. The construction of this new cistern will go far to make this result less liable, and shows a wisdom and foresight quite commendable in the said c. f's.

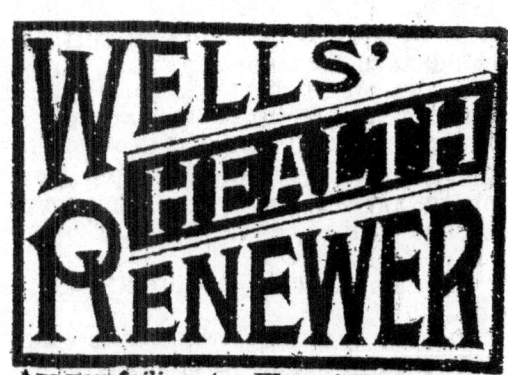

Are you failing, try WELLS' HEALTH RENEWER, a pure, clean, wholesome TONIC, For Brain, Nerves, Stomach, Liver, Kidneys, Lungs. An Unequaled Invigorant.

FOUTZ'S HORSE AND CATTLE POWDERS

No HORSE will die of COLIC, BOTS or LUNG FEVER, if Foutz's Powders are used in time.
Foutz's Powders will cure and prevent HOG CHOLERA.
Foutz's Powders will prevent GAPES IN FOWLS.
Foutz's Powders will increase the quantity of milk and cream twenty per cent., and make the butter firm and sweet.
Foutz's Powders will cure or prevent almost EVERY DISEASE to which Horses and Cattle are subject.
FOUTZ'S POWDERS WILL GIVE SATISFACTION.
Sold everywhere.

DAVID E. FOUTZ, Proprietor,
BALTIMORE, MD.

7/29/82 Washingtonian

[From the New York Sun.]

Another Duel in Virginia.

CHRISTIANSBURG, Va., July 25.—A duel was fought half a mile from here this morning at sunrise between Capt. John S. Wise, Mahone's candidate for Congressmen at Large and John S. Crockett, Commonwealth's Attorney for Wythe county. Both parties, accompanied by their seconds, reached here early this morning and at once made preparations to fight. Mr. R. Crockett of Wythe was Crockett's second, and G. Ward, editor of the Abingdon *Virginian*, acted for Wise. The parties met in an open field, half a mile from here, and were on the ground and ready for the hostile encounter before the village people were astir. They were accompanied by a surgeon.

Soon after leaving the train, both the principals and their seconds went at once to the field, where, without any useless talking and with few preliminaries, the preparations were made for the duel. This hurrying up of matters was necessary because a difficulty between Messrs Wise and Crockett has been apprehended for some days past, and the fact of the two men being together would have been sufficient to cause their arrest. In five minutes after reaching the ground, the principals were told to take their positions. The distance agreed upon was ten paces. The weapons used were revolvers of the regulation pattern.

"Gentlemen, are you ready?" asked the seconds.

Both combatants bowed in the affirmative.

"Fire—one—two—three."

At the last word, 'Three,' both pistols went off almost simultaneously, so much so that it was at first thought that only one weapon had been discharged. The fire was without effect. The men were about to take their positions, but as Crockett was raising his pistol it went off accidentally. The men were again placed in position, and at the command each raised his weapon and pulled the trigger. This time Wise's pistol failed to go off, but Crockett's was discharged without effect. Then Crockett said he was satisfied, and this ended the duel. The parties at once scattered. Crockett and his second took the train for home, and Wise's seconds also left. Capt. Wise came here and made a political speech to a large crowd.

The duel was another in that series of political affairs of honor which have been going on since State politics have been raging so hotly in Virginia. None have resulted fatally as yet, and it is a remarkable fact that during the period of four years in which duels have at different times been fought, the only one with fatal effect was that in which a lady was concerned—the Garland-Addison duel last week.

The difficulty which led to the Wise-Crockett duel began on the 17th of this month. It seems that when Wise was in Wytheville a few weeks ago, a conversation took place between him and Mr. Crockett, in which the latter alleged that Wise made use of the expression: "There is no honor in politics."—This Crockett had repeated as coming from Wise, and this fact had been reported to the latter. Meeting Mr. Crockett in the evening on the hotel porch at Marion, Wise called him aside and interrogated him about it.—Crockett acknowledged that he had made the statement and that it was true. Wise denounced it as false and struck at Crockett. Before the latter had time to resent the blow his arm was caught by Marshal Watts, who was standing close by, and then a policeman appeared on the scene and commanded the peace. Perhaps the difficulty might have ended here, but the next day the Richmond *Whig*, Mahone's organ, printed a telegram, in in which was the following:

A short time after Capt. Wise concluded his speech he met a Funder who had slandered him recently. He asked him if he had made certain statements, and the gentleman admitted that he had. Capt. Wise punished him severely on the spot.

When Crockett heard this and other reports to the effect that he had been beaten by Wise he and his friends regarded such assertions as imputations upon his courage. This feeling was aggravated when the Richmond *Whig* came out with a second article, which said:

The affair was much talked about yesterday, and the question was repeatedly asked, "What was the name of the man whom Capt. Wise drubbed so roughly?" A private telegram received here said it was John S. Crockett, Commonwealth's Attorney for Wythe county, and that Capt. Wise gave him three Sullivanian licks direct from the shoulder, and came out of the difficulty without a scratch.

Mr. Crockett at once prepared a card severely denouncing Wise and calling him a liar and scoundrel, but it was not published. When Wise left the city a few days ago and came to this section of the State, Mr. Crockett at once opened hostile correspondence with him, winding up by challenging Wise to a duel. The challenge was promptly accepted.

Later advices say that when Wise's pistol missed at the second fire Crockett asked that Wise be allowed another chance, when Crockett's second said that he was satisfied, and under the ruling in the code Crockett was

August, 1882

compelled to submit. The parties left the field with the question still unsettled. In Wise's party it is understood there were J. M. Browning, the Governor's private secretary; R. F. Walker, Superintendent of Public Printing; P. H. McCaul, member of the House of Delegates, and Asa Rogers, Railroad Commissioner, all Mahone's officials.

This is the first duel which has been fought here since the anti-dueling law was passed, and under its stringent provisions no person can hold office in the State who has fought a duel.

The grand jury on Wednesday indicted Capt. John S. Wise and Mr. John S. Crockett as principals in the duel. Indictments were also found against G. W. Ward and J. Stewart Crockett, cousin of John S. Crockett, as seconds, and Dr. Moore as surgeon. The other surgeon, being from Richmond and name not known, escaped indictment.

8/18/82 Telephone

The transformation which has lately taken place in the Bourbon press is amusing and ridiculous. A short time since they were all abusing Massey, now they are embracing him. Here are some quotations from the Richmond *State* before this change of heart took place.

"The creature Massey"—"this traducer of honest men"—"a disfrocked pulpiteer." "This vile Massey"—brutal and villainous"—"this dog"—"this mangy cur"—"this wretched liar"—"this creature who has forgotten every rule of right"—"the spawn of corruption"—a brute, a liar and a villain"—"the moral leper"—"upon whose forehead we have forever put a brand"—"this Reverend hypocrite"—"unmasked canting creature," &c.

FOR SALE IN HAMILTON by Baker & Co.
LINCOLN. P. JANNEY.

8/18/82 Telephone

TABLE ETIQUETTE

It is with a view of elevating the popular taste and etherealizing, so to speak, the manners and customs of our readers, that we give below a few hints upon table etiquette:

Macaroni should be cut into short pieces and eaten with an even, graceful motion, not absorbed by the yard.

Oranges are held on a fork while being peeled, and the facetious style of squirting the juice into the eye of your host is *au revoir*.

Stones in cherries and other fruit should not be placed on the table-cloth, but slid quietly and unostentatiously into the pocket of your neighbor, or noiselessly tossed under the table.

If by mistake you drink out of your finger-bowl, laugh heartily and make some facetious remark, which will change the course of conversation and renew the friendly feeling among the members of the party.

In drinking wine, when you get to the bottom of your glass do not throw your head back and draw your breath like the exhaust of a bath tub in order to get the last drop, as it engenders a feeling of the most depressing melancholy among the guests.

If you cannot accept an invitation to supper, do not write your regrets on the back of a pool check with a blue lead pencil. This is not regarded as "ricochet." A simple note to your host, informing him that your washerwoman refuses to relent, is sufficient.

On seating yourself at the table, draw off your gloves and put them in your lap under your napkin. Do not put them in the gravy, as it would spoil the gloves and cast a gloom over the gravy. If you have just cleaned your gloves with benzine, you must leave them out in the front yard.—*Cincinnati Fair Journal.*

THE COW-BOY.

[Wichita (Kan.) Cor. Chicago Tribune.]

The cow-boy of the great West is a distinct character and type of frontiersman, produced by the Texas cattle trade which began in Kansas soon after the war, with headquarters at Abilene, Kan. The trade originated from the necessity of having a good shipping point for cattle near the Missouri river, and at the same time contiguous to unlimited range, and, although since that time, as railways have been built, the cattle trade has shifted over the State, the cowboy, while increasing in numbers, has lost none of that distinctive character and method which has made his name a terror upon the frontier and linked him inseparably with all new cattle towns in the West. His reckless daring and deviltry have marked out for him a distinct and startling page in the history of the border. After a new town has got a good fair start and begins the boom, it only needs a cowboy raid to open a first-class and well stocked graveyard. The cowboy has no hopes of heaven or fear of hell.

Yet the real employment of the cowboy is innocent enough, and consists of riding a small, wiry mustang of bucking proclivities, and following an immense herd of cattle over an unlimited range, his special duties being to see that none of the cattle stray away, and to steal any stray animals which may be unbranded and brand them with his employer's name. When sober he naturally shuns civilization. He pursues his herds upon the plains of Western Kansas, among the gentle slopes of the Cherokee country, in the Indian Territory, along the lonesome deserts of the Panhandle, amid the foothills of Colorado, and in the wilds of New Mexico and Arizona, inured to the saddle, exposed to all kinds of weather, and all sorts of people, from the Greaser to the Apache. To all appearances the cowboy is "the mildest-mannered man that ever scuttled ship or cut a throat." But when their pay-day comes, and they reach the nearest town and imbibe some of their "liquid crime," then stand from under, for then they fight, gamble and shoot at friend or foe.

The typical cowboy wears a white hat with a gilt cord and tassel, high top-boots, leather pants, a woolen shirt, a coat and no vest. On his heels he wears a pair of jingling Mexican spurs as large around as a teacup. When he feels well (and he always does when full of what he calls "Kansas sheep-dip"), the average cowboy is a bad man to handle. Armed to the teeth, well mounted, and full of their favorite beverage, the cowboys will dash through the principal streets of a town, yelling like Comanches. This they call "cleaning out a town." After repeating this operation several times, and before the stampeded recover to repel the attack, they dash away and are seldom, if ever, captured. All frontier towns that have ever had any Texas cattle trade have had this same experience. In 1874 the cowboys in large numbers attempted to raid Wichita, and were only driven off by a very determined resistance on the part of our shotgun brigade. For a long time the cowboys held possession of the town of Abilene, Kas., until Wild Bill, the Indian fighter and scout, became Marshal of the town. Wild Bill killed six of the most desperate cowboys of Abilene in a single night. Thereafter he was respected and feared by the cowboy element. Wild Bill was at last murdered by a cowboy, who got the drop on him, and died as he had lived, "with his boots on."

November 1882

10/13/82 Telephone

Guilford whiskey nearly scored two more victims on Wednesday of last week. Samuel Jinkins, commonly known as "Long Sam" spent the day in Guilford, having a good time, I suppose he called it. He had with him a boy, eight or nine years old, who was obliged to sit on the wagon and hold the horses all day. After the poison had taken effect, so that it was unsafe for any person to pass by him, and those who had got his money had locked the door in his face, he finally started for home—about 5 P.M. He was found about an hour afterwards, fearfully mangled, but still living, and will probably recover. The boy was run over by the wagon, which was partially loaded with lumber. His injuries are internal and his recovery is doubtful.

Whiskey did it and nobody is responsible. Of course, gentlemen engaged in the lawful, honorable and respectful business of selling Hell fire cannot be expected to look after the consequences.

(Guilford is now Sterling.)

—"Westward the tide of rumfire takes its way."—Day after day men pass through our town so full of Leesburg grog that they bow to everybody on the street.

11/25/82 Washingtonian

A young man in a train was making fun of a lady's hat to an elderly gentleman in the seat with him. "Yes," said his seat mate, "that's my wife, and I told her if she wore that bonnet that some fool would make fun of it."

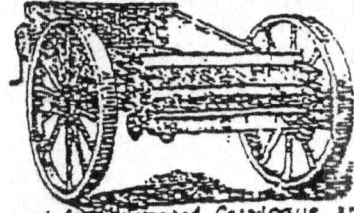

KEMP'S MANURE SPREADER, PULVERIZER and CART COMBINED. Greatest Agricultural invention of the age. Saves 100 per cent. of labor, and doubles the value of the manure. Spreads evenly all kinds of manure broadcast or in drill, in one-tenth the time required by hand. Send for Illustrated Catalogue and full particulars to KEMP & BURPEE MFG CO., Syracuse, Onondaga Co., N.Y.

The doctor and the letter-carrier are not talking about a case of serious illness. They have simply suspended work to discuss the merits of their shoes. The letter-carrier says the James Means $3 Shoe is the best in the world. The doctor denies it, and says that the James Means $4 Shoe is better. Considering the needs of each, they are both right.

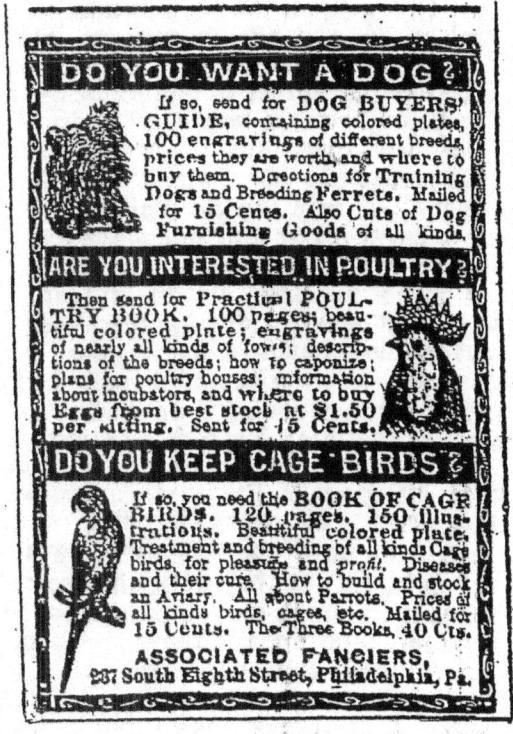

DO YOU WANT A DOG? If so, send for DOG BUYERS' GUIDE, containing colored plates, 100 engravings of different breeds, prices they are worth, and where to buy them. Directions for Training Dogs and Breeding Ferrets. Mailed for 15 Cents. Also Cuts of Dog Furnishing Goods of all kinds.

ARE YOU INTERESTED IN POULTRY? Then send for Practical POULTRY BOOK. 100 pages; beautiful colored plate; engravings of nearly all kinds of fowl; descriptions of the breeds; how to caponize; plans for poultry houses; information about incubators, and where to buy Eggs from best stock at $1.50 per sitting. Sent for 15 Cents.

DO YOU KEEP CAGE BIRDS? If so, you need the BOOK OF CAGE BIRDS. 120 pages, 150 illustrations. Beautiful colored plate. Treatment and breeding of all kinds Cage birds, for pleasure and profit. Diseases and their cure. How to build and stock an Aviary. All about Parrots. Prices of all kinds birds, cages, etc. Mailed for 15 Cents. The Three Books, 40 Cts.

ASSOCIATED FANCIERS, 237 South Eighth Street, Philadelphia, Pa.

November. 1882

11/23/82 Mirror

John L. Sullivan, the celebrated pugilist, and who is endeavoring to effect a ring meeting with Tom Allen, the English bully, in an interview with a STAR reporter the other day, gave the following account of how a prize fighter trains. He said—

"You want to know how a prize-fighter trains," said Sullivan, puffing away on a cigar which he held in his mouth at the angle approved by the "b'hoys." "Well, first he physics himself thoroughly; some use a black draught, and some use castor oil. I take a black draught. Then the man starts in working. He gets up at 7 o'clock in the morning and walks a mile leisurely. He eats breakfast at 8 o'clock—mutton chops or beefsteak, two cups of tea and stale bread, and anything salty. About half past nine he starts out on a twelve mile walk six out and six back. The last mile or mile and a half, he runs in, in pretty fast time. There's a man ready when he comes in to rub him down, and he is rubbed thoroughly until he is dry. He is rubbed again and again and then lies down with two quilts upon him.— When the perspiration comes, he is rubbed down vigorously again. Afterwards he stands in a shower and a pailful of salt water is thrown over him. If he is not training near sea water a half bag of common salt is dissolved in common water and that is used.— This hardens the man's skin and makes him. Every time the man comes in he is rubbed down. This gets all the flesh of him, so if he is struck in the eye he doesn't get bruised or cut. It is rubbed down to the bone. Well, he has his dinner at one o'clock—there are five hours between meals. For dinner he has roast beef, roast mutton or broiled mutton, one potato and no other vegetable except celery. A man can eat plenty of celery. I used to eat three or four bunches a day. It is good for wind and good for the nerves. He used a bottle of Bass' ale at dinner. He walks around leisurely during the afternoon. He must sit down as little as possible. When he feels best, later in the afternoon, he runs a hundred yards probably four or five times. When I was training I ran a hundred yards in 11 seconds with my clothing on, and I weighed 209 pounds then. A man has to do that sort of work for five weeks and keep it up until the last three days before the fight. Then they give him castor oil and about that much gin, (measuring off a couple of joints on his forefinger) in a glass. The reason they give the castor oil in the gin, is that men can't take castor oil without vomiting. Then it makes them feel cool and refreshed. Then, until the day of the fight, he eats gradually, and just enough to satisfy his appetite. A man don't fill himself up — He doesn't do any hard work at all during these three days. He does nothing but rest. Now he keeps at this course of training every day for five weeks. He is not allowed to drink anything, not even water, except the ale at dinner. He gets parched and dry, and cannot eat on account of it."

11/2/82 Mirror

THEY ARE STRANGERS NOW.— A Middletown young lady never tires of relating an amusing occurrence of one sleighing season last winter. She was enjoying a ride in company with two Hartford gentlemen, and she was driving. One of the gentlemen slyly inserted a hand in her muff and lovingly pressed her disengaged hand. She blushed and withdrew it just as the gentleman on the other side slipped his hand in the muff. She knew by the action of her adorers that the hand pressures were frequent and loving within the silk lining of the muff for first one face and then the other would bob forward to catch a look at the sweet face and eye which prompted, as they supposed the tender pressure of the hand. The by play lasted until the young lady quietly remarked, "If you gentlemen are through with my muff I will trouble you for it now, as my hands are getting cold."— And the gentlemen who had been comfortably warm up to this time suddenly felt an Arctic chill creeping up their spinal columns, and the mercury of their feelings dropped to 180 degrees below zero. The two gentlemen are strangers now.

AGENTS WANTED for the LIVES and ADVENTURES of the OUTLAWS, **FRANK & JESSE JAMES.** Complete Life of these Bold Highwaymen. Also of the Younger Brothers and other bold outlaws Elegantly Illustrated. Over 500 Pages. Beware of inferior editions.— COMPLETE OUTFIT BY MAIL, FORTY CENTS. TERMS LIBERAL.
FORSHEE & McMAKIN, 186 West 5th St., Cincinnati, O.

UP THE WASHINGTON MONUMENT.

A Fearful Ascent of Nearly 400 Feet Rewarded by a Magnificent View.

Washington Letter to the New York Sun.

If one feels a desire to sup full on horrors in Washington, there is no way in which success is so certain and so speedy as an ascent of the 275 feet of the unfinished Washington Monument. Although no accident of any kind whatever has happened since the work was begun, owing to the admirable precautions that have been observed the mere contemplation of the dangers to be avoided would give General Washington, if he were alive, the cold creeps. It must be remembered that the monument is already among the highest structures in the world, while the transportation of the gigantic blocks of stone to the top is something which has no parallel in the country and has seldom been equaled anywhere. Whether the ascent is calculated to inspire fear or not may be imagined from the reply made by one of the highest officials in Washington to the inquiry: "Were you not just a little frightened going up?"— "Frightened! I was perfectly terrified!" was the hearty response given with all the force of emphasis.

The ascent is made by the elevator which runs through the middle of the great obelisk. This elevator is a mere open platform, which does not deserve the name of the alleviator, as Mrs. General Giffory puts it; it is rather a terrifier. Every time it goes up it carries from five to ten tons of stone, and the only way for visitors to get to the top is to huddle around the immense mass of stone on the diabolical looking machine. The platform begins to move slowly and laboriously upward, grinding and creaking at every inch from the enormous weight it lifts. In half a minute the light of day totally disappears, and at that moment the horrors of the position suddenly swoops down upon one. To be dangling hundreds of feet above a chasm with only a rope between a fall to the bottom with 10,000 pounds of stone is enough to equal any imagination. Although the darkness is blackness inconceivable and the intense silence broken only by the groaning of the great mass feeling its way painfully upward, yet the frightful abyss appears to become of itself both audible and visible. The last 150 feet of balancing between heaven and earth is like hanging between life and death. Even the elevator man gives up his heroic efforts to keep up the courage of the party.

At length light from the top begins to appear, and in a minute or two a pallid party of pleasure-seekers step out on the platform at the top nearly three hundred feet in the air. There is an enormous iron structure running through the middle of the obelisk and around this the stone is blocked. Six feet are added every week in three tiers of two foot blocks. The structure is then six feet above the temporary platform, which is thereupon raised, and the work of bringing it six feet above the level is recommenced.

A net work of rope is securely fixed around the top of the shaft, extending several feet off, to catch any unfortunate man who might drop over—the workmen are compelled to be on the very edge in order to complete the outer layer of stone. A young lady not long since, in a spirit of bravado, threw herself into this life saving net. A weak spot in the rope would have sent her nearly four hundred feet to the earth. A contrivance like the rigging of a ship's is on the top of the shaft and the wind howls through it with enormous force. When a tier or two of stone is laid the workmen are protected in a measure from the violence of the wind, but they acknowledged that when they were working on the level it is something terrific.

If anything could repay one for the horrors of the ascent it would be the view after reaching the top. Even the most hardened sightseer must be enthusiastic at the great panorama spread out before him. The vast Treasury building looks like a Lilliputian house. The plan of Washington becomes as well defined as a checker-board. The full grandeur of the Capital is then for the first time realized.

When it is remembered that the Capitol is almost the identical dimensions of the great pyramid and of St. Peter's, being perhaps a few feet longer than either, it may seem that it has nothing to lose by looking at it from any point of elevation. Everything else grows minute from the top of the monument except the white splendor of the Capitol. It seems to be on a mountain instead of a hill, and amid the diminishing of every other object the great white dome stands grandly out, so high that it looked as though poised in air.

A look at the elevator and a proposition to descend is enough to kill any enthusiasm however. But it is by comparison with the ascent simply delightful. There is no mountain of stone to make one fancy how it would feel to go to the bottom of the hideous hole with it. To the simultaneous and earnest assurance made to the elevator man that nobody in the party would ever do so any more, he sardonically replied: "All of 'em says that!"

December, 1882

12/22/82 Telephone

SUNDAY LAWS.

As there has been much comment and discussion of the new penal code of New York City, we give the following editorial on that subject, taken from *The Independent*, which must be admitted as excellent authority!—ED.

The Penal Code of this state, that professes in one of its chapters to embody all the unrepealed legislation of the state in regard to the observance of the Sabbath, went into operation on the first day of this month. This Code makes "the first day of the week" to consist of "all the time from midnight to midnight" and defines any violation thereof to be "Sabbath breaking." The acts forbidden on this day, "except in a work of necessity or charity," are as follows: 1. All manner of servile labor, with the exception stated. 2. All shooting, hunting, fishing, playing, horse-racing, gaming, or other public sports, exercises, pastimes, or shows, and all noise disturbing the peace of the day. 3. All trades, manufactures, and mechanical employments. 4. All manner of public selling or offering for sale publicly of any commodities, except that meats, milk, and fish may be sold at any time before nine o'clock in the morning and except that food may be sold to be eaten upon the premises where sold, and dings, medicines, and surgical appliances may be sold at any time of the day. 5. All service of legal process of any kind whatever, except in cases of the breach of the peace, or apprehended breach of the peace, or when sued out for the apprehension of a person charged with crime, or except where such service is specially authorized by statute.

The penalty for a violation of the law in respect to any one of these specifications is a fine of not less than one dollar and not more than ten dollars, or imprisonment in a county jail not exceeding five days, or both.

12/29/82 Telephone

ANTHONY COMSTOCK has discovered that there are 550 places in New York where one can play policy, and it makes him faint to think of attacking such a combination.

(Comstock, the legendary bane of all civil libertarians created the New York Society for the Supression of Vice. His heavy-handed policing of public morals made him many enemies.)

Wanted,

A FRESH MILCH COW. Any one having such a Cow for sale will inquire at this OFFICE.

Cattle Wanted
TO WINTER.

I AM PREPARED to WINTER FIFTY HEAD of CATTLE on Fodder and Straw—best quality.
CHARLES FLETCHER,
on the Wildman Farm, near Leesburg.

Co-Partnership
—IN THE—
Butchering Business
IN LEESBURG.

J. ARCHY HAMMERLY and J. A. LOVELESS, on the 1st day of January, 1883, formed a Co-partnership, under the style of HAMMERLY & LOVELESS, to conduct the

Butchering Business

in Leesburg. They will keep constantly on sale, at their establishment on King street, the BEST MEATS the county can afford, such as BEEF, MUTTON, VEAL, PORK, &c. and ask a share of the public patronage.
HAMMERLY & LOVELESS
Leesburg, Va.

December, 1882

11/16/82 Mirror

A gentleman from Woodstock Va., to-day gives a lively description of a fisticuff and rough-roll-and-tumble fight that took place there the day before the election between Mr. Ned Dandridge, of Winchester, and United States Senator elect Mr. Riddleberger, in which the latter was considerably worsted.—

12/7/82 Mirror

A Duel Between Page McCarty and Riddleberger Probable

A Richmond dispatch, dated Nov. 30th, was published in the Baltimore papers last week, which states that—

"Some weeks since Captain Page McCarty, in his Washington letter to the Richmond *State*, mentioned that Senator Riddleberger had been whipped by Captain Dandridge, of Winchester on the occasion of public speaking. A few days since a Shenandoah weekly, of which Riddleberger is understood to be the owner and editor, commicated editorially upon the letters in the *State* signed "M," and said they were written by Captain McCarty. It averred that the statement therein, to the effect that Dandridge had whipped Riddleberger, was untrue, and proceeded to allude to Captain McCarty as a man of duelling notoriety, specifying his connection with the lamented McCarty Mordecai duel of some years ago, in which Captain McCarty was desperately wounded and his antagonist killed. The *State's* Washington letter, published Thursday evening, written by Captain McCarty, says:

Riddleberger, in imitation of his master, has an organ, in which the alleged gamecock advertises himself and abuses his enemies, and he has been lately denying that Capt. Dandridge whipped him at Winchester. It was not expected that after being denounced as a poltroon and beaten to emphasize the epithet, that Mr. Riddleberger could give a purely disinterested account of the affair. It was natural that he should be prejudiced and his moral and intellectual optic was in as bad a condition as his physical eye, when he proceeded in the "organ" to deny the statements in the newspapers which represented him by his accepted synonyms.

"Mr Riddleberger seems to be unaware of the fact that honorable men do not answer insults by abuse, and that he, after having boasted of the challenges he has sent, has merely imitated the school-boys who say "you are another" when they quarrel over marbles. His reference to a duel is unfortunate, for it recalls his own brilliant performance in challenging a gentleman and taking advantage of an accident to run from the satisfaction he had demanded and made such a ridiculous display of his vaunted chivalry that Bob Acres was eclipsed and a new exemplar of braggart and poltroon established in the person of Capt. Harry Riddleberger, the alleged gamecock of the Shenandoah. When by whiskey and persuasion he was gotten to another field of gore, his behavior excited the pity of his adversary, and the statement of his ludicrous bearing, made by me in the editorial of a Washington paper, passed without contradiction or denial.

Mr. Riddleberger's imitation of Gen. Mahone lacks two important features which practice cannot possibly supply. Gen. Mahone was a brave soldier and is a man of brains. His little imitator and coat tail attachment has only the slouch hat." M

Riddleberger chanced to be in Richmond when the above letter appeared, and Capt. McCarty was also understood to be in the neighborhood, for the purpose, it was later red, of giving Riddleberger an opportunity to communicate with him if he desired to do so.

Mr Riddleberger, a year ago, fought a bloodless duel with Congressman George D Wise, and had accepted a challenge to fight R F. Beorne editor of the *State*, on the same day; but, owing to an accident by which the caps were forgotten, the latter duel did not take place, Mr. Riddleberger declining to wait until they could be procured. It is to these duels that Capt. McCarty refers in his letter. Serious trouble is anticipated.

An intimte friend of Mr. Riddleberger says that he will fight no more duels not only on account of the considerations which every man should have for his family and his home, but also because he is convinced that this method of resort settles nothing that may be at issue.

(Virginia, like most of the solid south, voted democratic. At this time, through a complicated set of circumstances, there were two Republican senators. General Mahone from the Petersburg area was known as an arrogant political boss, but capable. Riddleburger from the valley was the more colorful. At one time, he was tossed in jail for disruptive behavior in the court room. He was sprung by a mob of his loyal followers. Another time he was escorted out of the U.S. Senate chamber by the Sergeant of Arms. Liquor probably played a part in all of this.)

December, 1882

12/21/82 Mirror

How It Feels to Wear a Coat of Tar and Feathers Next to the Skin.

From the Virginia City Chronicle.

"Most people," said a prominent Renoite to a CHRONICLE reporter to-day, "don't know what a terrible punishment tarring and feathering really is. They suppose that it is nothing worse than a badge of infamy, rather uncomfortable, perhaps, but not painful unless the tar gets into the eyes. This is a great mistake. I helped to daub Jones. He was a disgrace to humanity and he deserved what he got. But I had no idea until I saw that fellow plastered what a tough deal the process is We painted him all over pretty thick with a broom and some enthusiastic vigilante poured a few gallons of tar on his head. Then the feathers, taken from a big pillow, were dusted on him, and he stood out, white and fluffy, in the starlight, like some huge and grotesque looking bird. He had to put his clothes on over the whole mess, and then he was ridden on a rail for fifty yards or so, and we put him on board the West-bound train at midnight, with instructions not to come back on pain of being hanged.

"I saw him on the train. He was sitting with his head on his arms on the back of the seat in front of him. The tar was so thick on his head that it covered the hair out of sight, and his poll shone in the light of the car lamps like a black rubber ball just nipped in the water. The poor fellow was groaning, and I couldn't help feeling mean at having taken a hand in the job. You see the body is covered with short hair, and when the tar hardens a little the slightest movement causes acute pain, as if one's beard were being pulled out with pincers, hair by hair.— Then there is the stoppage of all perspiration, which would soon kill a man if he didn't make lively time in getting scrubbed.

"Besides, the smell of the tar turns the stomach, and about half an hour after a man has been coated he must feel very sorry he wasn't hanged. Then comes the scrubbing with oil. It took two Chinamen and a darkey three days in Truckee to reduce Jones to a mild brown. The rubbing makes the skin tender, and the body must be sore as a boil for weeks."

12/1/82 Telephone

DROP THAT HAT.

We were running through South Carolina when a great big giant of a fellow with a terrible eye and a voice like a fog-horn boarded the train at a small station. I think most of the passengers sized him up as a chap whom it would be dangerous to argue with, but the giant wasn't satisfied with that. He blustered at the conductor, growled at the brakeman, and looked around as if seeking some one to pick a fuss with. Every one answered him civilly, and he had two or three seats to himself, but the man who wants a row can generally find some pretext. About the centre of the car a pale-looking chap, about twenty-five years old, occupied a seat, and was reading a newspaper. After a time the giant rubbed along to where the young man sat and growled out:

"Stranger, what may be the first cost of such a hat as yours?"

The young man looked up with a flash in his big blue eyes, and then turned to his paper without replying.

"Hi! Did you hear me?" roared the other, as he leaned over the seat and lifted the hat off the young man's head.

Quicker than one could count six a shining revolver came from you couldn't tell where, lifed itself on a level with the big man's eye, and the white fingers clutching the butt never trembled a hair's breadth as a quiet voice uttered the words:

"Drop that hat!"

The hat fell from the giant's grasp, and the quiet voice exclaimed:

"Now you sit down, or I'll kill you!"

The muzzle of the weapon was not six inches from the man's eye, and I saw him turn from red to white in ten seconds. He backed away at the command, sat down in a seat opposite, and never stood up or spoke another word during the ride of twenty miles. He had a "navy" under his coat, but something in that quiet voice and blue eye warned him that the move of a finger on his part would crash a bullet into his head.—

December, 1882

THE HOLIDAYS AT Bassell's!

Extraordinary Additions being made to Stock

Novelties in Every Department!

NEW DRESS GOODS
NEW CLOTHS AND CASSIMERES,
NEW NOTIONS,
NEW Boots & Shoes,

NEW Hats and Caps.
New ULSTERS,
New Cloaks,
New Shawls,
NEW FURS,
&c., Etc.

FANCY GOODS! FANCY GOODS!
IN LARGE AND SPLENDID VARIETY.

In Casting About for Proper and Suitable

Xmas Presents,

LET THE PUBLIC REMEMBER THAT SOMETHING USEFUL IS ALWAYS THE MORE ACCEPTABLE. SOMETHING WHICH WILL CONTRIBUTE TO PERSONAL COMFORT—SOMETHING WE MAY ENJOYINGLY USE OR WEAR FROM DAY TO DAY. For illustration:—A *HANDSOME SUIT*, to order, SELECTED FROM OUR BEAUTIFUL

Foreign and Domestic Cloths,

CUT BY THE TASTEFUL *F. C. GRAHAM*, AND MANUFACTURED BY OUR CORPS OF SKILLED AND COMPETENT WORKMEN—ALWAYS A PERFECT FIT - and *always to be appreciated*

A Dress, A Cloak, A Shawl, An Ulster,
A Hat, A Fur Cap, A Pair of Hand-Made Shoes, (Ladies or Gents),
A Scarf, A Silk Handkerchief, a pair of Gloves,
A pair of Slippers, a ——— thousand articles that we have in

Great Profusion at *PRICES* always Attractive to the *Purchaser*.

We Are Never Undersold!

This business motto is nailed at our mast-head.

THE TELEPHONE.

FRIDAY .... DEC. 22D.

CHRISTMAS GREETING!

—Merry Christmas!

—A newspaper can't be run on promises.—Pay up.

—The comet is still visible between midnight and dawn.

—Wiley's Bakery is turning out lots of toothsome gooddies.

—The Potomac is frozen over. White's Ferry is running through a channel cut in the ice.

—The Supt. of the Penitentiary informs our Sheriff that the report about Edward Green having escaped from that institution is incorrect.

—Ice gathering has been a prominent part of this week's work in this vicinity. The quality has been good —from four to six inches thick, and a great deal has been housed.

—Apples are scarce and high in the Washington Market. A good article sells for $4 per barrel

January, 1883

1/5/83 Telephone

The Ford brothers, who killed Jesse James, together with a fat woman and one or two other monstrosities, are displaying themselves in a ten cent show. While exhibiting in Boston, recently, the bandit brothers became exasperated at some one in the audience and drew their large revolvers, which they carried in their belts, causing a general stampede.

It is a disgrace to our Country and a shame to our civilization that people will give ten cents to see such characters. The death of Jesse James was a good riddance, but the man who would partake of Jesse's hospitality and then at an unguarded moment shoot him in the back, deserves no praise nor patronage.

1/12/83 Telephone

The once famous William and Mary College has run its race, and now stands silent and lonely, food for worms and rust. There was too much of royalty about its name and, doubtless, too much of Bourbonism about its management.

(My son, who graduated from there, insists it eventually rebounded.)

GOODS
At J. R. BEUCHLER'S
BAKERY AND CONFECTIONERY,
LEESBURG, VA.

I AM JUST RECEIVING a large supply of Fresh Goods for the Holidays, such as Currants, Raisins, Citron, Oranges, Lemons, runes, Bananas, Figs, Canned Fruits and Vegetables, Pickles, and a Variety of Nuts.

Plain & French Candies,

TAFFIES, and a Full Assortment of SMALL CAKES and CRACKERS, PIES, BREAD, and FISHER'S MINCE MEAT—the best in the market—and a large supply of POUND AND FRUIT CAKE, nicely Iced—all of which will be sold at the very lowest prices.

☞ CAKES NICELY ICED AND ORNAMENTED, for Weddings, Parties, &c., on short notice.

J. R. BEUCHLER,
Leesburg, Va.

1/4/83 Mirror

SENATOR JONES AT POKER.

BEATEN BY WASHINGTON SHARPS, HE SHREWDLY TAKES REVENGE.

[From the Stockton Mail.]

George L. Waters, the colored janitor of the City Hall, related an incident to a Mail reporter concerning a big poker game in which Senator John P. Jones of Nevada was a player. Waters had been in the employ of certain Congressmen around the Capitol at Washington for many years, and his statement may be accepted as true. It was several years ago before the millionaire had become thoroughly posted in the ways of Washington society. Almost before he had thoroughly warmed his seat in the Senate, he was introduced into the District Club, of which Boss Shepherd was a prominent member. Poker at that time was a prominent recreation of the club, and Jones was induced to take a hand. Although a good poker-player, he retired from the game a loser to the amount of $70,000.

The Senator, having a few silver mines at his back for pocket money, was game and did not allow the least expression of chagrin or distrust to escape him. The next morning he telegraphed to one of the most expert card sharps in Virginia city. Eight days afterward the gambler arrived in Washington, dressed in a very expensive suit of clothes and sporting a small fortune in the way of diamonds. Jones introduced him to the members of the club as a mining millionaire from Nevada, and the Star Route frauds and Navy yard thieves immediately made arrangements to pluck him. He accepted an invitation to play. The stakes ran high, and the spurious millionaire was well supplied with Jones' money. At the end of the tournament the stranger rose from the table the winner of $100,000 of the money of the club. It was a severe blow to the ringsters, but they made the people of the United States pay it back to them indirectly and in short order. Jones divided the swag with his friends and never set foot in the club room again. It was not long after before the ringsters found out that they had been beaten at their own game, but they were not in a condition to make any fuss about it.

One must remember that a dollar then was worth $20 in today's money.

BREAKING UP A SCHOOL.

It was given out in church Sunday that school would open on Monday morning. After the evening service the boys got together and talked it over, and decided to give the new teacher just a week. It had been thawing for a day or two, and the boys were tired of skating, so they thought they could afford to spend a week educating themselves in how to break up a school. On that evening we were duly elected a member of the class of hard citizens, and we were to open the ball, and do something bad, get the teacher to lick us, and then the boys were to jump in and help. Monday morning the school commenced, and the teacher proved to be a sickly, slim sort of a fellow, a timid, nervous man, with a hand and face like a girl. Every time he looked at one of us boys there seemed to be an expression on his face as though he would say, "I hope you will be good." When he had anything to say to the scholars he said "please" and gave other evidences of being pretty soft, we all thought. That morning the weather changed, and it froze hard, and at recess the boys got together and said we would wind up the school before noon and go out on the ice. It was our turn to be bad and it commenced right off. The big boys had to carry in the wood and lay it down quietly by the stove. We took in an armful and dropped it on the floor so that it shook the building and loosened the stovepipe. The pipe came out of the chimney and filled the room with smoke, but it was put back, and the slim teacher reprimanded us, and said that it must not occur again. We just ached to go after some more wood, but there was no opportunity. Pretty soon the teacher said we might go and get a pail of water, and while at the well we decided to stumble on entering the school room, and spill the water all over the floor and thus give the sickly looking teacher a chance to show what he was made of. The teacher was near the stove, and we stumbled, and the water went all over everything, wetting his boots, and making him pretty mad. In sizing him up we had not noticed before that his eyes were as black as coals and that he seemed to be about eight feet high, but as he looked at us we could see it plainly. He seemed to read our thoughts and knew that it was done on purpose, and we have always thought he heard the boys talking it over at recess. Any way, he jumped clear across the room, grabbed us by the neck and sat us down in the water; and then he lifted us up and shook us so the teeth rattled, and then he seemed to grab us all over and just maul us. We got a chance, once or twice, to look around to the back seats, as he was revolving us around on our axis, to see if the other boys were coming to help us to put him out doors, but they were the most studious lot of big boys you ever saw. They had their heads down in their books, and their lips were moving in silent prayer. After the teacher had mopped the floor with us, he took us by the slack of the pants, just as a dog would carry a duck, and went to his desk and got a big hickory ruler, and proceeded to dry our pants. Well, it was the meanest way to dry pants that ever was, and while it dried them well enough, it left great ridges inside of them, made a corrugated chair almost a necessity. The boys did not fulfil their part of the programme, and when the teacher got through drying our pants, and said "please return to your seats," we felt as though his politeness was a perfect shamer. We looked at the boys as we went to our seat, but they never looked up. We have witnessed contested seats in the Legislature but never saw one that was so exciting as that one in the old white school house, at the foot of the hill. The teacher never spoke during the proceedings, and when it was over he looked even paler and more sickly than when he had one hand in the hair that once grew where we are now bald, while the other was at work in the vineyard. But none of the boys seemed to care to pitch on to a sick man, and he taught that school two terms, and never had to whip another boy. That was the last school we ever broke up. The slim, sickly teacher is an old man now living quietly in this State, with children as old as we are, and we occasionally see him and ask him if he remembers how we broke up the school. He is feeble now, and walks with a cane, but if we had to have a fight with him even now, we would hire a man to do it.—*Burlington Hawkeye.*

CARRIAGE, CARRIAGES

A SUPERIOR LOT FOR SALE.

I HAVE for sale, Carriages, Buggies, Wagons &c. All of the most elegant and durable workmanship, guaranteed if desired. ☞ Old Carriages and Buggies taken in exchange for new ones. All in want will give us a call and we will not fail to please you.

To be seen at Fadely's Livery stable.

FADELEY & CO.,
Leesburg, Va.

THE SEWING MACHINE AGENT.

The sewing machine agent is of all ages and sizes, and flourishes luxuriantly in all climes. He travels in a light spring wagon, drawn by two sore backed ponies. He carries "the best machine in the word" in his wagon, and has its name in gilt letters, painted on the sides of the vehicle. He inhabits the cities and towns, but is often found in rural districts. He knows that he is a great public benefactor, and is therefore not at all modest about forcing his family blessings on the people. When he rides up to a house he hitches his horse to the fence and instead of standing at the gate and shouting "Hello! Mister, does your dog bite?" as other travelers do, he boldly walks up to the house, and, if no one is around, takes a seat on the gallery and begins to whistle. He does not whistle to keep his courage up, for, confident that he is engaged in a good and noble cause, he does not fear dogs. He is there on a beneficent errand. His mission is to cheer the wife, comfort the daughter and make the old man buy them a new improved-scroll-spring, sidebar, adjustable servon wheel, lockstitch Grover and Singer sewing-machine. He tells the old lady that he sees her health is giving away, and that the old Wheeler and Baker machine that she uses is the cause of it. He has known fifty ladies whom that machine has hurried to an untimely end and an early grave. He tells the daughter that he is unmarried, going to settle in the county, and hopes she will let him call on her when he is in the vicinity. He informs the old farmer that he (the old farmer) has more good agricultural sense than any man he has yet met in the State. Then he tightens up the fifth wheel of the machine, and starts it to sew. He shows how much lighter it runs than any other machine, how easy it is to adjust, and how much superior the new turbine take-up is to the old four-motion crank still used in all the rival machines. He asks them to examine the mouldboard on the off stationary arm and the French burr take up on the stern, and then inquires if they do not think that the perfection of mechanism, and very unlike the cheap rattletraps that all the other companies are now making with a view to swindle the public; filling their coffers, while they ruin the health of thousands of mothers, and wear the bloom off the cheek of the fairest in the land.

A good sewing-machine agent's tongue will make seventy-five oscillations and three laps per minute and keep on the track nine consecutive hours without refreshments. It is not to be inferred, however, that the sewing-machine agent is indifferent to refreshments. His stomach is like his machine—always in order and adjusted to any size, style, thickness or quality of goods. He eats corn bread and fat bacon, when he cannot get chicken and cake.

THE "NEW HOME" IS POSITIVELY the Simplest and Lightest Running Sewing Machine ever invented, and we challenge comparison with other machines in these respects. In the construction of the New Home, we have aimed to reduce friction to the minimum. This we have been successful in doing, and the result is a machine unequaled for lightness of running and which DOES NOT FATIGUE THE OPERATOR!

The very low prices and liberal terms, on which these Machines are sold, puts it within the reach of all. Delivered to any part of Loudoun County, and guaranteed for 5 years.
E. WRIGHT, Agent, Leesburg, Va.

2/2/83 Telephone

Herndon Flashes.

WEDNESDAY, JAN. 31: —Scarlatina is raging in and about Herndon.— Thirty two cases are reported up to the present time. Two children have died with this dreaded disease since Sunday, and several more are very sick. Theadore Oliver's youngest child, aged about two years, died on Sunday and Cash Thomas' youngest, aged about six months, died on Tuesday. Mr. Averill's little boy is not expected to live. Earnest Roby is very ill with Typhoid Fever. The wife of Harvey Wiley died on Saturday last, with Pneumonia. Her remains were taken to Leesburg, on Monday. This makes three deaths in this usually healthy place within one short week. Dr. Choate, of Washington, Dr. Warner, of Guilford and Drs. Jack and Wm. Day of Dranesville are called here almost every day.

2/2/83 Telephone

—The most dilapidated yet congrous caravan that ever visited our Town passed through here on Monday. There were four men, four women, sixteen children, four ponies, five bears and two monkeys. The men and women (who were not attired in fashionable clothing) led the brutes and the children were packed in pockets upon the ponies. A child was born to one of the women at Leesburg, on Sunday, and on Monday she was tramping along the turnpike, carrying the infant and leading a pony. It was not possible to tell by their appearance to what nationality they belong—it is satisfaction enough to know that they did not originate in this country.

2/16/83 Telephone

Six medical New York experts examined a man as to his sanity, and were evenly divided. After they had wrangled about it for a week it was discovered that they had examined the wrong person altogether.

2/2/83 Telephone

Hillsboro, Va., Jan. 30.

Our Town is situated in the gap of the Short Hill Mountain, twelve miles west from Leesburg, the County Seat, ten miles south east from Harpers Ferry and five mile north of Purcellville, the nearnest station on the W. & W. R. R.

There are, in the Town, a large flouring mill, a large woolen mill, seven stores, a church, a large and handsome school house, with a graded school, (conducted by Prof Dowdy, assisted by Miss Hannah Grubb, three shoe shops, two harness shops, a blacksmith shop, a wheelright shop, a meat shop, a large Temperance Hall, a livery stable, a house of entertainment, a broom factory, two doctors, a postoffice and an undertaker's shop, but, thank God, no whiskey shop.

The town of Hillsboro, constricted on both sides by mountains, has expanded very little in the number of buildings. The number of businesses then is surprising. Today there is a deli, jewelry store; post office and little else businesswise. The reason for this sea change has to be one coming invention – the automobile.

TO WHOM IT MAY CONCERN:

LEESBURG, VA., Feb. 7th, 1883.

S. J. JOHNSTON having brought suit against me for slander, for saying that he, S. J. JOHNSTON, sold a brass watch for a gold one, I this day assert that I desire to RETRACT, and DO RETRACT, that assertion ; that I did not mean to harm said S. J. JOHNSTON in his person or business, and if any harm resulted from my said thoughtless assertion. I am sorry for it, and do hereby apologize for the same ; that I believe that S. J. JOHNSTON did never sell a brass watch asserting it to be gold, and that said JOHNSTON is an honest business man and, I believe, worthy the confidence of the people. And I further promise to pay the costs of said suit up to date. He, JOHNSTON, on the above consideration, dismissing the same.

J. T. RITICOR.

W. E. GARRETT.

A MINER'S STORY.

Game there was none. We could not break camp now with our weak men upon our hands, and it only remained for some one to attempt the desperate journey across the San Juan Range, by way of the Devil's Pass, to Animas, and return with food or a rescuing party. Failing in that, spring-time would find our cabin inhabited by corpses.

We drew lots among ourselves, therefore, we well men, to decide who should undertake this perilous journey, and the job fell upon me. It was best, perhaps, that it should have been so, for of all the party I best knew the trail. Without waste of words or time, I prepared myself for the journey, and, tho roughly primed, early one morning, before the pale moon had fallen behind the western mountains, I bade good bye to my comrades and started. Turning my back upon the camp, I settled my course by a star, and at a brisk pace southward. All day I continued on the trail, ever with a watchful eye for Indian signs—for I believed our old enemies still in the vicinity—but all day unmolested, and at last, weary and worn, as the chill shadows began to creep across the great white plain behind me, I saw looming up in front the San Juan range, gashed with a narrow gorge—once through this horrible grave—for it was little else, and the road to Animas was comparatively easy. My spirits rose hopefully.

As darkness came fairly down, I found myself just at the mouth of the canyon which led up to the pass, and deeming it a most sheltered place for a camping spot, I soon gathered a heap of dead limbs beneath an overhanging rock where the snow had not yet come, built a roaring fire, which warmed and cheered me, and I prepared for the night. I felt little fear, for the morrow, frowning canyon walls would hide the light of my fire from all the plain country. The only disturbance which I might look for would be the howling of the wolves, who threatened, but dared not attack me; and I cared not for them.

With these comforting reflections, therefore, I ate a hearty supper, drank a little melted snow water, lit my pipe, and rolling myself in my blanket, crowded close to the wall behind me, now well warmed by my fire. And so, in the flickering light, protected upon all sides, I gave myself unhesitatingly up to slumber.

How long I slept I cannot say. It was deep in the night when I woke with a sudden chill It was as if some one had touched me with a cold and clammy hand, but even before I was well awake my frontiersman caution returned, and I opened my eyes slowly, and didn't move

The fire was all but out and the ghostly light from its dying embers touched the snow and rocks and trees about with a strange color like thick blood. The air was growing chill and still, too, except for the cry of a coyote far up the canyon wall opposite, who whined and barked incessantly.

The was something almost oppressive about the silence to me, when suddenly from just beyond the smouldering fire the sound of a step startled me, and before I had time even to move there was bending over me a hideous, painted face—the face of a savage. And in his hand already creeping toward my heart, was his heavy scalping knife.

To describe my sensation is impossible. Some terrible spell seemed to bind me. Not only was I facing a danger which meant instant death, but I was unable to move, even in the attempt to save myself. It was as if I were fascinated.

I tried to reason with myself. This was but a single enemy—if I should spring upon him I might kill him and so be free; but although the reasoning was all right, the action I was unable to bring about, and all the time the terrible knife drew nearer. The redskin knew that I was awake, and that I saw him, but he gloated over my helplessness and delayed his fatal blow.

At last, however, I saw the gleam of his eye, the tightening of his muscles, and knew that in an instant more all would be over, when a harsh metalic rattle sounded, as if it were in my very bosom. I felt something glide from my side—a long, scaly, snaky body shot out to met the on coming arm. There was a blow, then a cry of horror, and, as the knife fell ringing to the earth, a rattlesnake crawled slowy away, and the Uncompahgre, with his now nerveless hand outstretched and the blood slowly dripping from his parted fingers, with a long wild, death shriek, turned and disappeared in the darkness. The rattler which my fire had drawn from his winter quarters had saved my life and the lives of my companions.

A week later, with a party of good fellows, I recrossed the San Juan range and rescued my party from starvation and the Indians; and it is because of what that snake did for me in Devil's Pass, nigh on twenty years ago that I let the critters live to day.

3/8/83 Mirror

AN ELEPHANT'S FIGHT.

Jumbo Enrages Pilot Who Charges on the Herd — Narrow Escape of a Keeper.

BRIDGEPORT, CONN, Mar. 4 — Elephants have a well known fondness for dogs and are invariably more easily managed and controlled when dogs are their companions. A large mastiff was recently purchased and imported as a companion for Jumbo and placed beside him yesterday, for the first time, and the other dog, a shaggy one, taken away. Jumbo immediately evinced his displeasure at the change by low grumbling, and suddenly catching the mastiff around the body with his trunk threw him nearly across the building with terrific force, striking another vicious elephant called Pilot, killing the dog instantly and enraging Pilot to such a degree that he broke the chain holding him and began fighting all the other elephants. For some time nothing was heard but the wild trumpetings of these huge beasts and destruction to everything in the building seemed imminent. The trainers and other hands employed made a rush for the doors and windows and succeeded in escaping but one, named Conrad, barely eluded the tusks of Pilot. Mr. George Arstingstall and Mr. Frank Hyatt, from the outside of the building, threw great ropes made into slip nooses on the floor of the interior and succeeded after about an hour in catching the legs of the animal and throwing him to the ground, when the employees came in and finally conquered the obstreperous beast, and not until after severe measures were adopted and considerable damage had been done — During all the excitement Jumbo, the originator of the disturbance, was quietly feeding, but Queen, the mother of the baby elephant, was much exercised on behalf of her young one. Chief, Mandria, Pilot and some others of the herd of elephants were much bruised by the repeated blows given by the maddened elephant. One employe, in his haste to get away, fell from a window to the ground and sustained slight injuries. Pilot is now heavily "handcuffed" and chained away from the other animals. Mr. P. T. Barnum was on the spot directing the movements of his employes.

3/7/83 Telephone

Cooking by Electricity.
Chicago Times.]

Some parties in Canada are reported to have invented a machine for cooking by electricity. It consists of a sauce pan or hot plate so isolated by non-conductors that the bottom forms the positive pole of a current. The other pole is attached to a movable point, which travels over the under surface of the pan in circles sufficiently quick not to burn a hole through. Some cakes were cooked in the apparatus and eaten by the inventor and his family, who are believed to be the first members of the human race who have eaten food cooked by the electric spark. One lady declared she tasted the flavor of electricity "quite strong."

4/12/83 Telephone

THE DEATH OF "PILOT." — Pilot, one of Barnum's largest elephants, became so dangerous that he was taken to Madison Square Garden, New York, last Thursday, and killed. George Arstingstall, the showman who shot the beast, said: that Pilot was one of worst elephants that ever lived under canvas. I noticed the fit coming on him down at Bridgeport and was pretty sure that in a short time he would help the violets to bloom. Pilot is an Indian elephant. He killed an Italian in London and seriously wounded Mr. Cross some time ago. He came to New York, April 15, 1877, and April 16 broke loose and drove off his keeper. An elephant may be killed very easily. I fired my first two shots into his heart and one into his eye. All Indian elephants are dangerous, I would not trust one of them ten feet away from me. Pilot was one of the largest elephants I ever saw; he was next to Jumbo in size, and weighed 9,175 pounds."

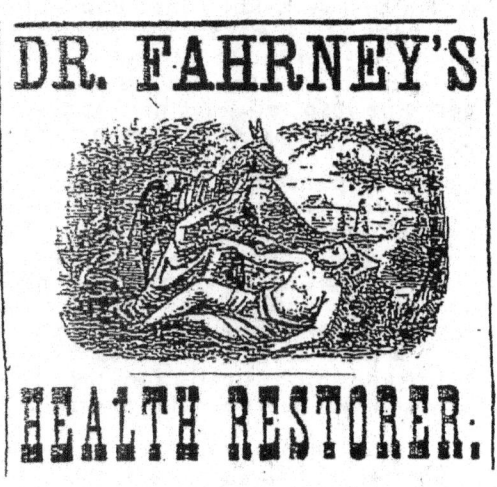

DR. FAHRNEY'S HEALTH RESTORER.

March 1883

3/8/83 Mirror

Death of Alexander H. Stephens.

This gentleman who for many years has held a conspicuous place in the political affairs of his State and nation, died at the capital of Georgia, at 3:15 on Sunday afternoon, March 4th, 1883. Mr. had S. been sick but a few days, and his death was peaceful and calm. He was unconscious since Friday.— His last official act was the signing of a pardon on Wednesday. He leaves $10,000 to the children of his brother, the late Judge Stephens, and the remainder of his estate to his nephew, John A. Stephens. The news of his death caused the profounded sensation in Atlanta, where the serious nature of his attack had not been realized by the people. The remains lay in State at the executive mansion all day Sunday, where they were viewed by over 20,000 people.

In announcing the death of Gov. STEPHENS the Baltimore Sun says "Hon. Alex. H. Stephens, who had been the Governor of Georgia for little over five months, but whose public life extends over a period of forty-six years, died yesterday morning at Atlanta. The career of Mr. Stephens was remarkable. Before the war he was, for sixteen years a leading whig Representative in the Congress of the United States. For eight years—1873 to 1881—he was a democratic member of Congress. Before the war he opposed secession, and during the war he became the Vice President of the Confederate States. He first entered public life as a member of the Georgia Legislature in 1836. That he had been for so many years in high official position is the best evidence of the high esteem in which he was held by the people of his State His popularity was such that factions opposition only served to strengthen it. It was his great merit that he deserved the confidence he inspired. At his bachelor home in Crawfordville he kept open house, where at all times when not engaged in his public duties he dispensed a liberal hospitality. Diminutive in person, of frail health almost from childhood, and in later years so crippled by rheumatism as to require the constant services of an attendant and the use of a wheeled chair, any one who saw him without close acquaintance with him, would have wondered how a man so insignificant is figure and so physically helpless could have so won the hearts of the people of his State.

THE death of ALEXANDER H. STEPHENS, Governor of Georgia, removes from the scenes of life one of its most active workers, and one of the most remarkable men of the present generation. With a frame weighing less then 75 pounds, and always laboring, to a greater or less degree, under physical infirmities sufficient to have dwarfed the intellectual powers of ordinary mortals, his mind was always clear, strong and vigorous, and enabled him to accomplish an unusual amount of mental labor much of which will live long in his country's history. From his often erratic course and self will in pursuing it, he was unfitted for a safe leader in politics, but upon the people of his native State, few men had a stronger hold, which was evidenced less than six months ago, when, notwithstanding his physical infirmities, he was elected Governor of Georgia by a majority of over 60,000

3/10/83 Washingtonian

In 1848 Alexander H. Stephens was rebuked in savage language by Judge Cone, of Georgia who stigmatised him as a traitor to the South. Stephens slashed his antagonist across the face with a cane. Judge Cone drew a knife, and inflicted eighteen or twenty wounds on his puny opponent. Finally, forcing him to the ground and holding him by the hair, Cone said; "Apologize, or I'll cut your d—d throat." Stephens coolly answered, "Never: cut away" Just as the knife was descending the combatants were seperated, but Stephens well nigh bled to death.

On February 21, 1878, the Mirror quotes from this former Confederacy Vice President who was once again a U.S. Congressman. The occasion was commemorating the large Franklin painting of the Emancipation Proclamation scene.

"I knew Mr. Lincoln well.— We met in this House in December, 1847.— We were together during the Thirtieth Congress. I was as intimate with him as with any other man of that Congress, except, perhaps, one. That exception was my colleague, Mr. Toombs. Of Mr. Lincoln's general character I need not speak. He was warm hearted; he was generous; he was magnanimous; he was most truly, as he afterward said on a memorable occasion, "with malice towards none, with charity for all."

In bodily form he was above the average; and so in intellect; the two were in sympathy. Not highly cultivated, he had a native genius far above the average of his fellows.— Every fountain of his heart was ever overflowing with the "milk of human kindness." So much for him personally. From my attachment to him, so much the deeper was the pang in my own breast as well as of millions at the horrible manner of his "taking off." That was the climax of our troubles and the spring from which came afterward "unnumbered woes."

March 1883

THE MIRROR.

VOL XXVII.   LEESBURG, VA., THURSDAY, MARCH 8, 1883.   NO. 39

Cigarettes and Small Boys.

Liquor and its terrible results have received the attention of the press and speakers, but the pernicious and unhealthy habit of cigarette smoking is fast keeping pace in its work of death and misery with the former. Especially does it ply its work with our young and rising generation who, instead of spending their pennies in cake or candies, as formerly, order a cigarette and strut around like lords with the exhilerating but deceptive little white role adjusted in their mouths, waiting to stop the first gentleman with "A light, Mister?" little knowing that they are filling their young pure blood with poisons, drying up their lungs, shattering their delicate nerves, and paving the way for an early but untimely grave. Even little children with the lisp of childhood still lingering on their lips, fall into line as readily as any. Look at their thin, wan faces, the circle of blue under the eyes which helps to tell the tale. Go to the cemeteries, and no doubt, if the dead could speak, they would say, "Inscribe upon my tombstone, as a warning to others, 'Died from cigarette smoking.'" If people must commit suicide in a respectable way, by smoking themselves to death, save the children, and enact some law for their preservation. Hoping this will not end in smoke.   A SUFFERER.

Sam. Medill's Faithful Dog.

A most pathetic and remarkable incident in connection with the recent death at Quincy, Ill., of Samuel J. Medill, late managing editor of the Chicago *Tribune*, is told by his brother-in-law, Mr James D. Carson, general manager of the Union Depot Company, Kansas City. Mr Medill had owned a pet dog of which he was extremely fond, but the care of which had been so great a burden to him in his condition of health that he had given it to a friend near Quincy. The animal had seemed at times restless, but ordinarily well contented in his new home. Of late it had apparently been espesially well domiciled and happy. Early in the morning of the day of Mr. Medill's death the dog suddenly disappeared from its home. At about 6 o'clock the dog appeared at the residence of Mr. John B. Carson, where Mr. Medill was already dying. It now howled piteously about the place until he was admitted, and instantly, with some unexplainable instinct, dashed to Mr. Medill's room, bounded upon the bed, and covered its dying master with its loyal caresses. It is stated that Mr Medill, although already almost unconscious, gave recognition of the occurrence.

TONSORIAL ARTISTS

B. ASHER & CO., respectfully inform the people of Leesburg and Loudoun Co., that they have opened a First-class SHAVING and

Hair Cutting Saloon,

AT THE REAMER HOUSE.

We have recently placed in position two handsome Barber's Chairs. Keen Razors, Sharp Shears and Clean Towels—in fact, everything first-class.

Your patronage is respectfully solicited.

B. ASHER & CO.,
(feb 8-1m.)   Tonsorial Artists.

George Campbell,
WHEELWRIGHT.

DESIRES to inform his friends, and the public generally, that he may be found at his Shops, in the North end of town, (near the old Foundry corner,) fully prepared to do any and all work in his line entrusted to him. He makes a specialty of

REPAIRING HEAVY ROAD WAGONS.

☞ Repairing of Light Work—such as Buggies, Carriages, &c., —promptly attended to. Terms reasonable.

☞ Well-seasoned TIMBER and COUNTRY PRODUCE taken in exchange for work. Give me a call before going elsewhere.

Respectfully,
GEORGE CAMPBELL.
feb 3-3m.

PEARCE'S IMPROVED

CAHOON

Broadcast Seed Sower,

SOWS ALL KINDS OF GRAIN AND GRASS SEED.

Does as much work as five men can do by hand. Does better work than can be done by any other means whatever. Worth its cost every year. Will last many years. Nobody can afford to sow grass seed or grain by hand. Price only $8.00.

3/15/83 Mirror

LAUGHABLE ACCOUNT OF YOUNG ALLAN ARTHUR'S BEHAVIOR AT PRINCETON.

Young Allen Arthur the son of the President, was not long since suspended by the authorities of Princeton College, in company with a son of General George P. McClellan and a son of Mr. Libbey, of New York, who has given so liberally to Princeton, on account of sportive tricks at a hotel. Several students from Harvard came to Princeton on a visit, and twenty Princeton boys, including the three above mentioned, arranged a wine supper for the Harvard visitors at one of the local hotels.

The proprietor of the hotel located the genial gentlemen in one of the wings of the hotel where their conviviality would disturb other guests as little as possible. When the supper had reached its conclusion the young men were in the usual happy frame of mind natural to the conclusion of a wine feast, where the guests are young and full of gay vitality of youth. Outside the night was cold and stormy. The guests concluded not to go home. To go down to the office and order rooms was altogether too tame a proceeding. Just above the upper room was a line of bed rooms assigned to the chambermaids of the hotel. It was thought to be a good lark to go up and drive out the girls and capture their quarters.

The frail doors were kicked in, and the girls fled shrieking down stairs. The jolly boys were only too contented in capturing the rooms to bother their heads about where the girls were afterward. The ancient housekeeper who slept at the end of the hall, awakened by the racket, came out just as the hall was cleared. She left her door open, and walked down the hall in her night-gown, hunting for the cause of the trouble. Two of the supper crowd came up near her room, supporting in their arms a very tired student. Seeing her room open, they ran in there and put their weary friend in the old lady's bed. As they came out of the door it slammed too and fastened with a spring lock. So, when the housekeeper returned she found herself locked out. Then she raised an outcry, which brought all of the students out of the rooms.

Young Arthur and McClellan came out with guitars and began to serenade the thinly attired housekeeper. She thought the young men were bringing disgrace upon the chambermaids and sounded a fire alarm. This aroused everybody. The students were captured. A small boy was put in over the transom of the housekeeper's room so that the students there could not escape. It was 3 o'clock before the housekeeper and her girls were restored to their quarters. All the students connected with the frolic were suspended, but as the escapade was really innocent, no complaints being made, the students were last week taken back.

3/8/83 Mirror

How Grant Escaped Assassination With President Lincoln.

(Washington Correspondence of the Boston Traveller.)

General Grant in a recent conversation said: "The darkest day of my life was the day I heard of Lincoln's assassination. I did not know what it meant. Here was the rebellion put down in the field and starting up in the gutters. We had fought it as war, now we had to fight it as assassination. Lincoln was killed on the evening of the 14th of April. I was busy sending out orders to stop recruiting, the purchase of supplies, and to muster out the army. Lincoln had promised to go to the theatre and wanted me to go with him. While I was with the President a note came from Mrs. Grant, saying that she must leave Washington that night. She wanted to go to Burlington to see her children. Some incident of a trifling nature had made her resolve to leave that evening. I was glad to have it so, as I did not want to go to the theatre. So I made my excuses to Lincoln and at the proper hour we started for the train. As we were driving along Pennsylvania avenue a horseman drove past us on a gallop and back again around our carriage, looking into it. Mrs. Grant said: 'There is the man who sat near us at lunch to-day, with some other men, and tried to overhear our conversation. He was so rude that we left the dining room. Here he is now riding after us.' I thought it was only curiosity, but learned afterward that the horseman was Booth. It seemed that I was to have been attacked, and Mrs. Grant's sudden resolve to leave changed the plan. A few days after I received an anonymous letter from a man saying that he had been detailed to kill me; that he rode on my train as far as Havre de Grace, and as my car was locked he failed to get in. He thanked God that he had failed. I remember that the conductor locked our car, but how true the letter was I cannot say. I learned of the assassination as I was passing through Philadelphia. I turned around, took a special train and came on to Washington. It was the gloomiest day of my life."

J. H. KUEHLING,

MANIPULATOR OF
Electrical and Mechanical
—BELLS,—

Burglar Alarms,
SPEAKING TUBES,
Iron Safes and Bank
LOCKS AND
All kinds of Electric
work executed in
scientific manner

March, 1883

3/15/83 Mirror

Dr. Mudd's Bitter Memories.

Dr. Samuel A. Mudd, of Bridgehampton, Charles county, Md., who died a few weeks ago, left in manuscript an interesting and instructive treatise on epidemic diseases, which was published in the Baltimore *Sun* of last week. In introducing his subject Dr. Mudd thus alludes to his imprisonment at the Dry Tortugas, and the bitter memories it entailed. He says:

"In July, 1865, I was sent a prisoner for life to the military prison at Fort Jefferson, better known as the Dry Tortugas, an island of coral formation in the Gulf of Mexico. Tried by a court martial, an unlawful tribunal constituted for the purpose of conviction the same that hanged an innocent woman. I was convicted on the testimony of paid and perjured witnesses of a crime the conception of which I never harbored or entertained. By such a tribunal I was pronounced guilty of complicity in the assassination of President Lincoln, when all the world knew, and the members of that iniquitous and law-defying military commission knew it as well, that my only offense consisted in setting the leg of a man whom I did not at the time know to be a fugitive from justice, and with whose insane act I had not the slightest sympathy. I had done merely an act of charity, from which no true physician would shrink, no matter what the consequences might be. For this I was banished under a life sentence from my wife and children, from home, friends and society and immured in the gloomiest and most distant prison in the United States. For this I was bound in chains like some savage brute, denied for a long time healthy sustenance, and forced at the point of the bayonet to perform menial and offensive offices which I will forbear mentioning. The iron entered my soul. Even now though, on restoration to my family and social circle, I am brought back to life and to some portion of all that which was lost by four years of banishment, the recollections of these years of mental and physical sufferings and the nature of what I endured on that barren coral reef, accursed and plague smitten, rises before me at times like a horror of great darkness, and will never be effaced as long as memory remains."

The yellow fever broke out in Aug. 18, 1867. "There were then at the Dry Tortugas," wrote Dr. Mudd, "five companies of the Fifth United States Artillery, a few civilians employed in the Engineer Department and about 200 'guard' prisoners. These last consisted of deserters from the Federal army, bounty jumpers, &c. The roll of State prisoners consisted of Messrs. Arnold, Sprangler, Cloghlin, and myself. There were also some Confederate prisoners, prominent among whom was Col. St. Leger Greenfel, sent there for life by sentence of a military tribunal for alleged complicity in the abortive attempt to release the Camp Douglas prisoners. It is generally supposed that he was drowned in the attempt he made to escape from the island." Dr. Mudd tells how the post surgeon, Dr. J. S. Smith was stricken with the disease. In his delirium he refused all medicine or treatment and died. Dr. Mudd was the only person on the island who possessed a knowledge of medicine. His fellow prisoners of State urged him to do nothing, one of them remarking, "The yellow fever is a square deal, in which the keepers take an equal chance at death with their prisoners, without regard to age, color, or previous condition of servitude." Dr. Mudd, however, offered his services to Major Stone, in command of the post. He remained in exclusive charge of the hospital for some time, and during that time he says he did not los a patient. He cited his experience in support of the doctrine which he advocated in his work. It is that epidemic diseases of infection are not propagated by floating germs, but by absolute contact with infected material, so that the isolation of patients is an absolute prevention of the spread of the disease.

(Mudd's guilt or innocence is still debated.)

BUCKEYE MOWER,

known the world over as the first and best Two-Wheel Mower made as well as the BUCKEYE TABLE RAKE & DROPPER, and Single Wheel 6 feet Reaper.

We carry a full line of REPAIRS for all these Machines, and can draw on the Manufacturers' large stock in Baltimore, at short notice, for Machines or Repairs.

Our usual stock of A. BUGGY RAKES, BARNEY OUTT GRAIN CRADLES, and other Harvest Goods, will be found full and complete.

Shroff & Co.,
LEESBURG, VA.

April, 1883

4/5/83 Mirror

Charles Wm. Beaner Hanged.

Charles Wm. Beaner, the colored youth who had been under sentence of death since last January, was hung in the jail yard of this county, last Friday morning. Up to Thursday he expressed his readiness for death, but protested his innocence of the crime for which he was to die. On the afternoon of that day, however, he sent for Mr. Matthew, one of his counsel, to whom he confessed his guilt, and signed the following

CONFESSION.

To the Public:

I Chas. W Beaner, now under sentence of death, in the jail, in Leesburg, Va., and fully expecting the sentence to be executed by the officers of the law on to-morrow, desire to say that, I am guilty of the crime for which I was tried and convicted, and I admit substantially, all the facts proven against me on the trial of my case, I desire to say further that I sincerely repent the wrong and injury done, and pray forgiveness of the injured ones as I have prayed forgiveness of my Heavenly Father, who, I feel, has freely forgiven all my sins. I thank my parents for their care over me, and regret that I have caused them so much sorrow, but hope to meet them in a happier world. I return my thanks to my counsel for their efforts in my behalf – also, to Sheriff Carruthers, and his assistants, and especially do I thank Mr. Nixon, my jailor, for his kindness to me while under his charge.

In jail, Leesburg, Va. March 29th, 1883.

4/7/83 Washingtonian

A WELL MANAGED EXECUTION.—The Washington *Star*, whose local editor witnessed the execution, thus compliments our officers upon the satisfactory manner in which they discharged their duty on the occasion referred to :

"But few executions have taken place in this section of the country where everything went off so satisfactorily as that of the boy, Beaner at Leesburg, Va., yesterday. As was stated in yesterday's *Star*, the prisoner was awakened at five o'clock and ate a hearty breakfast. The ministers called on him at six o'clock and remained till the execution; the rope was rigged on the scaffold and tested ; the prisoner heard the death warrant read; directed what disposition should be made of some of his effects; bade farewell to Col. Nixon, the jailer; went to the scaffold, and his body was lowered into the coffin fifteen minutes after the drop fell, then taken to the burial ground, half a mile from the town, and interred, with the rites of the Episcopal church, by 8 o'clock. There was no hitch or jar of any kind, and Capt. Carruthers, the sheriff, and his assistants are to be congratulated that the disagreeable duty was performed so well.

Actually, it was a tragedy in that the punishment was brutally excessive. What had occurred was not rape but fondling.

May, 1883

5/17/83 Mirror

A Colored Mass Meeting.

We, the undersigned Delegates in mass meeting assembled, in Leesburg, May 14th, 1883, were duly authorized by the said meeting to present this Petition:

To the Hon. James B. McCabe, Judge of the County Court of Loudoun:

We, the undersigned colored citizens of said county would respectfully call your Honor's attention to the following facts, namely, that twenty years have elapsed since the bondage of our people in the South was removed: then we were a people comparatively without property, without the means of acquiring it and business capacity to manage it. Then we were uneducated and but few of us could read or write. Time has changed and improved our condition.— Under the guarantees of the National and State Constitutions, and laws in execution thereof our people have made advances: our children are being educated, and knowledge is supplanting ignorance, and the many little homes show we are acquiring property. Thus we have become identified with the material interests of our State; we have homes to defend; lives and liberty to protect; children educated and to be educated; and in all that pertains to the order, peace and prosperity of society, we have a common interest in the general welfare. We were in a sad condition to have conferred upon us citizenship, but are now much better prepared to appreciate it and meet its responsibilities. We disclaim any reflection upon the administration of justice; we know that hitherto we were in such condition as not to expect to participate in the administration of either. But we respectfully submit that that time has past. Political society enjoins on us the same duties and requires of us the same that is exacted from its other members. For twenty years we have been trying to qualify ourselves for the duties of citizenship; we trust it is not presumption in us, to say, our efforts have not been unavailing; we desire in the future a fuller recognition of our rights and privileges which the laws of the land have guaranteed to us; hence we respectfully petition your Honor in the future, to recognize our rights, to serve as Jurors and Judges of Election.

The Judge granted all of the above Petition except the right of being Judges of Elections. He, the Judge said he did not know that we, the colored people, had any right to ask to be appointed judges of election, but we think we have that right too.— The meeting adjourned to meet at Lincoln, August 4th, 1883.

5/17/83 Mirror

Sullivan and Mitchell, the two noted pugilists, had a prize fight in New York on Monday, in which Sullivan came off victor. They had three rounds—In the first of which Sullivan was slighted worsted. In the second round Mitchell plainly felt the effects of his opponents blows, and was not near so smiling as in the first encounter. In the third round the excitement was intense.— Mitchell got in some sharp body blows on Sullivan, but the latter delivered his blows with great directness and force, and the Englishman was twice knocked down. The third time he rose quite groggy, when Capt. Williams rushed upon the stage and ordered the fight to be stopped. There was much confusion for a few minutes, but when order was restored both men removed the gloves, shook hands, and were presented with bouquets of flowers, and Sullivan was officially declared the winner of the match.

Mitchell was voted a game and clever boxer, but too light to cope with a heavy weight like Sullivan. The winner took 60 per cent. and the loser 40 per cent. of the gate receipts, which amounted to about $10,000.

The Big Bridge to be Opened May 24th.—The Brooklyn bridge trustees, at their meeting Monday, fixed the toll for foot passengers at one cent the fare on the cars at five cents, for one horse and man at five cents, one horse and vehicle ten cents, two horses and vehicle twenty cents, each additional horse five cents, and sheep and cattle five cents The protest from the labor unions of New York and Brooklyn against the opening celebration being on the Queen's birthday, May 24th, was laid on the table.— The financial report showed that the total receipts amounted to $14,689,905, and the disbursements to $14,627,879

A BARGAIN

IN A FIRST CLASS INSTRUMENT! I offer, at Private Sale, a very fine

Rosewood Piano

of the celebrated manufactory of STEINWAY & CO. It is nearly as *good as new*, as can be seen by examination.

CARRIE HAMMERLY,
Leesburg, Va.

P. S.—Will take pleasure in showing the Instrument to any one who may call at my home, and, if desired, will sell upon the *Instalment Plan*. C. H.

5/31/83 Mirror

Something About Our Opium Eaters.

"Do I sell opium?" remarked a druggist, on the west side, when asked the question. "Yes lots of it. I suppose I sell as much of it as anybody in the city."

"There is an old fellow calling regularly for his stuff. He is lame and very debilitated but he uses fifteen grains per day—morphia, of course. One quite prominent business man (I guess he is a speculator or something of that sort) uses two and a half grains per day, hyperdemically—has it injected with a syringe right under the skin. The effect is quicker. I believe men use it mostly that way. They all have excuses for using it.— One old woman who called here the other day said she wanted to make salve of it. I let her have the opium, however, because I could see that she was a habitual user; otherwise we don't give every one this drug that calls for it, only when we see they are used to it. I have a business man for a customer who uses eighteen grains per day. There is a young lady on the west side who claims to is very poor, and we let her have the opium at cost price. I don't know how she lives, but I know that she buys sometimes five and sometimes ten, and sometimes fifteen grains, and swallows it right here and it doesn't seem to make any difference with her either way. Then we have had an old woman customer, quite funny one. She must be in one of the city hospitals now, for I haven't seen her for several days. She is shrivelled and wrinkled, four drachms of morphia every two day. You can appreciate this better when I tell you that one grain of morphia is equivalent to six grains of opium or 150 drops of laudanum. One grain of morphine is enough to kill a man unaccustomed to its use. But those who have acquired the habit of opium eating can get away with almost incredible quantities of it."

"How about chloral?"

"A good deal of it used to be taken a few years ago, but it is mainly used by society ladies, when they want sleep which they can't get otherwise on account of excitement. One lady customer of ours, living on Prospect street, used forty grains of this at a dose but thirty grains is the usual allowance at one time. It used to be employed a great deal by physicians in cases of approaching or manifested delirium tremens, but the medical fraternity have lost faith in it and discounts once, its use for that purpose now instead of it chosing bromide of potassium or bromide velerian. There's one thing about opium it takes from two to three years to firmly acquire the habit. But the habit once formed never losses its grip till the victim sinks into the grave. All the pretended cures of the habit are tricks of quacks. The opium victim cannot survive the loss of the only thing which bids him to life."

"Do you have many such customers?"

"Many! Why its one of our most prosperous resources. There is a gentleman out on Euclid avenue that daily consumes twenty-five grains. Users of ten or fifteen grains in a single day are quite common. You know physicians often say that they could reveal secrets that would break up households. We could tell things that would smash society in general. It is none of our business, however. We get their money, and we don't have to beg for it either."

MY BABY USING DR. FAHRNEY'S
BEFORE — AFTER

TEETHING SYRUP.

IT has never failed to give the most perfect satisfaction. Thousands of mothers are using it all through the land, and all are pleased with its charming effects. IT MAINTAINS THE BABY'S HEALTHILY KEEPING IT FREE FROM COLIC AND DIARRHŒA. Do not stupefy your Baby with Opium or Morphia Mixtures, but use

Dr. Fahrney's Teething Syrup, which is always safe and reliable. It soothes and quiets the CHILD, RELIEVES PAIN and INFLAMMATION and gives SWEET, NATURAL SLEEP TO BABES AND REST TO MOTHERS. ALL DRUGGISTS AND MEDICINE DEALERS SELL IT.

TWENTY-FIVE CENTS A BOTTLE.
PREPARED BY
DR. D. FAHRNEY & SON,
HAGERSTOWN, MD.
June 9, 1883.-1y

June, 1883

6/7/83 Mirror

A Terrible Disaster on the Brooklyn Bridge — At about half past four o'clock on Wednesday evening, May 30th there occurred a most frightful tragedy on the new bridge between New York and Brooklyn. The bridge had not been open to the public quite a week, it having been opened May 24th, and immense crowds had been passing over it each day, and at the time of the accident there were rather more persons on it than usual. On the approach to the bridge from the New York side are two flights of stairs of seven steps each, connected by a landing about eight feet long. These steps are generally blocked with people, coming from the two cities, and at the foot of these steps the accident occurred. A woman fainted and fell, another woman screamed, and a man in attempting to pick up the fallen woman, was knocked down and several persons fell over him. Instantly there were a dozen piercing screams as men and women tripped over the prostrate ones. The cries seemed to completely demoralize the crowd on the structure, who, frightened at the idea of something horrible, the nature of which they did not know, began a regular stampede. In a minute's time the lower stairway and landing was filled with struggling persons and those on the top stairway were forced by those behind on the fallen victims. The scene that followed is described as a most sickening one, men, women and little children, being crushed and mangled in one promiscuous mass. The crash lasted for about twenty minutes and it was only by the combined efforts of militia and policemen that it was checked. When order was restored and the work of caring for the injured commenced, it was found that eleven persons had been killed outright and about twenty-five or thirty injured, more or less seriously, several of whom have since died.

Nobody seems able to assign with any certainty the reason for the disaster. Some attribute it to pickpockets and roughs causing a jam for the purpose of plunder; others to a want of police to keep the crowd moving — Whatever may have been the cause of it is to be hoped that ample precautions will hereafter be taken to prevent a similar occurrance in future.

6/7/83 Mirror

A Lively Day Among the Colored Troops. — Last Saturday in Leesburg appears to have been a sort of general field-day for a portion of our colored citizens, during which there was witnessed a lively profusion of pulled-hair, bleeding-noses, and "razors flying through the air." In the afternoon there was a base-ball match on the suburbs, between the Leesburg and Hamilton clubs, that resulted in favor of the former. During the progress of the match there were one or two fisticuffs, participated in by some of the female spectators. As this was but a prelude to that followed, little or no harm was done, and with the close of the game the bad blood subsided, and further proceedings were deferred until night, when a Fair at the colored M. E. Church, attracted quite a crowd—and the pleasures of the evening were enlivened by a sort of free-fight, within the "sacred precincts"—resulting in several battered countenances, and the great terror of the more timid attendants. Several arrests were made on Monday, and the additions made to the corporation exchequer testify that the outraged law was fully vindicated.

Later in the evening, an outbreak of a more serious nature took place. It appears that about 11 o'clock, as two colored men were leaving town in the direction of the Dry Mill, they were met on the railroad by another colored man, who with pistol and club made an assault upon them;—they ran, one of them taking refuge in the stable of Mr. Robert Davis, into which they were pursued by the infuriated darkie. Mr. D. happened to be in the stable when he entered, and probably mistaking him for his fleeing victim, the pursuer sent a bullet through Mr. Davis' hat. The latter immediately closed in on the intruder, knocked him down and secured his pistol; after which he turned him over to his brother and a negro man, who put him in a wagon and started for jail. Before reaching town, however, the supposed disarmed ruffian, drew a razor, and under the terror thus unexpectedly inspired, and the darkness of the night, made his escape. Sheriff Russell and Town Sergeant Head, were notified of the proceeding, and prompt chase given, but so far the rascal has eluded their vigilance and is still at large. None of the parties were able to recognize him.

June, 1883

6/22/83 Telephone

EDITOR TELEPHONE:—A few evening ago, I visited the Lincoln Cemetery or Friends burying ground. Marble stones mark the places where many loved ones have been quietly laid away. One tells the spot where the loved minister, S. M. Janney, is buried. How many love to visit that grave and call to mind his many noble deeds and the pure life he led. To the Society, that spot should almost seem like sacred ground, and should be kept in the best of order. The query arose in my mind, while meditating there, alone with the dead —are the surviving friends doing their duty towards keeping the grounds in order? The answer comes, *By no means!* While gazing over the grounds I saw a large flock of sheep, penned therein, looking like the picture of despair, with not a drop of water to cool their tongues. A feeling of sadness came over me. O that men would keep their sheep at home and be willing to destroy briers and weeds with their own hands.— A good deal of brain work, with a little labor and money, judiciously used, would fix the Cemetery, so it would be a credit to the Society and community, instead of a disgrace to such an intelligent and monied people. I was informed that the women were opposed to having sheep pastured there, but the men, with their quaint notions, overpowered them.— Bless the women!

Sheep Claims !

ALL persons who may have lost Sheep, Killed by Dogs, between the first day of February, 1882, and the first day of February, 1882, and who have not yet returned to me their Certificates of said loss, are notified that they must do so, on or before MONDAY, the 26th of JUNE, 1883. After that date the business of the above named year will be closed, and the surplus funds, if any, turned over to the School Fund of the respective Districts. Persons, therefore, who may have suffered loss by the ravages of Dogs will see the necessity for prompt action.

☞ This notice is simply a call for the evidences of Sheep killed during the year ending February 1st, 1883. The funds for the payment of losses are not yet in the hands of the Treasurer,—notice of that will be given hereafter. B. F. SHEETZ, Treasurer.
june 1

6/29/83 Telephone

In our last issue appeared a letter scolding the Friends for allowing their burying ground, at Lincoln, to remain in disorder and be used as a pasture for sheep. Two days after that publication we had occasion to visit the grave yard, and we admit that we were shocked and grieved to behold the damage which had been done, through somebody's carelessness. Almost every grave had been despoiled by the hoofs and horns of the sheep.

7/19/83 Mirror

Tom Thumb Dead.

MIDDLEBORO', Mass., July 16.—Charles Heywood Stratton, better known to the public as Gen. Tom Thumb, died at his residence here at 8:30 o'clock this morning of apoplexy. He had been slightly ill for a few days, but nothing serious was anticipated. The deceased was born in Bridgeport, Conn., January 4, 1838, and was consequently 45 years old. At the age of 14 he entered the service of P. T. Barnum, and has been before the public ever since. He leaves a widow, who has been on the stage with him since their marriage in 1863. She was the pretty and conspicuously petite Levinia Warren, sister of the equally pretty and still smaller Minnie Warren, to whom the late Commodore Nutt paid devoted attention for a long time, and whom he afterwards married. Tom Thumb's wedding, in Grace Church, New York, in 1863, was a famous event.

Probably the most popular performers in Barnum's shows, the largest and the smallest, the massive elephant Jumbo and the diminutive Tom Thumb.

Portrait of Garfield

SIZE OF SHEET, 19x24.

With his Autograph, acknowledged by himself to be the best likeness in existence.

$7.00 per hundred.
SINGLE COPIES, 25 CENTS.

Copy of Autograph Letter given with each picture. Address,
SHOBER & CARQUEVILLE LITHO. Co.,
119 Monroe St., Chicago, Ill.

ELAM SHOT BY BEIRNE.

The Meeting at Waynesboro'.

TWO SHOTS FIRED.

A special dispatch to the *Sun* from Staunton Va., says: "At exactly six o'clock Saturday morning the duel between Beirne and Elam came off two miles west of Waynesboro', in this county, on the farm of Philip Killain."

A correspondent of the New York *World* writing from Harrisonburg, gives the following account of the duel:

HARRISONBURG, Rockingham county, Va., July 1.—W. C. Elam, who was shot in a duel by Richard F. Beirne near Waynesboro' yesterday, is lying in a dangerous condition at the house of his friend, Lieut Governor John F. Lewis, Jr., near Lynwood, in this county, whither he was taken immediately after the fight.

Of course, he could not be seen today, but a son of Mr. Lewis, who lives here, returned home this evening from a visit to his father's. When called upon by the *World* correspondent he said that the ball was cut out of the inner side of Mr. Elam's left hip, which it had entered after passing through his right thigh, this morning. He is still attended by Dr. Wheat, who is of opinion that, unless blood-poisoning sets in, Mr. Elam's chances of recovery are good.

A physician just from Elam's bedside said tonight that he was dangerously wounded. The ball was found in the inside of his left thigh, having passed through the right leg, grazing the bone and cutting the tissues below the urethera.

Mrs. Elam reached husband's side today and will remain with him, as it is deemed inadvisable to remove him for several weeks.

MR BEIRNE'S PARTY AT BALTIMORE.

BALTIMORE, July 1.—Mr. Richard F. Beirne reached here late last evening accompanied by a party of friends, including his brother Andrew Beirne, of Lewisburg W. Va.; H. M. Smith and W. T. Chockly, of Richmond, Va.

The *World* correspondent had a talk with them on the train as they entered the city. On his knee lay one of Josh Billings's joke books, with which he had been amusing himself.

The travel stained condition of the party and their sunburnt faces would have led any one to suppose that they were a company of mountaineers coming to the city to see the sights and celebrate the Fourth of July. They were very reticent and were particularly indisposed to say anything about the duel.

"How is Mr. Elam?"

"We do not know," said another gentleman in the party. "We left him lying on the field in care of his surgeon and friends. We departed immediately after the affair."

The train had by this time reached Hillen Station, and the gentlemen took a carriage to Barnum's Hotel.

Mr. Beirne carried a stout oak stick which he had cut from a tree in the mountains. Although they had evidently endeavored to travel as quietly as possible and to avoid publicity, they were recognized by several persons on the train.

On reaching the hotel the party went immediately to their rooms, and Mr. Beirne declined to see any one during the evening. One of his companions, however, said that Mr. Beirne was satisfied; that he did not want to kill Mr. Elam, but was determined to vindicate his insulted honor. The gentleman added that two braver men never met on the field. Both were excellent shots and faced each other unflinchingly.

A SECOND'S ACCOUNT OF THE FIGHT.

Mr. Wright, one of Mr. Beirne's seconds, gave *The World* correspondence a thrilling account of the hostile meeting. He said that after the interruption by the authorities near Hanover Junction, Va., on June 23, which resulted in the arrest of Beirne and his subsequent escape, the parties travelled through the country. They kept away from the towns and villages, travelling as secretly and quietly as possible and spending their nights either in the woods or at farm-houses.

It was determined that the meeting should take place no matter how far they had to travel to find a place where they would be unmolested. The seconds on both sides had several conferences from time to time regarding a selection of the place for the meeting.

THE FIELD SELECTED BY ELAM.

Last Tuesday Beirne and his friends arrived at Ronceverte, Va., where they spent the day, and it was there that, in accordance with Elam's wishes, it was decided to have the meeting near Waynesboro. Accordingly, on Tuesday night, in the midst of a terrific rain and wind storm, Beirne, accompanied by his friends, started in a carriage on their long journey. Beirne travelled 124 miles in a carriage. Horses and conveyances were changed at different points on the route and several stops were made overnight. On Friday all the arrangements as to the exact

July 1883

place of meeting were completed and Mr. Chockly spent Friday night in Waynesboro.

Mr. Chockly, one of Mr. Beirne's seconds, went ahead, travelling by railroad to Waynesboro, to make arrangements for the duel and see if the coast was clear. As Beirne was proceeding from his retreat, about 300 miles distant in West Virginia, and Elam started from the neighborhood of Richmond, the two parties did not meet until they arrrived at the rendezvous. Much of the time the principals travelled alone, letting their friends go on before or follow behind to avoid suspicion.

JOKING BEFORE THE FIGHT.

It was about 4 o'clock yesterday morning, just as the sun was rising over the mountains, that the two parties came together at the appointed place of meeting, both parties having encamped in the woods over night. The principals appeared bright and cheerful and Beirne joked gayly with his seconds as they walked through the woods to the meeting place. The seconds at once proceeded to measure off the eight paces of distance, the principals meanwhile talking as gayly with their friends on either side of the field as though they were only going to have a little friendly bout, instead of a mortal combat. The weapons selected were Colt's five-barreled 32-calibre revolvers. The first shot to be between the count "one, two, three."

After the first fire the challenger was to say whether he was satisfied, and if not the parties were to advance and fire until they had emptied every chamber of their revolvers. At 6 o'clock all was ready, and the men took their positions. The friends of both stood on either side watching breathlessly for the word.

BEIRNE INSISTS UPON BLOOD.

At the word fire, both men discharged their pistols simultaneously, but neither was hurt. Beirne declared himself unsatisfied and after a few minutes of anxious suspense the word was given and they fired again. This time Elam fell, shot as we supposed, through the right thigh, as he said the ball had passed into his left leg. He raised his hand saying: "I am shot!"

Mr. Chockley went over to him while Dr. Wheat was making a hurried examination of the wound. After seeing the nature of the injury Mr. Chockley returned to Mr. Beirne. After a brief consultation Mr. Beirne, through his second, declared himself satisfied.

Mr. Elam was then removed to his carriage and Mr. Beirne and his friends entered their carriages and drove rapidly away.

Not a single person witnessed the duel except the principals, their seconds and the doctor.

In concluding his account of the affair Mr. Wright said: "We had some rough travelling, a variety of adventure, and I am glad it is all over."

Mr. Beirne attended service at church this morning and then returned to Barnum's Hotel, where he remained quietly in his rooms all day, seeing no callers.

To *The World* correspondent he said that he intended to return to his home at Ashland, Va., at 4 o'clock in the morning. He will at once resume his editorial duties at the office of the *State* in Richmond, and quietly await any action to be taken by the Virginia authorities. He did not apprehend any serious punishment.

7/6/83 Telephone

The ground selected was on a twelve-acre grove, not far from a milldam, and where the parties could not well be discovered. In this grove there was a slight depression, in that depression the men were promptly placed, facing each other. A toss for the choice of position and word of command had been won by Mr. Sheffey Lewis, second for Mr. Elam. He also staked off the ground and placed the men. The principals were eight paces apart, which is less than eight yards. The principals faced each other. Both appeared cool, and not in the least excited. Mr. Beirne looked haggard and pale, the result of a long and wearisome drive over the Alleghany mountains from Lewisburg, with the loss of sleep. Mr. Elam stood erect, and an eye witness says "as firm and as solid as an oak." He wore his spectacles, but so nearsighted is he that with his glasses he could scarcely recognize a person at a few paces from him.

Mr. Lewis, after the principals had each loaded their pistols. Both gentlemen gave assent, and tightly clutched their weapons. They were to fire between the words one—two—three. "One," said Mr. Lewis, in a tone that could be distinctly heard and not misunderstood. Quick as a flash Mr.

Elam's pistol went off, and the report from Mr. Beirne's pistol followed like an echo. The ball from Mr. Elam's pistol touched Mr. Beirne's vest and caused a change in his aim, which made the ball from his pistol go whizzing through the air over Elam's head. A second fire was then had. Again Mr. Elam fired a little in advance of Mr. Beirne, but harmlessly. The second shot from Beirne's pistol struck Mr. Elam in the upper portion of the right thigh, as he was standing with that side advanced.— Mr. Elam said, "I am hit," and cocked his weapon for another fire. His finger was on the trigger ready for another shot, but a parley ensued, resulting in Mr. Beirne's second saying that he was satisfied. The Beirne party then raised their hats courteously to the other side and left the field.

Strange to say the first Mr. Elam ever saw of Mr. Beirne to know him was on the field at Hanover. It is said they have never been introduced, and were never in each others company before the day they met at Hanover Junction. Passing day after day within almost a stone's throw of each other, they never met. All they knew of each other was from information derived from others.

"The Beirne Elam duel was the second one which has been fought since the enactment by the Legislature, in 1882, of the law requiring the oath of all State and local officers that they had not since the passage of that act fought a duel or accepted a challenge nor acted a a second in a duel. Elam, who was one of the principles in the affair of yesterday, was elected secretary of the Commonwealth after the passage of the law, and consequently was not required to subscribe as provided thereunder. Recognizing probably the fact that he was under a moral obligation not to participate in a duel while an officer of the State, he handed in his resignation of the office before he accepted Beirne's challange. No arrests except that of a colored man who drove Mr Beirne from West Virginia to Waynesboro have yet been made. It is stated that the Commonwealths Attorney of Augusta, the county in which the Beirne and Elam fight occurred will prosecute the case against them.

THE TELEPHONE.

FRIDAY.................JULY 6TH.

THAT DISGRACEFUL DUEL.

As will be seen elsewhere in this paper the two belligerant Richmond editors finally met and fought. It is with a deep sense of shame for Virginia, and especially the Press of the State, that we chronicle this affair.— It is a disgrace which should be rebuked by every good citizen in the State.

It Settled Nothing.

[From the Washington Critic.]

The trial by battle between Editors Beirne and Elam is over. The net results are a good deal of shoe leather worn out, a good deal of money wasted, a good deal of powder burned, and only one man shot, and a flesh wound at that.

And what has been settled?

Elam, though wounded, is as big a liar as ever.

Beirne, though unhurt, is even a worse man than before.

Elam is satisfied.

Satisfied about what?

That Beirne wrote truly?

Of course not.

Only that Beirne could shoot better than he could.

Beirne was satisfied.

About what?

Only that he had hit Elam and Elam had not hit him.

What was settled by the duel?

Nothing!

If Elam lied he still lies.

If Beirne lied he still lies.

Nothing was settled, except that shortsighted Elam could not shoot with dead-shot Beirne.

7/12/83 Mirror

A ROAD ENGINE.—On Saturday evening last one of these machines made its appearance on our streets, and as it was the first that had ever been seen in town it received no little attention. We were particularly struck with the ease and readiness with which it was managed and its almost noiseless movements. It ran at about the speed of a horse's walk and seemed able to go backward or forward, up hill or down, with equal facility. It appeared well adapted to the purposes for which it is intended and will doubtless prove a boon to threshermen and others in need of machines of its kind. The one on our streets was of the Cooper manufacture, and is sold by Mr. JNO. MILTON, of Hamilton, who is agent for Loudoun and Fauquier counties

The Latest and Best!

—C. & G. COOPER & CO'S—

SELF-STEERING

Traction Engines,

with *Link Motion*, reversing gear, with either Inspirators or pumps; the Strongest, Handsomest and Cheapest Traction Engines in the market. Also, Common Farm and Portable Engines — both side and centre crank. SAW MILL, and Cooper's New

VIBRATOR SEPARATOR.

☞ Keller Grain Drills, Corn Planters Cultivators, &c. Call on or address

JOHN MILTON,
Hamilton, Va.

RACES!

—AT THE—

Fair Ground

LEESBURG, VA.

—

ONE DAY ONLY!

JULY 4TH, 1883.

under the auspices of the

LOUDOUN AGRICULTURAL SOCIETY.

1st Race—Running—Purse, $125.
2d Race—Running—Purse, 75.
3d Race—Trotting, (2:50 class) Purse, 75.
4th Race—Running—Purse, 90.
5th Race—Hurdle—Purse, 125.

Races will begin promptly at 12 o'clock, M.

Admission to the Grounds, 50 cents.
Children under 10 years of age, 25 "
All Vehicles Free.

Special Trains

From Washington and Alexandria, and

ROUND-TRIP TICKETS

from Cities, and all points on Railroad, at GREATLY REDUCED RATES

☞ Can see the Races, and return same day.

W. D. HEMPSTONE, Sec'y.

May 31, 1883.

7/6/83 Telephone

—The racing celebration at the Fair Grounds, on the 4th was a failure, there were but two or three races and few people were in attendance.—A man who was present said there were only twenty-five persons there and twenty-four of them were drunk. It was lucky that he kept sober enough to count or we might have had no record of the affair.

7/26/83 Mirror

SIXTY-FIVE MILES AN HOUR

Fast Trial Trip of a Philadelphia Locomotive in the West.

[Chicago Herald]

The Shaw pulled out with one hundred and thirty pounds of steam, and sneaked out over drawbridges and through the outskirts of Milwaukee and with a kind of "oh just look at me" that suggested a school boy's innocent run from a melon patch. Word had been passed to Mr. Lockwoods's engineer and to Mr Hill of the Northwestern, that the first test might be made on the ten mile run between San Francis and the county line. At St. Francis the Shaw suddenly gathered herself up and with a low, deep snort shot by the station house like a flash. Her every movement was watched with the keenest interest by the railway officials. There was nothing of the jerking, thumping, vibratory motion other engines have, but the machinery worked smooth and regular. But for the roar of the wheels on the rails her movement would have been as noiseless as that of the finest stationary engine. A moment or two and Professor Dudley looked at his dynograph "She is running pretty sharp now," he said in a quiet way. "How much?" asked Mr Laying. "Sixty miles an hour" said the Professor Mr Laying looked satisfied, but Mr Dudley motioned to the engineer to let her out. A Herald man who was of the party sat in the front window and watched the furious steed as it shook itself and seemed like a living thing to reach out for rein and bit. Down at the side the cranks on the drivers were going in a perfect whirl—so fast the eye could not begin to follow them—and the great driving wheels spun like buzz saws.

"How fast?" said Mr Lockwood.

"The last mile in fifty four seconds. We are running now at sixty four miles an hour," said the Professor. The next mile was made in fifty five seconds, and the five mile out from St Francis was covered in four minutes and forty five seconds. Another very fast run was made from Lake Forest to Highland Park, and that distance was covered at the rate of 65 miles an hour, one mile of it being covered at the rate of sixty five miles an hour, one mile of it being covered in exactly fifty one seconds, or sixty eight miles an hour.

During that run the Herald man sat perched up in the cab of the engine, and the sensation of being hurled over the ground at that speed was terrific. Fences along the road seemed devoid of posts and the rails looked like a continuous blurr. A gang of track repairers were close to the track as the train shot by. The reporter had just time to see one knocked over by the atmospheric force created by the rushing engine and the others bracing themselves against it. At a little station called Highwood some ladies stood on the platform – a mere glance, in which not even the color of their dresses could be distinguished and they were gone. A few rods farther on a dog came bounding out. He gave one faint bark, barely heard, when he got caught in the atmospheric swirl and went rolling over and over heels over head. The grass along the road was laid flat by the rush, and even the trees waved as the monstrous force hurled by.

7/6/83 Telephone

GRANT ON LINCOLN:

I had never met him until I came East in 1864 to take command of all the armies. I had heard very much of him. I had heard much of his fund of anecdote. I was led to suppose that he was a man who passed away his time in telling little stories, and sometimes stories that it would not do to repeat except in society entirely composed of gentlemen. He spent a good deal of time with me at City Point, and I saw him on intimate terms. I never heard a word from Mr. Lincoln himself that could not be said in the society of a lady. He had a fund of anecdotes, and it was always to illustrate a point. I scarcely ever heard him talk in my life but that, after stating the case very clearly, he did not add some little anecdote to illustrate exactly what he meant and to give point to it.

7/14/83 Washingtonian

A Riotous Cowboy Shot Dead

DODGE CITY, KAN., July 10.—About six o'clock last evening a party of five cowboys, well under the influence of liquor, mounted their horses to leave the town. Approaching a dance-house, one of them rode up to the porch and fired off his six shooter. Two of the others then commenced firing, at the time putting spurs to their ponies. The city marshal and his assistants quickly arrived and sent a few shots after the three fugitives. When about three hundred yards away one of them fell from his horse and the other two made their escape across the bridge.

August, 1883

8/9/83 Mirror

Off the Track. The engine attached to the west-bound mail train on the W. O. & W. R. R. ran off the track just beyond Falls Church, on Saturday morning last, and turned completely over on its side on the bank. The accident caused considerable delay in the running of trains, and the track had to be shifted around the derailed engine. The accident, it is supposed, was caused by a buffer casting falling on the track from a freight train which preceded the mail, and when it was struck it threw the engine over on its side and also damaged the caboose and mail car. The engineer and fireman escaped injury by jumping from the engine just as it turned over. Several of the cars left the track but no one was hurt. Another engine was sent to the scene of the accident and took the cars on to Round Hill, returning to this city about half-past nine o'clock on Saturday night. The damaged engine was up-righted yesterday evening and brought back to this city, and to-day trains are running as usual.—*Alex. Gazette of Monday evening.*

Considerable inconvenience was occasioned to stock dealers by the mishap above referred to. There was no less then fourteen car loads of cattle and sheep lying at the depot in Leesburg, at 5 o'clock Saturday evening, most of them designed for the Queen town market of Monday. They left here about 9 o'clock Saturday night, and owing to the missing of connections were run into Washington city, from which point they had to be driven to the stock yard on Sunday—very much to the annoyance of the owners.

(It would be interesting to know in those days how they righted that heavy engine.)

8/10/83 Telephone

THE GREAT LITTLE JAY GOULD.

The country is full of the doings of this great little man. Personally he is one of the poorest specimens of the genus homo one would see in a day's journey on the streets of a large city. He is not much over five feet two inches in height, and weighs about 100 pounds. He is a sickly man, always taking medicine. He is unimpressive in manner, and has a dazed, shamed, look, as if he dreaded criticism. He is dark, swarthy, and his face has a Jewish cast. He was called on to speak recently at a railroad meeting in Boston, but he simpered and stammered like a schoolboy. He could only utter a few words, when he sat down confused. Yet this little, feeble, sickly-looking fellow is one of the most daring speculators of the age, and the most wonderful manipulator of stocks known to the history of Wall street. He controls properties estimated to be worth $400,000,000. Nobody, not even himself, can tell how much he is personally worth. But the disposition is always to exaggerate the fortunes of operators. In addition to his gigantic railway enterprises, this man owns the telegraphic system of the country, and through it has the press of the whole nation by the throat.—*Demorest's Monthly.*

Wm. G. BOPP,

Of Leesburg,

WOULD respecfully remind his old customers and the public generally that he is still prepared to do any work in his line, such as

PAPER HANGING, MATTRASS-MAKING,

UPHOLSTERING OF FURNITURE,

at short notice, and Reasonable Price.

☞ He can always be found on King St. J. W. Hammerly's Cabinet Maker Shop. Any order left there will receive prompt attention

---

MARK TWAIN'S NEW BOOK

"LIFE ON THE MISSISSIPI,"

Is proving the *grandest success* of all the Twain Series. A genuine bonanza to

BOOK AGENTS. For terms and territory, address DOUGLASS BROS., 53 N. 7th St., Phila., Pa.

August, 1883

8/10/83 Telephone

FASHIONABLE FOLLY.

HOT BLOOD OF TWO LOUDOUN MEN,

But None of it Spilled.

Quite a commotion was caused throughout the County, on Tuesday, by the announcement that two prominent men of the vicinity of Leesburg had indulged in the fashionable folly of a duel. It seems that hard feelings had, for some time, existed between Dr. Magill of Leesburg and Dr. West, who lives a few miles north of that town, resulting in a formal challenge being sent by the latter and accepted by the former and on early Tuesday morning they met on Harrison's island in the Potomac, (a spot made historic by the dreadful battle of Ball's Bluff) for the purpose of settling the difficulty with pistols. But both men have been seen since, with no evidence of violence and because of the reticence of the parties interested it is not known whether they exchanged shots, though report says they did, but somehow they succeded in adjusting matters without loss of blood. And if this was done without the burning of powder it is the more credit to the participants.

It is reported that Capt. Fauntleroy was second for Dr. Magill and Henry Selman for Dr. West.

It is bad enough when the hot blooded newspaper men, excited by fierce political controversies, indulge in pistol practice with each other as targets, but when the physicians, who should be the coolest-headed people in the land, resort to the duello, it seems that our civilization is progressing backward, and it is time to order a halt.

8/3/83 Telephone

Frank James is now on trial for murder and robbery and the evidence against him is strong, but we fear that the contemptible sentimentality which lionizes such characters as he is will be strong enough to turn him free without punishment.

The unqualified acquittal of Frank James, who was on trial for murder and robbery, was no surprise to us; indeed, such a verdict was foreshadowed in these columns. We do not know how far the jury was justified by the evidence in returning such a verdict, but it is well known that the man is guilty of the charges, and it is also well known that there are plenty of witnesses in Missouri to convict him; therefore the result of the trial is not only an outrage to justice but it is a great misfortune to Missouri. But if the people of that state are willing to give their sanction to such deeds of violence and crime as those of which Frank James is guilty, they deserve to be persecuted by the generation of outlaws which that verdict will foster.

But James is to be again tried, for participation in the Blue Cut train robbery, in which he is implicated by a posthumous confession of Clarence Hite, the youngest of the gang, which was published since the trial ended,

(Frank James was acquitted and spent his remaining 30 years out of trouble. He had several jobs and his last task was giving tours of the James farm for 25 cents.)

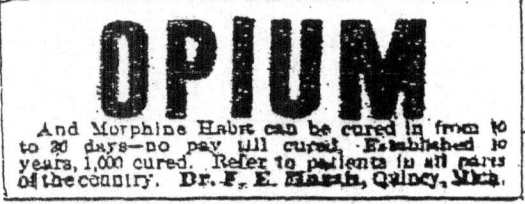

8/9/83 Mirror

Sullivan and Slade. These two representatives of the pugalistic fraternaty, had a bout with gloves in New York on Monday night last. Sullivan is the champion of the country and Slade is a Maori giant, brought here by old Jem Mace, for the express purpose of knocking the champion out. On Monday night, however, he, like many a man before him, went for wool and got wooled — Sullivan knocking him all around the ring, and finally sending him to "grass" too badly used up to respond when time was called — The fight took place in the Madison Square Garden, and the place was packed.

8/10/83 Telephone

On Wednesday morning a horse attached to a buggy in which Mrs. J. W. Deer and her little nephew were riding, became frightened near the colored school house and ran away, turning the corner at Harmony Church so shortly that the buggy struck the fence throwing it and the occupants nearly across the turnpike. We learn that they were badly bruised but not seriously hurt. The buggy looks like it had wrestled with a first-class cyclone.

—On Wednesday morning when just east of Town, a gentleman, whose name we could not learn, was thrown from his vehicle, caused by the latter breaking down, and had his arm broken. The Hamilton physicians being absent, he had to go Leesburg to get it attended to.

FRED. A NICOL.   RUDOLPH NICOL

NICOL BROTHERS,

Veterinary Surgeons,

LEESBURG, VA.

ALL DISEASES OF HORSES, CATTLE, and other Stock, treated in the Safest, Quickest and most effectual manner.

8/16/83 Mirror

Colored Troops from Washington. In addition to the crowd of persons from the county, who were in Leesburg on Monday, there arrived from Washington about twelve o'clock, A.M., a special train of 8 or 10 cars bringing Company B of the Capital City Guards, colored military organization of that city, and some 400 or 500 excursionists. The Company headed by a band of music after marching through the principal streets, drew up in front of the mayor's office where they went through some evolutions very creditably. They were received by Mayor Head in an address of welcome; they then marched to the Fair Grounds where they gave an exhibition drill and spent the rest of the evening in dancing and enjoying themselve generally, leaving about 9 o'clock — The company was under the command of Capt. W. P. Grey and presented quite a fine appearance.

8/3/83 Telephone

A Strange Story From Texas. GALVESTON, TEX., July 24.—A special dispatch to the News from Lampasas says a carriage containing the skeletons of three adults and two children, sitting bolt upright as if in life, has been found near a road in Piano county under a large tree. — The tree was shattered by lightning. It is supposed the carriage sought shelter under the tree and was struck, the bolt killing the inmates and the horses. The weather-beaten appearance of the carriage and its trimmings indicate that the event happened a year or two ago. In a small trunk was a letter addressed to "James G. Chamberlain, London, Eng." The remains were found by a ranchman driving cattle. The parties are supposed to have been tourists. The spot where they were found is very secluded, and far from any habitation.

8/10/83 Telephone

Agricultural Fairs.

[Episcopal Methodist.]

The original designs of these fairs was an excellent one. It was supposed that on the one hand the exhibit of farm and dairy products would tend to excite a spirit of emulation, which would result in more careful culture and better work; and the merit of improved stock would commend them to all farmers as promising far better returns than the ordinary breeds so common everywhere. On the other hand the exhibition of improved machinery would result in the introduction of labor-saving appliances, and enable the farmers to do better work and more of it at a minimum cost. And these results were for a time certainly secured, if indeed to some degree they are not now obtained. But the offering of large premiums made it necessary to add other attractions, so as to secure the largest possible number of visitors, that the gate-money might be sufficient to meet all demands. And instead of consulting together as to the means best calculated to elevate and interest the people, the effort was soon put forth to pander to human weakness and passions, and our agricultural fairs have become shamefully perverted from their original designs. Judges of horse-flesh soon demanded trials of speed to enable them to make proper awards, and then all the surroundings and evils of the race-track very naturally followed. Offers were also made to pay money for the privilege of having various shows, shooting galleries, games of chance, wheels of fortune, &c., which were gradually acceded to, because all these helped to pay the expenses, and lately some of the fairs have been more noted as resorts of fakirs, blacklegs and gamblers, than for anything else, the agricultural element becoming secondary, and the fair degenerating into a school of vice, where innocent country lads first saw the gilded temptations of sin. Balloon ascensions have proved a taking card, and the æronaut, who would ascend clinging to a mere bar, was more in demand than the one who used the safer basket. This picture is not overdrawn. The so-called Agricultural Fair of Loudoun County, Virginia, for the year 1881, answered the above description exactly, and we denounced the iniquity from our pulpit at the time. We distinctly remember that the exhibit of farm products, machinery and stock was very meagre at this fair, and that the evils we have referred to were most prominent. Now we call attention to this matter, and urge Methodist people to have nothing whatever to do with such legalized (?) iniquities. Your boys have temptation enough, without having an avalanche like this turned on them. It is the old story of going to the menagerie to see the animals and staying to see the circus. If Christian men will set their faces like flint against everything which has in it the appearance of evil, and will not only vigorously oppose the introduction of gambling in any form at our fairs, but, if despite their protest, these evils are allowed, they will conscientiously stay away from the exhibitions, and not only keep their own families away, but influence their neighbors to do likewise, the evil would soon be stamped out—

August, 1883

8/24/83 Telephone

Horse Stealing in Fairfax.

An account of the recent horse stealing in Fairfax county was published in yesterday's *Gazette*. A letter from that county received at this office today says: "Last Saturday night persons living in the vicinity of Fairfax Court House felt the effect of a sudden visit from horse-thieves. Messrs. John W. Graham and R. F. Broadwater, both of whom live right on the turnpike east of the village, had their stables entered and a horse from each taken out. Dr. F. H. Weltz had put his mare on pasture at Mr. Arthur Broadwater's Saturday afternoon and she fared a similar fate. A huckster from up the country passed through the Court House very early Sunday morning, and left word that a man passed through the toll gate near Ox Hill about two o'clock that morning, leading four horses westward. Parties from the Court House immediately put after the thief and there is no doubt but he will be taken, as those in pursuit mean business. The unanimous opinion is that if the man is caught and fully identified a piece of rope will be used, short and few the prayers said and a man will be seen standing under a tree with his feet about 30 inches from the ground."—*Alex Gazette, 21st.*

9/6/83 Mirror

Horse Stealing. For some time past there have been accounts of horse stealing in our neighboring counties of Fauquier and Fairfax, the latter county apparently having been especially visited by the thieves. It was, however, not until last week that we had to chronicle an occurrence of this kind in Loudoun, when we noticed the stealing of a horse from Mr. Whaley and one from Mr. Wm. Young, the latter of which was recovered. On Sunday night last the thieves again plied their vocation in this vicinity, stealing a horse, saddle and bridle from the stable of Mr. Jas. Thomas, a few miles west of town. Search was instituted on Monday, which resulted, toward night, in the finding of the mare, turned loose in a field a few miles from where she had been taken—the thief either having ridden her to his satisfaction, or become alarmed at the fear of capture. The frequency of these occurrences, and the boldness with which they are done should put our citizens on their guard. The crime of horse-stealing is a peculiarly mean one, and is heavily punished by the statutes, and we opine, should the rascals, who have been practicing it so boldly in this and the neighboring counties, be caught, there would be no hesitancy on the part of a jury in giving them the full benefit of the law

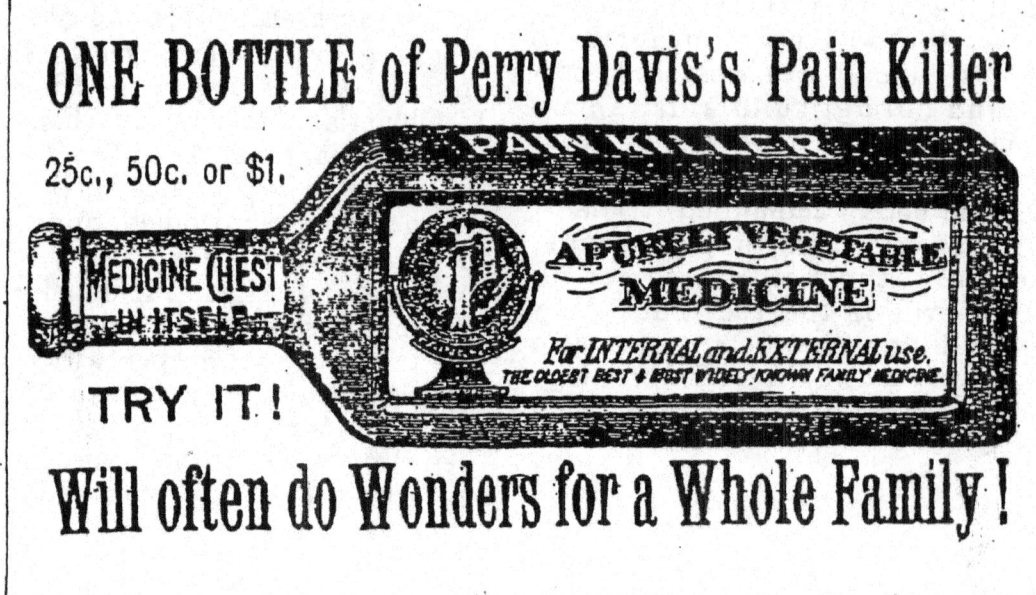

8/9/83 Mirror

A Child Outraged by a Tramp.

A special dispatch to the Baltimore *Sun* from Hagerstown, Md., says that Friday Gertrude, a nine year old daughter of Mr. Cornelius Virtz one of the prominent citizen of the neighborhood of Sandy Hook, Washington county, Md, accompanied an elder sister, Miss Pearl Virtz, on a part of the way to Sandy Hook. As she was returning to her home she was met by a tramp, who forced her into an adjacent cornfield of Mr Jacob A. Miller, where he outraged her. The child attempted to make an outcry, but the wretch prevented her from so doing by biting her lips, which show the marks of his brutality. After the occurrence in a dazed condition the child made her way toward Sandy Hook, where she was met by a colored woman and taken to the house of Mr. John Smith, where she was seised with convulsions and was for a time unable to give any statement of the cause of her condition. As soon as it was known men on horseback and on foot turned out in search of the perpetrator of the outrage, and no neck or corner was left unexplored. While drinking in a saloon in Harper's Ferry, W. Va., the man was arrested by Mr. George Bancroft, and with the aid of other citizens, and without waiting for authority of law, hurried across the river and taken before Justice Preston E. Miller, who, upon the evidence before him, sent him to jail for the grand jury. He is a man twenty five or thirty years of age, and gave his name as Edward Carr, but refused to give any further account of himself. The justice, hearing that violence would be offered the prisoner if taken from his office in front, secured the services of Rev. J. G. Butler, of Washington, who was visiting at his home, to attract the attention of the excited crowd outside while he sent the prisoner on from the rear in charge of deputized officers. At different points along the railroad men were waiting to lynch the villain, but he was removed by carriage. At Garrett's station the prisoner was placed on the train. Then the lynchers demanded the prisoner, and while the officers were trying to protect him, and while everything was in a state of excitement, the prisoner jumped out of the car window while the train was running about fifteen miles an hour and escaped.

RECAPTURED — Edward Carr, the perpetrator of the outrage upon little Gertie Virtz, was recaptured about ten o'clock Sunday night at the base of the Stone Mill mountain, near Knoxville, Frederick county, Md., about two miles from the scene of the crime. His captors, George Bancroft and Link Reed, fearing he would be lynched, hid him in a school house, and Monday morning lodged him in the Hagerstown jail. Carr confessed his crime, but says he was under the influence of liquor. The next influence brought to bear on him should be good hemp.

8/10/83 Telephone

The body of the lynchers consisted of forty masked men. They carried revolvers and were a determined and desperate set of men, and freely spoke of their intentions of lynching the tramps should they get them in their power. The lynchers demanded the surrender of the prisoners, and while the officers were trying to protect them and everything was in a state of excitement, the prisoners became greatly frightened at the demonstrations of the mob, and one walked quickly to the door and jumped from the train. His companion jumped through the window but alighted on the ground unhurt. The train was running at the rate of thirty miles per hour at the time of their escape. The lynchers were much chagrined at the escape of the prisoners, and quickly stopped the train and endeavored to recapture them.

LATER: One of the villains, named Edward Carr, has been recaptured and the other will, most likely, be; and the demonstrations of the people of that locality evidence that the dastardly fiends will never be troubled with a trial—except the trial of a rope.

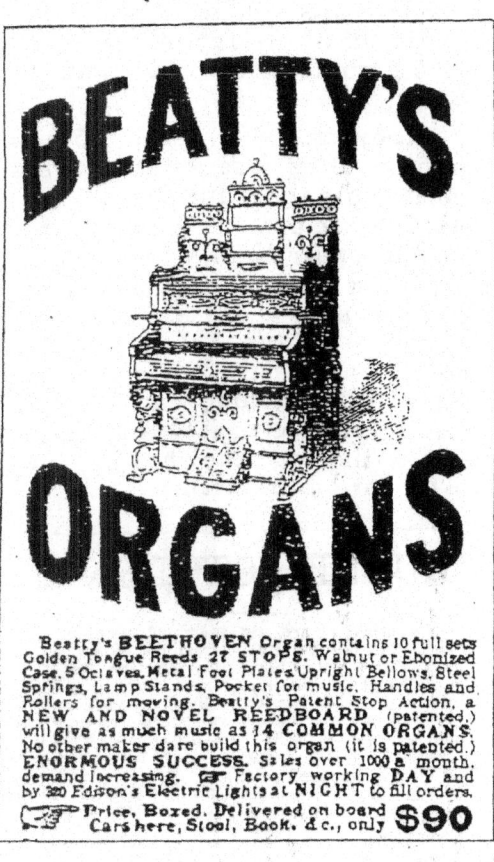

September, 1883

THE TELEPHONE.

FRIDAY.......... SEPT. 28TH.

—We had a slight frost last week.

—Send us notes—both news notes and bank notes.

—Threshers report that wheat is turning out first rate.

☞ Go to T. A. Schooley's shop and get heavy hoop iron for your cider barrels.

——Mason Throckmorton has rented the Osburn house here and will open a livery stable and hotel soon.—— Jonah Thomas threshed 990 bushels of wheat from 30 acres. Who can beat this?——Farmers will begin seeding this week.

—J. F. Dodd, Esq., took a barrel of flour to the Fair and got first premium on it, but he lost the flour.— He left it in the building, where it was exhibited, for a few days, and when he went after it, behold it had crawled out a window and escaped. Mr. Dodd could have no better recommendation, for surely we have no man in Loudoun who would steal a barrel of *poor* flour. Mr. Dodd should institute search in the houses of the committeemen who examined the flour.

—BLOOMFIELD, VA., Sept. 25th.— As the result of a series of meetings held at Ebenezer, during the past week, fourteen persons were baptized in the dam near Moor's Mill, this A. M.——Miss Aurie Brown, now staying at her uncle's, (R. C. Littleton) is quite ill.——Miss Fronie Gill was quite seriously hurt one night last week, whilst returning from church, by some boys riding into the buggy and upsetting it, the horse's foot striking her on the head.

HORSE STOLEN!

A light bay mare, six years old, weighing about 1000 lbs., was stolen from the subscriber's pasture, near Purcellville, sometime Wednesday night. She was marked as follows:— White stripe in her face a light diamond on her nose, a white mark about two inches long on the outside of her left leg near the hock joint and slightly capped on right hip. She is quite fat and well gaited.

A liberal reward will be given for information which will lead to the recovery of the animal or apprehension of the thief.
BETTIE COPELAND,
P. O.—Purcellville, Va.

The Winchester Fair.

The Fourteenth Annual Fair of the Shenandoah Valley Agricultural Society will be held at Winchester, Va.

COMMENCING WEDNESDAY, OCT. 17, 1883, and continuing four days. The regular premiums have been supplemented by many valuable individual subscriptions, among them TWO magnificent SILVER CUPS AS FIRST AND SECOND PREMIUMS FOR SADDLE HORSES, presented by Col. E. P. C. Lewis, of New Jersey. These Cups are both superior to the one presented by the same gentleman last year, which was worth $100, and will beyond doubt induce the finest show of Saddle Horses ever seen in Virginia.

ONE HUNDRED DOLLARS FOR THE BEST HERD OF SHORT-HORNS, of five or more, offered in cash or plate by Col. U. L. Boyce, of Clarke county; (besides Society's cash premium.) And numerous other valuable special premiums in every Department, for details of which write to the Secretary.

THE CADETS OF THE VA. MILITARY INSTITUTE WILL ENCAMP UPON THE GROUND DURING THE FAIR.

Trials of Speed Every Day, for Large Purses.
ARRANGEMENTS FOR A GRAND TRADES DISPLAY,

Representing all the varied industries of the Valley of Virginia, have been perfected. It will occur on Thursday, October 18, and will be a most novel and interesting feature.

ATTRACTIONS AND AMUSEMENTS for visitors are numerous and varied. The most liberal arrangements have been made with the Railroads for the transportation of Visitors, and Exhibits of every description; and every facility for the comfort and entertainment of patrons has been proved.

For further particulars address the President,
MAJ. H. L. D. LEWIS, Berryville, Va., or
E. G. HOLLIS, Sec'y.

(Winchester is in the county adjacent to the southwest corner of Loudoun. It changed hands more than about any other town in the war. The former "apple capital of the world" and the former home of Senator Harry Byrd and Patsy Cline.)

Let Us Have Light.—Since our street lamps have been provided with the new arrangements for lighting, we have been enjoying the pleasure of unusually well lighted streets and congratulating ourselves that at last we had a light that did more than make the darkness visible. But, on Monday night there was not a light on the streets and the town was shrouded with a pall of darkness equal to the fabled stack of black cats. As a result of this the foot of many a belated pedestrian was dashed with more or less violence against unexpected rocks, while owing to the rains of Monday there were pools of water standing on the pavements and every loose brick responded to the tread of the passer-by with a deluge of mud and water very trying to good clothes, clean linen and the christian character of the luckless individual who happened to plant his foot squarely on the one or the other,—and we fear the language used in many instances was more expressive than elegant.

The town is lighted with gasoline, under a contract with a Philadelphia company, and the mishap of Monday night was caused by the failure of their lamp-lighter, from sickness or some other cause, coming to time.— On Tuesday the company sent an employe from headquarters to look after the matter, and we presume that hereafter things will be better managed; as they will have to be if the party of the first part would live in peace with the party of the second part.

FRESH FISH.

WE desire to inform our customers and the public generally, that we are still engaged in the Fish Business, at Steadman's Corner, (corner Loudoun and King Streets,) Leesburg, Va. We are now prepared to furnish FRESH

Herring and Shad,

by the hundred or thousand, to all who may favor us with their orders, and

AT THE VERY LOWEST PRICES.

We are thankful for past patronage, and solicit a continuance of the same.

JAMES F. FRANKLIN,
H. CLAY RYON,
Leesburg, Va.

THE TELEPHONE.

FRIDAY............SEPT. 28TH.

It was the true spirit of noble humanity which prompted the New England veterans to visit the Confederate cemetery, at Winchester, when on their recent visit to that vicinity, and offer a floral tribute to the bravery of their fallen foes. It was a sight of which the prejudiced minds of that locality had never dreamed; and when they beheld it they were overwhelmed with amazement if not remorse. One old confederate exclaimed: "I have never been in the Yankee cemetery, [near by] but this thing has brought the tears to my wicked old eyes, and I am going to visit that graveyard tomorrow."

That expression, such as makes the whole world kin, will do much to melt the feeling of prejudice and resentment which had long been fostered in the bosoms of many who beheld it, regarding the people of the North. If the men who met each other on the awful fields of battle can drop a flower on the grave of a foe, surely the citizen who did no fighting can afford to put away the hatred of the past and let the spirit of neighborly kindness control his intercourse with these around.

ROAD ENGINES.

THRESHERMEN, save yourselves, and the vexations delays in moving; largely increase your earnings, with but a small increase of investment!

C. & G. COOPER & CO'S.,

SELF STEERING,

TRACTION ENGINES,

with Link-Motion, Reverse Gear. The best and cheapest 10 Horse Power, all complete, $1,225.00.

I am now ordering a number of these splendid Machines for Threshing and Sawing.

9/14/83 Telephone

Railroad Accident.

Engine No. 1 (in ante bellum days known as the "Lewis McKenzie") and two cars of the passenger train on the Washington, Ohio and Western Railroad due here at 7:15 a. m. yesterday, were thrown from the track between Hunter's Mill and Thornten's by the engine striking some cattle which were standing in a curve of the track, preventing the engineer from seeing them in time to stop the train. The engine turned completely over and went down the embankment, followed by the two cars, one of which was wrenched from the trucks which were left on the track. Fireman Beard had one leg broken and his shoulder dislocated, and baggage master Meaks was slightly hurt, though able to walk to his home after arriving in this city. The remainder of the crew of the train and the passengers, though jarred and shaken up considerably, escaped with slight bruises. As soon as the news of the accident was received here a wrecking train was sent out, the track cleared and the passengers and injured persons brought to this city.— Persons who visited the scene of the accident and beheld the almost inverted position of the train were astonished and glad to learn that no one was killed, as from the spectacle presented it seemed that it was only through a merciful interposition of Providence that any one in the accident escaped instant death or serious injury. It is also a strange fact to note that notwithstanding the manner in which the cars were piled up by the accident, they were damaged but comparatively little. They have been righted and brought to this city, and the engine will be raised to the track and brought here by tomorrow.

THE PROPOSAL.

He.—My darling, you look irresistibly lovely tonight!

She.—Do I? Thanks very much! you are handsome as a Prince, Charley, in your dress suit.

He.—Give the credit to the DIAMOND Shirt, my love, which I wear for the first time to-night; it is that which gives tone to my toilette. Here is its prototype (slipping the Diamond engagement ring on her finger).

She.—May our love be as enduring as the fame of
"The DIAMOND Shirt."

Tableau.

CRUDE PETROLEUM
—FOR—
Throat & Lung Diseases
THE GREATEST MEDICAL DISCOVERY OF THE AGE.

The Consumptive's Hope!

No secret. Formula sent free to any physician. Relief from the first dose. Miraculous in its effects. Cures 99 cases in 100. A noted physician says he regards it as the only remedy that can be relied upon for healing Tubercles on the lungs. Another says that from his experience he is satisfied beyond all doubt of its power in curing consumption.

☞ The afflicted are requested to send to us FREE OF CHARGE. ENCLOSE STAMP.

WATTERS MEDICAL CO.,
Box 651,   Bradford, Penna.

October, 1883

10/12/83 Telephone

ANOTHER HORSE STOLEN.

Mr. B. F. Dove who lives in Fairfax county, near Burke's station, had a fine horse stolen from his farm last night about 10 o'clock, but has been unable to obtain any traces of it, though he reported the case to the police authorities of this city and Washington early this morning. It is supposed that the horse was stolen by the same gang of thieves who have been operating in this neighborhood for some time.

A man named John Wilson was arrested in Frederick county, Md., on Friday charged with horse stealing which it is said may furnish the clue to the band which have been plying their vocation in this section of country, if there is any truth in the prisoner's statements. The band, he says, is bound by oaths not to divulge secrets or betray a confederate, and a violation of their obligation is severely punished when the opportunity offers. Its present field of operation is from Luzerne county, Pa., down through Maryland and Virginia.— Horses stolen in these States are taken when necessary to Southwestern Virginia, Tennessee, North Carolina and Kentucky, to be sold or exchanged with a gang operating in a similar way in those sections. In other words, an exchange system is carried on largely, the object being to elude pursuit or detection by getting the stolen property as far from the vicinity of its ownership as possible. He stated to some of the officials that if a guarantee was given him that he would not be prosecuted for the offense for which he was now imprisoned he would reveal the names and rendezvous of the gang with which he claims to be connected, and give information that would lead to the recovery of a number of horses. An opportunity to do this will probably be given him. Before being taken to Hagerstown the prisoner was called on by Mr. J. W. Ashton, of Falls Church, who is in search of three horses valued at nearly $500, which were stolen from his farm on the 26th ult., and which he succeeded in tracing as far as Montgomery county, but although some knowledge of the matter was indicated by Wilson, he would say nothing positive or satisfactory unless first promised a release from his present confinement. He would say this much, that ten horses recently stolen in Virginia and Pennsylvania are now in possession of two of the gang named Johnson and Baird.—*Alex. Gazette.*

DODD'S
TWO MILLS!

'TIS SAID THE MILLS OF THE GODS
grind slow, but grind exceeding fine!
The MILLS OF DODD GRIND FAST,
YET GRIND EXCEEDING FINE!

THE OLD WATERFORD MILL

is in perfect order and turns out daily the best quality of FLOUR. ☞ TRY IT! WE GUARANTEE SATISFACTION! The

Virginia Mill,

(or WOOD'S MILL), is ready at all times to do first class work, and our Miller is expert and accommodating.

☞ WE ONLY ASK A TRIAL,
WE KNOW WE CAN PLEASE ☜

These Mills have undergone thorough repairs, and the public may rest assured that at either they will receive fair treatment and always get the worth of their money.
☞ REMEMBER WE ARE RUNNING TWO MILLS to accommodate the public, and ask a liberal patronage. We are determined to please. Give us a call.
J. F. DODD,
sep 20, 1883 tf   Waterford, Va.

The Waterford Mill, still standing and apparently in good shape from the outside, was regarded as old, even in those days.

10/25/83 Mirror

October, 1888

POCKET-PICKING AS AN ART

A Millionaire Pickpocket and His Exploits—Training Boys in the Science of Abstracting.

There may be persons who, like the Queen of France, rather admire a great thief on a gibbet, but have a high disdain for such a petty offender as a mere pickpocket. On the stage *Pistol*, *Nim* and *Bardolph* are amusing, and audiences smile as these worthies steal whatever they can lay hands on. But when the play is ended the careful man buttons his coat over his watch-pocket and leaves his sympathies with the stage rogues behind him in the theatre. Yet, philosophically as well as practically considered, there is after all, a tinge of romance connected with the profession of picking pockets. It is only a big city that can furnish one of this craft with his daily supply of purses and pocket books, jewelry and small wares. Only amid great wealth and a vast population could such a profession be carried on with success, and it surely requires great adroitness to escape detection.

"Pickpockets are a class of thieves who must be specially fitted for the business," said a headquarters detective to a Chicago *News* reporter. "They go through a course of instruction, as a general thing, and learn it as a child learns to read. But no instructors will accept as a pupil any one with short, stumpy fingers. It requires for pickpockets, just as it does for playing the violin, long, lean, flexible, and even sensitive fingers."

"Do you mean to say that there are regular instructors in the art of digital appropriation?"

"Oh, yes; old experts who have reduced it to a science. Some of them who are advanced in years, or otherwise incapacitated for active work on their own hook, devote all their time to instructing thieves and putting up jobs for them. It is a peculiar profession, and requires peculiar talents, as well as peculiar surroundings and circumstances to make it a success. The pickpocket, out of a large city, ceases to be a great artist, and in a poorer town or a village, would degenerate into a mere burglar, or even become honest or prosperous. The pickpocket never commits violence, as the footpad, the burglar or the garroter does. He performs his work unostentatiously, unobtrusively—I might say delicately. He is a judge of character, too. He is a sort of detective in his way, knowing at a glance the kind of a man whose which is likely to be solid and valuable and not belonging to the order of flash jewelry. Long experience has made him about as good a judge of the value of a thing as a jeweler or pawn-broker. There is a daily danger in his mode of life, which no doubt has attractions for the adventurous—He goes forth with his liberty in his hand—He lives in the face of danger. He sees companions and friends perpetually struck off the roll of gentlemen-at-large. He knows not when his own day of doom may arrive."

"Does his business pay, generally speaking?"

"Hardly. That is to say, there are very few rich thieves of any description. They nearly all die paupers, or in prison, or in their boots; many at the hands of their comrades. Fear and guilt are the passions that sway them. There is no such thing as honor among thieves. Some have amassed wealth, but to how many of them has it been of use? You remember Joe Parrish, who was arrested here in Chicago last February by Detective Elliott and taken to Syracuse, N. Y., where he was wanted for picking a man's pockets of $500? He was one of the most adroit pickpockets in the country, and his similar operations of the few months preceding his arrest would reach an aggregate of several thousand dollars. Parrish has grown rich from his multitudinous robberies and owns valuable real estate in Chicago, New York, and many other large cities. He is widely known among the crooks of every city in the country, by whom he was given the title of the "King of Pickpockets." His career of crime has been a long one, and he is supposed to have stolen about $1,000,000. He is not over 45 years of age, yet he has committed more robberies and escaped scot free oftener than any man in America. Then there was Dan Noble, another famous pickpocket, who recently died in a London prison. He was about the age of Parrish, and was quite as well known at one time on this side of the Atlantic but he graduated into a bank-sneak before his final arrest."

"Do professional pickpockets usually operate singly or in gangs?"

"Some of them prefer to go it alone, but as a general thing they travel in organized mobs of three. It takes three men to do a neat and safe job, except in dense crowds, where the usual precautions are not necessary, but even then, they nearly always work in gangs. In the parlance of the craft these three individuals are known respectively as the 'wire,' the 'stall' and the 'cover.' The 'wire' is the pickpocket himself; the stall does duty by attracting the man's or woman's attention while the operator's fingers are in the pocket; the 'cover' places himself in a position so that the movements of the wire cannot be observed. It is very often the case that the wire is a boy, while the other two are men. For the mere business of relieving pockets of their contents boys are the ablest adepts. Many a street Arab has been driven to the work by want and bad company at a very early age, becoming a professional long before he has attained his growth."

"I have heard also that women are very smooth at the business?"

"So they are. They frequently travel with male pals, and always do the delicate and risky part of the work. You seldom hear of one being caught. This is not so much owing to their superior cunning as the fact that they are carefully covered and protected by their male confreres. I have noticed that when a female pick pocket travels alone she preys upon her sex almost exclusively. When pickpockets are working in a great crowd, as I said before, they go in gangs -- The chief manipulator goes ahead. He selects a victim, fans his pockets to see if there is anything in it, then slips his hand daintly into it and takes out the purse of money, which he passes back to one of his comrades. Sometimes it changes three or four times in as many seconds, and even if the operator is nabbed immediately after the work is done nothing is found on his person to convict him of the theft."

"What do you mean by 'fanning'?"

"That is simply the slang for feeling it in the light cautious manner which is learned by training. A sharp thief never puts his hand into a man's pocket at random, but goes through the fanning process at first, and locates the object he desires to 'pinch.' A clever boy, gaining a character for a light and successful hand, is well cared for by his older pals. With such a lad it is well worth their while to behave fairly and give him a liberal share of the spoils. I heard of a case not long ago where a boy, being detected by one of his victims, was got away by two of his comrades, one of whom was arrested, tried and convicted, and sentenced to six month's imprisonment. During the circus season swarms of pickpockets follow the travelling shows about the country, plying their trade in the vast crowds of people that are attracted by the exhibition. In the past few years, however, the proprietors of some of the leading circuses have abated this nuisance to a considerable extent by employing an efficient corps of special detectives to accompany the show and protect its patrons."

11/2/83 Telephone

Rev. De Witt Talmage, in a sermon, said of tobacco as follows:

"One reason why there are so many victims of this habit is because there are so many ministers of religion who smoke and chew. They smoke until they get bronchitis, and the dear people have to pay their expenses to Europe. They smoke until the nervous system breaks down. They smoke themselves to death. I could name three eminent clergymen who died of cancer in the mouth, and in every case the physician said it was tobacco."

—Farmers, now is the time to do your hauling. Dont wait till you are able to cut the roads with your heavy wagons.

MOTHER NOBLE'S HEALING SYRUP.
20 Million Bottles sold in 16 years. A certain Cure for Dyspepsia, all Diseases of the Kidneys, Liver, Stomach, Blood, Skin and Bowels. Can Produce Thousands of Letters proving its Curative Powers. AN OLD AND LONG TRIED REMEDY.
77 AMITY STREET, NEW YORK CITY.
FOR SALE BY ALL DRUGGISTS.

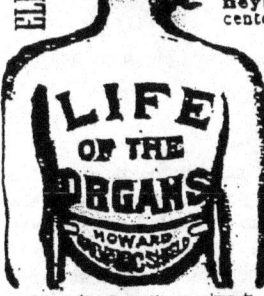

Nerve-Life and Vigor
— RESTORED —

This cut shows the **Howard Electric AND Magnetic Shield** as applied over the Kidneys and Nervo-vital centers. The only appliance made that fits every part of the body, and the only one needed to POSITIVELY CURE **Kidney Disease, Rheumatism, Dyspepsia**, the worst cases of **Seminal Weakness, Exhaustion, Impotency**, and all Diseases and Weakness of the Urino Genital Organs.

(Patented Feb. 25, 1879.)

YOUNG MEN, from early indiscretion, lack nerve force and fail to attain strength.

MIDDLE-AGED MEN often lack vigor, attributing it to the progress of years.

The MOTHER, WIFE and MAID, suffering from Female Weakness, Nervous Debility and other ailments, will find it the only cure.

To one and all we say that the Shield gives a natural aid in a natural way WITHOUT DRUGGING THE STOMACH.

Warranted One Year, and the best appliance made.

Illustrated Pamphlet, THREE TYPES OF MEN, also Pamphlet for Ladies only, sent on receipt of 6c, sealed; unsealed, FREE.

American Galvanic Co.,

OFFICES: 134 Madison St., Chicago.
1103 Chestnut St., Phila.

November 1883

(This was a state election. The presidential election would occur in 1884.)

THE MIRROR

BENJ. F. SHEETZ, Editor.

Thursday Morning, Nov. 8, 1883.

BOSSISM CRUSHED

BOTH BRANCHES OF THE LEGISLATURE DEMOCRATIC.

THE TELEPHONE.

FRIDAY............ Nov. 9th.

VIRGINIA A LITTLE OFF!
BUT SHE WILL COME IN ALL RIGHT NEXT TIME.

VIRGINIA

THE BOURBONS VICTORIOUS.

Some comments regarding the confusing political scene in Virginia:
The critical issue of the day concerned the method of paying for the state prewar debt. The Conservative party (later the Democrats) became split into two factions: the Funders and the Readjusters with the latter eventually gaining control. Ex-Confederate General William T. Mahone was one of the founders of the Readjuster movement. He was elected U.S. Senator in 1881 but to the dismay of many Virginians turned Republican and was later state Republican chairman.

The term Bourbon was a derisive term that the Republican press applied to Democrats. According to local historian Wynne Saffer, the term was derived from the French Royal family. "A Bourbon never forgets anything or learns anything."

12/7/83 Telephone

Sojourner Truth, a noted colored woman, died at Battle Creek Mich. on the 26th ult, aged, as she claimed, 108 years. She was a woman of strong mind and upright character. Most of her life was devoted to the elevation of her race. She was, doubtless, the most noted and influential colored woman in America— We heard her speak several years ago and we were impressed with the strength of her untutored mind and her untiring fidelity to her oppressed race. An exchange speaking of this remarkable woman, said:

She was born a slave in New York state and when she was nine years old she was sold on the auction block with a lot of sheep, she and the sheep bringing $104. She was owned by Colonel Ardinburgh, but in 1827 she was emancipated. Her life us a slave was a hard one, her labor being almost endless, and she was under no improving influences. She never learned to read or write. At an early age she experienced religion, and, as most colored people do, she became very enthusiastic over it, never missing an opportunity to attend a camp-meeting. By her lectures in various parts of the country on slavery, temperance and other topics, and her services as a hospital nurse during the war, she gained much notoriety, but she ever sought to do conscientiously what she considered to be her work, and did not seek the applause of her fellow-beings. Previous to the war Sojourner held a series of meetings in Northern Ohio. She sometimes made strong points in her speeches which she knew would hit hard those who apologized for slavery. At the close of one of these meetings a man came up to her and said: "Old woman, do you think that your talk about slavery does any good? Do you suppose people care for what you say? Why, I don't care any more for your talk than I do for the bite of a flea!"— "Perhaps not," Sojourner said; "but the Lord willing, I'll keep you scratching!"

December, 1883

Christmas Goods,
—AT—
Beuchler's BAKERY,
LEESBURG, VA.

I HAVE just received a large lot of Goods for the HOLIDAYS, which I offer at the following prices:

LONDON LAYER RAISINS,	20 cts	per lb
LOOSE MUSCATEL	15 cts	" "
VALENCIA	13 cts	" "
SEEDLESS SULTANA	18 cts	" "
CITRON	25 cts	" "
CURRANTS	10 cts	" "
MIXED NUTS	20 cts	" "
MIXED CANDY, 6 lbs for	100 cts	
MINCE MEAT	13 cts	" "

CHRISTMAS IS NEAR AT HAND.

And as usual NIXON is the first in the field, with a fine line of fresh new pack goods, consisting of Leghorn Citron, Valencia, Sultana and London Layer Raisins, Currants, Olives, Nuts, French Candies, Prunes, &c., all of which are at bottom prices. A full line of the celebrated Houston Canned Vegetables which are delicious in flavor and full weights.

A handsome line of Glass and Queensware, consisting in part of French, English and American Tea Sets, newest styles Majolica ware, ornamented China, &c., suitable for christmas presents. All of these goods were bought low and will be sold accordingly.— Continue to keep a full and complete stock of Standard Groceries, best quality guaranteed, no off goods handled. Remember Nixon's the only store in the county that deals largely in Fancy groceries, both foreign and domestic.

Jersey Lily and Silver Lake Flour always on hand. Pure grain Pepper Sifted, only 20c. lb.

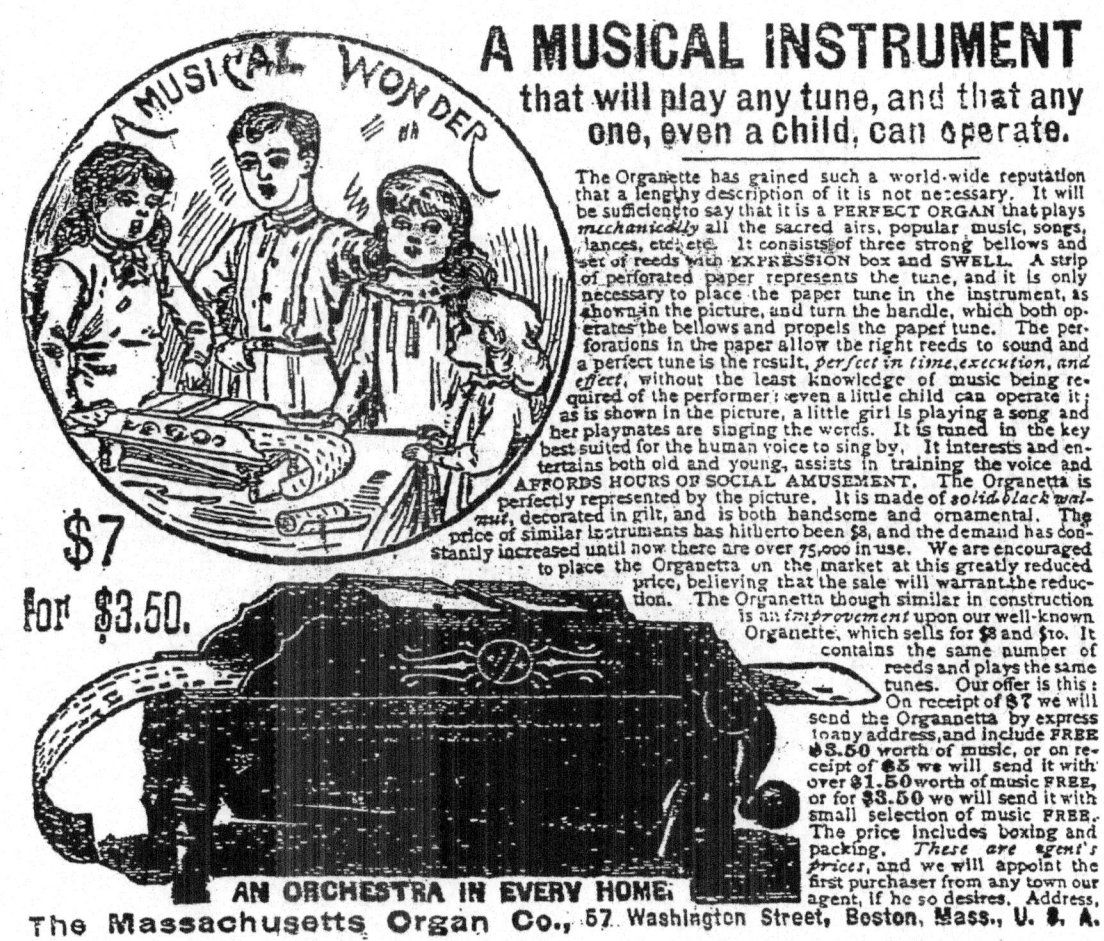

A MUSICAL INSTRUMENT
that will play any tune, and that any one, even a child, can operate.

$7 for $3.50.

The Organetta has gained such a world-wide reputation that a lengthy description of it is not necessary. It will be sufficient to say that it is a PERFECT ORGAN that plays mechanically all the sacred airs, popular music, songs, dances, etc., etc. It consists of three strong bellows and set of reeds with EXPRESSION box and SWELL. A strip of perforated paper represents the tune, and it is only necessary to place the paper tune in the instrument, as shown in the picture, and turn the handle, which both operates the bellows and propels the paper tune. The perforations in the paper allow the right reeds to sound and a perfect tune is the result, *perfect in time, execution, and effect*, without the least knowledge of music being required of the performer; even a little child can operate it; as is shown in the picture, a little girl is playing a song and her playmates are singing the words. It is tuned in the key best suited for the human voice to sing by. It interests and entertains both old and young, assists in training the voice and AFFORDS HOURS OF SOCIAL AMUSEMENT. The Organetta is perfectly represented by the picture. It is made of *solid black walnut*, decorated in gilt, and is both handsome and ornamental. The price of similar instruments has hitherto been $8, and the demand has constantly increased until now there are over 75,000 in use. We are encouraged to place the Organetta on the market at this greatly reduced price, believing that the sale will warrant the reduction. The Organetta though similar in construction is an *improvement* upon our well-known Organette, which sells for $8 and $10. It contains the same number of reeds and plays the same tunes. Our offer is this: On receipt of $7 we will send the Organetta by express to any address, and include FREE $3.50 worth of music, or on receipt of $5 we will send it with over $1.50 worth of music FREE, or for $3.50 we will send it with small selection of music FREE. The price includes boxing and packing. *These are agent's prices*, and we will appoint the first purchaser from any town our agent, if he so desires. Address,

AN ORCHESTRA IN EVERY HOME.
The Massachusetts Organ Co., 57 Washington Street, Boston, Mass., U. S. A.

December. 1883

(It is amazing that just a few years after Edison's patents on the phonograph, these toys would appear.

THE TELEPHONE

FRIDAY, ... JAN. 4TH.

—1883 is not.

—Lookout for ice!

—Look before you leap—this year.

—The high wind of last Thursday night moved a car on the switch at Purcellville, so that the morning train struck it, badly damaging the sides of two coaches. We hear that a similar accident occurred at Leesburg, but without doing much damage.

—Last Thursday night was a howler! The wind shook everything to its foundation, dispelling sleep and causing the would-be sleepers to get up and prepare for the general crash which seemed imminent. But it did not worry the individual who was raised on the western prairies.

THE TELEPHONE.

FRIDAY .... JAN. 18TH.

—Sleighing has been good this week.

—Most ice houses are full of the best ice put up for years.

—The friends of Thomas Hatcher will be grieved to learn that he is quite low with Consumption.

—BLOOMFIELD, VA., Jan. 15.—The dreaded measles has at last reached us, and, in connection with colds, has nearly broken up the public school.

—On Wednesday the Loudoun Valley was beautiful as Fairy Land. A soft, fleecy snow had fallen and thawed just enough to fasten it to whatever it touched, then followed a mist and all was solidly fixed by a good freeze Tuesday night; and when the great luminary peeped o'er Catoctin's crest on Wednesday morning, it illuminated the delicate drapery of the landscape and made the Valley glorious.

—Mr. John Frasier, of the Trapp, left last Thursday for Texas, in quest of the dear object of his affections. Jno., we wish you a safe journey and may the day never come that you will regret going so far after a companion for life.

1/18/84 Telephone

THE STAGE-COACH ROBBERS.

There was an army officer, a sutler, a surveyor and two men who might have been mine inspectors in the stage when it drew up at Burt Hill to take on another passenger.

"Howdy," said the new passenger as he crowded in.

As he stood for a moment in the light of the station lamp, all saw that his left eye was gone. He wore no shade or patch to conceal the loss, and those who gave him a second look felt that the fire in his remaining eye was bright enough to answer for two. Dark as it was in the stage he seemed to have "sized up" every man inside of a minute, and, seeming to be satisfied regarding the crowd, he settled himself back in his seat, and had no remarks to make.

By and by the army officer mentioned something about road-agents, and directly the conversation became interesting. Coaches had been stopped at various points on the line within a week, and it was pretty generally believed that a bad gang had descended on the route and were still ripe for business. The man with one eye had nothing to say. Once or twice he raised his head and that single eye blazed in the darkness like a lone star, but not a word escaped his mouth. The captain had said what he would do in case the coach was halted, and this brought out the others. It was firmly decided to fight. The passengers had money to fight for and weapons to fight with.

The man with one eye said nothing. At such a time, and under such circumstances there could be but one interpretation of such conduct.

"A coward has no business traveling this route," said the captain in a voice that every man could hear.

The stranger started up, and that eye of his seemed to shower sparks of fire, but after a moment he fell back again without having replied.

"Pop! pop! halt!"

The passengers were dozing as the salute of the road-agents reached their ears. The coach was halted in a way to tumble everybody together, and legs and bodies were still tangled up when a voice at the door of the coach called out:

"No nonsense, now! You gentlemen climb right down here and up with your hands! The first man who kicks on me will get a bullet through his head!"

We had agreed to fight. The captain had agreed to lead us. We were listening for his yell of defiance and the click of his revolver when he stepped down and out as humbly as you please. The sutler had been aching to chew up a dozen road-agents, and now he was the second man out. The surveyor had intimated that he never passed over the route without killing at least three highwaymen, but this occasion was to be an exception. In three minutes the five of us were down and in line and with hands up, and the road agent had said:

"Straight matter of business!—First one who drops his hands won't ever know what hurt him!"

Where was the man with one eye? The robber appeared to believe that we were all out, and he was just approaching the head of the line to begin his work when a dark form dropped out of the coach, there was a yell as if from a wounded Tiger, and a revolver began to crack. The robber went down at the first pop. His partner was just coming around the rear of the coach. He was a game man. He knew what happened, but he was coming to the rescue. Pop! pop! pop! went the revolvers, their flashes lightning up the night until we could see the driver in his seat.

It didn't take twenty seconds.—One of the robbers lay dead in front of us—the other under the coach, while the man with one eye had a lock cut from his head and the graze of a bullet across his cheek.—Not one of us had moved a finger. We were five fools in a row. There was a painful lull after the last shot, and it lasted a full minute before the stranger turned to us and remarked in a quiet, cutting manner:

"Gentlemen, ye kin drop yer hands!"

We dropped. We undertook to thank him, and we wanted to shake hands, and somebody suggested a shake-purse for his benefit, but he motioned us into the coach, banged the door after us and climbed up to a seat beside the driver. His contempt for such a crowd could not be measured.—*M. Quad.*

January 1884

1/18/84 Telephone

A Reminiscence of Fred. Douglass.

In a lecture on the anti-slavery movement in Lynn, Mass, last week, Mr. J. M. Buffum related the following:

"About this time the mob was after Fred. Douglas, and I told him he was not safe in New England, and on the 16th of August, 1845, Mr. Douglas and myself sailed in the steamship Cambria for England. The captain would not allow Mr. Douglass in the first cabin, and so we were obliged to take the after cabin. When the Irish coast was reached the captain gave the first cabin passengers a complimentary dinner. After the dinner was over Captain Judkins came to me and said some of the passengers desired to hear Douglas speak.— Mr. Douglass complied and as soon as he began to speak there was great excitement, and cries of 'Throw him overboard,' 'Kill him,' and other threats were made. The crowd became so boisterous that Capt. Judkins came on deck and said that he (Douglass) must stop, as he (the captain) wanted to speak. The captain said that he had made it pleasant for the passengers all the way over, and that some of the passengers wanted to hear Douglass speak, and he should speak: then, said the captain, 'Give it to them, Douglass, like bricks.' After listening a few minutes a little man from Connecticut spoke up and said that he would be one of six to throw Douglass overboard. A big Irishman spoke up and said, 'You will throw him overboard, will you? Did it ever occur to you that you might go over yourself? Douglass has as many friends as you have.' Capt. Judkins told the boatswain to go down below and get the irons, and said that he would put them all in irons if they made any more disturbance. Upon reaching the wharf the captain was handed a card from one of the passengers, challenging him to fight a duel."

2/1/84 Telephone

FRED DOUGLASS
Marries a White Woman.

On the evening of the 24th ult. Fred Douglass was married to Miss Helen M. Pitts, of Avon N Y., who is an intelligent lady, 35 years of age. For some time she has been a copyist in Mr. Douglass' office. Colored circles of Washington are thrilled from center to circumference by the sensation.

1/3/84 Mirror

Stonewall Jackson and His Slaves.

A correspondent furnishes the Pittsburgh (Pa) *Commercial* with some letters written by Stonewall Jackson, including the following, which may have general interest even at this late day:

"WINCHESTER, December 3, 1861.

"My Dear Friend,—Yours of the 28th ultimo has come to hand, and I am much obliged to you for your kindness in taking such good care of my lot. Any expense that you may be at for keeping up the fences, &c, let me know, and I will settle it. I did not expect to hear of the grass having taken well. Please sell the wheat and deposit the proceeds in the Bank of Rockbridge. You can retain Cy another year on the same terms as at present; and should you desire George, you can also have him on your own terms. Please let me know whether you desire him, and what he is worth in the event you keep him. Should you not need him please hire him to some suitable person, with the condition that, if near or in town, he is required to attend Sabbath School, and wherever he may be, let him be required to attend church at suitable times, as I am very desirous that the spiritual interests of my servants be attended to.

"Very truly, your friend,
T. J. JACKSON."

"WINCHESTER, December 12, 1861.

'My Dear Sir,—Yours of the 10th instant is at hand, and I am much obliged for your kindness. Keep George at the price named. I am glad to hear that both the boys are well, and I trust that, through the blessing of an overruling Providence, they will serve you faithfully. It is gratifying to know that they are in such good hands as yours. Your much obliged friend

"T. J. JACKSON."

"CAROLINE COUNTY VA,
December 20, 1862

3/1/84 Washingtonian

The Strange Story Told by Senator-Elect Blackburn at a Dinner Party.

[Special to the World.

WASHINGTON, Feb. 24 —At a dinner party given during the past week Senator-elect Blackburn, of Kentucky, told the following interesting story, which he says was told him by Gen. Garfield, at a social gathering at which Alexander H. Stevens and other prominent Democrats were present. The stirring events of the closing days of the session of 1876-77 were the topics of conversation, and some of the party were commenting on the narrow escape of the country from a bloody struggle. It was agreed by all that if it had not been for the great self-control of the members of both parties, and the real patriotism of the Democrats, a civil war would certainly have broken out. Gen. Garfield here came in with a high compliment for the Democrats. He said that perhaps none of them really knew how great the danger was at that time. He added that he thought he had been the means of breaking up a foolish programme which some Republicans had actually arranged, and which, if carried out, would certainly have resulted in a bloody outbreak. "Now," said Gen. Garfield, "as we are talking among ourselves as gentlemen, and not as politicians, I have no hesitation in telling you what that programme was." Instantly there was the most profound attention. Gen. Garfield continued, after a moment's pause, in which he lighted a fresh cigar, to say that there was nearly a panic among the Republican leaders during the days immediately preceding the passage of the Electoral Commission bill. It was believed by some that the filibusters would be able to defeat the count and leave the country, on the 4th of March, without an Executive. Late on the last day of the debate Garfield was summoned to an important conference of the Republican leaders. Garfield did not say who were present, or where it was held, but from what followed it was inferred that the President and his Cabinet, and the General of the Army were there. Garfield said he arrived very late. The conference had just concluded its work. Upon his asking what subject had been discussed and what conclusion reached, he was told that those present believed the filibusters in the House had the power to defeat the count unless extraordinary measures were employed. It had been agreed, therefore, to march 600 men from the Arsenal at 3 o'clock the next morning to the Capitol, and station them in the basement of the House ready to be marched up into the House lobby and upon the floor itself if necessary, when the House met. The filibusters were then to be notified by an order from the President that persistent filibustering in the face of the situation would be treated as an act of rebellion, and the objecting members would be arrested and carried out.

Garfield said that he denounced this programme and opposed it to the extent of his ability. said such an act would arouse the country to a pitch of madness, and that blood would flow in the street of every city in the country. His objections were not listened to until he said that if this resolution was persisted in he should go to the telegraph office and denounce the whole thing to the country.

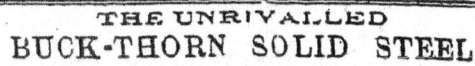

THE UNRIVALLED
BUCK-THORN SOLID STEEL

BARBED FENCING.

MANUFACTURED by the BUCK-THORN FENCING CO., (late the T. V. Allis Mfg., CO..).Trenton. N. J., who will send samples and circulars to all applicants.

LEESBURG ADVERTISEMENTS.

READY for 1884!

I AM now in receipt of a full line of the celebrated

GOLDEN STAR

OIL COOKING STOVES AND RANGES.

They are a household necessity.—Will do the work of your Cooking Stoves, with one-half the expense, and without heating the house, and no dust,smoke or smell from them.—I have been selling them for two seasons; they have given entire satisfaction to those who have used them; they have been greatly improved for '84; they are now actually safe and durable.

Leesburg References:
Mrs. Matt. Harrison.   Mrs. R. E. Divine
Mrs. Janet Harrison.   Mrs. Meade & Worsley.   Mrs. C. D. Hammerly.   Mrs. Geo. W Brooks.

I invite an inspection of them at my Tin and Store House, Leesburg, Va.

M. T. WHITMORE.

CONGRESSMAN WISE

Declares that He will Not Fight Capt. McCarty.

[Baltimore Sun.]

RICHMOND, VA., March 5.—Under date of March 2, Mr. John S. Wise published in the Whig of this city this morning a card to the public, in which he says:

"About twelve months ago, as is well known to many persons, I resolved never again to recognize the practice of dueling. A few weeks ago my political disabilities, incurred under the dueling act, were for the second time removed by the Legislature. The above conclusion was stated under oath, on Monday last. My reason for so deciding were satisfactory to myself. Those of a private nature are of no concern to the public. The public consideration most potent in my decision was that I am satisfied public opinion will not sustain a duelist in any civilized community at the present day.

"Henceforth, therefore, I wish it publicly understood that I will not fight a duel or be party to one.

"I make this declaration public because some persons may expect me to resent several assaults of late appearing in newspapers, especially in the paper called the "Campaign." If I had intended to recognize the editor of that paper I would have done so long ago, for the article last appearing are no worse than many others that have been published. W. Page McCarty can have no difficulty with me. If the Commonwealth's attorney of the town where that paper is published had done his duty, McCarty would have been in jail long ago as the utterer of criminal libel. A poor man here in Richmond was sent to jail some months ago for an offense much less than his.

"Since McCarty killed Mr. John B. Mordecai he has been going about smelling the blood on his hands and panting for more apparently.

"Without stake of any sort, he has maliciously sought to provoke difficulties; first with General Mahone, then with Senator Riddleberger, and next with myself. Some months before he said aught against me I was informed that he declared his purpose, in a public place, to seek difficulty with me next. General Mahone and Riddleberger failed to notice him, and I propose to do likewise. What satisfaction can I secure from McCarty? I would not fight a duel. I do not wish his blood, and would be as miserable as he is now if I shed it. If I were to sue him for slander and give the money to some charitable institution, I could not make anything out of him on execution.

"With a sweet home filled with merry children, with enough to live comfortably, with a paying profession, I am happy and want to live. In God's name what would a man like Page McCarty put in stake against this when we stood at ten paces with pistols? His abuse of me has no more effect than a dog's barking at the moon. His invitation comes too late. Time has been when I might have been fool enough to indulge in such folly, but with age, and its responsibilities and duties, I have bidden farewell forever to the McCarty type of manhood.

"What people may think of my courage, by reason of this letter, I cannot say. If they do not think me courageous, duelling would never convince them. I know what my friends will say. I sometimes think I would rather risk the charge of cowardice than that of murder. I have tried not to be too severe upon poor McCarty, whose wasted talents and miserable life I truly pity!"

Mr. Wise alludes in this letter to an editorial published in Capt. Page McCarty's paper, the "Campain, last Friday, which contained the following language: "How characteristic of the individual is Mr. Johnny Wise's stump speech on the witness stand. A man occupying a seat in Congress, stolen with manufactured votes, himself the very exemplar of Virginia prejudice, braggart and bully, the hero of thirteen bloodless duels, kicked out of the democratic party, and selling his little stock of brains to Mahone, frozen out of recognition by honest men, and relegated to the association of the negroes whom he derided, and who are his superiors in all that make even a pretense to manhood. Johnny Wise, forsooth, talking about vilification, when he and his gang never had any other capital but vilification, prejudice and falsehood."

WHITE HOUSE CRANKS.

Crazy Callers on the President---The Red Man of Revelations.

(Cor. Pittsburg Commercial Gazette.)

The White House is a very popular resort with cranks. Every crank who comes to Washington imagines he has some important business with the president. Some days the lynx-eyed sergeant on guard at the White House door turns away ten or twelve crazy people. The sergeant was asked how he managed to distinguish the cranks from the ordinary business callers. "It's not much trouble," he said. "But since the shooting of Garfield we have been especially watchful of all the president's visitors. Usually we spot a crank on sight. There is a wandering of the eyes, or an abruptness of speech, or a wildness of gesture, or some peculiarity of dress or manner.

"This, however, is not always the case. I remember a short time ago I was on duty in the grounds one night when a reception was going on. I was approached from the White House portico by a tall, clean-shaved, middle-aged man, neatly dressed in a black walking suit, who asked in a tone as if he merely wanted a chat with some one: 'Are you a watchman here?' 'In that line,' said I. 'The president is giving a reception, I believe?' 'I believe he is,' said I. 'A public reception, isn't it?' asked the stranger. 'I don't know anything about that,' I answered. 'Would you take me to be a respectable citizen?' was the next question. 'Hardly able to judge on so short an acquaintance,' said I. The stranger chuckled quietly at this and said, 'Quite right; but from my general appearance now, my manners and conversation, would you set me down as respectable or otherwise?' 'Respectable,' said I. 'Just so. And yet, in this great and glorious land of the free,' sarcastically said he, 'a respectable citizen is suddenly turned away from the door of the executive mansion by flunkeys when he simply seeks, with other citizens to pay his respects to the officer they have chosen by ballot to preside over them; at a time, too, set apart, it is understood, for the purpose.' 'But perhaps,' said I, 'there must have been a reason. Perhaps you are mistaken, and this is not a public reception.' 'Asked if I had a card,' continued the stranger, indignantly (ignoring my last remark); questioned and cross-examined as if I was a felon or conspirator, and the door then shut in my face. All right, if this is St. Petersburg, and this is the palace of the czar,' pointing to the White House. 'Infamously wrong if this is Washington and that is the White House.'

"So far there had not been anything in the man's manner or talk to indicate that he was anything more than a visitor to the city, disgusted and indignant at his disappointment at being summarily deprived of what he perhaps considered his only chance while here to see the president; but suddenly changing his manner after his last remark, he abruptly asked me in the sepulchral tones of the ghost in 'Hamlet,' 'Do you ever read the bible?' 'Sometimes,' I answered. 'Did you ever read the book of Revelations?' 'Yes.' 'Do you remember the red man in that book?' 'I can't say that I do.' 'Well, read it again, guardian of the night, read it again,' said the stranger, adding quickly, 'I am the red man there mentioned. I hold in my hands the fates of nations and their rulers. I make and unmake presidents—Washington, Jefferson, Jackson, Lincoln, Grant, and this man Arthur. They were elected, yes, but elections can not change destiny. That I control. Let the present occupant of the White House beware,' and with a threatening shake of his long forefinger at the mansion, the man started down the flag sidewalk toward the gateway. Now, if that fellow had got in he might have behaved as well as anybody. But in case he had got started on the book of Revelations there is no knowing what might have happened."

March, 1884

3/28/84 Telephone

REMINGTON STANDARD TYPE WRITER,
In Washington.

On previous occasions we have made mention of this more than useful machine. It is asserted, and the statement is well founded, that no one invention has ever met with greater favor amongst well informed people, than the type writer. At this session of Congress, the Washington agent of the company has introduced them in the Capital with most flattering success, and today there are standing on the order books several unfilled orders, and not a day passes that more are not added. Canvassing for the sale of them has for a time been suspended as volunteer orders are sufficient for the business. The great question now is, who will be kind enough to wait a few days and let some pressing demand be supplied first? Today an order could not be filled at double the price of a new machine and so it has been for the past two weeks. The office is kept open from 8 o'clock A. M. until 9 P. M. for the accommodation of young ladies learning to use the machine.

Remington Standard
Type Writer.
WICKOFF, SEAMANS & BENEDICT,
SOLE AGENTS.

Branch Office, LeDroit Building,
Washington, D.C.,
A. BAKER, JR., MANAGER. [1-25-y

A FINE FARM
AND PERSONALTY
AT PUBLIC AUCTION
NEAR HAMILTON, VA.
WEDNESDAY, APRIL 2ND. 1884.
COMMENCING AT 10 O'CLOCK A. M.

The undersigned, executors of the late Wm. Tavenner, will offer at public sale on the farm of the decedent, located one-half mile south of Hamilton, on the road leading to Lincoln, all the personal property of the decedent, consisting, in part, of

THREE GOOD WORK HORSES,

Two of them mares, one of which is with foal, and one colt, 2-years old next Fall.

THREE COWS, one of which is fresh, 3 fat Hogs, ten very fine Ewes with lambs, 1 4-horse Wagon, 1 two horse Carriage, one Sleigh, double carriage harness, light single, Harness, 2 pairs hind Gears, 2 pairs fore Gears, plow bands and traces, check lines, and halters, bridles and collars for four horses, 1 3-horse iron Plow, 2 single and 2 double shovels, a lot of old plows, 1 Corn Coverer 1 nearly new AA Harrow, 1 wheat Fan, 1 wheat Drill 1 Cutting box, 1 corn Sheller, single double and tribble trees, Log chains, short chains, breast chains and a pair of stretcher chains, one sack of Salt, Grindstone, a lot of Fencing Boards, half-bushel measure, 1 barrel Vinegar, 1 cowbar, iron Wedges, mowing scythe, grain cradle and other farm tools, 40 Barrels Corn, 1 Stack Hay, some Fodder, and about 14 Acres of Wheat.

HOUSEHOLD AND KITCHEN FURNITURE:

Two Bureaus, 3 Falling leaf Tables, 2 Cupboards, 2 Washstands, Safe, Chairs, 2 feather Beds, Boulsters, Pillows, Blankets, Comforts, Carpets, Oil Cloths, Mirrors, 8 day Clock, Cook Stove and utensils, Dishes, Churn, Lamps, Lot of stone Jars, 1000 lbs Bacon, keg Lard, 15 bushels Potatoes, 1 Beehive &c.

TERMS: All sums of $10 or less cash; over that amount a credit of six months will be given, the purchaser to execute bond with approved security, with interest from date and waiving homestead exemptions.

This Valuable Farm

(Which will be sold about 1 o'clock) consists of about 71 acres, divided into four fields (all of which are well fenced and contain running water) a meadow orchard &c. There is no waste land and the quality of the soil is No. 1. There is enough timber for the farm. The buildings consist of a Frame Dwelling, containing 7 rooms a barn and other out-buildings. This is a very desireable property being located near the town of Hamilton hence convenient to all public affairs.

TERMS:—One fourth the purchase money cash on day of sale; the remainder to be payable in three equal annual installments, the purchaser to give bonds for the deferred payments, with interest from date, and the title to be retained until all the purchase money be paid.

3-7-ts. E. H. & G. O. TAVENNER, Ex'rs.

March, 1884

3/27/84 Mirror

The Washington Monument.

PREPARATIONS FOR PROSECUTION OF THE WORK.

A force of seventy men are at work on the Washington Monument grounds, cutting and dressing the stones preparatory to placing them in position on the monument. These men have been at work, when practicable, since the suspension of setting stone last winter, when the structure had reached a height of 410 feet. It is not intended to resume the work of setting until the 1st of May, although there is a sufficient quantity of stone now dressed and ready to be placed in position to raise the monument thirty additional feet. It is absolutely necessary, however, to have plenty of material on hand when the work is once commenced, to preclude the possibility of it being stopped for want of material, and therefore by the first of May it is intended to have stone enough prepared to raise the monument to 470 feet. Nearly enough stone is already on the grounds to do this. The Lee company, of Massachusetts, who were at first awarded the contract last year, succeeded in supplying but twelve suitable blocks, and at an expense of $16,000. Owing to their failure to furnish a sufficient quantity, their contract was annulled and was awarded to Hugh Sisson, of Maryland. He expects to supply about two hundred blocks per month, and at that rate there will be a sufficient quantity on hand to make the monument's height 500 feet, and if this is accomplished it is expected that all of it will be set by the middle of August. All that will remain then will be to erect the pyramidal marble summit of 50 feet, making the monument 550 feet high.— When the structure reached 470 feet there will be a change in the manner of setting the stone, in order to prepare sure foundation for this summit. Instead of being set with a smooth interior surface the blocks will be bracketed. The first course above four hundred and seventy feet will jut about six inches, and these corbels or projections will be increased gradually up to the height of 500 feet. There will be then a firm foundation for the summit, which will be upheld by arches resting upon these corbels. When the whole work is completed, it will doubtless be considered one of the engineering feats of the age.—*Star.*

ROCKFORD WATCH.

The man who did buy a Rockford watch. (On board)

The man who did not buy a Rockford watch (He got left)

J. J. STANSBURY,
JEWELER,
LEESBURG, VA.

HANG IT, MARIA!

Why don't you buy my shirts ready-made? What's the use of wearing your eyes out over fine needle work, and breaking your back trying to save a few cents? I don't see the savin' of it. Why, you can buy shirts now-a-days for very little more than the cost of material. Look at this "Diamond" I've just bought.

THE WASHINGTONIAN

LEESBURG LOUDOUN COUNTY VA
SATURDAY........April 12, 1884

A CARD.

EDITOR WASHINGTONIAN: My attention has been called to what appears as an editorial in your last issue, in which you have seen fit to characterize that portion of my remarks made at the last meeting of the Farmers' Club, which appeared in the *Telephone*, as communistic. Regarding your attack as gratuitous and the manner of it more sensational than courteous, I shall ask sufficient space in your paper to present some views on the point to which you have given such prominent notice.

Let us look at the communism in my little agricultural speech.

"Has a man like Vanderbilt the right to control his $100,000,000, while another works for 50 cents a day? I question whether a man has a right to lord it over 400 acres, and have those around him working for a pittance a day.

A CARD.

LINCOLN Va., 4, 18th, 1884

MR. LYNCH:—

Is it not a fair inference that a cause which needs to be sustained by unfair means, is weak? You assailed some utterances of mine, found in another sensational, rather than argumentative, editorial, printed so as to be readable. I replied in an article written in chaste language in such manner as suited myself. You printed in type scarcely legible a fraction of my article. You must be aware that I was very conscious that in replying to an editor, I was putting myself in his power, but I did expect fair editorial treatment. The opinions of the man who differs from me should be as sacred in my hands as though they were my own. Though he differs from us he has rights that I am bound to respect. But it is true that the man who lives upon the plane of statute law lives miserably low. In an intercourse with editors, stretching over 25 years, I have not known similar treatment.

Will you publish this?

J. B. WILSON.

The Editor replies

You have been fairly and properly dealt with, much more leniently than your obnoxious and revolutionary sentiments deserved. Every word you wrote, in support of your communistic sentiments, was published, and in the usual type of the paper; but we did not deem it proper to have mixed up in this discussion, your vagaries on slavery, polygamy and temperance, totally irrelevant to it. This paper is free to the discussion of subjects of public interest, when properly and respectfully presented. As a specimen of your best language, and, we presume, sentiments you deem highly proper, we take the following from the above; "*It is true that the man who lives upon the plane of statute law lives miserably low.*" We do not believe we have a man in this county, but the one, who expresses the vicious doctrines you did at Lincoln, could be guilty of such an utterance, so pregnant of mischief, demoralization and danger to the social order of the community. Two unfortunate men, near this place, a short time ago, doubtless, thought it was "miserably low to live upon the plane of statute law," and thought they would move upon a higher plane—concluded that they had a right to divide out the money of one of our citizens, and relieved him of his cash on the highway. They have been given fourteen years in the penitentiary, to reflect which is the wiser and more honorable way to live, as you phrase it, "miserably low" by the statute law, or to move upon your higher plane, which leads to brigandage and a short life time in prison. Doubtless, you have not the discretion to give such sentiments their true meaning, as men of your superficial mode of thought are not given to the habit of sound reflection, and are led more by the shadow than the substance, but you have in the case cited, what may be the outcome of the sentiments you express, as your thoughtful neighbors will tell you, to whom it would be wise for you to go for advice. We think one so wanting in common sense and so reckless of the rights of society, as to be guilty of such utterances, should be placed in the hands of a committee of sensible men to guide and control him.

May, 1884

5/1/84 Mirror

The advent of a "white elephant" could hardly have attracted a larger crowd than did the arrival at the depot on Sunday evening last of engine No. 6, the new passenger engine recently purchased by the W, O. & W. R. R. Co. It was her first trip out on the road and she was much admired by all who saw her, and, indeed, would strike one unskilled in such things as a splendid specimen of locomotive mechanism.

5/8/84 Mirror

To the Surviving Soldiers from Virginia in the Confederate Armies.

The undersigned has been charged by an act of the General Assembly with the duty of enrolling the names of all the soldiers and sailors contributed by Virginia to the armies of the Confederate States. It is required that this enrollment shall show, as far as can now be ascertained, "the name, age, place of enrollment and residence at time, company and regiment or battalion, battery or squadron, to which each such person belonged, or position held by same as general or staff officer, or, if in the navy, to what vessel attached or to what duty assigned; with statement also as to wound or wounds, when and where received, character of present disability, imprisonment, death and where buried, discharge or surrender of such person at the end of the war, and any other particulars in regard to any such persons which in his [the Adjutant General's] judgment should be recorded."

All the military rolls and records of the State having been destroyed in the great fire that attended the evacuation of Richmond by the Confederate forces and those of the Confederate government and armies that were turned over to the United States authorities at the surrender being unavailable for lack of adequate means at my command to meet the cost of the work required for the purpose, there is nothing left to me but to apply to the surviving soldiers and sailors of the State for the assistance needed, and which I cannot doubt they will cheerfully give.

5/8/84 Mirror

Gen. U. S. Grant has sent his check for $500 to the R. E. Lee Camp for the Confederate Home. The contribution was made on Wednesday through the New York committee.—*State*.

5/1/84 Mirror

Mr Edward Wright, as will be seen by advertisement in another column, has returned to Leesburg and resumed his old business. He left here a few months ago for Marysville California, but like many another who has gone west, he found not the Eldorado that had been described to him, and lost no time in returning to his old home and friends, and declares that hereafter old Virginia is good enough for him. We are glad to welcome him and his family back into our midst, and bespeak for him a return of the patronage he enjoyed in his business before his departure. He is a good mechanic, an upright man and is worthy of public confidence.

Cheap Homes in Texas.

GOOD, rich Land—Good Water—Good Schools—Good Churches—Good Health—A Delightful Climate—on the T. & P. R. R., in Mitchell county, Texas.

128,000 Acres,

in a solid body twenty-six miles long and eight miles wide, in Hockley and Lamb counties.

23,000 ACRES,

in a solid body, on the Double Mountain Fork of the Brazos river. Twelve miles of running water and three good springs on said land.

51,000 ACRES in a solid body, on the Plains in Howard and Martin counties, four miles west of Big Springs, on the Texas and Pacific railroad.

30 SECTIONS of School Lands, in Mitchell and Scurry counties. These lands will be sold at from $1.75 to $3.50 per acre; one-half cash, balance in eighteen years with eight per cent per annum interest on the same, with privilege of paying the entire amount at any time.

1280 ACRES adjoining Colorado City, including the lately discovered COAL MINE. On the land, near the mine, are two lasting springs of water. This tract of good, rich land, including the mine, can be bought for $10 00 per acre, cash. Numerous small tracts of from 80 to 640 acres, near Colorado City, ranging in price from $2.00 to $3.00 per acre.

TOWN LOTS, in Colorado; also, lots in the town of Snyder. Ten-acre lots on Lone Wolf creek, in sight of Colorado City.

Business and Residence Houses for Sale or Rent. THURMOND & CHAMBLIN,
Big Springs, Howard Co., Texas.
McGINNIS & SON

5/15/84 Mirror

GEN. GRANT'S MISFORTUNES.—One of the lessons taught by the recent failures in New York, and the developments which have followed them, is that Gen. Grant, notwithstanding his hard-earned reputation as a man of war, is not a safe man to trust with the direction of important business interests, either private or public. The revelations so far made in connection with the failure of Grant & Ward do not necessarily fix any criminality upon Gen Grant, but they do show that he was guilty of gross negligence and inattention to the interests entrusted to his firm. He was only a special partner, it is true, but it was his name and influence which gave the firm its prominence and prestige, and which inspired the confidence of hundreds of trusting customers. The liabilities of the firm, it is thought, will reach $10,000,000, and the losses, it is stated will fall principally upon individuals who have put their money in the hands of the firm. Gen. Grant's friends may and do plead that he was entirely ignorant of the state of affairs, and that he was the innocent victim of "wicked partners." How far this claim may be justified by the facts it is not necessary to discuss, but whether he was totally ignorant or not, he deserves censure for lending his name to bolster up a business necessarily involving the financial interests of many hundreds of people, and then leaving it to take care of itself or to be conducted at the pleasure of his partners. Of late indiscreet friends of Gen. Grant have been endeavoring to bring his name before the public in connection with the presidential nomination, and but for this failure the country might have been inclined to forget the signal business incapacity and loose administrative methods which he displayed during his former terms in the White House. But this failure, luckily for the country and unluckily for him, emphasizes afresh the unfitness of General Grant for the position to which some of his friends are again urging him—His transactions in Wall street are simply a repetition in another field and on a somewhat smaller scale of the methods which characterized his administrations at Washington. In both cases, it is claimed, he was personally innocent of wrong doing, but in both he managed to surround himself by false friends and had advisers, who, when he was President, robbed the government, and when he was in Wall street fleeced the customers of the firm. Gen Grant may be as upright as the day is long but the country cannot afford to see again in the presidential chair, in control of the great interests of fifty millions of people a man whose whole history shows that he is peculiarly apt to become the victim of pretended friends and "wicked partners."—*Balt. Sun.*

5/22/84 Mirror

As President of the United States his salary was increased from $25,000 to $50,000 per annum, and at the close of his eight years service, he had bestowed upon him a fortune that nobody could touch, which is still yielding him $15,000 a year. And now, after becoming a Wall street broker, and in the course of two or three years, sunk about $14,000,000 of other people's money—congress retires him with full pay as a general of the army, and the hat is being passed round for another relief fund. The N. Y. *World* says that the assertion that Grant was blameless in the failure, "is worse than fustian—it is false"—and continues. "Grant was not blameless and simple when he upheld BELKNAP and BABCOCK and stood between them and justice. He was not blameless and simple when he made the Black Friday pool with FISK and GOULD. He was not blameless and simple when he accepted gifts from people who would be certain to want favors in return. He was not blameless and simple when he held the Presidency for eight years, defying public sentiment and debauching public virtue. He was not blameless and simple when for years and years every Republican organ puffed him to the very skies as a great, shrewd, keen, wise man. He was not blameless and simple when he degraded his office and disgraced his country by stepping from the Presidency and the supreme command of a nation's armies into a Wall street broker's business to gamble in stocks.

5/29/84 Mirror

General Grant's Unhappy Lot.—A personal friend of General Grant, who saw him in New York last week, says that his experience in Wall street has cost him not only his fortune but ten years of his life. He seems broken in body and mind. He is not allowed to read the newspapers, so that he probably does not know half that the rest of the world now knows about the firm of Grant & Ward, but he knows enough to give him a keen sense of his humiliating position.

He thinks he has earned the condemnation and contempt of his friends, forfeited the confidence of the country, and tarnished his hard won fame. He is a wretched old man. He takes no interest in politics or anything else, except his ruined fortunes. All his thoughts are given to plans for their restoration in such a way that in his latter years he may have peace with honor.

May, 1884

THE TELEPHONE.

FRIDAY............ MAY 2D.

Senator Mahone possesses, in a high degree, the characteristics of an able commander and on the field of battle he could win great distinction; but as a political leader he is a failure. He is so proved by his record and he stands condemned in advance by his methods - which belong to a system of politics that does not and cannot prevail in this Country. Love of independence and tolerance and the weakening of party ties have made it impossible for one-man power to stand in this land of political freedom, and Mahone shows great lack of discretion in not recognizing this potent fact.

This thing, his reliance on the so-called "boss system," is Mahone's one great failing. By it he has lost the greatest opportunity any man ever had in this State, or, perhaps in any other state, of making himself—*or of being made by the people*—the one great power of the State, for years to come.

"The Telephone" which supported Republican candidates, finally broke with Mahone for the reasons given.

5/1/84 Mirror

Base Ball.—The base ball fever which has been epidemic in the U. S. for the past two years has recently struck our youth pretty hard, and daily numbers of them may be seen on the Academy grounds pursuing or pounding "the leather" with a vigor and energy rarely exhibited in other directions. The attack is by no means confined to the younger "boys," but many an old stager, who possessed quite a local reputation on the diamond in the days before the advent of "curves" and when heavy hitting was the order the day, may be seen on the field.

6/3/84 Mirror

The return game of base ball between the Aldie and Leesburg Clubs was played on the grounds of the latter at the Fair Grounds on Saturday afternoon last, and resulted in a defeat of the home club by a score of 39 to 27, the Aldieans not playing their half of the last inning as they had the game already won. The game which was called at half-past one—occupied about four hours in the playing, and was marked by heavy hitting, loose fielding, wild throwing and accidents, of which latter there were no less than four, two of which were to players on the home team and necessitated their retirement from the game; of the other two, one was to the umpire and the other to an outsider.—Fortunately none of them resulted very seriously though any of them might easily have proved so. The utmost good feeling prevailed throughout the game and the defeat of the home club may be attributed to the superior base running of their opponents and to the effectiveness of their "battery." The game was witnessed by quite a large crowd among whom were many ladies, who seemed to greatly enjoy it, though totally unable to understand "why the men would not hold the stick still when the other man threw the ball at it."

Gen. Lee Declined to Sell his Fame.

WASHINGTON, May 30.—Gen. Lee, at the close of the war, received innumerable offers to engage in commercial enterprises. Insurance companies, railroads, and many large corporations at the south were anxious to pay him any salary he might demand solely for the use of his name, without any labor on his part, or the incurring of any responsibility whatever.

Gen. Lee left three sons. They, too, received many offers of a similar kind, and likewise declined them.

Two of Lee's sons and one nephew became generals during the War. The youngest son joined late and became captain. After the War, one became Governor of Virginia in 1886, another a U.S. Congressman and a third took over the presidency of Washington College succeeding his father who died there.

May, 1884

5/16/84 Telephone

A TREMENDOUS CRASH.

FAILURES IN THE EAST AND WEST.

A PANIC IN WALL STREET.

Financial circles have been greatly shocked during the past week. First the banking firm of Grant & Ward suspended with liabilities beyond their assets estimated to be as great as $10,000,000. Following close upon this came the suspension of the Northwestern Car Company, of St. Paul Minn., of which Sen. Sabin is President. It is reported, however, that this suspension will not prove a failure. These occurences, together with the general decline in stocks, caused wild excitement in Wall St., on Wednesday, resulting in the closing of two banks, numerous brokers offices and far-reaching complications there and in other cities. It is not probable that a general panic will result, but the crash may be very disastrous in some quarters.

5/17/84 Washingtonian

BLACK WEDNESDAY PANIC IN WALL STREET.

Wednesday last, was a dark day for Wall street. The financial storm which has been gathering for some time, and which gave the first sound of its approaching thunder, by the failure of Grant's firm last week, burst in its fury upon Wall street last Wednesday. Bankers and brokers—some of the largest, and, supposed to have been, the strongest firms in the city, went under, threw up the sponge and passed into the ranks of broken firms. Stocks, bonds and all kinds of securities, went down, causing a wreck almost as great as the historic Black Friday.

What is the cause of these panics and crashes in financial circles, at a time when the country is full of money—the treasury of the government burthened with surplus revenue, and the elevators and grain depots overflowing with wheat and corn, and the markets falling in prices by the number of cattle for sale?

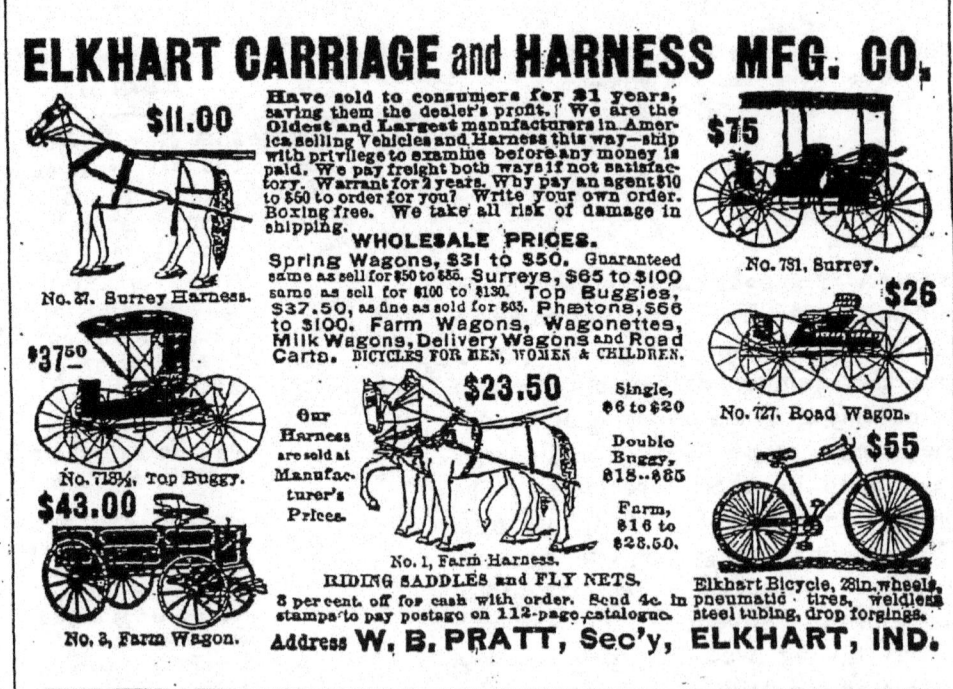

May, 1884

5/16/84 Telephone

News Notes.

Cyrus H. McCormick, head of the great harvester manufacturing company which bears his name, a native of Rockbridge county, Va., died at his home in Chicago last Tuesday. He was a zealous member of the Presbyterian Church, devoting much of his time and means to church extension.

(The reaper was patented in 1834 and was of enormous importance as the grain field of the west opened up.)

(His successful company in 1902 became part of the International Harvestor Corporation.)

5/29/84 Mirror

CYRUS H. McCORMICK'S MILLIONS

His Estate Valued at $32,500,000—The Provisions of His Will

A Chicago telegram of Monday, says: The will of the late Cyrus H McCormick was admitted to probate this afternoon, and Mrs. Nettie Flower McCormick and Cyrus H. McCormick, Jr., were given letters testamentary on furnishing a bond of $20,000,000. The heirs are Nettie F. McCormick, widow; Cyrus H McCormick, Harold F. McCormick and Stanley R. McCormick, sons; Mary V McCormick and Anita E McCormick, daughters. The trust estate consists of real estate in this city and county, improved and unimproved; also real estate in Virginia, Wisconsin, Iowa, Nebraska and Minnesota, of value of $25,000,000, and the personal property, including nearly three-quarters of the stock of the McCormick Harvesting Machine Company, and other stocks, bonds, securities, &c., amounting to $7,500,000.

THE BEST IN THE WORLD.

THE McCORMICK

HARVESTER AND TWINE BINDER

THIS Machine may well be styled the King of Harvesters, for it has from the beginning asserted and steadily maintained its supremacy over all others.
The improvements of the new angle iron cutter bar, adjustable reel for picking up fallen or lodged grain, adjustable table for binding tall or short grain always in the middle of the sheaf, and table trip which prevents any choking of the binder in lodged or tangled grain, together with the other improvements the past season, have satisfied and delighted every purchaser. Never since we first engaged in this business have we made a record that we are prouder of than that of 1883. Indeed, so remarkably and uniformly superior to all others has been the work of the McCormick, that we fail to see wherein any radical change could be made that would improve its cutting or binding, under any conceivable condition. The Binding Mechanism is of the simplest, most effective and reliable character, and as it binds tight and cuts off the twine close to the bundle, with no *possibility* of the knot slipping or the bundle getting loose, until the band is cut for the thresher.

☞ We have now our Ware Room full of BINDERS REAPERS & MOWERS, having bought them by the quantity, we are enabled to offer them to the farmers of Loudoun, at the very lowest possible prices. We also keep the Repairs on hand in Lovettsville, which is an advantage to every purchaser, and we ask every farmer who wants a Binder to come and see the "KING HARVESTER" which is up, and ready for operation. We insist upon the farmers giving their orders as early in season as possible, so that it will give us time to have every Binder put up and ready to start, when Harvest is at hand. All persons desiring any information in regard to our machines, please correspond with us, and we will furnish circulars Books &c., free.

CHINN BROTHERS, Lovettsville, Va.

P: S —Agents wanted in the County, apply to CHINN BRO.

June, 1884

THE TELEPHONE.

FRIDAY.......... JUNE 20TH

—More boarders.
—Raspberries ripe.
—Harvest next week.
—Clover is now being cut.

—Quite good bass fishing is reported in the Potomac and Shenandoah.

—A new and beautiful soda fountain at J. W. Wiley's, the finest in the county, and it will only cost you 5 cents to take a trip so near the polles that you can imagine you feel the breeze. Soda Water, Tonic Beer and Vichy Mineral Water always on draught. No extra charge for ice cream in soda. Come and try it.

FRIDAY.......... JUNE 27TH

—Wm S. Roose, of Washington father of Mrs. Dr. Connell, expected to construct a telephone line from Waterford to Clarks Gap, in the early part of this week. It will be the Bell Electric Telephone, and is to be put up by experienced linemen, hence it will be first class in every particular. He will charge, at first, ten cents for a message, but may reduce the rate if he can afford to do so.

—The sound of the reaper was heard throughout all the countryside in the early part of this week and perhaps half of the crop was cut—some farmers having cut some last week. It is probable that much of the grain has been cut too green; and should we have much damp weather, some of it will be damaged. The yield is, perhaps, above the average and the quality good. Laborers have been scarce, although many new self-binding harvesters have been put to work.

—This vicinity was visited by a heavy rainstorm, or succession of showers, on Wednesday, about noon, and continued till Thursday morning. A great deal of water fell and doubtless much damage was done to the grain and property along the streams.

J. H. Paxson met with quite a loss in having a valuable mare so badly kicked, that it became necessary to kill her.

—The ladies of Farmwell will give a strawberry and ice cream festival at the school house, on Wednesday June 11th, beginning at 5 o'clock P. M. A cordial invitation is extended to all.

BY ORDER OF COMMITTEE.

—There will be a strawberry festival held in the Grove, near Lemon's Blacksmith Shop, on Tuesday 10th inst., in the afternoon and night.

(For a time, strawberries had replaced oysters as Loudoun's favorite food.)

—The Good Templars will hold a festival at Lincoln tomorrow (Saturday) from 3 to 10 o'clock P. M. Ice cream, strawberries, cake.

—ALDIE VA., June 4th '84.—The strawberry festival of last night, for benefit of the new church, was quite a success.

—A strawberry festival will be held at Catoctin Free Church, next Thursday commencing at 2.30 P.M. for benefit of the church.

WATERFORD DRUG STORE,

Dr. G. E. CONNELL, Prop'r.

A complete stock of Drugs, Chemicals, Dye Stuffs, Spices, Fine Teas, All kinds of Patent Medicines, Fine Cutlery—Penknives. Razors, Scissors &c.

TOILET ARTICLES AND PERFUMERY,

HAIR BRUSHES, COMBS, SOAPS, POCKET BOOKS, PORTEMONAIES, DIARIES, BLANK BOOKS AND A LARGE ASSORTMENT OF

FINE STATIONERY.

BLUG SHOT.

A FINE ASSORTMENT OF BEAUTIFUL LAMPS!

THE WONDERFUL DANFORTH'S FULID.

EQUAL TO GAS!

GEORGE W. BROOKS

HAS just received from Baltimore a nice assortment of

GROCERIES,

consisting of Sugars, Coffees, Teas, Molasses, Syrups Spices, Mace Peppers, Soaps of all kinds, Coffee Essence, Gingers, Concentrated Lye, Blacking, Brooms, Blacking Brushes, Buckets, Selves, Soda, Blueing, Lamp Burners, Chimneys, Matches, Cream Tartar, Wash Boards, Rice, Crackers, Candles, Candies, Cakes, Cheese, Butter, Eggs, Clothe Pins, Raisins, Mustards, Cinnamon, Twine, Flour, Meal, Salt, Starch, Coal Oil,

BACON, FISH, MACKEREL, LARD, Essence of all descriptions, such as Lemon, Cinnamon, Peppermint and Vanilla, Inks, Nutmegs, Yeast Powders, Shoe Strings, Pocket Books, Baskets, Lamp Wicks, Stove Polish, Potatoes, Hominy, Canned Tomatoes.

Also,

TOBACCO,

both Chewing and Smoking;

CIGARS,

Snuff, Pipes, Pipe Stems, &c., &c.

☞ Don't forget the place, one door East of the Book Store, on Market St., Leesburg Virginia. GEO. W. BROOKS.

7/31/84 Mirror

The Moving of Engines.—We have noticed recently several accounts of accidents occasioned by horses becoming frightened on the highways by the moving of steam engines. A few weeks ago an accident of this kind occurred in Loudoun, and more recently one in Fauquier, both attributed to a steam engine. That parties owning these engines may fully understand what is required of them, and also the penalty imposed upon them for a failure to observe certain precautions, we publish the following from the acts passed by the last Legislature of Virginia.

Approved March 13th, 1884.

Be it enacted by the General Assembly of Virginia: That any person who shall move an engine with steam on any turnpike or county road of this state, shall first send one hundred yards in front of his engine, a messenger, whose duty it shall be to notify persons of the approach of the steam engine, and if necessary, to assist them holding their horses until it shall have passed by. Such engine shall be provided with a good spark arrester in proper order and place, to prevent spreading fire.

2. Any person who shall fail to conform to the requirements of the preceding section shall be liable to a fine of five dollars, to be imposed as like fines, on conviction and judgment before a justice of the peace. The offender or offenders shall be liable for damages to any persons aggrieved.

For one month preceding last Thursday, scarcely water enough fell in this county to lay the dust. Corn, grass, vegetation generally, and even the springs in some localities, were beginning to feel the effects of the long continued "dry spell." On Thursday, however, we had a fine rain which was repeated almost every day up to Wednesday, rejoicing the hearts of the husbandman, and infusing new life, and vigor, and beauty to all nature.

A telegram is going the rounds of the paper, dated Washington July 23d, which says: Hiram Beans, Postmaster at Waterford, Loudoun county, Va. has informed the Post Office Department that unknown persons fired ten shots into the Post Office on Sunday morning, breaking glass and doing other damage. The Postmaster says that the local authorities do not show a disposition to investigate the affair.

ALL MAY READ
This and be Benefitted

HAVING just returned from the east with a very large and well assorted stock of the LATEST STYLES in

Furniture,

consisting of BUREAUS, WARDROBES, SOFAS, LOUNGES, TABLES, CHAIRS, Wash-stands, Towel-Racks, Mattresses; Most Beautiful Sets of COTTAGE FURNITURE, all of which I offer at Prices as Low as the LOWEST anywhere, (cities not excepted.)

Undertaking

in all its branches promptly attended to and at moderate rates. My experience in this line extends over a period of twenty years. An excellent Hearse and everything necessary to this department of my business.

Repairing

done Shops, Tow Country, at low rates and promptly. A ask is a call from those who desire anything in my line satisfaction guaranteed. Respectfully,
JNO. W. HAMMERLY,
Leesburg, Va.

CHAS. T. BIRKBY.   LLOYD SLACK

Furniture. Furniture.

WITH many thanks to our friends for their past and highly appreciated patronage we still offer at our

Furniture Store

Large and increased STOCK, embracing Walnut and Poplar Chamber Sets, Bedsteads, Bureaus, Washstands, Lounges, Tables and Chairs, of every description. Hair and Husk Mattresses, Feather Pillows and Bolsters, Window Shades and Picture Frames

UPHOLSTERING & REPAIRING
Old Furniture a Specialty—City prices guaranteed.

UNDERTAKING

With considerable experience in this branch of the business, and the latest facilities for conducting it, we offer our services with a Complete STOCK of Rosewood, Walnut, and Poplar COFFINS and Caskets, have also just added to our Stock

Metallic Coffins

and CASKETS, of Best Quality, from the New York Metallic Burial Case Co. Calls will be carefully and promptly attended to at Moderate Rates.
BIRKBY & SLACK,
Leesburg, Va.

(These two undertakers, plus another who also advertised all had a carpentry business.)

THE TELEPHONE.

FRIDAY............... AUG. 1ST.

—Diurnal showers.

—This is August 1. Yet summer seems scarce begun.

—The city boys who are sojourning in Town will play a match game of base ball with the Hamilton nine tomorrow afternoon.

—The traveling public will be glad to learn that a number of ugly obstructions in the shape of large stones have been removed from the turnpike between Hamilton and Clarks Gap. But O! how rough the pike is, since the recent rains.

—The roads are all in bad condition, having been badly washed by recent rains; the overseers should attend to them at once. There is a great deal of travel at this season of the year and our roads should be *kept* in good condition *now* if at no other time.

—Last Saturday Mr. Albert Scanland, of North Fork, drove a young horse to Lincoln and left him stand, without tying, in front of P. Janney's store. Thus left at liberty the horse started off and ran a few hundred yards, through the woods, then broke loose from the buggy and went homeward at a lively gait. The buggy, which we understand was a very good one, was literally ruined.

—I desire to state to the vast crowds who will be at the Bush Meeting that I have secured the exclusive privilege to furnish ice cream, soda water, confections, fruits &c., on that occasion; and that I shall be on the grounds well prepared to fully supply the people with the very best quality of goods that I can procure which I shall sell at popular prices.

J. W. WILEY.

—In response to an inquiry relative to an item we have seen in the city papers, stating that the Waterford post office was fired into last Sunday week, a gentleman of that vicinity informed us that some drunken individuals did fire at least twenty shots into the store of Mr. Aaron Beans, where the post-office is kept. And, he further said that though the names of the parties are known, no efforts have been made to punish them for the damage to property and danger to life which they occasioned.

Oehm's Acme Hall.

Three hundred thousand dollars, worth of superbly made clothing, due to our large facilities in buying and manufacturing, (second now to none in America) enables us to offer the largest, the richest and the most varied stock in Spring and Summer Clothing, at prices simply inimitable.

MEN'S SUITS.

Every mill of worth, at home and abroad, is represented in our stock of Clothing.

Business Suits $7.50 to $30.00.
Working Suits $5.00 to $18.00.
Dress Suits $10.00 to $40.00.
Spring Overcoats $6.00 to $30.00.

Juvenile Suits.

Our Boys' Department never was so beautifully and bountifully stocked as at present. Extraordinary values, $2.00 really for $1.00, are bound up in many of our offerings.

Norfolks, Plain Blouses Sailor Blouses, Pleated Suits, Plain Kilts, Braided Kilts, Short Pants and long Pants Suits $2.00 to $18.00

Baltimore, Md.

August, 1884

8/15/84 Telephone

THE CLEVELAND SCANDAL

No paper that supports Blaine for the presidency has published the details of the Buffalo story concerning Governor Cleveland. It was printed by Independent and Democratic journals, and by these alone spread before the country. It has since been widely commented upon, and is now occupying a large share of public attention. And very properly so. The New York Sun, a Democratic paper, is urgently demanding an investigation. It neither affirms nor denies, but it refuses, under the circumstances, to ignore the matter. It very properly says it can not be ignored. It claims that Governor Cleveland owes it to himself, and to the party whose candidate he is, that it be met and refuted, if it can be.

8/16/84 Washingtonian

As Republicans and Independents residing in Buffalo, and having peculiar means of knowledge, we have been called upon by private letters and otherwise for information in regard to the scandals which have been put into circulation respecting Gov. Cleveland's private life. We have felt it to be a duty imposed on us by circumstances to examine these stories in detail and to make a formal statement of the results.

The general charges of drunkenness and gross immorality which are made against Gov. Cleveland are absolutely false. His reputation for morality has always been good. There is no foundation for any statement to the contrary. He was sought out and nominated for the Mayoralty against his will and was supported for that position by the larger portion of the educated, intelligent and moral citizens of Buffalo, without regard to politics and on purely purely personal grounds. After he had gone through this contest he was again put forward as one of the most distinguished citizens of Buffalo as a candidate for the Governorship and again received the support of the same class of his fellow citizens. In this community, where he had lived for twenty-nine years and where his life was known, and his character well understood, this support would not have been given to him had he been either a drunkard or a libertine. We are able to speak from personal knowledge as his acquaintances of long standing, and to say that his general private life has been that of a quiet, orderly, self-respecting and always highly respected citizen.

(It was a rough campaign. Both Cleveland and Blaine were severely and unfairly attacked by the opposite party.)

8/29/84 Telephone

MARIA HALPIN TELLS ALL.

The Story of Her Wrongs Heard From Her Own Lips.

The Evening "Telegraph" of Buffalo, N.Y., published on Thursday evening an interview held by a member of its staff with Maria Halpin at New Rochelle. Following is a synopsis of a statement of which the "Telegraph" claims to have attested proof. Mrs. Maria Halpin said to the reporter:

"I was employed at Flint & Kent's when Grover Cleveland persistently sought and finally made my acquaintance. I was not as stout as I look now, being tall and slender, and it is a wonder that I endured all I suffered in the years from 1874 to 1877.

"My child, Oscar Folsom Cleveland, was born September 14, 1874. Grover Cleveland is his father, and to say that any other man was responsible for his birth is infamous. The attempt to connect the dead Oscar Folsom with me or my boy, of which I hear, is cruel and cowardly. I had but a very slight acquaintance with Oscar Folsom.

"It does not seem possible, after all I have suffered for Grover Cleveland and for my boy's sake, that an attempt will be made to further blacken me in the eyes of the world. No one knows the extent of my sufferings.

"After my child was taken from me I begged Cleveland on my knees to let me have a sight of my baby. He was immovable. I found where the boy was, however, and one day I rushed in upon his keeper, snatched him up and ran away before they could stop me.

"My sufferings subsequently, my fruitless efforts to have Cleveland fulfill his promise of marriage, his neglect of myself and our child, my abduction and violent treatment by his hired tools, are truthfully but only partially told in the Buffalo "Telegraph" of July 21.

"It would be impossible to cover the events that made up those years of shame, suffering and degradation forced upon me by Grover Cleveland."

The "Telegraph" adds: "The gentleman to whom she made this statement says that, in the course of a long interview with her, she wept bitterly as she told of her wrongs. Her manner and appearance enforced a conviction of sincerity. When told that it was reported she had made, or was about to make a statement exonerating Governor Cleveland, Maria Halpin drew herself up as if preparing for a supreme effort, and replied in a most impressive and earnest manner: 'Me make a statement exonerating Grover Cleveland?'

Every amateur historian knows the partisan Republican refrain "Ma Ma, where's my Pa? Gone to the White House, ha-ha-ha"

August, 1884

8/14/84 Mirror

August Court.—Monday last was an occasion of Loudoun's time-honored August Court. As the years go by this court seems to be losing its pristine greatness, and gradually coming to be no more than an ordinary term of the County Court—still, however, there were many features noticeable on Monday that would have been recognized by an old timer. The crowd, in point of numbers was hardly so large as that of last year, though there was a goodly assemblage present. It was, as for the most part are all Loudoun crowds, good natured and well behaved,—and we heard of but one arrest during the day. The day was pleasant and, strange to say, was without rain, a rare occurrence for an August Court. The melons, yellow-legged chickens, &c., were in abundance, and their merits were lustily proclaimed by the vendors, who seemed excellently well pleased with small returns for a vast expenditure of breath. The crowd dispersed toward sundown, and but for the ball held by the colored folks in Hammerly's Hall, the town relapsed after night fall into its usual quiet—Monday was the regular grand jury term and they were in session nearly the whole morning, finding in all fourteen indictments, seven of which were against persons for selling liquor at the recent Temperance Bush Meeting.

8/15/84 Telephone

THE HIGHEST IN THE WORLD.

The Washington Monument Shaft to be Finished Today.

[Special to The American.]

WASHINGTON, Aug. 8.—Col. Casey, the superintendent of the Washington Monument, expects to finish work on the shaft of the monument tomorrow. By the close of working hours tomorrow the last layer of stone will have been put in position, and the work of removing derricks and other machinery will immediately begin.—Photographs are to be taken of the monument at this stage of its construction, and the work of erecting the immense derrick for placing the stones on the roof in position will begin at once.

8/15/84 Telephone

August Court.

As usual every hill and dale of Loudoun was represented in Leesburg last Monday "August Court" day, though the crowd was, probably, not so large as on most former occasions. A great many colored people, the festive watermelon, the depressing ginger cake, the customary array of grain drills and other implements, the vender of fertilizers and "forty rod whiskey" were all present as usual—and most of them busy, especially the latter.

But it was noticable that the whole affair was tame. There was no political speaking to stir up the crowd, and, indeed, politics was scarcely mentioned. This may be accounted for by the fact that the crowd was largely Democratic, and they are not anxious of late, to say much about their ticket. There being nothing else exciting, some of the crowd turned their attention to "Red-eye;" and those who remained in Town till late, report that the result was disastrous.

8/15/84 Telephone

A Horse Homily.
[Texas Siftings.]

The bad boy had no kindly feeling for the poor old horse.

But the poor old horse felt for the boy, all the same.

August, 1884

8/15/84 Telephone

Hillsboro Flashes.

HILLSBORO, Aug. 13th, '83:—If the citizens of Hamilton are sorely agrieved (and we hear some are) by the rigidity and enforcement of corporation laws relative to stock running at large in the streets, we will say for their consolation that Hillsboro has, also, the same laws; but the city fathers are so kind hearted and lenient that, notwithstanding the many complaints and entreaties for the protection of flower and vegetable gardens, they still allow the depredations to continue. Therefore we invite all who have been grieved past endurance by the stringency of Hamilton laws to drive their stock to Hillsboro, where they can get abundance of street pasture, free of charge and a guarantee that the brutes will not be molested. The fertilizing qualities of stock furnish ample compensation, in the estimation of the corporate authorities, for the little annoyance that a few people suffer; therefore, send on your animals.

8/15/84 Telephone

A Mr. Myer of New York, is sojourning here at the Hammerly House. He is one of those enterprising, active men who are always making discoveries, and a few weeks ago, while strolling on the summit of the mountain, about three fourths of a mile from Town, just above the Wolf's Den, he observed an opening between two massive rocks. He determined to further investigate the place; so, on the following day, in company with a friend, Mr. Tho. Spats he returned to the place and after moving obstructions from the opening, they entered a narrow passage which they followed about 75 feet, descending at an angle of 45 degrees. Here they stopped for the day; but Mr. Myer, determined to explore this subterranean passage, procured the assistance of his companion's son, Walter Spats, and T. H. Everhart, two daring young men like himself, and again repaired to, what is now known as, The Diamond Cave. Equipped with lanterns &c., they descended the first incline and came to a beautiful hall about 30 feet long 5 or 6 feet wide and about 12 feet to the ceiling, with perpendicular walls on either side, of solid granite encrusted with most beautiful crystal formation, which, in the light of the lanterns, glittered like myriads of diamonds. At the further end of this hall they came to a perpendicular passage way, 12 feet to the bottom, which was so small that Mr. Myer, who is somewhat corpulent, could not get through until some small obstructions were removed.— Here they entered another beautiful hall 45 feet in length 5 or 6 feet wide and 25 feet high, with walls like the first, perpendicular and glistening with crystals. At the extreme end of the hall a few small satellites hang from the ceiling. Here the explorations ended until last Wednesday, when with the assistance of two colored men and a little powder an entrance was made to the third hall of still greater magnitude, where these daring men found themselves 125 feet below the surface of the mountain.

This is destined to be a great place of resort.

(Still a mystery. Perhaps the present owner, whoever it is, would want it to remain so. Maybe it was a hoax to begin with.)

OLIVER R. DAVIS

PRACTICAL  JEWELER

HIGH St., LINCOLN VA.

SEWING MACHINES, CLOCKS, WATCHES, SPECTACLES, ACCORDEONS MUSIC BOXES, VIOLINS AND JEWELRY REPAIRED NEATLY AND DURABLY AT SHORT NOTICE.

WORK WARRANTED—CHARGES MODERATE—TERMS CASH.

8/15/84 Telephone

DARING DEVILMENT
AT THE BUSH MEETING.

LIQUOR AND GAMBLING.

SOME OF THE OFFENDERS CAUGHT.

AND A GRAND STAMPEDE OF THE OTHERS.

AN IMPORTANT LAW.

Last Wednesday, while the Temperance Bush Meeting was in progress, signs of a "dirty camp" in the vicinity became apparent, and on following up the trail, some of the members of the Bush Meeting Committee succeeded in finding a small camp and very leniently gave the parties the privilege of leaving or going to jail. Of course they left—but, perhaps, they only changed base.

On Thursday it was again rumored that a similar, but more extensive, camp was located in the woods north of the Depot. On investigation the rumor was established in fact, and the authorities proceeded to capture the crowd.— Sheriff Carruthers, with his deputies Shawen and Bussard, and Justices of the Peace Gaver, Vandevanter and Throckmorton, proceeded to the designated locality and found a crowd of gamblers from Alexandria and elsewhere and a number of liquor venders, mostly from Leesburg, who were plying their vocations in a wholesale and shameless manner. About one hundred and fifty persons, about equally divided between white and colored, were present. The coming of the officers was announced by the spies and accomplices of the law-breakers, consequently a number of them got away by precipitate flight. It was a general stampede, but the officers succeeded in arresting some of them. Notably among those who were restrained by the arm of the law were F. M. Boswell, who said he was from Baltimore, (but some say he belongs to a respectable Washington family,) and his chum and partner E. B. Shock, of Alexandria. They were immediately tried by Justices Gaver, Vandevanter and Throckmorton, and fined $100, and costs. Their paraphrenalia, including a magnificent Wheel of Fortune, was taken in charge by the Sheriff and he ordered that it be burned as the law, in its majesty, directs. Deputies Shawen and Bussard said they would conduct the burning on Wednesday. Another Alexandrian by the name of F. A. Church, was also convicted and contributed $10 (toward paying off Virginia's State debt,) beside the costs. The whole guilty clan were so thoroughly alarmed, that they ran in every direction, forgetting their bravery, and some even forgetting their clothes, for one man left his hat, coat and vest, the pocket of the latter containing some money. Two of them made for the Manassas R. R., one took the train at Hamilton next morning and one at Leesburg. The Alexandria papers report them as returning, haggard and forlorn, indeed; as being "foot sore, brier torn, mud-bespattered and unhappy." They are, doubtless, all willing to vote these Loudoun County Temperance Bush Meetings as great nuisances, and as being altogether too "sumptuary" in their operations.

It is reported that the Bush Meeting Committee express great regret at not getting the Ex-Detective, S. T. Taylor, from Alexandria.

None of the proprietors of the jug taverns were arrested until last Monday, which was Grand Jury day for Loudoun County, and which Jury found true bills of indictment against seven parties who violated the revenue law, during the Bush Meeting, four from Leesburg, and three from outside the County's Capitol.

August, 1884

8/22/84 Telephone

Telephone in Waterford.

When in Waterford recently Dr. Connell kindly invited us to go into his store and see the telephone which he had put up, making connection with Clarks Gap. Hanging on the wall we found a very handsome instrument, and a turn of the call bell crank and a "Hello" quickly brought a response from "Al" Bowie, the operator at Clarks Gap, three miles distant. We very quickly pronounced it the best telephone (excepting the Loudoun, of course,) that we have ever tried, being much more clear and distinct than those we have used in Washington, on shorter distances. The Doctor explained that it is a new instrument, in fact the two which he procured was the first and only pair then completed by a new company which has been formed for the purpose of operating the new instrument—one of the company being an intimate friend of the Doctor.

Mr. Roose, father-in-law of Dr. Connell, originated this telephone line and had most of the work done, when unfair treatment by the Bell Telephone Co., whose instruments he expected to use, caused him to suspend operations and he then sold out to the Doctor, who completed the line, which will be a great convenience to the two points connected; and the gentlemen who have accomplished this thing deserve more than the thanks of the community, for this expression of public spirit.

8/29/84 Telephone

—The celebrated Vienna Base Ball Association with King, their noted curve pitcher, will visit Hamilton some day during the coming week and play a game with our local club. Turn out and encourage the boys to take the conceit out of these Fairfax youths.

9/4/84 Mirror

Buried Alive.—Monday afternoon Mr. LYNS, who resides on the farm of Mrs. HATTIE B GLASSCOCK, near Snickersville, sent one of his hands to a field not far from the house to clean up some briars, and who while thus engaged, was attracted by the crying of a child in a strip of woods in one corner of the field. Investigation revealed the presence of a white female child, about two months old, regularly entombed among the rocks—the sides of which were carefully filled in with leaves and dirt, and a large flat rock placed over the grave thus improvised. The little thing was robed in its ordinary clothing with a handkerchief around its neck. The supposition, is that it had been drugged with laudanum, and under the impression that life was extinct, this inhuman expedient was resorted to for the purppse of getting it out of the way and possibly to conceal a crime. The supposition that laudanum had been administered was strengthened by the fact that the handkerchief about the neck was saturated with vomit, which probably saved her life. The little creature is supposed to have lain in her cold and rugged grave since the preceding Saturday—and when found she was fearfully emaciated and almost dead for the want of nourishment. Medical skill was called to her aid, however, and a lady who saw her on Tuesday morning, informs us that she was greatly revived, and under tender, careful treatment, was likely to servive after her miraculous escape from a horrible death. We learn from the same source that the footprints of a man and a woman were detected in the earth about the grave. The child is said to be quite interesting in appearance, but that notwithstanding she had been visited by scores of people in the neighborhood among whom the burial of a living child in their midst had naturally aroused a deep feeling, no clue to her parentage, or the authors of the "deep damnation" of its attempted taking off has yet been discovered.

Leesburg, Monday, Sept. 15th.

JOHN ROBINSON'S
10 BIG SHOWS COMBINED. 10

Menagerie, Museum, School [Trained Animals, Calisthenic Exhibition, Aviary]

3 CIRCUSES IN 3 RINGS,

at one and the same time, and an Enormous Elevated Stage for Bicyclists, Skaters, Olympian Games and Dramatic Entertainments.

$300,000 NOVELTY STREET PARADE,
CONSISTING OF.

50 Cages, 2 Steam Organs, Herd of Elephants, 8 Brass Bands, Steam Caliopes

15 Trumpeters, 4 Steam Musical Wagons, 31 Sun-Bright Chariots, Drum Corps

12 DISTINCT KINDS OF MUSIC. Female Brass Band of 15. Troupe of Colored Jubilee Singers. Droves of Camels, Ostriches, Giraffes, Elks, Buffaloe, Elands, Llamas, and Zebras Led Untrammeled in the Streets. 300 Horses. 100 Ponies, 100 Mounted Knights
500,000 YARDS OF CANVAS MADE RADIANT BY ELECTRICITY!

TRAVELING BY ITS OWN SPECIAL TRAIN OF 60 CARS.

A FEW OF OUR LEADING FEATURES AND NOVELTIES

ZENOBIA Hurled 200 Feet by the CATAPULT.	$45,000 DROVE OF GIRAFFES.
OX WITH 3 Separate Horns and 3 Distinct Eyes.	—AIDA— Dives from Apex of the Canvas, 100 Feet.
GRACE, TATTOOED WOMAN, With over 500 Separate Animals and Pictures Tattooed into Her Flesh.	Giant Ox, larger than an Elephant. $30,000 FLOCK OF
COLORADO WHITE BUFFALO	OSTRICHES

50 CAGES AND DENS 50
Containing over 1,500 WILD BIRDS, BEASTS AND REPTILES from every clime.

GIANT HORSE, 21 HANDS HIGH.	FEMALE GIANTESS! Weight, 720 Pounds.
HINDOO FEMALE SNAKE CHARMER.	LONG-HAIRED BELMONT SISTERS Length of Hair, 86 Inches.

PAIR BABY ELEPHANTS 2 YEARS OLD.

CLARA! Rolls and Balances a Globe on a 3-4 inch Wire 100 feet High	Band Zulus! Troupe Arabs. Tribe Indians! Tribe Hindoos Pair Cannibals! Band Fejees
FEMALE SAMSON. Outpulls a pair of Elephants.	ZOLA! Rides a Bicycle on a 3-4 Inch Wire Elevated One Hundred Feet.
Zenals Startling 353-Feet stair Slide from Top of Canvas	Pair of Sacred BURMESE CATTLE. Two and one-half Feet High.

SACRED WHITE DOUBLE-HORNED RHINOCEROS!!
ELLA ZOLA walks on stilts upon a frail wire 100 feet high. 9 Female Bicycle Riders
9 Siberian Roller Skaters. $10,000 White Nile Hippopotamus, Monster Herd of Elephants all ages, Sizes and Kinds.

110 Male and Female Artists.

We never advertise an Act, Feature or Performance That We Do Not Exhibit.
TWO PERFORMANCES DAILY. Doors open at 1 and 7 P. M.
DON'T FORGET THE DAY KEEP YOUR EYE ON THE DATE AND PLACE
CHEAP EXCURSIONS on all Railroads leading into the town. (sept. 4, 1884)

September, 1884

9/26/84 Telephone

The following letter, which will explain itself, should be heeded by the people who may, through carelessness or otherwise, pollute the waters of the Potomac. Remember, the people of Washington are at the mercy of those who live along the Potomac and its tributaries.

HEALTH DEP'T, DIS. OF COLUMBIA.
Washington, Sept. 18th, 1884.
To the Sheriff of Loudoun County, Va.:

SIR: I am reliably informed that hogs in considerable numbers dying from cholera in the counties of Maryland and Virginia, bordering upon the upper Potomac River, are deposited in this stream, thereby rendering possible the contamination of the water from which the supply of the City of Washington is drawn.

If it be a fact that the carcasses of dead hogs are thrown in numbers into the Potomac above us, it becomes at once a matter of serious consequence to our two hundred thousand inhabitants and in the interest of their health and lives, I would ask your assistance to the extent of warning the people of your own county against this practice.

Very Respectfully &c.,
SMITH TOWNSHEAD, M. D.,
Health Officer.

JOHN ROBINSON'S Ten Big Shows, Combined, exhibited at Leesburg, on Monday last to a vast crowd. The Canvas was unusually large and everything connected with the exhibition most admirably arranged. The canvas covered two rings and a platform for the equestrian and gymnastic performances. The programme, as published, was carried out, to the pleasure and satisfaction of all present. The performance was admirable and performed in the most artistic manner.

10/2/84 Mirror

As John Robinson's circus was entering Portsmsmith, Va., on Sunday morning last, two black tigers broke out of their cages, and after killing two trained goats, escaped in the direction of the Dismal Swamp. A throng of hunters with packs of hounds started in pursuit, but so far the animals have not been captured.

9/26/84 Telephone

—The *Washingtonian* of last week announced the death of Mr. Hyram Tavenner, of our Town. This was a surprise to Mr. Tavenner, who was just on the eve of starting on a visit to the Wooden Nutmeg State, where he is now sojourning.

10/3/85 Telephone

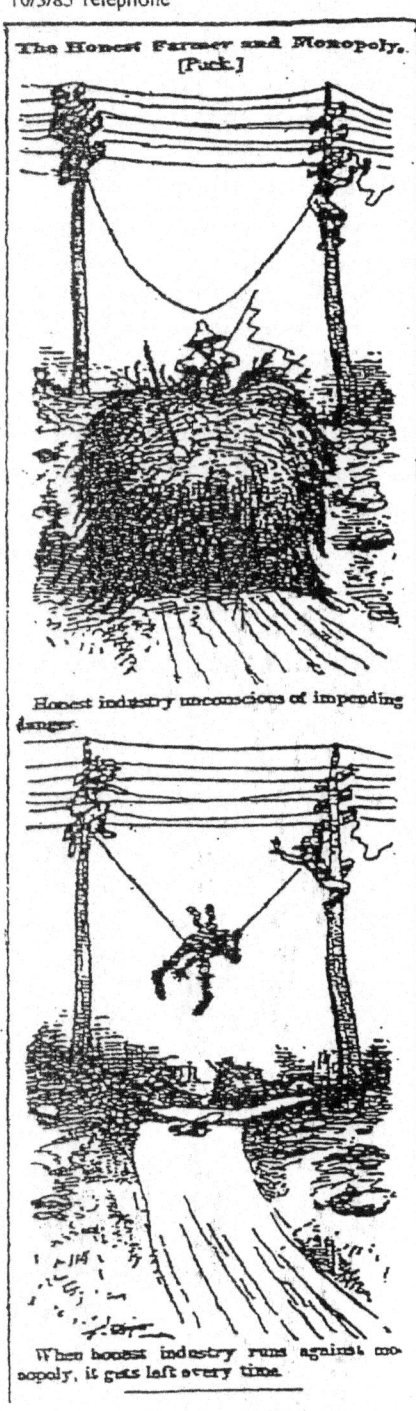

The Honest Farmer and Monopoly. [Puck.]

Honest industry unconscious of impending danger.

When honest industry runs against monopoly, it gets left every time.

September, 1884

9/25/84 Mirror

THE DROUGHT —The heavens continue as brass and the sun as a ball of fire. The earth and the fulness thereof is pleading piteously for rain. Streams are running low and the mill wheels are unable to perform their accustomed labor. The cattle on a thousand hills are nibbling at the parched grass, and plaintively lowing for a refreshing shower. The growth of vegetation generally is stunted and stopped, and the drought of nearly two months duration, still continues.— the highways are filled with dust, likewise the eyes and lungs of man and beast. The noble stream that for nearly a half century has supplied this community with an abundance of the purest and best of water, is yielding to the inevitable, and its fountain head, where there is usually a depth of from four to five feet, has been reduced to less than sixteen inches, compelling our city Fathers to appeal to our citizens to be mindful of its waste. Fall seeding is retarded— the stalks of unmatured ears have dried up and been cut off, and the universal cry of the human soul hereabouts is for rain, rain, rain.

9/26/84 Telephone

Although the clouds were dark and lowering on Monday last there was no rain. Fully one month has elapsed since this vicinity was favored with a good shower. Vegitation has suffered considerably from the dry weather. There will be a light corn crop which will rate far below an average. Our town is poorly watered. In both cisterns and wells the water is getting quite low. Many of the people here go out to the suburban springs to get their daily supplies.

9/25/84 Mirror

Owing to the parched condition of every thing caused by the excessive drought, much inconvenience is being occasioned to persons along the line of the railroad by sparks from passing engines. We have heard of numerous instances of considerable fencing having been burned, and we are informed that a few days ago several hay stacks, belonging to Mr. H. S. Smith and Mr Robt. Clowe, two farmers living near Guilford, were in this way set on fire and some thirty tons of hay destroyed; also that about two thousand rails on the farm of Mr Jno. W Hammerly, near Farmwell, were destroyed in the same manner. Of course such accidents occasion much inconvenience and loss to those who fall victims, but we suppose it would be unreasonable to think that their occurrence could be prevented in the tinder-like condition which all things are at the present time.

NEW ADVERTISEMENTS.

An Ordinance.

BE IT ENACTED by the MAYOR, RECORDER and COMMON COUNCIL of the town of LEESBURG in Virginia. That whosoever shall hereafter wash tubs, clothes, Carriages, or any other article whatever, or water horses or other stock at a Pump or Hydrant in this corporation. He or she shall for such offence forfeit and pay to the use of the Corporation two dollars and fifty cents, to be recovered before the MAYOR or RECORDER with costs.

2. That it shall be unlawful for any person to fasten back by any means any cock to Hydrant, within this Corporation, or to cause the water to flow from said Hydrant unnecessarily or be waste, or to use from any of the Cisterns for any purpose whatsoever except in case of fire or for the purpose of exercising the Fire Engines. Whosoever shall be guilty of either of said offences, shall for any such offence forfeit and pay to the use of this Corporation the sum of not less than two dollars nor more than ten dollars, with costs, at the discretion of the MAYOR or RECORDER.

RINKER ON THE ROAD AGAIN!
MEAT TO EAT!

HAMILTON, LINCOLN and PURCELLVILLE, On Tuesdays and Fridays.
WHEATLAND and HILLSBORO On Wednesdays and Saturdays.
WATERFORD Four days in each week.

C. W. RINKER, Waterford, Va.

October 1884

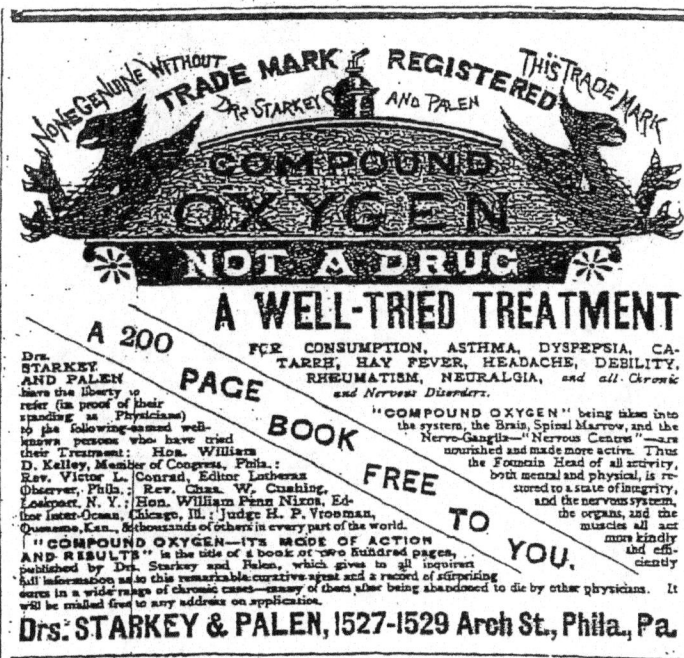

10/9/84 Mirror

Last Monday Mrs. Clark, mother of a section boss on the W. O. & W. R. R., aged about 60 years, living at Vienna, was burned to death in her house, which was entirely consumed. She was killing waspes with a torch, which came in contact with a coal oil can that was hanging on the wall, when an explosion occurred, throwing oil over her instantly, enveloping her in flames. Her body was rescued but not till life was extinct. The building might have been saved but for the scarcity of water.

Mr. H S Smith had about 30 tons of hay burnt, by sparks from a locomotive, about two weeks ago. Messrs. C. F. Bridges and Walter Hummer had 10 tons burnt, the fire being communicated from an engine which was running the hay press. The press, owned by Mr. Coleman, narrowly escaped. Mr. Lynn had a large amount of fence and about 50 cords of wood burnt, the fire originating from locomotive sparks.

The drouth here is terrible, cattle have to be driven miles to water, pastures are perfectly bare and stock have to be put on winter rations.

There have been three horses gored to death, by bulls in this vicinity, within a fortnight.

10/11/84 Washingtonian

A RUNAWAY AT POINT OF ROCKS.—Mr. George W. Compher, of Taylortown, Va., is having a carriage repaired by S. W. Kable, at Middletown, and Mr. Kable recently took a fine Buggy to Taylortown to endeavor to make a sale. Tuesday morning Messrs. Kable and Compher started out from Taylortown, for Frederick en route to Middletown in the carriage. When near Point of Rocks the horse took fright and ran away. After coming in contact with a number of telegraph poles, fences, etc., the vehicle was a total wreck. The two gentlemen where thrown out and slightly bruised. Mr. Kable took the train and arrived here Tuesday night in deplorable condition. After regaining possession of the horse Mr. Compher rode the animal to town where he arrived with no further accident. He says there was not enough left of the carriage to bring along.—

November 1884

THE MIRROR
BENJ. F. SHEETZ, Editor.

Thursday Morning, Nov. 13, 1884

DEMOCRATIC VICTORY.—The founders of this Government intended, and so declared, that this should be a Republic, every citizen of which should be free and independent—and every State co-equal with its sister. But it needs no elaborate reasoning to convince the people of this section, at least, that such has not been our status in all the twenty-five years of Republican rule. True once in four years the democrats have been accorded the privilege of going through a form of voting for President—but it has only been, when the contest was over, to witness the blasting of our hopes, either by the corrupt use of money and the unwarrantable exercise of power of those who held the federal reins or, to meekly behold a victory won, stolen from them by agencies such as in any kind less conservative than our own, would have deluged it with blood.

But that condition of things, thank God, has passed into history. Our noble standard bearer of to-day—with that coolness and firmness, and dignity of character that has characterized his conduct throughout the canvass just closed, has declared, "I believe I have been elected President, and nothing but the grossest fraud can keep me out of it, and that we will not permit." Therefore in view of the glorious results of the 4th of November we can almost forgive, if we cannot forget, the outrages of the past, in contemplation of the brightness and glory of the dawning future.

RING OUT THE GLAD SOUND.

CLEVELAND IS PRESIDENT.
THE DEMOCRATS HAVE
THE NEXT HOUSE OF
REPRESENTATIVES

Official Vote of Loudoun.

Below we publish the vote of Loudoun (official), as cast on last Tuesday week:

Precincts	For President		For Congress	
	Grover Cleveland	Jas. G. Blaine	Jno. S. Barbour	Duff Green
Leesburg Dist.				
Leesburg	507	265	506	264
Goresville	149	65	149	65
Mt. Gilead Dist.				
Hughesville	56	85	56	84
Silcott Springs	58	78	58	78
Snickersville	158	41	157	38
Mt. Gilead	67	32	68	32
Hamilton	109	108	109	106
Philomont	62	51	62	51
Jefferson Dist.				
Hillsborough	150	90	150	91
Waterford	93	150	93	149
Purcellville	78	83	78	82
Woodgrove	69	24	69	24
Mercer Dist.				
Middleburg	104	76	103	76
Aldie	103	105	105	88
Powell's Shop	75	33	75	33
Unison	148	99	148	92
Mountsville	64	15	64	15
Lovettsville Dist.				
Lovettsville	98	291	99	290
Waters'	56	59	57	58
Lucket's Store	58	101	58	101
Broad Run Dist.				
Guilford	131	75	131	75
Gumspring	237	60	236	60
Farmwell	165	42	165	42
Total	**2795**	**1978**	**2797**	**1971**

November, 1884

10/24/84 Telephone

Guilford Flashes.

GUILFORD, Nov. 6.—Election passed off quietly in Guilford. Out of a possible 85 Republican votes, 77 were cast, one of which was thrown out because two were polled together, one Republican sold out, one was bribed to stay away, two were sick, two were not registered and two failed to appear.— The officers were all Democrats but our lines were so well guarded that they could find no pretext for refusing a vote, except in one instance they attempted to defraud one man of his vote on the most flimsy pretext imaginable, so that we were put to the trouble of getting Captain Foster's opinion, which, of course, admitted the vote. The Guilford bosses expressed rather a contemptuous opinion of Captain Foster's decision, which proves that it was a sound one. The Democratic heelers and strikers all got gloriously drunk by the time the polls closed and made the night hideous with their howlings. There was a row at the station at about 8 o'clock, in which John Burr cut a colored boy named Robert Jackson, seriously, with a pruning knife I am unable to learn the details of the affray and have heard of no steps being taken towards a legal investigation. About 12 o'clock, on receipt of some news supposed to be favorable to the Democrats, a delegation of them were so kind as to treat your correspondent to a characteristic serenade. It was not the first time I have rested serenely with a pack of howling wolves around the door.

A GRAND DEMOCRATIC
JUBILEE
WILL BE HELD IN
LEESBURG, FRIDAY, NOV. 14

Celebrating the election of

CLEVELAND AND HENDRICKS,

AND THE OVERTHROW OF MAHONEISM!

At night, a MAMMOTH

Torchlight Procession,
ILLUMINATION
AND PYROTECHNIC DISPLAY!

CLUBS from all parts of the County, mounted or on foot, will take part, bearing TRANSPARENCIES, TORCHES & BANNERS. The old Town to be in holiday attire.

☞ Every Democrat in Loudoun invited to take part.

The whole to be Marshaled by Col. HENRY E PEYTON. Assistant Marshals and Route of Procession will be made known Thursday morning.

BY ORDER OF COMMITTEE.
nov. 13, 1884.

Chinese Lanterns,
—AND—
LARGE AND SMALL
FLAGS,

Will be sold at low prices, at Loudoun Book Store.

nov. 13 H. W. CLAGETT.

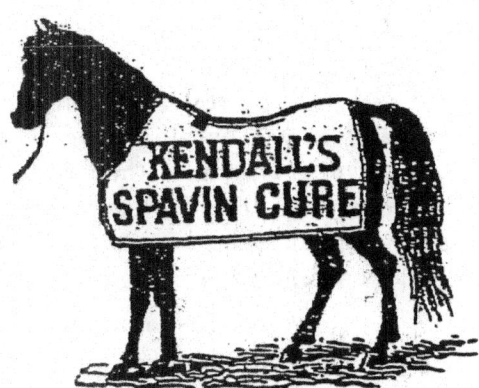

The most successful remedy ever discovered as it is certain in its effects and does not blister.

November, 1884

11/20/84 Mirror

The Grand Jubilee!

FRIDAY NIGHT'S DEMONSTRATION

Leesburg in a Blaze—The Town Hidden by People.

Nothing Like It Ever Seen by the Oldest Inhabitant

The Democratic Jubilee over the election of Cleveland and Hendricks, held in this town on Friday night last, was the biggest and grandest affair of the kind ever seen not only in this county, but we believe in this section of Virginia. The ratification meeting of a few weeks ago was generally considered a big success, and so it was, but it was tame by comparison with the monster demonstration of Friday night. The town people and the country people with one accord seem to have laid themselves out to make it the biggest thing of the season, and the way they succeeded can be understood when we say that there were from 2500 to 3,000 stangers in town, which with those here made a crowd on the streets, but little short of 5,000 persons.

Betimes on Friday morning the stir began in town; the committee of the club had advertised that the town would be in "holiday attire" and every one went to work, determined that as far as possible the terms of the announcement should be carried out to the letter. And all day long the preparations went on, until toward evening even the "oldest inhabitant" could hardly recognize in this gaily and beautifully decked masquerader, the usually staid and prim old burg.— From one end of town to the other, confined to no particular street, but on all, yards upon yards of gay bunting hang in graceful festoons over the houses, thousands of flags fluttered gaily in the evening breeze, countless Chinese lanterns, with their kaleidoscopic colors swung in arches over the doors. Just as their efforts were completed and they were viewing with admiration the splendid results, the crowd began to come in, at first singly, then in twos and threes, then in squads and finally in a steady stream, until at dusk it seemed as if "everybody and his wife" had come in, and by six o'clock the streets were packed with an immense but at the same time jolly, good natured Democratic crowd.

THE ILLUMINATION, PROCESSION, &c.

As the shades of evening began to fall, a huge bon-fire was started on Fort Johnston, and as its glare fell athwart the heavens, visible for miles around, the lights in town began to be set going, and soon the gaudy lanterns had taken a new beauty from their enclosed lights, the torch-lights that swims across the streets blazed forth, while nearly every house in town and even some on the outskirts were aflame from turret to foundation stone. By the time the town had gotten thoroughly illumninated the scene was one of magnificent grandeur.

As the hour for the procession to move drew near the uproar on the streets increased, mounted men and men on foot thronged the streets, passing to and from the headquarters from which the torches were given out, and as they were supplied they moved off to the depot lot upon which the procession was to form and ever and anon through this throng a mounted marshal, with his silver colored sash streaming in the wind, would pass at full speed as if upon his individual efforts depended the fate of the whole arrangement. About this time

THE POOLESVILLE BAND,

which had come over earlier in the evening, formed in front of the Reamer House, and followed by the Poolesville and Goresville contingent on horseback, started for the depot. The first note from the band was the signal for the small boy to let himself out, and from that time until the procession disbanded, pandemonium was loose, using the tin horn, the kazoo, the squee-dunk and every device for making hideous noises. Soon the

LEESBURG BAND

appeared and at the head of the Leesburg Club and other footmen, marched to the depot; arrived there the procession was formed as follows:

In the lead and about a block ahead was sent a wagon containing a large bell which was rung continuously; then came the chief marshal, Col. H. E. PEYTON and aids, followed by the Poolesville Band at the head of the mounted clubs from Poolesville, Goresville, Hillsboro, Round Hill, Purcellville, Hamilton, Waterford, Farmwell, besides numbers of other men who did not come as organizations—behind these came the Leesburg Band followed by Capt W. W. Athey, marshal of the home club, and aids, and bringing up the rear was a piece of artillery brought from Pursellville, and Capt Cockey's Float, mounted on wheels, and drawn by a traction engine, consisting of a huge frame, sixteen feet high, of obelisk shape, on one side of which was the Tattooed Knight, on another old Ben Butler, on a third Belva Lockwood, and on the fourth a representation of Billy Mahone, swinging by a rope, thrown over the limb of a tree and a little bull pup pulling at the farther end. On the four sides of the base upon which the obelisk rested, were inscriptions suitable to the several figures represented—was the most elaborate, as it was perhaps the most attractive of the many striking transparencies that figured in the procession. In addition to the horsemen from Hamilton, Pursellville and Round Hill, they brought several wagons loaded, a traction engine drawing three, and two pieces of artillery.

The procession was formed in column of fours and stretched over a third of a mile and as this huge line of not less than 1,200 to 1,500 men, bearing torches, transparencies, &c., moved through the brilliant streets the sight was wierd and beautiful. As it moved it was accompanied by fire works, booming of cannon, martial music, huzzas from the crowds that lined the streets, the ladies being as enthusiastic as the men, the screeching of steam whistles, the yells of the leather lunged and brazen throated small boy, who fell in line and shouted to the music such couplets as

"Blaine, Blaine, James G. Blaine
The biggest liar in the State of Maine"

As the procession wheeled from Church St. into Market it was greeted from the stand in front of headquarters by a perfect shower of rockets, Roman candles, Greek fire, &c. It seemed as though the whole street was a sheet of flame. As one stood and watched the long line of torches as they bobbed up and down along the radiant streets, and saw the different colored lights, the burning Greek fires cast upon the whole, he realized that the town was more than "painted red," and almost imagined that some artist had upset his paint pots all over her, or that the enthusiastic Democrats had borrowed a rainbow from some summer sky, and illuminating a section of it had robed the old town with that and then invited the world to see the splendid effect. After marching through all the principal streets the procession was halted on King street, and disbanded.

(The enthusiasm which seemed excessive was explainable. The first Democratic president had been elected since before the war and rightly or wrongly the party felt that they were cheated out of the '76 Hayes Tilden election.)

11/21/84 Telephone
Bourbonism Broken Loose.

The only excuse that charity can find for the unusual and unwarranted behavior of the Loudoun Democrats, for the past week, is, that they have gone roaring crazy because of Cleveland's election. Last Friday a great crowd of them congregated in Leesburg and shook the old town up so badly that some of the moss fell off the roofs (not off the backs) and no grass has grown in the streets since. It is said to be a fact that Leesburg never knew such a racket before. Two or three regiments of cavalry, two batteries and several ambulance trains (to bring home the disabled) passed through Hamilton. Among the horsemen was one lonely colored man, who seemed to be ashamed of his company, for he rode by himself. Of course the "best people" of the crowd were proud of the "cullid pusson's" presence, but no one of them rode by his side.

When we were boys we used to give the other fellow a game now and then just to keep him from giving up in despair, and thus putting an end to the fun. The Democrats were getting so out of heart that we had to let them have an inning this time, for they were becoming so discouraged that we feared they would all want to join us.—We could'nt stand that.

January 1885

1/1/85 Mirror

GEN. GRANT'S DIFFICULTIES.

His Property to be Sold Under the Vanderbilt Mortgage.

An attorney who asserted that he was acquainted with the facts said to a N. Y. *Tribune* reporter Saturday that an inventory had been taken of all Gen. Grant's possessions, under the judgment entered against him in favor of William H. Vanderbilt for $150,000 and interest, loaned to him when he was trying to save the firm of Grant & Ward from failure. The inventory and executions under the judgment were taken, he said, to protect Gen Grant as well as Mr. Vanderbilt. The executions cover houses in Washington and Philadelphia, and farms near St. Louis and Chicago. The farms alone are valued at $65,000 and $25,000 respectively, and, with the other property, are ample to secure Mr Vanderbilt, as Mrs Grant joins with the general and gives up her life interest in the property mentioned. The inventory includes all the presents of weapons, bric-a-brac and rare articles made to the general at different times by friends at home and potentates abroad, the swords and medals awarded him by Congress, his pictures and books, his relics of the war, and even the engraved cards ordered struck to express the thanks of Congress.

The *Tribune* says: Gen. Sherman, on his visit here, learned of the possibility that Gen. Grant might lose all these articles. Indeed it is said that Gen. Grant called a council of war with his old comrade in arms over the situation. The result has been that steps are being taken to relieve the property. Gen Sherman left the city yesterday for Philadelphia, and will afterward visit Washington.

Cyrus W. Field said to a *Tribune* reporter: "Gen Grant's swords, medals and relics of the war may be sold at any moment under a mortgage to secure the debt of $150,000 which he borrowed from Mr Vanderbilt to help the firm of Grant & Ward, and for which he has confessed judgment. This ought not to be. I received a message from Gen. Sherman last night informing me of the fact. It was the first I knew of it. This morning I went to see Mr. Vanderbilt about it and he promised to throw off $60,000 of the total amount, which is now about $160,000 with interest, if the remaining $100,000 was paid. I have taken the matter in hand and I think I shall have no difficulty in raising the money."

1/9/85 Telephone

QUITE A RACKET.

A LIVELY BUT INNOCENT EARTHQUAKE.

LOUDOUN THE CENTER OF THE SWELL.

Three Shocks Felt in This Vicinity

Last Friday night at about 9:15 P. M., a very decided earthquake shock startled, and in some cases frightened, the people of this vicinity. A rumbling noise was first heard sounding very much like a chimney afire, followed by a very perceptable ground swell — The noise and shaking together were very similar to the sensation caused by a heavy wagon passing over the frozen ground, and many persons thought the commotion was caused by a vehicle of that kind.

Many persons were quite badly frightened by the peculiar commotion, and ran out of their houses. About an hour later another shock, though not so severe as at first, was felt by some persons and again at about two o'clock a third shock, more forcible than the second, was noticed by those who chanced to be awake at that time. It was, indeed, a shocking night.

It was amusing to hear the experience of the people next morning. Some had thought the commotion was caused by one thing and some another. Some declared that the noise was in one direction while others that it seemed to be elsewhere. Mr. John Hughes said, when he heard the noise, that he was sure that a rain barrel which he had near his house had been bursted by Jack Frost Esq. Mr. E. H. Tavenner said he ran out of the house expecting to see fire blazing out of a chimney, and many others did the same.

January 1885

1/8/85 Mirror

WALT WHITMAN ON CLEVELAND.

"Grover Cleveland stands out in strong colors in a clear light as a safe and a strong man—one with a purpose. No man before the people ever stood up and took the blows of the press with better welcome than did Cleveland. He bids fair to bring the old-time Democracy back to the days of manifest destiny and human progress. In Cleveland there is a combination of Scotch-Presbyterianism added to his early self-education which would make a statesman who will be governed by good sense and patriotism. Under Cleveland, who has what is rarer than genius in our public men, old fashioned horse sense and a splendid solidity of personal character, there is a very likelihood of the Southern problem reaching a satisfactory solution in the next eight years.

1/29/85 Mirror

Sullivan in a Free Fight.—John L. Sullivan became engaged in a free fight in an Eliot street barroom in Boston Thursday night, where he had been drinking with his companions most of the afternoon. Sullivan was offended at a man named Hodgkins, whose opinion on pugilistic matters differed from his own, and, after some words, the champion caught Hodgkins by both arms and with his head struck the latter between the eyes. Another of the party, named Deliere, swore at Sullivan and said he was no man.— Releasing Hodgkins from his grasp Sullivan, who was mad with rage and liquor, struck Deliere, felling him senseless to the floor— Friends of the latter interfered, and the fight became general. The melee had progressed but a short time when the bar-tender, named Maguire, it is alleged, drew a revolver, the sight of which together with the prompt arrival of a detail of eight police officers, restored quiet, but not until all those present were more or less hurt. At sight of the officers Sullivan was hurried from the saloon through a rear door by his friends. Deliere, who was quite badly hurt, declares that he will procure a warrant for Sullivan's arrest.

LIME! LIME!
—AT THE—
Leesburg Lime Kiln.

THE TELEPHONE.
FRIDAY..................JAN. 16TH.

A GREAT MISTAKE.

There are hundreds of farmers in Loudoun, at this very time, making a serious blunder; but one which, strange to say, they make every year and yet never seem to learn by the things they suffer.

What we mean is this: Every farmer has a certain amount of hauling to be done between this time and May, and many of them are devoting their attention to other minor affairs which could well be put off till a rainy day, and are letting their teams stand in the stable now, while the roads are comparatively good. But by and by, when the frost and rains of Spring have made the roads almost impassable, they will realize that the hauling must be done, and with roads so bad that it takes half of the team to pull the empty wagon, they go at it. What is the result? They flounder about in the mud; get everything begrimed; keep their teamster in ill humor; pull their horses down badly; spend about twice as much time in making a trip as they would when the roads are good; only haul half a load at a time; and cut up the roads so badly that they do not get smooth again before midsummer.

AYER'S
Ague Cure

IS WARRANTED to cure all cases of malarial disease, such as Fever and Ague, Intermittent or Chill Fever, Remittent Fever, Dumb Ague, Bilious Fever, and Liver Complaint. In case of failure, after due trial, dealers are authorized, by our circular of July 1st, 1882, to refund the money.

Dr. J. C. Ayer & Co., Lowell, Mass.
Sold by all Druggists.

February, 1885

THE MIRROR
BENJ. F. SHEETZ, Editor.

Thursday Morning, Feb. 19, 1885.

INAUGURATION preparations are being rapidly carried forward in Washington just now, and it is thought everything will be gotten in perfect order in ample time. The work of putting the wooden roof on the new Pension building where the ball is to be held, is progressing very satisfactorily, six of the sixteen trusses to support the roof over the interior hall which is 116 feet wide, were gotten in place in a couple of days, and the others will be as rapidly gotten ready — Twenty five hundred tickets for the ball have already been sold and distributed for sale —

THE TELEPHONE.

FRIDAY................FEB. 27TH

—Light vehicles have been crossing the Potomac on the ice at Pt. of Rocks. Herds of cattle have also been taken across on the ice bridge.

—We desire to state that the story published in our paper last week about Miss Mary Cox, of West Virginia having been buried alive was a senseless hoax. We beg pardon of all those who lost any sleep after reading the sensation.

—HILLSBORO, Feb. 25.—Messrs. J. Matthews and Dave Thompson had some sheep killed by dogs last week. On the following day they had some dogs killed.

2/20/85 Telephone

The Washington *Star* of last Saturday states that on Friday evening about 6 o'clock Butler Mahone, son of Senator Mahone, entered the bar at Welcker's Hotel (where the Mahones were stopping) and ordered something to drink; which was refused, because he was already intoxicated. He then became angry and violent but soon left and returned again about 11 o'clock. He started to go up the elevator and a colored porter, John Willis, was deputised to look after him. On the way up he quarreled with the negro, who descended by the stairs soon after getting out of the elevator. Young Mahone followed the porter down to the parlor, where Willis and several gentlemen were, and it is said, exclaimed "Where is the d— nigger? I want to kill him. He then drew his pistol and fired, one ball striking Willis' finger, and another passing through Mr. John Welcker's hair. After reasserting his intention to kill the negro, Mahone left the hotel and was arrested about 2 o'clock in a saloon, and taken to a station house, where he left $50. collateral for his reappearance at the police court next morning. He did not appear however, but on a warrant procured by Willis he was re-arrested, and subsequently bailed by Postmaster Windsor, of Alexandria, in the sum of $1,000.

The *Critic* of Saturday says:— After the shooting last night, Mrs. Felter, the wife of the proprietor of Welckler's, informed the Senator that he and his son would have to secure quarters elsewhere. She gave them till Monday to leave. The Senator was enraged when he heard that an officer had been sent to arrest his son, and said, addressing Mrs. Felter, "No power on earth can be brought to bear to remove my son from this house, and if any one harms him I will kill him."

But on Monday the General and his young hopeful removed to the Ebbitt House.

March, 1885

3/7/85 Washingtonian

ROAD MACHINES.

The right of the Road Board to purchase machinery for use on the public roads, was decided, by the Commonwealth's Attorney, before the purchase was made, the expediency of this act has been endorsed by the public, so far as the *Mirror* and WASHINGTONIAN reflect public opinion. A Rock Crusher, and Lamborn Road Machine now await the open season, to attest their usefulness, and power for good, to the cost of the Road District—some $300. The unanimity of sentiment, regarding the capacity of these Machines to do what is claimed for them, expressed by the Road Boards, who have adopted them, and by individuals who have traveled the roads worked by them, is too strong for any reasonable being to doubt, that if the true purpose for which the Road Tax is levied, is to make the roads durable and smooth, the best means to attain that end, is to give a fair and impartial trial here, to these machines, that have been fully tested elsewhere, and not found wanting. An impression seems lately to have spread, that this introduction of machinery militates against the interest of the working man,—we think this unfounded—it is equally of interest to rich and poor,—he who rides and he who walks; that the roads they travel are in good condition, the horse must flounder through the mud, and the footman take to the fields to escape it—thus rendering himself liable to fine and imprisonment for trespass, as a recent decision has settled; for it is the duty of the public to find right of way, and make it accessible to all, mounted and foot. This, the public can do in the near future, if rich and poor now join to adopt this, to us, novel, to others, a tried and approved plan,—work your roads with the help of machines. These machines are a help, not hindrance,—they require man's aid, as do the plow and scoop already used; only more men than they do. We believe there will be more hands employed on the roads than ever before; and that their work will be blessed as never before to rich and poor alike.

3/19/85 Mirror

Old Daniel Tucker, colored, the most notable character on Chincoteague Island, died last week. He claimed to have had many hairbreadth escapes by field and flood. He also claimed to be the man that "the song was writ about."

3/5/85 Mirror

There is something peculiarly sad in the condition of Gen U. S. Grant. While it has for sometime been known that the General was a great sufferer, few supposed that his infirmity is of the aggravated and fatal character now ascribed to it—cancer of the throat: which has been and is gradually gnawing upon his vitals. His physicians say there is no remedy—no medical skill that can afford him relief, and that death, in a few months at the farthest, is inevitable. Death in any form whether from lingering disease, or sudden attack, carries with it greater or less terror,—but to be the victim of an incurable malady—with mental and physical power sufficient to pursue ordinary labor and at the same time to be conscious of impending doom, dying as it were daily, before the hour of final dissolution arrives, is sad in the extreme. And whatever may have been the differences between Gen. Grant and his fellowmen while he was in the vigor of health, and the plentitude of his power, they will be forgotten in this hour of his physical suffering, and the great heart of a nation will swell with sympathy for him in this season of sore distress.

3/6/85 Telephone

GENERAL GRANT.

The announcement made public a few days ago that General Grant's condition is such that he cannot get well though he may live for some time, will spread a shadow of sadness over all the land. The trouble at the root of his tongue which was thought to be yielding to treatment has at last been pronounced a cancer, and it is so located that an operation is not considered possible. The disease is supposed to be the result of the General's habit of smoking, to which he has seemed to be a slave.

THE TELEPHONE.

FRIDAY............ MARCH 6TH

Mr. Cleveland's inaugural address is creditable to him in one respect at least — he evidently wrote it himself.

Well, Mr. Cleveland,
We tried to defeat you,
 But failing in that
We are willing to seat you

A great many persons went to Washington on Wednesday to witness the abdication of President Arthur. It was a big time. May the Ex-President live long and catch many fish.

3/12/85 Mirror

Notwithstanding the remarkable good order observed at the inauguration last week, Washington appears to have been infested with an unusual number of the light-fingered gentry and pocket book lifting, watch snatching, room robberies and almost every other species of thievery was everywhere prevalent, and the papers gives long lists of losses.

3/26/85 Mirror

SURGERY WITHOUT PAIN.

Wonderful Success of the New Anæsthetic — A Great Demand for Cocaine.

A prominent eye surgeon was removing the bandages from the eye of a patient at the Post Graduate School of Medicine yesterday when a *Tribune* reporter entered the room and asked "Do you still use cocaine as an anæsthetic?"

"Well, I should say so, in operations upon the eye I feel now that I could not get along without it. In general practice it has driven ether and chloroform out of the field.

3/19/85 Mirror

Stunning Sensation at Miss Cleveland's Reception.

WASHINGTON, March 14.— Miss Cleveland's reception at the White House this afternoon was well attended. Dr. Mary Walker created the sensation of the afternoon at the White House. She called early, and was dressed in a new suit — Prince Albert coat, buttoned up high dark trousers and stout, heavy boots of calfskin. A high standing collar and black tie gave a very masculine expression to her thin face.

Dr. Mary entered the reception-room carrying a new silk tile in one hand and a small umbrella with a silver handle in the other — She walked towards Miss Cleveland with a long, sweeping stride.

Marshal McMichael, who was prepared for almost anything, turned pale as Dr Mary approached

"Heavens!" he ejaculated, "what am I to do?"

He didn't have long to consider.

"Please present me to Miss Cleveland," said the Doctor sharply, taking him by the arm.

Miss Cleveland knew nothing about the Doctor's strange peculiarity of dress, and when Mr. McMichael presented "Dr. Walker," she said pleasantly :

"I am glad to meet you, sir"

"I would have you know that I am not a sir," said she, drawing herself up to her full height. "I am a woman, but I have advanced ideas about dress"

"So I perceive," said Miss Cleveland, trying hard not to smile.

"I understand that you are one of us and belong to the advanced thinkers in our sex?"

Miss Cleveland made no direct reply, but simply said that she thought the cause of womanhood was not suffering.

"You ought to be on our side," continued Dr. Mary, to the great annoyance of the people waiting for her to pass on, "for I elected your brother ; but for me he would not be in the White House to-day."

"Indeed !"

"Yes ; I know that I influenced more than enough votes to have turned the scale against him in New York State."

At this point the pressure in the rear became so strong that she was forced into the next room, not without assuring Miss Cleveland, however, that she would call again and often.

(Dr. Mary Walker might have been eccentric, but because of her work as a surgeon with the troops in the Civil War she is the only woman to receive the Medal of Honor.)

March, 1885

3/7/85 Washingtonian

INAUGURATION

A Day of Grandeur and Demonstration at the National Capitol.

President Cleveland

The President and Vice-President Installed in Office With the Usual Ceremony

THE GRAND DEMONSTRATION

Imposing Exercises at the Capitol and a Brief and Effective Inaugural Address.

An Imposing Procession.

Mr. Stephen Grover Cleveland of New York, is President, and Thos. A. Hendricks of Indiana is Vice-President of the United States. The inauguration and the administration of the oaths of office were accomplished at noon to-day with the formalities and ceremonies usual on such occasions from time immemorial and with a grand military, civic and popular demonstration unequalled in the history of the city. The weather could not have been more perfect, a bright sunny sky and gentle breeze combining to render the temperature as favorable as possible on a March day.

The city presented an animated and attractive appearance, nearly every building along the long route of march showing evidences of the decorator's art, and the entire route resembling a vast pathway of flags and buntings, banners and decorations of all descriptions. That the city never before contained so large a number of persons is an unquestionable fact. Every available place for the accommodation of visitors was utilized.

3/6/85 Telephone

GROVER IN CLOVER!

HENDRICKS FEELS BLEST!

THE AGONY'S OVER!

NOW GIVE US A REST.

Last Wednesday was undoubtedly the biggest day Washington City ever experienced or tolerated. To say it was full of people does not express the fullness unless the streets be considered sleeping places and ginger bread stands recognized as breakfast tables. From the four quarters of the whole Country a stream of the "hungry and thirsty" had been pouring constantly for many days, and on the 3d and morning of the 4th the adjacent country and neighboring cities seemed to disgorge the entire population into the Nation's Capitol. Of course most of the Republicans remained at home out of consideration of their Democratic neighbors, because each one of them was expanded to about twice his normal size. A great many persons went from Loudoun, especially from Leesburg, where Sheriff Caruthers organized a company of white horse cavalry, composed of men from all parts of the County. They formed a part of the 219th battallion in the inaugural procession.

Travel by rail in the vicinity of Washington, was simply a wild rush and jam. Every road leading to the City was literally crowded with trains. All the regular trains were run in sections and extras were thrown in between. Trains from Baltimore arrived every ten minutes. The Sixth Street Depot was overrun with trains, and passengers on the W. O. & W. had to find their train down at Maryland Avenue—or get left.

The City was decorated from end to end with banners and bunting and everything abandoned to the grand frolic.

March. 1885

Some of the Most Important Scenes in Washington
on That Memorable Day

3/6/85 Telephone

TO THE CAPITOL

The sight which was witnessed on Pennsylvania avenue last Wednesday was one of the most gorgeous and brilliant ever seen in the nation's capital. In some respects it eclipsed the pageant of 20 years ago, when the historic avenue resounded to the tramp of the thousands of battle-scarred veterans who passed in review before Gen. Grant at the close of the war. From an early hour on Wednesday morning Washington looked as if it were an armed camp. At every street corner could be seen military organizations on the qui vive, and anxiously awaiting the command to move. There were the familiar blue of the line regiments, the various colors of the state militia, the peculiar and rich uniform of the Continental's, the trim and handsome looking cadets from West Point and Annapolis, dressed respectively in gray and blue; the artillerymen sitting stiff and upright on their gun carriages and tumbrils, the mounted men of the signal corps, the blue jackets and the "lobsters," as the marines are familiarly called; the glittering scarlet tunics, laced with gold, of the Marine corps band, while ever and anon staff officers, resplendent in gold laces and bright, broad sashes, dashed hither and thither, rapidly bringing the various bodies into required positions. That day will not be soon forgotten by those who saw it. At every hundred feet or so came a band, which filled the air with blares of martial music.

A HOTEL CORRIDOR THE NIGHT OF THE THIRD.

There was a humorous side to the inauguration ceremonies. Once in every four years Washington hotel keepers expect to make a fortune—and they generally realize their expectations. A place to sleep in, no matter whether it be big or little, is worth during the week of March 4 as much as would pay the rent for a year of very handsome apartments at other times. Fortunate is the person who has a place to lay his head when the excitement of the day is over, and if he has to make his bed on a billiard table, or in a bath tub, or on the piano, he laughs and consoles himself with the thought that inauguration only comes once in every four years. Hotel corridors look like the wards of hospitals.

The Forty-eighth Congress having expired on March 4 at 12 noon, the President (Arthur) previously issued an Executive proclamation convening the Senate in special session, so that the Cabinet of the incoming President might be confirmed. The ceremonies in the Senate are brief and simple. As the hour of 12 draws near the galleries are filled with distinguished spectators. The Vice-President then makes a brief farewell speech, and at its conclusion announces that he is ready to administer the oath of office to the Vice-President-elect. As Senator Edmunds said this he introduced Vice-President Hendricks who was received with applause, and made a brief address. The oath of office was then administered to him, after which Mr. Edmunds announced that the time for the expiration of the Forty-eighth Congress having arrived he declared the Senate of the United States adjourned sine die. As he uttered these last words he rapped on the desk with his gavel, descended from his chair and the Forty eighth Congress had passed into history. For a minute there was a pause—a pause which marked the death of the old Congress and the birth of the new. Then, hardly before the echoes of the sound of the gavel had died away, Vice-President Hendricks mounted the desk, gave a sharp rap on it, and exclaimed: "The Senate will come to order." The executive proclamation was then read convening the Senate in special session. The roll having been called, the new Senators having been sworn in, the Senate awaited the coming of the President and President-elect. When they had arrived a procession was formed, consisting of the Cabinet, Diplomatic Corps, Supreme Justices and others, to the east front, where the President took the oath of office.

The administering of the oath is a simple although impressive ceremony, from its nature. The oath of office is prescribed by the constitution, was slowly read by Chief Justice Waite of the supreme court of the United States. At its conclusion President Cleveland swore to keep its provisions and then kissed the open Bible which was extended to him. Then thousands of throats yelled out a hoarse hurrah, salvoes of artillery rent the air and Grover Cleveland, twenty-fifth president of the United States, smilingly bowed his acknowledgements to the people who had witnessed the ceremony. The procession was then reformed. The senators returned to their duties the president entered his carriage, and surrounded by his military escort, clattered up Pennsylvania avenue to the White House—his home for the next four years.

At the White House the new President and the outgoing Executive partook of lunch. When this interesting event had been concluded the President, accompanied by distinguished guests, took his stand on a pavilion which had been erected on the White House lawn, overlooking Pennsylvania avenue. Again the crowd broke forth into cheers as they recognized him. Necks were craned down the avenue to catch the first glimpse of the procession as it swung up Fifteenth street into Pennsylvania avenue. Every ear was at the highest pitch of tension to catch the first sound of martial music. Hark! There it comes. The policemen push back the crowds on the sidewalks. There is a moment of expectancy. Then comes a platoon of mounted police, followed by a band playing a lively air. And now in rapid succession the procession sweeps by. As the stand is neared commanding officers roar out hoarse commands, subordinate officers take them up, there is a sharp rattle of rifles, the sunlight gleams on the officers' swords, the batons of drum majors are cast high up in the air and dexterously caught as they come down, and as the column proudly marches on the honor of a marching salute is paid to the new President. Civic organizations pay their tribute of respect, and the bands fill the air with music while the spectators gaze and applaud, too much interested to feel weary. This ends the day part of the inauguration ceremonies.

PRESIDENT CLEVELAND AT THE INAUGURATION BALL

The inauguration ball caps the climax to Washington's great day. The ball was held in the new pension office, a magnificent structure not yet completed. Decorators and artists had done heroic work on it during the last few weeks, and when the Marine band struck up "Hail to the Chief," which was the signal for the entrance of the President, the sight was indeed a brilliant one. Thousands of dollars had been lavished on this part of the pageant, and the result showed the money had been well spent. The capitals of the lower columns round the hall were embellished with handsome colored shields, representing the arms of the several States and territories, draped on either side with three handsome American banners, with silver plated spear points on their shafts. Superb eight-foot banners, made of the finest silk, were suspended from the ceiling, while from the center of the roof to either side hung in graceful festoons colored streamers, which were so numerous as to completely hide the bare wood of the construction. The eight immense pillars which divide the ball room into three sections were covered with white muslin, and twining evergreen garlands were wound round the shafts. Silk curtains were drawn across the windows. The decorations were loaned, and the cost for hiring them amounted to $5,500. The President received on a dais under a canopy of real roses, standing in front of a chair made of similar flowers. In the canopy and chair were 800 roses, which cost ten cents apiece.

VISITORS IN THE EAST ROOM

The East Room of the White House is a portion of the Executive Mansion always open to visitors. It is an apartment of noble proportions, and about the only room suitable for large public gatherings. It is in this room that the presidential receptions are always held, and if the walls could talk many a tale could they tell of the lovely women and brave, handsome men who have gathered there. Imposing columns support the finely frescoed ceiling, while three magnificent crystal chandeliers shed light. In this room hung the portrait of Mrs. Hayes, in the frame which has provoked so much criticism, but the picture has now been moved to the Blue Room. During the last few days the East Room has been overrun with visitors, who desired to take a peep at the famous place before returning to their homes

April, 1885

Health Ordinance!

WHEREAS, there is felt throughout the land a universal and well grounded apprehension of the approach of Asiatic Cholera in the coming Summer, which threatens to scourge the country, unless it be averted by rigid and searching sanitary precautions such as are being now actively inforced elsewhere.

Therefore we, the Mayor and Common Council of Leesburg, do most earnestly invoke the citizens to look to the cleanliness and healthfulness of their premises, and to remove all offensive or unwholesome matter. And especially do we earnestly request all good citizens, for this critical period at least, to dispense with hogs—sources of much unwholesomeness and great complaint while scarcely profitable to the owners. Therefore

BE IT ORDAINED, by the Common Council of the Town of Leesburg

1. That the Council shall elect two discreet citizens of the town of Leesburg, who, together with the Town Sergeant, shall constitute the sanitary Committee of the Town.

2. That said Committee shall proceed to the with, and fortnightly thereafter between the 1st day of April and the 1st day of November of each year, to visit and inspect all the premises within the corporate jurisdiction, and to notify and direct the occupant of each lot (or the owner thereof if it be vacant) as to what is required of him to put and keep his premises in proper condition; and said committee shall make report of its proceedings from time to time to the Mayor.

3. Upon complaint made by any one to the Mayor, or to a member of said Committee, the said Committee shall be required to make special inspection of any premises complained of.

4. If any person shall fail or refuse to do what is required of him by said committee under the provisions of the 2d and 3d Sections of this Ordinance, within such time as said committee may specify, he shall be fined not exceeding five dollars for each day he may be in default, and in default of payment of the fine imposed, may be confined in jail not exceeding 30 days.

5. It shall be the duty of the Town Sergeant to see that the requirements and directions of said Committee in each case be fully and promptly executed, and shall report any failures so to do to the Mayor, who shall immediately summon such person to appear before him, to be dealt with according to the provisions of the foregoing section

6. The Mayor is authorized to contract for such teams, labor, &c., as may be requisite, for the period referred to in the second clause of this ordinance, to remove to the place, he shall designate, and at such periods as said committee may direct, all garbage night-soil, &c., from the premises of such persons as are not able to have the same removed.

PASSED, April 10th, 1885.
H. O. CLAGETT,
Recorder.

☞ The Inspectors provided for in the above Ordinance, will make their first visit on FRIDAY, APRIL 17th, 1885.

apr 16, 1885.

4/3/85 Telephone

A young man of Hamilton, who is evidently enthusiastic in behalf of the local churches, sends us the following interesting item:

"An exchange says that hugging parties for the benefit of churches are a recent importation into the South, but they are becoming very popular in some sections, especially in Virginia. The prices are as follows: Girls under fifteen, thirty-five cents for a hug of two minutes; from fifteen to twenty years of age, from thirty-five to seventy-five cents; another man's wife, $1; widows according to looks, from ten cents to $2; old maids, three cents apiece or two for a nickel; and no limit as to time.

We warn the aforesaid young man that, in a town where are domiciled over two dozen widows and ———— maidens who, by the unexplainable mutations of fate, got left over, it would not be safe for him to be known in the inauguration of any such an innovation as is mentioned above. It would be safer for him to engage in a sparring match with a ton of dynamite. We promise him to keep this matter profoundly confidential; but if he is determined to move publicly in this project, we beseech him in behalf of his own scalp, to readjust the price list and time table.

4/10/85 Telephone

Be it known to the credit of the good people of Philadelphia that the prize-fighters Sullivan and McCafferty were put under arrest and bound, over to keep the peace in instead of being allowed to make a brutal exhibition in that city. The Mayor had refused to interfere but some of the citizens finally succeeded in preventing the fight.

NOTICE.

HAVING LOST by the severe fire in Middleburg, Va., on the 4th of April, nearly all my personal property, as well as my house, dwelling, &c., I am compelled to ask my old customers to come forward and aid me, by either paying the whole, or at least a portion of their dues. I have been a very lenient creditor, and trust now, some reciprocity will be shown in my great misfortune. My most important papers and books were saved.
CHAS. A. SMITH.

apr. 9, 1885-4t.-(Wash. copy.)

GEN. GRANT'S FAITH.

How He Kept it to Gen. Lee and His Officers.

Prof. R. S. McCulloch, of Baton Rouge, La., for some time an associate of Gen. Robt. E. Lee in Washington and Lee University, Lexington, Va., writes as follows to the New Orleans *Times-Democrat*:

The present is perhaps the fit moment to make public the following statement. In the year 1867 the undersigned spent an evening with the late John W. Garrett, Esq., then President of the Baltimore and Ohio Railroad who made to him the following communication:

After the assassination of Mr. Lincoln the cabinet met in the Treasury Department and passed a resolution to arrest and try by military commission the leading men of the Confederacy, beginning with such as Mr. Davis, Gen. R. E. Lee and others; and meaning thereby to strike terror into the hearts of the Southern people, suspicion of complicity in that crime being the ground for such intended trials. They concluded that to carry their resolution into effect Gen. Grant must give the requisite orders. Tired of war he was seeking repose on the banks of the Delaware. He was therefore telegraphed to come immediately to Washington and the railroads were ordered to bring him without detention.

Mr. Garrett was at the moment in Washington and was instructed by Mr. Stanton to go forthwith to Baltimore in a single express car, there to meet Gen. Grant and bring him to Washington as quickly as possible. He was also told by Mr. Stanton to inform Gen. Grant of the resolution passed, which he was expected to execute, and that the cabinet would be in permanent session until his arrival. When the message was delivered in the car Gen. Grant said:

"These gentlemen do not reflect that such action would be a stain upon the escutcheon of this nation which could never be wiped out. The assassination seems to have unsettled their wits. Tell me that such men as Gen. Lee and Mr. Davis had anything to do with a murder, gentlemen whom I have known and esteemed for years, and who are incapable of crime. As well suspect myself."

The response was: "Well, General, the cabinet are waiting only for you to give the orders; and you will go into their meeting as soon as you get there. I hope when you do that you will speak to them just as you have now done to me."

Then came the noble reply: "I shall go further, Mr. Garrett. I shall tell them they must take my sword from me."

Upon their arrival Gen. Grant went directly into cabinet meeting, and Mr. Garrett remained in the corridor. After some time the Postmaster General came out. Approaching him Mr. Garrett said: "I do not wish to pry into that which is confidential or secret, but you know the message with which I was charged. When I delivered it Gen. Grant said he would tell you gentlemen that you must first take his sword from him." The answer was: "He has done that very thing, Mr. Garrett."

Lower and lower settles the shadow of impending sorrow as the grand old hero of the civil war grows weaker and frailer under the oppressing hand of fatal disease. That same spirit of quiet bravery which roused him to heroic action throughout his eventful life now sustains him in the trying hours of approaching dissolution. Not many days hence Death will relieve him from his suffering.

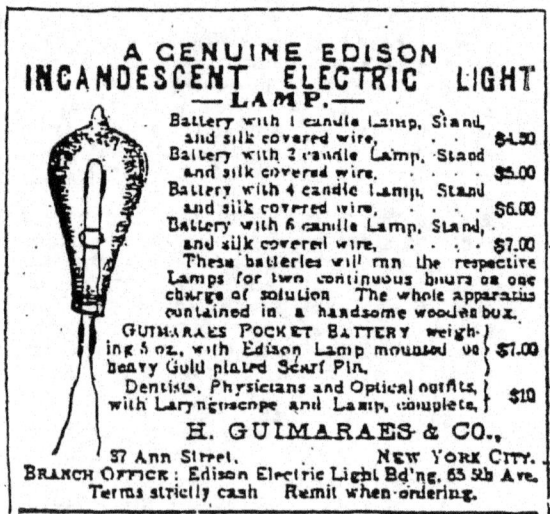

6/4/85 Mirror

Marriage of Gen. Stonewall Jackson's Daughter.

RICHMOND, VA., June 2 – The event of Richmond society this season was the marriage here this evening of Miss Julia T. Jackson, the only child of the late Gen. Stonewall Jackson, of Confederate fame, to Mr. Wm. E Christian, of this city. The ceremony took place from the Second Presbyterian Church and was performed by the pastor, Rev. Dr. Moses D. Hoge, assisted by Rev. Wm. H. Christian, of the M. E. Church South, father of the groom. The church was filled to overflowing with the leading people of this city and surrounding country. The bride is a petite and beautiful blonde, with the deepest of blue eyes golden hair and a delicate, soft tint on her cheek — She looked unusually pretty on this interesting occasion, in white satin, with point lace trimmings and diamond ornaments. The latter was the gift of the groom. The bridesmaids who wore white muslin, were Misses Lilia Branch, Frances Scott, Sue Mawry and Miss Christian, of Richmond; Miss Niven, of New York, Miss Irwin, niece of Mrs. Jackson, of North Carolina; Miss Bruce, of Tennessee; Misses Witherspoon and Junkin, of South Carolina, and Miss Prince of N. C. — The groomsmen were Carter Branch, John K. Branch, John Scott, Col. Chas. E. Anderson, Thos. N. Page and John Randolph Tucker, Jr. of Richmond, MacGrame Cox and Philip Bruce, of Baltimore; Douglas Shirley of Ky., Dr. Garnett, of Washington D. C., and Wm. Ryan of Richmond.

The bridal presents are of the most elegant and costly kind, and are so numerous that only a few of the more conspicuous can be given. These include one hundred dollars by J. A Early, of Virginia; a splendid silver ice cream service and gold spoons by W. W. Corcoran, of Washington; a superb gold and silver bowl, with medallion portraits of Gens Lee and Jackson, and a Confederate flag, by a Louisian. Confederate regiment; a elegant set of hand-painted plates, by the Mobile Rifles; a handsome satin banner, with names inscribed, by the Stonewall Brigade of Staunton, Va; handsome silver spoons and forks, by Third Alabama Regiment; elegant silver service, by Gen. James B. Johnston; rich silver service, by Gen. Custis Lee besides a variety of other wedding gifts some of which are of great beauty and value.

(Apparently, the social event of the year in Richmond. Those present besides Jubal Early and the other illustrious generals were Congressman Tucker, author and diplomat Thomas Nelson Page, Thomas Corcoran, later the art gallery benefactor, and many others of note.)

"You needn't stop for me; I'm not an old woman."

"Can't see why an able bodied man wants to stop a car before he gets off."

"Two souls with but a single thought, two hearts that beat as one."

THE MIRROR
BENJ. F. SHEETZ, Editor.

Thursday Morning, JUNE 4, 1885

The Nation's Troublesome Wards.—The nation's unruly wards, the western Indians are beginning to become troublesome again, as they have a way of doing each year just as soon as the weather begins to get warm. This time the vindictive Apaches are the promoters of the difficulties, speaking of which, in a despatch, Gen Crook says, "the outlook is very bad and the troubles will be exceedingly difficult to suppress." The present outbreak is by Indians belonging on the San Carlos reservation in Arizona, and is the most determined of any within late years. Numbers of ranchmen and their families have been murdered in the most brutal manner. Col Phillips and his family, consisting of a wife and daughter, were slain and their bodies horribly mutilated. Several companies numbering 1200 or 1500 soldiers have been put in the field, but can do little towards chastising the Indians, who, divided up into small bands, keep close among the hills when they find the soldiers on their track. Great dissatisfaction is felt among the people who say they are tired of the government's dilatory policy. They do not appreciate Gen Crook's Indian fighting qualities and say that if the military again fail them they will adopt their own remedy, which it is understood will be based on the rule that there's no good Indian but the dead Indian."

6/26/85 Telephone

An Aeronaut's Fall.

A great crowd of people, composed not only of the citizens of Charlestown, W. Va., but from all around the country within a radius of twenty miles, gathered at the opening performance of Richards & Leon's circus yesterday afternoon. Before the circus performance began there was a number of sideshows to attract the curiosity and the quarters of the country folks. The big balloon was the centre of attraction, and William Patterson, the handsome young aeronaut, in his fancy dress, was watched attentively by the crowd as he superintended the arrangements for his first ascension. He was a strong-looking, plucky young fellow, and only smiled at the spectators when they expressed their fear of going up in a balloon, and looked with awe upon one so daring. Finally, all was ready. The balloon was swelled out to its full capacity.— The aeronaut, with a flag in his hand, leaped lightly into the little basket, and with a wave of the flag gave the signal to let go. Just as the ropes were cut, one of the workmen accidentally overturned a hot air stove used in inflating the balloon. Instantly a tiny flame and a puff of smoke appeared at the bottom of the balloon as it shot upwards. A cry of horror burst from the crowd. The aeronaut had not at first noticed the accident. He heard the shouts of the crowd. The cry of fire called his attention to the flame rapidly spreading towards the inflated portion of the balloon. He was then about one hundred feet in the air. He looked down and dropped his flag. The crowd saw the look of terror that overspread his face. The men who had been inflating the balloon, and others, as soon as they saw the balloon had caught fire, shouted to Patterson to jump. But he had not at first recognized the cry of alarm in the shouts that attend the ascension. The people below saw him hurriedly turn around in the basket, and then reach out with a knife, as though he would try and cut away the burnt portion of the balloon, but that was impossible. Then he appeared as though he would jump. He hesitated, looked down and wildly gesticulated. He raised himself up and clung to the ropes that held the basket. Just then a cloud of smoke almost enveloped the balloon; it gave a lurch, and the next instant collapsed at a height of over three hundred feet. Down shot the body of the aeronaut, swifter than the upward flight of the balloon had been. Over and over it turned, and struck the ground and rebounded. The body was picked up. Several of the muscles twitched slightly, but life was extinct.

July, 1885

BUCKEYE TWINE BINDER!!

It gives us much pleasure to again offer the Farmers of this section of Virginia, this CELEBRATED MACHINE, and after two years experience in the sale of them, we unhesitatingly pronounce them the very BEST BINDER now made.

SHROFF & CO.,
LEESBURG, VA.

The picture tells the story. The binder is a machine that cuts the crop (usually wheat) and wraps it in a bundle. These are stacked to await the arrival of the threshing machine which literally separates the wheat from the chaff. Today all of this is done in one operation by the modern combine.

IMPORTED "MATCHLESS," OF LONDESBORO.

A RARE opportunity is offered to the Farmers of Loudoun and adjoining counties, to breed to this magnificent specimen of Yorkshire Hackney, the winner of 16 first prizes in England, among them the Royal of 1885; and The Grand International at Brussels, over twenty two competitors.— No horse of his age has such a record in the show ring.

He is a five year old—a dark chestnut, with white points, 15¾ hands high, and weighs over 1,300 lbs.

As roadsters, many of them have records of from 15 to 20 miles an hour; while bred on half bred mares the produce make fine saddle horses.

THIS YOUNG HORSE will stand the following season at "OAK HILL," and then be sent to New York. So this will be the only chance parties from this section will have to avail themselves of his services.

For particulars, apply to
HENRY FAIRFAX,
Aldie P. O.,
Loudoun Co., Va.

F. P. MILLER   JOHN L. MICHAEL.

MILLER & CO.

Contractors for Drilling and Equipping

Artesian Wells,

of any required depth. Boring of old Wells, without removing the walls. Drilling new Wells from the surface and inserting the finest

ARTESIAN WELL CASING,

excluding all foul surface waters. Have all the Improved Steam Appliances for Drilling and Reaming in hard or soft rock, from four to eight inches in diameter. Agents for Pumps for pumping water. Address, Frederick city, Md.

REFERENCES

C. R. Paxton, S. S. Lutz, Dr. S. Carter, Leesburg, Va., A J. Souder Taylortown, Va. Kingsley & Bro., Hamilton, Va. And hundreds of farmers everywhere.

All orders left with E. E. THOMPSON, Leesburg, Va., will be promptly attended to. All work Guaranteed.

July 1885

6/26/85 Telephone
A Splendid Place.

There are few, if any, places in Loudoun where the city people can find more of the solid comforts of country life than at T. Brown's, near Lincoln—where a few more persons can secure quarters. A commodius, cool house; plenty of shade, abundance of fruit, splendid spring water, amply-filled ice house, proximity to daily mail and beautiful surroundings make it a very attractive place.

7/10/85 Telephone
Creamery at Round Hill.

It is announced that the farmers of Round Hill will hold a conference with Kingsley Bros. tomorrow week (18th inst.) for the purpose of arranging for establishing a branch of the Hamilton Creamery at that place. We understand that the farmers of that vicinity are alive to the importance of the creamery business, some of whom are now hauling their milk all the way to headquarters, at Hamilton.

(The above two paragraphs illustrate two burgeoning industries for Loudoun county: The accommodation of summer boarders who desired to escape the Washington heat and the beginnings of an efficient means of marketing milk. Both were abetted by recent rail connections.)

7/25/85 Washingtonian

LEESBURG has an admirable water supply, from a never failing source but should a long continued drouth diminish the water in Rock Spring, there is another good spring near the Railroad above the water tank, which might be utilized, and only requires bricking up and being properly enclosed to be made available.

7/31/85 Telephone
That Affair of Honah!

In another column of this paper will be found mention of a difficulty between Dr. Noland, of Farmwell, and Mr. Summers, of Guilford. On our return to Farmwell we heard some additional statements relative to the affair.

On Tuesday the parties were brought together for the purpose of effecting a reconciliation, when Dr. Noland insisted on an apology from Summers; the demand was refused and a worse quarrel than ever precipitated, both parties drawing their pistols. At this juncture Mr. Cleve. Coleman, (who was probably acting the part of peacemaker) rode between them and prevented hostilities. But this did not settle the matter and another meeting of a sanguinary nature is threatened.

It is a shame that such an affair as this should occur in our usually orderly community—and that between two public officers, a deputy sheriff and treasurer and a clerk of a district school board. It is to be hoped that cooler heads will prevent any gory proceedings.

THE drouth still continues unbroken in this section,—the last week being the hottest we have had,—literally drying up the fields and gardens. Our farmers, in some places, are driving their stock off the farms to get water. We have had no rain, to mention, since about the 1st of June. The early corn is pretty well destroyed, but the late corn may make good crops if we have rain soon.

A prayer meeting for rain was held in the M. E. Church South, (yesterday,)

7/24/85 Telephone

July 1885

GENERAL GRANT GONE.

The Grand Old Hero Passes Away Peacefully.

[Washington Star.]

MOUNT MCGREGOR, N. Y., July 23.—General Grant died at 8:08 a. m., surrounded by all his family. He passed out of life peacefully and without evident pain.

A few minutes before 8 o'clock the physicians noticed upon the face of the patient sufferer the unmistakable imprint of the Pale messenger and directed that all the family be quickly summoned, and soon they were gathered about the sick man's cot.

The colonel seated himself at the head of the bed, with his left arm resting upon the pillow above the head of the general, who was breathing rapidly and with slightly grasping respirations. Mrs. Grant, calm, but with intense agitation, bravely suppressed, took a seat close by the bedside. She leaned slightly upon the cot, resting upon her right elbow, and gazing with tear-blinded eyes into the general's face. She found there, however, no token of recognition, for the sick man was peacefully and painlessly passing into another life. Mrs. Sartoris came behind her mother and leaning over her shoulder witnessed the close of a life in which she had constituted a strong element of pride. Directly behind Mrs. Grant and Mrs. Sartoris, and at a little distance removed stood Drs. Douglas, Shrady, and Sands, spectators of a closing life their efforts and counsel had so prolonged. On the opposite side of the bed from their mother, and directly before her, stood Jesse Grant and U. S. Grant, jr., and near the corner of the cot on the same side as Jesse and near to each was Mr. N. E. Dawson, the general's stenographer and confidential secretary. At the foot of the bed and gazing directly down into the general's face was Mrs. Col. Fred. Grant, Mrs. U. S. Grant, jr., and Mrs. Jesse Grant, while somewhat removed from the family circle Henry, the nurse, and Harrison Tyrrell, the general's body servant, were respectively watching the closing life of the patient. Dr. Newman had repaired to the hotel to breakfast and was not present, and the general's little grand children, U. S. Grant, jr., and Nellie were sleeping in the nursery room above stairs. Otherwise the entire family and household were gathered at the bedside of the dying man. The members of the group had been summoned not a moment sooner than was prudent.

The doctors noted on entering the room and pressing to the bedside, that already the purplish tinge—one of the signals of final dissolution—had settled beneath the finger nails. The hand that Dr. Douglas lifted was fast growing colder than it had been through the night. The pulse had fluttered beyond the point where the physician could distinguish it from the pulse in his own finger tips. The respiration was very rapid and was a succession of shallow painting inhalations; but as the respirations grew quicker and more rapid they also became less labored and almost noiseless. This was a comfort to the watchers by the bedside, to whom was spaired the scene of an agonizing or other than a peaceful death.

The wife almost constantly stroked the face, forehead and hands of the dying general, and, at times, pressed both his hands, and leaning forward, tenderly kissed the face of the sinking man. Col. Fred Grant sat silently, but with evident feeling. U. S. Grant, jr., was deeply moved, but Jesse bore the scene steadily, and the ladies, while watching with wet cheeks, were silent, as befited the dignity of a life such as was closing before them. At seven minutes after eight o'clock, and the eyes of the general were closing. His breathing grew more hushed as the last functions of the heart and lungs were hastened to the closing of the ex-President's life. A graceful expression seemed to be deepening in the firm and strong-lined face, and it was reflected as a closing comfort in the sad hearts that beat quickly under the stress of loving suspense.

A minute more passed and was closing as the general drew a deeper breath. There was an exhalation like that of one relieved of long and anxious tensions. The members of the group were impelled each a step nearer the bed, and each awaited another respiration, but it never came. There was absolute stillness in the room and a hush of expectant suspense, and no sound broke the silence, save the singing of the birds in the pines outside the cottage and the measured throbbing of the engine that all night had waited by the little mountain depot down the slope.

In April last, when the death of Gen. Grant was momentarily expected, a correspondent of the Boston GLOBE wrote to Jefferson Davis asking him to give his views of Gen. Grant's military career. The following is Mr. Davis reply, never made public until since the General's death:

"BEAU VOIR, Miss., April 2, 1885.

"SIR: Your letter, asking me to give my views on the subject of Gen. Grant's military career, has been received. With most respectful consideration for you and the influential paper you represent, I must decline to comply with the request, for the following reasons;

Gen. Grant is reported dying. Although he invaded our country with ruthless track, it was with open hand, and so far as I know, he abetted neither pillage nor arson: When his armies were so successful that Gen. Lee's army had not even the power further to retreat, Gen. Grant gave terms both liberal and courteous, and has since the war I believe shown no malignity nor perpetuated slanders against the Confederates, either of the military or civil service. Therefore, instead of seeking to disturb the quiet of his closing hours, I would, if it were in my power, willingly contribute to the repose of his mind and the comfort of his body.

"JEFFERSON DAVIS."

August, 1885

8/13/85 Mirror

"It is Finished."—Gen. Grant died and is buried. Last Saturday the great metropolis of the nation was crowded with a dense mass of sorrowing humanity, drawn from among the people of every nation, tribe and tongue, and of every condition in life, either as participants in the funeral ceremonies or as mere "lookers on" of the grand civil and military display, surpassing anything of the kind ever before witnessed on this continent.

With such surroundings, and amid the melancholy sounds of muffled drums,—the sorrowful dirges poured forth by hundreds of brass bands—the rattling of musketry and the thunders of cannon, the mortal remains of Gen. U. S. Grant were laid at rest in Riverside Park. To attempt a description of the grand parade would require more space than we have at command; but it is unnecessary. As a national funeral it was eminently successful. Nothing that the ingenuity of man could devise or money contribute, toward rendering the occasion impressive, was lacking, and hereafter the 8th day of August, 1885, will take its place in the records of American history, as marking one of its most memorable events.

8/14/85 Telephone

REMARKABLE INCIDENTS.

While the body of General Grant was lying in the cottage where he died, the house was struck by lightning. Several of the family were stunned.

Soon after the old Hero's burial place was selected in Riverside park a tree near by struck by lightning.

An editor in North Carolina wrote an abusive editorial about General Grant, and as soon as it was finished fell dead.

On the day the General was buried a horse which was wounded under him on the day before Vicksburg died.

8/13/85 Mirror

The Funeral of Gen. Grant.

NEW YORK, Aug. 8 —The casket containing the remains of Gen. Grant was placed on the catafalque at 9:50 a. m., at which time the procession started for Riverside Park. One thousand persons were at the City Hall waiting their turns to view the corpse at one o'clock this morning. They were allowed to enter and soon hustled past the casket, after which the building was closed to the public. The undertaker then closed the lid over the glass plate, forever sealing from view the face of the dead General, and the coffin was left in the charge of a guard. The floral displays on and around the casket were of a gorgeous nature. At 9.25 this morning an imposing funeral car, drawn by twenty four jet black horses in black trappings, halted on the plaza in front of the City Hall, and shortly afterwards the casket containing the remains, borne by twelve men, emerged from the hall, and was placed upon the dias of the mounted catafalque. In the meantime the procession began to form, the numbers of organizations which were to take part in the parade and funeral ceremonies rapidly assuming their positions in the line, and in a short time the funeral cortege, doubtless the largest ever witnessed in this country, began winding its slow length along toward Riverside Park — The crowd in the streets by this time had grown into immense proportions, and windows, balconies and housetops were black with people, as were the pillars, cornices, &c., with the sable emblems of mourning. As the procession moved it passed between solid walls of myriads of human beings. The booming of minute guns, the doleful dirges of the bands and the measured tread of the military and other organizations, and the surgings of the innumerable throng which followed, were sounds and sights never to be forgotten. Colored men, attired in mourning livery, walked beside each of the twenty-four horses which drew the funeral car. Carpenters during the earlier hours of the morning improvised stands along the proposed route of the procession for the benefit of those who desired to witness the pageant from elevated positions, seats on which were rented at prices ranging from one to ten dollars each. The carriage containing President Cleveland and Cabinet was drawn by six horses. At 12:30 p. m. the procession entered Riverside Drive, about 2¼ miles distant from the park, and at twenty four minutes past one o'clock the head of the pageant arrived in front of the tomb, where according to the published programme, the remains were placed with impressive ceremonies. The multitude in and around the park was the largest ever assembled in New York, the sea of heads extending for miles in all directions.

Mrs Grant did not attend the funeral, being too weak to leave Mt McGregor.

July 1885

7/30/85 Mirror

He was a soldier, with the requisites of a soldier. It was his duty to carry the armies of his nation to success—and he planned and fought as much or more from this sense of duty than from any mere hunger for personal glory. But war never made him hate his enemies, nor thirst for their blood or destruction—it never converted him, as it did many of his comrades, with their lower natures, his hounds, caring less for the successful performance of duty, than for the gratification of a malignant craving to rend and destroy their quarries. He was one of the few men of exalted station, who fully comprehended the situation, and the true northern object of the war—as a war for the Union;—and he believed the sincerity of the South, as shown by its sacrifices;—he respected courage and skill, and realized that a mere political Union would be worthless without a re-union of the hearts of its people. As a victorious soldier his nature made him ready to stretch out a friendly hand to the conquered, when resistance was over. As a statesman, he saw and seized the moment for reconciliation. Nobly he treated the Confederates in the surrender, and nobly he protected them against the malice and vindictiveness of narrower minds and lower natures. Gen. Grant, by his terms at Appomattox, and his subsequent conduct, probably did more to quiet the southern people—to incline to reconciliation, and to bring about unity, than any man—and the confidence he inspired neutralized the effect of the antagonistic policy of the reconstructionists. The whole Union is his debtor.

8/6/85 Mirror

At the request of Mrs. Grant, President Cleveland last week appointed the pall-bearers for Gen. Grant's funeral. The President asked if Mrs. Grant had any preferences in the matter, to which she replied, that the only suggestion she would make was that in case any prominent Union officer like Gen. Sherman or Lieut. Gen. Sheridan be selected, a leading Confederate officer like Gen. Johnston or Gen. Buckner be also included in the list. In accordance with which, Gen. Joseph E. Johnston, of Va., and Gen. S. B Buckner, of Ky., were named to act with Gens. Sherman, Sheridan and eight other stanch friends of the Union cause.

7/25/85 Washingtonian

Virginians, especially, have cause to be touched with a feeling of sorrow at his death—to him, we are indebted for the most invaluable services, at a time the most critical in the history of this Commonwealth—When the present State constitution was submitted to our people for its adoption, there was a provision in it which would have disfranchised a large portion of our people, had it been adopted. A committee of our citizens called upon President GRANT, and asked him to appeal to Congress, in our behalf, to give us the right to vote separately on that provision. True always, we believe, to the demands of duty, he did so, and we were saved the dark fate which awaited us

---

In researching the several months after the Civil War, I was surprised to find an August 1865 *Mirror* article reporting the shocking news that property belonging to all who supported the rebellion could be confiscated. My Confederate ancestors, the Hutchisons, were on that list. Thankfully, this did not happen, because it would have further divided the nation and promoted everlasting enmity.

Occasionally, given time, attitudes can change for the better. Twenty years after the war, former enemy General Grant was referred to above, not just with total respect, but with **genuine** affection.

8/7/85 Telephone

Ex-Pres. Arthur's Arrest.

AN EXCEEDINGLY DIFFICULT STORY TO BELIEVE, BUT AN AMUSING ONE TO READ.

[Toledo Blade.]

Now that the majesty that doth hedge an executive is being dissipated in Mr. Arthur's case by his retirement, says the San Francisco "Call," his ex-cabinet, is beginning to let out a good many little incidents of the reign of one who will deservedly go down in history under the sobriquet of "the jolly President." For illustration, one of his constitutional advisers, in a recent letter to an old crony in this city, says:

"Did I ever tell you of the fun we had during the visit of the Presidential party to Florida summer before last? You must know that besides being a confirmed practical joker, Chet is quite an adept at certain sleight-of-hand tricks, a proficiency in which he has kept up from boyhood. He flatters himself he can remove a handkerchief or watch from a pocket with as much adroitness as a professional 'nipper.' He has perpetrated many a queer joke in this way, the exalted position of the perpetrator naturally protecting him from suspicion. While at Jacksonville the 'White House gang determined to attend a monster darkey camp-meeting about ten miles back in the country, and, to avoid the eternal 'reception' nuisance, we went incog. When we left the train, and were awaiting for conveyance at a small tavern, Chet noticed a fat planter dozing in the bar-room, and displaying a preposterous bunch of seals on his fob-chain. Arthur watched his chance, snaked out the man's watch, and hid it in the saddle bags of another traveller, that was hanging on the wall. Now, Bill Chandler had been waiting for a chance to get back on Arthur for several days, so he in turn collared the planter's property, and slipped it into the breast pocket of Chest's big duster. Then he quietly led each member of the party aside and let them into the conspiracy, to their great delight. When the vehicles returned from the camping ground, Arthur was immediately collared by the planter who savagely demanded his property.

"'What do you mean, fellow?' said the President, trying not to laugh, and winking at his staff—all of whom, however, remained suspiciously indifferent.

"'Oh, you can't come any funny business with me. One of these gentlemen saw you steal my watch and put it in your pocket. Here, constable, I want this man searched!'

"'Very well, then, search me,' said our first citizen, almost exploding with laughter.

"'I thought so,' said the constable, and, and, to Chest's petrification, he fished out the watch from the first pocket he dived into. 'I'll just slam you into the caloboose, my fine fellow.'

"'You will, eh?' said the President, with a chuckle. 'Here, Mr. Frelinghuysen, just tell this man who I am.'

"'Did you speak to me, my good man?' said the secretary of State, innocently.

"'Yes, yes. Hurry up and explain this thing,' said Arthur, as the constable began taking out a pair of handcuffs.

"'Explain what? I don't know you, sir,' and the state department walked off.

"'Great Scott!' stammered Arthur.—'Say—you there—Chandler! What does all this mean?' Tell these people who I am—quick!'

"'If you are addressing me,' said the secretary of the navy, putting on his glasses and taking a benevolent survey of the prisoner, 'my name is not Chandler, and I never saw you before.'

"'Great heavens! this is outrageous!' screamed Arthur, fighting desperately with the constable. 'I tell you I am the president.'

"'The most impudent rascal I ever saw!' said Folger.

"'Hard looking face,' chipped in Bob Lincoln.

"'Don't be rough with the old man,' said Teller kindly. 'Perhaps he's a little gone in the——. What are you president of, my good fellow?'

"'I'm President of the United States, as you'll pretty soon find out'' gasped the prisoner furiously.

"'Tut, tut, tut!' murmured Chandler, pityingly. 'Clean gone, clean gone! Intelligent-looking man, too. Escaped from some asylum, likely.'

"And to his unmistakable horror, Arthur was loaded into a wagon and carted off to the county bastile, where he was kept almost an hour, until, in solemn caucus, the cabinet voted for his release. To Chest's credit, however, be it said, that although he was extradited in a white rage and vowing to smash the entire household slate, he cooled down before we reached Jacksonville, and concluded to 'set 'em up' for the crowd in true White House style. But the joke business had a rest after that."

August 1885

8/14/85 Telephone

WHAT BASEBALL COSTS.

Of the thousands who daily witness a baseball match, very few have any idea of the actual cost of maintaining a first-class professional club during a season. Very few ever stop to inquire about the expenses or receipts of a club during the seven months in which the games are in progress, but are apparently contented in paying their money to see the high-salaried men play for their amusement. This is probably just as satisfactory, as managers as well as players, are not over-anxious to give any approximate figures as to the loss or gains of the speculation.

When engaged to play ball for the season each player is compelled to sign a contract, in which the amount he is to receive, how it is to be paid and other important points, are clearly stipulated. The contents of these documents are known only to the parties interested unless it is desired to make the agreement known.

The lowest estimated cost of running a first-class baseball club is, as nearly as can be estimated, about $65,000 a year. The salary list of the clubs vary somewhat, but a representative nine, such as the team of New York, Providence, Boston or Chicago, average between $35,000 and $40,000 annually. The average salary paid to individual players is between $1,500 and $3,500. Some of the men, however, receive more than this. In addition to this extraordinary salary list, the expenses of the players while they are traveling is fully covered by the club, as the men are only taxed fifty cents a day. This includes first-class board and other hotel accommodations, as well as various expenses on the road. The expenses for travelling annually foot up to about $10,000, and the number of miles covered by each club is about 7,500. The next large item on the expense list is the renting of suitable grounds. As many of the clubs renting, however, of grounds amounts to about $10,000 a year. In addition to this the services of the gatemen, ushers, ticket takers, and other attendants amount to $8,000. Advertising and various other items will bring the total for the club fully up to $65,000, the amount stated, if not more.

Each player in the League is compelled to furnish his own uniform, as well as the bats he plays with. In the American Association, however, the club furnishes the uniforms. The first year or two a club seldom more than pays its expenses. To start a new club requires additional expense. The expense of securing the release of a good player from the club he previously played with must be taken into consideration and a higher salary must be offered to induce him to make the change. When the release is secured, advance money is paid in order to prevent his signing with another club. The advance of money is often a mere speculation, as the players subsequently prove unsatisfactory and the club is so much out. Thousands of dollars are paid out through the advance system every year. When a good nine becomes a drawing card it pays well, but not before that. The salaries of the best paid men run about as follows:— First and third base men average from $2,000 to $3,000; second base men, $2,500; shortstop, $3,000; outfielders, from $1,500 to $3,500 according to their ability at fielding and batting. A good catcher rarely receives less than $2,000 and often as much as $5,000. The pitchers are the most expensive players in a club. The position is the most difficult to fill and the game depends largely upon the power of his delivery. Radbourn, the champion pitcher of the League last year, is contented to remain with his own nine at $3,500.

The aforementioned pitcher was known then as Ol Hoss Radbourn and his 1884 total of 59 wins in a season was a record that will forever stand. He finished with three victories in baseball's first World Series despite a sore arm.

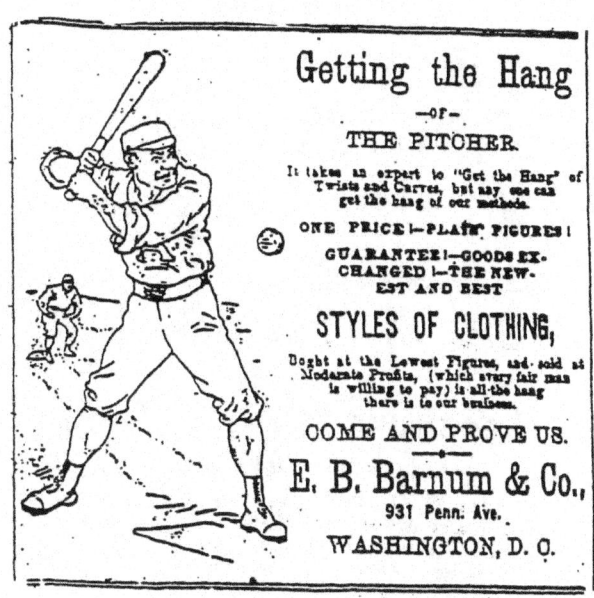

Getting the Hang
—of—
THE PITCHER.

It takes an expert to "Get the Hang" of Twists and Curves, but any one can get the hang of our methods.

ONE PRICE!—PLAIN FIGURES!

GUARANTEE!—GOODS EX-CHANGED!—THE NEW-EST AND BEST

STYLES OF CLOTHING,

Bought at the Lowest Figures, and sold at Moderate Profits, (which every fair man is willing to pay) is all the hang there is to our business.

COME AND PROVE US.

E. B. Barnum & Co.,
931 Penn. Ave.
WASHINGTON, D. C.

8/22/85 Washingtonian

A New War Story.

"The last day of the fight I was badly wounded. A ball shattered my left leg. I lay on the ground not far from Cemetery Ridge, and as Gen. Lee ordered his last retreat, he and his officers rode near me. As they came along I recognized him, and though faint from exposure and loss of blood, I raised upon my hands, looked Gen. Lee in the face and shouted as loud as I could, "Hurrah for the Union!" The General heard me, looked, stopped his horse, dismounted and came toward me. I confess that I first thought he meant to kill me. But as he came up he looked down at me with such a sad expression upon his face that all fear left me and I wondered what he was about. He extended his hand to me, and grasping mine firmly and looking right into my eyes, said:

"My son, I hope you will soon be well."

"If I live a thousand years I shall never forget the expression in Gen. Lee's face. There he was defeated, retiring from a field that had cost him and his cause almost their last hope, and yet he stopped to say words of comfort like those to a wounded soldier of the opposition who had taunted him as he passed by. As soon as the General had left me I cried myself to sleep upon the hard and bloody ground."

8/28/85 Telephone

Not Always a Sure Guide.

Jinks—"Do you think Miss Labelle is pretty?"

Minks—"No, she is not pretty."

"I must consent I think her beautiful"

"Well, I did too; but I asked my wife and she said I was mistaken."

DAILY STAGE LINE
FROM
Leesburg to Pt. of Rocks.

close connection made between Trains, on the W. O. & W. R. R. and B. & O. R. R. both east & west. COMFORTABLE COACH, good Team, and quick time. Freight and baggage carried at reasonable Rates and prompt delivery guaranteed.
GEO. B RINKER, Proprietor
Leesburg, July 13, 1885.

8/28/85 Telephone

AUG. 24 '85.

MR. Y. BROWN

Dear Sir

I write this to you personaly. I few weeks ago you seen fit to publish a communication from this locality on P Office and and other matters, that article being a libel from beginning to end your publication of such an instrumment must show after your refusal to give its authorgh that you are a Dam scoundrele and schoose to take the a the authorship which must render you a direct Liar, and and a poltroon.—that article reflects on me in the most dastardly and cowardly insinuation that could be used by a brainless school-boy, quit probably endorsed by older heads who should have better sense than give such stuff to the public. I desire that you give this a place in your nose rag Otherwise I shall have you you noticed in other journals as as a pooltroon and dastardly liar.

CHAS. J. BROWN.
Lovettsville.

Yes, indeed! Mr. Brown, we comply with your request to publish your letter, with the greatest pleasure, except that we do not like to have such aesthetic language in our paper—our readers, generally, are of such an ordinary cast of intelligence that they do not understand or appreciate such expressions; furthermore, they are wholly unaccustomed to your style of phraseology. To make sure that you may not be misrepresented, we publish your letter *verbatim et literatim*.

August, 1885

8/28/85 Telephone

Mark Twain on Child Government.

[Mark Twain, in the Christian Union.]

For whippings are not given in our house for revenge; they are not given for spite, nor even in anger; they are given partly for punishment, but mainly by way of impressive reminder, and a protect for against a repetition of the offense.— The interval between the promise of a whipping and its infliction is usual an hour or two. By that time both parties are calm and the one is judicial, the other receptive. The child never goes from the scene of punishment until it has been loved back into happy heartedness and a joyful spirit. The spanking is never a cruel one, but it is always an honest one. It hurts. If it hurts the child, imagine how it must hurt the mother. Her spirit is serene, tranquil. She has not the support which is afforded by anger. Every blow she strikes the child bruises her own heart. The mother of my children adores them—there is no milder term for it; and they worship her; they even worship anything which the touch of her hand has made sacred. They know her for the best and truest friend they have ever had, or ever shall have; they know her for one who never did them a wrong, and can not do them a wrong, who never told them a lie nor the shadow of one; who never deceived them by even an ambiguous gesture; who never gave them an unreasonable command, nor ever contented herself with anything short of a perfect obedience; who has always treated them as politely and considerately as she would the best and oldest of the land, and has always required of them gentle speech and courteous conduct toward all, of whatsoever degree, with whom they chanced to come in contact; they know her for one whose promise, whether of reward or punishment, is gold, and always worth its face, to the uttermost farthing In a word, they know her, and I know her, for the best and dearest mother that lives —and by a long, long way the wisest.

You perceive that I have never got down to where the mother in the tale really asks her question. For the reason that I cannot realize the situation. The spectacle of that treacherously-reared boy and that wordly, namby-pamby father, and that weak, namby-pamb mother, is enough to make one ashamed of his species. And, if I could cry, I would cry for the fate of that poor little boy—a fate which has cruelly placed him in the hands and at the mercy of a pair of grown up children, to save his disposition ruined, to come up ungoverned, and be a nuisance to himself and everybody about him, in the process, instead of being the solacer of care, the disseminator of happiness, the glory and honor and joy of the house, the welcomest face in all the world to them that gave him being—as he ought to be, and would be, but for the hard fortune that flung him into the clutches of these paltering incapables.

THE RASIN FERTILIZER COMPANY,

C. C. HOMER, Sec'y & Treasurer.   PROPRIETORS OF   B. W. RASIN, General Manager.

We Employ the Most Eminent Agricultural Chemists,
AND PRODUCE
STANDARD FERTILIZERS ONLY

SEA-WALL GUANO WORKS
SITUATED ON THE PATAPSCO RIVER
AT SEA-WALL ANNE-ARUNDEL COUNTY, MD.

CORRESPOND WITH US
BEFORE MAKING YOUR PURCHASES
In a Perfectly Dry Condition for the Drill.

(Guano, composed of bat and bird droppings, had been for many years a leading fertilizer.)

September 1885

9/3/85 Mirror

The much talked of glove fight between John L. Sullivan, of Boston, and Dominick McCaffrey, of Pittsburg, came off at the Driving Park near Cincinnati, on Saturday last, and was witnessed by upwards of 15,000 persons. It seems to have been a most unsatisfactory affair all the way round, and at the close came near ending in a general row. The conditions were that the men should fight "six rounds or to a finish;" at the end of the seventh round the referee, who was selected by the Sullivan party, remarked that "Sullivan has the best of it" and the fight ended, though neither man was in any sense "finished" or indeed showing any signs of punishment or exhaustion. McCaffrey made a better showing before the Boston man than many thought he would and on the strength of it his friends claim that he could have beaten him. Sullivan and his friends are equally confident and another meeting is likely to take place between the men. Whether it was a fair fight or a "hippodrome" it was a brutal and disgraceful affair and that it should have gone on unmolested is no credit to the authorities of the Queen City.

9/3/85 Mirror

Well Boring.—Several of our citizens have, within the past few months, provided themselves with convenient supplies of water by boring wells in their yards. The wells, which are bored by means of apparatus arranged here, are from four to six inches in diameter and furnish an abundant supply of fine water. Where rock is struck the caliber of the hole is very much lessened and the boring done with an iron drill. Of the three or four we know of, water has been struck, at an average depth of 40 feet in great abundance, and in one instance the stream was so strong as to flow over half way up the shaft and to defy any attempt to lower it by pumping. When completed, the dirt portion of the shaft is cased with iron, a pipe inserted, to which is attached a suction pump and the work is done. The cost of these wells is so small and the results obtained so satisfactory that they must soon become general.

9/12/85 Washingtonian

"What brought you to prison, my colored friend?" said a philanthropic visitor to a New York prisoner. "Two constables, sah." Yes; but I mean had intemperance anything to do with it?" "Yes, sah; dey was bof of 'em drunk."

Hammerly's Hall,
LEESBURG,
MONDAY, SEPTEMBER 14th, 1885.

The wonderful Negro Boy Pianist

BLIND TOM,
—THE—

Musical Phenomenon of the Age.

Renowned throughout the world. *The Greatest Natural Pianist Living*, The exhibition of whose marvelous gift has gained him world-wide celebrity and has both astonished and delighted the greatest masters of music, will appear as above for

POSITIVELY ONE NIGHT ONLY

admission 50 cts. Gallery 25 cts. reserved Seats 75 cts.

Seats secured at Mott & Pursel's
CONCERT AT 8 O'CLOCK.

9/12/85 Washingtonian

Blind Tom will give a concert at Hammerlys Hall, Leesburg, on Monday evening next, at 7½ o'clock. He fame as a performer on the Piano, is known wherever the science of music is taught. This wonderful musical prodigy attracts large crowds wherever he goes. When at Leesburg last—in 1877—he had a large and appreciative audience.

At least one recent biography has been written commemorating this remarkable man.

7/25/85 Washingtonian

FEET DOWN.

"Charles," said a sharp-voiced woman to her husband, "do you know that you and I once had a romance in a railway car?"

"Never heard of it," replied Charles in a subdued tone.

"I thought you hadn't, but don't you remember that it was that pair of slippers I presented to you seven years ago last Christmas—the Christmas before we were married—that led to our union? You remember how nicely they fitted, don't you? Well, Charles, one day when we were going to a picnic you had your feet up on a seat, and when you wasn't looking I took your measure. But for that pair of slippers I don't believe we'd ever been married."

A young, unmarried man sitting near by immediately took his feet down from a seat.

September, 1885

9/19/85 Washingtonian

Care of Milch Cow.

Kind and careful treatment of animals may be laid down as one of the prime conditions of success in dairying and stock-raising. In vain are cattle warmly housed through the winter and supplied with abundant pasture during the summer if they are at the same time subjected to kicks and blows in the stables, beaten with stones in the yard, or harried to and from the pastures by noisy and savage dogs. Cattle thus treated will not thrive in flesh and milk, even though they feed in clover up to their knees. There is, in fact, no class of domestic animals more responsive to kind and gentle treatment than cows. They are naturally slow and deliberate in their movements and need to be humored in this respect. Cows hurried and fretted by shouting boys and barking dogs are sure to be wild, nervous, ugly, giving little milk, and that of an inferior quality. When coming home from the pasture at milking time it is specially needful that cows should be permitted to move leisurely, to drink by the way if they desire to do so, and rest if the way is long and they are likely to become tired and heated. In short, they should be allowed to take time both in coming and going being under the care of some one who has sense and discretion enough to know that nothing is gained but much loss by hurry and worry. The difference between cows that are maltreated and otherwise misused and those that are treated kindly, is often noticeable in a herd where one or more are singled out as favorites or pets. These favored individually are generally in better flesh and give more and better milk than the others, and that for no other reason than that they are treated as all cattle should be, with care and consideration.

BLIND TOM'S CONCERT.—A large crowd —as is usually the case when this wonderful musical prodigy gives an exhibition—attended his concert on Tuesday evening last, at Hammerly's Hall, Leesburg. All were delighted. A musical critic has given us the following comments on his performance:

The rendering of the classic compositions, "The March From Taunhausen," by Wagner; "The Wanderer," by Schubert, transcribed by Liszt, and the "Polonaise," by Weber, were the most remarkable features of the entertainment. The imitation, upon the piano, of unmusical sounds, such as produced by the drum or cannon, is far more easily accomplished than the reproduction of the subtle ideas of master minds in the musical science.— One strange freak of his was the finishing of his variations on "Honu," with the minuet from the Moonlight Sonata by Beethoven. Whether the performer from whom he learnt the piece, or he himself is at fault there, would be hard to decide. Most likely the blame would fall upon the former.—His own productions and imitations were also given in the most perfect manner. The Battle of Manassas, introducing various national airs, was a grand success. The "Preparation for Battle," composed by himself—a musical poem of singular beauty and sweet pathos.

☞ Jumbo the mammoth elephant was killed by a locomotive on the Grand Trunk Air Line R. R., in Ontario. He was valued at $30,000.

Thousands of children in America will lament the untimely death of Jumbo. He was the "biggest of beasts" patient, docile and good tempered This great and good elephant—whom has had thousands of children on his back—will be sincerely mourned.

PARSONS' PURGATIVE PILLS

MAKE NEW RICH BLOOD

And will completely change the blood in the entire system in three months. Any person who will take 1 Pill each night from 1 to 12 weeks, may be restored to sound health, if such a thing be possible. For Female Complaints these Pills have no equal. Physicians use them for the cure of LIVER and KIDNEY diseases. Sold everywhere, or sent by mail for 25c. in stamps. Circulars free. I. S. JOHNSON & CO., Boston, Mass.

October, 1885

Waterford, Mills

WATERFORD, VA.,
J. F. DODD, Proprietor,

FULL ROLLER PROCESS!

THIS ILLUSTRATION represents one of six Patent Roller Process machines now used in the Waterford Mills, where they are running quietly, smoothly and beautifully day and night, turning out a great amount of BEAUTIFUL and perfect flour, which is pronounced by experts to be

The Very Best Flour.

THESE MACHINES operate so radically different from the old burr system that they revolutionize the milling business. The primary principle of this process is to *crush* the flour out of the grain and not *rub* it as with the old process, thus getting

The Very Best Results

—Therefore—

IF YOU WANT THE VERY BEST BREAD,

Buy the Waterford Roller Process. It will make bread almost as white as snow. The Waterford Mills "Family" flour will also be sure to please, being equal in quality to the "Process," but not quite as white.

I respectfully solicit the patronage of all who are in search of best returns for their money, and who feel disposed to encourage this enterprise, which has occasioned much labor and expense; but which will be, I trust profitable to the community as well as myself.

TERMS OF EXCHANGE.

Our terms of exchange, with the FARMERS, is, 1 bbl "Roller Process and 40 lbs of bran for six bushels of wheat. One bbl "Family" and 40 lbs bran for 5 bushels wheat.

NOTICE:—All persons are hereby notified that they must not use sacks, bearing my name, as I shall take possession of them, with contents, wherever I shall find them.

J. F. DODD.

Over 70 mills in Loudoun County. Steam was beginning to replace unpredictable streams as a dependable power source.

9/19/85 Washingtonian

A runaway occurred in this town on Wednesday morning. A horse and skeleton wagon, without a driver, dashed down the main street, leaving portions of the vehicle scattered en route, and winding up by coming in contact with Schiller's corner, leaving the remainder of the wagon a total wreck. The only casualty being that Wm. Allen a youth, who was knocked down and stunned, his injuries, however are not serious.

10/23/85 Telephone

An Unfortunate Loss.

"That durned speckled critter with the broken horn," said an exasperated farmer. "makes more trouble than all the cows I've got put together. If I could give her away I'd do it. I'd sal her for beef, but she'd cost more'n she'd be wuth."

That same night a railroad train ran over her and killed her, and the farmer, with tears in his eyes, told the official of the road who was prepared to remunerate him for his loss, that if it had been any one of his other cows he wouldn't care so much, but to lose that valuable animal, the only thoroughbred he ever possessed or expected to possess, was a misfortune almost beyond money reparation.

DIED.

At her residence, Balfield, in Loudoun Co., Va., on Tuesday, the 15th of September, 1885, Mrs. Elizabeth O. Carter, in the 89th year of her age.

Mrs. Carter had been for several years past, oppressed by the increasing infirmities of her very advanced age, and for the last year or two, almost confined to the house. But till long past three score and ten, she retained her vigor of mind and body, and managed her affairs with the practical judgment for which she was remarkable. She was a person of excellent sense and warm affections, a true friend and kind neighbor. As a church member, she was, for many years, a liberal supporter of the Churches at Leesburg and Upperville; and, while her health permitted, a devout and regular attendant upon the services of the sanctuary.

Mrs. Carter was twice married. Her first husband was Major Lewis, who, for a number of years represented the Loudoun District in Congress. She married, the second time, George Carter, of Oatlands.

In the hall of the Oatlands mansion, where, before the war, she long presided, her funeral services were conducted by Rev. Arthur Johns, and in the family vault, whose doors had not been opened in 20 years past, her remains were laid.

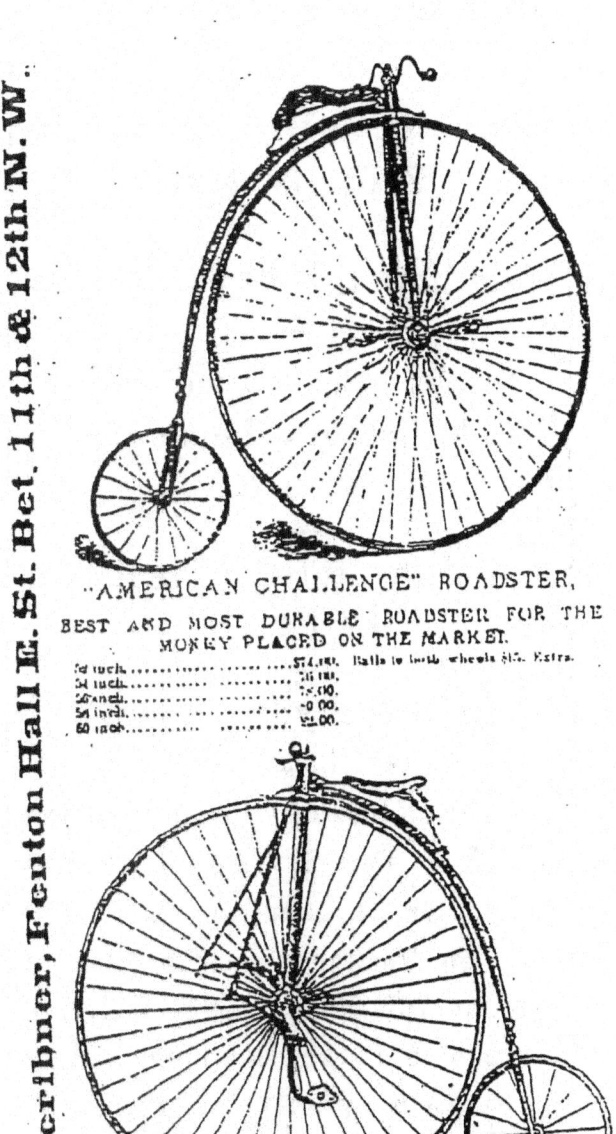

Wm. C. Scribner, Fenton Hall E. St. Bet. 11th & 12th N.W.

"AMERICAN CHALLENGE" ROADSTER,
BEST AND MOST DURABLE ROADSTER FOR THE MONEY PLACED ON THE MARKET.

"AMERICAN SAFETY BICYCLE."
THE CHEAPEST "SAFETY" ON THE MARKET.

Repairing faithfully Executed. Bicycle Sundries of every description.
SECOND HAND MACHINES AT LOWEST PRICES.

October 1885

10/9/85 Telephone

WISE IS COMING!

The People's Champion will Visit Loudoun.

Hamilton the Favored Spot.

Herald the Good News Throughout the Country-side.

An Unexpected Treat for the People.

And Don't you Forget It.

We take pleasure in announcing that Hon. John S. Wise will address the people of Loudoun at Hamilton, on Wednesday, the 14th of Oct., at 1:30 P. M. This will give the people of the Loudoun Valley an excellent opportunity to hear the issues of this campaign discussed by this brilliant orator and brave defenders of the people's rights.— The meeting will be held in the woods, hence all who come will be able to hear the speaking.

10/16/85 Telephone

A GREAT DISAPPOINTMENT,

CAPT. WISE FAILED TO REACH HAMILTON.

A SPLENDID AUDIENCE WAITED HIM.

NOTHING BUT THE GOOD NEWS FROM OHIO KEPT THEIR SPIRITS UP.

The failure of Hon. John S. Wise to appear at the Republican meeting held in Hamilton, last Wednesday, was one of the greatest disappointments ever realized by the Republicans of Loudoun. Everything up to the hour of the meeting had been so propitious and expectation ran so high that the disappointment was keenly felt. Being in the midst of a delayed seeding time it was expected that very many interested persons would be prevented from attending; but a soaking rain on the previous day made it too wet to seed, hence a large crowd was in attendance, aggregating about a thousand persons. And considering the intelligence and respectability of the crowd, it was, doubtless one of the finest audiences that has congregated anywhere in Virginia.— We had heard that a few roughs might be present, but such was not the case; we saw no man in the crowd, either white or black that did not deport himself as becomes a gentleman—there was nothing boisterous or rude about the place. And it may be said to the credit of the Democrats present that they, as well as the Republicans were very much disappointed by the failure to hear Mr. Wise.

To miss a promised speaking engagement was not a good way to win elections. To be fair, travel in those days was often difficult and uncertain.

THE WASHINGTONIAN

LEESBURG, LOUDOUN COUNTY, VA.

SATURDAY............October 3, 1885

Democratic Ticket.

FOR GOVERNOR,
Gen. FITZHUGH LEE,
OF STAFFORD.

FOR LT.-GOVERNOR
JOHN E. MASSEY,
OF ALBEMARLE.

FOR ATTORNEY GENERAL,
RUFUS A. AYRES,
OF SCOTT.

FOR STATE SENATE,
District Composed of Loudoun and Fauquier.
HENRY HEATON,
OF LOUDOUN.

For Floater for the Counties Composed of Loudoun and Fauquier,
Col. THOMAS SMITH,
OF FAUQUIER.

FOR THE HOUSE OF DELEGATES,
JNO F. RYAN,
OF LOUDOUN.

Public Speaking in Leesburg.

On MONDAY, OCTOBER the 12th, (County Court day), the Hon. DANIEL VOORHEES of Indiana, will address the citizens of Loudoun, at the courthouse in Leesburg. He is one of the most distinguished Democratic orators in the country. Don't fail to come and hear him.

The Superintendent of the W. O. & W. R. R. will run extra trains, to meet the convenience of those who may wish to attend.

10/31/85 Washingtonian

Fitz Lee in Petersburg.

PETERSBURG, Va., Oct. 25.—Gen. Fitzhugh Lee, the Democratic candidate for Governor of Virginia, spoke at Farmville on Friday night and on yesterday at Blacks and Whites, a hamlet of two hundred souls, about forty miles from Petersburg where four thousand persons from the surrounding counties gave him an old-time Virginian welcome. In the afternoon a committee with a special train brought him from Blacks and Whites to this city. When the train reached the depot there was another enthusiastic multitude waiting to greet him. Some were mounted on horseback and some were in carriages. Gen. Lee's appearance was the signal for a tumultuous outburst of applause. It was some time before he could make his way through the crowd, so eager were the people to shake him by the hand. As soon as he did so he mounted his horse and took his position at the head of the procession, which passed through the principal streets and was witnessed by about 15,000 people. The many ladies on the street and in the windows waved their handkerchiefs, and the General rode most of the time with uncovered head, bowing to right and left.

☞ Come Democrats. WAKE UP! If ever you did work for the cause you have stood by in the past, and believe is for the present and future welfare of your State, do so now. We will want your vote, and the votes of all you can get to the Polls. Our opponents are secretly at work with influences, which tell, as we learn, and we must meet them, or we will fall short of the majority we expect. The result of this election depends mainly on the work we will do from now until Tuesday next. We have no votes to lose and we must each one of us do all we can for the cause. Defeat can only come of our indolence!

November, 1885

THE WASHINGTONIAN.
LEESBURG, LOUDOUN COUNTY, VA.

SATURDAY......... November 7, 1885.

The Election——A Grand Victory!

The election is over! A splendid victory for the people has been achieved! It is a victory which carries with it much more than a partisan triumph, upon which hangs the disposal of the spoils of office. It is a victory which will date a new era in the politics of this State. It is one which has put an extinguisher upon the leadership of one of the most shrewd political party schemers and unscrupulous partisan tyrants, who ever struck for the rule of a State, by the blind submission of a party or faction. It has closed the reign of Bossism, and asserted the controlling power of the people, through the ballot-box. It has effectually wiped out Mahone, as the embodiment of Republicanism in this State, and will leave parties to divide and contest elections upon issues designed for the popular welfare instead of wrangling over the programme marked out by a self-imposed leader.

Lee has given us a canvass unequalled in the history of parties in this country, and has achieved a victory from which will flow results essential to the good order and wise government of this State. His election will secure us a judiciary equal to any in this country, in point of ability, and of the highest standard of moral and official integrity and worth.— It has saved to us a State Government which will be the choice of the people, and which will represent the interests of all, in the enactment of wise and needful laws such as the growing prosperity of the State demands. It will hush the cry of factions, by winning the confidence of the people by its judicious acts, and not leave them to the mercy of a Legislature which merely reflects the wishes and dictates of the leader of a party. It effectually crushes this attempt to introduce sectional animosities to consolidate the colored vote of the South, and stimulate the bad elements of the North. It has shown to the country that the day of carpetbagism is gone, and all its kindred elements for sectional mischief, with Mahone, will be gone with it.

It has shown that the colored people of this State have begun to think, act and vote for themselves, as FREE men should do, and that Mahone and his henchmen can no longer herd and drive them to the polls to vote as they direct. They have voted, in this election, largely for Lee, and the Democrats will see that they are protected in the exercise of their opinions, and guarranteed all the rights of citizens before the law.

The result is grand and glorious—

A SECOND WATERLOO.

The Entire Bottom Knocked Out!

Lee, Massey and Ayers, Elected!

20,000 MAJORITY,
OF WHICH LOUDOUN GIVES 900!!!

THE LEGISLATURE OURS.

VIRGINIA REDEEMED!

THE LAST OF BILLYMAHONE.

THE ENSANGUINED GARMENT DIDN'T PAN OUT!

Call Again, Mr. Sherman!

Over Two-Thirds on Joint Ballot of Both Houses in Virginia Legislature!!!

(The Democrats depiction of General Mahone ("the Confederate hero of the Crater") as an arrogant political boss was probably correct, but allowance must be made for political hyperbole. It is interesting that in this predominantly democratic state, there were at this time two republican senators. This happened as a consequence of a long controversy of how to pay the war debt, a complicated history we will leave to other historians.)

(The other Republican Senator, Riddleburg, from Woodstock, was quite a "character" in his own right, as we shall see.)

11/27/85 Telephone

From Hamilton to Washington.

[Editorial Correspondence.]

As we stood on the platform of the W. O. & W. R. R., at Hamilton last Tuesday, the east bound train rolled up to the station, drawn by that fine new engine recently put on the road. It was indeed a gratifying sight to see that grand, huge, 40-ton monster standing in the place of the old and disabled locomotives which have caused so many delays on the road, because of their inefficiency.

We boarded the train and started off, over the improved track which has been re-built near Hamilton Station during the past week. The improvement consists of cutting the defective ends off the otherwise good iron rails and relaying them with an improved connection, which makes them about as good as new; and the repairing of the ties and grading.

At 4:10 we halted in the spacious train shed of the B. & P. Depot in Washington; and as we passed along by the new engine, we admit we felt not a little proud of it, as it stood by the side of the mighty motors of the Penn. system, in size and finish comparing quite favorably with them. There is a good day coming yet for the W. O. & W.

11/7/85 Washingtonian

Hard to Suit.

"Mother," said a young wife, "would you mind cooking the dinner today? It would please John, I know. He complains so much of the new girl that I shall discharge her the moment I can get another."

"Certainly," replied the old lady cordially.

At dinner John said to his wife:

"Mary, that new girl seems to be getting worse and worse."

5,000 AGENTS WANTED TO SELL THE
LIFE OF GARFIELD!
His early life and career as soldier and statesman; his election and administration; his assassination; his heroic struggle for life; wonderful medical treatment; blood-poisoning; removal to Elberon; death, etc. Profusely illustrated. Splendid portrait of Garfield, his wife and mother; scene of the shooting; the sick chamber; Guiteau in his cell, the surgeons, and the Cabinet. The only complete and authentic work. There is a fortune for agents first in the field with this book. Outfit 50c. Speak quick. Address HUBBARD BROS., 723 Chestnut St., Phi Pa.

W. O. & W. Railroad.

TAKE EFFECT SUNDAY, AUG. 30th.

LEAVE Washington at 9 00 a. m. and 4 35 p. m. and Alexandria at 9 10 a. m. and 4 46 p. m. Pass Leesburg, going westward, at 11. 01 a. m. and 6 36 p. m., and arrive at Round Hill at 1. 43 a. m. and 7. 18 p. m. Leave Round Hill at 6.03 a. m. and 4 30 p. m. Pass Leesburg, going eastward, 6 42 a. m. and 5 18 p. m., and arrive at Alexandria at 8 25 a. m. and 7. 00 p. m., and at Washington at 8.35 a. m. and 7.10 p. m.

ON SUNDAYS,

The Morning Train, which leaves Washington at 9 and Alexandria at 9:10, goes no further than Leesburg, where it arrives at 11:01 — as on other days of the week.

All trains daily, affording parties an opportunity of visiting Belmont Park on Sunday.

☞ Passengers from Washington will take the Washington. Ohio and Western cars at the Baltimore and Potomac Railroad station at 9:00 a. m. and 4:35 p. m., and go through to Round Hill without change of cars.

The 9 10 a. m. train from Alexandria and 4:39 p. m. train from Round Hill connect at Round Hill with Daily Line Coaches for Snickersville, Beryville and Winchester; also with line of coaches which leave Leesburg daily for Aldie and Middleburg.

Both trains westward, make close connections at Vienna, with Sisson's Line of Stages for Fairfax Court-House.

One thousand mile commutation tickets $20.

ALEXANDRIA, August 30, 1885.

B. M. BROPHY, Supt.

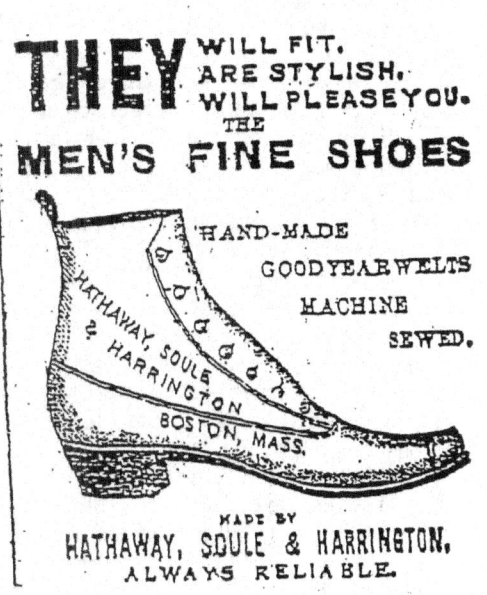

THEY WILL FIT.
ARE STYLISH.
WILL PLEASE YOU.
THE MEN'S FINE SHOES

HAND-MADE
GOODYEAR WELTS
MACHINE
SEWED.

MADE BY
HATHAWAY, SOULE & HARRINGTON,
ALWAYS RELIABLE.

November, 1885

THE TELEPHONE.

FRIDAY............Nov. 6TH.

LOUDOUN LOCALS.

—New Moon tonight.

—Local news is very scarce.

—Road officers, look to your duties.

—Now for de shucken ob de co'n.

—Protracted meeting will begin at Harmony Church next Sunday night.

—The colored people are getting ready to plaster their new church, in Hamilton.

—Some contemptible curs killed five sheep belonging to Eli Hoge Esq., last Tuesday night.

—Rev. J. R. Bridges will preach at Cool Spring School House, Sunday, Nov. 8th, at 3½ P. M.

—Say, city fathers, hurry up the posts for the street lamps. The lamps are ready and waiting.

10/16/85 Telephone

A Mississippian's Little Artifice.

A few days ago a rich planter boarded a steamer off Natchez. He purchased a paper from a newsboy and was soon lost in its perusal.

"Colonel," said a bland young man, a few moments after, "you have just dropped this," handing him a fifty-dollar note.

"I reckon not," said the old gentleman, as he overlooked his spectacles.

"I just picked it up under your chair," replied the young man, "and see no other way to dispose of it. However, since it belongs to neither of us, we might just as well divide it."

The plan worked well. The old gentleman passed over $25 in change, and the young man carelessly sauntered out on land. A few minutes after the vessel had taken to water the old gentleman presented the $50 note to the clerk in payment for his fare.

"Counterfeit," exclaimed the clerk, and then for the first time the whole truth dawned upon the old man's mind.

11/5/85 Mirror

His First Day at Sing Sing.—Ferdinand Ward, of the late firm of Ward, Grant & Co. bankers, in New York, was last week sentenced to ten years imprisonment in Sing Sing prison for obtaining money under false pretenses, and such like crookedness during the existence of the late firm. Last Sunday was his first day behind the bars. A despatch says he was awakened after a good night's sleep at 6.30 and told to dress. At 7.30 he was marched out to breakfast, and ate his hash, bread and coffee the same as the other convicts. He was then marched to the chapel and listened to a sermon by the chaplain, Mr. Edgerton. At 10.30 he was marched back to his cell, having his bucket on one arm and his pan of apple sauce and bread on the other. This was to serve as a dinner and supper combined. He spent the afternoon alone in his cell.

A young woman in Detroit, who signed herself "Mary," put this personal in the *Free Press*: "Dear Ned: Come back; all is forgiven. Pa kicked the wrong man and didn't know it was you. Come immediately."

W. H Brown, a colored porter, of Pittsburg, Pa., has been notified that Col. Spangler, a confederate officer who died recently, has willed 150 acres of land in Warren county, Mo. During the war Brown found Col. Spangler severely wounded after the capture of Fort Harrison. He conveyed the wounded officer through the lines to friends, and has never seen him since

---

11/13/85 Telephone

—WATERFORD, VA., Nov. 1st:—A grand demonstration of christianity transpired recently at the Methodist meeting (colored) in this place; J. T. Moten, P. C., opened meeting by reading the third chapter of the Gospel recorded by St. John, followed with prayer by Rev. F. B. Skinner, of Middleburg, after which Mr. Beverly Hough came forward, and in a very feeling speech, informed the congregation of having been authorized by the white Baptist church of Waterford; to present us a beautiful communion set, which he placed in the hands of the pastor, who extended a vote of thanks which was manifested by the congregation rising to their feet.

November, 1885

11/27/85 Telephone

HENDRICKS GONE.

SUDDEN DEATH OF THE VICE PRESIDENT.

INDIANAPOLIS, Nov. 25.—Hon. Thos A. Hendricks, Vice President of the United States, died very suddenly at his residence in this city at 4.45 o'clock this evening, under circumstances that were particularly distressing to his family and friends, insomuch as they had not anticipated a fatal termination of his brief illness and nobody was with him when the end came. He returned from Chicago on Saturday last and since then had been complaining somewhat of pain in his head and breast, but nothing serious was thought of it.—

He remained in his room all afternoon, occasionally rising from his bed, to which he was compelled to return by the recurrence of the abdominal pains. To all callers who came, and they were numerous, he sent word that he was indisposed, but would be glad to see them tomorrow.— About 4:30 o'clock Mrs. Hendricks, who had been at his bedside all day, went down into the parlor to see a caller.

Tom, a colored servant, and Harry Morgan, Mr Hendricks's nephew, and page in Washington, remained with him. The servant went out and Mr. Morgan stayed. Mr. Hendricks tossed uneasily in his bed and complained of great pain, but suddenly it seemed to cease, and he said to his nephew: "I am free at last: send for Eliza," meaning his wife, and these were his last words, for the young man, not realizing the urgency of the message, did not deliver it at once.

Just before 5 o'clock Mrs. Hendricks came into the room and found that her husband was dead.

Mrs. Hendricks became almost distracted with grief, and it was an hour or more before she became sufficiently composed to give any information about her husband's last moments. The family servants, two of whom had lived with Mr. Hendricks for years, ran about the house crying and moaning, and there was the utmost confusion for a time. When the news was bulletined down town it was generally discredited, yet in a very few minutes a hundred or more of Mr. Hendrick's close political and personal friends had hurried to the house. Very soon a great crowd collected around the entrance and on the street, and it was found necessary to refuse admission to any and all comers except the immediate relatives.

11/27/85 Telephone

The sudden and unexpected death of Vice President Hendricks is indeed a sad incident to all our Nation. In an hour like this the passions of political warfare are subdued by the bond of sympathy which makes the whole world kin; but to the near friends of Mr. Hendricks, the pangs of disappointed ambition mingled with the throe of personal affection must prostrate them with great grief. To see him stricken down, like Moses, just on the threshold of the promised land is, to them, a great disappointment. Let us trust that he celebrated this Thanksgiving day with joy that "the world knows not of."

11/20/85 Telephone

A Message by Mr. Lincoln That was Never Sent.

Hon. John Usher, of Lawrence, Kansas, who was Secretary of the Interior under President Lincoln, writes to the St. Louis Globe Democrat in reference to a message said to have been prepared by Mr. Lincoln on his return from the Hampton Roads conference in February 1865: "Soon after his (Lincoln's) return from the James river the cabinet was convened, and he read to it for approval a message which he had prepared to be submitted to Congress, in which he recommended that Congress appropriate $200,000,000 to be apportioned among the Several States in proportion to slave population, to be distributed to the holders of slaves in those States, upon condition that they would consent to the abolition of slavery and the disbanding of the insurgent army, and would acknowledge and submit to the laws of the United States. The members of the cabinet were all opposed. He seemed somewhat surprised at that and asked: 'How long will the war last?' No one answered, but he soon said: 'A hundred days. Well, we are spending now in carrying on the war $3,000,000 a day, which will amount to all this money besides all the lives.' With a deep sigh he added: 'But you are all opposed to me and I will not send the message.'"

1/8/86 Telephone

IT WAS A SUCCESS IN ALMOST EVERY RESPECT.

The entertainment given by the Hamilton Literary Society, last Friday night in Kingsley's Hall was, to say the least, a success; and that impression on the part of the TELEPHONE'S representative was confirmed by the applause and subsequent remarks of the audience.

It had been advertised that the doors would be opened at 7.30 o'clock; but so early did the crowd gather, that the doors had to be opened much sooner; and every seat in the house was occupied at the hour above-mentioned. All the standing room was also occupied.

Prof. Scharf's full orchestra, comprising 5 violins, 4 back-action fiddles of divers sizes, picelo, flageolet, triangle, organ and piano, rendered a fine program in excellent manner. Some of the boys have evidently made rapid and reliable progress.

The performances were concluded with "Cousin Jedidiah, a rollicking, laughable solo and chorus, participated in by nearly all the company of performers, after which the audience was dismissed with a semi-promise of a similar occasion at some future day.

MUSICAL AND LITERARY ENTERTAINMENT,
AT
KINGSLEY'S HALL,
HAMILTON, VA.,
FRIDAY, JANUARY 1st, 1886.—7.30 P. M.

PROGRAMME:

Star of the West,	Orchestra.
Gipsy Countess,	Tableau and Duet.
Polish Battle Song,	Orchestra.
Mother Says I Mustn't,	Vocal Solo.
Dame Blanche,	Overture—Piano and Violin.
Well of St. Kean,	Recitation and Tableau.
Polacca,	Orchestra.
Sale of Old Bachelors,	Recitation.
Medley of American Songs,	Orchestra.
Borrowed Plumes,	Farce—One Act.
Dixie,	Orchestra.
Mother's Dream,	Tableau.
Mr. & Mrs. Snibbs,	Duet.
Richmond Waltz,	Orchestra.
Three Fishers,	Tableau.
We'll Have to Mortgage The Farm,	Mus. Pec.
Salute to Prague,	Orchestra.
Cousin Jedidiah,	Solo and Chorus.
Soldier's Song March,	Orchestra.

The Committee.

1/7/86 Mirror

Telephonic.—Quite a spirit of telephonic enterprise has developed itself in this section of the county recently, which promises ere long to give our people all the advantages of this rapid, convenient and satisfactory method of communication. There are already one or two lines in successful operation in Loudoun—one from Clark's Gap to Waterford and one from Lincoln via of Purcellville to Berlin, we believe, and one from Middleburg to the Plains Station, Manassas Gap railroad. We understand that it is the intention of the Middleburg and Plains Company to extend their line to Aldie there to connect with the line to Leesburg, thus giving to the citizens of Loudoun a direct communication between its most northern and southern borders—which, with the telegraph wires connecting the eastern and western sections of the county, will give our people ample facilities for rapid communication in almost every direction.

Wheat Wanted!
—AT—
WATERFORD MILLS.

We are paying from 2½ to 5 cts per bus. over the market price for good wheat.

CHAS. R. PAXTON & CO.

January, 1886

1/15/86 Telephone

The Weather.

Within the past week the weather has been a legitimate and prolific topic. About dark last Friday night the snow began to fall thick and fast, directly from the North... late in the evening the wind slowly changed until in the morning it came from the Northwest with some snow still falling. The wind increased in velocity hurling the light flakes in clouds and piling the drifts so high that some of the the few people who ventured out upon the roads were made to reach their destinations—the north and south roads all being badly drifted. This state of affairs continued until Tuesday, part of the time the wind blowing a furious gale, consequently the roads were piled high with drifts. The road on the mountain is so badly drifted that communication with Leesburg has been cut off except on horseback—and even that way it is difficult.

Together with this fierce storm of snow and wind the cold has been very severe, recording in some places, as low as 6 or 7 below zero, early Wednesday and Thursday mornings. Fortunately mercury did not get down to zero (though quite close to it) while the wind and storm were raging.

1/22/86 Telephone

MILLTOWN VA., Jan. 16:—From present indications, it seems the delightful "Polar wave" which visited us last week intends to stay, as the mercury is hovering about zero, occasionally getting a majority of six degrees. And yet the "Dudes" are not happy, as the genial zephyrs last Saturday and Sunday gathered the beautiful snow from the fields and groves and deposited it in the roads, and did not preserve much regularity in the distribution, as, in some places, it gives a good representation of the "Sierra Navadas." The Mugwumps, half-breed Republicans and Bourbons have all united in heroic attempts to clear the roads.

1/22/86 Telephone

LOVETTSVILLE, VA., Jan. 18.

EDITOR TELEPHONE:—We wish to sound a blast in praise of the Lovettsville ministers, doctors, merchants and business men generally.

Boreas swept the fields clean of the snow that fell on the night of the 8th inst, and filled the roads from fence to fence. Travel and traffic were suspended, and the farmers, who heretofore have been active and energetic in opening the thoroughfares when blockaded with snow, seemed on this occasion to have lost all energy, and made no effort to open communication with the outside world. The mail carrier failed to get here with the "precious freight" on Saturday, and everybody suffered from a dearth of news.

On Monday morning a "Council of War" was held, and soon detachments of L—— men, armed with saws and shovels attacked the drifts on the main road leading from Lovettsville to Berlin. With vast labor the road was opened to the river and the denizens of our village had the satisfaction of receiving intelligence through the medium of the U. S. mail the same evening.

Another detachment was set to work on the road to Bodington and a road shoveled through drifts on an average, five feet deep for a mile and a half. Another force opened the road to the New Jerusalem Lutheran Church, and the cemetery, and thus to a considerable extent relieved our "snow-bound" condition.

1/22/86 Telephone

—TAYLORTOWN, VA., Jan. 18.— Winter has arrived at last and awakened us from our sleepy state. The farmers have been busy filling their ice houses with beautiful ice; which is from 6 to 8 in.—— The young gentlemen of the neighborhood have been trying to sleigh, but they are making slow progress.

1886.

JANUARY and FEBRUARY are always very quiet months in my business. I propose trying to make them more busy by offering the following special discounts on all

Agricultural Implements

bought in
JANUARY, FIVE PER CENT.
FEBRUARY, THREE "

and offer the following seasonable goods:—

A Full Stock of all sizes of

Fish Bro's WAGONS,

Road Carts,

SULKIES.

(A Carload just received.)

ENSILAGE HAY, STRAW AND FODDER CUTTERS, FROM $5.00 TO $100.

Corn Shellers,

Hand and Power, from $6 to $15.

Cooley Creamers,

From $15 to $75.

Reid's Butter Workers

DAVIS SWING CHURNS,

A few good SECOND-HAND

Reapers and Mowers

At One-half Their Value.

Corn & Cob Mills

at UNPRECEDENTEDLY Low Prices.

"New Things"

GORTON'S

CATTLE FOOD STEAMER

WHEEL ROAD SCRAPERS.

CHAMPION

Corn Planters

—AND—

DRILLS.

F. L. MOORE,

3147 M St. N. W.,

West Washington, D. C.

January, 1886

1/15/86 Telephone

HE WAS WITH GRANT.

The Tramp Who Came to Sleep by the Tomb at Riverside Park.

Boston Herald: "Home? I guess not. Haven't seen one since '72, an' that's quite a while, I reckon. I'm what they call a Wandering Jew, I suppose. I've been through the states half a dozen times, down to Mexico twice and on the continent once. I have slept on the steps of the centennial building at Philadelphia, in the gallery of the capitol at Washington, in the Yosemite valley, and in lots of other famous places. Now I've come to sleep in Riverside park near Grant's tomb. It will be a cool place' I suppose, there tonight, but I've slept in cold places before. I marched under Gen. Grant once in Mexico. He was a young man then, and hadn't won his laurels, but he was brave and true as steel even then to his poor friends. I was in my young manhood, too, and could boast of what you asked me about just now—a home. But I got on the downward path, and soon hurried from bad to worse. I'm now a total wreck, past all redemption, and just able to carry on a weary existence. Everybody despises me, and yet I had as good a start in life as he did. I've often thought of the difference in our two stations now, and then remembered him as he was in Mexico when we both fought for the same flag. I was in California when the news of his death reached me. I have been coming to New York ever since. It seems a long while just to travel that distance, don't it? But then a tramp don't travel like a millionaire. We steal a ride on the first freight train that is going our way, and remain there till we get put off. Then we stop and beg, or work for something to eat. Sometimes we work for a week at a time in one place, and then go off on a week's spree. This, of course, takes time, and where you would make a journey in a day it would take us a week or two. I've been a good while coming from California to New York, but now I'm here and I'm going to sleep near Grant's tomb to-night. I'll be orderly and do no harm."

HAMMERLY'S HALL.

Two Nights Only

—MONDAY AND TUESDAY,—

JANUARY 18th and 19th.

TEN NIGHTS IN A BAR-ROOM.

The Worthington Dramatic Co.,

1/14/86 Mirror

QUEENSBERRY.

He Tells How He Came to Write His Well-Known Prize-Ring Rules.

"What is the true history of your famous prize-ring rules?"

"Well, John Chambers and I wrote them while I was attending school at Cambridge. When there I held for two years the light weight championship in the ring. The amateur cups of the annual sparring matches were prizes that many boxers sought. We then had no definite rules of boxing. Chambers and I were delegated to draft a set of rules. We did so, and I afterwards revised them. Hitherto it was difficult to decide, when two men fought, which got the better in scientific points. The rules were written to cover not only scientific points, but any questions that might arise as to which was the best boxer.

"America has much to be proud of in fine boxers. It is carried on to a greater extent, and the people patronize and encourage the art. In San Francisco I witnessed a sparring match. I was surprised at the science displayed. Even the amateurs did remarkably well. I have never seen John L. Sullivan box. From what I hear I rather think he has a great deal of science with his sledgehammer blows. He makes a rush at his opponent and beats down his barriers of defence. Then, if his opponent could knock him back while he is thus exposed, giving him terrible blows, and at times leaving himself unguarded, no doubt the tide would change. Reverse the method of fighting now, and attack Sullivan for all that can be gained. The onslaught which he has never been used to astonishes him, and puts him in an attitude of defence, something he never contemplated. The rusher is met by a rusher, and the tug of war is more uncertain than ever. But as I have not witnessed his sparring, I cannot enter into any analytical discourse about it. It was the old tactics to stand wary and defend until the party attacking was wearied out. The victory was then easy. Sullivan has reversed the order, and has the physical prowess to make it effective.

February, 1886

2/18/86 Mirror

The ice blockade of the Potomac was broken all along the line last week. On Friday night the break up occurred on that portion along our borders. The ice was from 10 to 14 inches in thickness and the noise of its disruption was terrific. It passed off rapidly and with little or no damage that we have heard of. On Saturday the river rose very rapidly and serious fears of a flood were entertained, for finally they were not realized, and early on Sunday the waters began to recede. The stream is now almost entirely free from ice.

2/18/86 Mirror

A Practical Joke. — The Warrenton *Virginian* says:

"Mr S. B. Chilton brought a large bushy black tail into town yesterday and hanging it up in a conspicuous place directed attention of all passers to it as a black fox tail. Of course it was an object of great interest and everybody went up and felt it, while Mr. C. smilingly looked on. But he stopped later in the day, when half the population of Warrenton was looking for him with hands that had been caressing the business end of a polecat, and if he had not made his escape, he would have been hung up by the heels on the same nail with the black fox tail."

2/18/86 Mirror

R E Lee Camp Confederate Soldiers, at Richmond, Va., passed resolutions expressive of their sorrow at the death of Gen Hancock, and on Saturday, the day of his funeral. Gov. Lee ordered the flag on the Capitol to be displayed at half-mast. The dead hero was a warm personal friend of Gov. Lee.

2/18/86 Mirror

The Funeral of Gen. Hancock was attended by a large number of distinguished people, headed by the Secretary of War.

The body of the dead General preceded by three batteries of the Fifth Artillery and followed by mourning relatives and the personal and general staff, was taken from the house on Governor's Island and conveyed to the barge office. There it was met by the pall-bearers and delegations from military and civic bodies. In the midst of a drizzling rain the procession moved to old Trinity, where the impressive burial service was read. After which the remains and the funeral cortege proceeded by special train to Norristown.

No long lines of troops, no sound of dirges no trappings of woe marked the funeral of Gen. Hancock. The man who had received the nomination of a great party for the highest honor in the nation's gift, he who had turned the fortunes of many a battle and whose calm courage in the midst of death had so often inspired the faltering regiments, was laid at rest quietly without pomp or vain show. A small escort of regular troops and a few devoted friends gathered before a tomb on a wind-swept hillside at Norristown and heard a blue-coated bugler sound "taps," the soldier's last good night. There the remains of Winfield Scott Hancock were placed beside those of his father and his beloved daughter. The firing party fired the military salvos and the Bugler sounded the taps and the simple ceremonies were ended.

Dr BIGGERS HUCKLEBERRY CORDIAL
FOR THE BOWELS & CHILDREN TEETHING

It is THE GREAT SOUTHERN REMEDY for the bowels. It is one of the most pleasant and efficacious remedies for all summer complaints. At a season when violent attacks of the bowels are so frequent, some speedy relief should be at hand. The wearied mother, losing sleep in nursing the little one teething, should use this medicine. 5 cts. a bottle.

TO RENT!
—THE—
WATERFORD TANNERY.
Will be to Rent AFTER MAY 1ST, '86.
For a Reliable and Energetic Party this is a good chance, as
EASY TERMS
Will be made, by applying to
SARAH H. BOND,
Waterford, Loudoun Co., Va.

SAKS & COMPANY, 308, 310, 312, 314 and 316 Seventh St., WASHINGTON CITY.
CLOTHIERS, HATTERS, TAILORS and FURNISHERS.
Good Articles and Lowest Prices.

3/4/86 Mirror

SAM SMALL'S CONVERSION.

Sam Jones's Able Lieutenant Tells his Own Story to a Chicago Reporter.

From the Chicago Inter-Ocean.

"It was this way. The 13th day of last September (Sunday) I took my wife and children and went from Atlanta, my home up to Cartersville, fifty miles away, to hear Sam Jones preach in a big camp meeting. It was a kind of a Sunday excursion. Any change of life up to that time? No, there had been no change of life up to that time—but for the worse. I heard Sam Jones preach, and I was convicted of my sins. I was awakened. This was on Sunday. I went home and got drunk again, and I stayed drunk until Tuesday afternoon. Then I went into my library at about 4 o'clock, and I prayed until I felt that I saw my way clear. I had been thinking about my condition, and I felt that the time had come to stop. I was getting over my depth. I looked the thing in the face, and I surrendered to the Lord. Then I went out and had 3,000 circulars printed, announcing that I would preach that evening at the corner of Marietta and Peachtree streets. The first job printer that I went to thought I was crazy. You see I had been on a drunk, and my friends had often thought that I would go crazy from drink, and so this man thought the same and wouldn't print my bills. So I went to another place and I got them printed at last. I had them distributed, an' at the place mentioned a great crowd assembled when it came for me to speak. I told them what had happened, what I was going to do, and told them I meant business. They could stand off and see me do it.

"As soon as Jones heard about what had happened he telegraphed me to come up to Cartersville and speak for him. Well, I preached the next two nights in local churches, and on Saturday I went up and preached for Jones. From that day to this I have lost about a dozen days, speaking some days from one to four times. Yesterday," and here was another complete overturning of the erroneous theory of his being converted some time ago, studying with Bishop Beckwith, &c. "yesterday I was five months old in the Gospel."

"How are you satisfied with your work?"

"Thoroughly, thoroughly. My best friends said I ought to have been in this work long ago. My mother prayed and prayed for it till her death. I fought it as long as I could. My work has been uniformly pleasant, and I feel that it has been blessed with success."

"Now, how many have you converted?"

"Well, you mean the two of us, since I have been working with Jones? It's hard to tell; it can't be told, but I can give you the estimates of our work together.— In St. Joseph Mo., 2,200; in Birmingham, Ala., 1,800; in St. Louis, well, we can't tell, but by the best calculation by those in the churches, about 1,600; in Cincinnati—there's absolutely no telling. The names of probably 2,000 people in Cincinnati were handed in, but there were many, many people who had been formerly connected with churches who did not care to have their names given. It is thought that the lives of from 20,000 to 30,000 people were affected.

3/4/86 Mirror

THE SMOKERS.

Smoke, do you? Well, then, sir, you know
How fast and firm these habits grow.
You've often doubtless sworn to quit,
And then forgot it till you'd lit
A fresh cigar and caught the smell
Of that which pleases you so well.

You've doubtless looked into your purse
And counted cost with many a curse,
And read the dread diseases caught
By smoking oftener than you ought,
And vowed at least that you'd curtail
The cost and danger, but to fail.

You buy two where 'twas six before—
But go more often to the store;
You storm and reason with yourself,
And put your box back on the shelf,
But, in whatever place you are,
Your thoughts are with your shelved cigar.

How weak this proves strong men to be!
Free, in helpless slavery!
The thought is madness to the mind—
We'll burst these galling chains that bind!
But ere, my friend, we go too far,
I'll thank for a fresh cigar.

April 1886

Base Ball.

4/2/86 Telephone

EDITOR TELEPHONE:— Nine Hillsboro dudes came down in a rattling vehicle from their "hard scrabble hills," to gobble up the "Little boys" of Alder's school house, in a match game of base ball, on the 19th inst. The Dudes had accepted the challenge of the "Little Boys" to a test of superior skill in that manly game; and came down with smiling faces and joyous hope to do the work. The game commenced with the "Little Boys" at the bat; the Dudes in the field, which they had to keep until the "Little Boys" scored twenty-one; then the Dudes came to bat, to show their master strokes, but in a few moments, where were they? O gentle shepherd tell me where.—They were skunked quicker than a wheelbarrow struck by lightning. They went to the field again, and the "Little Boys" took the bat, and had made five scores, when Heaven and earth shook!— the giant Dude sent in a ball with such force that it struck his hind-catch in the mouth, spoiling his countenance, and, as we thought, sending him to the land where they play base ball no more forever, until he began to dig one of his front teeth out of the roof of his mouth, and draw his nostrils down, out of the way of his bangs. That ended the game. The disheartened Dudes, with their wounded comrade loaded themselves into their wagon, and left!

3/18/86 Mirror

OLD SORREL DEAD —Stonewall Jackson's warhorse, familiarly known as "old sorrel," and the same that the General rode up to the time he was mortally wounded at Chancellorsville, died of old age at the Soldiers Home near Richmond on Sunday. He was 32 years old. Mr. Norman V. Randolph, president of the board of the soldiers' home, wishing to save the remain of the old horse preserved, is summoned Taxidermist Webster of Washington, to Richmond to mount them. Mr. Webster will bring the skeleton and skin to that city and do his work there.

The flag of the Soldiers' Home was displayed at half-mast, in honor of the old steed's memory. It is said that no one had ever been on his back since his gallant rider received his fatal shot twenty-three ago.

4/9/86 Telephone

The soul of William Broyles has also been removed from this earth, to the Limbo of Oblivion, by a broken fence stake, in the hands of one, Thomas Oldham, a wicked companion, assisted by Forty Rod Lightning Whiskey. Broyles; Oldham; Shed Bolyn and Buster Jones (all colored) left Middleburg on Sunday morning some time between the hours of one and three o'clock, and proceeded westward up the Little River Pike. Bolyn and Jones were in front, and after going as far as the old toll gate, they heard the sound of a blow, which Bolyn describes as being sufficient to fell an ox. Returning to the scene of the tragedy the said Jones and Bolyn found Broyles on the ground and Oldham standing over him. The three companions then left the victim to his fate and went homeward. Broyles lay there with his head crushed, while the rain pelted him, nor was he removed until death, which took place probably on or after 3 o'clock P. M. when the gory corse of the inebriate was taken to the Shiloh church, where a post-mortem examination was made by Dr Cochran, on Tuesday morning at 10 o'clock.

The verdict of the coroner's jury implicates Thomas Oldham, and as he is still lingering in the neighborhood he will be arrested in a day or two from date of warrant.

Broyles was a harmless man, but addicted to drink, and was very noisy when under the influence of intoxicants. He had twenty-two cents in hard cash on his person, also some matches carefully put up in a wallet; but, poor fellow, while his toes are turned up to the daisies and his soul no one knows where, he will never want those lucifers. Score another for middleburg.

April. 1886

4/15/86 Mirror

Another Jail Delivery. Three Prisoners Make their Escape from the Jail of Loudoun.—Wednesday was set for the hearing by the County Court, of the case of the Commonwealth vs. John Banister and others, charged with stealing, a short time ago, $200 from the house of Mr. Mort. Thompson, near Round Hill. Banister was in jail, and Grace Cooper and Beverley Jackson, whom he charged with being his accomplices in the theft, were out on bail. The witnesses were all summoned, and everything was ready for a hearing of the case.—But on Wednesday morning, when the jailor visited the cell occupied by Banister to furnish breakfast, he discovered that during the night, that accomplished young scoundrel had removed two sections of the iron bars in the window and made his escape.—two other prisoners—Harvey Gray and ——— Pinket—both confined for minor offences, and whose terms of service in the county jail, were nearly up had gone with him. Before leaving they had made a long rope of their bed-clothing, at one end of which was a large stone, by the assistance of which they designed to scale the outer wall. Once in the yard however, they found its use unnecessary as a large opening under the yard gate, furnished them a more convenient mode of egress. The removed steel bars are about 1¼ inches square, which of course had to be sawed in four places, and from the skillful manner in which the work was done, it is evident they had the necessary implements for the job. Where, when or how they got them will probably never be found out. Up to the hour of going to press no tidings have been heard of the fugitives.

Luther Paine the colored man, whose trial on Monday, is noticed elsewhere, was in the same cell with the absconding prisoners, and when asked Wednesday morning why he didn't go along replied that he was "too much of a man for that" Luther is evidently a "biger" man than either of those who escaped through the small hole in the wall—but it is more charitable to suppose that Luther determined to take his chances for liberty through a jury of his countrymen, than the somewhat hazardous risks of a fugitive from justice.

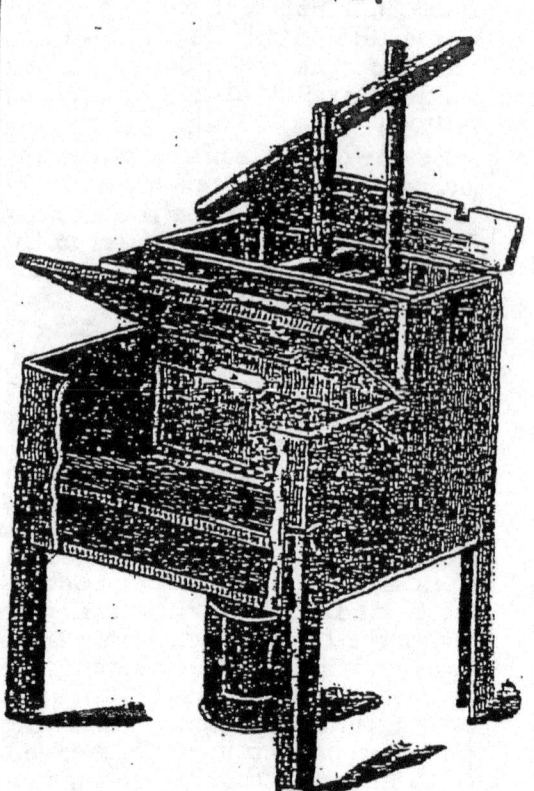

WOMAN MADE HAPPY AT LAST.

OF the 8,000 washing machines patented none have given perfect satisfaction until the King of all Washing Machines was invented, which is an improvement over all washing machines and of an entirely new principle from anything of the kind ever before invented. It washes by force of air and water, and removes all streaks of dirt out of collars and cuffs of dirty clothing which farmers and mechanics and laboring classes generally wear. It breaks no buttons and does not tear or rub the clothes. It soaps itself, it is easily and rapidly operated, washes everything from a lace collar to a bed quilt.

The Leesburg Laundry.

THIS LAUNDRY is now in operation at Birkby's Old Stand, ready to do all kinds of Laundry work on the following terms:

Plain family washing, without starching, 60 cents per dozen; with starching, 75 cents per dozen. Rough dry, without starching, 30 cents per dozen; with starching, 40 cents per dozen.

These prices will be reduced to families of large washings. Other washing proportionately cheap.

march 6— WRIGHT & BROTHER.

4/23/86 Telephone

PROF. AUBREY DELEMAIN.

Worse Than a Humbug.

Last Friday and Saturday nights, a man calling himself Prof. Aubrey Delemain, "the celebrated electric marvel" gave exhibitions of his magical (?) powers in Kingsley's Hall, to good houses. His performances consisted of many very clever tricks and imitations of mesmerism, ventriloquism, mind reading, electrical force &c. The entertainments were well received by the audiences and were altogether too good to be spoiled as they were by subsequent developments. He stated at the beginning of his Friday evening performance that he intended to humbug the audience, which was all very well, for that was what they expected; but it was something else for him to play the swindler as he did by sneaking away from Town and leaving divers debts unpaid. He announced Saturday night that he would leave Hamilton Monday noon; but about nine o'clock Sunday morning a Waterford team appeared, and having his effects all ready, he stepped in and was away from town in a hurry. It was soon found out that he had failed to pay several small bills—$6.50 due Mr. Silas Kingsley for assisting him &c., $2 due the editor of the TELEPHONE for printing and $2 each to four small boys, whom he hired at $1 per night to play dummies on the stage and assist in his humbuggery. Perhaps there are other debts that have not been reported.

The meanness of the man and the audacity of his behavior was such that, with Mr. Kingsley, we concluded that if he attempted to exhibit at Lovettsville, as he said he would, he should be taken in, brought to account and exposed.— To this end Mr. Kingsley and Warner Brown, one of the TELEPHONE boys, appeared in Lovettsville about 7 p. m. Monday and found Mr. Delemain at the hotel. Upon the boys presenting their bills he declared that he had sent by mail the amount due the TELEPHONE and possitively repudiated Mr. Kingsley's bill. As he persisted in his refusal to square up, the boys left him and proceeded to a magistrate (Stone,) who issued an attachment on his effects. Delemain proceeded to the hall, where he opened his performances, and just as he dismissed the audience the Constable arose and read the attachment levying on the receipts of the evening in the money drawer of the store keeper who sold the tickets.

The Professor (?) subsequently appeared on the sidewalk and furiously berated the boys and making many threats. He, of course, decided to stand trial which was set for tomorrow (Sat.) but on Tuesday morning he sloped, crossing the Potomac at Berlin, leaving his appointment to show in Lovettsville that night.

Mr. Kingsley secured some of the Kingsley's Hall tickets which the fellow had carried off with him.

We learn that he also swindled the people of Waterford in like manner, though probably worse. He spent Sunday in that place where, it is reported, he was decidedly drunk.

Evidently Professor Delemain thought there is no spunk in the people of this part of the country, but he will not be apt to fool with this section again soon. The recovery of a little filthy lucre is a small affair but the capture and exposure of such a scamp is a good thing.

FITS STOPPED FREE
Marvelous success.
Insane Persons Restored
Dr. KLINE'S GREAT NERVE RESTORER
for all BRAIN & NERVE DISEASES. Only sure cure for Nerve Affections, Fits, Epilepsy, etc. INFALLIBLE if taken as directed. No Fits after first day's use. Treatise and $2 trial bottle free to Fit patients, they paying express charges on box when received. Send names, P. O. and express address of afflicted to DR. KLINE, 931 Arch St., Philadelphia, Pa. see Druggists. BEWARE OF IMITATING FRAUDS.

4/24/86 Washingtonian

THE PRESIDENT'S BRIDE

President Cleveland's approaching marriage is now regarded as a certainty. All his friends agree that he would have been very prompt to deny the story of his marriage coming in as positive a form as it has in the last week or ten days, if he had not fully made up his mind on the subject. He has kept the secret very well from even his most intimate associates. It is understood that the engagement took place during Miss Folsom's last visit to Washington. If Mr. Cleveland is married at the White House in June it will be the second marriage of a President during his term of office. Mr. Tyler was married while he was President, but his marriage took place in New York.

Miss Folsom's visit to Washington last spring was as a school girl enjoying her vacation. She accompanied her mother and the two were guests at the White House some ten or twelve days. They were here again very quietly in the fall, just before sailing for Europe.

4/23/86 Telephone

Instead of the Telephone.

[New York Sun.]

An Ohio man has invented an electrical type-writer which transmits messages by wire long distances, and it was exhibited to a number of capitalists, electricians and newspaper men, at 145 Broadway, on Saturday. It is a simple arrangement with a keyboard, which, when a key is touched brings the right letter down on a sheet of paper which moves along automatically at one side, so that words are printed as by an ordinary type-writer, and the machine at the other end of the wire acts in unison, printing the message in the same way. It does all the work of the operator at the ordinary telegraph instrument. It is intended by the National Printing Telegraph Company, which own the patent, to put it in use in the manner of the Bell telephone instruments, connections to be made at a central office. Mrs. Jones, of New York, will be able to call up Mrs. Brown, of Philadelphia, and while Mrs. Jones is talking Mrs. Brown can be dressing the baby and reading the message from the machine. Every reader of a message has it duplicated for himself.

4/15/86 Mirror

Gipsies.—A company of these strollers were encamped a mile or so east of town for several days but left on Monday last. They were engaged in the usual gipsy avocations of begging, fortune telling, &c., on the part of the females, while the men, with the *Rumany Rye's* accustomed improvidence employed themselves in "swapping" horses and doing nothing, or worse, though we have not heard of any depredations of consequence that they have committed. It was rumored that one of the children of the band was very sick with some malignant fever.

PLYMOUTH ROCKS.

200 Cockerels & Pullets.

BRED FROM CHOICE STOCK.

INTENDING to remove from where I now live, I will sell my entire stock of Plymouth Rocks, consisting of 200 Cockerels and Pullets and one breeding pen of 20 Hens and 2 Cocks.

I have made Plymouth Rocks a specialty for 6 years, and have spared neither time nor expense to get the best blood. Will sell the entire lot at a bargain.

J. R. BARNHOUSE.
Goresville, Va.

May, 1886

1886 SPRING AND SUMMER 1886
DRY GOODS.

LARGEST DRY GOODS HOUSE —IN— Loudoun Co.

LARGEST STOCK —OF— DRY GOODS, —AND— NOTIONS IN LOUDOUN CO.

WILDMAN & SONS,

Have just opened, and are now offering, the largest and most attractive stock to be found in this part of the country, at prices to suit the present hard times. Our

DRESS GOODS DEPARTMENT,

Embraces all the Novelties of the season, consisting partly of Canvas Cloths, both plain and plaid, Homespuns, Etamire Stripes, Satin Berber, Cashmeres, &c., &c.

A CHOICE SELECTION OF LAWNS FROM 5c. UP.

PRINTED INDIA LINENS, Seersuckers, Ginghams, Calicos, &c., in endless variety;
—a stock of—

DOMESTICS AND HOUSEKEEPING GOODS,

An examination of which will convice you that they are lower in price than the lowest and in great variety.

SHOES, SHOES.—The best hand and machine made Shoes for ladies and children to be found. Warranted to give satisfaction.

Give us a call or send for samples. Respectfully, WILDMAN & SONS.

This rather interesting old building is still occupied in historic Leesburg diagonally across from the Courthouse.

5/14/86 Telephone

BY MISTAKE.

HOW HORACE GREELEY CAME TO BE NOMINATED INSTEAD OF DAVID DAVIS.

"Did you know," said a New York member of Congress, "that the nomination of Horace Greeley for the Presidency in 1872 was the result of a blunder, and that those who were surprised the most were the very people who had done the most to bring it about? It is an interesting story. If you remember, it required great effort on the part of Lyman Trumbull, Carl Schurz and the other friends of the liberal movement to enlist Mr. Greeley's sympathies in the cause. When he did so, however, we Democrats felt that we had secured a powerful ally, and our hearts warmed, as it were, to our old enemy of the "Tribune." Shortly after this the Democratic Liberal convention was held at Cincinnati. The New York delegation was not pledged to any candidate, but the prevailing sentiment was that David Davis, of Illinois, would be the most acceptable man to put against Gen. Grant. Mr. Davis was very popular with the moneyed classes of the East. He was a man of high character and broad attainments, and we believed his candidacy would give us a good fighting chance of securing the electoral vote of Illinois. But we felt very grateful to Mr. Greeley. We decided, therefore, that we would give him a complimentary vote in the convention as an expression of our kindly regard. We went out to Cincinnati in a special train, with drums beating and flags flying, 72 delegates, and probable 200 others who had no business there, but wanted to see the fun. As soon as we arrived we began talking Greeley. This was done for a lark, you must remember, but we talked about him so much that we soon started a great boom for him. We concluded, however, that this would do us no harm, and that, at the proper moment, he could be quietly set aside, when we would bend our energies, first, to the nomination of David Davis, or, failing in that, the nomination of Charles Francis Adams. The Kentucky delegation was headed by Cassius M. Clay. They had no candidate, but they had heard so much talk about Horace Greeley around New York headquarters that they believed we were honestly in favor of the old man, to our horror, when that state was called, what did Clay do but announce that Kentucky cast her 26 votes for Horace Greeley. As we had pledged our first vote to Mr. Greeley we were bound to make good the promise, and when New York's 72 votes followed Kentucky's 26 the Convention became wild with excitement, and from that time until the roll-call was finished nothing could be heard but shouts for Greeley. We attempted to check the tide on the next ballot, but it was too late. Greeley was nominated on the second ballot, and the maddest set of men in Cincinnati that night were the members of the New York delegation, whose choice was David Davis of Illinois."

5/6/86 Mirror

Tight Lacing to be Fashionable Again.

"Is it true," was asked one of our best known modistes, "that tight lacing is coming into fashion again?"

"Yes, it is true. You see, it is fashionable for ladies to be broad-shouldered and small-waisted, and customers of mine, whose clothes I used to make from twenty-three to twenty-seven inches, waist measure, now have them fully five inches smaller. Only a year ago a natural waist, measuring any from twenty-five to twenty-seven inches, was considered graceful and pretty, which it really is, but now it is not fashionable to measure more than from eighteen to twenty-three. Of course the lacing is done by means of the corset, but sometimes I nearly break my fingers trying to fit and close basques that are so tight they will not meet without an effort.

EFFECT OF TIGHT LACING.

There was a young masher called Pacer,
Who waltzed with a very tight lacer;
  When he pulled her in two,
  She said, "Thanks, that will do,
For you dance in a very rough way, sir."

6/10/86 Mirror

A CARD.

I desire to return to the citizens of Leesburg, my sincere thanks for the prompt and efficient services rendered on the occasion of the fire last Thursday afternoon, at my home. For their noble efforts in preserving my furniture from destruction and also for the timely and generous contributions, to aid in the repair of damages, I tender the deepest expressions of heartfelt gratitude on the part of myself and family.

May 31, 1886.   JAMES BYRNE.

So Far and Yet So Near.—Leesburg and Aldie were brought into very close communication by the putting in place one day last week of the instruments on the telephone line just completed between these two places. Since the phones have been in place the jingles of the call-bell have been frequent and boys have kept up quite a chatting. The line works remarkably well.

5/29/86 Washingtonian

Quite a Run.—On Tuesday last lawyer Edward Nichols, of Leesburg drove up to his farm, near Wheatland. On his return while driving through a muddy place in the road, the swingle tree broke and the mare attached to the vehicle being startled by the snap, sprang quickly forward, dragging Mr. Nichols, who had her well in hand, over the dash board into the mud. Happily he received no injury. The mare became disengaged entirely from the buggy and ran straight ahead to Leesburg, a distance of about 7 miles, plunging through the streets and finally to her stable unhurt, and in good condition.

> Runaway horses and torn up buggies seem to be frequently mentioned. Fortunately, the traffic accidents then happened at only one-fourth the speed of today's collisions, but still there were injuries and an occasional fatality.

ONE DOLLAR

Will Buy 100 FEET of BOARDS

AT WILLET & LIBBEY'S,

WASHINGTON CITY, D. C.

6/17/86 Mirror

The Wheelmen.—At precisely 6 o'clock Sunday evening last ten members of the Capital Bicycle Club of Washington, D. C., rolled into town and deposited their weary forms at the Reamer House. That is nine of them rolled in, one coming in a vehicle, which he had luckily met between here and Edward's Ferry, carrying his disabled machine; he had encountered a festive mule on the ride up the tow path of the canal and the result was an uninjured man and mule but a badly broken 'cycle which compelled the rider to return on Monday morning's train. An additional Sunday evening member arrived on the train, and the twelve spent the night in town. They left Washington Sunday morning at 7 o'clock, and the nine who had ridden the whole route were pretty well jaded when they reached here and described their ride over the road from Edward's Ferry, in the intense heat, as very severe work. When they left early Monday morning, however, they were moving gaily enough and seemed entirely fit for the 40 miles that lay before them.

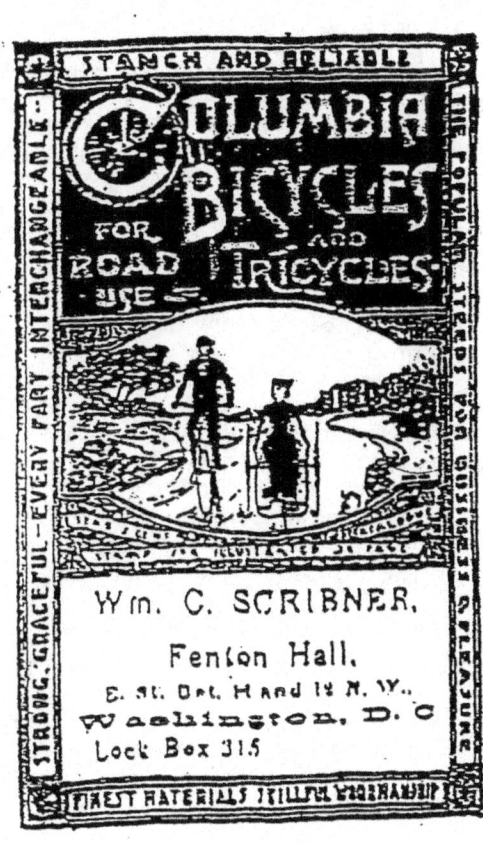

PRESIDENT CLEVELAND.—MISS FOLSOM.

Hear the mellow wedding bells, Golden Bells.

6/10/86 Mirror

THE INVITATIONS.

The following is said to be the form of invitation sent by the President to the members of his cabinet

Executive Mansion, May 29, 1886.

My Dear Mr. ———— : I am to be married on Wednesday evening at seven o'clock at the White House to Miss Folsom. It will be a very quiet affair, and I will be extremely gratified at your attendance on the occasion

Y'rs. sincerely,   GROVER CLEVELAND.

To the members who are married the invitation includes their wives. Three of the members of the cabinet are widowers— Messrs. Bayard, Lamar and Garland.

Miss Van Vechten, who is the particularly intimate friend of Miss Cleveland, and who, rumor says, was preferred by the latter for the spouse of the President, is not among those mentioned as likely to be present. As she has been a frequent visitor at the White House, there is some comment over this, although it has probably no significance.

SCENE OF THE WEDDING

It is said that the ceremony will take place in the Blue Room, which in some respects is the handsomest of the suite of rooms leading from the East Room. It was in the Blue Room, only a few weeks after President Cleveland's inauguration, that, at one of the first Saturday afternoon receptions of Miss Cleveland, Miss Folsom stood with her and assisted in receiving the guests. She was then making her first visit to the Executive Mansion. The whole scene was new to her and she, like a frank, young girl, made no disguise of the interest which it created in her. She was really more interested in watching the long line of new faces, as it swept by in its waving course.

WASHINGTON, D. C., June 7, 1886

The much-talked of marriage of the President and Miss Folsom of Buffalo, is now a thing of the past. The ceremony took place at the White House, Wednesday evening, and was performed by the Rev. Dr. Sunderland of this city. It was in every respect a quiet, unostentatious affair. The guests numbered only thirty five but the curious assembly in the White House grounds, was estimated at three thousand. Upon reaching the station a special car carried the bride and groom to Deer Park, which is a delightful resort, located far up upon the crest of the Alleghanies.

In order to avoid any possible interruption during the honeymoon, twelve detectives have been stationed about the cottage.

During the week, Col. Lamont received nearly five hundred messages of congratulation. One of the first to arrive was a cablegram from Queen Victoria.

7/17/86 Washingtonian

Interesting Facts of the War.

During the civil war President Lincoln never faltered nor became discouraged but once. That was just after the second battle of Cold Harbor, June 3, 1864. The Union army was terribly beaten. In less than half an hour of fighting on that awful morning there were more killed and wounded on the Union side than was lost at Gettysburg, and for the first and only time in its history was the army of the Potomac so crushed that it would not obey orders to renew the fight. In one month's campaign Grant had lost a greater number of men than Lee had commanded.

At a Cabinet meeting soon after the battle of Cold Harbor, President Lincoln is said to have used nearly the following words: "This thing has been going on about long enough. Grant the man I had the most confidence in, is whipped; our money is badly depreciated, and I think it is about time to stop."

With the exception of Mr. Stanton every member of the Cabinet was in favor of recognizing the confederate states. Mr. Stanton at once protested, urged the non-consideration of the subject secured the postponement of any action, and it went over until Sherman's victory at Atlanta lifted the gloom and restored hope and confidence. Had not Jeff Davis removed that Confederate General, Joe. E. Johnston, during the summer of 1864, it is probable that the rebellion would have been successful if Stanton had been removed by death or otherwise.

I am aware that this is a startling statement, and will awaken incredulity in the minds of many. I gained my knowledge while assisting my deceased brother, John P. Polk who was for thirty years a clerk in the diplomatic bureau of the State Department, and Mr. William H. Seward was responsible for what I have stated of the Cabinet meeting.

My brother and myself supposed that we were the only persons, outside of the Cabinet, who had any idea of the Cabinet meeting until "Swinton's Army of the Potomac" was published. To our surprise, however, the secret had got out, and Swinton gives it nearly as I do except he does not tell that it was Stanton, who, in that gloomy period, prevented the recognition of the southern confederacy and saved the Union. Greeley, in his "History of the Rebellion," also refers to this Cabinet meeting, but does not give the just credit to Stanton.
C. G. POLK, M.D.
2219 Catharine street.

(Is it possible that this man, at this point in time, by himself, was responsible for the preservation of our Union.)

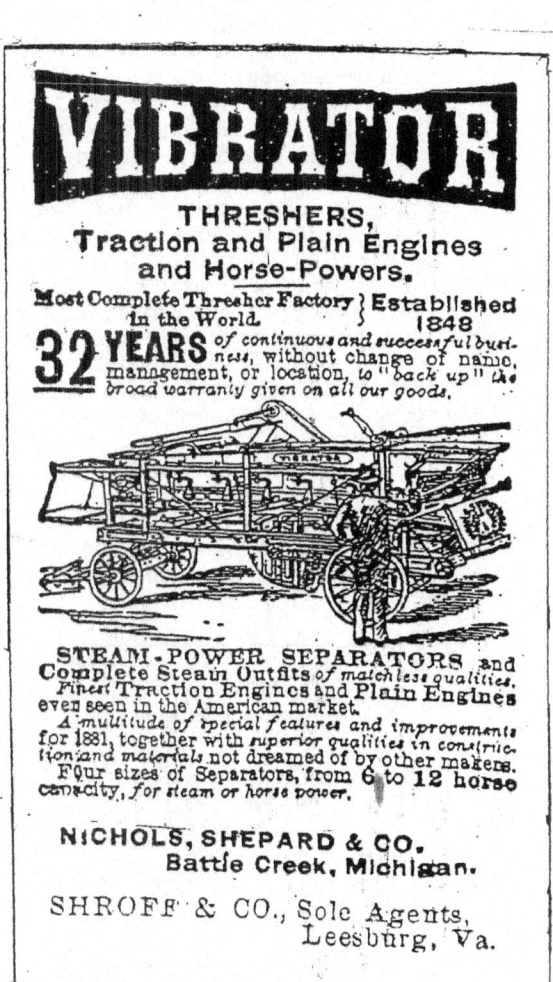

August, 1886

8/13/86 Telephone

August Court, Loudoun's oldest and most noted institution, was attended by quite a large crowd last Monday; but judging by the sighs and witched remarks of more aged citizens, it was "no circumstance" to the crowds that used to attend in "ye good old times". But this fact is gratifying to those who think it is not very profitable for the men of Loudoun to loaf around the streets of Leesburg all day, eating melons, ejecting tobacco juice, injecting bad whiskey and talking amateur politics. Verily the world progresses.

Of course there was a general celebration at the bar rooms, of the recent "wet" victories in Leesburg and Mercer districts, which, as a natural consequece, resulted in considerable drunkenness and disorder, several citizens, both white and colored being sent to jail. It was a disgusting sight to the law-abiding, sober people to see one set of Leesburgers licensed to make men drunk and another set duly authorized to run them in. To draw it mild, this drink business is a disgrace to our enlightened people and a festering sore in the body politic of our County.

The climax of the day's doings was reached when a Mr. Edwards and a Mr. Lowe indulged in a fight, which was an ugly and dangerous affair. We did not see the fight but it is reported that Edwards knocked Lowe down and pounded him considerable and cut him badly with a knife. It seems that the assailant was allowed to depart in peace, though two of his kinsmen were arrested and fined. This is a joke on the police of Leesburg.

8/20/86 Telephone

Thomas Edison is still busy. Although a millionaire, with a beautiful wife and an eighty thousand-dollar house, he goes to his laboratory with a lunch basket, because he hasn't time to go back home to dinner.

Annual Statement

OF THE

EXPENDITURES AND RECEIPTS

OF THE

County of Loudoun,

FOR YEAR 1885-6.

THE following is a full exhibit of the Receipts and Expenditures of the County of Loudoun, for the year ending July 1886:

Judge County Court Salary	$560.00
Commonwealth Attorney	600.00
Clerk County Court	500.00
Clerk Circuit Court	180.00
Sheriff	309.00
Superintendent Poor's salary, and to meet arrearages and future expenses	820.00
Members of Board of Supervisors	153.56
Physician at Poor House	125.00
Comm'r Revenue, assessing taxes	420.00
Stationery for Circuit and Co. Courts	100.00
Books and fuel for Clerk's Office	100.00
Fuel for Jail, cleaning Court-House	313.75
Attorney to Board	10.00
Sheriff attending Board	12.00
Clerk of Board	30.00
Overseers Poor salary	120.00
Commissioners and Clerks of Election	160.90
Repairs to Jail and Court House	61.95
Books & Stationery Treasurer's office	50.00
Physicians and medicine for Poor	430.60
Printing	87.97
Surveyors and Comm'rs laying new road	37.75
Defending criminals	35.00
Coroner and constable (inquest)	4.50
Registration	95.00
Burying Paupers	310.00
Reward for Foxes	716.00
Appropriation to meet arrearages and future expenses of foxes and hawks	350.00
Room rent and Justices' court and elections	100.50
Expenses cleaning Court House yard	40.00
Examining Lunatics	30.00
New cases in Clerk's Office	69.25
Dr Taylor and Ransom in Reed prosecution	200.00
Stove Clerk's Office	23.00
Jurors for 1886-7	440.00
Leesburg District Poor	725.00
Mt. Gilead " "	632.00
Mercer " "	500.00
Lovettsville " "	350.00
Broad Run " "	200.09
Jefferson " "	550.00
Small claims	8.30
	$10,051.13

8/26/86 Mirror

TERRIFIC TORTURE.

I had some fun this morning. Some time ago, on discovering that I had a bad tooth that sooner or later would make trouble, I went to a dentist and had it filled. The dentist was honest enough to tell me that the tooth wasn't worth filling as it was too far gone; but I knew better, so he filled it with cheap material, and I departed happy. But the other day at dinner I tackled a plum pie, and in the sad attempt to bite a stone in two, all that was visible of my bad tooth broke off short—never to crack stones again. Since then the root of the minus tooth has kept up a steady growling, until last night, just after midnight hours, it ceased to growl and commenced to rave and jump in the maddest kind of a way. It riled me so that I jumped out of a bed, and for nearly an hour I walked the floor clad only in my innocence and a twenty cent cotton undershirt. Then my better half came to my relief, and with the aid of camphor, clove oil and nearly a pint of brandy succeeded in quieting my tooth to some extent. Still it kept up a steady rumbling until daylight, so that I got cheated out of my sleep. I had an idea that on reaching my office I could throw myself so completely in my work as to forget the kickings of my tooth; but, alas for me, I had no sooner commenced my work than my tooth opened battle on me in its terrific madness. I said "dang it," slammed my desk shut and rushed off to the dentist. I found him. Did you ever know a dentist to be out of his office when you wanted a tooth pulled? Never! The boss dentist of the concern was absent, but he had a fellow in his place who kindly informed me that he was well up to the business. I said: "Go ahead!" He did. He first invited me to sit in a real nice cushioned chair. He next asked me if I'd be kind enough to open my countenance. Then with one hand he held on to my nose, while with his other hand he held some sort of a do-funny instrument, which he used in fishing for the whereabout's of the bad root inside my mouth. At last he got his eye on the root, and then he got another kind of an instrument. I said: "Will it hurt me?" "Oh, no," he said, and I was glad I had come, as he appeared to awfully clever. But, good-bye to all his cleverness. I never met such a honey tongued, cold-blooded murderer in my life, and heaven knows I never want to meet the likes of him again. Why, that cuss took that instrument, and in trying to get a hold on the root jammed it into my gums with all his might. I didn't holler, I couldn't; but the torture I underwent completely out-pictured any description of hades I've seen yet. And then to think, that after he had succeeded in getting a hold on the root, he should miss fire—'Twas too much. After I had come to he said: "It kind of hurt some." "A little," I said. I meant it as red-hot irony, but the cuss failed to recognize it as such.— Then another big, chunky chap came in from the back room and remarked that I had some pluck. I wanted to kick him, but I felt too weak for the business, so I simply smiled. Once more the murderer went for me. It was a war of physical force. I never knew what strength there was in a jawbone before. I am able to comprehend now how Samson got in his work on the Philistines with the jaw-bone of an ass. There was nothing small about my murderer. He put his whole strength, his very life, into the business. My murderer took a short rest. Poor fellow, I pitied him, he was so tired. As for me, I rested too. I couldn't well do any thing else, as I was too near played out to think of even raising my head from the cushioned back where first it was placed. By and by my murderer again proceeded to business. I saw by his eye, that was red with fire, that there was victory in the air for him. He placed a sort of base by the side of my chair, then he stepped on it and looked at me with a sort of utter contempt and air that as much as said: "I've played with you long enough, but I mean business now." I have only a faint recollection of the last tussle. I remember seeing the murderer swoop down on me like a hawk goes for a spring chicken; next I felt the hot iron digging into the flesh of my jaw, then as the torture forced me to raise myself up, I felt the heavy weight of the chunky chap as he bounced himself into my lap and grasped my hands in his iron grip. This is all I recollect of the affair. When it was all over and I had regained my senses, the murderer remarked that he had never met with such a trying case during his long years of active experience, and that I stood it bravely, and then he smiled on me. But I was too far gone to smile back, and after telling him I'd see him again when I had some loose change about my person, I managed to stagger out of the room, through the street, to my office. When I get the next tooth pulled I won't know it.

DR. L. A. BROWN,

DENTIST,

OFFERS his professional services to the public. Eight years practical experience.

WASHINGTON REFERENCES.

Bishop E. O. ANDREWS, Cor 18th and H. Sts., N. W.
G WYTHE COOK, M. D., No. 3 Thomas Circle, N. W.
JOHN WINTER, M. D., 1523, 9th St., N. W.
Dr JAS B. HODGKIN Cor. Vermont Ave and 15th St
S B MUNCASTER, M.D. D.D.S., 1405 N Y Ave N W

☞ PURE GAS ADMINISTERED.

OFFICE.—Rooms formerly occupied by Dr. H. G. WEST, opposite EDWARDS & Son's Drug Store. [Aug 5, 1885-1y]

September, 1886

8/27/86 Telephone

Misfortune To a Native of Loudoun.

A private letter to the editor of the TELEPHONE from Winfield, Iowa, makes the sad announcement that Charles Fox, a former resident of this vicinity, has recently become deranged and has to be closely watched. It seems that he has become melancholy on account of his spiritual welfare. He declares that he is lost, and deplores the fact that he has not given more attention to this matter. Mr. Manly Fox, his nephew, who recently left here, is with him. A few days ago Manly and another man were watering some stock at a well, and while their attention was turned elsewhere "Charlie" suddenly vanished from sight. They looked down the well and found him standing about 30 feet from the surface with the water up to his neck. He dropped his head under the water several times but failed to keep it there, and soon called to the men at the top to help him out. They dropped him a rope and pulled him to the surface. He had slipped off most of his clothing before leaping into the well.

Charlie Fox will be remembered by many of our older people in this vicinity, where, for years, he conducted the farm for "Aunt Sallie" Brown—the place now owned by W. F. Mercier, near Hamilton Depot. The writer knew him well in the West, where he has always been much esteemed by his neighbors. He never had any family, hence it is fortunate that Manly went to him when he did.

PIANO TUNING.

AFTER an absence of 10 years from the county it gives me great pleasure to state that I have been very kindly received by my old customers and the public generally, and in consequence have determined to continue as formerly my yearly visits to LEESBURG to TUNE and REGULATE the PIANOS of this and the adjoining counties.

☞ All orders left at this office will receive prompt attention.

Very Respectfully,
J. F. LUCAS,
Washington, D. C.

9/30/86 Mirror

The Toughs and President Arthur.

The toughs of the town have small respect for eminent men. While Gen. Arthur was president, he came on to New York and registered at the polling place nearest his residence. It was a small cigar store near Twenty-eighth st. on Third avenue, a neighborhood of average respectability. I chanced to pass it election day on my way to the elevated road, when I saw the tall and imposing figure of Gen. Arthur swing around the corner, and I stopped to see a president of the United States cast his ballot. He was alone, clad in the most fashionable attire, erect, composed, dignified and handsome. There was a group of half-grown boys, hulking roughs and slatternly women around the door, and as the president walked through them one or two of the small boys gave a feeble cheer, and half a dozen of the men raised their hats. The president lifted his hat courteously and stepped into the little shop. Here he answered the usual questions about his name, nativity, residence and so on in a deep-toned voice, bowed to the clerks and inspectors and began to make his way out.

"It seems ter me," a flabby looking woman with a babe at her breast remarked shrilly as the president brushed by her, "as ow 'is legs is givin' somewhat ter bowin' Jemimer."

"Yis mam, perhaps they does; but his whiskers," said the woman addressed with an expression of engaging candor, "his whiskers is what I calls puffectly elegint."

Upon this, one of the half-grown boys said confidentially to the president:

"Say, Chet, yuv got er mash! Y'ave, fur a dead cold fac'. She's stuck on dem sideboards. Give 'er one fur a philoppener, won't yer?"

There was a roar of laughter, which did not subside until the chief magistrate disappeared around the corner.—His demeanor was as composed, sedate and polite under it all as though surrounded by his own family.—N. Y. Cor. Chicago Times.

September, 1886

The Loudoun Telephone.

HAMILTON, LOUDOUN COUNTY,   FRIDAY, SEP. 24, 1886.

A LIVELY RACKET.

GAMBLERS GOT TO GO.

"Dick" Vandevanter Cleans out the Fair Grounds and Makes Rome Howl.

Last Thursday Justice D. H. Vandevanter created considerable excitement on the Leesburg Fair Grounds by setting the heel of the law upon the gambling establishments which were plying their infamous vocations there. We understand that Mr. V. had given the officers of the Association warning that if they allowed gambling upon the grounds he would see that it was routed. Therefore, on Thursday he appeared upon the grounds and found various gambling devices doing an open and unrestricted business. He therefore applied to Justice Hempstone for a warrant for the arrest of the offending parties but that officer refused to issue the paper. Then seeing Justice Milton, of Hamilton, on the grounds, he applied to him and received the desired document. In the meantime the offending parties "got wind" of what was going on, and, believing it would be more healthy elsewhere, suddenly sloped. However, the paraphrenalia was left behind and Justice V. proceeded at once to dispose of the same according to law. He procured a wagon and loaded all the plunder into it and hauled the same outside of the Fair Grounds, where he made a fire and burned the whole business.

Death of "Aunt" Maria Streams.

Last Friday night "Aunt" Maria Streams, a very worthy colored woman, living at the residence of I C. Hoge, died very suddenly, of some unknown cause, supposed to be Apoplexy. About eleven o'clock a colored man came home and on his way up to his room noticed a light in "Aunt" Maria's room, which being unusual at that hour, he thought something might be wrong, so he called to the colored woman, but got no response. He then tried the door, which refused to open, being obstructed, as was afterward discovered by the prostrate form of the woman. He then called Mr. Hoge, and together they pushed the door back and gained an entrance, when they found the woman lying dead upon the the floor, having been there probably an hour. She had been unusually active that day, gathering winter supplies from the garden &c., and she had taken a lot of beans to her room and was hulling them, and she had just reached over and secured a handful of the beans, when she fell forward and died, still holding the beans in her hand.

Her Last Long Sleep.

By a communication to the TELEPHONE which was unaccompanied by the writer's name, and an item in the city papers, we learn that Cora D. Fry, daughter of Peter W. and Mary E. Fry, died at the home of her father, near Bethel, last Friday, aged nearly 15 years. She is the same person who was recently mentioned in the TELEPHONE as experiencing a remarkably long sleep. Her first sleep lasted sixty-six hours. After she awakened, it seems that she plead with her friends to keep her from going to sleep again, but unable to counteract her drowsyness she again slept and so continued for nine days, when the vital spark of life fled, and her long sleep ended in death. The newspaper reports say the doctors prnounce it a case of starvation while asleep, but the communication referred to pronounces it a case of conjestion of the brain. It also says that she opened her eyes a few moments to close them in death.

THE "SPEEDY" CORN SHELLER!

A NEW COMPACT and EFFECTIVE SHELLER. Strongly constructed of metal, easily attached to the grain receptacle, be it barrel, box or tub. Shelling corn green or dry, ears that are long or crooked. Takes less power than any other machine, shells a bushel of ears in five minutes, takes little room to use or store it. It is cheap and effective.

☞ GET ONE AND BE HAPPY.
"CLINE'S HARDWARE HALL."

11/20/86 Telephone

DEATH OF EX-PRESIDENT ARTHUR.

He Has a Stroke of Apoplexy Tuesday Night and Never Regains Consciousness.

NEW YORK, Nov. 18.—Ex-President Chester A. Arthur died at 5 o'clock this morning at his residence, No. 123 Lexington avenue. He had been ailing for some time from a complication of diseases, principally kidney affection. He had spent the summer at a watering place and it was supposed that this had strengthened somewhat his enfeebled constitution. His death was unexpected, it not being supposed outside of his house he was in any immediate danger.

APOPLEXY THE IMMEDIATE CAUSE OF DEATH.

As soon as the news of Mr. Arthur's death was made public many flags on public and private buildings were placed at half mast. Mr. Arthur had lived at No. 123 Lexington Avenue for twenty years or more. A stroke of cerebral apoplexy sudden, but not wholly unexpected by the attending physicians, terminated his life. The stroke came in his sleep, between Tuesday night and Wednesday morning, and he did not rally thereafter. His death was painless, like the slow going out of a burned-down candle, and for hours before the end came he was unconscious to his surroundings. His son and daughter, his sister, his former law partner, Sherman W. Knevals, and his closest friend, Surrogate Rollins, were at his bedside.

(It seems strange, the rather meager mention of former President Arther's death, even by the Republican TELEPHONE. By most accounts, he did a rather decent job as Chief Executive.)

THE LOUDERBACK
COMBINATION TOOL.
Each Part a Practical Working Instrument.

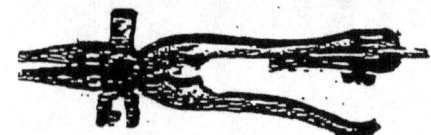

Comprising Ten Useful Tools, as follows:
A. Adjustable Screw Driver. F. Hammer.
B. Hand Vise. G. Leather Punch.
C. Wrench. H. Wire Cutter.
D. Nail Puller. I. Small Gas Plyers.
E. Large Gas Plyers. J. Pincers.
PRICE $1.50.

11/18/86 Mirror

DR. WOODROW FOUND GUILTY. The Georgia Presbyterian synod, at Speria, last Friday night sustained the decision of the presbytery finding Dr. Woodrow guilty of heresy in his evolution belief and trusts. Dr. Woodrow on Saturday gave notice of an appeal to the next general assembly against the synod's decision.

John Jacob Astor is now the richest man in America, counting up some $150,000,000. Jay Gould is worth $100,000,000, and William Astor, Cornelius Vanderbilt, Russell Sage and John Mackay in the neighborhood of $60,000,000 each.

CAPT. COCKEY had the fire-company out a few days ago for a test of their engine, and it was not until three or four efforts had been made, consuming 20 or 30 minutes time, that it could be gotten to work properly. Such a delay at a fire would be irremediable and only shows the wisdom of Capt. C. in making the trial of the machine, for, as the saying is a "stitch in time, &c." At this season of the year, when the danger of fires is greater than at any other, nothing is more desirable than that the machinery and appliances for combating them be in the most perfect order.

Sullivan and Ryan the ancient pugilistic rivals, met in San Francisco for a three round mill on Saturday night. Sullivan completely knocked out his opponent and was awarded the fight. It really looks as though the Boston man was without an equal in the fistic art on the globe.

THE first Confederate monument at Gettysburg is to be dedicated next Friday, upon which occasion a large number of ex-confeds, especially, are expected to be present.— In view of this and for the accommodation of those wishing to be present, arrangements have been made for the sale of round trip tickets from Washington to Gettysburg and return, for $3.

November, 1886

11/19/86 Telephone

Homes and Employment Wanted For Boys.

The Children's Aid Society, of New York, has been engaged for over 30 years in finding homes for homeless children. The Society gathers into its Industrial Schools and Lodging House children who have never been committed for crime and seeks good homes for them, and at regular intervals sends them in charge of an agent into communities desiring them. The Society proposes to send a company of homeless lads, from 14 to 16 years of age, to Hamilton Va., for the purpose of finding them homes and employment. They will arrive at Hamilton on Wednesday, Nov. 24th, at 11:30 A. M. Farmers and others desiring to take one or more of these boys are requested to make application at once to the following gentlemen, who have kindly consented to act as a committee:

JOHN MILTON, } Com.
H. R. HOLMES. }

TERMS:—The boys will expect to work for about one year for their board and clothes; after that they are at liberty to make their own arrangements. If a removal becomes necessary, it can be done either through the Committee or by writing to

A. SCHLEGEL, Agent,
Box G., Station D.,
New York

11-12-2t.

11/26/86 Telephone

Last Wednesday, in response to an advertisement in the TELEPHONE, twenty or twenty-five gentlemen from the surrounding country congregated at Hamilton Depot to meet the company of boys to arrive from the Childrens Aid Society, of New York. Nobody realized before that there was such a demand for boys in this community. Farmers, millers, blacksmiths and others were on the hunt for help. Finally the train rolled up to the station and an agent of the Aid Society stepped off, accompanied by *two* boys. The waiting crowd looked for the others to come, but when it was evident that all were out, the situation was so ludicrous that the crowd laughed in concert. The boys were taken into the Depot where the Agent addressed the crowd, explaining the reason for the small number of boys accompanying him, he said the scarcity of applicants and the proximity to Thanksgiving Day were the causes: but assured them that after the Holidays they would continue to send more boys until all were supplied.

After a conference with the local committee—Messrs Milton and Holmes—and various applicants, the two boys were confided to the care of Dr. Chancellor, of Silcott Springs, and Mr. Albert Vandevanter, near Hamilton.

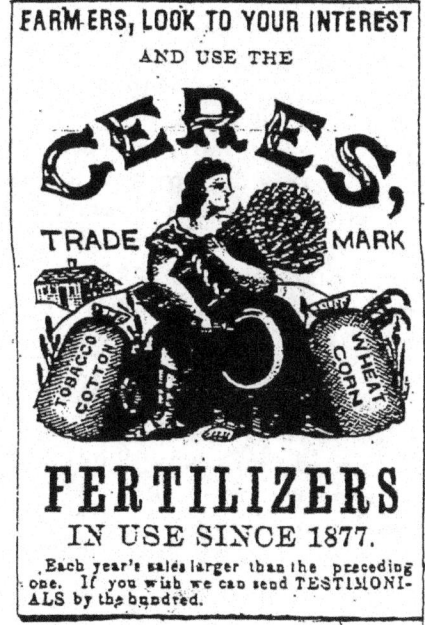

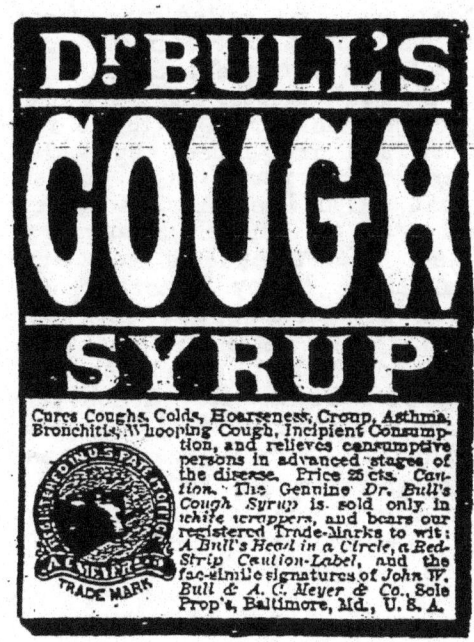

December, 1886.

11/26/86 Telephone

Col. John S. Mosby.

Col. John S. Mosby is a slight, bent, blonde man, with a cold gray eye containing no more expression than a boy's marble. He talks slowly, never gets excited, and does not know what fear is.— He loves his friends and hates his enemies, and he carries his fight to the death. I heard a story from a captain in the Union army of a scene in which Mosby took part during the war. A union force had driven him and a small body of his men into a ten-acre field about which was a high fence. They could see him plainly within it, and they surrounded the field and began to close in upon Mosby. They wanted to capture him, as he had already killed nearly half their regiment. They closed in upon him slowly, his handful of troops still firing. They had backed him up close to a fence, and they apparently had him in their grasp, when he drove his spurs into his horse and went over the fence like a flash, and as he did so, turned in the air upon his saddle and shot a soldier through the head with his revolver. There are few such shots as Mosby, and during the war he shot to kill.

At the close of the war Horace Greeley wanted Mosby hung. He denounced him as a guerrilla and murderer, and published article after article calling upon the President to hang him. Mosby fled to the mountains and he told me he intended to fight to the last. Gen. Grant was in Washington at the time. Mrs. Mosby came here with a sucking baby on one arm and these papers of Horace Greeley under the other. She called upon Grant and laid the papers before him. Grant told her to go to her husband and to tell him that he would protect him if he would surrender, that he should go to the nearest station and give himself up and he would protect his parole as much as he would that of Gen. Lee. Mrs. Mosby carried this news to John S. Mosby in the mountains. He surrendered and Grant protected him. Mosby never forgot it, and when the campaign of 1872 came around, in which Greeley was pitted against Grant, Mosby stumped the State of Virginia for Grant. He carried Greeley's papers around and told the people how Grant had treated him. The result was he carried Virginia for the Republicans, the first time in its history.

12/16/86 Telephone

McCLELLAN's BOOK.

The late Gen. Geo. B McClellan's story of his connection with the civil war is soon to be placed before the public.

Considerable space is taken up in detailing his entrance into the struggle from civil life, his campaign in Western Virginia, and his labors in organizing the Army of Northern Virginia. He pays warm tributes to the gallantry and capacity of Gens. Hancock, Sedgwick, Reynolds, Meade, Fitz John Porter and others. The following extracts in regard to his troubles with party leaders and his arraignment of Secretary Stanton will be read with interest:

"I have already stated in a general way what occurred between myself and some of the radical leaders shortly after I reached Washington. They then saw clearly that it would not be possible to make a party tool of me, and soon concluded that it was their policy to ruin the ——— ——— ——— ——— object ——— ——— ——— ——— restoration of the Union, but the permanent ascendancy of their party, and to this they were ready to sacrifice the Union, if necessary. They committed a grave error in supposing me to be politically ambitious, and in thinking that I looked forward to military success as a means of reaching the presidential chair. At the same time they knew that if I achieved marked success my influence would necessarily be very great throughout the country—an influence which I should certainly have used for the good of the whole country, and not for that of any party at the nation's expense. They therefore determined to ruin me in any event and by any means: first by endeavoring to force me into premature movements, knowing that a failure would probably end my military career; afterwards by withholding the means necessary to achieve success. That they were not honest is proved by the fact that having failed to force me to advance at a time when an advance would have been madness, they withheld the means of success when I was in contact with the enemy, and finally relieved me from command when the game was in my hands. Taking both

December 1886

East and West, and counting the losses alas by disease, I do not doubt that more than 500,000 men were sacrificed unnecessarily for the sake of insuring the success of a political party.

"I do not base my assertions as to the motives of the radical leaders upon mere surmises, but upon facts that have frequently come to my knowledge during the war and since. For instance, Major Charles Davies, once professor of mathematics at West Point, told me, and at a different time told General Joseph E. Johnston, the following story: During the very early part of the Peninsular campaign he was one of a commission sent from New York to urge more vigorous action in supporting me. They called upon the President, and found Mr. Stanton with him. In reply to their statements of the purpose of their visit Mr. Stanton stated that the great end and aim of the war was to abolish slavery. To end the war before the nation was ready for that would be a failure. The war must be prolonged and conducted so as to achieve that; that the people of the North were not yet ready to accept the view.

"From the light that has since been thrown on Stanton's character, I am satisfied that from an early date he was in the treasonable conspiracy, and that his course in ingratiating himself with me, and pretending to be my friend before he was in office, was only a part of his long system of treachery. I had never seen Mr. Stanton, and probably had not even heard of him before reaching Washington in 1861. Not many weeks after arriving I was introduced to him as a safe adviser on legal points. From that moment he did his best to ingratiate himself with me, and professed the warmest friendship and devotion. I had no reason to suspect his sincerity, and therefore believed him to be what he professed. The most disagreeable thing about him was the extreme virulence with which he abused the President, the administration and the republican party. He carried this to such an extent that I was often shocked by it. He never spoke of the President in any way than as the 'Original Gorilla,' and often said that Du Chaillu was a fool to wander all the way to Africa in search of what he could so easily have found at Springfield, Ill.— Nothing could be more bitter than his words and manner always were when speaking of the administration and the republican party. He never gave them credit for honesty or patriotism and very seldom for any ability.

"At some time during the autumn of 1861 Secretary Cameron made quite an abolition speech to some of the newly arrived regiments. Next day Stanton urged me to arrest him for inciting to insubordination. He often advocated the propriety of my seizing the government and taking the affairs into my own hands.

"As he always expressed himself in favor of putting down the rebellion at any cost, I always regarded these extreme views as the ebullitions of an intense and patriotic nature, and sometimes wasted more or less time in endeavoring to bring him to more moderate views, never dreaming that all the while this man was in close communication with the very men whom he so violently abused. His purpose was to endeavor to climb upon my shoulders and then throw me down."

Mr. Stanton's action at the time of his appointment is thus described: "Before I had finished my toilet Mr. Stanton's card came up, and as soon as possible I went down to see him. He told me that he had been appointed Secretary of War and that his name had been sent to the Senate for confirmation, and that he had called to confer with me as to his acceptance. He said that acceptance would involve very great personal sacrifices on his part. If I wished him to accept he would do so, but only on my account; that he had come to know my wishes and determine accordingly. I told him that I hoped he would accept the position. Before he was in office he constantly ran after me and professed the most ardent friendship; as soon as he became Secretary of War his whole manner changed, and I could no longer find the opportunity to transact even the ordinary current business of the office with him. It is now very clear to me that, far from being, as he had alway represented himself to me, in direct and violent opposition to the radicals, he was really in secret alliance with them, and that he and they were alike unwilling that I should be successful. No other theory can possibly account for his or their course, and on that theory everything becomes clear and easily explained."

After the seven days' fight McClellan wrote to Stanton: "In addition to what I have already said, I only wish to say to the President that I think he is wrong in regarding me as ungenerous when I said that my force was too weak. I merely intimated a truth which to day has been too plainly proved. If, at this instant I could dispose of ten thousand fresh men I could gain the victory to morrow. I know that a few thousand more men would have changed this battle from a defeat to a victory. As it is, the government must not and cannot hold me responsible for the result. I feel too earnestly to-night. I have seen too many dead and wounded comrades to feel otherwise than that the government has not sustained this army.— If you do not do so now the game is lost. If I save this army now I tell you plainly that I owe no thanks to you or to any other person in Washington. You have done your best to sacrifice this army"

Of "Old Brains" Halleck, McClellan says:

Of all men whom I have encountered in high position Halleck was the most hopelessly stupid. It was more difficult to get an idea through his head than can be conceived by any one who never made the attempt. I do not think he ever had a correct military idea from beginning to end.

When he arrived at Washington, he says a panic prevailed, the capture of the city was deemed inevitable, and "there was a war steamer anchored off the White House, with steam up, ready to take off the President, Cabinet, etc., at a moment's notice

He was now put in command of the fortifications of the Capital, and that seemed to limit his authority, for he was told that the commander of the army had not been chosen; but hearing that Lee was marching into Maryland, he says:

"I determined to solve the question for myself, and when I moved out from Washington with my staff and personal escort I left my card with P. P. C. written upon it, at the White House, War Office and Secretary Seward's house, and went on my way. I was afterward accused of assuming command without authority, for nefarious purposes, and, in fact, fought the battles of South Mountain and Antietam with a halter around my neck; for if the Army of the Potomac had been defeated and I had survived I would, no doubt, have been tried for assuming authority without orders, and in the state of feeling which so unjustly condemned the innocent and most meritorious Gen. F. J. Porter I would probably have been condemned to death. I was fully aware of the risk I ran, but the path of duty was clear and I tried to follow it."

McClellan virtually charges Pope with cowardice, and speaks of Burnside with ill-disguised contempt. This paragraph hints at some of the sinister influences by which he was surrounded:

"Stanton came to caution me against trusting Halleck, who was, he said, probably the greatest scoundrel and most barefaced villian in America; he said that he was totally destitute of principle, and that in the Almaden Quicksilver case he had convicted Halleck of perjury in open court. When Halleck arrived he came to caution me against Stanton, repeating almost precisely the same words that Stanton had employed"

A popular pundit of today has regarded him as our worst General.

12/30/86 Mirror

NEW STATES.—It is understood in Washington that Representative Springer intends to do all he can to pass this session, his bill to enable Dakota, Montana, New Mexico and Washington Territories to enter the union of states, and he thinks he may succeed The STAR says: It is not proposed to admit them at once, but enable them to elect delegates next fall to draft constitutions to be submitted to the people at the time of the presidential election, and let them all into the Union the year following. He thinks the idea of admitting all at once will prevent opposition on party grounds, as they will be equally divided as to politics, and the fact of their not having any voice in the presidential election of '88 will silence some opposition also.

December, 1886

11/26/86 Telephone

Our roads are everywhere made worse than they should be by the existence of myriads of miserable, back breaking, vehicle-smashing, horse-jerking breaks; and it is surely enough to tolerate them on the hills; but a break occured in a mudhole, half a mile south of town, a few days ago. As Dr. Stone was passing through that miserable little run near Mr. Gabrael Warner's, he broke a spring of his buggy—a spring that had stood the wear of the roughest roads, for years—but broke in a contemptible little mudhole which, in the light of human reason and economy has no excuse for existence. There is never any high water at this place hence a small and inexpensive culvert would suffice to abolish a nuisance and leave that beautiful stretch of road unbroken, so that a team could glide gracefully along without losing time and energy to say nothing of the damage to vehicles.

12/10/86 Telephone

PURCELLVILLE VA, Dec. 8th.—
Dear Telephone: Your last issue contained a notice of a funeral cartege passing through Hamilton, and told your readers of the sad bereavement of Mr. Daniel Ayres and wife, of Purcellville, in the loss of their two babes.

If you will kindly allow me—who had the mournful privilege of being present, many times, during their illness—I would like to supplement your notice with the mention of a little incident that occured in the presence of three or four persons. Gracie Martina, the elder, and familiarly known as Tina, a bright and beautiful child of about three and one fourth years, had been complaining for some three weeks, but was not seriously ill, till about ten days preceding her death, when she was seized with a violent attack of Croup, which yielded to no remedies. On Saturday preceding Tina's death, her baby sister, Laura, aged about one and one fourth years, was stricken with the same remorseless disease, and died on Monday evening. Still Tina lingered; her fond parents and anxious friends "hoping against hope," for her recovery until Wednesday morning, when it was evident the angels were come to bear her hence. She called a lady present to her side and whispered, "Tell Mattie (an older sister) to tell Laura to wait for me. I am going too." Upon being asked where she was going, she answered, "I am going to Jesus." In a little while she stretched out her hands, and looking intently, said: "Laura is there;" and with a smile, unspeakably sweet, illuminating her face, her spirit joined her sister.

Who can say that Laura was not waiting, and that Tina did not see her?   Yours Sincerely,
                                    N.

Thomas & Whitmore

WOOD PUMPS!

Something New.

PORCELAIN LINED CYLENDER, with Rubber Plunger or Sucker, Iron Spout, Iron Brackets for handle Bolted on. This is the most durable Pump in use, cannot get out of order as the Cucumber Pumps did. They are 6 inches square, Suction Pipe 4 inches. Steam tested 80 lbs. pressure to the foot, good for Wells from 5 feet to 100 feet. All Pumps Warranted delivered and put up.

FOR REFERENCES:

At Leesburg, F. W. Shaffer, John V. Tavenner, J. R. Rhodes, W. Clements, L. W. S. Hough, H. C. Gist, C. Hempston, James Reamer, W. N. Wise, W. P. Smith.
At Lincoln: L. Nichols, E. Fenton, J. W. Jewett.
At Snickersville: R. M. Johnson.
Round Hill Depot: H. Heaton.
At Lovettsville: W. T. Crusen.
Hamilton, W. Vanderventer.
Wheatland: Mr. Jenkins.
Waterford: F. Schooley, J. Adams.
Gortsville: Wm Clowe, James Kidwell.
Woodburn: T. Titus, J. Lack.
Oatlands: G. F. Smallwood, J. L. Rawling.
Mountsville: J. Weadon, Dr. Mount.
Middleburg: S. F. Carter.
Arcola: Cud Hutchison, M. Lane.
Guilford: B. Bridges, Mr. Wills, Thomas Mikel, C. Hutchenson, P. Moran.

WATER COOLERS,

and Cream Freezers, Preserving Kettle, deep Milk Cans, at

THOMAS & WHITMORE,
Leesburg, Va.

HEADQUARTERS
— FOR —

Sleigh Goods,

ASSORTMENT LARGE.

PRICES LOW.

IRONED SWELL CUTTERS,

WITH SHAFTS, No Paint,

Substantial, Stylish, Superior.

Write for Prices.

SWELL CUTTERS, Not Ironed.

SLEIGH BASKETS,

Two and Four Passenger.

SLEIGH RUNNERS,

One to Two Inches Square.

Sleigh Bells.

Plumes, Plushes, Cloths, Carpets, Couplings, Shoes, Irons, Bolts, etc., etc.

QUOTATIONS CHEERFULLY MADE.

J. B. Kendall,

618 Pa. Ave. 619 B. St., N W.,
WASHINGTON, D. C.

nov. 4, 1886.

12/10/86 Telephone

—The young fellow who has a sleigh and a girl and did not take her out sleighing Wednesday evening has no soul in him and should be promptly mittened. The girl cant afford to trust her future to such a creature.

JOHNSON'S ANODYNE LINIMENT

THE MOST WONDERFUL FAMILY REMEDY EVER KNOWN.

FOR INTERNAL AND EXTERNAL USE.

December 1886

SANTA CLAUS

Has found the reindeer business too slow and weak for this age, and has therefore employed the

MIGHTY LOCOMOTIVE

and railroad cars to carry joy to the people. His trains are now arriving daily at Hamilton, loaded with splendid supplies for

J. W. WILEY,

Who has a big assortment of Holiday goods to select from.

ELEGANT ARTICLES IN CHINA WARE, such as vases, toilet sets &c.

BEAUTIFUL BOXES OF PAPATERIE, Xmas Cards, Picture Books, Toy Books, and larger illustrated book for presents

SPLENDID ASSORTMENT OF WAX AND CHINA DOLLS. Toys of every description.

BEAUTIFUL TOILET BOXES, in plush and leather Ladies work boxes, writing desks &c. Boys Sleds and wagons Shoo Fly Horses and Doll Baby Carriages.

GOOD LINE OF FIREWORKS.

OLD KRIS KINGLE

Has given up the retail business and now devotes his attention to selling at wholesale to

J. W. WILEY,

Who has agreed to fill every stocking in this part of the country, and for that purpose he has received an IMMENSE SUPPLY of useful, beautiful and delicious things.

Cords of Confectionery,

Of almost every description are piled up in his storeroom.

BUSHELS AND BUSHELS OF NUTS, COCOA NUTS, Cream Nuts, Almonds, Filberts, Pecans, Peanuts &c.

BAGS AND BOXES OF FRUITS, Such as dates, figs, raisins, oranges, lemons &c., &c., &c.

BARRELS AND BARRELS OF OTHER THINGS which it is not possible to enumerate

All of Which will be Sold at Low Prices.

HOLIDAY GOODS

OYSTERS, OYSTERS, OYSTERS, In any Quant

J. W. WILEY, HEADQUARTERS FOR Holiday Goods.

W. & W. R.R.

at J. W. WILEY'S

January, 1887

1/1/87 Washingtonian

COMMUNICATED

ROUND HILL, VA., Dec. 22, 1886.

EDITOR OF "WASHINGTONIAN."—Winter came in with December—and we had several cold and blustery days with a good deal of snow, enough to make the sleighing good for several days, and ice formed to a good thickness—a good deal being gathered and housed. Since then the weather has been more moderate. A good deal of farm work has been done during the month—most of our farmers are prepared for the early winter, but as usual some few had not finished their busy fall work of gathering their corn and fodder.

Stock of all kinds have gone into winter quarters in good condition. Most of our farmers are well supplied with plenty of fuel. Many farmers have built large barns to winter their stock in where they are put every night, and during the day when stormy, with plenty of good feed and good bedding, quite an improvement to what it was a few years back—when a good cow was thrown a little feed in an out place, and she to look to the cold side of an old straw rick for shelter and protection from our heavy storms and cold weather. I hear little or nothing now of the hog cholera, which disease played havoc here early in the season. Some farmers lost nearly all their hogs, and will be compelled to buy their pork.

Produce very low—chickens only bring 4 to 5 cts. per pound gross; turkeys not much better. An old saying when corn is plenty, poultry is plenty too, and of fine quality and might add low prices, for this is the way we are realizing it here.

Our Creamery is still in operation. They are not receiving as much milk as did during the summer, but price much better, paying $1 ten cent per hundred pounds for this month, for those who have fresh cows. It is paying well. It would be much better if our farmers would have their cows to be fresh in the fall instead of spring—as it takes very little more feed to keep a fresh cow through the winter than to winter a dry one properly, when the pay from a good wintered cow would be double that of the summer cow then when the winter cow goes on grass she will give nearly as much milk as when fresh.

As a rule our farmers have been very well pleased with the prices received for milk—bringing them in money every month.

FAIRMOUNT POULTRY YARDS.
EGGS FOR HATCHING,
FROM CHOICE WYANDOTTE AND
BROWN LEGHORN FOWLS.
EGGS $2 A SETTING.
BROWN LEGHORN FOWLS FOR SALE.
I Guarantee Satisfaction.
T. M. TALBOTT, M. D.
Falls Church, Fairfax Co., Va.

NEW YORK OBSERVER.
(Established 1823.)
UNDENOMINATIONAL, EVANGELICAL,
UNSECTARIAN, AND NATIONAL
A Safe Paper for the Family.
THE NEW YORK OBSERVER
CAN BE TRUSTED.
It Stands by the Old and Tried Truths
in Religion, Morals, Education, and in all Public
and Private
Matters.

It is Conservative of all Good Things. It steadily Opposes Evil and Sin in every form. The OBSERVER is the well-known enemy of

INTEMPERANCE,
INFIDELITY,
AND ROMANISM.

Price, $3.00 a year, in Advance.
Clergymen, $2.00 a year.
$1.00 commission allowed on New Subscribers. Send for Sample Copy, free. Address,

NEW YORK OBSERVER,
NEW YORK.

LOGAN CAFE
(LATE FORSYTH CAFE)
No. 518 Tenth Street, N. W.
Washington, D. C.

We give the best 25 and 15c meal in the city. Nothing but first-class articles used, and cooked properly. The best Coffee made in a French Drip Glass Lined Urn. Oysters in every style—Lunch at all hours. Dining Room for Ladies—Polite waiters in attendance.
29 25-CENT MEAL TICKETS, $8.00
7 15 "   "   " $1.00
No Liquors.—Call and be convinced.
W. E. LOGAN, Prop.

1/13/87 Mirror

A Singular Accident on the Shenandoah Valley Road.

A Hagerstown special of January 7th says A singular accident, which has just come to light occurred early last Tuesday morning on the Shenandoah Valley railroad. As the north bound passenger train No. 2 was nearing Buchanan's station, a station this side of Roanoke, Va., about 5 o'clock, some one noticed that the hose attached to the air brakes was leaking. The train was stopped, and the entire crew left the train for the purpose of repairing the leak, leaving on board the passengers, the express messenger, the postal clerk, and the newsboy. The brakeman was sent back to flag a freight that was coming in the rear. The freight soon made its appearance, and, not having been notified in time to stop on the heavy downward grade, plunged into the hindmost car of the passenger train, which was a Pullman, wrecking the greater part of it and badly injuring the rest of the train.

The concussion was so great that the throttle valve of the passenger engine was thrown wide open, and its train leaped forward with an impetus of over a mile a minute. So sudden was the start that the crew was unable to board. The wildcat train ran at a fearful rate of speed until the steam became exhausted when it came to a standstill about fifteen miles from the place of the collision. During its flight the passengers were thrown about in their seats and were almost wild with terror. Apprehending that some south bound train might collide with the runaway after it had stopped all the passengers left the cars and built fires in the fields to await the freight, which they thought would bring up the crew of their train. After the lapse of over an hour the rear train hove in sight, and the passenger engineer and fireman were soon at their places. The brakeman, who had been sent back to flag the freight no sooner saw that a collision was inevitable than he struck for the woods, and has not yet turned up.— Several of the passengers received severe bruises, but no one was seriously injured by the collision. The crew of the runaway train have been ordered to Roanoke on a special, where their conduct will be investigated by the officials of the road.

1/13/87 Mirror

A Disappointed Editor.

The editor of The Blue Knob Eagle came to town the other day purposely to make the acquaintance of the editor of The Daily Advocate, Col. Brooks. Brooks had copied so many items from The Eagle that the editor of that sheet knew that he would be a welcome guest. When he entered the office of the great daily, instead of introducing himself to the editor, he sat down carelessly, chuckling inwardly at the surprise which he would create. After a while he said:

"I see that you copy a great deal from The Blue Knob Eagle."

"Yes."

"Rather like its matter, eh?"

"Oh, it doesn't amount to much. You see I copy it because The Eagle has so bad circulation that no one has seen its stuff, which is consequently new when I get it. If the paper had any circulation I wouldn't clip a line from it."

The disappointed editor did not introduce himself.

Wildman & Co.,
—ARE OFFERING—

THE BEST HAND-MADE AND MACHINE SHOES TO BE HAD IN THE COUNTRY.

GIVE US A CALL, AND IF WE DO NOT SELL YOU WE WILL MAKE SOME ONE ELSE SELL YOU LOW.

BIG BARGAINS
TO REDUCE THEIR IMMENSE STOCK OF
DRY GOODS,
Before Making Their Regular Spring Purchases

They consist of Black Goods, Cashmeres, Silks, Colored Dress Goods; Woolen Goods of all kinds. A COMPLETE ASSORTMENT OF NOTIONS, Shirtings, Shirtings, Cheviots, Damasks, Tickings, and a large lot of DOMESTICS, Bought before the recent Advance in Prices.

WILDMAN & CO.

January 15th, 1887.   Leesburg, Va.

THE PERKINS WIND MILL.

Buy the Best And Save Money.

It has been in constant use for 16 years, with a record equaled by none.

WARRANTED
not to blow down, unless the Tower goes with it.

February, 1887

THE TELEPHONE.

FRIDAY............ FEB 4TH

Lincoln as a Lawyer.

His weak as well as his strong qualities have been indicated. He never learned the technicalities, what some would call the tricks, of the profession. The sleight of plea and demurrer, the legerdemain by which justice is balked and a weak case is made to gain an unfair advantage, was too subtle and shifty for his strong and straightforward intelligence. He met these manoeuvres sufficiently well, when practiced by others, but he never could get in the way of handling them for himself. On the wrong side he was always weak. He knew this himself, and avoided such cases when he could consistently with the rules of his profession. He would often persuade a fair-minded litigant of the injustice of his case and induce him to give it up. His partner, Mr. Herndon, relates a speech in point which Lincoln once made to a man who offered him in objectionable case: "Yes, there is no reasonable doubt but that I can gain your case for you. I can distress a widowed mother and her six fatherless children, and thereby get for you six hundred dollars, which rightfully belongs, it appears to me, as much to them as it does to you. I shall not take your case, but I will give a little advice for nothing. You seem a sprightly, energetic man, I would advise you to try your hand at making six hundred dollars in some other way."— Sometimes, after he had entered upon a criminal case, the conviction that his client was guilty would affect him with a sort of panic. On one occasion he turned suddenly to his associate and said, "Swett, the man is guilty; you defend him, I can't," and so gave up his share of a large fee. The same thing happened at another time when he was engaged, with Judge S. C. Parks, in defending a man accused of larceny. He said, "If you can say anything for the man, do it, I can't; if I attempt it, the jury will see I think he is guilty, and convict him." Once he was prosecuting a civil suit, in the course of which evidence was introduced showing that his client was attempting a fraud.— Lincoln rose and went to his hotel in deep disgust. The judge sent for him; he refused to come. "Tell the judge," he said, "my hands are dirty; I came over to wash them." We are aware that these stories detract something from the character of the lawyer; but this inflexible, inconvenient, and fastidious morality was to be of vast service hereafter to his country and the world.

The Nemesis which waits upon men of extraordinary wit or humor has not neglected Mr. Lincoln, and the young lawyers of Illinois, who never knew him, have an endless store of jokes and pleasantries in his name; some of them as old as Howleglass or Rabelais. But the fact is that all his stories and jests, his frank companionable humor, his gift of easy accessibility and welcome, he was, even while he traveled the Eighth Circuit, a man of grave and serious temper and of an unusual innate dignity and reserve. He had few or no special intimates, and there was a line beyond which no one ever thought of passing. Besides, he was too strong a man in the court-room to be regarded with anything but respect in a community in which legal ability was the only especial mark of distinction. Few of his forensic speeches have been preserved, but his contemporaries all agree as to their singular ability and power.

Sometimes he disturbed the court with laughter by his humorous or apt illustrations; sometimes he excited the audience by that florid and exuberant rhetoric which he knew well enough how and when to indulge in; but his more usual and more successful manner was to rely upon a clear, strong, lucid statement, keeping details in proper subordination and bringing forward, in a way which fastened the attention of court and jury alike, the essential point on which he claimed a decision. "Indeed," says one of his colleagues, "his statement often rendered argument unnecessary, and often the court would stop him and say, 'if that is the case, we will hear the other side.'"

Whatever doubts might be entertained as to whether he was the ablest lawyer on the circuit, there was never any dissent from the opinion that he was the one most cordially and universally liked. If he did not himself enjoy his full share of the happiness of life, he certainly diffused more of it among his fellows than is in the power of most men. His arrival was a little festival in the county-seats where his pursuits led him to pass so much of his time. Several eye-witnesses have described these scenes in terms which would seem exaggerated if they were not so fully confirmed. The bench and bar would gather at the tavern where he was expected, to give him a cordial welcome; says

February, 1887

one writer, "He brought light with him." This is not hard to understand. Whatever his cares, he never inflicted them upon others. He talked singularly well, but never about himself. He was full of wit which never wounded, of humor which mellowed the barshness of that new and raw life of the prairies. He never asked for help, but was always ready to give it. He received everybody's confidence, and rarely gave his own in return. He took no mean advantages in court or in conversation, and, satisfied with the respect and kindness which he everywhere met, he sought no quarrels and never had to decline them. He did not accumulate wealth as Judge Davis said, "he seemed never to care for it." He had a good income from his profession, though the fees he received would bring a smile to the well-paid lips of the great attorneys of to-day. The largest fee he ever got was one of five thousand dollars from the Illinois Central Railway, and he had to bring suit to compel them to pay it. He spent what he received in the education of his children, in the care of his family, and in a plain and generous way of living. —February installment of The Century's Life of Lincoln.

2/26/87 Washingtonian

Thousand of Cattle Dead on the Ranges.

Special dispatch to the Star.

LINCOLN Neb., Feb. 20.—As the trains came in yesterday, passengers and trainmen saw cattle in the draws buried to their heads in the snow. As hardly a cow was to be seen elsewhere, it is evident that many are entirely covered. Most of those seen will perish. In fact, all except the few that can be found and dug out by the small force available for that purpose will be lost. The losses of cattle will be something appalling.

(Edmund Morris describes in his celebrated biography of Theodore Roosevelt, how half of Roosevelt's cattle were saved by placing them in a wooded area. Many ranchers lost entire herds in this horrible western winter.)

2/25/87 Telephone

There is one vast mudhole between Hamilton and Waterford, at this time, but the worst of it is at the two ends i. e, between our town and the depot and over Walker's Hill.

Walker's Hill is a long, hard pull on either side when the roads are good, and the soil is of such nature, that when it is muddy a trip over that particular eminence is a fearful ordeal - an abomination! to any man who has any regard for his time and his beast.

2/18/87 Telephone

A False Statement.

I am informed that a certain man publicly made the assertion, in the store of Mr. McFarland, in Hamilton, that I had sold wine to "Pack" Bean's son and made him drunk. I positively declare that assertion to be false, and without foundation in fact. I make this statement public because I am above any such business and do not intend that such reports shall go unchallenged. I wear no cloak to hide rascality and do not propose to let rascality cloak me with falsehoods.
It.   JOHN T. CUMMINS.

PUBLIC NOTICE!
To whom it may concern:

This is to certify that I, GEORGE SPRANSY, of the city of Washington, U. S. A. am fully prepared to furnish all the people with the BEST OF CLOTHING AT THE LOWEST PRICES, (and at one price only.) And be it understood that the present general depression in business has seriously effected the clothing trade, and caught dealers with large supplies on hand which must be sold.— Therefore, this is the time to buy goods at less than their true value. In order to conform to existing circumstances my goods are all marked down to lowest prices —and all MARKED IN PLAIN FIGURES, WITH ONE PRICE TO ALL. Do not fail to visit my store and I shall do you good and make you happy. Respectfully,
GEO. SPRANSY,
507. 7th St. N. W. Washin'g D.C.

— It is reported that all the dogs in the northern end of the County have barked themselves to death— caused by the numerous visits of the countless candidates.

March 1887

3/11/87 Telephone

The death of Rev. Henry Ward Beecher, which was caused by apoplexy, at his home in Brooklyn, at 9.30 last Tuesday morning, ends the career of one of the ablest and most noted men of America. As a preacher, he had no peer in this country and, probably, in all Christendom. Like all other men, he doubtless had his faults, and some of them may have been nothing short of crimes; but over his cold clay the people of today will spread the mantle of charity, and strive to remember only his good deeds and great ability.

4/1/87 Telephone

BOB INGERSOLL ON BEECHER.

"Manhood Is His Forte"—A Touching Tribute Paid in 1880.

New York Herald.

Do you want to know what Bob Ingersoll thinks of the great man who lies dying in Brooklyn?

Would you like to know what the renowned infidel wrote with his own hands of Henry Ward Beecher?

It was the fall of 1880.

Mr. Beecher had introduced the infidel orator to a great political gathering in the Brooklyn Academy of Music, saying that the colonel was the most brilliant living orator in any tongue.

A day or two afterward the colonel was asked by a reporter what he thought of Mr. Beecher. He at once sat down and wrote as fast as his pencil could trot over paper thus:

"I regard him as the greatest man in any pulpit in the world. He treated me with a generosity that nothing can exceed. He rose grandly above the prejudices supposed to belong to his class, and acted only as a man could act without a chain upon his brain and only kindness in his heart.

"I told him that night that I congratulated the world that it had a minister with an intellectual horizon broad enough and a mental sky studded with stars of genius enough to hold all creeds in scorn that shocked the heart of man. I think that Mr. Beecher has liberalized the English speaking people of the world. I do not think he agrees with me. He holds to many things that I most passionately deny. But in common we believe in the liberty of thought.

"My principal objections to orthodox religion are two—slavery here and hell-hereafter. I do not believe that Mr. Beecher on these two points can disagree with me. The real difference between us, is, he says God, I say nature. The real agreement between us is we both say liberty."

"What is Mr. Beecher's forte?" the reporter asked.

"He is of a wonderfully poetic temperament. In pursuing any course of thought his mind is like a stream flowing through the scenery of fairyland. The stream murmurs and laughs, while the banks grow green and the vines blossom

"His brain is controlled by his heart. He thinks in pictures. With him logic means mental melody. The discordant is the absurd.

"For years he has endeavored to hide the dungeon of orthodoxy with the ivy of imagination. Now and then he pulls for a moment the leafy curtain aside and is horrified to see the lizards, snakes, basilisks and abnormal monsters of the orthodox age, and then he utters a great cry, the protest of a loving, throbbing heart.

"He is a great thinker, a marvellous orator, and, in my judgment, greater and grander than any creed or church. Besides all this, he treated me like a king. Manhood is his forte, and I expect to live and die his friend."

Henry Ward Beecher, along with his sister, Harriett Beecher Stowe, who authored <u>Uncle Tom's Cabin</u>, had been strong supporters of the abolition movement.

2/18/87 Telephone

A Warm Choice.

There is a story told that one day, not far from Atlanta, a young man, after listening to a certain preacher pound and expound the scriptures for two hours, arose and started to leave the church.

The preacher stopped short.

"Young man!" he said.

The young man stopped.

"If you'd rather go to hell than to hear me preach, just go on!"

"Well," replied the young man, after a pause, "I believe I'd rather!" and out he went.—Atlanta Constitution.

3/24/87 Mirror

LEESBURG, VIRGINIA.

The intelligent and observant Conference reporter of the Baltimore *Sun*, who knows how to appreciate an inviting place when he sees it, wrote to that paper from Leesburg as follows:

LEESBURG, VA., March 15.—This town, which is one of the oldest in this section of Virginia, and one of the most beautiful in the State, is at present enlivened by the presence of the Baltimore Conference of the Methodist Episcopal Church, South, which has quite a large membership here. This is the county seat of Loudoun county, and is 37 miles from Washington by way of the Washington and Ohio division of the Richmond and Danville Railroad, the terminus of which branch is at Round Hill, twelve miles northwest of this town. The Potomac river is a few miles distant. From Round Hill is a stage route through Snickersville Gap, in the Blue Ridge mountains, to Berryville, Clarke county, and another stage line runs northerly to Point of Rocks, on the Baltimore and Ohio Railroad. The surface of the town, partaking of the nature of the surrounding country, is slightly rolling, and at this season, when almost continuous rains and melting snows have rendered the roads wellnigh impassable, the streets, which are laid out at right angles with each other, cannot deny their kinship with the well-known Virginia spring roads. The streets, however, are paved with cobblestones or are macadamized, and are lined with brick pavements, and a large force of men are employed by the corporation to scrape the streets frequently, so that, with the exception of rainy weather, they are exceptionally clean at all times. Gasoline lamps, placed at convenient intervals light the street, and excellent water is piped all over town without machinery from the never-failing and ever-pure Rock Spring which is situated on a little knell near the western corporation limits. The public schools, one for white and one for colored children, are situated here and are well-attended.

The town government consists of Hon. Jos. L. Norris, mayor; Capt. H. O. Clagett, recorder; twelve common councilmen, and Benj. F. Head, town-sergeant. The council meet at the mayor's office, but $15,000 have been voted to build during the coming summer a town hall. The Loudoun county courthouse, two stories high built of brick, with a lofty pillared portico, and surmounted by a small wooden belfry, stands at the corner of Market and King Street, in the middle of a well kept lawn, and surrounded by tall, rugged and well-developed maples. The lawn, which is fenced with an iron railing, is the pride of the town, and citizens claim that it is the finest of the kind in the State. In the rear of the courthouse is the clerk's office, also a two story building with fire-proof annex for the preservation of records, &c.

3/11/87 Telephone

—Guilford, as one of the towns of Loudoun, is no more. It will hereafter be known as Sterling.

Mastering a Mule.

The other morning a mule attached to one of George B. Newton's coal wagons fell on Chestnut street above Sixteenth.

The cars were blocked for at least half an hour. All the efforts of some twenty car drivers and conductors were of no avail in trying to get him on his feet.

At last a darkey who had been watching the proceedings announced that he could raise "dat ere mule."

He was given the field.

Entering Thompson Black's grocery, he procured two lumps of sugar, which he gave the mule.

The mule's keen relish of the sweets, as he lay in the snow with his head on a blanket, was ludicrous in the extreme.

No sooner had he licked his chops after his dainty lunch than up he jumped to his feet.

The several hundred pedestrians who had gathered to witness the feat of the darkey made the welkin ring with their loud cheers in honor of the man who mastered the mule.—

May, 1887

5/19/87 Mirror

BROKE JAIL.—When jailer Nixon made his usual round on Sunday morning last he found that during the preceding night three of his wards had effected their escape and were "over the hills and far away." The three prisoners, all of whom were negro men, were confined in one of the lower ironed cells thought to be the most secure of any in the building. There was, however, a hole in the ceiling, through which a stove pipe had passed to heat the upper cell during the winter. This hole they enlarged by sawing sufficiently to admit a man's body and passed into the upper cell, which was unoccupied from thence they readily got into the corridor and then prying open the door leading into the hall of the jailer's house, they quickly made their way into the open air. The instrument with which the sawing was done was a piece of sheet iron which the prisoners had stripped from the side of their cell window, and in which by rubbing on some hard surface, they had made rough teeth. The escape was made perfectly noiselessly and doubtless quickly— a feat not hard of accomplishment in the present state of the county prison.

The men who thus freed themselves were Lewis Curtis, sent up for stealing a watch from a colored man in this town; John Thomas, who stole a horse from Mr. W. H. Havener and some money from Mr. Everhart on the same night not long ago, and ——— ——— who was sent up for obtaining money by raising a check of some one near Middleburg;—as stated above, they were all colored. The community is well rid of the lot, especially Curtis, who is an accomplished villain, but it does not accord with one's ideas of the fitness of things that it should have gotten rid of them just in this way.

GOING! GOING!!

ALL THE STOCK of the late ALFRED CLINE, embracing

Saddles, Bridles, Harness,

Whips, Trunks, Satchels, Blankets, Robes, and all kinds SADDLER's HARDWARE and TOOLS, Shoemaker's Stock, Platform Scales, &c., &c., must be sold—at cost, or less. Call and secure bargains at once.
MARY A. CLINE, Executrix,
Leesburg, Va.

5/19/87 Mirror

COLOR LINE IN THE CHURCH—The Episcopal Convention of South Carolina, in session last week at Charleston, was nearly disrupted over the question as to whether colored clergymen should be admitted to the floor as delegates. Bishop Howe, who was presiding, virtually decided in one of his rulings that they should be, whereupon a lengthy discussion arose and much feeling was manifested. An appeal from the Bishop's decision was made but the convention refused to sustain it; this brought matters to a head, and the delegates from fourteen parishes withdrew. There were enough delegates left, however, to form a quorum and the convention continued its session. Overtures were made to the seceders to induce them to re-return, with, it is hoped, good prospects of success. The bishop pronounced it the most serious break that had occurred during the hundred years of the existence of the diocese.

5/19/87 Mirror

NARROW ESCAPE.—Rev. C. M. Brown, recently rented the residence of Col. L. Chancellor in Middleburg. Two of his little children found some old bottles in the house, one containing strychnine, which they emptied in the well bucket and drank the water. As soon as it was discovered, Dr. Luck was summoned and administered an emetic, which prevented serious consequences. A very valuable and highly prized Newfoundland dog belonging to Mr S. Carroll Chancellor, of this town, drank some of the water and died within about fifteen minutes.—

PEERLESS PAPER MEAT SACKS

Prevent Skippers in Meat.

May, 1887

5/19/87 Mirror
Wild Days in California.

"Do I remember the work of the vigilance committee of 1856?" said an old Californian. "Well, I should say so. I was right on the spot. Thousands of dollars had been distributed among the rough element to influence the election of mayor.— Murder, riot and arson were common. A few days before the election I was sitting in one of the leading hotels of San Francisco. Dr. Randall, a popular physician, entered and went to the counter. As he stood there an English money lender, named Hetherington, a desperate fellow, entered, and, without a word, stepped directly up to the doctor and drove a long knife almost to the hilt into his left breast. It was instant death, and one of the most cold blooded murders ever committed in the city. Hetherington was arrested promptly, and that night he was hanged by the vigilance committee on the open street. It seemed that the doctor owed Hetherington some money and had refused or delayed payment. Hetherington was worth over $100,000, and had murdered another doctor some time before. He got free by paying $7,000.

"But this example was not sufficient to put a stop to the lawlessness, and the committee decided that something more decisive must be done. Jack Hayes was the sheriff then. He was sent out of the city on a false scent. The committee then went to the jail and took out seven murderers, hustled them to a gallows on the street and strung every one of them up. I remember when the committee was being quietly formed two desperate characters tried to kill me in court. Two of my friends, big, strong, muscular fellows, stepped up and cowed the desperadoes by showing fight. Then I suggested to the judge that my assailants should be bound over to keep the peace. This was done, and they gave bonds, but followed me to my office. They said they wanted to talk with me. When we reached my rooms they said they heard I had influence with the vigilance committee that was being organized, and, fearing they would be hanged, they wanted me to save them.— They promised to behave themselves, and the next day I succeeded in saving their necks.

"I remember when the committee went to get the seven murderers they found a woman in the jail who had kept a grocery store in the cellar of which a number of skeletons had been found, believed to be those of murdered persons. The committee was undecided whether to hang her with the others. Finally, as there was some doubt about her having actually committed murder, though there was no doubt she had been accessory to more than one, it was decided to send her adrift on the ocean in a small boat. After the men had been disposed of she was taken to the shore and put in a boat. Some provisions were put in with her and she had on her person $30,000 in money. Then the boat was sent adrift.

5/5/87 Mirror
Rosser on Sheridan.

WINCHESTER, VA., May 3 —The following letter from Gen. Thos. L. Rosser will appear in the Winchester TIMES to morrow:

"*University of Virginia*, May 3 —Major Holmes Conrad, Winchester, Va.—My Dear Major: I have seen it reported recently in the newspapers that Gen. P. H. Sheridan, U. S. A., contemplates at an early day another ride up the Shenandoah valley. I had hoped that our beautiful valley should never again be desecrated by his footprints. Cold, cruel and brutal must be the character of this soldier, who fondly cherishes memories of the wild, wanton waste and desolation which his barbarous torch spread through the valley, laying in ashes the beautiful and happy homes of innocent women, young and helpless children and aged men, and who over these ruins boasted that now a crow cannot fly over this valley without carrying its rations. Gen. Sheridan has done nothing since the war to atone for his cruel barbarism during the war. We have not forgotten that during his reign in New Orleans he asked that our fellow-citizens of Louisiana might be proclaimed banditti in order that he might set the dogs of war on them. I have forgiven the brave men of the Union armies whom I met in honorable battle, and who finally triumphed over us in the great struggle.— Among them I can now name many of my warmest and truest and most prized friends. They are good and true men, and think none the less of us for having fought them. Indeed, they esteem him highest amongst us who fought them the hardest. Sheridan is not one of this kind, and he has never accorded to us that peace which Grant proclaimed. I now say to you, my dear Major, and to our gallant comrades who are now in the valley, that I hope you will allow this man to make his triumphant ride up the valley in peace, but have him go like a miserable crow, carrying his rations with him.— Yours, truly, THOS. L. ROSSER."

5/19/87 Mirror

GRANT'S ORDERS TO SHERIDAN.

The Stripping of Loudoun County Directed by the Lieutenant-General

GIVE THE ENEMY NO REST, BUT PROTECT UNION MEN AND PAY THEM FOR SUPPLIES TAKEN.

From the Washington Star of the 13th.

In view of the criticisms made by Gen. Rosser on Gen. Sheridan for the work he did in Virginia during the closing days of the rebellion, and of the statement of the latter, in an interview with a STAR reporter, that he had nothing to say about the matter, as he was simply carrying out his orders from the lieutenant-general in what he did in Loudoun County, the dispatches printed below will be of interest. A dispatch from Utica, N. Y., to the New York SUN says: They are copied from the originals, which are now in possession of William Blaikie of that city. They were transcribed into cipher and sent by S. H. Beck with of that city, who at this time was in the secret service of the United States.

CITY POINT, VA, Aug. 16, 3:30 p. m., 1864.
Major-General Sheridan, Winchester, Va.

If you can possibly spare a division of cavalry send them through Loudoun County to destroy and carry off crops, animals, negroes, and all men under fifty years of age, capable of bearing arms. In this way you will get many of Mosby's men. All male citizens under fifty can fairly be held as prisoners. If not already soldiers, they will be made so the moment the rebel army gets hold of them.
U. S. GRANT, Lieutenant-General.

H'DQ'RS, ARMIES OF THE UNITED STATES.
CITY POINT, Aug. 21, 1864.
Major-General Sheridan, Charlestown, Va.

In stripping Loudoun County of supplies &c., impress from all loyal persons so that they may receive pay for what is taken from them. I am informed by the Assistant Secretary of War that Loudoun County has a large population of Quakers, who are all favorably disposed to the Union. These people may be exempted from arrest.

U. S. GRANT, Lieutenant-General.

H'DQ'RS. ARMIES OF THE UNITED STATES.
CITY POINT, Va., Aug. 26, 2:30 p. m., 1864.
Major-General Sheridan, Halltown, Va.:

Telegraphed you that I had good reason for believing that Fitz Lee had been ordered back here. I now think it likely that all troops will be ordered back from the valley except what they believe to be minimum number to detain you. My reason for supposing this is based upon the fact that yielding up the Weldon road seems to be a blow to the enemy he cannot stand. I think I do not overstate the loss of the enemy in the last two weeks at 10,000 killed and wounded. We have lost heavily, but ours has been mostly in captures when the enemy gained temporary advantages. Watch closely and if you find this theory correct, push with all vigor. Give the enemy no rest, and if it is possible to follow the Virginia central road, follow that far. Do all the damage to railroads and crops you can. Carry off stock of all kinds and negroes, so far as to prevent further planting. If the war is to last another year, we want the Shenandoah Valley to remain a barren waste.
U. S. GRANT, Lieut.-Gen.

H'DQ'RS, ARMIES OF THE UNITED STATES.
CITY POINT, Va., Sept. 4, 10 a. m., 1864.
Major-Gen. Sheridan, Charlestown, Va:

In cleaning out the arms-bearing community from Loudoun County and the subsidence for armies, exercise your own judgment as to who should be exempt from arrest and as to who should receive any for their stock, grain, &c. It is our interest that that county should not be capable of subsisting a hostile army, and at the same time we want to inflict as little hardship upon Union men as possible.
U. S. GRANT, Lieutenant General.

CITY POINT Nov., 1864.
Major-Gen. Sheridan, Cedar Creek, Va:

Do you not think it advisable to notify all citizens living east of the Blue Ridge to move out north of the Potomac all their stock, grain, and provisions of every description? There is no doubt about the necessity of cleaning out that county so that it will not support Mosby's gang. And the question is whether it is not better that the people should save what they can. So long as the war lasts they must be prevented from raising another crop, both there and as high up the valley as we can control.
U. S. GRANT, Lieutenant-General.

June, 1887

6/17/87 Telephone

THE TELEPHONE

FRIDAY............JUNE 10TH

LOUDOUN LOCALS

—Shoot the fly.

—County Court next Monday.

—Boarders are coming to town.

—Currant worms are ruining the currant and gooseberry crop in this locality.

—There are some fences in Hamilton that badly need some paint or whitewash.

—Look at the date on your paper! Many of our subscribers should make us a call with cash in their pockets.

—One of the old land-marks of Leesburg, "Boss' Corner" is being cleared away, to make a place for the proposed town hall.

—Mr. Israel Warner is reported to be very low this morning.— About noon yesterday, believing that he was about to die, he bade farewell to all those who were about him.

—Do not forget the festival to be held in Hillsboro this evening and tomorrow evening. In addition to other attractions the cascade at Janney's Mill will be illuminated with Greek Fire, producing magical effect.

Rev. David Updegraff preached two able sermons here last Sunday. The congregations were not as large as usual as it was not generally known that the Rev. gentleman would preach.——Mr. Gill still lingers in a critical condition. There is no hope of his recovery.

—ALDIE, VA., June 7, '87.—The festival and lecture was not so well attended as was expected owing to bad weather &c., yet a snug little sum was realized, supposed to be enough to pay the remaining debt on the church. Maj. J. Mort Kilgour delivered two lectures, which were highly enjoyed by his hearers. His subjects were "Good People," and "The Battle of Life." The Maj. has many warm friends in this neighborhood, and it is to be hoped he will come again.—— The Rev. S. L. Baily fell from his horse some days past and sprained his leg so that he has to use a crutch.

Last Monday week Mr. B. H. Hammerly, liveryman, of Hillsboro, hired Maggie and a buggy to a colored man to drive to Harpers Ferry. The man drove to the River, and, leaving the horse and buggy on the Loudoun side, walked across the bridge into the town. In the evening he returned to the place where he had left his turnout, but failed to find Maggie and the buggy—they had left for parts unknown. He and his lady love then boarded Walker's train en route to Hillsboro, where he reported to Mr. Hammerly the unaccountable departure of his horse and buggy. Mr. H., accompanied by Capt. Spates immediately started for Harpers Ferry in search of the missing Maggie, but failed to find any clue to her whereabouts. Next morning, however, about daylight, the mare came into Hillsboro, from the direction of Morrisonville, unattended by a driver, and bringing the buggy home all right. Mr. H. then started out in search of the party who evidently had been enjoying a ride at another man's expense. He was not long in learning that Maggie was driven past Kalb's nursery, near Lovettsville, on the previous day, by a young man who lives near Morrisonville. On further inquiry he learned that the said young man started from Harpers Ferry with the rig and took the river road towards Lovettsville, and on to Morrisonville, where he turned Maggie loose to go home, which she did, without injury to herself or the buggy. Further developments are expected.

PUBLIC SALE.

BY virtue of a decree rendered in the chancery cause of Fry vs. Ayers, in the Circuit Court of Loudoun County, Va., at the April Term, 1887, I will sell, in Leesburg, on

Monday, July 11th, 1887,

Court-day, about 12 o'clock M., the following MACHINERY, viz:

1 Traction Engine,
1 FARM ENGINE, 1 SAW MILL,
1 Threshing Machine,
1 VIBRATOR SEPARATOR.

TERMS.—One-half Cash, remainder in two equal payments, six and twelve months, purchaser to give bond, with interest and security, payable in Loudoun National Bank.
J. E. CARRUTHERS, Sheriff,
Commissioner of Sale.
JOHN A. RINKER, Auctioneer.   june11

Specialties for this season
—AT—
WHITMORE'S!

IRON-CLAD MILK CANS & BUCKETS. Water Coolers, Refrigerators, Plain and Fancy Toilet Sets; Preserving Kettles (brass and porcelained); The Power Fly Fans FRUIT CANS, glass and tin; Jelly Glasses

TINWARE
of all kinds, factory and custom made.

GOLDEN STAR

OIL COOKING STOVES & RANGES.

Paynes' Automatic Farm Engines
OF ALL KINDS.—Established 1840.

2 to 100 Horse Power.

Our 10-Horse Spark Arresting Threshing Engine has cut 10,000 feet Pine Lumber in 10 hours. Will burn wood 6 feet long, coal, Straw and corn stalks. Send for Price List and Catalogue G.
B. W. PAYNE & SONS, Box 1400, Corning, N. Y.

June 1887

LINCOLN—HATCHER.

An Incident Before the War.

From the Richmond State of Friday.

"I was at the first reception President Lincoln gave," said Hon. George D Wise, who was, with others in THE STATE office today, talking about the war, "and I will tell you an incident which came directly under my observation. It was in 1861. Being in Washington on the day of the reception in company with a tall and handsome man by the name of Hatcher, whose home was in Loudoun county, Va. we determined to attend the reception. Hatcher was at least six feet 5 inches tall and was elegantly proportioned. While on our way to the reception Hatcher asked, 'Are you going to shake hands with Lincoln?' 'Why not?' I replied 'What are you going there for?' Well, I am not going to shake hands with him said Hatcher. It was the custom for the marshal to introduce the visitors to the President and when I reached Mr. Lincoln, the marshal who was well acquainted with me, said 'Mr. President, this is Mr. Wise, of Virginia.' The President had a few words to say and gave me a cordial handshake. I was ahead of Hatcher and I thought I would look back to see if he was going to keep his word about not shaking hands with Lincoln. As I looked back I saw Hatcher deliberately pass the President holding his hands behind him. He passed on by without taking the slightest notice of the President. Mr Lincoln saw him, and turning to the marshal asked, 'Who is that tall man that has just passed me?' 'It is Mr. Hatcher, of Virginia.' 'Ask Mr. Hatcher to come back' said Mr. Lincoln; 'tell him I wish to see him.' The marshal overtook Mr Hatcher, and told him what the President had said. Hatcher went back and President Lincoln extended his hand to him. Hatcher accepted the President's hand, and then Mr Lincoln asked 'How tall are you, Mr Hatcher?' 'I am six feet five inches,' he replied. 'Well,' said Mr. Lincoln, with a smile, 'I believe you top me a few inches.'—And what do you reckon," continued Mr. Wise; "Lincoln and Hatcher actually stood back to back and measured, and Hatcher was at least a half a head taller. When they parted Hatcher had a better opinion of Lincoln than he had before, but he did all he could to help the southern cause. Hatcher was a brave soldier, a handsome man, and was killed by a Federal bullet at Ball's Bluff.

(The fine points of this meeting are debated. Other historians say that the encounter occurred on a city street. Curiously, at the Ball's Bluff Battle, this six-foot-five Loudoun native had been a flag bearer, which made him a more accessible target.)

Letter from Aldie.

Our public school taught by Miss Lilly Saffer closed last Wednesday. Miss Saffer proved a most thorough and efficient teacher as well as firm desciplinarian, and needed but the support and encouragement of the patrons to make the school a success. We regret that she declines the school for the coming year, having accepted a much more pleasant and lucrative position in the Hagerstown Female Seminary.

J. E Douglas has commenced building, in connection with his large flouring mills, a saw mill and corn crusher. A circular saw, of the latest and most improved design will be used, while a 23 horse power turbine water wheel will run the works.

Chicken thieves raided the premises of Mr Ed. Russell one night last week, capturing about 30 fowls which they sold for $1.50. Mr. Russell and others followed on their trail, and succeeded in capturing them in the northern part of the county. They were tried before Justice Hempstone who promptly committed four of them to jail for six months, and the other two for two months.

Gentle Woman's Revenge.

Husband and wife had had a little tiff. He buried his nose in a morning paper, while she gazed out the car window with persistent intentness. Thus an hour and thirty miles passed. A lady entered the car. Husband dropped his paper and looked at her admiringly.

"Ah," said he, "that's a fine woman. And a widow, too. Don't you think she's handsome?"

"Yes, rather. You seem to like widows."

"Indeed I do. They're just charming."

Husband evidently thought this would pique his partner. But it didn't.

"Alfred," said she, tenderly, and placing her hand softly on his arm, "Alfred, I guess I was in the wrong a little while ago, when I became angry at you, and I'm sorry, so sorry. Will you forgive your little wife?"

"Certainly. Don't say another word about it."

"And will you grant a little request I have to make of you, hubby dear?"

"Of course. Anything that lies in my power."

"You say you think widows are so charming?"

"Yes, I did say so, but—"

"Then make me one; that's a good husband mine. Oh, I shall be so happy."

6/16/87 Mirror

A Prize Fight in Loudoun.

BALTIMORE SPORTS ENGAGE IN A "MILL" WITHIN OUR BORDERS.

On Monday last a party of ten or a dozen sporting men and newspaper reporters accompanied Pete Lally and Al Hartman, two Baltimore middle-weights, to a point on Catoctin Creek, some distance from Pt. of Rocks, where the two men engaged in a prize fight for the rich take of $130, the winner, Lally, taking $90, and Hartman $40. The party reached the Point of Rocks about 12 o'clock and the reporter of the Balto. *Sun* who was with them, says, "they were ferried across the river into Virginia without creating any suspicion as to their object. On reaching the Virginia shore however, the stage driver bothered the crowd considerably by his importunities to convey them to Leesburg. He was given some money, however, and sent on a wild goose chase, and the party then proceeded to find a spot suitable for the fight. It took a three mile tramp over a mountain before they could find a level piece of ground that was not covered with rocks. When all were discouraged. one of the party discovered a meadow, but it was on the wrong side of the Catoctin river; but the gang were not in a humor to be baffled, and immediately began to strip to reach the other shore. The lighter members were carried over on the backs of the big fellows, and the principals ordered to strip, or rather dress for the fight. It required but a few moments to get in shape, and, with the spectators sitting on a rail fence, some with and some without clothing, making themselves as comfortable as a split rail fence would allow, prepared to see the fight. No ring was pitched, but the shade of a tree was all the ring required. A referee was selected from among the newspaper reporters. The two principals put on two ounce gloves and announced themselves ready. Each were stripped to the waist. Hartman wore white tights and brown stockings and belt. He weighed 145 pounds and looked in good condition. Lally wore blue tights and stockings and weighed 148 pounds. At 2:50 p.m. the men shook hands and then began the fight."

Only two rounds were fought the battle lasting six-and-a-half minutes during which time, however, so the same authority says, some severe fighting was done. Hartman was considered the better man of the two and was in much the finer condition, but just at the close of the second round, Lally let his right fly in a swinging half upper cut that caught his opponent with terrific force on the point of the left jaw. Hartman's eyes rolled, he became dazed, he reeled and fell to the ground like a log. Lally drew back and waited to see what he would do. The timekeeper, meantime, had his eyes on the second hand. Under the Queensberry rules, which governed the fight, Hartman was allowed ten seconds to recover. When eight points had been passed the fallen man, although unconscious, endeavored to raise himself on his elbow, but fell back more exhausted than before. Lally made a rush at him as he attempted to rise, for the purpose of again knocking him down, but nature saved him the trouble. The time-keeper then gave Lally the knock out and the fight. Hartman was carried to his corner, and every effort was made to revive him, but it was several minutes before he completely recovered. He then said his face did not hurt him and he did not remember of having received the blow.

At the conclusion of the fight the party made their way back to the Point and returned to Baltimore on the 6:18 train, having been entirely unmolested.

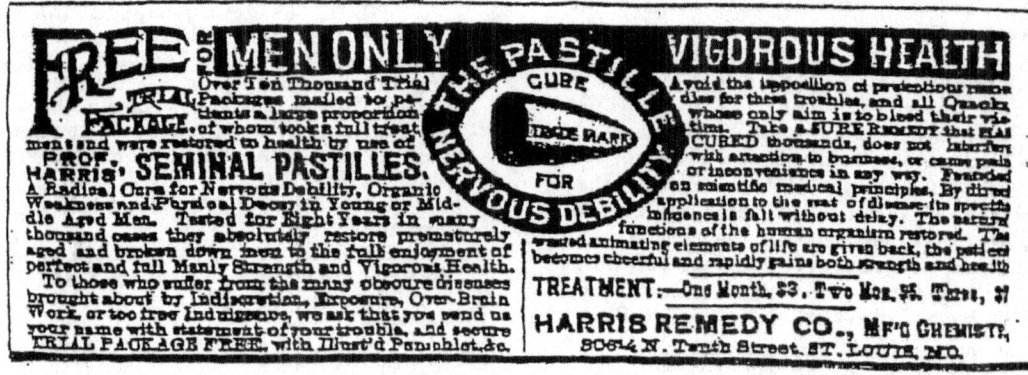

July, 1887

THE WASHINGTONIAN

LEESBURG, LOUDOUN COUNTY, VA

SATURDAY............ July 9

THE FOURTH OF JULY.

This national holiday was more generally observed last Monday than at any previous recurrence since the war.— North, South, East, and West, the people celebrated it, and gave expressions to their devotion to the Union in ways without number. Many reunions of the soldiers of the late war were had, and speeches, full of patriotic devotion to the flag and the country, were made. This was pleasing to see, but there are bounds beyond which good sense and becoming propriety should not go. Too much gush and too much expressions of affection is not a true indication of the sentiments of the people, but partakes more of demagogism than genuine fraternal feeling and true patriotic sentiment. The growing interests in unity, comity, and good feeling will make us all cling firmly to the Union and its sheet anchor, the constitution, and we do not see why our budding Ciceros should be called upon to spend, annually, so much eloquence in letting our brethren of the North and South know how much they love each other. More consideration should be had to questions of practical utility, and the discussion of the great causes which should be advanced and promoted looking to the permanency of our institutions, and in aid the prosperity and happiness of the country. They should have more of the elements of instruction to the masses than platitudes descriptive of the burning love of the soldiers of the sections for each other, which is more in sound than substance.

GETTYSBURG REUNION.

VICTOR AND VANQUISHED VIE IN FRIENDLY EXPRESSIONS.

GETTYSBURG, PA., July 2.—The Philadelphia Brigade of Union Veterans, which had invited the survivors of Pickett's Division of Lee's Army to a reunion on this historic field of contest, reached here about 6 P. M. to-day, and Pickett's "boys" arrived about 8:35 p. m. fifteen of them bringing their wives and daughters with them. Mrs. General George E. Pickett and her son accompanied the party, which numbered over 100. The Southerners were warmly received by the Philadelphians, and were escorted from the depot to the Eagle Hotel, where a standup lunch was given them, after which all proceeded to the county Court House, where the first camp-fire of the Blue and the Gray upon the historic ground of Gettysburg was held. Here John W Frazier called the meeting to order, and suggested that these fraternal meetings would do more to create and maintain a sincere and lasting fellowship among the people of the whole nation than anything else that had taken place since the war for the preservation of the Union ended, and he hoped to see them held all along the line from Gettysburg to Vicksburg. He then presented Comrades W. S. Stockston as the presiding officer of the meeting with the statement that to him more than to any other was due the credit of bringing the reunion about.

Col. A. K. McClure made the welcome speech to the southerners present. It was a warm and generous welcome very elegantly and eloquently expressed.

The veterans' reunions had begun and the encouraging sign was that each side was inviting their former opponents.

Just Received

MOSBY'S "WAR REMINISCENCES & STUART'S CAVALRY, by JOHN S. MOSBY.

PRICE 50 CTS., BY MAIL 55 CTS.

☞ Send orders to Loudoun Book Store, Leesburg, Va.   H. W. CLAGETT.

may 14.

July 1887

7/21/87 Mirror

From almost every section came accounts of the fatal effect of the heat on Sunday and Monday. At Richmond for the two days, there were twelve deaths, evenly divided between whites and blacks. At Fortress Monroe, the baker at the Hygeia died on Monday, and at Hampton three elderly ladies died on Monday. In Philadelphia on Monday forty-eight persons were overcome, 31 of whom died. Seventeen deaths occurred at Pittsburg and as many more were prostrated. In Cincinnati there were 48 cases of sunstroke and 18 deaths—there were eight deaths in Louisville. In Chicago twenty deaths from sun stroke were reported on Sunday, and as many more on Tuesday morning, and 263 babies less than a year old fell sick.

RENTING OF PRIVILEGES.—The renting of privileges for the Temperance Bush Meeting to be held at Purcellville during the first week in August next, which took place on the grounds on Tuesday, was well attended and the bidding spirited. The successful bidders with their privileges were: ——— Bradley, of Washington, merry-go-round; J. W Wiley, ice-cream; C. C. Bell, confectionery and notions; L. F. Hough, cigars and tobacco; A Zerega, ice-water and lemonade; Carter Monroe, watermelons; Wm Layton, barber shop; Wm. Matthews, horse pound; C. Hampton, photographs; A. W. Smith, carriages, and T. C. Baker, harness—the total sum realized was $339.80 being about $36 in excess of last year's renting. The committee announce that they have made special arrangements for having water furnished upon the grounds free.

7/14/87 Mirror

BUFFALO BILL'S TRIUMPHS.—According to a letter received from Buffalo Bill (Wm. F. Cody) by a friend in New Orleans, that distinguished American has achieved both financial and social success in England — With a frankness characteristic of his western training, Mr. Cody states that he has captured England from the "Queen down, and is doing them to the tune of $10,000 a day." He confesses that it "is pretty hard work with two and three performances a day, and the society racket, receptions, dinners. etc. No man, not even Grant, was received better than your humble servant. As a proof of this Mr. Cody says he has "dined with every one of the royalty from Albert Prince of Wales down. —

7/8/87 Telephone

Hysteria is a form of nervous disease not yet thoroughly understood. It was once believed to be peculiar to women, but there are well-authenticated cases of men being afflicted with it. Its manifestations are various, from hysterics in which the sufferer laughs and cries uncontrollably, to convulsions. Firmness and gentleness are indispensible in dealing with hysterical persons. Reasoning is wasted, as if not incapable of attending they generally pay no attention to it. The clothing should be loosened, the room darkened and only one person allowed to stay with the sufferer unless another is absolutely required to assist. A warm foot bath sometimes gives relief, and a mustard plaster, or a flannel wrung out of boiling water and sprinkled with turpentine may be applied over the seat of the supposed pain. There are few diseases which have not been simulated by patients suffering from hysteria and sometimes without any wish to deceive; they are the victims of their own imaginations. *Globus hystericus* is a distressing symptom. The sensation is of a ball rising in the throat and causing suffocation. It can be relieved by wringing a handkerchief out of ice water and binding it tightly round the neck. Asafoetida is the usual remedy, and occasionally the fear of having to take it will cut short a fit of hysterics. Sometimes doses of bromide of potassium will so quiet the nerves as to prevent an attack, and in the intervals the doctor usually orders some preparation of iron to be taken, or other tonic treatment. Young persons should be taught self-control and encouraged to practise it, and girls especially should be disabused of the idea that hysterics make the sufferer interesting.

6/24/87 Telephone

Young man (to sexton at church door)—Isn't the sermon nearly done?
Sexton—About an hour yet. He is only on his "Lastly."
Young man—Will it take him an hour to get through his "Lastly?"
Sexton—No but there's the "One word more and I am done," and the "Finally,"

WANTED

A Steady Neat Young Man

To learn the Dairy Business. No one who uses liquor or tobacco need apply.

15-july-tf.   S. L. CHAPIN, Aldie, Va.

August 1887

7/28/87 Mirror

A gang of hands commenced this morning making necessary repairs upon the Aldie & Leesburg Telephone line. It is proposed to substitute poles for trees, wherever needed, and put the entire line in first class order.

8/4/87 Mirror

Letter from Aldie

On Monday night of last week, NANCY THOMAS, an elderly colored woman living in the dusky settlement near here, retired at the usual hour, leaving her door unlocked for the other members of her family who were all out attending an entertainment of some kind. How long she had been asleep she cannot say, when she was rudely awakened by a masked man who dragged her to the floor and brandishing huge knife over her declared his purpose to kill her then and there. She screamed and begged for her life, when her assailant modified his purpose and contented himself with a rough beating dislocating both shoulders and bruising up her body in a painful manner. She claimed to recognize her assailant as a neighbor, and on Wednesday Justice Furr issued a warrant for Wm. Godfrey, charged with the offence. He was brought before the Justice when the above facts were brought out and he was bailed in the sum of $500 for his appearance in court.

Godfrey is a reputable, well to do colored man has a clean record and is well spoken of by his neighbors, both white and colored.— Much sympathy is expressed for him; he could easily prove an alibi by his wife, but her evidence was ruled out. But few believe him guilty; in fact, the opinion is growing that the woman was altogether mistaken in the man.

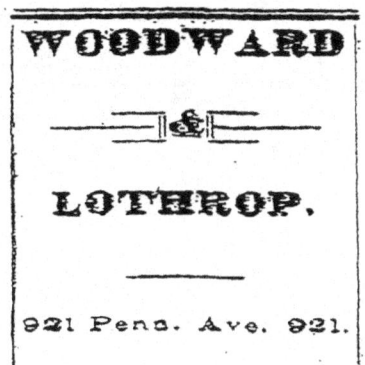

8/27/87 Washingtonian

H. M. STANLEY'S TESTIMONY.

In a recent interview between Mr. Stanley and a newspaper correspondent, the distinguished explorer said: "I have been in Africa for seventeen years, and I have never met a man who would kill me if I folded my hands. What I wanted, and what I have been endeavoring to ask for the poor Africans has been the good offices of Christians, ever since Livingtone taught me during those four months that I was with him. In 1871 I went to him as prejudiced as the biggest atheist in London. I was out there, away from a worldly world. I saw this solitary old man there, and asked myself, 'Why on earth does he stop here?' For months after we went, I found myself listening to him, and wondering at the old man's carying out all that was said in the Bible. Little by little his sympathy for others became contagious; mine was awakend; seeing his pity, his gentleness, his zeal his earnestness, and how he went quietly about his business, I was converted by him, although he had not tried to do it. How sad that the good old man died so soon!

This historic event was also commemorated by Hollywood with the popular movie *Stanley and Livingstone* (1939) starring Spencer Tracy.

August 1887

BUSH-MEETING.

THE GOOD TEMPLARS and W.C.T.U. of Loudoun county, will hold their 10th Annual "Bush-Meeting," for the promotion of Gospel and Temperance, on the old grounds at PURCELLVILLE, commencing TUESDAY, AUGUST 2d, 1887 at 10 o'cl'k. a.m., and continuing four days.

The following distinguished Ministers and Temperance Workers have been engaged:— Hon. J. R. MILLER, G.C.T., of Virginia; JOHN A. B. WILSON, D. D. of Delaware; Hon. LUTHER PERSON, of Indiana; Mrs. C. R. BUELL, Secretary of Nat. W.C.T.U.; Mrs. M. A. GOODALE, of Louisiana; Col. W. E HALL, of Philadelphia; Rev. L. C. MILLER of Harrisonburg, Va., and others.

All Ministers of the Gospel in the County are cordially invited to attend and participate in the meeting.

In addition to the Temperance addresses, there will be devotional and praise services each day conducted by the ministers present.

Vocal and Instrumental Music will be provided to enliven the occasion and everything done as far as possible for the comfort and pleasure of those in attendance.

An efficient police force will be on hand, thus insuring good order.

Refreshments for man and beast will be amply provided.

SPECIAL EXCURSION TRAINS will be run over the W. O. & W. Railroad, at very low rates, leaving the City at 8 A.M. and the grounds at 6.30 P.M., and extra coaches will be put on regular trains to accommodate excursionists.

The public is cordially invited to attend and hear the great moral truths and principles discussed which have taken such a firm hold upon the people of the entire country, and now agitates the public mind to a greater extent than ever before in the history of America. A question of more vital importance to a larger proportion of her people than any other issue, either moral or political.

FRIDAY, the 4th day of the meeting, is especially intended for our colored citizens, who will be addressed by Prof. D. N. Vassar of Richmond, Rev. Walter H. Brooks and Rev. Wm. H. Draper, of Washington, D C.; Rev. J. S. Cooper, of Leesburg and others.

All the colored Ministers in the County are cordially invited to be present.

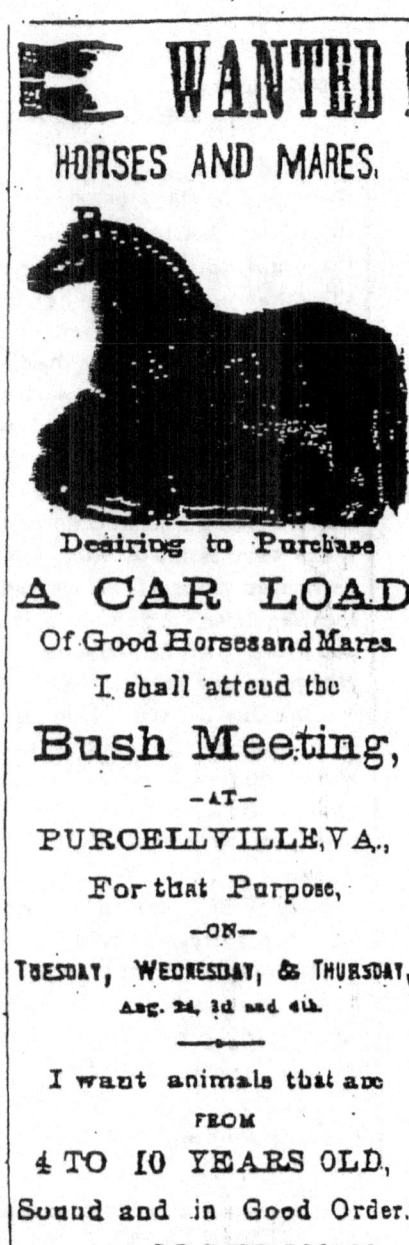

WANTED!
HORSES AND MARES.

Desiring to Purchase
A CAR LOAD
Of Good Horses and Mares,
I shall attend the
Bush Meeting,
—AT—
PURCELLVILLE, VA.,
For that Purpose,
—ON—
TUESDAY, WEDNESDAY, & THURSDAY,
Aug. 2d, 3d and 4th.

I want animals that are
FROM
4 TO 10 YEARS OLD,
Sound and in Good Order.
M. BERGMAN.

8/5/87 Telephone

ENCAMPED IN THE WOODS.

A MIGHTY HOST OF TEMPERANCE PEOPLE

Again the great institution of Loudoun, the annual Bush Meeting, held under the auspices of the I. O. G. T., and W. C. T. U., convened, at the usual place, near Purcellville, last Tuesday. Yes, it has become the great institution of Loudoun; for it has taken the place of the camp meeting and actually lays August Court in the shade. It has become a very popular place of resort, not only of the denizens of Loudoun but of the people in numerous adjoining counties and states.

And while these meetings have become, to a large degree, times of social intercourse and pleasure, yet the great attendance and deep interest manifested must be recognized as evidences of a great growth of public sympathy with the cause of Temperance. It shows that the public conscience is aroused to a degree which forbodes the annihilation, in the near future, of the greatest of all evils, the drink traffic.

THE FIRST DAY.

After about three long weeks of sweltering heat, that was almost unbearable, Tuesday morning, the time was set for the opening of the great Bush Meeting, was ushered in with a more kindly temperature, as though the hand of Providence was guiding and directing the efforts of his people to the best affect —as it has seemed, on similar occasions in the past. At an early hour signs of activity pervaded the beautiful grove where for a year scarcely a leaf in the brown carpet had been molested. The booth keepers were busy putting the finishing touches on their respective stands and making all ready for the grand rush. They had erected quite substantial sheds for the various branches of trade giving the grounds somewhat of an air of civilization. The stands for the speakers and choir was conspicuous because of its increased size—being about one half larger than heretofore. The part of the stand devoted to the speakers was handsomely decorated with evergreens and flowers, making it quite attractive. The seats for the audience had been all arranged, a rope was run around the part of the grounds devoted to the meeting, the water wagon arrived with a load of spring water.

(Rather than summarize the speeches of numerous orators over a period of three days, we will proceed to the last one.)

HON. LUTHER BENSON

of Indiana was then presented to the audience, which quickly moved up closer and jammed in together, to hear the man whom the beloved Bain told them a year ago, was "a regular cyclone" on the temperance platform.

Mr. Benson had arrived the day before, sick, and had been indisposed ever since but if his effort on that stand was the work of a sick man, what in the name of all the giants at once would he do when feeling well?

With the average address, it is possible for the reporter to give an outline sketch of the thought expressed that may be interesting to the reader, but it is as possible to bridle a thunderbolt and harness a tornado as to do justice to such a speaker as Mr. Benson with anything short of a sterographic report. And even that would not suffice —cold types cannot portray the fire, the intensity, the eloquent utterance with which the "cyclone" poured forth from the lips of Col. Benson, while assaulting the rum traffic, which he seems to hate from the bottom of his soul. He assailed it with indictment after indictment, charge after charge, and proof after proof; tearing the cloaks of hypocrisy from its face driving it from one refuge to another, and leaving no place, no earth or under heaven large enough for it to hide the ugliness of its horrid form.

He convulsed his great audience to shouts of applause then swelled the hearts and moistened the eyes of every hearer as he told the sad, sad story of ruined homes, blasted hopes and blasted lives. It was such a speech as few had ever heard and none will ever forget!

8/20/87 Washingonian

RIDDLEBERGER

THE SENATOR SENT TO JAIL AND RELEASED BY A MOB.

[Special telegram to the Dispatch]

WOODSTOCK VA., August 13 — Senator Riddleberger's committal to jail, as wired you last night, was brought about by the following causes: Senator Riddleberger appeared on Thursday morning in the County Court here, in connection with four other lawyers, to defend W. W. Jones in a trial for misdemeanor. The whole morning session was consumed in wrangling. By noon one of the lawyers, to the great indignation of Senator Riddleberger, who immediately withdrew from the case, asked the Court to appoint counsel for Jones. The Court replied it thought the prisoner well represented. Then all the lawyers who had been consuming the time of the court in behalf of Jones withdrew. The Court appointed the Hon. H. C. Allen attorney for the defendant and proceeded with the case. While Judge Allen was conducting the case Senator Riddleberger and several of the other lawyers who had appeared for Jones in the morning returned and resumed connection with the case. The jury decided that

JONES WAS INSANE.

and he was discharged. Jones was a client of Senator Riddleberger's, and the verdict made the Senator angry. He was accused of writing a placard and giving a boy two dollars to haul Jones up and down the town, the latter displaying the placard meanwhile, which had written on it:

"Verdict — Bill Jones not guilty but insane, jury insane, lawyers insane, court insane in the main."

Senator Riddleberger was summoned before the Judge at 5 o'clock on Friday evening, and the following scene took place: The Court told the Senator that he had been summoned to show cause why he should not be fined and committed to jail for contempt of court. The Senator said he had not seen the warrant. The Commonwealth's attorney read the return for the warrant.

"SIT DOWN," RIDDLEBERGER.

The Senator claimed the Court had no jurisdiction. The Court said it had fully decided it had. The Senator attempted to make a speech and the Court told him to sit down; that argument would not be heard until the evidence was in. The Senator still persisting in making a speech, the Judge fined him $25. The Senator still persisting in speaking, the Court said it would send him to jail if he did not sit down.

"TAKEN TO A COUNTY JAIL."

Senator Riddleberger then said: "I won't be sent to jail, and I'd like to see the damn man that will take me there." The Court ordered the sheriff to take him, and Senator Riddleberger resisting, the Court ordered the bystanders to assist the sheriff, when the bystanders and some of the deputy sheriffs began to jump out of the window. The sheriff took the prisoner to jail.

Senator Riddleberger bought the cardboard used in the placard. The confinement of Senator Riddleberger in jail caused great excitement among his followers.

The jail is an old-fashioned solid stone structure, standing on a grassy lawn shaded by large locust trees. It is situated in the centre of the town. The jailer was sick in bed, and Deputy Sheriff Hottel was placed in jail with the Senator. About 2 o'clock Mrs. Shull, wife of the jailer, was awakened by some one trying to get in jail. She refused admittance, and they threatened to use force. Mrs. Shull told them it would be on their own responsibility. She ran to Senator Riddleberger's cell and asked him to appeal to the mob. He asked her to let him out. She refused, as she did also to let the deputy sheriff out, who requested it. In the meantime the mob broke into the kitchen, and Mrs. Shull, who was in her night clothes, ran in her room. A key was found which let the Senator out through the jail-yard in the rear.

Riddleberger, on Monday, voluntarily returned to the jail to serve out his sentence — the most sensible thing he has done for some time. A motion was made by his friends to have the judge resind his order of imprisonment, which he refused.

August, 1887

THE TELEPHONE.
FRIDAY............AUG. 26TH.

—Ice is scarce in Hamilton. Wiley's supply is exhausted and Kingsley Bro's will not have enough to last till cool weather.

—The road officers should see to it that the turnpike, between Hamilton, and Clarks Gap is put in passable condition at once. It is simply horrible at present. This important highway should have due attention before the time for holding the Leesburg Fair.

—An item stolen from the TELEPHONE last week by the *Alexandria Gazette*, appeared in the *Mirror* yesterday credited to the *Gazette*.— That's a fine chance for fairness.

8/18/87 Mirror

THE scene last week, at Woodstock, in Shenandoah county, the home of U. S. Senator RIDDLEBERGER, was a rather humiliating one to the people of Virginia. But from the newspaper accounts of the affair, Riddleberger's conduct made it next to impossible for the Judge to do otherwise than he did, and retain his seat on the bench.

When the offender who insults the court for administering the laws he himself has helped to frame, is a Senator of the United States, representing the people of a great State in the highest representative body in the world, the reflection affects each individual citizen of the land.

HUMPHREYS'
HOMEOPATHIC VETERINARY SPECIFICS
For Horses, Cattle, Sheep, Dogs, Hogs, Poultry.
500 PAGE BOOK on Treatment of Animals and Chart Sent Free.
CURES—Fevers, Congestions, Inflammation.
A.A.—Spinal Meningitis, Milk Fever.
B.B.—Strains, Lameness, Rheumatism.
C.C.—Distemper, Nasal Discharges.
D.D.—Bots or Grubs, Worms.
E.E.—Coughs, Heaves, Pneumonia.
F.F.—Colic or Gripes, Bellyache.
G.G.—Miscarriage, Hemorrhages.
H.H.—Urinary and Kidney Diseases.
I.I.—Eruptive Diseases, Mange.
J.K.—Diseases of Digestion.
Stable Case, with Specifics, Manual, Witch Hazel Oil and Medicator, $7.00
Price, Single Bottle (over 50 doses), .60
Sold by Druggists; or
Sent Prepaid on Receipt of Price.
Humphreys' Med. Co., 109 Fulton St., N. Y.

8/25/87 Mirror

WHEN BARNUM PAID FOR DRINKS.— At a recent dinner, by the way, a story was told of Barnum. "He is a temperance man now," said one of the party, "but I remember when he set up the drinks for a distinguished crowd. He didn't do it out of pure good nature, either. It was twenty-six years ago, at the Profile House in the Franconia Mountains. Barnum was feeling pretty smart in those days, and he had been playing his jokes and cute tricks rather freely about the house. A lot of guests sat on the piazza of the hotel. Among them were Commodore Vanderbilt, W. H. Vanderbilt, another of the family, Gov. Gilmore's son, John Hyde, the artist, Barnum, and a number of others, including myself. Young Gilmore was a lively young chap then, but he has changed and become a minister since. Gilmore put up the job and let us all into it. He twisted the talk around to physical prowess, and got Barnum to brag about how fast he could run. Across the plateau in front of the hotel was a rail to which horses were tied. Gilmore proposed that we all start from the piazza and run to the rail and that the last man to touch the rail with his hand pay for the drinks for the crowd. Everybody agreed and we got into line, all except the Commodore, who sat on the piazza, and gave the word —P. T. was lively and confident and waited impatiently for the word. The Commodore said 'Go!' and away went the greatest show on earth like Jumbo in a sprint race. He took the lead right away. Everybody else pretended to run for all that was in them, but took care not to get ahead of P. T. The showman got there in great style, put his hand on the rail, and turned round in triumph. There stood the rest of the crowd in line behind him, not one touching the rail. When he heard the Commodore roar he took in the situation.— He was the only one who put his hand on the rail at all. Barnum set them up, but he was so mad that he couldn't tell a plausible fairy tale for a week."—*Albany Journal*.

September, 1887

9/17/87 Telephone

INSANE PEOPLE LOCKED UP IN COUNTY JAILS.

RICHMOND, Sept. 11.—Charles Herbschleb, a German, who is worth $10,000 in Richmond real estate, has been adjudged insane by a commission, and is now confined in the miserable city jail here, awaiting room in an asylum. He is an old man, having no relatives near him, but it is said that he has a sister in Philadelphia or New York. His property is in the hands of a commission by the court, but why he is locked up in a jail, which is no place for the incarceration of a human being, is not explained.—N. Y. Tribune.

Humanity cries out against the Bourbon Democratic *regime* which allows lunatics to remain in county jails, for want of accommodations at the asylum. What sight is so sad as the form of one so unfortunate reclining upon the floor of an ill-kept jail—in a felon's cell—with poor accommodations at best and little or no curative treatment. Pity weeps at such a sad sight, and Justice arises in righteous wrath and demands that these unfortunate people shall be cared for decently, if not tenderly.

For more than a year efforts have been made to have an insane woman (who might be permanently cured, with proper care) removed from Loudoun to an asylum; but instead of being thus provided for, and possibly cured, she is confined, month after month, in our County jail —which, instead of curing her of her malady, is enough to make a sane man crazy.

9/1/87 Mirror

Mr. F W. Harper, of Kentucky, owner of the famous race horse and sire, Ten Broeck, has ordered a handsome and costly monument of white marble to be erected over the grave of the great horse. The shaft will be seven feet two inches tall and surmounted by an urn it will bear the date of the horse's birth, death and his records.

(Bluegrass musician Bill Monroe also commemorated this horse with his rendition of the ballad "Molly and Ten Broeck".)

9/22/87 Mirror

OIL BURNING LOCOMOTIVES.—Capt W. H. Brooks Thursday made a trip over the W and O. railroad, from this city to Round Hill, on his patented oil burning locomotive, during which trip his locomotive accomplished all that is claimed for it. He left here in the morning ten minutes behind the regular mail train, and returned in the evening ten minutes after the arrival here of that train, having kept the same time throughout the trip. During the run to Round Hill and back, a distance of 110 miles, the locomotive consumed two and a half barrels of crude petroleum, and Capt. Brooks says he will yet lessen the consumption of oil by his locomotive. He is confident that in time oil will be used exclusively as fuel for locomotives, and thinks his patent will be generally adopted.—

—BALTIMORE—
UNITED OIL CO.
—REFINERS OF—
PETROLEUM
AND ITS PRODUCTS
DEODORIZED GASOLENE,
For Stoves.
Alta Safety Oil,
For Lamps.
Lubricating Oil,
For Machinery.

BEDRIDDEN

for the Regulator. I recommend it to every woman I hear of who is suffering with any womb trouble, no matter of what description, and I have yet to hear of a single failure to cure."
Send for our Book on Diseases of Women, which is mailed free.
Address BRADFIELD REGULATOR CO.,
Atlanta, Ga.

MRS. ANNA LAND, of Belair, Ga., under date of Nov. 6, 1884, says: "I have been using your wonderful remedy, Bradfield's Female Regulator, in my family a long time, and I would to God that every afflicted woman in our land knew of its wonderful virtues and curative powers as I do; there would be a great deal less suffering among our sex. I am sure I would have been *bedridden for life* had it not been

FOR LIFE!

October, 1887

10/31/87 Mirror

The Monument to Gen. Lee.

In spite of the rain the laying of the corner-stone of the Lee monument at Richmond last Thursday, was the most imposing event of the kind ever seen in that city, the attendance of people to witness the ceremony and the pageant attendant upon it exceeding any similar demonstration ever witnessed in the State. It is estimated that the crowd of visitors exceeded 25,000. Almost every house on Main, Broad and Franklin streets along the line of march was decorated many of them with great artistic skill. On two or three houses along the line old battle-stained war flags were prominently displayed. The procession was nearly an hour passing a given point.

FOR SALE

—AT—

LEESBURG, LOUDOUN CO., VA.,

at Public Auction,

Tuesday, November 15, '87

The Splendid Estate of

OATLANDS,

containing

700 ACRES,

more or less. One of the finest old Mansions in the State of Virginia—handsome Grounds, Terraced Gardens, Hot and Green Houses.— The Lands are first-class Loudoun Land.

Will be sold one-third cash, balance in one, two and three years, with interest, secured by deed of trust.

Two Tracts of Land, each with a TENANT HOUSE, 100 ACRES OF CLEARED LAND, and 25 ACRES OF WOOD, may be offered separately, leaving between four and five hundred Acres to be sold with mansion.

Mr. GEORGE CARTER, who lives on the place, six miles from Leesburg, Post Office Oatlands, will be glad to show the place to parties wishing to purchase the whole or sub-divisions.

ARTHUR HERBERT, Trustee
sep17.   KATE P. CARTER.

Oatlands is now supported by the National Historic Trust and is open to the public. It is just down the road from President James Monroe's home, which is privately owned.

10/22/87 Washingtonian

A REMARKABLE INVENTION.

AN ELECTRIC TYPE-WRITER THAT WILL BE A RIVAL OF THE TELEPHONE.

A Washington dispatch to the Baltimore SUN says:

There is considerable talk in the Patent Office just now concerning an invention patented recently, which, in the opinion of some, will be a formidable rival of the telephone, Mr. Bell's monopoly. The invention is an electric type-writer. The instrument in appearance somewhat resembles an ordinary mechanical type-writer. It has a key-board, and the types are placed on steel bars, which play upon a common centre, as is the case with the type-writer. The motive power used is electricity.

10/14/87 Telephone

BASEBALL GOSSIP.

The success of some of our great pitchers of today comes mainly from the secret signs which they give to the catchers. Some of the heaviest punishment inflicted on pitchers this season has been caused by some one in the opposing team discovering the system of signs, and in return using a sign to tell the batsman what ball is about to be pitched for him. To prevent an opponent discovering his signs a pitcher will sometimes give two or more signs to his catcher at one time. From this one can see that a catcher must have a head on him as well as the pitcher.

Al Spalding, of Chicago, is already on the warpath for 1888. He has secured Pat Tebeau, third baseman of the Denver Baseball club, considered the best of the young talent of the Western league.

10/7/87 Telephone

—The boarders have nearly all left town. This has been a very busy season among the boarding houses. Over 500 strangers were reported in town at one time.

10/28/87 Telephone

No we shall not reply to the long and labored letter in the *Washingtonian*, last week, mainly devoted to the TELEPHONE, signed "E. L. S."—Emil Ludwig Scharf.

The game is too small.

November, 1887

10/28/87 Telephone

On the Verge of Marriage.

Once engaged the happy pair should avoid all public demonstrations of affection, except that they may walk together arm in arm, and the young lady may drive out with her affianced with a servant behind. She must not, however, go to the opera or theatre with him alone; she must have a chaperon if she would consult the prejudices of society.

While it is delightful to see a young couple really in love they should not go to the theatre to show it. All unsophisticated human beings are fond of this egoisme a deux, but it is most painful to the lookers-on. These lovers should remember that people are observing them, laughing at them; and if they make love on a stage-coach drive, a picnic, a lawn-tennis party, the whole pleasure of the party is spoiled. A woman loses her dignity by this process, and nothing is finer in a young woman than a sweet, maidenly reserve.

When an engagement is announced the family of the lover all call on that of the lady. The announcement should come from the mother of the gentleman; as soon as is convenient and proper there should be an invitation extended by the family of the young man to that of the young woman. She then becomes an autocrat; everything is referred to her. She goes out with her future mother-in-law or sisters, and is one of them in fact though not in name; she can visit them at their country house; but she must never travel alone with her lover. Our language is singularly deficient; we have no word to represent fiance and fiancee; "my daughter's engaged" is a very awkward phrase; "my daughter's young man" is very countrified; "my daughters's lover" is scarcely a proper phrase.

12/1/87 Mirror,

THANKSGIVING DAY last Thursday, seems to have been more generally observed throughout the country, than usual. In Leesburg, however, the day passed pretty much as other days, except that the Bank was closed, and services held in the Episcopal Church, where Rev. Dr. Davis preached an admirable discourse.

11/2/87 Mirror

Panic at a Funeral.

TIFFIN, Ohio, Oct. 27—At a funeral near Sycamore to day the team attached to the hearse ran away and the vehicle was reduced almost to kindling wood. The coffin was dashed to the ground, the lid torn off, and the corpse rolled into a ditch by the roadside. Other teams took fright and a general panic ensued. Women fainted, men jumped from carriages, wagons were overturned, horses became entangled in the general wreck, and several persons were more or less seriously injured. Rev. Mr Howells, who was to have conducted the funeral exercises, was perhaps fatally injured.

11/10/87 Mirror

SMART BOYS.—The town of Woodstock in addition to being the abiding place of Virginia's picturesque Senator, seems also to be blessed with a goodly supply of sharp boys.—It appears that on Halloween these youths turned out and celebrated the event in the most approved or more properly, disapproved style, and nineteen of them were threatened with arrest for their pranks of removing signs, taking gates off their hinges, &c. They were prepared, however, and hired counsel, refused arrest without warrant, lodged complaints with the town council against the mayor and plaintiff for obstructing the streets with various property, which ought to be removed, and demanded a separate trial. The plaintiffs, figuring up the probable costs, dropped the prosecution.

A. E. Dinsmore,

Purcellville, Va.

I desire to announce to all the people of the surrounding county that I am permanently established in Purcellville, and well equipped with excellent facilities for doing everything in the line of Carriage

CARRIAGE PAINTING

and Trimming.

IN FIRST CLASS MANNER.

Keeping in stock various grades of materials, I can do all work to suit the purses of my customers, but I especially desire the patronage of those who want

FIRST CLASS WORK,

November 1887

11/17/87 Mirror

Look Out for Them.—Horse thieving has again broken out in Loudoun. One night last week a fine young stallion belonging to Mr. Geo. C. Royston, living on the farm of the late A. T. M. Rost, was stolen from the stable. The next morning Mr. R. had a lot of bills printed which he industriously circulated and they led to the recovery of the animal near Dranesville, which point the thief reached about daylight the morning following his theft, and being accosted by a gentleman whom he passed on the road, and questioned about his early ride, he said he was going for a physician; but evidently becoming alarmed he shortly after dismounted, and slipping the bridle from the horse turned him loose in the road. Later in the day the animal was turned into a pasture field, where he remained until the handbills revealed his ownership, and Mr. Royston notified. Mr. R. went down last Monday and returned in the evening with his property.

11/17/87 Mirror

A Man Who Rode Into the City on a Borrowed Horse—At an early hour this morning a man about thirty years old entered this city on horseback, having ridden across the Long Bridge. He rode a fine-looking animal, which he offered for sale to Wm. Kearney, a horse trader, for $40.— Kearney suspected something wrong, and made the purchase, in order to secure the animal, and paid the stranger $1 in order to bind the bargain, the latter agreeing to return later in the day for the remaining $39. As soon as the stranger left the stable Kearney turned the animal over to the police of the first precinct and gave a description of the man, who was subsequently arrested by officer Kenny. When taken to the station he gave his name as Henry Jewell, and afterwards said his name was James Goings. He claimed that the animal belonged to him and he had a right to sell it, but when about to be put behind the bars he confessed that he had stolen the animal from the stable of Wm. A. Smoot, a coal merchant in Alexandria. He signified a willingness to return to Virginia, and this afternoon he was turned over to Capt. Webster of the Alexandria police, who took him back to Alexandria. The penalty for horse stealing in Virginia is ten years imprisonment.—Wash. Star

12/1/87 Mirror

PROFESSIONAL PALLBEARING.

A Gloomy Trade, but Very Easy and Eminently Respectable.

He was a gloomy looking sort of person and his face wore an expression of woe that made one think he had it stamped there as a sort of trade mark. He was clad in garments of the somberest hue, and from the wide weed on his high hat to the dead polish on his broad soled shoes he looked for all the world like a man in whose family there was a death at least once a year. When he came into the street car a sort of hush fell upon the passengers out of respect for his placarded sorrow. By and by the gloomy man was asked if he had met with a bereavement lately.

"No, indeed," he replied. "there has not been a death in my family for years."

"Why, then," asked his neighbor, with more curiosity than politeness, "do you dress in such deep mourning?"

"Oh, that's on account of my business."

"You are an undertaker, then?"

"No, I am a pall bearer," and noting the look of surprise in his interlocutor's face he went on: "Some years ago there was a strike in my trade. I am a carpenter and during one of my idle days I passed a house where there was a funeral. Stopping to watch it I was approached by the undertaker, who asked me if I was going to the funeral. I said no, that I knew no one there. He then asked me if I had any objection to being a pall bearer. I said I had none, provided I was paid for it, and we finally struck a bargain. I made as much that afternoon as I would had I worked all day at my trade, and since then I have adopted pall bearing as a means of livelihood. I dress in black, as you see, and each morning look over the death notices. I generally seek out the undertaker and make my bargain with him, and I average about two funerals a day.

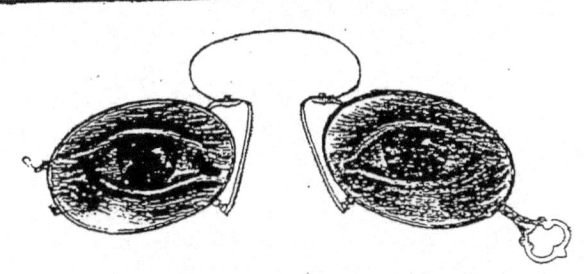

READ, REFLECT AND ACT.

IN PURCHASING PRESENTS FOR THE HOLIDAYS,

SPECTACLES a specialty.

dec. 17, 1887. **C. E. EVARD**, Leesburg, Va.

HE COURTED DEATH IN VAIN.

The Career of a Most Noted Duelist in the Gulf States.

Mrs. Clement C. Clay, widow of the noted Alabama Senator captured with Jeff Davis, was concerned with the most famous duelist the South ever produced, in the person of Alexander McClellan. He was a native of Kentucky, and for many years was prominent in politics and society. He was an exquisite in dress and manners, a brilliant speaker and a writer of tremendous power, possessing the keenest wit and sarcasm. His attacks on the Van Buren Administration gave him a national celebrity.

He killed a great many men during his career. As an instance of his deadliness, for he always killed the man he fought, may be mentioned his duel with General Allen of Mississippi. He had heard that Allen made some slighting remark about him. After Allen had accepted his challenge McClellan declared that he would shoot out the tongue that made the remark. The duel was fought at forty paces with rifles, and he literally cut Allen's tongue out, as he threatened.

One instance exhibits his courage. One day he rode up to an inn in a little Mississippi town. While he was dismounting, a notorious bully and desperado of that country, who had killed many men and was the terror of the region, was on the inside, with his revolver cocked and a watch in his hand. He had ordered the room cleared in five minutes, and every man had gone, although all were fighting men. When McClellan entered the bully faced him and with a big oath informed him of the facts and that there were only three minutes left before he should kill whoever remained. McClellan, without moving a muscle or drawing a weapon, produced his watch, glanced at it, and said:

"My name is Alexander McClellan. I give you ten seconds to leave the room or you are a dead man."

The fellow yelled out:

"By thunder, Colonel, one-half of that time will do!" and he was out in two seconds.

Later on in his career he was haunted by remorse. Man-killing had left its pains. His light was never out of his room at night, and men said he slept not. When the Mexican war broke out he told the Rev. Peter Donan, father of the now only Colonel Pat, that he was weary with life, that he had never found any one who could kill him, and he was going to battle to seek death on the field, as he did not want to commit suicide.

He entered the service as a volunteer, and from the first placed himself in the front point of danger, commanding attention for his absolute bravery. He was promoted again and again until he reached the head of the regiment, when he was shot through the body. Then he returned home saying he couldn't be killed and hazarded his life in several duels thereafter. He grew more and more eccentric, and thought his opponents abused his confidence by not killing him. Then he met Mrs. Clay, a beautiful girl of her time.

She describes him as the most fascinating man to women she ever met, possessing that serpentine power over women which historians and romancers attribute to Aaron Burr. McClellan proposed marriage to Mrs. Clay, but her friends objected on account of his excessive duelling propensities and the fear that she would never be happy with him. She asked him to wait six months before replying, and during the interval did not dare to meet him on account of his power over her. In the meantime she met Clement C. Clay, and was satisfied that he was her destiny. Shortly after the engagement was announced she got a note from McClellan asking for an interview. Being afraid of his spell, and that he might kill her, she declined. It was only a few days later when McClellan rode into the then little pine town of Columbus, Miss. He was shown to a room at an inn, the floor of which was irregular, like those of all such places. He poured water on the floor and observed which way the incline ran. Then dressing himself with the greatest care and exquisite neatness, he lay down with his head inclined with the floor. He placed one hand across his breast, and with the other the muzzle of his favorite duelling pistol at the base of the brain where death is instantaneous. He was found there dead, without a stain of blood on his scrupulously clean, perfectly arrayed person, having realized his superstition at last—that finding no one else who would kill him, he became a *felo de se*.

January, 1888

THE TELEPHONE.

FRIDAY............JAN. 20TH.

REPUBLICAN TICKET.
1888.

FOR PRESIDENT OF UNITED STATES

JAS. G BLAINE

FOR VICE-PRESIDENT,

J. B. FORAKER.

OUR PLATFORM.

PROTECTION OF AMERICAN HOMES, against the Saloon.

PROTECTION OF AMERICAN BALLOTS, against Fraud and Violence.

PROTECTION OF AMERICAN LABOR, against Foreign Labor.

PROTECTION of AMARICAN INDUSTRIES against Foreign Greed.

Death of Wm. W. Thompson.

The entire populace of Hamilton were shocked and grieved last Monday morning by the report, that quickly sped from house to house, announcing the sudden death of Wm. W. Thomson, Mayor of the town. The shock was so sudden and unexpected that it was difficult for anyone to belive the report at first.

On the day previous, Sunday, Mr. Thompson, accompanied by his wife and daughter, visited their daughter and family, at North Fork. He returned in the evening and retired apparently in usual health. About four o'clock in the morning his wife awoke and hearing him snoring, as she thought, made some jocular remark to him about it. Receiving no response she asked him why he did not speak to her, but still no answer came. She then placed her hand under his head and raised it up, when his breathing immediately ceased and he was dead. Just at this juncture, their daughter, Miss Belle, having heard the noise, entered the room ; and they were horrified with the terrible truth that they were at once widow and fatherless. Under the shadow of night the Pale Messenger had invaded their happy home and, with no sign of warning, like a lightning flash from a clear sky, took away its head and its support. The physician who was soon summoned, announced that death was caused by Apoplexy. He had peacefully passed from the physical rest of sleep to the spiritual rest of eternity.

William W. Thompson was born in Fairfax County, in October, 1831 but spent most of his life in Alexandria, where he learned and worked at his trade, as tinner. About sixteen years ago he moved to Hamilton and opened a tin and stove store, in a modest way, which, by his dilligence in business and upright dealing with his fellow men, has grown in value until, during the past few years, he has been doing a profitable business—and, we trust, has laid by something for those who were dependent upon him. In this connection it may be proper to state that his prudent regard for his loved ones had prompted him to have his life insured—for what amount we are not informed.

1/28/88 Washingtonian

Senator Heaton, in a conversation Saturday, spoke enthusiastically of the future of that part of Virginia adjacent to Arlington and Alexandria. He is not only in favor of Mount Vernon avenue, but he is a strong believer in a branch from the Washington and Ohio R. R., starting at Falls Church and Running to the end of the Aquduct bridge, which he thinks, would take a great deal of summer travel out through Virginia and up as high as the Blue Ridge mountains. He says the suburban growth of Washington is certain to be on the Virginia side of the Potomac, for there can be found not only an abundance of room but the finest views of Washington and the beautiful Potomsc. He thinks Memorial bridge an absolute necessity.

1/21/88 Washingtonian

A FATAL BLIZZARD.

ONE HUNDRED PERSONS PERISH.

Many others Reported to be Missing.

ST. PAUL, Jan. 16.—The terrible snowstorm which has swept over the Northwest, blockading railroads in five States is now over, and the victims of its fury are being counted. The pitiful list is growing almost every hour. It is not improbable, when the record is complete, it will show a hundred lives sacrificed to the awful fury of the blizzard. Next to this the worst blizzard that the Northwest ever experienced occurred January 9, 8 and 9, 1873. In that storm seventy people were frozen to death and thousands of dollars worth of propery were destroyed. The present storm proves to even more terrible in its results. It came without warning. At sunrise last Wednesday Dakota never had more lovely winter weather. The air was clear as crystal, and every object about the harrizon was distinctly vissible. The wind was from the south warm and balmy, and before the sun was high in the sky a decided thaw had set in. Farmers took advantage of the beautiful weather to go to town, to draw wood, hay, &c. About noon a cloud was seen along northwestern horrizon, lying close to the ground, but stretching from the west to the north in a dark semicircle. Little attention was paid to it, but in an hour the cloud had swept over the country, the sun was obscured, the snow was falling fast, and a gale sweeping from the northwest with terrible fury.—the blizzard had begun. The murcury fell rapidly, and by 5 o'cl'k it was degrees below zero, and the next morning registered 30 degrees below. All the while the wind increased in fury, the snow fell thicker, and the large amount of snow that was already on the ground was blown into powder and hurled along by the wind. On the prairie an object forty feet distant could not be seen. A man's voice could not be heard six feet distant. The air was full of snow as fine as flour, and the roaring of the wind and the darkness caused by so much snow in the air made the scene the most dismal drear and forsaken that man ever looked upon. Every railroad in Dakona, Minnesota, and many Iowa Nebraska and Wisconsin railroads were blockaded. Telegraph wires everywhere were down, and it was not until Saturday that the full extent and awful results of the storm became apparent. The telegraph hourly brings the most pitiful stories of suffering, terribly struggles for life and heroic deeds by the brave men and women of the storm stricken sections that have never been equaled.

TEACHER AND PUPILS PERISH.

ST. PAUL, Jan. 18.—The report of the death of a school teacher and sixteen children at Clear Lake Township, in Eastern Edmund County, at first discredited, is probably true. Parties who came from Warner, Dak., state that the teacher and six children have been found. H. H. Chapin, of Minneapolis, supposed to have been lost, arrived in Aberdeen last night

The Druse family live on a farm 9 miles south of Woolsley. Katharine Druse, with a sister, were at the barn, about 60 rods from the house, when the storm came up. Katharine started for the house, but lost her way. The next morning her body was found 40 rods from the house.—Those reported most severely frozen are improving and may recover.

SNOW DRIFTS THIRTY FEET HIGH.

A Yankton, Dak., correspondent says: Only two deaths are reported so far in Yankton County and two in Clay. In Bon Homme County nineteen deaths are reported. From South Dakota 104 deaths are reported. In Bon Homme County 200 head of frozen cattle were counted in one place and 140 at another. Dead cattle and hogs may be seen along the road from Yankton to Springfield. The snow drifts are said to be 30 feet deep. Some persons missing are yet unaccounted for.

FIFTEEN PERISH IN ONE NEBRASKA COUNTY

LINCOLN, NEB., Jan. 18.—A dispatch from O'Neill, Neb., says: Fifteen persons perished in last Thursday's storm in Custer County alone. The loss of stock is said to be enormous. Particulars are not obtainable.

HIS TWO BOYS FROZEN TO DEATH.

DUBUQUE, Jan. 18.—The fatalities of the late blizzard on the prairie districts of Iowa are being gradually made public.—Byron Cleveland, of Manchester, Delaware county, has received information

January 1888

that his two sons, aged fifteen and seventeen, were frozen to death during the storm, together with ninety head of cattle. The two boys were driving the cattle to water, about a mile from the house, when the blizzard struck them, and their dead bodies have just been found. The cattle were frozen stiff.

COWARDLY CONDUCT OF TWO YOUNG MEN.

Miss May Henning and a boy named Julius, twelve years of age, started in a sleigh to attend a party in company with two young men. When the storm struck them they lost their way, and the young young men deserted the lady and the boy, and reached a farm house in safety. The deserted pair remained out in the storm all night, and in the morning they were found partially covered with snow. The young lady will lose both legs, and the boy's hands and feet were badly frozen.— He was saved from death by the brave girl, who wrapped him in the only blanket left them.

A SCHOOL TEACHER'S HEROIC STRUGGLE TO SAVE HER PUPILS.

Miss Loule Royce, a school teacher eight miles from Plainview, had but three pupils on the day of the storm. She started at 2 o'clock with the children for a house about twenty rods distant, but lost her way. All lay down in the snow, and Miss Royce wrapped up the little ones as best she could. Early in the night one child died, and later a second one, and just as morning broke the third child succumbed to the cold. Miss Royce then managed to reach the house, less than twenty rods away. Both her feet are badly frozen, and they will probably have to be amputated.

EIGHT SCHOOL CHILDREN AND FIVE BROTHERS PERISH.

A school teacher and eight children, names unknown, are reported from Neligh to have perished. Five men named Stickle, brothers, are reported from the same place to have been frozen to death. Also an old man named Glose and a boy named Miller. Mrs. Miller, the boy's mother, was also badly frozen and will lose both legs. She was returning from the funeral of another son when caught in the storm.

(This storm, so terrible in its suddenness and severity, was recently mentioned by several journalists including George Will)

The Blizzard Succeeded by Terribly Severe Weather all Over the West.

CHICAGO, Jan. 16.—The great storm which swept over the entire country from the northwest last week has been followed by a freeze, the like of which has not been experienced since the memorable winter of 1864. The area of unusual cold has been general, extending from the extreme northern line of telegraphic communication as far south as Texas and the Gulf States. Extreme suffering is reported from all directions, especially in Minnesota, Dakota, Montana, and Nebraska, where many lives have been lost. In Kansas thousands are suffering from want of both fuel and food, and in some counties aid is needed to save many.

1/28/88 Washingtonian

The Western Blizzard.

The blizzard last week, over the Western States, will mark an important event in the history of that section. Such losses and suffering have never occurred in this country before, and if that vast section is to be doomed to these tempestous storm periods in Winter and the destructive tornadoes in summer, it will become a question, whether it will be a country in which the people can live in safety and comfort—or will it pay, as the enterprising American first asks, when entering upon a new enterprise? For several winters and summers its blizzards and tornadoes have scourged its inhabitants to a most severe degree.

1/20/88 Telephone

An Ice Time.

We may have plenty of cold weather yet, but those who have not yet filled their ice houses should not let this present opportunity pass. The ice is now thicker than can usually be secured in this locality and of fine quality. But do not hurry the ice in so fast that you cannot do it properly. The important part of the work is properly packing the ice in the house. It should be piled up as carefully as a stone wall, filling in every little hole, making the whole mass a solid pile of solid ice. If carelessly placed (or dumped in by the cart load, as some do it) the air will get through and the ice will melt.

1/28/88 Washingtonian

The Rush to Florida.

Jacksonville is now on a regular boom and the streets present a more animated appearance than they have for several years in the midst of the season.

January, 1888

1/20/88 Telephone

MAKING A TOWN.

A LIVE NEWSPAPER MAN MADE THE WILDERNESS BLOSSOM.

After the war Maj. Adams, of the Webster (Dak.) "Farm and Reporter," was prominent in Iowa politics, but finally determined to move to Dakota. He settled in Day county, took up a claim, and built himself a sod shanty. He was a printer by trade, and a newspaper man by instinct, and took a printing outfit with him to his claim. He finally went to amusing himself by getting out a paper. He was twelve miles from a postoffice, and 38 from a railroad, but he issued a paper filled with accounts of the occurrences which would ordinarily take place in a town of 3,000 or 4,000. He described the firmen's parade, the concert by the band, lectures by prominent people in the town hall, church sociables, and so on. After printing a few hundred copies of these papers the major would drive over to the postoffice and mail them to various offices in the East and West for general distribution.

One day the editor of this strange sheet was standing in front of his sod shanty when he saw a horse and buggy coming across the prairie. As it drew nearer he observed the figure of a man in the buggy, and he noticed that every now and then the vehicle stopped and the man stood up in the buggy and looked anxiously about him. At last he stood up on his seat, shaded his eyes with his hand and scanned the horizon in every direction. Then he sat down and drove straight to the sod shack.

"Hello!" said Adams, "how are you?"

"Howdy do," replied the stranger.

"Won't you get out and come in and rest," said the major.

"Yes, I will," responded the traveler, and he did.

He took a stool and looked around the shack curiously, taking in the printing outfit with the other furniture. Then an idea seemed to strike him.

"Look here," he said, "do you print the Western Chief here?"

"Yes," said Adams. "Would you like to look at one?"

"Look at one!" exclaimed the stranger; "look at one! No, thank you! I've looked at it a good many times."

"What do you think of it?" inquired Adams.

"You want me to tell you?" responded the stranger.

"Certainly," replied the editor.

"Well, then, I think you are the d—dest liar I ever knew."

"Why, you didn't take my fun in earnest, did you?" inquired Adams.

"Fun nothing!" said the stranger.— "Why, I came out to your infernal place to start a hardware store."

Adams tried to prevail upon the stranger, whose name was Lawrence, to stay and start the store anyway. But it was no use. But it was no use. He went back to Iowa. But four months from that date Mr. Adams stood in the door of his shack and counted 120 houses in sight. The boom edition had brought others in who staid. Now railways traverse the region, and a short distance from that first dwelling stands the thriving town of Britton, in Marshall county. Day having been divided and a new county formed of that name. "If Lawrence had staid and started the hardware store," says Adams, "he would now be worth $50,000."

2/24/88 Telephone

BOLINGTON, Feb. 21, 1888.—The Rev. C. F. Beales, of Morrisonville, was made the recipient of a nice donation on Wednesday evening, of last week, by the congregation at Shinar, as an appreciation of his services rendered since the resignation of the regular pastor, last Fall. On the evening mentioned the good people of that society began to gather at his residence, nor did they stop until the house was full, bringing with them the good things of life, in almost every conceivable shape, replenishing the family storehouse generally, making glad the hearts of the good brother and his lady, who entertained their guests in the best manner. After spending a pleasant evening all departed for their homes, with glad hearts, feeling assured that their gifts were appreciated. But the end was not yet. On the next morning a four-horse load of wood was driven to the front door and unloaded—a much needed article, as the supply had grown short during the recent cold weather.

There are several articles regarding poorly paid preachers receiving similar surprise parties from appreciative congregations. Most of them happened at Christmastime, however.

February 1888

2/9/88 Mirror

THE COWBOY.

From Theodore Roosevelt's illustrated article in the Mid-winter CENTURY we quote the following:

"Singly or in twos or threes, they gallop their wiry little horses down the street, their lithe, supple figures erect or swaying slightly as they sit loosely in the saddle; while their stirrups are so long their knees hardly bent, the bridles not taut enough to keep the chains from clanking. They are smaller and less muscular than the wielders of the axe and pick; but they are as hardy and self-reliant as any men who ever breathed—with bronzed, set faces and keen eyes that look all over the world straight in the face without flinching as they flash out from under the broad-brimmed hats. Peril and hardship, and years of long toil broken by weeks of brutal dissipation, draw haggard lines across the eager faces, but never dim their reckless eyes nor break their bearing of defiant self-confidence. They do not walk well, partly because they so rarely do any work out of the saddle, partly because their CHAPARAJAS, or leather overalls, hamper them when on the ground; but their appearance is striking for all that, and picturesque too, with their jingling spurs, the big revolvers stuck in their belts, and bright silk hankerchiefs knotted loosely round their necks over the collars of the flannel shirts. When drunk on the villainous whiskey of the frontier towns, they cut mad antics, riding their horses into saloons, firing their pistols right and left, from boisterous light-heartedness rather than from any viciousness, and indulging too often in deadly shooting affrays, brought on either by accidental contact of the moment or on account of some longstanding grudge, or perhaps because of bad blood between two ranches or localities; but except while on such sprees they are quiet, rather self-contained men, perfectly frank and simple, and on their own ground treat a stranger with the most whole-souled hospitality, doing all in their power for him and scorning to take any reward in return. Although prompt to resent an injury, they are not at all apt to be rude to outsiders, treating them with what can almost be called grave courtesy. They are much better fellows and pleasanter companions than small farmers or agricultural laborers; nor are mechanics and workmen of a great city to be mentioned in the same breath."

Waterford Waifs.

2/10/88 Telephone

WATERFORD, Feb. 8.—Two little colored children were brought to town on the morning of the 3d, in a dreadful condition, having their feet, and the stomach of one, badly frozen. Mr. Roe Hough interested himself and raised money to get some necessary clothing. Kind people of the town soon furnished them suitable garments and Dr. G. E. Counell promptly administered medical aid.

Loudoun Book-Store.

PRICES OF

Public School Books

Reduced,

On and after JANUARY 1st, 1888, the price of Public Scool Books will be reduced as follows:

McGuffey's 1st Reader 17c. former price, 20c.
" " 2d " 30c. " " 33c.
" " 3d " 42c. " " 44c.
" " 4th " 50c. " " 55c.
" " 5th " 72c. " " 80c.
" " 6th " 85c. " " 94c.
Eclectic History $1.00 " " $1.11
Graphic Copy Books, 10 " " 11c.
Worcester Dictionaries, 48c. " " 50c.

H. W. CLAGETT,
Opposite the Bank, Leesburg, Va

A TERRIBLE TRAGEDY.

TWO YOUNG VIRGINIANS SHOOT TO KILL.

One is Dead and The Other May Die.

The most dreadful tragedy that has occurred in this section of Virginia for some time took place in Culpeper on the morning of the 1st inst., resulting in the death of Ellis B. Williams, son of the editor of the Culpeper "Exponent," aged 21 years, and the serious, and perhaps, fatal wounding of Edwin Barbour, editor of the Piedmont "Advance" aged 18 years. The trouble seems to have grown out of an article in the shape of a letter from Washington, published in the "Advance" which contained some caustic allusions to Mr. Williams, which occasioned the following correspondence:

CULPEPER, Feb. 17.—MR. EDWIN BARBOUR—Sir: I am informed that in your paper of yesterday is a communication signed "Jack Clatterbuck," containing offensive allusions to me. You will be kind enough to give me the name of the author in writing. Respectfully, &c.
GEO. M. WILLIAMS.

The following reply was sent to Mr. Williams:

SIR: I will not disclose the name of the author of the letter signed "Clatterbuck," and consequently make myself personally responsible for anything said in his letter. Respectfully,
EDWIN BARBOUR.

Then followed a deal of words in the two papers, in which bad language was used, resulting in young Williams going to Culpeper on the morning of the 1st inst., on the hunt of Barbour.

After some ineffectual efforts at getting Mr. Barbour to come down from his office, Williams, accompanied by a friend, went up, and on entering, demanded: "How do you propose to settle this difficulty—fist and skull or with pistols?" Barbour said, or intimated, that the matter could be settled by friends of both parties.— Whereupon Williams said it must be settled now, and struck Barbour with his fist. At this point both drew their revolvers and began firing at each other at six paces. Some nine or ten shots were fired in all.

Barbour's first shot, it is thought, struck Williams in the region of the heart. Williams, after emptying his revolver, sank to the floor helpless. Barbour was found to have been dangerously wounded in the lower part of his body.

Williams soon died without recovering consciousness. Latest reports say that Barbour is still living but dangerously wounded in the abdomen.

IT IS DELIGHTFUL
YOU KNOW,
TO DO YOUR SPARKING
JUST SO,

—BUT—
There is nothing yet that comes up to a nice Buggy ride in
A FIRST CLASS RIG.
This point is important—you must have a vehicle that is gilt-edged, if you would be supremely happy on such an occasion.

Loudoun Valley
Carriage Factory.

March. 1888

3/2/88 Telephone

—Tom Olden, alias Thomas Jackson (colored) was arrested on Saturday at Fox Mountain ore bank, in Rockingham county, by Sheriff J. N. Chapman, of Page county, upon the charge of killing William Broyles (colored), near Middleburg, in the spring of 1886. Olden has been around Milnes, in Page county, for a week or more past, where he went by the name of Jackson. He was seen and recognized by a colored resident of Milnes, who formerly lived in Loudoun county, and who knew both the prisoner and his victim. This discovery led to the arrest of Olden, who made no resistance. He was given a hearing before a justice in Milnes and admitted the charge, but stated that he killed Broyles in a drunken row or difficulty by striking him over the head with a tick.

3/16/88 Telephone

Last Monday was March Court day, but the bizzard put a "wire edge" on the atmosphere which almost destroyed all semblance of the pristine glory of that famous fete day. Of course but few people were in town, hence business was quite dull excepting in the saloons, which did a booming business. So great was the rush that they did not seem to have room for loafers as was evidenced by pitching divers patrons headlong out into the street, one of whose head was badly cut on the curb stone. As the weather was cold everybody made that an excuse for filling up with liquid fire and Jersey Lightning, hence nearly everybody was drunk, presenting a disgraceful spectacle. A gentleman remarked to one of the editors of that town, who poses as an advocate of temperance, that there as a subject for an editorial.

"O no," said he, "I'll not say anything about that."

That's the kind of a temperance man he is.

3/21/88 Telephone

The beauty of a typewriter is the legibility of the copy and the easy facility with wich it is madee. We are surprised and pleased at the ease with witch a typeriter can be operated We had umuderstoood it was guite difficult to operate these intricat little machinaes but we find no troubble what everr. We operate our machine with easy grrace and make no miiistaks. Nothengg llooks so slovenly as bady copy. We abhor bad copy ourselvess and never make it. Ase beautiful as our coppy ss when written with a goose quill, we are sure the printers and our correspondents will be pleased with our typa whitingz. We are ourselves much pleased wishitt.

3/22/88 Mirror

She—I hear that you have lost your valuable little dog, Mr. Sissy.

He—Ya'as, in a railroad accident. I was saved but the dawg was killed.

She (shocked)—What a pity.

THE SPIRAL SPRING CART.
A WONDERFUL VEHICLE!
A BOON TO THE HORSE AND A BLESSING TO MANKIND.

This Is Unquestionably the KING of all Carts.

T. C. BAKER Purcellville, Va.

KINGSLEY BRO'S
PROIRIETORS OF THE
LOUDOUN VALLEY AND FAUQUIER
CREAMERIES,
MANUFACTURERS OF
Fine Butter and Cheese,
— ALSO —
COMMISSION MERCHANTS
And Wholesale Dealers in
Butter Eggs & Farm Produce.

FIGHTING HORSES.

THEODORE ROOSEVELT is contributing a series of separate papers on Ranch Life to THE CENTURY which Frederic Remington illustrates from his own experience. From the "Home Ranch" in the March number we quote the following: "Some horses, of course, are almost incurably vicious, and must be conquered by main force. One pleasing brute on my ranch will at times rush at a man open mouthed like a wolf, and it is a regular trick of the range-stallions. In a great many—indeed, in most—localities there are wild horses to be found, which, although invariably of domestic descent, being either themselves runaways from some ranch or indian outfit, or else claiming such for their sire and dams, yet are quite as wild as the antelope on whose domain they have intruded. Ranchmen run in these wild horses whenever possible, and they are but little more difficult to break than the so-called tame animals. But the wild stallions are, whenever possible, shot; both because of their propensity for driving off the ranch mares, and because their incurable viciousness makes them always unsafe companions for other horses, still more than for men. A wild stallion fears no beast except the grizzly, and will not always flinch from an encounter with it; yet it is a curious fact that a jack will almost always kill one in a fair fight. The particulars of a fight of this sort were related to me by a cattle man who was engaged in bringing out blooded stock from the East. Among the animals under his charge were two great stallions, one gray and one black, and a fine jackass, not much over half the size of the former. The animals were kept in seperate pens, but one day both horses got into the same enclosure, next to the jack-pen, and began to fight as only enraged stallions can, striking like boxers with their fore feet, and biting with their teeth. The gray was getting the best of it; but while clinched with his antagonist in one tussle they rolled against the jack-pen, breaking it in. No sooner was the jack at liberty than, with ears laid back and mouth wide open, he made straight for the two horses, who had for the moment seperated. The gray turned to meet him, rearing on hind legs and striking at him with his fore feet; but the jack slipped in, and in a minute grasped his antagonist by the throat with his wide open jaws, and then held on like a bull dog, all four feet planted stiffly in the soil. The stallion made tremendous efforts to shake him off; he would try to whirl round and kick him, but for that the jack was too short; then he would rise up, lifting the jack off the ground, and strike at him with his fore feet; but all that he gained by this was to skin his foe's front legs without making him loose his hold. Twice they fell, and twice the stallion rose, by main strength dragging the jack with him but all in vain. Meanwhile the black horse attacked both the combatants with perfect impartiality, striking and kicking them with his hoofs, while his teeth, as they slipped off the tough hides, met with a snap like that of a bear-trap. Undoubtedly the jack would have killed at least one of the horses had not the men come up, and with no small difficulty separated the maddened brutes."

4/14/88 Washingtonian

April 1888

Moody in Louisville

For weeks, every day, and twice every day, except Saturday, has stood and preached in the great tabernacle built for him, the famous evangelist Moody. Day after day crowds of five and six thousand people came to listen. The huge building could not hold all that flocked to it, for of the throngs that poured through the gate, thousands had to be turned away at nearly every service.

His speech was not polished, he did not even speak the English language correctly; but no word of his was lost on the listening throng. From the farthest outskirts of the great congregation, ears were strained, and eyes were gazing to catch every word and motion. Ministers, eminent men of every denomination sat around him, leaning to hear, with earnest eyes fixed on his face, eager to lose no word that fell from his lips. Only those near him could see the kind expression of his plain face, or the loving look with which he regarded the sea of faces turned to him.

His words, his manner, his appearance were so homely that at first we wondered in what lay his power to attract those listening multitudes, who never seemed to become weary and whose attention never for one moment flagged. The wonder ceased, however, when after opening his Bible and reading a portion, he proceded to apply the practical lesson it contained, often giving additional meaning to old familiar passages; or to take some Bible character, who before had been to us not much more than a name, bring him with his surroundings as they were before our eyes, and make him say and do before us what he said and did thousands of years ago.

Everything was made so real that the old scenes seemed to pass before our eyes, and meanings that we had never perceived before shown out from the passages in the Bible he read or quoted. He has a thorough knowledge of Holy Scripture, and a poets imagination to clothe in all with reality.

His theme was always the love of God, man's estrangement from him, and his willingness to pardon and receive him. Punishment was lightly dwelt on; only that of absence from God mentioned. The horrors of hell he seemed never to think of, to be cast out from the presence of the Savior he loved with such burning fervor was punishment enough; and it seemed as if his ardent spirit and loving heart yearned to take every creature before him in his arms and carry them to Christ.

When he prayed it was as if his heart was too full to express what he wanted to say; and sometimes, as if overcome with emotion, he would pause and wait, as if the Lord understood and would hearken and do; then he would say, "Speak Lord" as if he knew he was there, and expecting to manifest himself to the hearts of the multitude bowed before him.

There was no excitement, no noisy declamation; only a plain statement of man's obligations to God, and of his offers to man and for every statement he had a proof of its truth ready in the Bible which he held in his hand.

To the dishonest man he said that restitution was the first thing required of him; to the drunkard, or he that dispensed liquor to others, he said that no drunkard could enter the kingdom of heaven. To each and every one he declared and proved that sin, in whatever shape was hateful to God and that he who rejected his Son was a sinner with the rest.

Thousands are said to have been converted, and hundreds have been added to the different churches during and since his visit, and many instances are spoken of where money has been restored which had never been suspected of having been taken.

The sincerity, the earnestness of the man, his passionate convictions of the truth and importance of his message, could not fail to have their effect, and though at first many objected to his methods, and would have nought to do with him, some accusing him of mercenary motives, at last every tongue and pen spoke and wrote in his favor.

(Moody was probably the most famous evangelist of the century.)

April, 1888

4/20/88 Telephone

CONKLING CONQUERED

HIS PROUD SPIRIT YIELDS TO THE PALE MESSENGER.

The Great Statesman's Death Mourned Throughout the Country.

Ex-Senator Roscoe Conkling died at his home in New York City, at 1.50 o'clock Wednesday morning, after an illness of a little more than two weeks.

4/21/88 Washingtonian

This distinguished statesman and lawyer, who had the confidence and esteem of all parties in the country, by his pure and untarnished public life—and whose splendid abilities had won the admiration of the public, died at his hotel in New York, on Wednesday morning last about 2 o'clock. At his bedside were Mrs. Conkling, Judge Coxe, Dr. Anderton, Mrs. Oakman, and the professional nurse. His vitality had been gradually wearing away, so that when the moment of dissolution came Mr. Conkling passed away with scarcely a sign save a little gasp.

4/19/88 Mirror

Mr. Conkling's death was not altogether unexpected but its announcement will be received with unaffected sorrow by men of all parties. He was a bitter partisan but detested shams. He was a man of massive intellect and a lawyer of extraordinary ability whose death will be looked upon as a loss to the country at large.

4/19/88 Mirror

MR. CONKLING'S FEE.—There is a story of two Rochester men who lately were in New York on legal business. It occurred to them to consult Mr. Conkling, and they did so at some length and very much to their satisfaction. As they rose to go the spokesman said: "Mr. Conkling, we thank you for your advice, which is very valuable to us. When we get home we will send you a check for $500." "Oh, no, gentlemen," said the ex-Senator, "don't do that I'm only too happy to be of service to you and make no charge. You are quite welcome, but when I do charge, my fee is $5,000."—ROCHESTER UNION, Apr. 14

Hamilton Creamery
HAMILTON, VA.,

KINGSLEY BROTHERS,
PROPRIETORS.

CHOICE CREAMERY BUTTER ALWAYS ON HAND.
SWEET CREAM AND MILK SUPPLIED PROMPTLY ON ORDERS.
ALSO
SALT and FEED KEPT IN STOCK.

ICE CREAMS
—AND—
WATER ICES,
—AT—
BEUCHLER'S!

FAMILIES SUPPLIED at SHORT NOTICE, at $1.25 Per Gallon.
april 29.

ICE CREAM.

I WILL supply the families of Leesburg, at their homes, during the season with Ice Cream, rich and pure, made and flavored to their orders; or will supply them at my residence, near the Toll Gate, on Aldie Turnpike. Fresh Milk furnished morning and evening.
JAMES BURNS,
Leesburg, Va.

5/3/88 Mirror

BROOKLYN BRIDGE.

A Steady Stream of Shop Girls, Working women and Men, Morning and Evening.

The day on the bridge begins early. At 6 o'clock in the morning the cars begin to run under a minute and a half headway. The crowds pour in and what is known as the "rush hours" begin. These are hours of hard work for every one, from the superintendent of the road down to the humblest brakeman. The little dummy engines that run the three car trains from the station out to the point where the cable connects with the grip rush backward and forward puffing and snorting and making a tremendous amount of noise.

This is at 7:30 on the Brooklyn side. About 75,000 New York business men and workmen, who use Brooklyn as a bedroom, are getting ready to launch themselves into New York. At 7:45 the stream is at high tide. At two glass covered boxes within the spot where three men are laboring with frantic energy to give out tickets and make change, two stalwart men stand to see that every passenger deposit a ticket. These men need to be alert and quick eyed, for 200 persons per minute are passing by these two glass ticket boxes. It may seem easy work to watch 12,000 tickets per hour dropped into a glass box but the guards say it has the effect of giving one the vertigo.

From 7 o'clock until 8:30 the stream of humbly clad shop girls and working women and men is kept steadily up, and some twenty odd thousand passengers are carried over the river. Three cars start each minute and a half, but in the seconds that they are at a standstill each of the cars is amply packed with ten tons of humanity. This rush is kept up until 9:30 o'clock, after which there is a lull, the number of passengers passing the ticket offices falling gradually from 12,000 to 6,000 per hour. Approaching noon it is even less on the Brooklyn side, but after the hour on the New York side the thousands that thronged to New York are hurrying back again, and after 4 o'clock Brooklyn begins to regain its population at the rate of from 200 to 300 per minute.

Of course these figures deal simply with the railway. The footpath is less patronized now than formerly. There were 354,304 less persons who used it last year than the year before, despite the fact that any one who wishes to buy tickets by the bunch to walk over the bridge and get the finest views imaginable for the not astounding sum of one-fifth of a cent. The footway is popular only on very mild days when it is the resort favored of good looking nurses with distracting French cars, who wheel baby carriages and admire the big policemen. The receipts of the footway last year amounted to something over $16,000, which would scarcely pay its expenses, and it has been proposed to make it free. This will scarcely be done, for making it free would be throwing it open to tramps or worse characters, and making an increase of police necessary.

(The Brooklyn Bridge, one of the wonders of that century, was open just four years previous.)

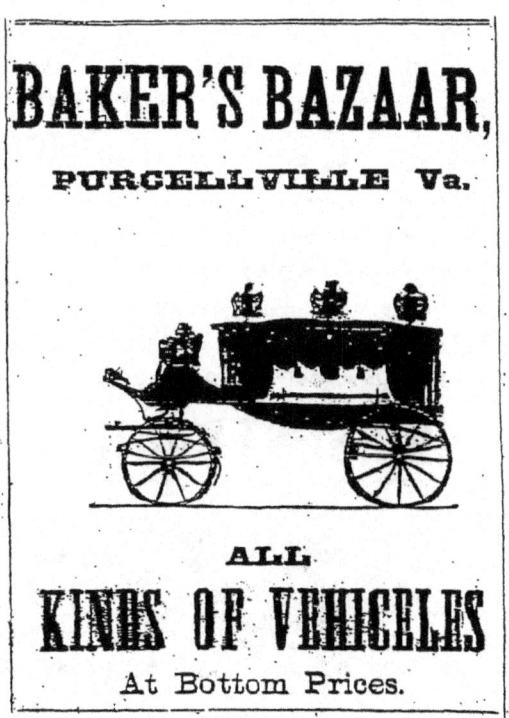

BAKER'S BAZAAR,
PURCELLVILLE Va.

ALL
KINDS OF VEHICLES
At Bottom Prices.

5/19/88 Washingtonian

LEESBURG ENTERPRISES.—The new town hall is fast approaching completion, the auditorium presents a fine appearance, with excellent acoustic qualities.

The building of the new jail is progressing, being already several feet above the ground.

The foundation of the "Peoples National Bank building" will soon be laid, workmen now being engaged in digging the cellar.

The Reamer House will soon be torn down to be replaced by a new and handsome hotel.

All these improvements show a commendable spirit of enterprise and will add greatly to the appearance of the town,—increase the value of other property—and doubtless add to business prosperity.

5/17/88 Mirror

The six-day's walking match that opened in Madison Square Garden New York, on Monday morning week closed last Saturday night. Seven out of the forty five starters continued to the end, of whom five made the necessary number of miles, 525, to share in the gate receipts, which were about $18,100. Littlewood the English champion, got first place, with 611 miles to his credit, and Guerrero, the Mexican, was second with 586 miles. The winner's earnings amounted to something over $4,000.

HORSE TRAINING!

I AM now prepared to take COLTS TO BREAK, or HORSES TO DRIVE, at my Stable in LEESBURG, Va.
My Terms are moderate, and I guarantee satisfaction. Any one having work of this kind that they want done, will please leave word at Mr. W. H. THOMAS' Tin-Store, Leesburg, where it will receive prompt attention.

J. D. ROGERS.

5/25/88 Telephone

The Arkansas Traveller.

Two small tented wagons, one drawn by a pair of little white oxen and the other by a span of poor horses, accompanied by a little "yaller dog" under the wagon, passed through Luray last Thursday and attracted the attention of all who saw them. The wide-awake reporter of *The Courier* saw in them a good local, and joining himself to one of the drivers soon learned his history. His name was Howard, from near Little Rock, Arkansas, had with him his wife and five children and all his worldly effects. He had traveled that way all the distance from that State, had been twelve weeks on the road, and was *en route* to Loudoun county, his old home. Eight years ago, he said, he went West with $5000 in his pocket, all of which he had spent in doctor bills and medicine for his family, who had been sick nearly all the time with ague. His story altogether was a pretty sad one.—*Page Courier.*

5/11/88 Telephone

Death of Maggie Norris.

Died, on the afternoon of the 9th, inst., at the Norris farm, Bureau Co., Ill., of Diptheria, Margaretta R., daughter of the late Isaac and Rachel N. Hoge, of Loudoun, and wife of Clarkson Norris, aged about 38 years. The sympathy of a large circle of early associates, friends and relatives goes out to the bereaved families. Less than 10 years since the deceased went out from us a happy bride, with the hue of health upon her cheek.

Two little girls, her daughters, have, within a few months, preceded her to the tomb, smitten also by Diphtheria. Another is now ill with this dreadful disease and one only remains in health.

—It is reported that one of the ex-mayors of Hamilton is putting up a corporation ticket pledging to no taxation. If he will guarantee the expenses of the town out of his own exchequer, his ticket will be elected unanimously.

June, 1888

6/14/88 Mirror

CLEVELAND AND THURMAN.

THE PRESIDENT NOMINATED BY ACCLAMATION.

Platform Adopted.

The Platform of 1884 Reaffirmed and the President Indorsed.

6/14/88 Mirror

MAHONE IS BEATEN!

Wise Wins the Virginia Contest.

A HOT FIGHT ENDED.

6/23/88 Washingtonian

Harrison Nominated.

THE NOMINATION FINALLY MADE ON THE EIGHT BALLOT.

MORTON FOR SECOND PLACE.

The Convention Completes Its Business and Adjourns.

The republican national convention, which has been in session at Chicago since the 19th instant, completed its work Tuesday by the nomination of Benjamin Harrison, of Indiana, for President and Levi P. Morton, of New York, for Vice-President. When the convention met in the morning, Mr. Boutelle, of Maine, read two cablegrams from Mr. Blaine, in which he said that he thought his Paris letter should be respected, and that he had the right to ask his friends to regard his wishes and refrain from voting for him.

Fourth of July
—AT THE—
Fair Grounds, Leesburg, Va.

GRAND
Demonstration.
Tournament & Racing.

ON THE FOURTH OF JULY, 1888, a most attractive entertainment will be given, at the FAIR GROUNDS, near Leesburg, Va., consisting of a

Tournament, Dancing and Racing.

The Tournament will commence at 11 o'clock, a. m., a number of Knights are expected to enter for the Prizes, and the charge to the Knights and Coronation address, will be delivered by parties who will be duly advertised later. The Knights will contend for the following prizes: The successful Knight will receive an English Saddle. The 2nd a fine Bridle. The 3rd a Riding Whip. Crowns will be provided for the Queens of beauty.

Dancing will commence after the Crowning of the Queens, and will continue during the evening in charge of the Committee on dancing. A handsome pavilion has been erected for the occasion. The music for the dancing will be given by a fine orchestra.

RACES.

The Races will commence immediately after the Tournament, about 1½ o'clock, p. m. 1st Purse, $25.00 open to all horses owned in the county—Trot or Pace. HAZEL BARHAW BARRED. Best 3 in 5—Entrance 10 per cent.

Running Races.

Second Purse $15.00 2-5 mile heats, open to all horses in the county. 3rd Purse, $15.00 half mile heats. 4th. Purse, $20.00 mile heats, open to all horses in the county. Entrance Fee to running 5 per cent.

All Purses divided as follows, 50 per cent to first, 25 to second, 15 to third, 10 to fourth.

JUDGES—H. J. Fadeley. Wm. Clemens, and James McDaniel.

A fine BAND OF MUSIC will be in attendance. Refreshments served on the Grounds. Admission to the grounds 25c. Children, 15 cts. All Vehicles Free.

Privileges for the sale of refreshments, such as cigars, Lemonade, Ice Cream, Confectionery, &c., will be let on Monday, the 25th of June, at the Fair Grounds.

june 16. LOVETT & SMITH.

July 1888

7/19/88 Mirror

THE ANNUAL TOURNAMENT ON THE RAPPAHANNOCK.

The Great Event of the Year—Calling the Roll of Brave "Knights"—Glory and Shame—"Queen of Love and Beauty" Crowned.

At last the hour of the tournament draws near, and all the vehicles are ranged in line around the field where the contest is to take place—and all are filled with happy occupants; pretty girls in ravishing costumes, young men of every type old men who recall the days when they contended in knightly lists, and old ladies who remember when they were honored with the crown.

The field, about which all are crowding, is a long, level stretch of pasture land, across which has been marked out a straight course, and at intervals of about 100 yards across it are built three frame structures, which strongly remind one of gibbets. A stanch upright is set in the ground, and to its top is nailed a cross bar extending over the course while from the end of this bar hangs a ring upon a hooked wire. The object of the contest is to take off those rings upon the point of a lance while riding at full speed. At one end of the course is a platform for the judge.

At length a bugle call summons the knights, and they are seen approaching at the far end of the field. Slowly they ride up to the stand—ten of them—and, reining up their horses, form into a line, facing the judges, ready to answer the roll call. A fine looking set of men they are and mounted upon superb horses. And now the call begins. The Knight of the Golden Key, cries the herald, and a young man wearing a wide blue sash, and bearing a lance tied with the same color, answers "here." Next "the Knight of the Locust Grove," and a small, dried up looking man, decked in red responds. Likewise are called "the Knight" of Sleepy Hollow," "the Knight of Walnut Hill," "the Knight of Chincapin." and others.

The roll being over, all fall into an attitude of attention, while the orator of the day delivers the "Charge to the Knights," reminding them of the joustings of old, and in many a flowing period urging them on to win glory and fame for the sake of their fair ladies. This ends the preliminaries, and there is a general stir among the crowd in the effort to get good positions from which to view the riding.

A RUSH OF EXPECTANCY.

Now, all is ready and the hush of expectancy falls upon the people. Suddenly the bugle call bursts out amid the silence, and the herald cries, "The Knight of the Golden Key." At the word he leaves the ranks and fixing his lance, spurs his horse into a rapid run, and, his eyes upon the first ring, rushes toward it. On flies his steed, sending the loose earth in showers behind him, and as he passes the first support, the knight carries away the ring upon his lance. In a moment he is upon the second but misses it by a hair's breath sending it spinning far into the crowd; the last he takes, and rides slowly back, flushed with his triumph, amid the cheers of the crowd.

The rings are replaced, and the next in order essays the feat, but fails to take a single ring. And so in turn all try, each making a striking picture as his stout steed bears him on like an arrow, and he sits firm and erect in his saddle, his lance straight before him, his gay ribbons streaming in the wind, his eye fixed upon the coveted ring. It needs a stout heart, a steady hand and a true eye to succeed at such work, for the slightest false motion may not only miss the ring, but throw the luckless knight headlong from his horse.

At length each knight has thrice essayed the run; some are covered with glory and some with shame. And now comes the most exciting time, for three knights have each the same score and must ride out the tie. By this time the horses have come to understand what is required of them, and the spirit of the sport has seized upon each man's heart. The riding is superb. Again and again they run, each taking all the rings each time, until at last one of the knights misses and retires. Now

July 1888

comes the struggle of the champions. The crowd is wrought up to the greatest enthusiasm, and watch with breathless interest each knightly contestant, and break in to deafening cheers at each success. At last another ring is missed, and the "Knight of the Golden Key" stands victor. As he rides for the last time down the field toward the judges' stand—his horse flecked with foam, his face blazing beneath his broad brimmed hat—the people burst into louder cheers, girls wave their handkerchiefs boys throw their hats in the air, and all is confusion.

CROWNING THE QUEEN.

And now he reaches the platform and salutes the judges. The crown is hung upon his lance's end. Then slowly he rides along the outskirts of the crowd, until he comes to a carriage where sits the lady whose colors he wears, and whose face is now radiant with smiles for her knight's success. Reaching her he dismounts and drops the crown at her feet, thus choosing her "Queen of Love and Beauty" while the acclamations of the crowd attest their approval of his choice. Meanwhile the knights who have won the second and third places have received smaller crowns, and hasten likewise to bestow them upon their ladies, making them "Maids of Honor."

And now for an hour is a pause, while the crowd breaks up into groups and discusses the riding and its results. As it is growing toward evening many seize the opportunity to eat the lunches they have brought with them, or are carried off by friends to sup in the neighboring farm houses.

At length the bugle call rings out once more and the crowd reassemble near the stand. "The Knight of the Golden Key" leads his lady upon the platform, while the "Knight of Walnut Hill" and the "Knight of Warsaw" follow with their maids of honor. They are met by the judges and by the most famous speaker of the country, who proceeds to make a long and flowery oration, ending by crowning the ladies, amid the plaudits of the crowd.

A local historian has described the tournament, sometimes called jousting, as Loudoun's most popular sport of that century. Baseball was coming on strong however.

7/13/88 Telephone

Washington on Swearing.

This was an order issued from general headquarters, Moore's House, West Point, July 29th 1797:

"Many and pointed orders have been issued against the unmeaning and abominable custom of swearing, notwithstanding which, with much regret, the General observes that it prevails, if possible, more than ever; his feelings are continually wounded by oaths and imprecations of the soldiers whenever he is in hearing of them.

"The name of that Being from whose bountiful goodness we are permitted to exist and enjoy the comforts of life, is incessantly imprecated and profaned in a manner as wanton as it is shocking. For the sake, therefore, of religion and decency, the General hopes and trusts that the officers of every rank will use their influence and authority to check a vice which is as unprofitable as it is wicked and shameful.

"If officers would make it an unavoidable rule to repremand, and if that does not do, punish soldiers for offences of this kind, it could not fail of having the desired effect."

VICTOR

15 CENT

POULTRY POWDERS

CURE AND PREVENT CHOLERA

GAPES, ROUP, LICE, EGG EATING,

Laying of Soft Eggs, &c.

Without Parallel as Egg Producer.

PREPARED ONLY BY THE

VICTOR REMEDIES CO., FREDERICK, MD.

Ask your dealer to write us for Circulars and fuller facts. A trial will prove our assertions.

8/30/88 Mirror

They wondered what he was like, whether his manner would be pleasing, whether he was as good looking as his portraits make him. And then, in a saucy tone of voice with a little sly tremor in it, too, one of the young girls (who could not have been more than thirteen) said: "Oh, see here, I've torn my glove, do you think he'll notice it?" "Take it off," said another; "he'll sooner hold your hand." At this moment the folding doors opened, and two gentlemen in plain frock coats came out and stood before it. A moment later, and there stepped into the reception than the portly form of Mr. President Grover Cleveland. He is a man of perhaps five feet nine inches in height of immense breadth of shoulder and very stout. But he carries himself so well that he gives one the impression of possessing great muscular strength rather than mere adipose. His head is firmly fixed on a large neck, which at first appears so short as to create fears of apoplexy, but when he bows and stands with his head inclined to one side (evidently a favorite pose) it is seen that the neck is quite proportionately long with the rest of the body. His head is well shaped—a high forehead with slightly overhanging brows, which slopes very gradually back till it merges into a peculiar angular ridge across the top, so often found in men of strong character.

He had something to say to every one—a word only or a little sentence, an expression of pleasure or only "How do you do, sirs." When a child came along he stooped down, and taking the little one's hand, looked right up into its rather frightened or awed face with a reassuring smile as though to say: "I want you to take away a pleasant thought of your President." I saw an old, old couple totter up to shake his hands and pass on. The people behind crowded them somewhat—and held hers while she said something I could not hear, but her face beamed with delight, and when the old man came the President's face was suffused with kindly smiles as he glanced over his shoulder at her retreating form and whispered to the old gentleman. I am told that President Cleveland possesses the faculty said to belong in a marked degree to our own royal family of never forgetting a face. There was nothing unpleasant in the genial, kind look he gave me as I passed, but it was evident that he was "taking stock" in that brief moment of every lineament on my face and possibly making mental estimate of my character. I felt certain that he would not forget me, as I shall certainly never have his face obliterated from my memory.

8/23/88 Mirror

BASE BALL.

Lenah and Farmwell played their second match at Lenah on Saturday last, resulting in a second victory for Lenah. The Eagles played with hard luck. Hanes pitched a very wild game and their fielding was very unsatisfactory. Their best score was in the third inning. Alexander went to the bat and sent a ball between 3rd base and short stop; then Higgins strove to belt the booming ball, mauled the atmosphere twice, then Mr. Ambler sent him a red hot ball, which raised a red hot blister on his right shoulder, and he was presented with his first base as a mark of esteem. Dr. Noland, Watson, Hanes, Bentley and A. Hanes scored on a run each—Alexander scored two, then Noland and Watson thinking they had made enough for one inning, went out. During this inning the decisions of umpire Garrett were disputed by some of the Eagles, and his refusing to officiate any longer, was succeeded by Mr. R. L. Sanford, who appeared to give satisfaction to both clubs. Lenah was thinking things looked rather squally for them, but Ambler picked up his piece of ash in the fourth inning like he meant business. Hit safely—bungled a second, and gradually arrived at the third base. Polen succeeded him and accumulated a one-bagger; then Mr. Saunders, Lenah's clever catcher, jolted merry thunder out of the horse hide—tore the tar out of the willow, smashed the leather, and then while Bentley was muffing the orb, Ambler and Polen straightened themselves out like long-waisted jack rabbits, and shoveled sand at a two-forty gait towards home base which they reached, just as Mr. Sanders fell about nine feet horizontally and caught hold the second base with his front teeth—and the spectators cheered. Things were now looking squally for the Eagles and when Cather, Lenah's particular "Star" made a three base hit, the brave Eagles folded their wings and played with little or no energy the remainder of the game. The score follows:

Lenah.. 27
Farmwell... 17

An unusual large crowd witnessed this exciting game.

"JIM THE PENMAN."

August 1888

8/23/88 Mirror

JOHN M. LANGSTON, one of the most respectable, and probably the best educated negroes in Virginia, recently announced himself a candidate for Congress from the Petersburg District, which has brought down on him the severest denunciation of Mahone & Co., and last week a sharp circular was issued from headquarters arraigning J. H. Brady for his support of Langston. And Fred. Douglass is induced to publish a letter, giving his reasons why the colored voters of the District should not support Langston. The fourth District is one of the few in Virginia where it is even possible for the colored people to chose one of their own race for Congressman, and they and Langston are not made of the material of which they are credited, if they quietly succumb to such dictation.

(A man of many accomplishments. Although he won this election, he was not seated for two years because of a voting irregularity controversy. During the war, he was a recruiting agent for Negro servicemen. Later, he served as inspector-general of the Freedman's Bureau, and then as Dean and Vice President of Howard University. In 1877, he became Minister-Resident of Haiti. After his return to the U.S., he was named President of Virginia Normal and Collegiate Institute before his congressional bid.)

9/28/88 Telephone

AN OVATION TO LANGSTON.

Petersburg Pays Tribute to the Anti-Mahone Candidate for Congress.

[Baltimore Sun.]

PETERSBURG, VA., Sept. 20.—John Mercer Langston, who was nominated for Congress at Farmville yesterday in opposition to Judge R. W. Arnold, Mahone's candidate, arrived here tonight, accompanied by Hon. Ross Hamilton, Scott Wood, R. H. Hampton, and other leaders of the anti-Mahone people. Mr. Langston was met at the depot by a crowd numbering about one thousand persons, chiefly colored men, and a band of music.

After getting from the train Mr. Langston and party took a carriage, to which four horses were hitched. The heads of the horses were gayly decorated with flags. Following in the rear of the procession were carriages containing well-known colored politicians. As the line marched through the streets the men cheered themselves hoarse for Langston and set off fireworks.

The procession came to a halt in front of Langston Hall, on Union street, where were assembled a crowd estimated at over 2,000. Speaking took place from the balcony of the building, the street in front of which was literally packed with people, white and colored. There were a hundred or more of the best colored woman in the city in attendance upon the meeting, who accepted seats in the hall.

The principal speaker of the evening was Mr. Langston, whose appearance evoked the most prolonged applause. He began his speech by saying that the colored people were now fighting despotism, and that they wanted liberty for themselves and a good and strong government for all. He said: "No man shall dictate to the voters of America. No man is so white in this country that he shall oppress a colored man, and no colored man is so black that he shall be oppressed by any white man." Mr. Langston thanked God that he had not been nominated by a bogus convention, and in this connection was very severe on Mahone, whom he termed "the little man who represents a dying tyranny, which makes tonight its last kick." Mr. Langston said that while in Congress he should make no discrimination on account of color, but should do all he could for the good of the district and the State. In speaking of Judge Arnold, Mahone's candidate for Congress, Mr. Langston said he was without reputation as a lawyer, and on the night of the 31st of July, in a dark place, somebody put his hand on him and he became the tool of Mahone. He, (Arnold,) like Boss Mahone is preparing to give up the ghost. Mr. Langston was heard with attention by the large crowd.

Langston has, heretofore, been one of Mahone's faithful followers, and he would doubtless have so continued had Mahone granted him what he had a right to demand, i. e., the right to secure the nomination for Congress if he could. Mahone's purpose to crush this laudable ambition is, as we understand, the cause of the trouble.

(The only political opinion The Telephone shared with the two Leesburg papers was a deep antipathy toward William Mahone.)

9/8/88 Washingtonian

A PERILOUS SITUATION.—Mr. George W. Survick and his wife had a very narrow escape from drowning on Friday night of last week. They were returning from Frederick, Md., and left the Point of Rocks in their buggy about 7 o'clock. It was very dark, and as a storm was approaching Mr. Survick borrowed a lantern at the Furnace, and proceeded on his way. Soon the rain fell in torrents. The road was flooded as they could see by the incessant flashes of lightning. When near a little branch, which runs across the road, through the farm of Mr. C. E. Ahalt, and which can be stepped across usually, the horse was found to be swimming. Soon getting into the current of the stream, both horse and buggy were carried down, and against the log crossing the stream, and the fence. Here the buggy was overturned, Mr. S. thrown out, and Mrs. S. caught between the buggy and the log and fence, being held there by the bows of the buggy which had been broken. Being utterly unable to release either his wife or horse, Mr. Survick did what he could to help, and encourage his wife, until the storm abated and the waters ran off somewhat. Then leaving her in the darkness, the lantern having been lost, he repaired to Mr. Ahalt's, awoke him, and returned with the hands on the place, to the assistance of his wife. She was found to be in a very critical condition, and Mr. S. says could have held out but a little while longer. But both she and the horse were quickly disentangled from the wreck, and carried to Mr. Ahalt's, where every kindly attention possible was rendered, and she revived, and was brought home the next morning, and is now all right again. Their escape was truly remarkable, as Mrs. Survick was in her unaided condition for nearly three hours, Mr. Survick being unable to release her, alone, and only able to encourage her by his efforts, and counsel, to hold out, till he could summon aid.

9/13/88 Mirror

THE ANNUAL FAIR

of the Loudoun Live Stock Exhibition, advertised to begin on the grounds near this town on Tuesday, was sadly marred by unprecedented rain storm that has prevailed for the last ten days. The exhibition, with fair weather, would have surpassed in point of excellence any previous one held under the present management.

The various departments were well filled, the entries of stock of all kinds were very numerous, particularly those of horses and cattle, while the number of racers was large and of better class than ever.

In the ladies department there was a full list of entries and despite the beastly weather.

When we came to make our exit from the building our observation had to stop, for outside there was nothing to be seen but driving sheets of rain, wet and forlorn looking cattle and horses, a sodden and water-covered field, and a track that would have furnished excellent material for the potter's wheel.

MRS DART'S TRIPLETS.

President Cleveland's prize for the three best babies at the Aurora County Fair, in 1887, was given to these triplets, Mollie, Ida, and Ray.

Lactated Food

Is the best Food for bottle-fed babies. It keeps them well, and is better than medicine when they are sick.

At Druggists, 25c., 50c., $1.00.

September, 1888

9/27/88 Mirror

A NARROW ESCAPE.— On Friday morning last Mr. F. C. Reamer, after having delivered the mail at the postoffice, attempted to turn the stage in the street. The front wheels became locked under the body of the vehicle and the horses started to run. Mr. R. was thrown forward and fell across the double tree and in this position was dragged some yards when the stage striking an obstruction in the street was overturned and the horses became detached.— The only other occupant of the stage was Jimmie, a three year old nephew of Mr. R. who, when it went over, rolled under the seat and escaped without a scratch, Mr. R was somewhat bruised though not badly hurt, but it was a close call for them both The horses, after tearing out one of the awning posts at Wallace's old corner, were soon stopped.

9/27/88 Mirror

BUFFALO BILL.— Col. Wm. F. Cody—Buffalo Bill—opened his Wild West Show on Monday last, at the driving park, immediately opposite the Washington Junction on the W. O. & W. Railroad. A correspondent of the Sun says:

The most thrilling ride since the organization of the company was accomplished by Tony Esquival on the black bucking horse Jubilee. Before Esquival had fairly mounted the vicious animal, he started for the fence separating the infield from the track, bucking rearing and kicking as he went. Esquival tried to turn him, but without avail, and Jubilee made a tremendous leap, clearing the fence but falling on his knees as he landed When he regained his feet the rider was still with him, and remained upon his back, until he had made the circuit of the track, rearing and jumping until exhausted. The crowd arose to their feet in excitement, and broke into loud applause when they saw that Esquival was unharmed.

Wanted a Man!

ONE who can furnish Horse and Harness, to sell the New V. S. & J. F SINGER MACHINE, in Loudoun County, for terms, Address with reference,
THE SINGER M'F'G CO.,
Alexandria Va.
C. J. HAMMERLY, Agent.

9/28/88 Telephone

Judge Thurman made a speech, a few days ago, to a delegation of colored men who called on him, in which he said that neither his father nor himself ever owned a slave. Then a little further on he said: "The most intimate companion of my boyhood days was a colored boy, given me by my father, as a companion and not as a slave."

In the name of common sense, how could the father give to his son a thing he did not possess?— And if he owned the negro, was he not his slave? And how could young Thurman own a companion who was not a slave?

(Copyrighted.)
"Stop That Man"

I WANT TO TELL HIM
ABOUT THE

BARGAINS IN OVERCOATS
—FOR—
MEN AND BOYS.

The handsomest Men's Blue Beavers at $12 and $15.

The most stylish Men's Cassimere and Cheviot $12 and $15.

The newest and best Small Boys' at $5.

ABSOLUTELY ALL WOOL

E. B. Barnum & Co.,
931 Penn. Ave.
WASHINGTON, D. C.

September 1888

ROUND HILL Aug 16th.—Last Tuesday Mr. Thos. Wynkoop, living near Silcott Springs, sent his little boy to drive up some horses. While doing so one of the animals turned and kicked him, both feet striking square in his stomach. He was carried to the house unconscious and Dr. Chancellor immediately summoned, but surgical skill was unavailing, and the little sufferer was relieved by death last night

It is said that the father was so crazed by grief that it required the strength of four men to keep him from taking his own life.

Mr. Wynkoop had but two sons and it will be remembered that some time ago one of them was scalded to death and now this.

WYNKOOP.—Richmond Hunton, son of J. T. and Fannie Wynkoop, Born April 16, 1875, died at his home near Silcott's Springs, Wednesday, August 15th, 1888, at 10 o'clock, P. M.

"In the midst of life we are in death."

In the bloom of youth Hunton was suddenly stricken and cast upon a bed of unspeakable pain. For thirty hours bravely he bore his suffering and struggled with the angel—Death. At last, as death was claiming her own peacefully and calmly, the little fellow gazed into the eyes of his loving father, and in response to his call, he breathed the word "Sir,"—faithful to his father's call in life—he was faithful, also, in death. His spirit then fled home to the God who gave it.

A boy who was always polite, courteous, and accommodating, he was universally loved, and his death is not only regretted, but mourned, by all who knew him. Among his schoolmates he was ever the same brave, high-spirited, true Hunton— a favorite with them all. Loving his parents, their slightest desire was always a command to him, which he delighted to obey. Loving his sisters, he was willing to sacrifice his own pleasure for their happiness. But infinite wisdom has taken him from us, and we bow to his stern decree, realizing that "all things work together for our good." Let us all hold him in sweet remembrance, and let father, mother, sisters and schoolmates, remembering the uncertainty of life, so live that when our Father shall come to call them home, He may find them waiting—yes, longing for the blessed reunion above.

"HIS TEACHER."

9/29/88 Washingtonian

A LARGE FUNERAL.—The funeral of the late Rev. William O. Robey, a colored Minister of this town took place on Sunday last, from the colored Methodist Church. He was in every respect a most worthy and highly esteemed man. Modest, and unassuming in his demeanor to all, he was a devout and earnest Christian, and walked "humbly before his God," His influence was always for good, and he exerted all his powers for the welfare of his race. He was a teacher also, in the public schools of this County

9/27/88 Mirror

DEATH OF WM. O. ROBEY.—Rev. W. O. Robey, a colored minister, died at his home in Leesburg, on Friday, Sept. 21st, 1888, in the 68th year of his age. Wm. Robey had spent the greater portion of his life in this town. He was well-known to this community, whose confidence he enjoyed to the fullest extent, and by every member of which, both white and colored, he was held in the highest esteem.

At 2 o'clock Sunday afternoon his remains were taken to Zion M. E. Church, and in the presence of a crowded house, the Rev. J. S. Cooper, pastor, delivered a funeral discourse in every way worthy of the life and character of the deceased. It was carefully prepared, and well delivered. In addition to a thorough elucidation of the text, the discourse was marked with flashes of eloquence and touches of tender pathos, that fell with visable effect upon his hearers. At the conclusion of the services at the Church, the remains were borne to the burying-ground of the Presbyterian Church, and laid at rest, in the presence of one of the largest congregations of people we have ever seen assembled in this town on a similar occasion. Peace to his memory.

October 1888

THE WASHINGTONIN
LEESBURG, LOUDOUN COUNTY, VA

SATURDAY............October 6, 1888

DEMOCRATIC TICKET

FOR PRESIDENT,
GROVER CLEVELAND.
OF NEW YORK.

FOR VICE-PRESIDENT,
ALLEN G. THURMAN,
OF OHIO.

FOR CONGRES
8th Congressional District of Virginia,
GEN. W. H. F. LEE
OF FAIRFAX.

PUBLIC SPEAKING.

GEN. W. H. F. LEE, our representative from this district accompanied by other good speakers, will address the voters of Loudoun on the issues of the day at the following places and dates:

FARMWELL...............October 8th.
LOVETTSVILLE............ " 9th.
HILLSBORO'................. " 10th.
UNISON........................ " 11th.
MIDDLEBURG............... " 12th.

These meetings will be held as near 2 p. m., as practical and active Democrats at these places will please exert themselves to secure a good attendance.
T. L. WORSLEY,
Chairman Com.

The Election is Approaching.

As the election approaches we have most encouraging reports from all sections. Our leaders are most flattering in their reports of the movements and working of the party in all the States, and they predict success to the cause.— But they tell us, we must do our best— do all we can to have our full vote polled. Virginia is looked to with much interest, and many, not farmiliar with the sentiment of our people, are doubtful of the result here. But there need be no doubts entertained, as we believe the democrats of the State are aroused from the mountains to the waters of the Chesapeake, and if we be faithful, and see to it that our vote is cast we may look for a majority of from 15 to 20,000. This will depend upon every man in the party doing the best he can to have our vote polled. Do not let Loudoun lag in the work—do not let her, by our lethergy and want of active effort, step down from the head of the column of Democratic counties in the State. We must poll our vote, to do that, see to it that every democrat in your neighborhood is registered and provide means to have them at the polls on Tuesday, the 6th of November. Let us wake up to our duty and do it.— Register and vote is now the work to do. We have talked and written and now we must act.

10/20/88 Washingtonian

The Outlook for the Election.

The reports we have from all sections of the county, indicate the election of Mr. Cleveland, with much more certainty than did the outlook preceding the last presidential election. There is scarcely a dark spot upon the political horizon.

11/1/88 Mirror

THE DAY AND HOUR DRAW NEAR.

In less than one week from to-day, the American people will have decided at the ballot-box which of the two great political parties of this country shall control its destinies for the next four years.

Presuming, therefore, that every citizen interested in a fair, honest, and economical administration of the government, has fully informed himself upon the issues involved, we appeal to them to come forward, like men and patriots, and on the 6th of November, record their judgment at the ballot-box, feeling assured that if the great masses of American people thus vote—uninfluenced by demagogues and designing politicians—the result will be the triumphant election of Cleveland, Thurman and Lee.

November 1888

11/9/88 Telephone

LOUDOUN COUNTY, VA., FRIDAY, NOV. 9, 1888.

AFTER ELECTION.

Questions Set at Rest by Yesterday's Returns.

INDIANA IS REPUBLICAN.

Both Parties Still Claiming California.

CONNECTICUT GOES DEMOCRATIC.

Details of the Vote in These and Other States.

REPUBLICANS CLAIM CONGRESS.

Illinois Taken from the Doubtful List. An Increased Vote Polled Everywhere. Only Partial Returns as Yet from Many States, but Enough to Tell Pretty Accurately How They Have Gone—Figures on Which the Republicans Claim the Next Congress—Election Day Events.

BEN HARRISON!

The Man Who Will Live in the House Uncle Sam Built.

THE VOICE OF THE PEOPLE

Is Heard in the Land for Harrison Triumphed O'er Grover Cleveland; Free Trade Has Been Beaten, It Was a Great Rout; Hurrah, All Republicans, Now We Can Shout.

This is the house Uncle Sam built.

THE TELEPHONE.

FRIDAY................ NOV. 9.

HURRAH!

We go to bat!

Glory enough for once!

It was worth four years of waiting.

The firm of Fisk & Brooks has failed.

Hurrah for Harrison, Morton and Protection.

We feel sorry for Mrs. Cleveland. She is doubtless a nice lady.

This lesson should teach the democratic party that this government does not belong to them.

Election Day In Hamilton.

Everything passed off quietly and orderly in Hamilton. The most striking feature of the occasion was the apparent heartlessness of the democrats and the confident air of the republicans. This was remarked by republicans generally. One democrat said that when he arose in the morning and saw the bright sky he felt fearful of the result. A not very creditable admission this, for a good day brings out the better class of voters.

A full vote was polled.

P. S. A few minutes after writing the above, and just before time for closing the polls, we stepped out upon the street, just as two colored men, in a buggy, hurried by, as fast as their horse could carry them—which was not very rapidly, although the whip was vigorously and constantly applied, for the poor animal was reeking with perspiration and almost ready to drop. The sight of the drunken drivers and their inhuman treatment of the horse was revolting. They drove directly to the polling place, where they were quickly recognized as Will Laten and "Webb" Valentine, of Leesburg—the latter formerly of Hamilton. They hurried to the window where Laten blusteringly provided his political *protege* with a democratic ticket, which he deposited in the ballot box. At the sight of this, the members of the "White Mans Party," cheered lustily. They then got into their buggy, where, with the usual brag, bluster and profanity Laten harangued the crowd, in a disconnected, senseless manner.—Some of the colored men present gave him replies that made it rather warm for him in that vicinity, and he drove on westward, just in time to evade the arm of the law. An hour later they came back through town, with Valentine as driver, for Laten was doubled up on the buggy seat, disgustingly drunk.

The democrats are welcome to all the satisfaction they can get out of this new convert. They take great delight in calling the republicans the "nigger party;" but here we see them exulting over the only disgusting demonstration of the day. All the other colored men who appeared at the polling place had voted the Republican ticket, and did it as orderly and respectfully as anybody; and it was left for the great "White Mans Party" to poll the only discreditable vote of the day, that of a democratic darkey—who was made a democrat between Leesburg and Hamilton, by the influence of democratic whiskey, procured at a democratic saloon!

PRESIDENT BENJAMIN HARRISON.

November 1888

11/9/88 Telephone

Paralyzed Democrats, journalists all,
Hopes they have cherished have taken a fall.
They tried very hard, but they couldn't make
  out;
The fat man was routed—he's got to get out
To make room for the man who will live in
  house
      Uncle Sam built.

This very fat fellow has suffered a rout,
And much to his sorrow will have to get out
To make room for the man who will live in
  the house
      Uncle Sam built.

This is the editor, smiling so grim,
Who declared that G. Cleveland would never
  suit him,
And helped in his own way to bring on the
  rout
Of the very fat man who will soon toddle out
To make room for the man who will live in
  the house
      Uncle Sam built

Uncle Sam and his nephews that won in
  the race.
That the old man is happy is shown by his
  face.
G. Cleveland is packing his goods to get
  out.
Protection has triumphed—it was a great
  rout.
Hurrah! hip! hurrah! and hurrah once
  again,
The country is safe in the hands of our
  Ben,
The man who will live in the house
      Uncle Sam built

12/6/88 Mirror

WALKING THE ROPES.

Blondin Writes About Himself and His Risky Profession.

From Blondin's paper in *Lippincott's Magazine* it can be learned that a rope-walker is like a poet, born and not made. I myself, he says, began to toddle along a rope when I was only four years old, and in my eighth year I gave a special exhibition before the King at Turin. It is a usual thing, no doubt, for the apprentices in a circus to be taught rope-walking among their other lessons, but only a few of them ever get beyond the rudiments of the art. The usual system of teaching is to make the pupil walk along a narrow board the width of which is daily decreased until it is barely thicker than an ordinary rope. Posturing and the assumption of graceful attitudes are taught in this manner and finally the pupil is introduced to the rope itself.

The apparatus which a leading rope-walker uses appears in the public eyes to be simple enough, but in reality it has to be constructed and arranged with the greatest of care. The rope I generally use is formed with a flexible core of steel wire, covered with best Manilla hemp, and is about an inch and three quarters in diameter. It is several hundred yards in length, and the cost may be $500. The rope is coiled from either end on two large windlasses and when supported by two high poles the windlasses are turned until the rope is stretched perfectly taut. It takes me, as a rule, several days to adjust this simple apparatus to perfection—a fact which caused me to abandon my performances at Staten Island, where it was necessary to remove the rope after each exhibition. At the top of each pole is a small platform, for the purpose of resting; and on one of these platforms I usually place a temporary dressing-room, where I can make necessary changes of my attire. I may mention here that the suit of armor in which I first appeared is of great weight and exquisite workmanship, the gauntlets having once belonged to the celebrated tenor, Mario. As a rule my other costumes are of the least possible weight, while the shoes are an ordinary pair of fine leather ones with soft soles. It is, I think, a popular error to suppose that a rope-walker's feet are exceptionally large or muscular. Mine, I am told, are rather below than above the ordinary size.

The balancing pole, I suppose, fairly comes within the classification of apparatus. In my own case it is made of ash, is about twenty six feet long, and weighs some forty or fifty pounds. It is made of three pieces, so as to be easily taken apart and to occupy but little space when I am traveling. Naturally, my journeys in every quarter of the civilized world have taught me to reduce my baggage to the smallest possible dimensions; but, as it is, I am forced to carry a great deal, and when I visited Australia years ago I remember I carried over sixty tons of baggage with me.

I am often asked as to my sensations when walking the rope; but if by that is meant whether I feel fear or nervousness, I must answer decidedly in the negative.— When walking I look some twenty feet ahead of me. I also invariably keep time in my step to the music the band is playing and I find that helps me wonderfully in preserving my balance. With my own weight and that of the balancing pole, there must be about 230 pounds bearing on bly, this sagging being one of the chief difficulties we have to encounter in keeping up our balance.— I prefer to perform in the open air; for in the hall or a theatre, even of the largest dimensions, the vitiated air found at the elevation at which my rope is always stretched is most unpleasant to breathe.

Nowadays, I never practice, and even my most difficult tricks, such as turning a summersault over a chair placed in the middle of the rope and landing with my feet on the other side of it, are usually performed without meditation, just as the whim seizes me. This enables me without effort to vary my programme at every performance, and prevents them from becoming monotonous to me. I could remain a year or even longer, without ever setting foot on a rope and then go on and tread it as safely as though I had been in constant practice. As an illustration of the slight amount of practice I require for a new trick, I may mention my bicycle act. Some years ago when bicycles were somewhat of a novelty, it struck me I could utilize one in my performance, and I accordingly had one constructed according to my directions —with a groove in the wheels to fit the rope, but otherwise of ordinary fashion. I ordered it to be sent to me sometime before the performance, so that I could try it, but it came just as I was making ready to appear. I was as pleased as a child with a new toy, and, mounting it at once, I rehearsed successfully in view of a large audience, who probably thought I had been practicing for months

I never take any stimulant before walking the rope, and take no special pains to keep myself in good condition. My attendant rubs me down carefully when my journey is ended, and then I take some light refreshment. Otherwise I only live plainly and regularly, merely avoiding eating too much meat shortly after a performance. Finally, I may say that I prefer exhibiting without a net stretched below me. I think it would make me so nervous as almost to lead to the accident against which it is intended as a safeguard.

If I myself do not feel nervous, I am afraid the many persons who I have carried on my back across the rope felt a trifle perturbed, save when they have been professional assistants. In reality there is nothing in the world for them to be afraid of. All they have to do is to sit perfectly still, refrain from clutching me too tightly around the neck, and leave the rest to me. When I am carrying any one over for the first time, I chat to him continuously on as many different subjects as I can think about, and try in this manner to relieve his anxiety, and I always caution him about looking downward when in mid air. Somehow, though, he never feels quite happy, and I always detect a gasp of relief when the end of the rope and the platform are reached. More than once the victim has devoutly exclaimed: "Never again!"

(Blondins most famous feat was crossing Niagara Falls on a tightrope. On occasion, he would walk these ropes blindfolded or with stilts. He died a natural death in 1897.)

12/1/88 Washingtonian

THE POINT OF ROCKS BRIDGE.—The Frederick, Md., *News* says that the work on the Loudoun County and Frederick Bridge across the Potomac at the Pt. of Rocks, is progressing most favorably.

Now let us have a turnpike from Leesburg to the Point, or better still a railroad. Either will much enhance the value of the land along the route and be of immense advantage to the entire Public. Then too the bridge at Berlin should be rebuilt.

(Both bridges were destroyed in the Civil War.)

(Berlin, Maryland is now Brunswick, Maryland.)

12/6/88 Mirror

LANDON T. LOVETT was arraigned before the Circuit Court of Jefferson County, last week, on the charge of horse-stealing. He plead guilty and was sentenced to the penitentiary for five years. Lovett, who is well-known in Loudoun, appears to be a perfect monomaniac on the subject of horse stealing. He was twice convicted in this county, and served two terms in the Virginia penitentiary for like offences. The FREE PRESS thinks "if he gets through with the five years in the West Virginia penitentiary he may be regarded as prison-proof." In early life Lovett was a man of fine address, and respectable habits—and having inherited quite a handsome property from his father's estate, he had it in his power to become a useful citizen. But in an evil hour he yielded to temptation, and the best years of his manhood have been spent behind the prison bars—his offending in each case being the appropriation to his own use, of horse flesh that belonged to others.

—Our New Jail is completed.— Deputy Sheriff, Chas. F. Laycock, is in charge, and the establishment is now ready for the incarceration of evil-doers. On Tuesday, Judge Tebbs issued an order remanding to the new prison here, the Loudoun criminals confined in the Alexandria jail.

December 1888

12/27/88 Mirror

CHRISTMAS DAY of 1888, will probably, long be remembered as one of the most beautiful days ever seen in this quarter of the globe at that season of the year. The ground was free from snow, the sun shone brightly and the air was as soft and balmy as on a day in spring. In Leesburg the day was observed very quietly, though universally. Services were held in the morning at the M. E. South and Episcopal churches, and good congregations gathered at both houses of worship — On the streets the best of order prevailed; there was no boisterousness, no arrests, and by 10 o'clock in the evening the town seemed to be sweetly dreaming with never the voice of a tired or belated citizen to disturb her slumbers.

12/27/88 Mirror
A Dinner With Stonewall Jackson.

Dr. Hunter McGuire, of Richmond, related to a DISPATCH reporter the other day the following reminiscence: December 25, 1861, is a memorable Christmas to me.— During the winter of 1861-'62 the little "Army of the Valley" was encamped near Winchester, and my father on Christmas day gave me a dinner party. About twenty-five guests were at the table. Among them were General T. J. Jackson, Majors Pendleton, Hawkes, Harman, Jones, Botts, Marshall, Kent, Colonel Allen, Dr. Harvey Black and others.

Although the table was abundantly supplied with the good things for which that section was famous, General Jackson dined on buttermilk, corn bread and butter. At this time he lived very abstemiously. It is a solemn and melancholy fact that of all the twenty-five people at the table that day, I am the only one now alive, and when I related this to my children a few days ago one of the little rascals kindly suggested that my turn was next.

Wiley's Twin Stores.
HAMILTON, VA.

Wiley's Is Headquarters again for XMAS GOODS.

TOYS! TOYS! TOYS! TOYS! TOYS! And no end to them.

DOLLS! DOLLS! In Great VARIETY.

Bisque Figures In Beautiful Designs.

China Cups and Saucers, Mugs, Mustache Cups &c. in variety.

Beautiful Goods in Plush and Leather, Games, Picture Books and Cards.

My stock of Confections, Fruits and Nuts are unsurpassed in variety in the County.

Should you wish something substantial for Xmas presents, you will find it in my Shoe and Furnishings Store, where you will find the finest assortment of Boots, Shoes and Gum Goods in this section, besides, a full line of Hats Caps and gents Furnishings and Notions.

If you want anything for Christmas, do not buy till you see my stock.

J. W. WILEY.

SANTA CLAUS' HEADQUARTERS.

January, 1889

1/10/89 Mirror

"Then this is your final answer, Miss Stubbles?"

"My final answer."

"Nothing can move you?"

"Nothing."

"Then my life will be a lonely one, and my fate a harsh one, for my uncle with whom I lived has just died and left me——"

"Just died?"

"Yes, and left me——"

"That fact somewhat alters the case, Henry. I cannot be to harsh to one who has sustained such recent bereavement.— If I could believe that you are sincere——"

"Sincere! Oh, Miss Stubbles!"

"You have certainly made an impression on my heart. Give me time to think of it."

"How long?"

"After all, why think of it? Henry, I am yours."

"Oh! Genevieve!"

* * * * * * *

"Do not squeeeze me so hard, Henry.— Your poor Uncle! Was he long ill?"

"Three days."

"It is too bad! You say he left you?—"

"Yes, he has left me."

"How much?"

"How much! I said he had left ME.— He had nothing else to leave. I am alone in the world now, homeless, penniless, but with you by my side——Gracious, she's fainted!"

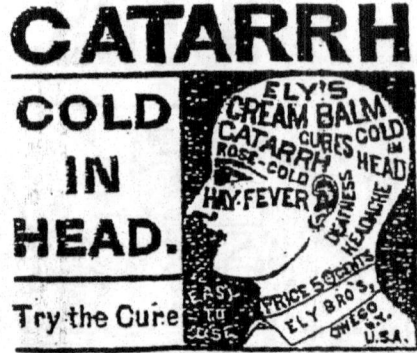

CATARRH COLD IN HEAD.

Try the Cure

Ely's Cream Balm

Cleanses the Nasal Passages. Allays Inflammation. Heals the Sores. Restores the Senses of Taste, Smell and Hearing.

1/17/89 Mirror

LONGSTREET'S RECONSTRUCTION.

Why He Accepted Office Under a Republican Administration.

"While at the Capital I met Gen. Grant. I think he had just been elected, but had not taken his seat. He said to me that he wanted me to call on him as soon as he was inaugurated and let him know what he could do for me, adding that he wished to appoint me to some pleasant position. That was all that passed between us on the subject. Shortly after the inauguration I was in Washington and started up to the White House to call on the President. On the way I met Mr. Corey, Gen. Grant's brother-in-law. He asked me where I was going. I told him, and he said I needn't trouble myself; that the President, a day or two before, had sent my name to the Senate to be Surveyor of the Port at New Orleans. That was the first I had learned of it. The nomination hung fire in the Senate for quite awhile.— One day I went to the President and asked him to withdraw the nomination as I feared it might embarrass him. I told him he had shown his friendship, and I had shown my willingness to accept office under a Republican Administration, and inferrentially my honest acceptance of the results of the war, by remaining in Washington while the nomination was pending. The President told me not to let the delay in confirmation bother me. The nomination, he said, would go through all right.—

'Those fellows up there,' he added, nodding toward the Capitol,' have got a good many more favors to ask of me than I have of them. Shortly after that I was confirmed and took the office. There were two reasons why I accepted. One was because I needed the office. The other was because I had to do it to be consistent with my position. I had said publicly that I was going to abide by the results of the war; that I accepted reconstruction and reconciliation. If I had refused to accept office, when I needed it, at the hands of a Republican Administration, I should have belied my word."

James Longstreet, along with Rosser Moseby and a few others would incur the wrath of some diehard southerners for turning Republican.

FASHIONABLE MILLINERY

AND DRESS AND CLOAK MAKING,

—AT—

MISSES ALDER & EVANS,'

ONE DOOR WEST OF THE "TELEPHONE" OFFICE, HAMILTON, VA.

February, 1889

2/1/89 Telephone

LOUDOUN RANKS FIRST,

AS A STOCK-RAISING COUNTY.

The TELEPHONE hereby acknowledges receipt of a copy of the first report of the State Board of Agriculture, which was appointed by the Governor, under the act of March 5th 1888, composed of one member from each congressional district.

Number of dairies and creameries, 10. Average price of farm labor, $10 per month. State of fencing, good. Number of grain mills, 55. Agricultural societies, clubs &c., 4. Canning establishments, 1. Number of tanneries, 5. Kind of minerals, copper and iron. Stone quarries, granite and marble. Average price of mechanical labor, $2 per day. Character of public roads, good. Number of toll turnpikes, 5; merchantile establishments, 150; liquor establishments, 12; distilleries, 2; churches, eighty; denominations, 7.

Thirty acres devoted to vineyards. Three fifths of land under regular rotation of crops, including improved pastures; one third in original timber. Lowest sale of farm land with buildings, $5 per acre; highest, $200. Lowest price of arable land without buildings, $3; highest, $100. Raising of horses, cattle, sheep, poultry and vegetables increased — p o u l t r y largely increased.

As a horse-raising county, Loudoun has first rank among the counties of the State, with 8,835, valued at $595,683. Augusta stands second, with 8,801, valued at $549,303.—The number a little more than in Loudoun, but the value considerably less. Rockingham stands third, with 8,674, valued at $453,336.

In cattle Loudoun comes second with 23,724, valued at $473,571. Fauquier has only 465 more, valued at $495,850. Augusta ranks third, with 21,035 valued at $332,904.

In sheep, Loudoun is way at the front, having 13,444, valued at $38,930. Augusta, second.

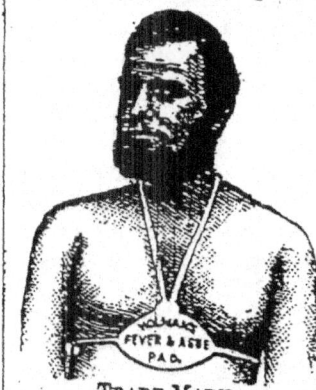

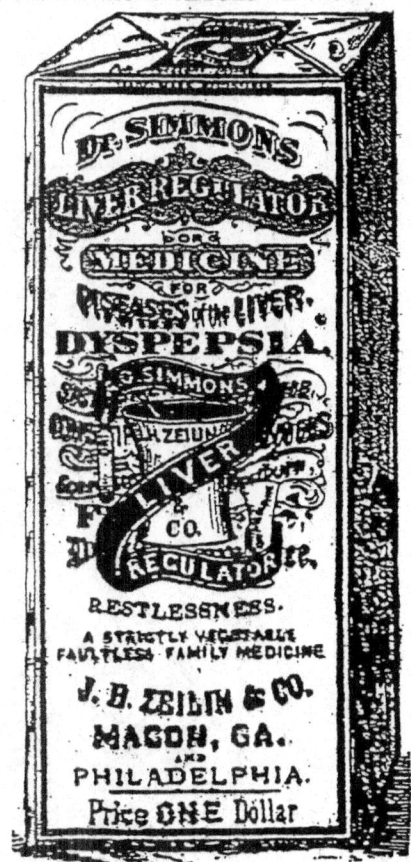

2/8/89 Telephone

DUTIES OF FERRYMEN AND RIGHTS OF THE PUBLIC.

EDWARDS FERRY, Md., Feb. 1st '89
EDITOR LOUDOUN TELEPHONE,

DEAR SIR:— I read in your paper that my Ferry had closed for the Winter. You will please correct it, as I have a No. 1 Ferryman and prepared to cross any one when the River is in condition.

Yours very Respectfully,
E. E. Jarboe.

The TELEPHONE based the statement referred to on a little personal experience. We had an appointment to meet a Loudoun man at Rockville Md., and he was almost prevented from keeping the appointment. After a hard drive over a bad road, he arrived at the Ferry, late in the evening, only to be informed that the boat was taken out of the River for the winter. He, therefore, had to go by way of White's Ferry, thus causing delay.

We cheerfully oblige Mr. Jarboe by publishing his note and giving him this free advertising; but we shall take this opportunity to say, that men who attempt to serve the public should permit no one to be disappointed or inconvenienced It is Mr. Jarboe's business to advise the public, at any time, of his inability to serve them. In his note he says that he is "prepared to cross any one when the River is in condition". But how are the people to know when he considers the River in condition? Why, by going to the Ferry perhaps many miles travel, and then, perchance he unable to cross, because of some little difficulty, which some more enterprising ferryman would have overcome. This kind of thing might have been pardonable a century ago, but not at the present time.

But Mr. Jarboe may ask, what can he do?

Do?

Why does he not know that there are newspapers published on both sides of the River, and that the people read them? There are three in Loudoun and soon there will be three in Montgomery — It is therefore, his business, to notify his patrons, through these papers, of any inability on his part to serve them. Thus they would often be saved great inconvenience and annoyance, as in the case mentioned.

And in writing this we have in mind not only Mr. Jarboe; for it applies, as well, to every other ferryman. For instance, we have, on one or more occasions, driven a dozen miles to Snickers Ferry, only to turn around and return, because the boat was not running — and had not been for several days. These things are great inconveniences to the public. And if the proprietors of ferries have not sufficient enterprise in their business or interest in the welfare of the public, on which they are dependant, to use the means at their disposal for the information of the people regarding their business, they should be compelled, by law, to do so.—

White's Ferry is still there — and busy.

Attention.

HAVING Rented EDWARDS' FERRY and supplied myself with good BOATS and attentive and polite ferrymen, patrons can rely upon being waited on promptly
R. H. COLLIER

2/15/89 Telephone

March, 1889

3/1/89 Telephone

The six days bicycle race which has just ended here was one of the most novel sights of the season. No one supposed there were as many female bicyclists, or rather bicyclisennes, in existence until this race begun. There were eleven good-looking young women riding around hour after hour for six days and nights competing for a portion of the gate receipts. It was a curious sight that met my eyes on entering the Madison Square garden at the closing hour of this contest. The audience was made up of the

MISS LOTTIE STANLEY.

most mixed set of people I ever saw under one roof. Foreign notables, professional men, crooks, merchants, and the many queer characters of the big city were mingled together enjoying themselves in a free and easy way while the girls, attired in bright costumes, were noiselessly adding miles to their scores.

Almost all the fair contestants have made excellent records on the wheel previous to this race and they came from all parts of the country to strive for the big prize awaiting the one who would cover the longest distance in one week.

For the Year 1889.

Farming Implements

—OF—

AL KINDS.

—OF—

W. H. LUCKETT,

CALLS the attention of farmers and others to his stock of FARMING IMPLEMENTS, such as SYRACUSE STEEL and IRON BEAM PLOWS, BRADLEY Chilled PLOWS, WIARD CHILLED PLOWS.

LATEST IMPROVED
BUCKEYE CULTIVATORS,
BUCKEYE GLASS FEED
CENTRE GEAR GRAIN DRILLS,
BUCKEYE FORCE PUMPS and
CHAIN PUMPS,
BUCKEYE CIDER MILLS,
AND DOG CARTS.

1/31/89 Mirror

A Lasting Feud

From the Detroit Free Press.

"What's the matter between you and Johnson? he queried as they dropped off the car.

"Oh, we don't speak," was the reply.

"Money matters?"

"No."

"Politics or religion?"

"No. You see we were both after the same girl. I drew off and let him marry her, and he has never forgiven me for it."

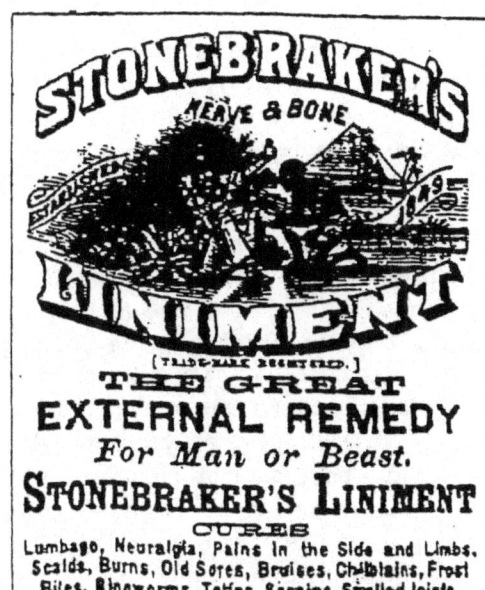

INAUGURATION.

Excursion Rates on the W. & O.

Excursion tickets to the inauguration, good for all trains on the W. & O., will be sold from today until Monday morning, at half fare for the round trip, and valid until the 8th inst.

A special train will be run on Monday; leaving Round Hill at 7.15, Purcellville 7.25, Hamilton at 7.36, Clarks Gap at 7.43, Leesburg at 7.56 and Farmwell at 8.12. Returning the train will leave Washington at 9.40 p. m. which will enable persons to see the fireworks.

3/1/89 Telephone

JEFF DAVIS AT HOME.

A Visit to the Ex-President of the Confederacy.

Beauvoir is not a city, nor even a village, but a little way station located in the pine woods in the extreme southern part of Mississippi, and nearly a half mile back from the shore of Mississippi sound, which is in reality a part of the Gulf of Mexico. The station is not large enough, commercially speaking, to demand the service of a telegraph operator, but in addition to several regularly stopping passenger trains each day the fast express trains are frequently stopped there to take on passengers, provided the latter have made previous arrangements to that end.

The Davis home is situated but a few rods from the sound, where often the roaring waves dash high only to be calm again and leave a smooth and silvery surface with a low shore lined by white sand and myriads of curious shells. From the front porch you look out on the sound, peering through the thick foliage of live oak, cypress, magnolia, pink oak and other trees, which are festooned with the low-hanging gray moss. Mr. Davis became the possessor of this fine homestead some ten or a dozen years ago, it having been left to him in a will by Mrs. Dorsey, a wealthy widow, who formerly made this Marine Villa her own home.

The home life of Mr. Davis and his family is something pleasant to look in upon and long to be remembered. Mr. and Mrs. Davis and a daughter, Miss Winnie, constitute the immediate family. Another daughter is married and lives in Colorado. A body of well trained servants attends the house and grounds and, contrary to the rule in southern homes, the servants are white instead of colored. Besides those whom I have mentioned as composing the family circle, it is rarely the case that there is not some one to occupy one of the guest cottages, close by the mansion, and add one or more to the number about the dining table. It may be a relative or it may be a friend, perhaps claiming little right to hospitality, but offered the benefit to health of a winter in the south. Perhaps it is only a caller, who steps off the train at the station, wishing to pay his respects to the Davis family. He finds when he has done so, that his host anticipates his inability to obtain accommodations elsewhere, there being no public house, indeed, scarcely a house of any sort in the vicinity, and he is cordially made welcome until such time as he takes the train to depart. All visitors are made perfectly "at home" for the time being; the whole household, from the master to the wee little servant girl who stands smilingly at the door to receive guests has caught the spirit and mastered the fine art of entertaining. You feel, when you hear the order given for the carriage to save you a half mile walk in the heavy sand, almost as though you are parting from friends of long standing, who will follow you with their interest, instead of from the acquaintance of an afternoon.

Although his hair is white and his voice not so strong as in the prime of life, Mr. Davis is intellectually as clear and bright as ever, and his fund of humor, instead of diminishing, seems to be growing greater. His knowledge of men and affairs is very extensive, and he converses freely about them, but in a quiet way. When asked by the writer if he would give expression to his views on certain public questions for publication, he firmly but politely declined to do so.

Mr Davis spends but little time anywhere else than at his Beauvoir home, where when he feels well, he does considerable reading and writing. He has a plantation up the Mississippi river in the state of Mississippi, and occasionally he goes there to see how things are running. He receives invitations to visit many points, here and there in the south, but very few of them are accepted. A short time ago he came over to New Orleans to attend a meeting of confederate veterans. He had but little to say, although given an opportunity to make a speech. The hardest task of the evening for him was to put his autograph on some 300 menu cards at the banquet. Mr. Davis is just as fond as ever of his friends, and here in the south, he has hosts of them.

Among the incidents of his life over which Mr. Davis becomes animated in relating is the part he took as an officer in the regular army of the United States. He graduated from the West Point military academy in 1828, and was sent at once to do duty on

March, 1889

the frontier. During the Black Hawk war of 1831-1832 he was in command for some time at Prairie de Chien, Wis., and from there he went down the Mississippi to Dubuque with a small squad of soldiers, encamping on the east side. His mission there was not only to protect the miners from the Indians, but to keep the miners from trespassing on what was then Indian territory in Iowa. The bluffs where the city of Dubuque now stands were full of the richest kind of lead ore, and there it was the miners went without permission, but Mr. Davis managed affairs very skillfully, and the whites were induced to withdraw without the necessity of a conflict

Mr. Davis has indeed had an eventful life. It has been crowded full to overflowing with much that has entered into history. Those now living who were with him in the Black Hawk war, in the Mexican war, and in the senate of the United States are few in number. Today he stands by far the most conspicuous figure of them all.

A CART LIKE THE ABOVE **FOR SALE--Cheap.** For particulars inquire of EDITOR TELEPHONE.

Wagons! Wagons!!

ANOTHER CAR LOAD of those celebrated WEBSTER WAGONS, just receiv and for sale low
SHROFF & CO.

3/22/89 Telephone

THE SAME OLD TOWN.

LEESBURG WILL HAVE ITS LIQUOR.

The District Declines to go Dry.

Yesterday was a wet day in Leesburg District, in every sense of the term. All day long a disagreeable drizzle of equinoxial characteristics pattered upon the voters who gathered about the polling places to decide the question of license or no license for the County Seat district; and an unlimited supply of bottled dampness, clandestinely supplied, made the occasion a "wet" one indeed.

Furthermore, it is reported that the district has declared for the "wet" ticket.

3/22/89 Telephone

All About a Postoffice.

There has been war in Lovettsville; at least there have been "rumors of war." These rumors, which may not be correct in details, indicate that Messrs C. W. Johnson and J. Buryer, both republicans, assisted by their sons, indulged in an ugly fight a few days ago. It is reported that Mr. Johnson met Mr. Buryer upon the street and accused him of being a party to a scheme recently worked, by which M. Chinn the democratic postmaster at that place resigned and a republican was appointed — presumably for the purpose of keeping the office in Chinn's store. To this Mr. Buryer made certain admissions, whereupon Mr. Johnson berated him so severely that blows and a scuffle followed and very quickly the two were lying in the gutter with Johnson on top. The latter was proceeding to punish his adversary when Mr. Buryer's son rushed up with a stone, with which he struck Mr. Johnson on the head, causing the blood to spurt in a stream from the wound. At this juncture Mr. Buryer was seen to get out his knife, but before he could use it the men were separated by others who had been attracted by the affair. All this happened in less time, perhaps, than it takes to mention it, but it was a serious and unfortunate affair. And it is hoped that the reports of it are exagerated.

March, 1889

3/8/89 Telephone

OUR NEW GOVERNMENT

The Inauguration of Harrison and Morton.

AN IMPOSING CEREMONY.

Conducted in Open Air in Spite of Rain.

THE INAUGURATION.

The inauguration was a grand success, so far as it effected the national weal.

It was a great failure, so far as the bodily comfort of the vast crowd of people congregated in the Capitol City was concerned. Nevertheless, the patriotic zeal and proverbial good nature of the American people were equal to the emergency, and there was very little variation from the programme.

On Saturday evening the rain began falling and continued in an almost incessant drizzle until Tuesday morning. But for this unfortunate feature, the inauguration would have been simply immense. However, it was pronounced the greatest demonstration of its kind

THE INAUGURAL ADDRESS.

President Harrison's inaugural address is just what those who knew the man expected. Mild but firm in its tone; plain and explicit in its expression of public policies; with no hypocritical pledges and promises; it at once commands the admiration of all men who are fair enough to appreciate the honesty of such a man as Harrison.

His expressed policies toward all important governmental affairs are simply the policies of the republican party —above which he does not attempt to set himself and toward which he does not assume to play the role of dictator.

INAUGURATION NOTES.

—— Had the weather been fair the number of Loudouners in Washington would have been doubled.

—— Excepting the President elect and the Monument, the most conspicuous object in the City was W. S. Beaty, formerly of Hamilton.

—— Wm. Hamlet, a colored man of Hamilton, came home without his overcoat. He said he simply laid it down.

—— Waterford was quite well represented.

—— Senator Heaton went down on Saturday and saw the whole thing through. He deported himself so well that he might easily have been mistaken for a republican. This is probably due to the part that Cos. James G. Blaine plays in the new administration.

—— John Ryan was also in the City.

—— Capt. Carruthers black horse cavalry, of Loudoun, so conspicuous four years ago, was not in the procession.

—— Nor was Gov. Lee on the ground to divide the honors with the new President, as he did at the previous inauguration.

—— But Gov. Foraker was a conspicuous feature of the parade, and loudly was he applauded.

—— Buffalo Bill, riding at the head of the Cow Boy Company, attracted much attention and received much applause.

—— It was a good day for one thing i. e., democratic whiskey. Evidently it was assumed that the condition of the weather justified a "glorious drunk," and many there were who indulged.

—— In spite of the disagreeable weather the parade was said to be the greatest one ever known; and yet it was reported that about 20 organizations, which were listed, did not appear in the line.

Goodbye Grover,
Your time is over,
We need your service no more.
With gracious "thankee,"
A smile for Frankie,
We respectfully show you the door.

Yes goodbye Stephen,
We now are even,
For here's the last of your pay;
Your service is o'er,
You're needed no more.
So goodbye Grover, good day.

A reason, you ask?
Quite an easy task,
For we do not wish to be rude.—
As a president,
You're equivalent,
To your own "innocuous desuetude."

You're quite too small
For a place so tall,
And your qualifications few—
No more nor less,
You're not a success,
So we bid you a final adieu.

March, 1889

3/8/89 Telephone

MR. RIDDLEBERGER DEFIANT.

He is Ejected From the Senate and Sends His Resignation to Gov. Lee.

(Special Dispatch to the Baltimore Sun.)

WASHINGTON, March 3.—The Capitol today was crowded. The galleries of both houses were packed, and the occupants were almost altogether strangers. In the Senate they had an opportunity to witness a spectacle altogether unprecedented in the history of the American Congress, if not in that of any respectable legislative body. It was the forcible removal of a Senator from the chamber by the sergeant-at-arms and his assistants for conduct disorderly and disgraceful in the extreme.

Mr. Riddleberger came into the chamber early in the afternoon and in a more oblivious condition than usual, and his interruptions of the proceedings by maudling remarks, interspersed with frequent hiccoughs, exceeded any of his previous performances of this character. He made constant motions for an executive session, he objected to every bill that was brought up, interrupted every speaker and evinced a determined purpose to run the whole proceedings on his own hook. The chair ignored him as far as possible and rushed business through, while Riddleberger swayed to and fro on his feet, gesticulating in the wildest manner and constantly exclaiming in thick and choked utterance. Finally the President pro tem. notified him in decisive terms that if he did not desist the rules of the Senate would be inforced and the sergeant-at-arms directed to remove him. This quieted him for a few moments and he disappeared, evidently in search of further refreshments. Then he reappeared and again rose to inform the Senate that his rights as a Senator had been so grossly inveiled that he had telegraphed his resignation to Gov. Lee and would now turn his back in gladness on the spot where he had met with so much bad treatment.

As his term has only a few hours left the point of his resignation was not apparent. He then resumed his position of interfering with the business, when the sergeant-at-arms was directed to take him in custody. The sergeant-at-arms took his position just behind, and stood there with one of his assistants, Mr. Wm. H. May, a man of powerful strength and resolution. It was not ten minutes before Riddleberger was up again, and the patience of President pro tem. Ingalls having been utterly exhausted, he directed the sergeant-at-arms to remove the Senator from Virginia from the chamber.

Col. Canaday promptly proceeded to execute the order, but when he laid hold of Riddleberger the latter held on to his desk by both hands and planted his feet firmly. At a nod from Col. Canaday Mr. May took hold of him on the other side, and Riddleberger was carried bodily from the chamber into the cloak-room, just behind his seat. Riddleberger ceased to struggle when he found himself in the hands of two men who meant business, but when he was set down in the cloak room he took his revenge in denouncing Mr. Ingalls in loud terms in the most violent and furious style. Finally he consented to go to his hotel, and in the charge of some friends he was taken down to the street, put into a carriage and sent home.

3/14/89 Mirror

Pleading for Riddleberger

A Washington dispatch says: "Before the adjournment of the Fiftieth Congress Senator Riddleber was restored to all the rights and privileges of a Senator, and although he did not choose to avail himself of them Monday, it will be a satisfaction to his friends and possibly to him in the future to know that no mention of the unfortunate occurrence appears on the Senate records. At one o'clock Monday morning the Senate went into executive session to consider Mr. Riddleberger's case. The motion was made by Senator Edmunds at the request of M. Daniel, of Virginia. — It was a pathetic feature of the Riddleberger incident that two of the Senator's daughters, sitting in the gallery of the Senate, were witnesses of his arrest and ejectment from the Senate. Mr. Daniel knew it, and when Mr. Riddleberger had been taken from the Capitol he went to Mr. Edmunds, and at his suggestion the Vermont Senator asked for an executive session. When the doors had been closed Senator Daniel made a pathetic appeal on behalf of Senator Riddleberger's wife and seven children. He asked unanimous consent to have the whole matter expunged from the records. Mr. Riddleberger was his enemy politically, but personally he looked upon him as a friend. Mr. Daniel's appeal was so pathetic, his delivery so effective, that the eyes of several of the Senators were wet with tears. There were tears in the speaker's voice and tears on his cheeks. — He said he had no criticism to pass on Senator Ingalls. He had done his duty as a presiding officer. A democratic Senator raised the point that the granting of the request of Mr. Daniel might be looked upon as a condemnation of the presiding officer. Mr Ingalls said he was willing to accept the judgment of those who had witnessed the scene from the galleries and the floor of the Senate. He had no objection to interpose. The request was accordingly granted, and the record of Mr. Riddleberger's disorder and arrest was expunged.

THE TELEPHONE.

FRIDAY .... APRIL 12.

It is probably not necessary for us to inform our readers that the editor has not been able to give much attention to his work this week. Nor would a rail-splitter or horse jockey have done much under similar circumstances. A man who is compelled to lie flat upon his bed with the worst cold east of the Alleghanies and other ailments of divers kinds and incomprehensible combinations; with a head at one time splitting with pains and at another feeling large as a tub and light as a gourd; with a whole apothecary shop cavorting about his prostrate form in uncorked fiendishness, supplemented by every home-made mixture of four generations—with three or four special inventions for the occasion; with the bursting, blooming beauty of Springtime shut out and the immediate vicinity hung 'round with the gloomy reminscences of departing Winter—a man, we repeat, who is thus compassed about is not in condition to do much work.

However, we may report the editor to be improving.

He Was Going to Washington.

[Washington Post.]

Three Philadelphia card sharps entered a train yesterday in that city and succeeded in getting seats alongside of a green-looking fellow whom they knew had a big wallet. They were very polite; he was genial. He explained that he was going to Washington; they were, too; so lucky, etc., etc. A little game was proposed and started. The countryman played awkwardly, but was evidently enjoying the fun. High stakes followed; very high. They let the countryman win, of course. Suddenly he started up. "I must get off here," he said; "I am on the wrong train."

"Eh! What!" they ejaculated. "You said you were going to Washington."

"Yes, I am," he replied, "to Washington, Penn. Good day."

The green countryman was not so green as he looked, and was not going to Washington, Penn. He took the next train to this city

Frederick Douglass in the South.

THOMASVILLE, GA., April 11.—Frederick Douglass has arrived here from Florida. Said he:

"My reception has been courteous. I have no trouble in getting on with the better element of the whites.

"Are you satisfied with the progress of your race since the war?"

"I amazed that it should be so great. No people were ever emancipated under more unfavorable circumstances. The Israelites were told to borrow what they needed, and they did borrow, and have made good borrowers ever since. When 20,000,000 Russian serfs were emancipated, they were given thee acres each and supplies, but my people were simply turned loose to starve.

"What about the Southern policy and the race problem?"

"I don't like either expression.—There should be no Southern policy or Western or Northern policy, and there is no race problem. All that is neccessary is to live up to the Constitution. It is not a question of social rights. I have nothing to do with that. If civil rights are secured, all minor question will settle themselves."

"What about building up a Republican party among the whites in the South?"

"The best way to do that is for the Republican party to do its duty, see that the law is impartially administered, and put good men in the public offices according to fitness. In distributing the public patronage, let Mr. Harrison have but one object in view, and that is fitness for the place, regardless of politics or race."

"Do you think the sectional feeling is dying out North and South.

"In a few more years it will be almost like the Wars of the Roses in England. We will not care which side our ancestors were on so we are Americans. My belief can be put in one word—unification."—*N. Y. Tribune.*

April, 1889

A FEUD ENDED.

4/19/89 Telephone

LANCASTER, KY., April 7.—Another historic Kentucky feud has ended. Tuesday Dr. Evans gave Dr. Hill the right of way along the Lexington pike and Dr. Hill touched his hat to Dr. Evans in recognition of the courtesy. Then the two horsemen separated, with the tacit understanding that the vendetta of which they are the sole survivors was at an end.

Since August, 1838 ninety odd men and boys have died with their boots on for thrashing one of his (Hill's) female negro chattels, a likely yellow girl known as Maria. Less than a week after the initial rencontre some person unknown pumped a load of buckshot into the physician's back as he was riding along an obscure bridle path. The body was taken home, there was a gathering of the clan, a general furbishing up of firearms, a chivalric warning sent the other side to "look out," and the half century's warfare began. The present representatives of the depleted families did not meet for the decade ending in the fall of 1888, for the reason that the Hills went to Oregon, returning to their old home only last year.

Six months ago the present Dr. Hill's family consisted of a wife and two sons, George and Samuel, one of the boys being 18 years of age and the other 16. Dr. Evans had one son and two nephews, besides more distant relatives. Several miles from Lancaster is the little crossroads hamlet of Lawville, and here the Hill lads stopped one day to get a saddle repaired. They noticed a group of their hereditary enemies lingering about the entrance of the grocery, so George went into the harness shop with the saddle, leaving Sam to guard the horses. An outcry arose, and George on rushing from the store saw his brother prostrate on the brick walk, while half a dozen men were hacking at him with knives and others inciting the murderers to finish their bloody work. George at once "turned loose" with a brace of double action revolvers, and soon dispersed the assailants, all save those who were stretched along the ground. Then he carried his bleeding and unconscious brother to a neighboring house. Sam was literally covered with wounds. One ferocious stab began in the right eyeball, went clear through the bridge of the nose, and tore open the left cheek.

Some hours after the affray he regained his senses for a brief period. He uttered no complaint; he knew he was on his deathbed, and he summoned all his strength for a final query. His gashed and bleeding lips framed the one word—
"George."
"Yes, brother," responded the 16 year old lad who stood at the side of the couch.
"Get any?"
"Got four for sure and winged some of the others."
"Bully!"
A gasp, a sigh, a smile, and Samuel Hill was a corpse.

Then George went out to wreak further vengeance. He was amply successful, and he breathed his last, knife in hand, as he fell across the body of one of Dr. Evans' nephews.

There are only the two old men left now. Both families have been exterminated by the feud which began with the "licking" of Maria fifty years ago, so these two bereaved and grim old warriors have concluded to let each other alone and change the tradition of their clans by dying natural instead of violent deaths.

4/13/89 Washingtonian

ELLISON HATFIELD TELLS A TERRIBLE STORY OF CRIME.

WHEELING, W. Va., April 8, 1889.—Ellison Hatfield, one of the participants in the Hatfield McCoy feud, who is confined in the Pike County Jail, in Kentucky has made a confession to State Attorney Lee Ferguson.

"I was present," he said, "and participated in the murder of the three McCoy brothers—Tolbert, Farley and Randolph.

About fifty feet from the river Carpenter tied them to a pawpaw bush and hung a lantern over their heads. Anse Hatfield then said to them, 'Boys, if you have any peace to make with your Maker you had better make it.' Tolbert and Randolph began praying, but Farley did not. Before the boys had time to finish their prayers John Hatfield shot Farley dead. Anse then gave the order to fire and shot as he gave the word, killing Tolbert and then emptying the contents of his revolver into the dead body. Alexander Musser fired and killed Randolph McCoy. The others followed suit and all the bodies were riddled with bullets. After the boys were killed Wal Hatfield administered an oath to all of us binding us to take the life of the first who divulged the name of any who were along.

Captain Hatfield said that he and Tom Wallace shot Jeff McCoy after he had escaped from them. The prisoner also gave the particulars of the murder of Alifera and Calvin McCoy, in which he took part.

4/19/89 Telephone

THE CAPITAL'S EASTER.

THE CHILDREN'S EGG ROLLING ON THE WHITE HOUSE GROUNDS.

Why the Young Ones of Washington Prefer Easter Monday to Christmas—Curious Features of a Picturesque Assemblage of Children—The Capitol Grounds.

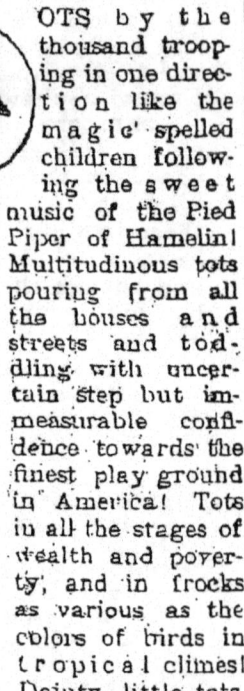

TOTS by the thousand trooping in one direction like the magic' spelled children following the sweet music of the Pied Piper of Hamelin! Multitudinous tots pouring from all the houses and streets and toddling with uncertain step but immeasurable confidence towards the finest play ground in America! Tots in all the stages of wealth and poverty, and in frocks as various as the colors of birds in tropical climes! Dainty little tots, with faces that have been scrubbed into a shiny redness, and in immaculately white and stiff pinafores that will be sadly discolored and limp before the day is done! Tots in patched dresses and little pink toes peeping through their shoes, but happy as chipmunks on an autumn day! Pickaninny tots, with faces as black as Michigan soil, hopping and skipping with unrestrainable glee! Smutch faced tots! Garterless tots, with stockings hanging down! But all of them deliriously happy tots!

It is Easter Monday in Washington, and the children are on their way to the White House grounds to spend the day.

The children of Washington have a more genuinely enjoyable time on Easter Monday than during all of the Christmas holidays. They look forward to it as the greatest event of the year. True, during the Christmas season they are given any amount of plum pudding, mince pie, turkey and pink and yellow candy, but the close of the festivities usually finds them in a condition of satiated disgust and they secretly wish the thing were over.

Easter Monday does not consist in the munching of indigestibles. It is simply a grand romp on the undulating lawns surrounding the mansion of the nation's president.

Washington is always beautiful in the Easter season. The rains of the early spring have ceased, and tree and flower have suddenly burst into bloom. The air is filled with the perfume of the hyacinths that are so plentiful in the parks, and the lilacs, dandelions and snowballs insert their rich colors in the most radiant spring kaleidoscope to be seen in the United States. The grounds surrounding the White House are beautiful in design and coloring, and the spectacle of thousands of children dancing over them, bathed in the warm light of the spring sun, is one of exquisite picturesqueness. The groups of toddlers extend as far over as the Washington monument, which looks like a gigantic marble finger pointing into space. Most of the children are with their parents or nurses, but it requires the most careful watching to keep the young ones from getting lost in the ever moving crowd. The children, most of of variously colored eggs, roll them down the slopes of the many mounds on the grounds, and when they are broken they distribute them among the numerous ragged bootblacks and homeless urchins who stand around and eat an enormous number of eggs without turning a hair.

In this common playground all distinctions of race, color and previous and present condition are razed to the earth. The before mentioned affluent tots will roll and romp and crack eggs with the contingent from Toddledom in Swampdoodle (one of Washington's rough spots), and before the day is over their mothers are talking confidentially together, comparing the various points of their progeny.

The lady of the White House usually mingles with the children for an hour or so on Easter Monday. Nellie Arthur, the daughter of the late ex-President Arthur, used to take part in the egg rolling games herself. Mrs. Cleveland always made it a point to be among the children on the White Lot on Easter Monday, and would amuse them and coddle and coax them with a skill that was the admiration of all the newspaper correspondents in Washington.

The spectacle of this most beautiful of White House mistresses carrying a little ragged girl on her shoulders, or taking a bunch of violets from her dress to give to a little boy who asked for them, would make striking enough pictures to hang on the walls of the executive mansion. When Gen. Grant was president he used to stroll out to a bench in the White Lot, where he would sit, puffing at a cigar and watching the antics of the children. The fun is kept up without cessation from early morning until darkness begins to fall, when the children, thoroughly played out, but with a healthy glow in their cheeks, are marched off to home and to bed. It takes some days for the gardeners of the White House to clear the grounds of egg shells.

It is not in the White Lot alone that these Easter egg rollings take place, but in all of the larger parks of the city. The spacious grounds surrounding the Capitol used to be a great place for the children, but the great marble terrace which is now being completed has spoiled the hill for egg rolling.

A Wise Egg.

To the Editor of the Washingtonian:—Allow me to speak a word concerning our Easter Services to the public through your valuable paper.

The church was tastefully decorated on Saturday evening, and on Sunday morning flowers of varied hues surrounded the pulpit. The pastor, Rev. J. S. Cooper, gave us a delightful sermon from the text, "But now is Christ risen from the dead and become the first fruits of them that slept," 1 Cor. 15-20. At 2 p. m.—the Sunday School assembled and many visitors who were much interested in the services of that hour. A nicely arranged programme was carried through, that was carefully prepared for Easter. Among the many who took part in the exercises were a few persons who prepared essays for the occasion. Mrs. E. Diggs' Subject, "Lessons which we may learn from Easter;" Miss A. Washington—"Flowers of Easter," after which the pastor and Supt. made a few remarks and the whole School gave a liberal Easter offering which was much needed. Mr. Thos. T. Robinson, a barber, who has lately come among us, was of great help to us in preparing the music for the occasion. He presided at the organ while Mr. R. H. Tyler led the singing. We wish to see the day when our white friends, to whom we are much indebted for many deeds of kindness, shall visit our school occasionally, and our religious services and lend us a helping hand that we may be able to head the army of the Living God aright.

JESSE MOTEN, Supt.
Mt. Zion S. S., M. E. Church,
Leesburg, Va., April 22nd, 1889.

WAYS OF THE RUSTLER.

"The rustler himself is a product of the west and his name originated in Dakota, where the very alacrity of his movements is supposed to produce a noise like that which the wind makes in the long dry grass of the prairies. He comes under all guises, from the local preacher with sanctimonious tones, the business man with silk hat and jerky manner, to the simple rustic in jeans and top boots.

"I remember one little town, however, Prospect Heights they called it, that sprang up in a night almost, thanks to a rustler, on the outskirts of Winnipeg, Canada, when people in that city went crazy over the opening of the great prairie lands to the west of it by the Canadian Pacific railway. The city was full of American real estate agents who had come up to help the Canadians appreciate and purchase their own land. Several of these wide awake fellows laid their heads together and bought 320 acres of farm land three or four miles out of the city, on a little knoll that rose a few feet above the dead level of the prairie. They plotted the place off in town lots, advertised it freely as the coming site of suburban homes for city dwellers, and formed a construction company to erect houses thereon. Great quantities of lumber and other building material were carted out to the site, over roads of almost bottomless mud, carpenters and masons were employed, and work was begun simultaneously on a town hall, several saloons, an academy of music, a grist mill, a number of small cottages for renting purposes, a postoffice, several stores and two or three more pretentious houses.

"All this was duly heralded in the papers and by small bills thrust into the hands of the new arrivals, who were then pouring into the city from eastern Canada and Europe at the rate of 500 a day. Even the wildest enthusiast in the city was astonished at the phenomenal growth of this suburban town. While vacant lots were changing hands in Winnipeg, here were buildings of many kinds going up on all sides. True, no one of them had gone up far, but a beginning had been made, and material was lying around in profusion, with more coming in every hour. Two saloons in tents were doing a good business with the teamsters, workmen and visitors, and at the real estate office over the way, surrounded by maps, pens, pencils, paper, plans and other implements of his trade, sat the bland agent of the ostensible owner. Every now and then a new comer would visit this office, when something like the following would occur:

"'Excuse me a minute, says the rustler, 'that's the telephone bell.' He puts his ear to the receiver and after a moment shouts: 'Can't say till I look at the books.' Then to his caller: 'Gentleman at the Victoria in the city wants to know if lots 9 to 12, block E, in Skinner's addition, can be had at $450 each.' Then the rustler rustles the leaves of a big book, consults a bogus sale list, and shouts into the telephone: 'Sold this morning to a Toronto syndicate to build gas works on. Very sorry. Good-by. What's that? The same numbers in the next block, do you say? Hold on, I'll see.' More rustling of the leaves of the ledger. Then he shouts again. 'Yes, they're gone too. Montreal man going to erect a brewery. You should have taken them yesterday when you were here. I'll bet you ten to one the whole plot is sold out before the week closes.' Then he talks a while to his visitor only to be interrupted by another ring on the telephone. 'Hello, who is it? The Albemarles. Oh, the Marlboroughs. Well, go ahead. Who are you? Oh, yes, you were out here this morning. Want those lots reseved for you. How long? Can't do it. Two days the outside. Well, I'll reserve four for three days, but not six. Not the corner one. Two or three people have been asking for it today. I might have sold it, but expected you to close to-night. That corner lot,' he adds, coming back to his visitor, to whom he has already made up his mind he will sell it, 'seems to be a favorite. The adjoining one on the north has been set apart by the owner of the plot for a church, the next one to the west was bought yesterday by a man whose stock of dry goods is on the way, and will be here before he can get his building up, I am afraid.'

"And so it went. He sold that corner lot, of course. He sold the who plot of 320 acres within a fortnight by the aid of consummate gall, a concealed battery in his desk that rang the telephone bell when he wanted it, and capital enough to get a lot of lumber on the land, hire a few men to dig foundation holes, lay bricks here and there and erect the framework of half a dozen buildings. His dupes did all the rest, supplemented his building operations and paid him their money. When he had sold it all, he sold the lumber too, and went away, and with the gentle rustler went the money and the boom. And now a fine growth of wild mustard fills the yawning cellars, oat crops are gathered on the town hall plaza, and the rest of Prospect Heights is buried among miles of tall prairie grass."

4/27/89 Washingtonian

OKLAHOMA'S GATES OPEN.

A Mighty Crowd Pours Through into the Land of Promise.

EVERY ACRE HAD ITS CLAIMANT LAST NIGHT—40,000 MEN SLEEPING IN THE OPEN AIR—LOTS OF RIVAL CLAIMANTS FOR TOWN LOTS AND QUARTER SECTIONS.

GUTHRIE, Indian Territory, April 22.—The gates of Oklahoma, the beautiful land of the Chickasaws, were swung open at noon today, and restless torrents of humanity began to pour over the soil. The hunting ground of the Indian is now the home of the white settler. The wilderness of yesterday is a populated Territory today. Every acre of land from the Canadian River to the Cherokee strip has a claimant. Every quarter section has its squatter. Around the boundaries and railroad stations whole colonies are camped on single quarter sections. Horsemen are racing in every direction to defeat the aims of rival homesteaders. The land offices here and at Lisbon are besieged by an army of eager, impatient men, who are fighting and struggling for a chance to file the records of their claims.

Down in Oklahoma City rival town site companies are preparing to enforce their respective claims with Winchesters and six shooters, and in consequence an additional large force of deputy marshals has been despatched there to help preserve order.

The scramble for land began promptly at 12 o'clock noon, and for hours crowds poured into Oklahoma over all the four borders. All were eager; all were determined.

Across the line they went altogether, great waves of cheering breaking upon the air. Guns were discharged, at first at irregular intervals, and then volleys that sent the horses prancing ahead faster than before. There was no halting, no hesitation. The wagons continued on over the level, green plain, until they were about half way across the northern tier of claims, and then upwards of a hundred of them were brought to a standstill. The others rolled on to the lower tiers.

Men, women, and children poured from the stationary schooners, and in an incredibly short time the foundations for the pioneer homes of Oklahoma had been laid by willing hands. Every farm had more than one claimant, some had two and three, and others as many as ten. They are all ready to swear that they crossed the border first, and that theirs were the first improvements. So it is all over the Territory, and especially on the sections adjoining Guthrie and Oklahoma City. The land offices will have many difficulties to decide before the week is over.

LIFE IN OKLAHOMA.

A Water Famine at Guthrie.

FIRST MURDER IN THE WESTERN EDEN.

KANSAS CITY, April 23.—The first homestead filed at Guthrie, the new Oklahoma city, was Mark S. Cohen, of Fort Smith, Ark. The first soldier to file a declaratory statement was Benton Turner, who was a private in Company I, Sixth Illinois Cavalry. During yesterday three town sites, Guthrie, Oklahoma City and Edmunds, three homesteads and twenty-one solders' declaratory statements were filed.

THE FIRST MURDER.

About five o'clock yesterday evening a pistol report across Cottonwood creek, west of the depot, outside of the town site reserve, attracted attention. It was found that S. T. Comppis had been shot dead in a dispute over a claim. This was the only murder near Guthrie up to midnight despite other reports.

WATER FIVE CENTS A GLASS.

After 4 o'clock yesterday and all night there was much suffering for water. The railroad company refused to let the settlers take from the railroad tank for fear of exhaustion. The water in the Cottonwood is red with mud and a water famine seems imminent. Hawkers went about the depot last night with buckets of water, charging five cents a glass. The water was poor, but found a ready sale. The engineers were besieged by thirsty people for drinks from the engine tanks and many were accommodated.

PREMATURE SETTLERS.

Up to midnight not a quarrel on the Guthrie town site had occurred. The citizens' 4 o'clock meeting adjourned to 6. The great anxiety of every one was information about the size of lots. There was great indignation over the fact that people had gone on the ground before 12 o'clock, and it was the general sentiment that all such should be singled out and debarred.

"Educate yourself for Business, the professions are full and the age demands it."

YOUNG MEN WANTED.

The business interests of the country demand wide-awake, energetic, enthusiastic, honest and *competent* young men. Thousands of young men are looking for situations, but it is difficult to find the right man when there is a place to be filled. Are *you* competent? Are *you* ready? The young men for whom the world is looking, and for whom there is always a place, are those possessing a *thorough business education*—those capable of doing their work in a business-like manner. If you lack this practical education, SADLER'S BRYANT & STRATTON BUSINESS COLLEGE, 10 and 12 N. Charles Street, Baltimore, Md., now in its twenty-fifth year, is prepared to furnish it. It teaches business methods in a business manner, on business principles. Its COURSE OF STUDY embraces thorough instruction in everything necessary for preparing young men to enter active business life.
There is no other Commercial Training School that is held in such HIGH ESTEEM by the better class of business men, that is PATRONIZED by so mature and cultivated a class of PUPILS, or has so large a number of GRADUATES in lucrative positions.

GIRLS IN BUSINESS.

The question is often asked: "What shall we do with our boys?" Why not "What shall we do with our girls?" Why should they not be fitted for some regular occupation as well as our boys?
Parents do not hesitate to give their daughters a finished education in music and the fine arts, but neglect to have them taught those things that will be of importance to them in time of adversity. The wheel of fortune turns swiftly 'round — the rich of to-day may be the poor of to-morrow. Should they not, therefore, be prepared for any emergencies that may arise by having a thorough business education?
The doors of the business world are now open to women equally with men, and merchants are ready to give them lucrative employment whenever fitted to do the work required. Girls with a good business education are in demand as bookkeepers, cashiers, private secretaries, stenographers, typewriters, &c.
Young ladies will find at SADLER'S BRYANT & STRATTON BUSINESS COLLEGE, Baltimore, refined and pleasant surroundings and an opportunity of fitting themselves for independence that will render them the equals of young men in similar walks, without unsexing them in the least degree.

THE COURSE OF STUDY AT

SADLER'S BRYANT & STRATTON

BALTIMORE, MD.

EMBRACES THOROUGH INSTRUCTION IN

BOOK-KEEPING, BUSINESS PRACTICE,
PENMANSHIP, COMMERCIAL ARITHMETIC,
CORRESPONDENCE, SPELLING,
COMMERCIAL LAW, SHORT-HAND,
RAPID BUSINESS CALCULATIONS, TYPE-WRITING, &c., &c.

For Terms, etc., and all other needed information, apply to

W. H. SADLER,

10 and 12 N. Charles St., Baltimore.   President.

May, 1889

5/4/89 Washingtonian

THE POINT OF ROCKS BRIDGE.— The new bridge at the Point of Rocks seems to have a hard time of it. Not long since a part of the new structure was washed away, and by the rains of the last week more damage was threatened. The Frederick NEWS of Wednesday says:

The Potomac raised about 20 feet at Point of Rocks bridge. The men worked very hard on Sunday until about 6 p. m., the trestle then being considered safe. A large amount of heavy drift had caught in the bottom of the trestle the night before and it seemed about 10 o'clock that nothing could be done to save its being washed out. But the brave men worked away risking their lives, and about 2 p. m. the water began to show an ebb. The water fell during the night about 6 feet and is now going out rapidly. The drift is now being removed and large trees 50 feet long and 18 inches at but were wedged in.

5/23/89 Mirror

W. A. Sunday, the center fielder of the Pittsburg baseball club, has taken up a new line of work and one that is very unusual for a man in his profession. On last Sabbath afternoon quite a crowd assembled to hear him preach in one of the Halls in Pittsburg. His theme was "Earnestness in Christian Work" and his address is well spoken of. The man's name bears a strikingly appropriate relation to his new work.

5/24/89 Telephone

New Civil Service Commissioners.

The acceptance by Theodore Roosevelt and Hugh Thompson of their appointment as civil service commissioners reorganizes the commission which has been in a comatose state since the forced resignation of Judge Edgerton. President Harrison appointed Governor Thompson as an endorsement of President

GOVERNOR THOMPSON.   MR. ROOSEVELT.

Cleveland's elections. Mr. Thompson has been governor of South Carolina and assistant secretary of the treasury. He is an able and thoroughly upright gentleman. Theodore Roosevelt is the well-known young Republican leader of New York city. He ran for mayor of New York in 1887 against Abram S. Hewitt, and was defeated. He is an impulsive young man, but is as bright as a new hat, and perfectly able to get good and honest men into public office. He owns a ranch in Dakota, and has written much about ranch and sporting life in the Far West.

HOTEL FOR RENT!

THE NEW HOTEL recently erected in this town by the "LEESBURG HOTEL & IMPROVEMENT COMPANY," is offered FOR RENT OR LEASE, for a term of years. The Building is 70x100 feet, with a Kitchen annex, and contains 50 Chambers, with handsome double parlors, a large airy Dining Room, &c., and is capable of accommodating 125 guests. The Southern exposure front on the Court-House green, a beautiful yard well shaded with sturdy elms, and it is altogether a most desirable location for summer boarders as well as transient custom. There are two daily trains or cars from Washington city.

There is connected with the Hotel, a fine Bar-Room, Barber Shop, with bath-rooms, and a large Livery Stable, 200 feet from main building.

Parties wishing to engage in the enterprise are invited to visit the town and inspect the premises for themselves. For further information, address

H. HEATON, President,

FRANK A. COE,
Photographer,
LEESBURG, VA.

PHOTOGRAPHS of all sizes taken in the best styles, by the instantaneous process.

PRICES TO SUIT THE TIMES.

SATISFACTION GUARANTEED.

Out-door work, houses, public buildings, animals, &c., taken in the best manner— Pictures copied and enlarged in Crayon, Oil, and Water Colors. The public is respectfully invited to call at my galllery (over Shroff & Co's Agricultural Ware-room,) Corner King and Loudoun Streets, Leesburg, and examine specimens of my work.

FRANK A. COE,

may 20-3m   Photographer.

June, 1889

THE MIRROR
BENJ. F. SHEETZ, EDITOR.

Thursday Morning, June 6, '89.

Entirely cut off from all mail facilities from Friday until noon Tuesday, it has been almost impossible to give anything like a connected account of the destructiveness of the great freshet. We, however, devote nearly all our space to such items as will at least afford our readers some idea of the magnitude of the storm.

OUR EPITOME of the recent flood conveys but a faint idea of its magnitude, or its horror. But while pecuniary losses, much suffering, and numbers of deaths marked its track wherever its billows rolled—in the presence of the Johnstown disaster, they pale into insignificance. The many thrilling incidents connected with that disaster would fill a volume. Men, women and children were seen floating on the turbulent waters shrieking piteously for help; but there was no hand to reach them, and all hurried on to a horrible death.—Family groups, peacefully sitting in their quiet homes, were startled by the roaring of the flood—their houses were set adrift—went to pieces, and in many instances the members of the household floated off in an opposite direction, only to be reunited in eternity.

UNPRECEDENTED!

The Freshet of 1889.

BRIDGES WASHED AWAY

Railroads Inundated!

Pt. of Rocks Bridge Gone.

Mason's Island Swept by the Flood.

Harrison's and other Islands Submerged!

Fearful Destruction of Property.

MILLS, STORE-HOUSES, DWELLINGS, CROPS, LIVE STOCK, &c &c.

The heavy rains of last week culminated Saturday and Sunday, in one of the greatest freshets ever seen in this section of the country, and unprecedented in its destruction of property. In Loudoun every stream and rivulet was swollen to unusual proportions, and wherever they coursed their way, the surrounding country bore painful evidence of its devastating power. Leesburg, rolled in angry torrents, flooding the railroad track in the vicinity of the station, sweeping through the store house of Jackson & Pleasants, though without doing much damage; Norris Bros. Lumber Yard and Cockey & Co's Foundry adjacent, were less fortunate, and the loss of the first named firm, in the carrying off, and otherwise damaging of lumber, &c., is estimated at over $500; the Foundry was flooded, and although sustaining no very serious pecuniary loss, was necessarily more or less injured.

The passenger train on the W. O. & W. Railroad, which left here at 2 o'clock Friday afternoon, proceeded as far as the bridge across Goose Creek; being unable to cross, owing to the insecurity of the bridge, it was compelled to return to Leesburg station, where it remained until Monday afternoon, when it again started on its downward trip. The road—notwithstanding the several washouts, mainly between Vienna and Alexandria—had been put in condition to admit the passage of trains by the afternoon of that day.

IN THE COUNTY.

From every section we have the same sad story of destruction, though of course we have only meagre and fragmentary accounts of its magnitude.

At Aldie and vicinity the streams rose several feet higher than they were ever known, doing much damage to gardens, wheat and corn crops, etc. The flouring mill of Mr. J. E. Douglas was pretty well flooded in the lower story, but while he loses something in that way, we are glad to hear the mill itself sustained no serious damage.

ALONG GOOSE CREEK

the damage was more severe. At Oatlands the water swept over the iron bridge without injuring it. The property of Mr. Chas. F. Riticor did not fare so well. Besides damage to flour and other mill stuff in the mill, his barn, stabling, &c., were swept away, entailing a loss of several hundreds of dollars. Considerable damage was also done at Evergreen mills. Lower down the creek, Lent's mill, a moderately sized frame structure,

WAS SWEPT AWAY BODILY,

and floated down stream until it came in contact with the bridge on the Leesburg and Alexandria turnpike, about four miles east of this town. The bridge resisted for awhile, but the weight of the mill, the accumulation of floating timbers and the rush of water was too much for it, and Saturday morning it was

LIFTED FROM ITS PIERS

and floated several miles below until it finally rested on Lowe's Island.

FEARFUL LOSSES ALONG THE POTOMAC.

The most fearful destruction, however, was wrought along the Potomac river, the waters of which, according to the testimony of the 'oldest inhabitants,' were

HIGHER THAN EVER BEFORE KNOWN.

The river, which had been rising for several days previous, took on a regular boom Friday night, from which time it continued to rise steadily and rapidly, up to about 12 o'clock Saturday night. All day Saturday and Sunday thousands of persons lined the banks of the river at every available point for observing the

GRANDLY AWFUL SCENE

presented by the river, which spread out to more than trebble its usual width, went rolling and roaring and rushing along, an irresistible torrent; bearing upon its angry bosom all manner of floating substances, lumber, fencing, uprooted trees, barrels, boxes, frame houses, canal boats, skiffs, chicken-coops, hogs, horses, cattle, and apparently thousands of rolls of pulp, supposed to have come from the paper mill at Harper's Ferry.

THE POINT OF ROCKS BRIDGE WRECKED

One of the most serious losses in this immediate neighborhood was the falling of one-half of the new iron bridge, connecting the Virginia and Maryland shores at the Point of Rocks. The bridge, which consisted of eight spans, was nearly completed, and was to have been turned over to the company last Saturday, June 1st. At the great flood in 1877, the water barely reached the top of the stone piers that had supported the old bridge. The present company had added five feet to the height of these piers, and from that to the top of the flooring was fully two feet more, and it was over all this that the water flowed Saturday night, evidencing at once that the river was fully

SEVEN FEET HIGHER

than in 1877, when it was higher than ever before known. The middle span, or the fourth one from the Virginia side, was at 6 o'clock Saturday afternoon the first to fall. It was followed between 10 and 11 o'clock that night by the three disconnected ones, thus making four spans, or exactly one-half of the entire structure destroyed. Two hours later, about midnight, the waters began to recede, and when we saw it on Sunday it had fallen about six feet.

Two men crossed the river at noon Sunday in a skiff to the Point of Rocks, which village they represented as almost entirely deserted—nearly every business and dwelling house being filled with water to the second story. They heard of no loss of life, but saw several houses that had been overturned by the flood. Mr. C. W. Mercer—a gentleman well known in Loudoun—was one of the heavy losers; his mill was carried away with 2000 bushels of wheat and 180 bushels of corn. The house of Mr. G. H. Hickman got a little start and began to float; the water went down and the house grounded and still stands.

On the Virginia side several houses were floated off without warning. The house of Tart Ridenbaugh went sailing away, and a small store, which was opened last fall by Charles Stream, at Taylortown, was destroyed.

Every island and all the river bottoms from Point of Rocks down were submerged, and the damage to growing crops, fencing, &c., has been very heavy, and as ALL have been losers to a greater or less extent, we have not the names of the sufferers, nor the space to enumerate them. The heaviest losers were of course on the islands—although hundreds of acres of wheat, corn, oats, grass, &c., along the river banks have been ruined.

HEATER'S ISLAND.

The home of Mr. Robert Conner, on Heater's Island, was soon filled with water. He had 75 head of stock—including horses, cows, and sheep—and these were all drowned and swept away. The only animal he saved was a colt that he took up stairs to the second story, where the waters, fortunately, did not reach. Mr. Conner remained so long on the island that he had to be taken out the second story window and ferried over to the Maryland shore.

MASON'S ISLAND.

owned by Dr. J. F. Mason, and tenanted by Mr. John Athey, was swept of everything—dwelling house, barn, stables, 8 or 10 head horses and colts, 6 or 8 milch cows, all the farming implements, and in short everything on the island—Mr. Athey and his family barely making their escape Saturday afternoon with the clothing on their persons.

HARRISON'S ISLAND,

owned by Mr. Henry Harrison and cultivated by Mr. Albert S Daily, is, we believe the largest island in the river, and is historic as the landing place of the Federal troops, from whence they crossed over to the Virginia shore to engage in the memorable Ball's Bluff engagement in October, 1861. Owing to its proximity to Leesburg, and the commanding view afforded by the steep bluffs facing it, it was the great centre of attraction for sight-seers.

Mr. Dailey, with his family, resides on this side of the river, and when the water began to rise Friday night the only persons on the Island was a colored woman (who lived there and cooked for his hands) with her two children, and two colored men. Mr. D. crossed over Saturday morning, and during the day was joined by Mr. John

Ault and one or two others, who busied themselves all day endeavoring to protect the stock and other property from destruction. In addition to six or eight horses, several milch cows, hogs, &c., there were 40 head of cattle on the island. The water continued to rise, until in the afternoon the two story dwelling was almost entirely submerged. By perseverance and hard work, all the cattle, cows, horses, etc., were driven up the cause-way into the second story of the barn. Late in the evening those who had gone to his assistance returned, leaving Mr. Daily, the two colored men, the woman and two children behind, all of whom sought safety with the cattle and horses in the *upper chamber of the barn*— Their presence was essential to the protection of the animals, and there, amid the neighing of horses, the lowing of frightened cattle, and the wild roar of the seething flood, they kept ceaseless vigil through all the long hours of that dark and dreary night. Toward day-break the water commenced falling, and by 10 o'clock had receded sufficiently to enable Mr. D. to cross over to the Virginia shore, and carry back provisions to the colored people, who like himself had had nothing to eat for the preceding twenty-four hours.

The loss on this island is hard to determine, but must be heavy. In addition to the growing crops of wheat, corn and hay, which a week ago promised a splendid yield, there was between 500 and 600 bbls. of old corn in the crib, which is of course greatly damaged. Nearly all the farming implements and other personal property were garnered in the barn and stable, before the flood overtook them, and are safe.— Saturday night eight head of cattle escaped from the barn and were washed away— one of which lodged in a lot of driftwood some distance down the river and was rescued.

SELDEN'S ISLAND,

was also submerged, and we understand, a large quantity of property, to say nothing of the crops, was destroyed, including several head of horses, cows and other cattle.

LOWE'S ISLAND,

further down the river, and owned by Mr. Isaac Vandeventer, was likewise overflowed, and it was here that the turnpike bridge this side of Frankville, found lodgement, after having floated several miles from its base. We have not learned the extent of the damage, but it must have necessarily been great. From the

UPPER PORTION OF THE COUNTY.

we have similar accounts of destruction.— The bridge over Catoctin, at Waterford, was carried away, and crops, fencing, &c., badly damaged. In short, as has been before stated, wherever there was a stream, the surrounding country paid tribute to its angry flood; and the loss to the county and individuals has been very heavy.

Losses Across the River.

The *Star* of Tuesday evening says: At Sandy Hook the loss to the railroad will probably amount to $150,000, while that sustained by the canal company, in the loss of buildings, will reach an aggregate of fully $100,000.

AT POINT OF ROCKS

Messrs. Hickman & Wright suffer a loss of about $5 000. The completion of the new bridge over the Potomac at this point will now be delayed at least three months. It was finished several days ago.

6/7/89 Telephone

A gentleman who was at the Great Falls on Sunday, reports that the Falls was not visible, owing to the great volume of water forced through the very narrow gorge at that place—it being estimated that the water was two hundred feet deep below the Falls. Another gentleman who drove up the River on Sunday, said the water ran over the floor on the Chain Bridge, which ordinarily hangs high above the water.

The Flood Elsewhere.

JOHNSTOWN, PENN., BLOTTED OUT.

10,000 PEOPLE KILLED.

2,000 Burned to Death.

At this writing, (Tuesday morning,) we are without information, save a New York WORLD of Sunday morning, from which we gather a few particulars of the most disastrous flood, possibly, that has visited this portion of the world for centuries.— From all sections, north, south, east and west, come tiding of the most miraculous water fall, and unprecedented loss, not only of the pecuniary treasures of earth, but of human life as well—the most dreadful and heart-rending of which comes from Johnstown, Pennsylvania, where by the bursting of a reservoir last Friday afternoon

FROM 6,000 TO 8,000 PEOPLE WERE KILLED, AND HUNDREDS BURNED TO DEATH.

Johnstown, like every other sections, had of course been subjected to the heavy rains of the preceding days. A dispatch says: The reservoir lies about two and a half miles northeast of Johnstown and is the site of the old reservoir which was one of the feeders of the Pennsylvania canal. It is the property of a number of wealthy gentlemen in Pittsburg, who formed themselves into a corporation, the title of which is the South Fork Fishing and Hunting Club. This sheet of water was formerly known as Conemaugh lake.— It is from 200 to 300 feet above the level of Johnstown, being in the mountains. It is about 3½ miles long and from 1 to 1¼ miles in width, and in some places is 100 feet in depth. It holds more water than any other reservoir, natural or artificial, in the United States. The lake has been quadrupled in size by artificial means, and was held in check by a dam from 700 to 1,000 feet wide. It is 90 feet in thickness at the base, and the height is 110 feet.— The top has a breadth of over twenty feet.

The steady rains of the last forty-eight hours increased the volume of water in all the small mountain streams, which were already swelled by the lesser rains earlier in the week. From the best information obtained at this time it is evident that something in the nature of a cloud burst must have been the culmination of the struggle of the water against the embankment." At all events the embankment gave way, and the immense body of water, rushed like a mighty avalanche upon doomed Johnstown, and almost in the twinkling of an eye, from 700 to 1,000 houses were washed from their foundations and their cargoes of human lives, swept into eternity. "Not only was thousands of persons drowned in the flood, but fire, even more dreadful to contemplate, aided in the destruction of precious lives. When the scores of houses had been torn from their foundations and were rushing down with the torrent, they were thrown together with many outbuildings and timbers, against the new railroad bridge in the town. This checked their onward course, and in less than an hour an immense heap of wooden structures was formed.

From some unknown cause, probably an overturned stove, the upper part of the wreckage caught fire. At first it burned slowly, and a long line of smoke was seen slowly mounting into the air. It looked to those who witnessed the scene from the opposite bank of the Conemaugh as if a funeral pyre had been lighted, and it was indeed that, for on the mass of houses and other wreckage were crowds of men, women and children. They had remained in their almost destroyed homes, thinking it was better to remain there than to trust themselves to the rushing waters. When they saw the timber on fire they realized their awful situation, and their screams were soon added to the awful chorus of horror. They were literally roasted on the flood.

Before the fire burned itself out other buildings and their half-drowned inmates were thrown against the mass. Thus the terrible scene was repeated. Then the fire suddenly went out, the ruins parted, broke up and were swept under the bridge into darkness."

GENERAL DESTRUCTION

was very great. Trees, canal boats, and all manner of drift struck against it with resounding force, until it was a wonder that the bridge remained in position.— Still the well built structure resisted the great pressure, and though considerably damaged it still stands.

AT GEORGETOWN.

Water street, in Georgetown is piled high with driftwood and timber, and will require considerable repairing. Along the Georgetown wharves, except in lumber and coal washed away, the damage is not very heavy. The property of the Transparent Ice Company has suffered more than any other, and the loss will exceed, it is thought, $30,000. The frame storehouse, which was swept away, is a complete loss.— It contained 1,500 tons of ice, all of which was swept away.

All through Washington, Frederick and Montgomery counties, Md., the loss was very great, and the damage to the B. & O. Railroad is the heaviest, perhaps, that that road has ever experienced, while the Chesapeake & Ohio Canal is a complete wreck, it being estimated that $1,500,000 will hardly repair it. Between Williamsport and Dam No. 6, more than twenty houses were swept away.

AT HARPERS FERRY

there were serious losses. The rise of the water was estimated at thirty-five feet. At about 3 o'clock Saturday afternoon, the railroad bridge spanning the Shennadoah river was completely destroyed, and this fact served to increase the interest in the magnificent iron structure across the Potomac, over the floor of which the water was pouring to a depth of from two to four feet. Its destruction appeared almost inevitable, notwithstanding the fact that it was heavily freighted down with nine large locomotives. The bridge, though damaged, still stands.

All the stock of the Shenandoah Pulp Company was washed out, and the warehouse of the mill owned by the Harper's Ferry Mill Company. The water was seven feet higher than it was in 1852.

Later From Johnstown.

A dispatch from Johnstown, Tuesday morning says that every hour reveals new horrors of the disaster. The total number of dead can not be less than 10,000, and may be more — To day the fear of pestilence has increased the horror of the situation. The stench from the putrefying bodies awaiting burial and those lying partially burned in the debris is terrible. Many men who have worked heroically for the past forty-eight hours are absolutely given out. The sight and smell of the remains have made them sick. Summing the whole situation up it may be said that at least ten thousand persons are dead and twenty thousand are homeless. It is probable that by evening there will be 8,000 new graves in the valley.

IN THE BURNT DISTRICT.

Amidst debris of the drift in various places could be seen the bodies of men, women and children, some of them partly buried by the timber and masses of rubbish. Other bodies are so badly charred by the flames that it will be impossible to recognize them. In one place a man's head was seen that had been torn from the body. The doctors are of the opinion that a mistake was made in putting out the fire. It will take a month to remove the mass of wreckage, and before that time the bodies will have been decomposed, and pestilence impregnated the towns along the way to Pittsburg with the germs of the epidemic. The general opinion among the doctors is that a large quantity of petroleum should be poured in the drift and set on fire, and in this way get rid of it in a short time."

Vandals Put to Death.

JOHNSTOWN, Pa., June 2 —Just as the shadows began to fall upon the earth last evening a party of thirteen Hungarians were noticed stealthily picking their way along the banks of the Conemaugh towards Saug Hollow. Suspicious of their purpose, several farmers armed themselves and started in pursuit. Soon their most horrible fears were realized. The Hungarians were out for plunder. Lying on the shore they came upon the dead and mangled body of a woman, upon whose person there were a number of trinkets of jewelry and two diamond rings. In their eagerness to secure the plunder, the Hungarians got into a squabble, during which one of the number severed the finger upon which were the rings and started on a run with his fearful prize. The revolting nature of the deed so wrought upon the pursuing farmers, who by this time were close at hand, that they gave immediate chase. Some of the Hungarians showed fight, but being outnumbered were compelled to flee for their lives. Nine of the brutes escaped, but four were literally driven into the surging river and to their death. The inhuman monster, whose atrocious act has been described, was among the number of involuntary suicides.

Another incident of even greater moment has just been brought to notice. At 8:30 o'clock this morning an old railroader, who had walked from Saug Hollow, stepped up to a number of men who were congregated on the platform station at Curranville, and said: "Gentlemen, had I a shot gun with me half an hour ago, I would now be a murderer, yet with no fear of having to suffer for my crime. Two miles below here I watched three men going along the banks stealing the jewels from the bodies of the dead wives and daughters of men who have been robbed of all they held dear on earth." He had no sooner finished the last sentence than five burly men, with looks of terrible determination written on their faces, were on their way to the scene of plunder, one with a coil of rope over his shoulder and another with a revolver in his hand. In twenty minutes, so it is stated, they had overtaken two of their victims, who were then in the act of cutting pieces from the ears and fingers from the hands of the bodies of two dead women. With revolver levelled at the scoundrels, the leader of the posse shouted: "Throw up your hands or I'll blow your heads off". With blanched faces and trembling forms they obeyed the order and begged for mercy. They were searched, and as their pockets were emptied of their ghastly finds the indignation of the crowd was intensified, and when a bloody finger of an infant, encircled with two tiny gold rings, was found among the plunder in the leader's pocket, a cry went up: "Lynch them! Lynch them!" Without a moment's delay ropes were thrown around their necks and they were dangling to the limb of a tree in the branches of which an hour ago entangled the bodies of a dead father and son. After the expiration of a half hour the ropes were cut and the bodies lowered and carried to a pile of rocks in the forest on the hill above. It is hinted that an Allegheny county official was one of the most prominent actors in this justifiable homicide.

6/8/89 Washingtonian

NEW FLORENCE, Pa., June 1.—The country people are coming into the news centres in large numbers, telling stories of disaster along the river banks in sequestered places. John McCarthy, a carpenter, who lives in Johnstown, reached here about four o'clock. He left Johnstown at half past four yesterday, and says the scene when he left it was indescribable.

The people had been warned early in the morning to move to the highlands, but they did not heed the warning, although it was repeated a number of times up to 1 o'clock, when the water poured into Cinder street several feet. Then the houses began rocking to and fro, and finally the force of the current carried buildings across streets and vacant lots and dashed them against each other, breaking them into fragments. These buildings were freighted with the poor wretches who so shortly before had laughed at the cry of danger. McCarthy says in some cases he counted as many as 15 persons clinging to buildings. McCarthy's wife was with him. She had three sisters who lived near her. They saw the house in which these girls lived carried away, and then they could stand it no longer, so they hurried away. The husband feared his wife would go crazy before he could drag her away, and they left the flooded district and went inland along the country roads until they reached here. It is said to be next to impossible to get to Johnstown proper today in any manner except by rowboats. The roads are cut up so that even the countrymen refuse to travel over them in their roughest vehicles. The only hope is to get within about three miles of Johnstown by special train or by hand car.

THE FATAL RESERVOIR

The reservoir lies about two and a half miles northeast of Johnstown, and is the site of the old reservoir which was one of the feeders of the Pennsylvania canal. It is the property of a number of wealthy gentlemen in Pittsburg, who formed themselves into the corporation the title of which is the South Fork Fishing and Hunting Club. This sheet of water was formerly known as Conemaugh lake. It is from 200 to 300 feet above the level of Johnstown, being in the mountains. It is about 3¼ miles long and from 1 to 1¼ miles in width, and in some places is 100 feet in depth. It holds more water than any other reservoir, natural or artificial, in the United States. The lake has been quadrupled in size by artificial means and was held in check by a dam from 700 to 1,000 feet wide. It is 90 feet in thickness at the base, and the height is 110 feet.

A CLOUD BURST

The steady rains of the past forty eight hours increased the volume of water in all the small mountain streams, which were already swelled by the lesser rains earlier in the week. From the best information obtained at this time it is evident that something in the nature of a cloud burst must have been the culmination of the struggle of the water against the embankment.

Mr. Crouse, proprietor of the South Fork Fishing Club Hotel, came to Johnstown this afternoon. He says that when the dam of Conemaugh Lake broke the water seemed to leap, hardly touching the ground. It bounded down the valley, crashing and roaring, carrying everything before it. For a mile its front seemed like a solid wall twenty feet high.

The warning given the stricken city was sent from South Fork village by Frieght Agent Dechert. When the great wall that held the body of water began to crumble at the top, he sent a message begging the people of Johnstown for God's sake to take to the hills. He reports no serious accidents at South Fork. Richard Davis ran to Prospect Hill when the water began to rise. As to Mr. Dechert's warning, he says just such messages have been sent down at each flood since the lake was made. The warning so often proved unnecessary that little attention was paid to it this time.

"I cannot describe the mad rush," he said. "At first it looked like dust. That must have been the spray. I could see houses going down before it like a a child's play blocks set on edge in a row. At it came nearer I could see houses totter for a moment, then rise, and the next moment be crushed like egg shells each other."

EXPERIENCE ON THE EXPRESS TRAINS.

Conductor Bell of the first section of the day express east, which laid at Conemaugh on the night of the disasters, said yesterday: "The first and second sections stopped side by side at Conemaugh Friday afternoon on account of the washout at Lilly. The second was next to the hill, the first on the outside. Suddenly I saw what looked like a wall of water. It was 30 feet high. We barely had time to notify the passengers and they nearly all fled up the hill side. One old man man, who with his son returned for some reason, was drowned. Two cars went down in the current. I do not know how many persons were drowned.

A MOTHER'S SAD STORY.

An utterly wretched woman named Mrs. Fenn stood today by a muddy pool of water trying to find some trace of a once happy home. She was half crazed with grief, and her eyes were red and swolen. She raised her pale and haggard face and said to a reporter:

"They are all gone. Oh, God, be merciful to them. My husband and my seven little children have gone down with the flood, and I am left alone. We were driven into the garret, but the waters followed us there It kept rising until our heads were crushed against the roof. It was death to remain. So I raised a window, and one by one, placed my darlings on some drift wood, trusting to the great Creator.

"As I liberated the last one, my sweet little boy, looked at me and said, "Mamma, you always told me that the Lord would care for me, will he look after me now,"

SIGHTS TO FREEZE THEIR BLOOD.

Thousands of people stood upon the river bank and saw and heard it all and still were powerless to help. They saw people kneeling in the flames and praying. They saw families gathered together with their arms around each other and waiting for death. They saw people going mad and tearing their hair and laughing. They saw men plunge into the narrow crevices between the houses and seek death in the water rather than wait its coming in the flames. Some saw their friends and some their wives and children perishing before them, and some in the awful agony of the hour went mad themselves and ran shrieking to the hillsides and stronger men laid down on the ground and wept.

All that night and all the next day and far into the morning of Monday these dreadful shrieks resounded from that place of doom. The fire burned on aided by the water underneath, added to by fresh fuel coming down the river. All that time the people stood helpless on the bank and heard those heart-rending sounds. What could they do? They could not fight the fire. Every fire engine in the town lay in that mass of rubbish smashed to bits. For hours they had to wait until they could get telegraph word to surrounding towns and hours more until the fire engines arrived at noon on Monday.

WRECKS OF FIVE IRON BRIDGES

The shrieks ceased early in the morning. Men had began to search the ruins and had taken out the few that still lived. The fire engines began to play on the still smouldering fire. Other workmen began to remove the bodies. The fire had swept over the whole mass from shore to shore and burned it to the water. A great field of crushed and charred timbers was all that was left. The flood had gorged this in so tightly that it made a solid bridge above the water. A tremendous, irresistible force had ground and churned and macerated the debris until it was a confused, solid, almost welded, conglomerate, stretching from shore to shore, jammed high up against the stone bridge and extending up the river a quarter of a mile, perhaps half as wide. In this tangled heap and crush of matter were the twisted wrecks of five iron bridges, smashed locomotives, splindered dwellings and all their contents; human beings and domestic animals, hay and factory machinery; the rich contents of stores and brick walls ground to powder—all the products of human industry, all the elements of human interests, twisted, turned, broken in a mighty mill and all thrown together.

Early in the morning a woman with her two children was seen to pass under the bridge at Boliver clinging to the roof of a coal house. A rope was lowered to her, but she shook her head and refused to desert the children. It was rumored that all three were saved at Cokeville, a few miles below Bolivar.

The original estimate of a ten thousand death toll was incorrect. Still, Johnstown's final accounting of roughly 2,200 dead was 400 more than hurricane Katrina's casualties.

6/14/89 Telephone

WASHINGTON FLOODED.

A FLOWING RIVER FROM THE WHITE HOUSE TO THE CAPITOL.

Curious Sights on Pennsylvania Avenue—Boats Turning Out for Street Cars

WASHINGTON, among the large cities of the country is the only one that suffered seriously from the recent floods. The loss here is estimated at $300,000, and the destruction up the Potomac and its effluent, the Shenandoah, is half as much more. At Fredericksburg, too, the loss is said to be a million dollars.

On Sunday morning when Washington woke up, it was found that, for the first time within the memory of man the Potomac had so far forgot its channel as to overflow the city and stand three feet deep in Pennsylvania avenue. Barrels and lumber, doors and furniture were afloat on that splendid thoroughfare, and for a few hours at midday street-car travel was entirely suspended. All the cellars and basements within two square miles were filled with water.

Five thousand tons of coal were washed out of one yard into the river; four thousand tons of ice were swept from an icehouse, and several thousands of barrels of flour were similarly destroyed.

Of course all Washington turned out to see the rare sight. Boats appeared on Pennsylvania avenue, and ambitious passengers were carried up street for a quarter a head. The side streets abutting on the great watery thoroughfare were thronged with curious thousands as during inauguration day.

Boys paddled up and down between the capitol and the White House on stray planks, on empty barrels, on rafts, and lucky was he who got a skiff to row. A few ventured out on high bicycles, and hundreds prudently rolled their trousers up to their thighs and then waded up to their waists.

During the prevalence of the waters the great Washington monument was in the center of an enormous gulf, which washed for days within its very shadow. Much apprehension is felt lest the tall shaft may have been fatally undermined.

6/20/89 Mirror

THE work of clearing away the debris at Johnstown and the search for dead bodies continues with unabated vigor, and considerable headway is being made toward straightening matters in that unhappy town. Business is gradually reviving, but it must necessarily be a long time before they can be put in proper shape. A recent dispatch says: "The guards at Camp Hastings, near the Prospect hill burying grounds, report that they are having great trouble with dogs that are constantly disturbing the dead interred there. Over one hundred dogs were driven from the place last night and several of them killed. The hastily dug graves there are shallow, and the dogs have been uncovering and devouring the dead. The Gautier wire people today put a large force of men to work cleaning up for the purpose of rebuilding. They will pay out $300,000 in wages on Saturday."

The Relief Committee have decided to erect 100 portable houses to shelter the survivors as soon as the buildings can be received from Chicago. The houses will be 12x26 feet, and will be large enough to accommodate six persons each. Each house will be furnished with a stove and utensils, six chairs, two beds and bedclothes, two spring mattresses, one pair pillows, two pairs of sheets for each bed, woolen blankets, a bureau, a table and tableware to set it. In fact a family will be given everything necessary to go to housekeeping and told to go ahead and paddle their own canoe. The object is to start the town on towards a rise from the ruins.

PENNSYLVANIA AVENUE FLOODED
(From a photograph by Bell.)

June, 1889

JOHN C. CALHOUN'S VISION

6/28/89 Telephone

The following most remarkable and singular story was furnished for the Philadelphia Quaker City, in the winter of 1849-'50, by its Washington correspondent, and was, at that time, quite generally copied into the leading papers of the day.

MR. CALHOUN'S DREAM.

Mr. Editor: The other morning at the breakfast table, our friend, the Hon. J. C. Calhoun, seemed very much troubled and out of spirits. You know he is altogether a venerable man, with a hard, stern, Scotch Irish face, softened in its expression around the mouth by a sort of sad smile, which wins the eye of all who converse with him. His hair is snowy white. He is thin, tall and angular. He reminds you very much of Old Hickory. That he is honest, no one doubts.

But to my story: The other morning at the breakfast table, where I, an observed spectator, happened to be present, Calhoun was observed to gaze at his right hand, and brush it with his left in a hurried and nervous manner. He did this so often that it excited attention. At length one of the persons composing the breakfast party, (Toombs, a member of Congress from Georgia,) took it upon himself to ask the occasion of Mr. Calhoun's disquietude.

"Does your hand pain you?" he asked.

To this Mr. Calhoun replied in rather a flurried manner, "Pshaw! It is nothing! Only a dream which I had last night, and that makes me see perpetually a black spot—like an ink blotch—upon the back of my right hand: optical delusion, I suppose.

Of course these words excited the curiosity of the company, but no one begged the details of this singular dream, until Toombs asked, quietly:

"What was your dream like? I am not very superstitious about dreams, but sometimes they have a good deal of truth in them."

"But this was such a peculiarly absurd dream," said Mr. Calhoun, again brushing the back of his right hand; "however, if it does not too much intrude upon the time of our friends, I will relate it.

"At a late hour last night, as I was sitting in my room engaged in writing, I was astonished by the entrance of a visitor, who without a word, took a seat opposite me at my table. This surprised me, as I had given particular orders to a servant that I should on no occasion be disturbed.—The manner in which the intruder entered, so perfectly self-possessed, taking his seat opposite me, without a word, as though my room and all within it belonged to him, excited within me as much surprise as indignation. As I raised my head to look into his features, over the top of my shaded lamp, I discovered that he was wrapped in a thin cloak, which effectually concealed his features from my view. As I raised my head he spoke:

"What are you doing, Senator from Carolina?"

"I did not think of the impertinence at first, but answered him voluntarily:

"I am writing a plan for the dissolution of the American Union!" (You know, gentlemen, I am expected to produce a plan of dissolution in the event of certain contingencies.)

To this the intruder replied, in the coolest manner possible:

"Senator from South Carolina, will you allow me to look at your hand—your right hand?"

"He rose; the cloak fell, and I beheld his face.—Gentlemen; the sight of that face struck me like a thunder-clap. It was the face of a dead man, whom extraordinary events had called back to life.—The features were those of General George Washington; yes, gentlemen, the intruder was none other than George Washington: He was dressed in Revolutionary costume, such as you see preserved in the Patent Office."

Here Mr. Calhoun paused, apparently much agitated. His agitation, I need not tell you, was shared by the company.—Mr. Toombs at length broke the embarrassing pause; "Well, well, what was the issue of this scene?" Mr. Calhoun resumed:

"The intruder, as I have said, rose and asked to look at my right hand. As though I had not the power to refuse, I extended it. The truth is, I felt a strange thrill pervade me at his touch; he grasped it and held it near the light, thus affording me full time to examine every feature of his face. It was the face of George Washington, gentlemen. I shuddered as I beheld the horrible dead-alive look of that visage. After holding my hand for a moment, he looked at me steadily, and said in a quiet way:

"And with this hand, Senator from South Carolina, you would sign your name to a paper declaring the Union dissolved?"

"I answered in the affirmative, 'Yes.'"

said I, if a certain contingency arises. I will sign my name to the Declaration of Disunion.' But at that moment a black blotch appeared on the back of my hand —an inky blotch that I seem to see now. 'What is that?' cried I alarmed, I know not why, at the blotch upon my hand.

"'That,' said he, dropping my hand. 'that is the mark by which Benedict Arnold is known in the next world.

"He said no more, gentlemen; but drew from beneath his cloak an object which he placed upon the table—placed it upon the very paper upon which I was writing That object was a skeleton.

"'There,' said he, 'there are the bones of Issac Hayne, who was hung at Charleston by the British. He gave his life in order to establish the Union. When you put your name to a declaration of dissolution, why, you may as well have the bones of Issac Hayne before you. He was a South Carolinian, and so are you.— But there was no blotch upon his right hand.'

"With these words the intruder left the room. I started back from the contact with the dead man's bones, and—awoke. Overworn with labor, I had fallen asleep and had been dreaming. Was it not a singular dream?"

> Former vice-president John C. Calhoun authored the nullification theory which many used as a rationale for secession.
>
> Robert Toomes became a Confederate cabinet member and later joined the army as a political general.
>
> The dream bears some resemblance to the hand-wringing episode in Shakespeare's *Macbeth*.

7/5/89 Telephone

The evening train on the W. & O. Wednesday evening last was one of the longest we ever saw on the road, and it was crowded with passengers, all of whom were bearing bundles suggestive of picnics and patriotism. Most of them were off for a little Fourth of July outing — away from the oppressive, soggy atmosphere of the City.

6/27/89 Mirror

UNLUCKY JOHNSTOWN.—Johnstown, the once busy little Pennsylvania city, seems to be pursued by the demon of disaster.— After its almost total destruction by the flood, the story of which has been heard all over the world, the portion that was left came very near being destroyed on Monday last by fire. The flames broke out in a school-building, near which were huddled about thirty buildings, and rapidly spread, burning over some three acres of the best portion of the city left by the waters. But for the adverse direction of the wind it is certain that the whole of the present city would have been swept by the flames. The Philadelphia firemen, however, at last succeeded in stopping the fire and Johnstown had again escaped destruction.

7/5/89 Telephone

SULLIVAN AND KILRAIN.

THEIR PRIZE FIGHT ON JULY 8TH NEAR NEW ORLEANS.

Who They Are — Their Size And Strength — Their Battles — Their Methods of Training — The Apotheosis of the Bruiser.

[Special New Orleans Correspondence.]

The fistic fraternity gather here. Scores come in every day from remote parts of the land. The friends of Kilrain have selected the ground, but its locality will be kept secret till the boat starts.

Most respectable people object to prize fights, but those who never read a report of their deeds of violence are few.

The fight arranged for John L. Sullivan and Jake Kilrain, near this city, on July 8, attracts deep and wide spread interest even among those who agree that such a spectacle of vulgar brutality ought to be prevented at any cost.

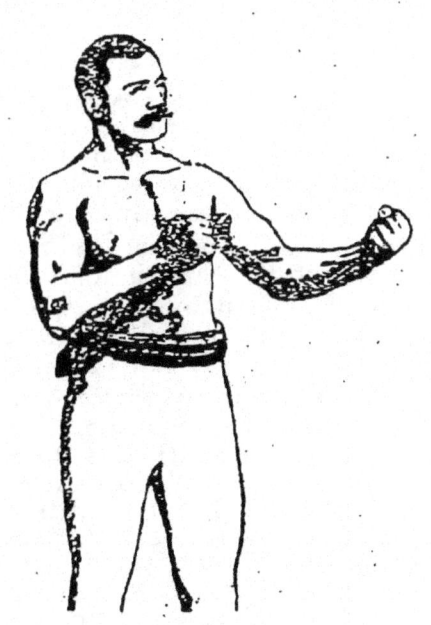

JOHN L. SULLIVAN.

John L. Sullivan was born in Boston in 1858 and is, therefore, 31 years old. He is in heighth five feet ten and a half inches, and a splendid specimen of physical manhood. He ordinarily weighs 220 pounds, but trains down to a fighting weight of 190 pounds.

At a very early age he developed great strength, and became expert with his "maulies" at 16. His muscular prowess soon gained for him the sobriquet of "The Boston Strong Boy." He early met and defeated with the gloves such men as Goss and George Rooke, having apparently no difficulty in knocking these worthies out of time. His first notable achievement, however, was a match with John L. Donaldson, a Cleveland hard hitter, to fight with hard gloves. The "Strong Boy" finished the westerner in eleven rounds. He next gave an exhibition at Harry Hill's, New York city. Sullivan offered $50 to any one who would spar four rounds with him under Marquis of Queensbury rules. The challenge was accepted by the notoriously hard hitter, Steve Taylor, of Jersey City. Sullivan knocked him out of time in the second round. John Flood then thought himself able to stand up against Sullivan, and matched himself against him for $750. The battle took place on a barge in the North river, where the police could not interfere. Sullivan finished Flood in eight rounds, lasting sixteen minutes. Among others who have succombed to Sullivan with hard gloves, are Dan Dwyer, of Springfield; Fred Crosby, of Philadelphia; Bryan of Michigan, and Stewart of Canada.

All this happened before Sullivan was 23, and he practically met no man he could not defeat in four three minute rounds. A fight was then got up for him with Paddy Ryan, the champion heavy-weight of the country. Sullivan defeated him near New Orleans, in 1882, knocking him out in 9 rounds and ten minutes, and winning $5,000.

Sullivan then gave exhibitions throughout the country, defeating the best pugilists all over the land in four three minute rounds. Then came his great contest with gloves with the Englishman, Tug Wilson, who escaped defeat only by his skill in keeping out of Sullivan's way. He next defeated Charlie Mitchell, the Englishman, and Slade, the Australian giant, in four rounds each. Sullivan's success turned his head, and he took to drinking heavily, disregarded the advice and the rules of trainers, and broke with his best friends. His "larks became notorious, and he was several times haled before police courts.

In March of last year Sullivan and the English pugilist, Charley Mitchell, between whom there had been much bad blood and frequent quarrels, met in France and fought a very severe battle to a draw. Sullivan was uninjured and almost untouched, and he could easily have won if he had not scorned to take advantage of "fouls" It rained piteously, chilling the champion, and then the agile Mitchell ran away from him and tired him out.

"My first encounter that really opened my eyes and perhaps the eyes of my friends, was an entirely impromptu affair that occurred in Boston Highlands, where I was at work on one of the city's sewers. I was a good deal of a youngster, and given to deserting my work for the ball field. This displeased the boss, and one day we had some words about it. I thought him entirely in the wrong, because he used the most brutal and insulting language to me. Before I knew it my temper had been aroused and I said some pretty sharp things in return. At that the boss attacked me, and I needed nothing more to pitch into him with might and main. There was no standing up for four rounds in first scrimmage. In less than a minute I had knocked the man out so completely that he had to be carried away by the others. I was sorry for it almost as soon as I saw how effective my blows had been, for it is never a pleasure to me to harm anybody. The only reason why I strike hard and heavy is to convince braggarts that they are no good and to show the public that the reports of my failing powers are false or mistaken.

JAKE KILRAIN.

Jake Kilrain has no such record as his noted antagonist. His name is John Joseph Killion. He was born in this country, of Irish parents, and is now 35 years of age. He began his sporting career as an oarsman, and was accounted a good one. His first pugilistic encounter was with George Godfrey, a colored boxer, whom he defeated. He next fought Jim Goode to a draw. He also met Charley Mitchell with gloves, and a draw resulted. He likewise fought a draw with Mike Cleary, and met Jack Burke, but the police interrupted the mill. He then defeated in turn Wm. Sheriff, Frank Herald, Denny Gallagher, and Joe Lannon. After Sullivan broke his arm, Kilrain challenged him, and, on his refusal to fight, assumed the title of "Champion of America." His last fight was with Jem Smith, Champion of England, which resulted in a draw.

Kilrain is a big, strong fellow, handsome in appearance, and noted for his good nature. He is a skillful boxer, and a plucky fighter. His friends say he has improved greatly, and hold him the superior of Sullivan in his present condition.

Sullivan has trained for his fight with Kilrain at the farm of William Muldoon, the champion wrestler, at Belfast, N. Y., on the Erie Railroad. It is very secluded. He is said to be in the pink of condition, and a spectator says that he has worked off the fat of dissipation and laziness, and in the healthy mountain air, under the scientific handling of Muldoon and his other trainers, is hardening his muscles and cooling off his nervous system with a rapidity that his friends believe will make him the most perfect animal in existence when he faces Kilrain.

Muldoon says: "Sullivan is the best developed man about the chest and arms of any in the world that I know. He strikes an 800 pound blow, and the man who conquers him must take awful punishment. I have no fear but that he will be victorious in the coming fight. Sullivan will win the fight, and if he continues temperate in his habits none will be found to stand in the rain of his master blows as long as he cares to follow up the business."

July 1889

THE TELEPHONE.
FRIDAY .... JULY 5.

—Wet!
—Clouds.
—More rain.
—Plenty of mud.
—Good weather for frogs.
—Ice cold soda water at Wiley's.
—The whole country has gone wet.
—Evidently the Moon is out of gear.
—It rains and it rains and it rains.
—The cutting of the wheat crop is done.
—And now that the wheat is cut there is danger of it being damaged in the shock or stack.
—The three men, Coes and Bradley, charged with assaulting Henry Haley, have been released on an aggregate bond of $2,450.
—The writer of an essay on "Flags" failed to send her name.— Will people never learn that anonymous communications are never published.

Either this evening or tomorrow a company of bicyclists will pass through Hamilton enroute to their homes in Washington. They attended the races at Hagerstown yesterday, and expected to leave that place this morning and travel by wheel via Williamsport, Martinsburg and Winchester to Leesburg, thence by rail to the City.— This will be the largest company of wheelmen ever seen in this section.

THE TELEPHONE.
FRIDAY .... JULY 12.

—Midsummer.
—Keep cool—if you can.
—This is hay harvest week.
—Blackberries are abundant.
—Wednesday was a scorcher.
—Local news is wofully scarce.
—Mercury got up to ninety six on Wednesday.
—See advertisement of meeting of Board and Supervisors.
—The year is half gone and yet many of the roads are in bad condition.
—The city people have been pouring into town during the past week, and Hamilton's several large boarding houses are being rapidly filled—but there's always room for more. Come on.
—It is reported that two or three cows in the vicinity of Round Hill have been worried to death by the dreadful little flies which infest the stock this season. They get in their work especially on the head near the horns, and eat holes into the flesh. These pests should have prompt attention. Tar or diluted carbolic acid are doubtless good preventives and these, or something else, should be applied promptly and frequently.

Commonwealth vs. Chas. E. Painter, for perjury, was tried. The jury rendered a verdict of guilty as charged and fixed punishment at nine months in county jail and $10 fine.

7/12/89 Telephone
Round Hill Rumors.

Our community is considerably agitated over the Sullivan—Kilrain bout, that was. So great is the interest manifested in it that the little urchins of sable hue may be seen on the way side personating "Sulven" and "Kilring."

One of our townsmen, "Tom" Trenary, went gunning a few days ago, but failing to see any game he became disgusted and started to return. He hadn't gone far when his foot caught in a grape vine throwing him, gun and all, about ten feet down hill; the gun struck against a stone and exploded. Immediately two squirrels came tumbling out of a tree killed by an accident. It's a fact. Who can beat it.
J.

[It is sad to see this young man who has a future before him, deliberately throw away a good reputation by working off upon a credulous world that twin squirrel racket. Such an outrageous job must not go unrebuked. Now, if he wanted to get off a genuine whopper, why did he not declare that Tree-nary was standing still in the woods when two squirrels ran up the bark of his limbs, and into his game bag and had made a nest and reared a litter of young before he could get home. Something like that would have been a romance worth reading; but for him to galvanize that old accidental shooting yarn, is simply unbearable. Chestnuts! Such an individual should not be allowed to run at large.]

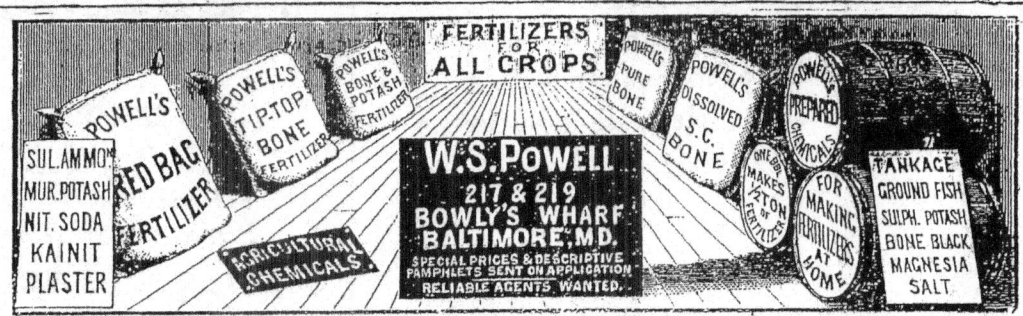

July, 1889

7/13/89 Washingtonian

SULLIVAN ARRESTED.

CAPTURED BY THE POLICE AT NASHVILLE, TENN.

NASHVILLE, TENN., July 11.—When the north bound Louisville and Nashville train pulled into this city at 10:83 this morning a crowd of people surged around the car to see John L. Sullivan, who was known to be on board. A rumor soon obtained circulation that a requisition was in the hands of the police, several of whom had boarded the car. Some discussion and finally a struggle was seen in the car, and an officer reached over with hand-cuffs in his hand and, seizing the slugger's arm, pulled him out into the aisle of the car. Sullivan resisted. Muldoon, who occupied the same seat, put his head out of the window and cried to the crowd: "Gentlemen, I demand American protection! His patriotic wail was greeted with a variety of responses. Some cheered Sullivan and begged him to knock the coppers out."

After a brief struggle Sullivan was taken from the car and hustled to a carraige.

In the scuffle he drew back to knock down a policeman, when Chief Clack stuck a pistol in his face and told him if he struck he (Clack) would kill him. The officers next grabbed Charley Johnson of Brooklyn, Sullivan's backer, who resisted vigorously, but finally began to cry with pain. Only Johnson and Sullivan were detained, though the others were wanted.

The arrest was made by authority of a telegram from Gov. Lowry of Mississippi to the Nashville chief of police. Sullivan has retained ex-Attorney General A. H. Washington, who says that the officers went beyond their authority and cannot hold their men.— An immediate attempt will be made to get the parties out on

A WRIT OF HABEAS CORPUS.

Gov. Lowry's telegram offers a reward of $1,000, and it is believed that if released on the present charge Sullivan will be rearrested in order to secure time for requisition to be obtained. The arrested belligerents are now at the police station in conference with their attorneys.

Sullivan was released upon a writ of habeas corpus by judge McAllister.

SULLIVAN said, after the fight with Kilrain, that he would never enter the ring again—that he had fought his last prize fight. He wishes to live and die a more respectable man. He will not, he says, fight the California darkie.

7/19/89 Telephone

EDISON'S QUEER MACHINE.

The Phonograph Enters on Its Practical and Useful Mission.

Seeing the sign "Phonographs and Phonograph - Graphophones" on the five-story brown stone mansion which is now the home of the Columbia Phonograph Company in Washington, I stopped to have a little chat with the president, Mr. E. D. Easton, who, before the advent of the new mechanism was a prominent stenographic reporter, he having acted in that capacity for many years, and reported, among other notable events, the Guiteau and star route trials.

"Is the talking machine really to supercede shorthand, Mr. Easton?" I asked.

"There can be no question of it," said he.

"Just think for a moment of the superiority of the machine over a stenographer. It doesn't take a vacation; it doesn't go out to lunch; it doesn't get cross, or drunk, or mad; it is always by your side; it is accurate: it has no limit as to endurance or speed. It will take a dictation at the rate of 250 or 300 words a minute as readily as a slower dictation, and as accurately; and of course some of this cannot be said of a stenographer," said Mr. Easton, with a smile.

August, 1889

8/2/89 Telephone

A STEP BACKWARD.

Subsequent events show that the late Sullivan-Kilrain brutality was a positive step backward in the march of civilization. This is particularly shown in the great number of similar affairs, which have taken place within the past few weeks, and the brutality which they have developed in the participants.

8/22/89 Mirror

FIVE men are to be hanged in New York to-morrow, (Friday). They will all drop at the same hour and place, but there will be two scaffolds. Three men are to swing from one, and two from the other. The crimes for which they are to hang, were committed before the passage of the law abolishing hanging—otherwise they would be sent into eternity by the new process—electricity.

8/2/89 Telephone

I understand, that a gentleman, residing below Gum Spring, states that he has missed a double shovel plow from his corn field. He talks of advertising for it, under the head of, "Lost, strayed or stolen.' It must have strayed off Mr. ——, as no one in your community would steal a plow to work with; and it is a settled fact, that the corn in your country never grows large enough to hide a plow.

8/2/89 Telephone

THE LASH FOR A WIFE-BEATER.

Forty Blows on the Back of C. A. Herbert, at Hagerstown, Md.

[Washington Star.]

HAGERSTOWN, MD., July 29.—By a law of 1882 wife-beating is punishable with at most forty lashes. C. A. Herbert, of Washington county, a man of huge frame, on Saturday came here and beat his wife, who is quite petite. He struck her repeatedly with his fist, and was about to brain her with a chair when his arrest.

He was brought here before Justice E. Britner, and was sentenced to fifteen lashes and five days in jail. This afternoon he was stripped to the waist and handcuffed to the iron grating of his cell. A strap bound to a stout stick had been prepared. One of the keepers brought the lash down with a will, but there was no cry for mercy. Each blow was accompanied by a low groan.

8/3/89 Washingtonian

A Pittsburg doctor says he can diagnose ailments by examining a single hair of the patient. Two young men, as a joke, took him a hair from a bay horse. The doctor gravely wrote a prescription, and said his fee was $25, as the case was precarious. They were staggered, but paid the fee, and after they got out laughed all the way to the apothecary's.—The latter took the prescription and read in amazement: 'One bushel of oats, four quarts of water, stir well, and give three times a day—and turn the animal out to grass. Then the jokers stopped laughing.

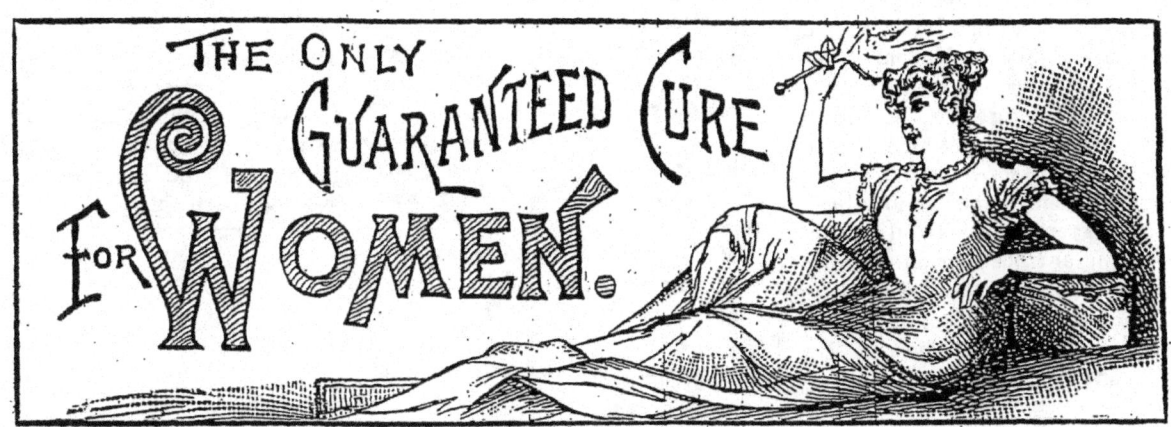

The only medicine for woman's peculiar ailments, sold by druggists under a positive guarantee, from the manufacturers, that it will give satisfaction in every case, or money will be refunded, is DR. PIERCE'S FAVORITE PRESCRIPTION. This guarantee has been printed on the bottle-wrappers, and faithfully carried out for many years.

THE TELEPHONE.

FRIDAY .... AUG 23

A BIG UNDERTAKING.

"We propose to drive him (the editor of the TELEPHONE) out of the party," is an expression which a friend of ours says was made to him, a few days ago, by Geo. W. Hoge.

Well really, this is amusing—it is racy and ridiculous! The idea of a man who has been a deep-dyed democrat nearly all his life declaring that another man, who has never voted anything but a republican ticket, shall be driven out of the Republican party is decidedly rich. For a man who has so little Republicanism in him that his nearest neighbors and kinsmen cannot tell his politics, to attempt to drive out if the Republican party a man whose earliest and latest political aspirations have been in harmony with the principles of the Republican party, is a roaring farce.

So preposterous is this proposition that we would waste no time or space upon it, were it not that we propose to use this to show the animus of the Mahone faction toward true Republicans.

This man Hoge proposes to drive us out of the Republican party because we do not agree with him in his subserviency to Mahone. We assume that it is a question of preference between us. He prefers to bow down at Mahone's bidding and wear his yoke—for a consideration; while we prefer to refuse to submit to the slavery of a political despot! In taking our position on this matter we have always *antagonized our own interests*, for Mahone is an almost omnipresent creature in Virginia affairs; and when we antagonize him in any way or cross his will, we know he will, *and does*, persecute us (and our friends through us) whenever he can get an opportunity. He has done this in the past and he will do it now, if he can. Why then should we oppose him, when, personally, *everything is to be gained by doing just the other thing?* Is it possible that we would do this thing out of pure mulishness?

No! We have reached our conclusions and taken our position in opposition to Mahoneism and, *in the face of proffered assistance*, from a sense of our DUTY TO OUR OWN MANHOOD AND THE REPUBLICAN PARTY—which we love so well that we are not willing to betray it, even for pieces of silver.

And who are the "we," who Friend Hoge says are to "drive" us out of the party? We presume he refers to Mahone's peculiar advocates in Loudoun, such as:

Chas. P. McCabe, who by the ~~assurance of Mahone secured the~~ ~~~~

O. W. Johnson, who recently succeeded in having two of his sons reinstated in the Government service—with Mahone's help we presume.

Dr. Buhrman, for whose sake Mahone turned out of the Waterford postoffice a tried and true old republican.

L. H. Potterfield, who is rewarded for his fidelity to Mahone by appointment as postmaster at Lovettsville—and for which purpose another, and possibly better, republican was tured out.

C. F. Myers, who says Mahone is going to take the Hamilton postoffice away from Mr. Willey and give it to him.

Mr. Spates who would never have been postmaster at Hillsboro without the potent influence of Mahone.

Now, are these the men who are going to "drive" us out of the Republican party—men who are bad ex-democrats and all the peculiar beneficiaries of Mahoneism? Are they the judge, jury and executioner of the Republican party? If so, all we have to say is, "Lay on Macduff!" We shall do our duty in defiance of their authority and threat to do an *impossible thing*—drive us out of the Republican party.

No, we have not been defeated by Bourbon Democracy and we certainly will not yield to the assaults of a few ex-democrats and their allies. WE CANNOT BE BRIBED NOR BULLDOZED.

Nor do we propose to allow these men, or any other, to dictate the sentiments or policies of THE LOUDOUN TELEPHONE. We established this Republican paper here without a penny or pledge from any man. With no other impulse than love of our party, we raised the republican banner, at a time when there was but one other color bearer in Virginia, and have battled for that banner fearlessly and honestly—even in the face of personal persecution and pecuniary loss. And having established this paper at our own risk and conducted it at our own expense, we shall not permit the party, much less a faction, to dictate its course and conduct.

8/30/89 Telephone

We understand Friend Hoge says he was only joking about driving us out of the Republican party. We feel better now.

9/13/89 Telephone

A FOOL-HERO OF THE AGE.

CARLISLE D. GRAHAM GOES OVER NIAGARA FALLS AND IS ALIVE.

Bolted and Barred in a Barrel of Chinese Locust Wood—A Quick, Awful Voyage in the Mass of Falling Waters—More Dead Than Alive He is Rescued Below.

[Special Niagara Falls Letter.]

The impossible is always possible! For 250 years white men have known this marvelous stream and never has any being human, or less than human, been known to go over the awful cataract alive until to-day.

At last a man has been able to go over Niagara Falls and live to tell the tale.

Carlisle D. Graham is the man who did it.

Graham is 35 years of age a cooper by trade. He was born on the Brandywine, near Philadelphia. He has made four previous and perilous experiments at the rapids and whirlpool. With his head out of the barrel he went through the lower rapids on June 15, 1887, and last Sunday he went through the whole length of the gorge below Niagara Falls. Sunday, September 1, 1889, will hereafter be a remarkable date in history, for then it was the perilous feat was performed.

Considerable secrecy was necessary, for the Canadian authorities threatened Graham with arrest, and he had to start from that side. The barrel is 6¼ feet long, 22 inches in diameter at the top and 15 at the bottom. The diameter at the bulge near the the top is nearly 27 inches. The barrel weighs 150 pounds. In it railroad iron was attached to a fifty-foot rope as a drag. Inside some canvas straps had been arranged to support Graham. These had not been deemed necessary in his trip through the whirlpool and devil's maelstrom, but this time Graham felt that he could not do without them.

Constable Horn of Niagara, and Constable Staley, of La Salle, towed the barrel out and set it adrift below the mouth of the Chippewa river. Graham had divested himself of everything except a pair of black trunks, two shirts and his shoes. He got into the barrel through the manhole and crouched down in the bottom fastening himself with three canvas straps, meanwhile the other men busied themselves towing the barrel out into the river. Graham had previously given his gold watch and $40 to Horn, with an injunction to give it to his family if he failed to come out alive. "I may be tempting God's providence," said Graham, "by trying to go over the falls, but it is the ambition of my life to do this. I am satisfied to die if it is necessary. Good by. Boys."

Constable Staley threw the iron drag into the river and the barrel boat started on its journey. The extra irons had been carefully fastened, the manhole cover had been buttoned with tarpaulin, and Graham was securely fastened. The barrel moved slowly down the Horse Shoe rapids. Suddenly it disappeared and the watchers thought it had gone under for good, but it reappeared in a few minutes and kept dashing on down the torrent toward the brink of the cataract.

Just twenty-five minutes after Graham had been cast adrift people on table rock who had watched an hour or more and were just ready to go away saw the barrel come swiftly down about 200 feet from the Canadian shore and well away from the inner horse shoe. The barrel swept down over the falls in the water and did not shoot out as was expected. This saved the shock of about two hundred feet of a fall.

The time was just 7:40. The mist of the morning had cleared away and the increased crowd around the banks watched anxiously for the barrel to reappear. In just one and one-half minutes it came bobbing up in the foam, circled around in the whirl and went into the bass rock eddy, only a few hundred feet from the foot of the falls.

Along the banks of both sides friends of the intrepid navigator waited to rescue him. Almer Jones and Michael Cahill finally lassoed the boat and took it ashore. Graham was more dead than alive. He was so limp that people thought his neck was broken. The rescuers finally revived him. He was badly bruised and will not get over his trip for some time.

"I was determined to make the trip this morning," said Graham, "because I was satisfied that I could do it safely. I notified all the people that I could trust and went ahead."

"What did you see?"

"Nothing. I was locked up in the barrel. I couldn't have gotten out to have saved my

C. D. GRAHAM.

neck. The irons on the bottom were all right, but those on top had to be movable, and Constable Horn locked them. That was the only way they could be fixed. I was

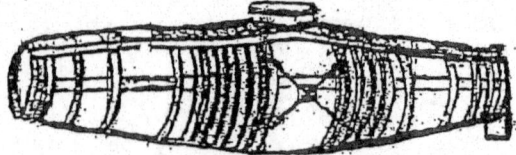

GRAHAM'S BARREL.

just as helpless as a dog would have been.

"I went down to the combing or reef where the Horse Shoe rapids start so quickly that I was hardly prepared. The fall there must be fifteen or twenty feet.

"The first thing I knew I seemed to be going into an abyss. Then I got a crack on the head, such as a policeman would give a drunken man. Then I didn't know much. I was tossed about like a feather. I couldn't get much air and I did not dare change my position.

"I had braced myself with the aid of the straps, so I was sure I would not strike my head again.

"The barrel was built of Chinese locust wood, the strongest kind of stuff, and I had given it the benefit of my experience on the Torpedo and other crafts that were wrecked in the cataract."

"What were your sensations when you went over the falls?"

"I cannot tell just when I did go over the fall," replied Graham. "The awful shaking up I got stupefied me. I felt happy. I felt like a man who has passed in the painless portion of a death by drowning. There was a sense of danger mixed with pleasure which then seemed more pleasant than I feel now, after accomplishing the feat.

"There were many shocks in the trip, but none so great as the first one, and the mere act of going over the fall did not make itself particularly felt. I was not entirely oblivious, but I felt helpless and voiceless. There was the terrible roar in the ears. I tried to speak aloud in the barrel to break it, but I couldn't.

"It was simply awful, yet I felt a contented resignation that I cannot now understand.

"The first time that I knew that I was really over Niagara Falls, was when the barrel went into bass rock eddy. I was in an almost insensible condition. They rapped on the barrel and shouted to me. I could hear them talk to me and I ried to answer but I couldn't. Finally they broke open the barrel. I didn't faint, but I don't know what happened for a while."

"Will you attempt the trip again?"

"Never. Once is enough.

"I came to Niagara Falls three years ago to go over the falls. People said all I had to do was to go through the rapids, then others followed me. Then I went through the whirlpool and they chased me there. Then I made a better trip than all of them, and escaped after I was drawn way down in the devil's maelstrom. To-day I have eclipsed everything. The falls have always been here and I have gone over them alive. Now let some of my detracters do the same. They usually follow where I lead, but if they take my advice they will never attempt it. I have had enough of it. It's taken ten years off my life, what I went through in half an hour this morning."

9/12/89 Mirror

ECLIPSING GRAHAM.— Last Friday, Steve Brodie, famous as a bridge-jumper and swimmer, went over the Horseshoe falls at Niagara, clad in an inflated rubber suit. Brodie entered the water 200 yards above the falls and was shot over the cataract, much to the surprise of every one, without serious injury. He was unconscious when taken from the water but soon revived and at last accounts was all right. His performance is considered to entirely eclipse that of Graham, who, it will be remembered, went over a week ago shut up in a barrel.

THE
Palace Hair Dressing Parlor,
Opposite Loudoun National Bank.
Thos. Lee Robinson,
PROPRIETOR and MANAGER

HAIR TRIMMING & HAIR DRESSING to harmonise with every difficult disadvantages of the features. LADIES AND CHILDREN'S HAIR NEATLY TRIMMED, BANGED and RENOVATED. Hair Dyeing and SHAMPOOING neatly executed.
N. B.—Shop kept strictly and stringently Clean—no dirty Towels, and positively no intemperance.

(The Robinson Barber Shop is still in operation.)

September, 1889

9/20/89 Telephone

A BICYCLING PARADISE.

Something about the Way They Go Wheeling in Washington.

[Special Washington Correspondence.]

Wheeling in Washington is always good. By that I mean bicycling, not the roads, though they are good, too. There are 5,000 bicycles in the capital city, and 500 of them belong to ladies, who ride as well as the men. It is hardly six years since the first wheel came to town. They all came from England for a time. Then the American manufacturers stirred themselves and the home-made bicycle took the lead. The English wheels cost at first from $150 to $200 with the duties. Now an upright wheel of the best make can be had here for $40 to $60. The low "safety" wheels command the high prices that were first given for foreign uprights.

It is strange how fashions rule in the matter of bicycling. High wheels are really seldom seen in Washington. There were 3,000 of them here two years ago. They have disappeared as the low wheels demonstrated their greater convenience. The low wheel, like the "Star," never gives you a "header" and runs quite as rapidly and easily as the larger machine. The beauty of the low wheel is that it is equally safe and available for ladies, and many an independent girl has invested her pin money in a wheel on which she conquers space at the rate of ten or fifteen miles an hour. Shopping, making calls, sight-seeing, the evening saunter, and even church-going are now done "by wheel."

There are half a dozen large bicycle schools as many machine shops and bicyclists' club-houses in Washington. The Capital City club-house is as fine as any in the city, though not as large. It faces the White House grounds from Fifteenth street, and is made of Ohio sandstone and pressed brick, three stories high. The ground floor has a spacious store-room for wheels; the second floor is devoted to parlors, reception-room, and library, while on the third are the billiard-room and the gymnasium. An accomplished steward is on duty day and night with an ample and well selected base of supplies. This describes all the club houses very well, except as to architecture, the rest not being quite as costly or imposing. Another exception, also, is the Ladies' club, which substitutes a sewing-room for the billiard-parlor.

THE CAPITAL BICYCLE CLUB-HOUSE.

New Rapid Safety.

THE FINEST ENGLISH WHEEL
With Improvements for '89.
THE RAMBLER.. With the finest spring frame in the world.
THE NATIONAL $75. Balls all over, $90.
WHEELS ON INSTALLMENTS.
BARGAINS in new and second-hand Bicycles. Write for Catalogue, and mention this paper.
THE CLARKE CYCLE CO.
908 Penn. Ave. Washington, D. C.
10 may 1y.

THE GOOD GRAY BARD.

A VISIT TO WALT WHITMAN AT HIS HOME.

Across the broad majestic Delaware on a Camden ferry, and a bumping ride uptown in the dingy little street cars that ply their crooked course through Camden town, bring the lover of Walt Whitman's verse to his door in Mickle street in less than half an hour from our new city hall. But if you ask boy, man, girl, or matron in Camden where the good gray poet lives, you will be hunting for him when night falls. Nobody seems to know anything either of the man or of his works.

"Does he live on Mickle street?" I asked.

"I don't know, but I dare say he does," was the only reply I could get.

So it is true of the poet as well as the prophet, that he is not without honor save in his own country.

However, after much fruitless search, I succeeded in finding the abode in which the poet dwells—a two storied cottage, No. 328, in "long, unlovely" Mickle street.

Armed with a letter of introduction from an intimate acquaintance and friend of Whitman, I inquired whether it would be possible for me to see him. After a brief delay I was informed that the doctor forbade too much talking and excitement, but that the poet would be glad to see me for a short space of time. I was then ushered into his bed-room where I found him seated amid a litter of books, manuscripts, and papers. He was dressed in a loose-fitting blue serge coat, and wore the large, soft drab cloth hat with which those who are acquainted with the portrait in "Specimen Days and Collect" are familiar.

WALT WHITMAN.

His reception of me was most kind and cordial. Without any unnecessary delay, or any beating about the bush, he proceeded at once to talk with the utmost freedom and ease about himself and the world at large:

"I am still very sick," he said. "For the last twenty years I have had attacks, what I call 'whacks,' of paralysis. In all I have had six of these 'whacks.' The others have lifted off after a while, but this is the most serious and obstinate of all; it has not lifted off yet, and does not seem like as if it would. My first attack came upon me when I was at Washington in one of the government offices nearly twenty years ago. By the way, few few people realize how near this country was to going to the devil in the early part of the war.

I was myself in favor of the Union and the war, but I had friends at the South of whom I was fond, and whom I liked very well. I went first of all from Brooklyn to Washington to nurse some of my friends. I went as a sort of amateur volunteer.

"I came originally," continued Whitman, "from Long Island. Paumanok, you know, is the old Indian name of the island. It was settled first by the Dutch and then by the English. I was born here, at Huntingdon," saying which Whitman drew a map of Long Island with his stick, and pointed out the relative positions of Huntingdon, Brooklyn, and New York. "From Long Island I went with my parents and settled at Brooklyn. I set up a paper of my own, and afterwards contributed to a larger newspaper. Well, I continued to live there for many years; in fact, till I went to Washington at the time of the war. But I made journeys, excursions, detours. I went to New Orleans and lived there awhile, and afterwards returned to Brooklyn by way of the great lakes, and Niagara Falls. It is at the West, in the States that border, or rather edge, on the Mississippi that the future of this country lies.

With us the mugwump is the most promising element in politics, but he is afraid to speak out his whole mind quite fearlessly on all public questions. Many people are afraid of the newspapers. Still, as I said, the mugwump element is the best we have got."

Here the caution came that there had been quite conversation enough for the old man's strength, and with a hearty handshake I departed, wearing all day the picture in my memory of his snowy, leonine head and kindly but dim eye.   J. H. BALLANTYNE.

The mugwumps represented the reformist wing of the Republican party which voted for Cleveland over Blaine in 1884.

October, 1889

10/5/89 Washingtonian

TO OUR GIRLS.

BY A LADY.

In the first place, I would counsel you—that is the girls—to be very careful about your conduct towards the young men you meet. I will take it for granted that you are pretty, and perhaps a little gay and thoughtless as well. If I have pictured you correctly, remember that to be thoughtless counteracts being pretty. You know the proverb—"As a jewel of gold in a swine's snout so is a fair woman without discretion."— And no modern proverb vendor or mender said a truer thing. Do be discreet; do not think that young men are the only delightful people in the world, or act as if you thought so. Keep them at a proper distance; no man likes or respects a girl who runs after him, defers to his opinion, lets him say rude things to her, and takes little liberties of speech or action.— Again, don't go out driving or walking or sailing alone with any young man. Perhaps you will tell me that girls all do it. Well that don't make it proper, if you have no real chaperone, take another girl with you.— Half the scandals and tragedies of women begin in their carelessness about this very thing. And over all, do be most particular about the young men with whom you associate. Avoid "fast" men as you would lepers.— Men who are dissipated are inherently low; no matter how rich, how handsome, how highly placed in what is called society, such men are no associates for a pure young girl. You do not know anything about their real lives and characters, and they know you do not; they take advantage of your natural and lovely innocence, not know anything about their real lives and characters, and they know you do not; they take advantage of your natural and lovely innocence, and admire it, though they know themselves they are not fit to touch the hem of your dress even. I must say something of your clothes. Don't be too fine; simplicity and exquisite fresh neatness are more attractive in a girl's costume than any extravagance of fashion or costliness of material; but even the plainest dress may be made flaunting by its immodest style.— Again, be just as careful with what young women you are friendly with as I would have you to be about young men. A girl is always judged by her friends; keep civilly aloof from the "fast," the slangy, the giggling girls you will too surely meet. Choose your company more carefully than your dress, for your friends are the true index of your moral and mental status. Nothing can ever retrieve the mistakes you make now in these respects, you are now "making history" —the history of your life.

9/20/89 Telephone

The Chief of Police of New York, says that three-fourths of the abandoned girls in that city were ruined by dancing. Young ladies allow gentlemen privileges in dancing for which, if taken under any other circumstances those gentlemen would be reported as improper persons. It requires neither brains, good morals, nor religion, to be a good dancer.

9/7/89 Washingtonian

Henry—"So you asked old Growler for his daughter last night, did you, Fred? And how did you come out?"

Fred—"It was a window, I believe, Henry. That was the best I could do.

10/25/89 Telephone

THE PENNANT WINNERS.

THE COMING FIGHT FOR THE WORLD'S CHAMPIONSHIP.

Who is the Greatest Player?—The Big Four—Interesting Points and Pictures—Specimens of Baseball Anatomy

[Special New York Correspondence.]

The baseball season is now over in both the league and national association. New York has had its share of victory, and now it is Brooklyn's turn. This is glory enough for the baseball cranks of this town, and its big suburb. The twin cities will now play off a series of games, probably consisting of eleven, for the world's championship, and the country will have a real deluge of baseball news.

The time is propitious for baseball chat. Who is the best player in the country? The sentiment on this island is all in favor of the great "Buck" Ewing. As captain, backstop, and batsman, he has few equals and no superiors, while he combines so many of the qualities of a great player that for the time being he has displaced "King Kelly," the great $10,000 Bostonian, from his throne of eminence. So, too, the contest for superiority in pitching which has been waged between the mighty Clarkson and the inimitable Keefe has been decided in favor of the latter, who leads the league in pitching, and is now recognized generally as the greatest pitcher that ever faced a batsman. What would New York have done without Ewing and Keefe? It is safe to say that they would have been fighting it out with the tailenders at the national capital for the "booby" prize.

The instantaneous photograph man has been after our great team, and here are some of the pictures he has taken. I am indebted to the Evening Sun for these pictures—the Sun has been the best baseball paper in New York this summer. Does anybody want to know how Buck Ewing stops Crane's lightning throws, or Keefe's terrific curves? The following picture, taken by an instantaneous flash, will shows how Buck's hands appear at that interesting moment.

EWING   KEEFE
KELLY.   CLARKSON.

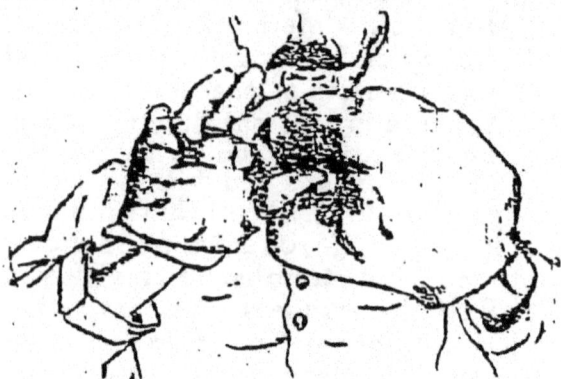

EWING'S HANDS.

The glove on the left hand is not pretty or graceful, but it is built for business. It is full of curiously arranged steel springs and wire, and is covered with the best buckskin. The fragment of a glove on the right hand is less elegant than the other, but it, too, has its uses, and the gallant captain of the finest baseball team on earth wears it with an easy grace which adds greatly to its beauty.

The following picture shows what an arm Ewing has. It is as hard as a bar of iron, but the skin is as soft and velvety as a boy's cheek.

October, 1889

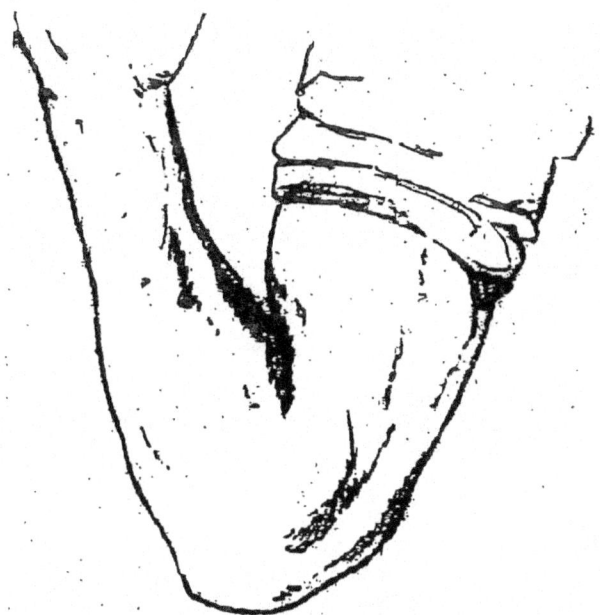

EWING'S ARM.

It is this arm which is used to make those marvelous throws to the bases when some opposing player is rash enough to try to purloin one. It is interesting to note here that only one of Ewing's fingers has been broken. That is the third finger of the right hand. It was broken in Philadelphia two years ago, and Buck was laid off six weeks in consequence.

Hank O'Day, New York's new pitcher, has become a favorite since he joined the champions, winning nearly every game he pitched in. He is a splendid athlete and a marvelous thrower. When he throws a ball he gives it swiftness by using the great length from the shoulder to his hand.

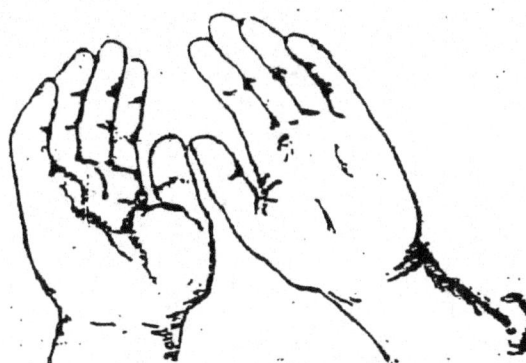

HANK O'DAY'S HANDS

Here are Pitcher O'Day's hands and very pretty hands they are for a baseball player. They are shown here as he holds them when about to catch a baseball, and they look as if they would hold on to it when it got there. Only the little finger of O'Day's right hand has been broken, and it is not preceptible except on very close examination.

If you want to see some out and out baseball hands just look at these. They are the property of Bill Brown, who catches for the Giants when Ewing is resting. On Brown's right hand the thumb has been broken twice and the third finger and little finger once each. The third finger of the left hand has

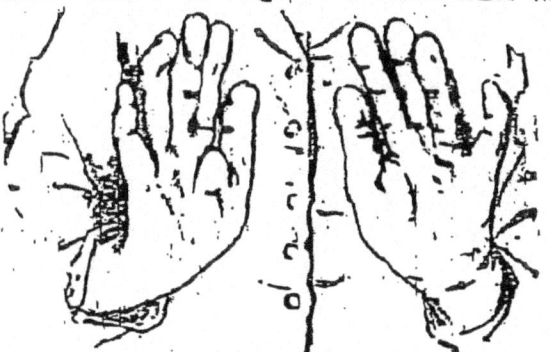

BROWN'S HANDS.

also been broken. This wholesale breakage gives Mr. Brown's hands a weirdly distorted appearance, but they are all right when it comes to catching a ball and holding it.

Pitchers also get their hands broken up. Here is another Giant's hand. It belongs to Hatfield. Hatfield is a pitcher, but he hasn't

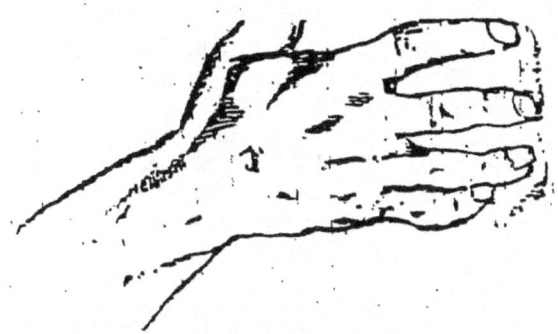

HATFIELD'S HAND.

been so lucky in escaping injury as O'Day has. The little and third fingers of his right hand have been broken and are very much out of shape.

There is another feature of the Giant's anatomy just now. It is Mutrie's smile. The popular manager of the New Yorks was never so happy before. It was the triumph of his life to beat the great Boston combination.

November, 1889

11/8/89 Telephone

MAHONE ARRESTED!

"Washington Star" announces that great excitement was created in that city Tuesday evening, by the arrest of Gen. Mahone on a warrant sworn out by C. M. Romaine, charging him with the unlawful and felonious shooting of Herbert P. Harrison of the firm of Gilian & Harrison, confectioners, of that city. The testimony at the preliminary hearing before Mayor Charles F. Collier was to the effect that a number of young men were firing off "baby wakers" and other fireworks near Gen. Mahone's residence in honor of the democratic victory when they were fired into by some parties in Gen. Mahone's front yard and that Gen. Mahone was seen with a rifle in his hands. Gen. Mahone testified that these young men shot off fireworks into his yard and believing that he had a right to protect his property he seized his gun and went out into his front yard, but that if any shot was fired it was before he came out of the house. Mayor Collier sent Gen Mahone on to the December term of the corporation court for trial and admitted him to bail in the penalty of $2,500. Mr. Walter S. Phillips became his bondsman.

Mr. Harrison, the wounded man, was shot through the leg. He is resting easy today and no serious results are entertained. Mr. Harrison says that he saw three men come out of Gen. Mahone's house and that the shot was fired after they came out. He could not say who fired the shot.

BELIEVE MAHONE FIRED THE SHOT.

RICHMOND, VA., Nov. 6.—Parties coming from Petersburg this morning say that it is generally believed in that city that Gen. Mahone was the person who shot Herbert Harrison last night.

11/14/89 Mirror

H. P. Harrison, the young man who is alleged to have been shot by Gen. Mahone on the night of the election, is slowly improving. The ball went through his overcoat, then through his leg and grazed the other leg— The court at which will be tried the case against Gen. Mahone—if one is made out against him by the grand jury—will meet on the third Thursday in December. Gen. Mahone is now under a bail bond of $2,500 for his appearance.

11/15/89 Telephone

John S. Wise on Mahone

John S. Wise, who ran for governor of Virginia on the Republican ticket a few years ago, and who is known as a red-hot anti-Mahonite, has been interviewed on the recent election in Virginia:

"Mahone's defeat was honestly gained," he said. "I must admit it was a great surprise to me as it must have been to all the rest of my Republican brethren. Yes, I am rather opposed to Mahone. In fact, I am an anti-Mahonite of the first water, although of the same political faith. There is one thing that I give Mahone credit for, and that is for shooting those ruffians who congregated in front of his house. Had I been in Mahone's shoes, and under the same provocation, I would have fired both barrels of the shot-gun into the crowd. I don't know who composed that crowd, but it must have been made up of some opposition political element." At this point the speaker became reminiscent. "I remember," he continued "when I was running for governor the same thing happened to me. I had been out hunting on this particular day. It was during the heat of the campaign. As I was approaching my home I saw a crowd assembled in front of my house. They were hooting and yelling and throwing stones up at the windows, and all the time singing out 'We will hang John S. Wise on a sour apple tree.' I had my dogs and shotgun with me, and sending the dogs into the crowd on a run I followed. My sudden appearance among them armed as I was took the fellows by surprise. The dogs put several of them to flight. When I had reached my stoop I wheeled around and aimed my gun at the nearest of the gang. The mob then fled in terror. I was afterward sorry that the gun was not loaded, or I would have sent a half dozen of these chaps home limping. I learned afterward that the gang were Mahone's heelers. The men whom Mahone shot at are a set of troublesome men of no particular political faith, whose whole lives are devoted to creating disturbances."

November, 1889

THE WASHINGTONIAN
LEESBURG, LOUDOUN COUNTY, VA

11/8/89 Telephone

WAR OF EXTERMINATION

Between the Hatfields and McCoys.

MILTON, W. Va., November 1. The Hatfield-McCoy feud appears to have become a war of extermination. The Blumfield family, frenzied by the murder of Al Blumfield and his wife, have joined the Hatfields, raising their number to 250 men. On Wednesday John and Charles Blumfield and George Hatfield went to Huntington, enlisted about a dozen of their relatives, who work in the Cincinnatti and Ohio shops, bought about one hundred repeating rifles, 125 revolvers and several thousands cartridges, and loading the goods into ten wagons started for the scene of the feud. While at supper that night near the farmhouse of Mrs. James Brown, who was born a Hatfield, the party was fired at from ambush. The Hatfields returned the volley, but in the darkness could not see the result. John Blumfield, their leader, was wounded, and after the firing Mrs. Brown was found lying dead in her house with a bullet through the neck. The excitement here is intense, and the Governor will be asked to send troops here.

DEATH OF JEFF DAVIS.

THE LEADER OF THE LOST CAUSE CARRIED OFF SUDDENLY BY A CHILL.

THE ENTIRE SOUTH IN MOURNING FOR THE PRESIDENT OF HER FALLEN CONFEDERACY—RESOLUTIONS OF SYMPATHY WITH MRS. DAVIS ADOPTED BY STATE LEGISLATURES AND FLAGS ON ALL SOUTHERN CAPITOLS HALF MASTED.

NEW ORLEANS, Dec. 6.—Jefferson Davis, the ex-President of the Southern Confederacy, died at 12:45 o'clock this morning, at the residence of his lifelong friend, J. U. Payne. The announcement of the event created a profound sensation in this city, although the death of Mr. Davis had been expected any time within the last month. Four weeks ago, while traveling on a river steamboat, he caught cold, and his condition became so serious that his physicians refused to allow him to return to his home in Mississippi. Mrs. Davis was sent for and immediately joined her husband and remained with him until the end. Mr. and Mrs. Davis were as devoted to each other as when in their youth.

At 6 o'clock yesterday afternoon, without any assignable cause, Mr. Davis was seized with a congestive chill which seemed to absolutely to crush the vitality out of his already enfeebled body. So weak was Mr. Davis that the violence of the assault soon subsided for lack of vitality upon which to prey. From that moment to the time of his death he sank gradually.

At 7 o'clock Mrs. Davis administered some medicine, but the ex-President declined to receive the whole dose. She urged upon him the necessity of taking the remainder, but putting it aside with the gentlest of gestures, he whispered, "Pray, excuse me."

These were his last words. Gradually he grew weaker and weaker, but never for an instant seemed to lose consciousness. Lying peacefully upon his bed, and without a trace of pain apparent in his features, he remained for hours. Silently clasping and tenderly caressing his wife's hand, he awaited the end.

MEMORY
DISCOVERY AND TRAINING METHOD

In spite of adulterated imitations which miss the theory, and practical results of the Original, in spite of the grossest misrepresentations by envious would-be competitors, and in spite of "base attempts to rob" him of the fruit of his labors, (all of which demonstrate the undoubted superiority and popularity of his teaching) Prof. Loisette's Art of Never Forgetting is recognized to-day in both Hemispheres as marking an Epoch in Memory Culture. His Prospectus (sent post free) gives opinions of people in all parts of the globe who have actually studied his System by correspondence, showing that his System is used only while being studied, not afterwards; that any book can be learned in a single reading, mind-wandering cured, &c. For Prospectus, Terms and Testimonials address,
Prof. A. LOISETTE, 237 Fifth Avenue, N.Y
Nov. 21, 1889·3m.

11/14/89 Mirror

LYNCHING IN LEESBURG.

A NEGRO ATTEMPTS RAPE.

He is Taken from Jail and Hung.

THE BODY PERFORATED WITH BULLETS—A TERRIBLE WARNING.

On Wedsesday evening, October 30th, 1889, as a fifteen year old daughter of a most respectable gentleman of this county, was returning to her home from the Academy at Hamilton, she was assaulted, at a somewhat secluded point in the road, with a villainous attempt at rape, by OWEN ANDERSON, a negro 19 or 20 years old.

The screams and stout resistance of the girl frightened her assailant, who fled, without accomplishing his purpose. When the child reached home she told the story of her assault, and said she believed her assailant was Orion Anderson. Anderson was immediately arrested, and taken before Justice Milton, but the little girl was unable to identify him, because he was disguised when the assault was made, and there being no evidence against him, he was released. During the next day, however, the friends of the injured child searched the ground in the vicinity of the assault and a short distance from where it was made they found an old guano sack, which was known to have been in Anderson's possession the day of the assault. Armed with this clue Anderson was again arrested, and in the absence of Justice Milton, he was carried before Justice F. M. Myers; when confronted with the sack and other suspicious circumstances,

HE CONFESSED HIS GUILT,

and was sent to jail in Leesburg. The knowledge of the fiendish assault aroused the wildest indignation in the community where it occurred, especially when it became known that Anderson had confessed his crime, and was securely ensconced behind the bars of our new jail. A feeling of violent indignation asserted itself, and a band of resolute men, determined, that however much their action might be deplored by those preferring that the law should take its course, they would themselves become the avengers.

THE MIDNIGHT RAID.

Accordingly, last Thursday night, between 12 and 1 o'clock, a body of horsemen, variously estimated by the few persons who saw them, at from 25 to 40, entered Leesburg through the most quiet and less frequented streets—stopping at Mr. Castle's blacksmith shop and providing themselves with two or three crow-bars, or other heavy pieces of iron, and a sledge hammer. Thus equipped, they proceeded on their way to the jail.

The one or two persons whom they happened to encounter on the street at that unseasonable hour, were halted, and detained until after the prisoner was in their possession, when they were released. The story of how they gained

ENTRANCE TO THE JAIL,

is best told by the testimony of the Jailor, Mr. C. F. LAYCOCK, given at the Coroner's Inquest.

CHAS. F. LAYCOCK, sworn—"I am the jailor of the Loudoun County Jail. I had as prisoner, Owen Anderson, colored, charged with attempt at rape, sent by Justice Frank Myers, about a week ago—the rape being attempted on Miss Mary Leith. About 1 o'clock this morning, Nov 8th, 1889, the jail bell rung; I put my head out of the window and asked what was the matter—I saw three men standing at the door, one of them said, "Mr. Laycock we have a prisoner for you." I came down with the keys of the jail. I opened the door and let them in the hall—I saw one with his hands tied behind him, whom I supposed was the prisoner—I unlocked the two first doors of the jail, and went to an empty cell at the back part of the jail, I unlocked the cell door for the prisoner to enter, and asked the man with the prisoner if he had him tied, he said yes, temporarily. I did not know the man; neither he nor the two with him were masked. they were all strangers to me. I knew neither one of them. One of the party said, "I guess we have gone far enough, we want that negro, Anderson." said I, "you can't get him," then they grabbed me, one on each side. I had the lamp in one hand and the keys in the other—the third man took the lamp and keys from me and went back through the jail to the front door and whistled, then others poured in like a swarm of bees. The fellows that caught me had a pistol, and disarmed me of keys and lamp. Then they went in, found Owen Anderson, put a rope around his neck, and left with him—that was the last I saw of them.— They left me then, and I locked up the jail, I then came out, and Dick Webb came and told me they had arrested him, and had taken Anderson down the road with a rope around his neck. I sent Dick to wake Mr. Russell, the Sheriff, I came to Ellmore's corner, and when Mr. Russell came, went with him to the jail, and saw that everything was right, and then went to the Depot, where I saw Owen Anderson hanging to the derrick dead. The last of the gang that came were masked, some with white, and some with black cloths, with holes cut for eyes and mouth, and some seemed to be painted. I did not recognize or know any one of the gang. I had never heard, or expected that anything of this kind was thought of, or intended. I did all in my power to prevent the capture of the prisoner from the jail—they did not threaten to take any other prisoner—they put two of their party at the door, as they said, to prevent any other prisoner from escaping. Any one in possession of the keys could open the cell doors—there is no combination lock to the jail at all. I could not recognize any of these parties now, if I should meet them—I know none of them

W. R. WEBB sworn.—I was the night police for the town on the 7th and 8th of Nov, 1889. I had been around town, and come to the Town Hall, at 10 minutes to 1 o'clock this morning, Nov 8, 1889—staid there about 10 or 15 minutes—I was on the pavement and saw three or four horses at the corner of Loudoun and Church streets, and two or three men with them.—I went there to see what they were doing there. When I got between Judge Tebbs' house and the corner, three men came from the corner and met me, one of them said "you are my prisoner for a while." I paid no attention to him, and went on down to the corner—when I got there 10 or 15 crowded around me one who seemed to be the Captain, picks out two men and put them guard over me. Then I saw three men with crow-bars, and one with a hammer. I asked what they were going to do—they said nothing. I saw the direction they were going, and said I suppose you are going to the jail to get somebody out, and said, "you will have a happy time getting in there"—they all left me, with the two men guarding me, and one boy with the horses — The mob stopped on the brow of the hill by Dr. Head's house — I suppose 25 or 40 of them. When some one came to the jail door and whistled, they all ran up there. In about 10 minutes they came back with the negro with a rope around his neck, and after they had mounted their horses they let me go, and I went to the jail. I asked Mr. Laycock if he was all right, he said he was, and told me to go and wake up Mr. Russell, the Sheriff. I went back to the jail with him, and then came with Mr. Russell and awoke you (Coroner) up. Went with you and him to depot lot, and saw Anderson hanging, dead. I did not know or recognize any one of the entire party, either at the corner or on the hill—all but one had their faces concealed, some with handkerchiefs and some with rags. Would not know any of the party if I were to meet him anywhere. Did not recognize the voice of any one, nor the horse of any one.

11/15/89 Telephone

LYNCH LAW.

The lynching of Orion Anderson, was an outrage upon the law and order of our County which all good people must deplore and condemn. If violence is to take the place of lawful procedure, civil enactments will soon become a mockery and the whole structure of society will be threatened. In our opinion, there can be no justification of lynching.

The offense charged against Anderson is the worst in all the category of crime, and if there is anything on earth that should be protected from harm, it is the virtue of womanhood; therefore, some more radical means must be found for suppressing this class of crime; and thereby putting a stop to this dreadful method of summary punishment.

December, 1889

12/6/89 Telephone

THE POPULAR INTEREST IN THE GAME OF FOOTBALL.

FOOTBALL, it is claimed by its devotees, is the coming American game. Baseball seems to have received a black eye through the warfare now inevitable between the national league and its star players. With two leagues in the field, one representing the brains and the other the playing skill of the profession, with no end of lawsuits and recriminations and bad feeling in prospect, the outlook for baseball next season is not very promising.

Certain it is, that football is enjoying prosperity at the present that it has never been favored with before. The recent Yale-Harvard game at New York attracted an amount of attention never surpassed by any sport in the country. At present it is the popular college game, and there is no doubt that

years, and as now played by the inter-collegiate association, it is really a game of science, in which brains count as well as muscle, and in which finesse and skill play the principal part. Small men have a chance to become expert at football, as is proved by the fact that several of the most noted players have been under 140 pounds weight.

a number of professional teams will be organized.

Football, as played just now in this country is thoroughly American, differing as much from the old English game as baseball does from "rounders." It has been reduced to a scientific pastime; the brutal features have been largely eliminated; and the game is not only one of skill and endurance, but it has the advantage of being absolutely under the control of the referees or umpires. As a matter of fact the game has been completely revolutionized in the past three

12/19/89 Mirror

FOOT BALL.

I mentioned in my last letter, I believe, that there was to be played on that day a game of football between the teams of the Univ. of Va and Wake Forest, N. C. Well, it was played, and what a game! As the hour for the contest to begin approached, I felt the partisan spirit for the Virginia boys rising within me and so boarding a go-as-you-please or don't go-at-all, electric car, I soon found myself at Boscheu's Park with the two teams lined up ready for work, before me. I had some sort of an idea of what the game was like, so got on pretty well; but for an old timer at the game, who was used to playing where every fellow kicked, like a spanker-boom in a hurricane, at the ball, whenever he found it, the game was not football at all — They played an hour and a-half and I have yet to see a Wake Forest man kick the ball a single time, and the Univ. boys kicked but little oftener. It is a game that in short looks like every man was trying to butt the brains or internal improvements out of his vis-a-vis or break his back on the ground. But all the same it was a great game and a glorious victory, the Virginia boys winning handily.

December, 1889

1889   **1889.**

CHRISTMAS !

WHERE MUST I GO?

To get a Dollar's worth of Goods for every dollar, is a question every one must ask in these times of scarcity of money. An inspection of our stock will

ANSWER

this important question. It is selected with the utmost care as to Style and Price, and we can suit all pocket-books, and the most fastidious taste. We invite attention

TO

THE FOLLOWING GOODS.

WATCHES—Gold, Filled, Silver, Nickle,
STERLING SILVER WARE—QUADRUPLE PLATED-WARE.
CLOCKS, from $1 up. Fine China and Glass-Ware
FANCY ARTICLES, in Silver, Plate, Brass, Nickel and Bronze.
Mirrors, remarkably low. Opera Glasses, Field Glasses.
PIANO LAMPS, ROCHESTER LAMPS,
Cheap Lamps, and Lamp Goods at

STANSBURY & KENT'S,

LEESBURG, VA.

12/28/89 Washingtonian

CHRISTMAS AT OUR CHURCHES.—The Churches of the town were all well attended at their Christmas celebrations. The Sunday School of St. James' Episcopal Church had their Christmas Tree on Tuesday night. The church, which had been most tastefully and beautifully decorated by the ladies, was brilliant with lights. The galleries were decorated with wreaths, the spaces between the pillars with arches of evergreens, the chancel with crowfoot, ivy and holly; over the arch of the chancel, in beautiful letters made of evergreens were the words, "Glory to God in the highest" while a large star of green hung from the apex, and directly in the middle of the chancel stood the tall and spreading "Christmas tree," laden with gifts for the scholars. After a short service by the children, the Rector, Rev. R. T. Davis, D. D., made a short address, well befitting the occasion, and Judge R. H. Tebbs, the Superintendent, after an affectionate and very appropriate talk to "his children," distributed the prizes given by himself to those successful in reciting the Church Catechism without error. Then the tree began to shed its fruits, and every one got something. Happy they seemed, and happy they were—for they said so.

On Christmas day the Rev. Dr. Davis preached to a good congregation. The music was most appropriately chosen, and beautifully rendered.

www.ingramcontent.com/pod-product-compliance
Lightning Source LLC
Chambersburg PA
CBHW060310240426

43661CB00059B/2711